BRITS

BRITS

The War Against the IRA

Peter Taylor

BLOOMSBURY

PICTURE ACKNOWLEDGEMENTS

British troops deployed in Londonderry (Popperfoto/Reuters); 'Bloody Sunday' (Belfast Telegraph Newspapers Ltd); Peter (David Barker); Lt-Gen. Sir Anthony Farrar-Hockley (David Barker); Donegall Street, Belfast (Belfast Telegraph Newspapers Ltd); William Whitelaw (Popperfoto/Reuters); Roy Mason (Pacemaker Press International); Lt-Col. Brian (private collection); George (David Barker); Michael Oatley (David Barker); Francis Hughes (Pacemaker Press International); John Boyle (private collection); 'Jim' (private collection); Warrenpoint wreckage (Pacemaker Press International); Mrs Thatcher (Pacemaker Press International): Stuart (private collection); The old German rifles in the hayshed (RUC); John Stalker ("PA" Photos); Colin Sampson ("PA" Photos); Kinnego wreckage (Pacemaker Press International); The Grand Hotel Brighton (Popperfoto/Reuters) Mrs Thatcher and Garret FitzGerald sign the Ango-Irish Agreement (Pacemaker Press International); IRA member shot dead at Loughgall (original source unknown); 'Frank' (private collection); The cake baked for the SAS (original source unknown); Pat Finucane (Pacemaker Press International); Brian Nelson (Pacemaker Press International); Sir Kenneth Stowe (David Barker); Sir Robert Andrew (David Barker); Ian Burns (David Barker); Commander John Grieve at the scene of the Docklands bomb (Metropolitan Police Service); James McArdle (Metropolitan Police Service): The waste ground in Barking (Metropolitan Police Service); David Trimble and Gerry Adams (Pacemaker Press International); Tony Blair and Bertie Ahern (Pacemaker Press International): Mo Mowlam (Pacemaker Press International); George Mitchell (Pacemaker Press International); The Northern Ireland Executive (Pacemaker Press International): Peter Mandelson (Popperfoto/Reuters); Gerry Adams and Martin McGuinness (Popperfoto/Reuters); Gunner Robert Curtis (Pacemaker Press International); Lance-Bombadier Stephen Restorick (private collection)

First published in Great Britain 2001
This paperback edition published 2002

Bloomsbury Publishing Plc, 38 Soho Square, London W1D 3HB

Grateful acknowledgement is made to the following for permission to reprint previously published material; Robert Hale for permission to quote from *Paying the Price* © Roy Mason (1999); HarperCollins Publishers Ltd for permission to quote from *John Major: The Autobiography* © John Major (1999); HarperCollins Publishers Ltd for permission to quote from *Margaret Thatcher: The Downing Street Years* © Margaret Thatcher (1993) Every reasonable effort has been made to trace copyright holders of material reproduced in this book, but if any have inadvertently been overlooked the publishers would be glad to hear from them.

The moral right of the author has been asserted

A copy of the CIP entry for this book is available from the British Library

ISBN 0 7475 5806 X

10 9 8 7 6 5 4 3 2

Typeset by Hewer Text Ltd, Edinburgh

Printed in Great Britain by Clays Ltd, St Ives plc

To Sue, Ben and Sam

Contents

Acknowledgements

I find acknowledgements almost the most difficult part of writing a book, not least because of the fear of forgetting to mention someone whose contribution or assistance was so vital. If I do, I hope they will forgive me and still accept my gratitude. These words are usually written when the long labour of writing is done – a task which, though lonely, is in reality the fruit of the labours and assistance of many. *Provos, Loyalists* and now *Brits*, which together make up the contemporary historical trilogy of the current Irish conflict, could not have been written without the enthusiasm and dedication of the team that I worked with in making the BBC television series on which the books are based. Sam Collyns was the best series producer I could have wished for, was great to work with and always believed there was light at the end of the tunnel if we just persevered; assistant producer Julia Hannis displayed her customary tireless energy in tracking down unfindable people as well as generously checking facts for the book; film archivist Stuart Robertson found revelatory footage to illustrate our theme, and executive producer Peter Horrocks kept the lightest touch on the tiller and always moved it in exactly the right direction. I'm also grateful to all my BBC colleagues for their support with the series and the book. At one stage I was minded not to write it but was told by friends, colleagues and others that I must, on the grounds that *Provos* and *Loyalists* were only two-thirds of the story. I hope they are not disappointed.

Thanks, too, to all those without whose remarkable interviews neither book nor series would exist. Many took great risks in co-operating with *Brits* both on and off the record and many of their names I cannot mention. They know who they are and I am deeply indebted to them. Many are featured in the book under pseudonyms marked by inverted commas. I'm also grateful to Brigadier Sebastian Roberts of the MOD who supported the project from the start and did all he could to assist despite the fact he was not able to help with Special Forces; and to RUC Chief Constable Sir Ronnie Flanagan and his colleagues who went out of their way to provide access to individuals who enabled us reflect such a vital part of the story.

At Bloomsbury, Bill Swainson was a cool and incisive commissioning editor who, when it became clear the book was going to overrun, encouraged me to get the story down first and worry about length later. *Brits* is much longer than originally envisaged and would have been even longer without the cuts overseen by Bill and Pascal Cariss, who brilliantly edited and improved the text. The book is infinitely the better for it and I am indebted to them both as well as to Edward Faulkner, who so meticulously put the jigsaw of text, changes and rewrites together and to Douglas Matthews for his excellent index. I'm grateful to my agent John Willcocks who sorted out the contractual side, leaving me free to get on with the writing, and also to David Hooper for his valued legal advice.

Finally, my thanks to my family, Sue, Ben and Sam, who supported me with love and patience throughout the long months and encouraged me to smile, 'chill out' and take Josh (our dog) for a walk whenever the clouds seemed to darken over the laptop. They assured me I would get there in the end. I did. I hope Northern Ireland does too.

Introduction

'Frank's' Story

14 Intelligence Company – known as the Detachment or 'Det' – is the army's most secret undercover surveillance unit in Northern Ireland, so secret that it doesn't exist. Its 'operators' have no names, identities or numbers. They are the eyes and ears of the SAS and the RUC's Special Branch – the men and women trained to gather vital intelligence by breaking into IRA men's houses, bugging or 'jarking' IRA weapons and vehicles and working undercover at huge personal risk. Regular soldiers call them 'The Muppets' because of their various disguises. Since its formation in 1973, 14 Intelligence Company's role in the 'war' against the IRA has been critical, latterly playing a vital – and unacknowledged – part in helping to bring the IRA to the negotiating table.

'Frank' is the only operator to have survived capture by the IRA – although he stopped three bullets in the process. He has no doubt about the 'Det's' impact on the conflict. 'It got to the stage where the IRA couldn't come outside their front door without being put under surveillance and tracked. We knew where they were going, what vehicles they were using, where they were getting their weapons from and where they were hiding them. By the end of the 1980s, they didn't know which way to turn because we were there all the time. Technology gave us the upper hand even more. We were able to watch them from a great distance, photograph what they were doing – and listen to them. We were a very small organization but we gave an awful lot. Over the years my particular unit lost nine operators, but we accounted for a lot more of the enemy.' The irony is that because 14 Intelligence Company's existence and activities are so sensitive, neither the army nor the MOD can publicly pay tribute to it.

Hanging on 'Frank's' wall is a graphic souvenir of his many years with the 'Det' in Northern Ireland. It shows four men wearing balaclavas, bomber jackets and trainers emerging from an old VW Passat, brandishing a Browning 9mm revolver, a machine pistol and an HK 53 assault rifle. Inscribed in a circle round them is the 'Det's': unofficial motto. 'Go out into the highways and hedges, and compel them to come in.' There's little doubt who 'they' are. When I asked where the words came from, 'Frank' left the room and returned with a large family Bible open at Luke 14 verse 23. It wasn't quite the context that Luke intended.

'Frank' first served in Northern Ireland in the late 1970s as part of the regular army but he grew bored and frustrated 'just wandering around, showing the flag, offering yourself as an occasional target and achieving very little'. He says he felt like a mushroom, being kept in the dark and never really knowing what was going on. On the rare occasions when soldiers did find a weapon, he felt they were being given it by other agencies just to keep them happy. Clearly his frustration showed – as did his potential. He finally escaped from the mind-numbing routine and became part of a Close Observation Platoon (COP), trained by the SAS, which was more exciting than engaging the locals in polite conversation. But he still wasn't satisfied and wanted to be closer to the action, to the sharp end of the 'war'. Some months later, an instructor asked him if he might be interested in 'a more specialist job, more to the cutting edge'. 'Frank' decided he had nothing to lose and applied for selection, although he had no clear idea of what he was being selected for or what the specialist unit was called. He discussed it with his father who advised him, 'Keep your mouth shut, do your best and get on with it.'

He arrived at a secret location in England and was shown into a hut with a blackboard on the wall. 'Frank' read the chalked-up words. 'Basically it was a declaration that you gave up all your human rights and they could do what they wanted with you. Your rank meant nothing and your name meant nothing. You were just a number from then on.' He was given a piece of paper to sign, signifying that he had read and understood the score. Then the psychological deconstruction began. 'They're only looking for a certain kind of person and they start weeding them out from the word go. Any Walter Mittys and James Bonds are soon on their way.' Each potential recruit had been given a kit list of things to bring. If he – or she – arrived with anything extra, like love-letters, they were immediately taken away. One of 'Frank's' intake, a Royal Marine officer, had a teddy bear in his suitcase. He never saw it again, and he didn't make it through the course. The three-week selection process, run by the SAS and experienced 'Det' operators, was the most physically exhausting and mentally draining experience 'Frank' had ever undergone. Of the 130 who had been accepted for selection, only 30 passed and were sent for 'continuation training' at another Special Forces' secret camp in Wales.

Although all the skills an operator required were taught in the six-month course – from how to remain anonymous in enemy territory to covert photography and electronic surveillance – the most important lesson of all was how to survive if your cover was blown. In that event, the IRA would show no mercy. The most harrowing part was being subjected to an IRA-style interrogation – although recruits were spared the full horrors. Because it was so realistic, they had to volunteer. 'Frank' was reluctant to describe what he went through on the grounds that 'it would detract from the training'. One can only imagine.

Even more critical were the drills on how to survive a fire-fight. Time and again, recruits practised with their partners – the 'Det' always work in pairs – until their reactions became second nature. 'We became like Siamese twins.' Every incident in which the 'Det' had been involved was replayed in 'situation awareness' training so lessons could be learned. From day one, 'Frank' was instructed to carry his Browning 9 mm pistol with him wherever he went. 'Every day we practised, drawing from a concealed position and engaging various targets.' In particular, he was taught what to do if confronted by the IRA. 'You make a decision, go for it and fight your way through. Our training is to ensure that you don't get taken away for interrogation. But if you are captured, you've got to make sure you stay alive as long as possible to give your back-up time to find you – for the cavalry to come steaming in.' Of the thirty potential recruits who had passed selection, only nine made it to the end of continuation training. The next stop was Northern Ireland.

The 'Det' operates out of three Detachments that cover the province: East 'Det' based in Belfast, South 'Det' in Armagh, and North 'Det' in Derry. Frank was posted to North 'Det' which covers some of the IRA's most active urban and rural areas, alive with some of the IRA's most experienced gunmen and bombers. From the beginning, he had to familiarize himself not only with the known 'players' or 'targets' but with the communities from which they came. To remain anonymous and avoid attracting attention, he had to look, dress and act like everyone else around. 'You would wander around Londonderry and see what people were wearing and you would style yourself to fit in. The same with your vehicles. You went with the fashion. It was during the early eighties so you could wear flares and your hair would be fairly long. At one time I had a beard. And you could wear plain-glass spectacles. Anything really to disguise what you looked like. Luckily, you could conceal all sorts of things under your flared trousers – your radio and spare magazines and various other things crêpe-bandaged round your legs. It was a sad day when flares went out of fashion.'

Mastering the local accent was more difficult. Those operators who came from Northern Ireland were at a huge advantage. 'Frank' had to improvise. 'You would pass the time of day – I wouldn't exactly call it speaking. You could grunt knowingly at them and even smile occasionally if you were in an area day after day, pretending to be a builder or whatever or just wandering around. When you were within speaking distance of some fairly well-known characters, the adrenalin was running and your heart was pumping. I must have bumped into the Minister for Education [Martin McGuinness] a few times.' If such encounters in the Bogside and Creggan became too close for comfort and the locals started paying too much attention, 'Frank' would radio for a replacement – or simply get out fast. Given the hazards, did he enjoy it? 'It was wonderful. Nothing like it. The buzz was fantastic. The best job in the world with a great bunch of people – comradeship you couldn't describe or get anywhere else.' And why did he do it? 'I think I was fighting for the right of people to live a normal life and hopefully defending them from terrorism. We were defending democracy.'

'Frank' has no time for the IRA. 'They're just a bunch of cowards basically. It's a bit rich they actually call themselves an army. They're Irish Republican terrorists and that's about it.' There is a personal reason for his contempt: while he was on one tour, the IRA planted a car bomb outside the army's married quarters in Londonderry. Most of the soldiers were out on duty, leaving only wives and children behind. 'The only way to get them out was to keep running backwards and forwards past the bomb before it went off.' With the quarters cleared and the bomb still ticking away, 'Frank' was told by one of the women that she'd left a young child behind. He dashed back and rescued the baby. Seconds later, the bomb went off. 'It devastated the houses – blew them to bits. They were going to kill wives and babies. And they call themselves soldiers.' The RUC Special Branch officers who helped 'Frank' clear the area were all decorated and 'Frank' was Mentioned in Despatches for saving the baby.

'Det' operators lived and breathed danger every day, trusting that if the showdown finally came and their cover was blown, months of training would maximize their chance of survival. 'Frank' knew in his bones that it was only a matter of time before it happened to him. It had already happened to several of his colleagues, not all of whom had lived to tell the tale. One rainy February night in 1984, 'Frank' and his partner 'Jack' were involved in an undercover operation centred on the tiny village of Dunloy in North Antrim, when the moment finally came.

At the beginning of 1984, there was intelligence that a new IRA Active Service Unit (ASU) was being formed in the village. The 'Det' knew the main players and where they lived. 'Frank' had even followed one of them onto a train from Derry and sat across the aisle from him as it chugged along the beautiful North Antrim coast. It was about as close as an operator could get. Meanwhile, the 'Det's' technical experts had apparently been busy sometime earlier, bugging one of the weapons that made up the new cell's 'hide'. 'Frank' wouldn't comment on the 'jarking', simply saying 'we had the weapons under control'. The Intelligence agencies had also been active and there was information that the new ASU was about to carry out a murderous operation. The 'Det' took steps to prevent it. 'Frank' and 'Jack' staked out the house belonging to the family of one of the suspects, twenty-year-old Henry Hogan. The family had moved into their new house three weeks earlier, having been intimidated out of Ballymena and then out of Ballymoney by loyalists who presumably knew the family's republican reputation. The house was one of the first to be occupied in a new development on the fringe of the village. Others were still under construction and the workmen's huts provided reasonable cover for surveillance.

On 21 February 1984, 'Frank' and 'Jack' took up position by the huts – about a hundred metres from the Hogan's house. It had been under surveillance for some time although this was 'Frank's' first night on the job as he'd just returned from leave. There was reliable intelligence that the attack might take place at any moment. A car was expected. 'We were in an advanced stage of thwarting the operation,' 'Frank' remembers. It was a filthy night, dark, misty, pouring with rain and blowing a gale. The operators were wearing donkey jackets and jeans 'so if we were seen, people would think we were nicking lead or bricks or just yobbos'.

But what 'Frank' didn't know was that they'd been spotted. It seems the ASU's suspicions had been aroused when the technical device bugging the weapon was discovered. The IRA also apparently received a report of a suspicious sighting by the sheds. That night, the ASU's leader ordered Henry Hogan and another member of the unit, eighteen-year-old Declan Martin, to check it out. Around 8 o'clock, they pulled on their masks and set out in full IRA combat gear, Hogan armed with a Vigneron 9 mm submachine gun and Martin with an Armalite assault rifle, which had been used in the killing of an RUC constable three months earlier. They planned to surprise the strangers from the rear. As the suspect car pulled up outside the Hogans' house, 'Jack', who had it in his sights, asked 'Frank' to confirm it was the right vehicle. 'Frank', who had been facing the other way to cover the rear as his training had taught him, turned to check. At that moment, Hogan and Martin appeared from the gloom. 'They got the drop on us,' 'Frank' admits. 'It was bad skills – and bad luck – on our part.

They were shouting and screaming, "Who the f***ing hell are you! What
are you doing here!" They clearly weren't sure who we were. They made
us stand up with our hands in the air – the classic cowboy position. It
seemed a bit bizarre at the time. For a split second I thought, my God, this
is a realistic training exercise!'

Either the IRA weren't absolutely sure their captives were soldiers and
didn't want to shoot dead burglars or local hoods, or their intention was to
take them alive and march them off for interrogation and certain death.
'Frank' and 'Jack' were standing a metre apart with their hands in the air.
Hogan and Martin stood three metres away, levelling the Vigneron and the
Armalite at the soldiers. 'Looking into the muzzle of an Armalite kind of
clears the mind a bit, knowing what it can do.' Months of training came
into play. 'You practise drawing and firing like in the Old Wild West
movies. 'Jack' and I just looked at each other, nodded and went for it.'

In a single movement, they whipped their Brownings from their duffle
coats and put several rounds into Hogan and Martin. 'Your instinct at the
time is survival. You've got to make a decision, go for it, put down as much
fire as you can and win the fire-fight. There's no such thing as a draw.' As
Hogan fell, he let off a burst of thirteen shots from his machine gun. 'I've
always thought of it as unlucky thirteen,' 'Frank' reflects. 'Three of them
hit me. They just went up my body in a line – one through the knee, one
through the thigh and one through the back.' Six rounds hit 'Jack' – two in
the neck, two in the trunk and two in the left leg. 'Frank' immediately
radioed a contact report to his back-up team and then pulled his partner
across and called his name. He got no reply. He checked his pulse but
couldn't feel anything. 'Jack' had been killed almost instantly.

Hogan and Martin were still alive, on the ground nearby, 'making a
noise'. 'Frank' says he then fired the couple of the rounds left in his
Browning into them. When the 'Det' back-up team – always stationed
nearby in case of emergency – arrived a few minutes later, they finished the
IRA men off in what 'Frank' euphemistically called 'a fire and movement
exercise'. I suggested the wounded IRA men could have been given first
aid – as soldiers had done before – but 'Frank' would have none of it. 'If
one of our guys had walked forward and said, "Excuse me young chap,
how are you feeling?" the guy could have turned round and blown him
away. That's not the way it's done. They were armed and minutes before
had been putting rounds down. You win the fire-fight. You make sure
you're not the one that ends up dead.' 'Frank' was piled into a car and
rushed to Coleraine hospital 'with blood squirting out and with one of the
operators with his fingers in the holes'. Today, 'Frank' looks back with a
mixture of emotions. 'I don't know whether the word "guilt" describes it.
I was alive and 'Jack' wasn't. It could so easily have been the other way

round. If he'd been on the right and me on the left, he'd have been alive and I'd have been dead. It's as simple as that.'

Sinn Fein erected a memorial to Henry Hogan and Declan Martin on the spot where they fell. The words on the black marble cross read 'Killed in action by British Crown Forces'. The Martin family did not know their son had joined the IRA until they heard the news of his death. They were devastated. 'It's sixteen years ago now,' his father told me, 'and I still feel it yet.' I asked 'Frank' if he had any feelings for the young men the 'Det' had shot dead. 'On reflection, I felt a bit sorry for them. At least they were dressed as "soldiers". Those who sent them out were responsible for their deaths. They should never have been out there. They should have been at home with their mummies, watching TV. I wasn't sad for them. They tried to kill us and we killed them. That's the way armies work.'

'Frank' spent a year recovering in hospital. By then, his first marriage was already in trouble due to his absence from home and the pressures of working undercover in Northern Ireland. Divorce followed. 'Frank' then married again. He finally left the army and tried to find a regular job that would suit his talents and experience but, like so many former members of Special Forces, found himself unable to do so. One of his former 'Det' colleagues, he says, is now stacking supermarket shelves. He did body-guard duties for a while but it wasn't what he really wanted. Frustration grew and the ghosts of Ireland would not go away. 'After what I'd been through, I treated all my enemies as the IRA,' he says. Breaking point came when he suspected his new wife of having an affair with one of her colleagues. 'Frank' went into 'operating mode' and placed both under surveillance as 'targets', using the training and techniques he'd been taught in the 'Det'. When he went away and left his wife alone, he bugged the house to see what she might be up to. In the end, he feared that he might do to his wife's suspected lover what he'd done to the IRA. 'It was a touch and go situation,' he remembers. 'It could have gone either way.' One weekend, after a blazing confrontation with his wife, he went to an army medical centre and asked for help. He talked for more than three hours to an army psychiatrist who realized that 'Frank' had come to him just in time. Together, they worked on his problem and, after many months of counselling, the psychiatrist finally helped put 'Frank' together again.

In wars like the Falklands or the Gulf, 'Frank's' breakdown would probably be known as post traumatic stress disorder. The stress that soldiers in Northern Ireland have suffered, in particular in the 'Det' and SAS, have not been considered in the same league. 'The problem is they build you up and fine-tune you into a killing machine – and then they drop you.' Fortunately, 'Frank' was caught before he fell. But he has no regrets. 'When the time came to leave the army, I was mortified. To this day I've never handed in my ID card. I would have carried on and on if I'd been able to. But then there comes a time when you realize your eyes aren't quite as good as they were and you probably wouldn't be able to fit into those jeans any more.'

Even at the beginning of the twenty-first century, Ireland does not go away. 'Frank', like most soldiers, feels intense bitterness about the direction of the peace process – especially about the way that prisoners have been released without the IRA handing over a single weapon. 'Terrorists we spent years putting behind bars are now out. The IRA is now back up to strength and fully armed. If they get a bit sad and throw their teddy bear in the corner, they can pick up their Armalites and AK 47s and pick up where they left off. There's got to be a peaceful solution but there can't be as long as they still have the tools of violence.' To 'Frank' and most of his colleagues, opening up dumps to independent inspection isn't the same as handing in weapons. Still, 'Frank' takes comfort from the fact that, despite almost three years of the IRA's ceasefire, 14 Intelligence Company has not let down its guard. 'The "Det" is still active,' he says with pride, 'still very, very busy.'

Chapter One

Into the Mire

1920–1969

For almost half a century since the partition of Ireland in 1921 and the establishment of the British statelet in the North known as Ulster, successive governments at Westminster had largely ignored the province, hoping to keep at bay the euphemistically named 'Troubles' out of which the new state had been born. Northern Ireland was a British province both in name and reality, in some respects not unlike those countless outposts of empire ruled by the Crown in days when most of the globe was coloured pink. It had a Governor General, complete with uniform, ceremonial and personal residence at Hillsborough Castle; its own parliament with upper and lower chambers housed in a magnificent neo-classical building at Stormont in Belfast's leafy suburbs; its own Government, Cabinet and Prime Minister – a mini-Westminster down to Speaker's mace and *Hansard* parliamentary record; its own police force, the Royal Ulster Constabulary (RUC), backed by an armed paramilitary wing of volunteers known as the 'B' Specials to defend the state from subversion; and a British army garrison for years nostalgically known to its occupants as 'Sleepy Hollow' – a prime location for hunting, shooting and fishing. But there was one crucial difference. This province was on Britain's doorstep, separated from the mother country at its narrowest point by twenty-five miles of Irish sea. Northern Ireland was so near and yet so far that, to most of the English, it was like a foreign country. A friend once confessed that when he first went there in the 1960s and left Belfast's Aldergrove airport in a hire car, he wondered whether he should drive on the right.

I must confess that in those early days, my own knowledge and understanding of the complex and violent history that had given birth to this part of the United Kingdom was no greater than that of most of the British public. I remember as a young journalist being despatched to Londonderry – or Derry as it is more generally known – on Sunday 30 January 1972 to cover the aftermath of the day that became infamous as

'Bloody Sunday'. I'd never been to any part of Ireland before, North or South, and had little idea where Derry was.

I was working for Thames Television's *This Week* programme at the time and we had been hoping to cover the civil rights march planned for that day with three camera crews as it was clear that the march was likely to be anything but peaceful, given the pitch at which emotions on all sides were running. The trade union that held much of ITV in its grip at the time demanded exorbitant 'danger money' from Thames, the company that made *This Week*, which Thames refused to pay. The crews were grounded and our three cameras were not there to record what happened that afternoon when, in highly controversial circumstances, soldiers of the Parachute Regiment shot dead thirteen unarmed Catholics who had been taking part in the march. When I heard the five o'clock news that Sunday afternoon, my emotions were a mixture of shock and anger: shock at the number of deaths, although few details were available at the time, and anger that an industrial dispute between union and company had prevented us from being there to record what had happened. I immediately rushed to the airport and met up with a camera crew. Now there was no dispute about danger money.

I got to Derry that night, feeling nervous, apprehensive and bereft of any historical bearing. Up to that point, I'd shut my eyes to the Irish problem, the only consolation being that I knew I wasn't alone in doing so. Early the following morning I walked into the Bogside, the nationalist area of the city that had been the scene of the shooting, and saw blood still fresh on the ground and hastily gathered flowers marking the spot where the dead had fallen. The air was eerily still and there was no one around. I started knocking on doors with some trepidation to find eye-witnesses to what had happened, expecting to have the door slammed in my face or be abused because I was a 'Brit'. I was astonished that neither happened. I was given tea and baps and biscuits by families grateful that a 'Brit' wanted to hear their account of what had happened. I found and interviewed a former British soldier, Jack Chapman, a Welshman living in the Bogside, the balcony of whose flat had afforded a grandstand view of what had happened. I thought it would have been difficult to find a more objective witness to an event that seems to throw objectivity to the winds. Jack had no doubt that the Paras had shot down his neighbours in cold blood. I was shocked to hear what he said and by his vivid description of 'bodies being thrown into the back of army vehicles like sheep'.

Although admittedly not knowing the full circumstances at the time, I felt guilty about what 'our' soldiers appeared to have done, and about my ignorance of the historical circumstances that had led not just to 'Bloody

Sunday' but to the re-emergence of the age-old conflict. I decided it was time to do something about it.

As Easter 1972 approached and the fall-out from 'Bloody Sunday' continued to dominate the headlines, I hit upon what I thought was a bright idea. At the weekly meeting of the *This Week* team, I suggested that one way of trying to help our audience understand the seemingly intractable problem was to take someone there who held the widespread view that Northern Ireland was more trouble than it was worth and that we should withdraw the troops and let the Irish sort it out. I thought that by engaging this person on the ground we would thereby engage the audience and perhaps at the end of the programme leave both parties the wiser for it. My suggestion was received with more merriment than journalistic enthusiasm. My editor, John Edwards, who was always game for trying something new, said if I could find my 'typical Brit', be he a bus driver, coal miner or whatever, I could do it.

I went North and in the end found a bus driver from Hull and his wife, called Tom and Doris. Tom was a television natural with opinions on anything and everything, not least Northern Ireland. The furthest Doris had travelled from her native Hull was a day trip to York, about an hour's drive away. I interviewed Tom in his bus depot surrounded by his mates. He was all for bringing the troops home and 'letting the buggers sort it out' and most of those around him agreed. We called the film 'Busman's Holiday'.

Tom and Doris had seen endless violence on the television news and been uncomprehending of it, knowing that it was taking place in a part of the United Kingdom but not really believing it. The only thing that brought it home was news of British soldiers being killed but, as far as they were concerned, they were dying in foreign fields. I remember driving into Belfast with them for the first time and sighting our first soldier. Doris was amazed and pointed him out to Tom saying, open-mouthed, 'Look, Tom, there's a soldier – and look he's got a gun!' They were amazed too when they walked through the city centre and saw Boots and Marks and Spencer. 'It's just like Hull,' Tom said. When a small bomb went off and left a shop front in ruins, Tom could not believe it. 'If that happened at home,' he said, 'the *Hull Daily Mail* would be running the story for weeks!' Gradually, as we introduced Tom and Doris to all shades of nationalist and unionist opinion, they began to understand the situation, although they could never accept a republican's insistence that Northern Ireland was part of Ireland and not the United Kingdom.[1] After a week, we returned to England and Tom and Doris went back to Hull, still confused, but certainly much the wiser. 'We can't just abandon them,' Tom concluded, 'we've got to stick it out.' That was almost thirty years ago and that's what the 'Brits' have done.

What is remarkable is that British ignorance of Northern Ireland in those early days extended to the highest levels of government. Junior civil servants who later became the senior mandarins, the Permanent Under Secretaries (PUSs), who had to devise policies and stratagems to deal with the escalating crisis, admit their own lack of knowledge when they occupied the lower rungs of the Whitehall ladder. In the late 1960s, Sir Brian Cubbon was Principal Private Secretary to the Home Secretary, whose department, the Home Office, had responsibility for Northern Ireland at the time. 'The Northern Ireland unit was very much a backwater,' he told me. 'Going back to the thirties, forties, fifties and early sixties, it just wasn't in the frame. It was a tiny bit of one of forty divisions in the Home Office and that unit also dealt with the Channel Islands – which were rather more hospitable – and other issues such as local authority bylaws. It was a very minor issue indeed. There was always a Northern Ireland civil servant sitting in the division as the liaison officer for the Northern Ireland Government so it was a very cosy relationship.' Ian Burns was Private Secretary at the Home Office in 1969. 'One of the problems was that one didn't know a lot about Northern Ireland and therefore you weren't in a position to form a judgment about it. There was a Government there – it was Her Majesty's Government – and there was a Governor. You assumed that matters were all right unless anyone told you otherwise. As a fairly junior civil servant I had no reason to think that the state of affairs was wrong in Northern Ireland any more than it was wrong in the Isle of Man.' Sir Frank Cooper, who was a Deputy Under Secretary at the Ministry of Defence between 1968 and 1970, echoed the sentiments.

> There was amazingly little knowledge in the rest of the UK of what Northern Ireland was like and there had been very little contact between the province and the mainland for many years past. It was a strange environment and although the army had a General Officer Commanding Northern Ireland [GOC], quite frankly it was regarded as a pleasant place to live and enjoy the delights of the countryside. But it was this terrible lack of knowledge which I found the most frightening thing of all at that time.
> **Did you lack knowledge of Ireland?**
> Oh yes. I don't know anybody who knew a great deal about Ireland. The Home Office knew virtually nothing and the British Government knew virtually nothing.

One of the lessons Sir Frank said he'd learned with hindsight was that to intervene in a place like Northern Ireland that had been given a large degree of self-government was a recipe for trouble. The problem was that although the province was effectively self-governing except for foreign policy and external affairs, the governing class, from the Cabinet and civil service to the judiciary and police force, was almost entirely drawn from the Protestant/unionist side of Northern Ireland's bitterly divided community. The province consisted of roughly a million Protestant unionists fiercely wedded to maintaining the union with Great Britain and half a million Roman Catholic nationalists, most of whom owed their allegiance to the Government of the Irish Republic.

The state of Northern Ireland had been founded by the Government of Ireland Act of 1920, a settlement designed to resolve the Irish Question once and for all. The Question – to whom did the island belong? – had bedevilled relations between England and Ireland since the twelfth century when King Henry II began the process of conquest and subjugation. As the centuries went by, the Question became more acute as successive English kings and queens ruled over their westerly neighbour with less than benevolent intent, crushing local resistance with a savagery that simply fuelled resistance to what most native Irish saw as the foreign invader. Since Ireland was also the back door to England through which her Spanish and French enemies sought to attack, the English Crown had powerful strategic interests for holding Ireland in the tightest of grips.

At the beginning of the seventeenth century, these strategic considerations made the Irish Question even more complicated. The Protestant King James I encouraged thousands of hardy Scottish Presbyterian settlers to make new lives in the north-east corner of Ireland in the ancient province of Ulster. The purpose of what became known as the 'plantation' of Ulster was to make the most troublesome corner of England's realm secure for the Crown. In setting up the colony, these Protestant settlers displaced most of the Catholic native inhabitants and took much of the best land, fuelling still further the resentment that already existed. Many of the million Protestants living in Northern Ireland today are descended from those who founded and defended England's Protestant colony in Ireland. This is primarily why the problem of Northern Ireland exists four centuries on: two communities, one Catholic and one Protestant, with different national identities, owing allegiance to two different states, both living in the same corner of the same island. Had the plantation of Ulster never happened, the Irish Question would have been solved years ago. Britain maintains her rule in the North primarily for two reasons: she feels she cannot betray a million of her fellow citizens who wish to remain part of the United Kingdom; and she fears that if she were to withdraw against the wishes of the Protestant majority, the long-uttered threat of armed resistance by so called 'loyalists' would become reality and civil war would follow, a bloody legacy as Britain left the province.

Ever since the conflict erupted once more in 1969, successive British governments have argued their case at the bar of both domestic and international public opinion that British policy is determined by the fact that in a democracy the wishes of the majority must prevail and in the case of Northern Ireland that majority is Protestant in faith and unionist in persuasion. But there is a central fallacy to that argument which is the result of history, not political inclination. Before the Government of Ireland Act of 1920, all thirty-two counties of Ireland were under British rule that the Irish Republican Army (IRA) had fought a determined campaign to break. The IRA sought to achieve the Irish Republic, a 'sovereign, independent, Irish state . . . established by Irishmen in arms', which Patrick Pearse, the leader of a small band of Irish rebels, had proclaimed outside the Post Office in Dublin at Easter 1916 after a suicidal rising against the British.[2]

With the Great War raging and thousands of Irish soldiers in the British front line, support for the rising was minimal. Dubliners spat at the rebels as British soldiers led them away. But when the British executed Pearse and the leaders of the rebellion for treason, in William Butler Yeats's immortal words, 'a terrible beauty' was born.[3] Support for the rebels soared as did support for the cause of Irish national independence for which they had shed their blood. Sinn Fein, the tiny Irish republican political party of which few had heard at the outbreak of the Great War in 1914 and which was to become the IRA's political wing, was the beneficiary. In the British general election of December 1918, a month after the ending of hostilities in Europe, Sinn Fein swept to a stunning victory across the whole of Ireland. Of the 105 Irish seats that constituted the country's political representation at Westminster, Sinn Fein won seventy-three, legitimizing its claim to represent the majority of people on the island of Ireland. Thus the seeds of partition were sown. The party's MPs refused to take their seats at Westminster on the grounds that it was a 'foreign' parliament and gathered in the Mansion House in Dublin, proclaiming themselves to be the legitimate government of the Irish people.

Over the next two years, the IRA fought a savage guerrilla campaign against British soldiers in Ireland and the native Irish police force, the Royal Irish Constabulary (RIC) who were their allies. Terrible atrocities were committed by both sides in what the Irish called the War of Independence and the British called the war against terrorism. To augment their forces, the British recruited hundreds of unemployed Great War veterans, dressed them in makeshift uniforms of dark green, black and khaki and sent them to Ireland to assist the beleaguered RIC and terrorize any local populations minded to give succour and support to the IRA. They became notorious as the 'Black and Tans' and to republicans were synonymous with British butchery. They were also aided by demobilized British officers known as the 'Auxiliaries' who enjoyed a similar reputation. To the British, the IRA excited the same feelings, not least when gunmen under the direction of the IRA leader, Michael Collins, effectively wiped out British intelligence in Dublin on 21 November 1920 by shooting dead fourteen of its key operators in the space of one night. Retaliation followed later the same day when a mixed force of soldiers, 'Black and Tans', 'Auxiliaries' and RIC opened fire on 15,000 spectators watching a Gaelic football match at Dublin's Croke Park. They were said to be looking for Collins's gunmen. The troops killed twelve civilians in a day that became known as the original 'Bloody Sunday'. As with 'Bloody Sunday' in 1972, the official account was that the soldiers had been fired on and shot back in self-defence.

The war became increasingly brutal and, as has happened in the current conflict, provoked a degree of outrage back home at what was being done in Britain's name. Herbert Henry Asquith, the former Liberal Party leader who had been Prime Minister at the time of the Easter Rising and who had been uneasy about the execution of the rebel leaders, although he had not stopped them,[4] declared, 'Things are being done in Ireland which would disgrace the blackest annals of the lowest despotisms in Europe.'[5] By the spring of 1921, both sides recognized that neither could be defeated, and negotiations followed, culminating in the Treaty of 6 December 1921 signed in Downing Street by the British Prime Minister, David Lloyd George, and the IRA leader, Michael Collins, who led the Irish delegation. The human cost of the war to both sides had been great, with over 500 soldiers and policemen and over 700 IRA volunteers killed.[6] But the Treaty, although repealing the 1801 Act of Union, fell far short of the complete independence that the IRA had fought for. It was, in the words of Michael Collins, a settlement that gave Ireland 'the freedom to achieve freedom'.

British prime ministers from Gladstone at the end of the nineteenth century to Asquith at the beginning of the twentieth had recognized the imperative of reaching a political accommodation with nationalist Ireland by granting a form of limited self-government known as Home Rule. Their efforts, however, were continually thwarted by an alliance of the Ulster Unionists who would have none of it, Southern Irish Unionists and the Conservative Party at Westminster who saw Home Rule as the thin end of the wedge of complete Irish independence. The situation was even more precarious because there were fears that if Home Rule were granted, Ulster unionists' resistance might be supported by sympathetic British army officers, some of whom, on the eve of the Great War, had indicated their potentially mutinous intentions should Ulster be coerced into a Home Rule settlement.[7] A compromise was eventually reached in the Government of Ireland Act of 1920 in which Ireland's thirty-two counties were divided into two separate political entities each with its own Home Rule parliament. It was known as partition. Twenty-six counties became the Irish Free State and the remaining six counties in the North became Northern Ireland. Elections to the new parliaments were held in 1921.

To create the new state, a new boundary was drawn around the ancient province of Ulster to guarantee that a majority of its citizens were Protestants. To achieve this end, three of Ulster's original nine counties were excluded.[8] To have left Ulster as it had been for centuries would not have guaranteed the Protestant majority that was the whole purpose of partition. From the outset, the new six-county state was a gerrymander. To the dismay of Irish republicans, the pens that signed the Treaty did not write out partition but institutionalized it. The sop to Irish republicans was that it gave the Irish Free State the Dominion status enjoyed by Canada, Australia, South Africa and New Zealand. This meant it no longer sent MPs to Westminster but elected representatives to its own parliament in Dublin known as Dail Eireann. What stuck in Collins's throat – and he had been forced to accept it at Downing Street – was that those elected to the new parliament had to swear an oath of allegiance to the Crown, modified though it was to 'fidelity' to the King.[9] Nevertheless Collins remained optimistic that the Treaty gave Ireland the 'freedom to achieve freedom' in the expectation that at some stage in the not-too-distant future the two Home Rule parliaments would become one and independence would not be far behind. This was the carrot that Lloyd George dangled before him, the stick being the threat of renewed war against a depleted and exhausted IRA.[10]

But Collins's expectation proved false. In the wake of the Treaty, the IRA split into two factions, one that endorsed Collins's signature and one that bitterly opposed it on the grounds that he had sold out. In 1922 the fledgling Free State was plunged into a murderous civil war that lasted for almost a year. It not only left 500 republicans on both sides dead but buried any prospect of the new Northern Ireland parliament and Dail Eireann ever coming together. It also had dramatic repercussions in the North where sectarian violence in Belfast resulted in the deaths of 257 Catholics and 157 Protestants. The Treaty had divided the two communities even more, with Protestants fearing that the next stop was Irish unity and Catholics bitterly resentful of being cut off from their nationalist brethren by partition. The British made sure the Treaty and with it partition survived by supplying the new Free State army, the pro-Treaty faction of the IRA, with 10,000 rifles to make sure that the IRA's anti-Treaty forces were defeated.[11] Collins never survived to see the outcome. He was shot dead on 22 August 1922 by the anti-Treaty faction in an ambush when he was thought to be travelling to a meeting to talk peace.[12]

With the civil war over and both sides left to count the fratricidal cost, the anti-Treaty IRA laid down its arms in recognition of the fact that the Republic it had fought for could not, for the moment, be achieved. Nevertheless, a rump of it was determined to fight on when the right moment arose to destroy the Northern Ireland state and British rule in the North and win Ireland's complete independence by force of arms. The IRA of today has fought its thirty-year 'war' in the hope of completing that unfinished business.

From the beginning, Northern Ireland had instability built into it. It was designed to be 'a Protestant state for a Protestant people' and was run as such. Nationalists, who made up roughly one-third of its population, were citizens of a state to which most had no wish to belong, and most of their leaders boycotted its institutions. With good reason, the Catholic minority regarded themselves as second-class citizens and were treated as such by the Protestant hierarchy that ran the state and its economy. Discrimination was institutionalized, most notoriously in the way that local government boundaries were rigged. The most blatant example was in Derry where, although Catholics were in a majority in the city, Londonderry City Council was run by Protestants. This perversion of the democratic principle was achieved by a gerrymander of the electoral wards whereby 14,000 Catholic voters ended up with eight councillors whilst 9,000 Protestant voters ended up with twelve.

Such practices extended into other areas too. Industry and business was run by Protestants and, again, most saw to it that jobs went to members of their own community. The most notorious example lay with the province's biggest employer, the giant Harland and Wolff shipyard that had once built the *Titanic*. It employed 10,000 workers, only 400 of whom were Catholics. There was also political discrimination that was unique in the United Kingdom. Many Catholics were not able to vote in local elections because the franchise only extended to ratepayers and to pay rates you had to be the owner or tenant of a house or flat. Since Catholics were not only the minority population but the poorest section of it, they were caught in a poverty trap that effectively denied them the vote and any access to political power.

This discrimination that permeated every level of political, social and economic life was no accident but designed to ensure that the state and its institutions were run by and for the Protestant majority for whom the political entity of Northern Ireland had been designed.[13] The fact was that many Protestants regarded many Catholics as a fifth column for the IRA and felt everything had to be done to ensure that the Trojan Horse remained outside the walls. This was to be achieved by a mixture of draconian legislation and practical steps. The Special Powers Act allowed the state to lock people up without trial and the Ulster Special Constabulary, the 'B' Specials, was constituted to nip subversion in the bud. To many of the loyalist 'B' men who volunteered their services, any Catholic was a potential subversive. It was not surprising that Northern Ireland was a society waiting to explode. What was surprising was that for so many years successive British governments did nothing about it.

Since partition, Westminster had kept Northern Ireland at arm's length with most of its politicians of the view that no good would come of interference in the internal affairs of a province that had the machinery to sort out the problems itself. The province's matters were matters for the province's parliament. There was even a convention at Westminster, in place since the Speaker's ruling in 1922, that questions relating to Northern Ireland could not be raised in the House of Commons. The result was that, from partition until the outbreak of serious rioting in Derry in October 1968, the time spent on Northern Ireland affairs at Westminster averaged less than two hours a year.[14] British politicians therefore could always blame the convention and the constitutional position of the province. The problem was that the levers of power at Stormont were in the hands of those who, far from wanting to change the status quo and the condition of the minority of its citizenry, had a vested interest in maintaining it. To the unionist establishment that ran the state, change was seen as an encouragement to nationalists to demand more that would eventually lead to the erosion of all that unionists held dear and perhaps even of the state itself.

That this state of affairs was tolerated for so long by Westminster was bad enough but that it was largely ignored by Harold Wilson's Labour Government in the critical years of the mid-sixties is a political disgrace. Wilson came to power in 1964 promising reform and change but clearly it was not to apply to Northern Ireland, despite the urgings of a handful of his left-wing backbenchers who visited the province in 1967 to investigate discrimination, electoral practice and unemployment. They returned appalled at what they had found and urged the Home Secretary, Roy Jenkins, to set up a Royal Commission to report on conditions in the province. Jenkins, the biographer of Asquith, knew more about Ireland than anyone else in the Cabinet and was loath to act on the grounds that, historically, any English attempt to solve the Irish Question had always failed. Northern Ireland was like Brer Rabbit's 'Tar Baby' – touch it once and you're stuck.[15] There was to be no Royal Commission.

One of the Labour MPs who visited the province was Paul Rose, who was also Parliamentary Private Secretary to Barbara Castle, a Minister in Wilson's Cabinet. Rose took his Minister to task and found his concerns lightly brushed aside. Government, Castle told him, had more weighty matters to consider.

I remember her patting me on the head and saying, 'Why is a young man like you concerned about Northern Ireland? What about Vietnam? What about Rhodesia?' I just looked at her with incomprehension and said, 'You'll see when they start shooting one another.' She was totally oblivious to this. I think their priorities were focused on other things to the extent that they were totally blinded as to what was going on in their own backyard.[16]

A better bet, the Government reasoned, was to pin its faith on Captain Terence O'Neill, who had been elected as Prime Minister of Northern Ireland in 1963, the year before Wilson came to power. There were good reasons for thinking that the strategy would work. O'Neill was a reformer and, in 1967, had even entertained the Irish Taoiseach (Prime Minister), Jack Lynch, at Stormont, facing down the wrath of the Reverend Ian Paisley, the Protestant fundamentalist preacher who denounced him from pulpit and platform as a traitor prepared to sell Ulster to the Irish Republic and the Pope. With the right encouragement, the Wilson Government surmised, O'Neill would lead Ulster into the light and the new era of equality the second half of the twentieth century demanded. But be it from ignorance or negligence, no realistic appraisal was made in London of the powerful forces ranged against O'Neill on his own home ground, not only from the legendary lungs of his arch enemy, Paisley, but from within his own Ulster Unionist Party. Paisley articulated what many Protestants felt, although not all were prepared to admit it.

It was only a matter of time before the explosion came. 1968 was the year of change as 1848 had been the year of revolution in the previous century. In America, blacks marched for civil rights fired by the powerful oratory of Dr Martin Luther King; in France and Germany, students took to the streets for a variety of causes, more for what they were against than what they were for; and in England, anti-Vietnam protests culminated in the violence of Grosvenor Square. The Rolling Stones' anthem 'Street Fighting Man' seemed to sum up the mood of the time. Nor was Northern Ireland immune to the spirit that defied authority and demanded change. Catholics led by a new generation of articulate and charismatic young leaders, from John Hume to Bernadette Devlin, insisted on equality of treatment and an end to their status as second-class citizens. In 1968, the civil rights movement was born, a mirror of its American counterpart and a reflection of the same issues. It even imported its anthem, 'We Shall Overcome'. Young Catholics, many now first-generation university students, had found a voice and leadership. Some Protestants too marched alongside them to show the world that civil rights was not a sectarian issue. Many of these protests across Europe and America provoked violence as demonstrators encountered state forces that were either resistant to change or insistent on maintaining law and order. In Northern Ireland, civil rights marchers clashed with the police. The Royal Ulster Constabulary and the 'B' Specials were arms of the Protestant state and as such were called upon to meet the challenge to the legally constituted authority of the Stormont Government.

Most unionists simply saw the civil rights movement as an IRA front. There is no doubt the IRA was involved in the Northern Ireland Civil Rights Association (NICRA) but it was not the driving force behind it. By then the IRA had changed tactics following the humiliation of its recent border campaign, known as 'Operation Harvest'. It began in 1956 with the bold declaration that this generation would be the one to free Ireland from the British and ended ignominiously in 1962 with an order to dump arms. The harvest was blighted. There was no decommissioning. Casualties were remarkably light. Only eight IRA men and six RUC officers were killed. Most of the IRA leaders had spent most of the campaign behind bars because internment had been introduced by both the Stormont and Dublin Governments. The campaign failed not just because of internment but because it never got beyond the border: the IRA had negligible support in urban areas and partition had long ceased to be a popular rallying cry. 'Operation Harvest' ended with a defiant statement from the IRA's ruling body, the Army Council, that future generations would carry on the fight. In the wake of the campaign's failure, the Marxists in the IRA gained the upper hand over the traditionalists, who advocated the use of physical force, and revolutionized IRA strategy, arguing that it was necessary to adapt to changing times.

The new Chief of Staff, the Dubliner Cathal Goulding, was realistic about the IRA's prospects. 'The notion that the IRA was going to rise up some day and free Ireland and get rid of the British was a ridiculous pipe-dream for the simple reason that we never had the support of the people North and South to do it.'[17] Although the IRA's Army Council did not rule out for ever the use of physical force to achieve its historic goal, it decided to concentrate on political agitation and mobilization of the masses in the hope of undermining the state in the North and gaining support in the South for its left-wing policies. It reasoned that with its arms now removed from the equation, support would flow to an IRA that had become a revolutionary political party, above all supporting the legitimate demands of the North's nationalist minority. But to unionists, it was still the IRA whatever its peaceful protestations. They claimed that the violence that erupted was orchestrated by the IRA whereas the reality was that IRA members acted as stewards on many of the marches to prevent not promote violence.

As the civil rights movement gained strength through 1968, most people in the rest of the United Kingdom were probably only dimly aware of what was happening on the other side of the Irish Sea. The Wilson Government too remained on the Westminster sidelines, watching and assuming that its liberal champion, Terence O'Neill, would respond to the challenge and introduce the reforms the demonstrators were demanding – one man, one vote and an end to discrimination. All would then live happily ever after. But it was not to be. O'Neill may have been a liberal in Northern Ireland unionist terms but his party certainly was not. For most, compromise was not a word in their vocabulary.

Then, on 5 October 1968, the rest of the United Kingdom suddenly woke up to what was happening on its doorstep. Television news brought dramatic images into millions of living rooms of the violence that flared during a civil rights march in Derry. Scenes of policemen charging into what appeared to be a peaceful crowd of demonstrators and batoning them over the head were shocking at the time and still appear shocking today. The image of the nationalist Gerry Fitt, the Westminster MP for West Belfast, holding his bleeding head seemed to say it all. Here was a Catholic Member of Parliament being beaten by what appeared to be a sectarian Protestant police force in part of the United Kingdom. Although these images were a propaganda gift for the demonstrators as they showed the state to be the repressive instrument they had always maintained it was, they increased unionist pressure on Terence O'Neill and the Stormont Government to resist and restore law and order to the province's streets.

Even with hindsight, William Craig, the hard-line Stormont Minister for Home Affairs who had not banned the Derry march but restricted its movement, had no regrets about the way the police handled the march. 'I was quite pleased with the way the RUC reacted,' he told me thirty years later. 'Maybe we'd made a mistake and we should have strengthened the RUC. The march was approached with a virtually certain knowledge that it would end in disorder.' Didn't he see anything wrong with scenes of policemen beating demonstrators over the head? 'They were a few that caught the attention of the media. I didn't see anything wrong with it. People were involved in violence, they weren't marching.'[18]

Craig had acted as he did to prevent a confrontation between the civil rights march and a parade planned by the Protestant Apprentice Boys of Derry for the same day. Many of the violent clashes that were to follow in the months and years ahead came in the wake of marches by Protestant Orangemen and other loyalist organizations.[19]

The events in Derry on 5 October 1968 were a watershed and the first of many to come. As the months went by, things went from bad to worse with protesters determined to march and Stormont determined to resist.

Violence flared time and again as the situation seemed to veer out of control. The situation became even more critical in mid-April 1969 when loyalist paramilitaries blew up Belfast's water supply and some of its electricity installations. They hoped to make the attacks appear to be the work of the IRA and thereby destabilize further the shaky position of Terence O'Neill.[20] The British Government responded by sending 1,500 soldiers to the province to guard vital installations. Paisley and the hard-liners in the Ulster Unionist Party demanded O'Neill's head and finally got it when he resigned on 28 April 1969.

By now, many Catholics had become totally alienated from the Royal Ulster Constabulary, which they had always seen as a sectarian force and which, with the exception of a tiny handful, they had never been prepared to join. The way that the police and their adjuncts, the 'B' Specials, conducted themselves in Derry simply confirmed what most nationalists had believed all along – that they were a Protestant force determined to keep Catholics in their place and, when necessary, beat them into submission.

By the summer of 1969, the explosion was ready to happen. Not surprisingly, it was ignited in Derry, swiftly spread to Belfast and then engulfed the whole province. There appeared to be a tragic inevitability to it all that neither the British Government at Westminster nor the unionist Government at Stormont seemed able to stop. By the time politicians woke up to what had to be done, it was too late.

Under growing pressure from the British Government, 'one man, one vote' and the reform of local government boundaries had been introduced by O'Neill's successor, Major James Chichester-Clark, shortly after he took over as Prime Minister on 1 May 1969, beating his hardline opponent, Brian Faulkner, by a single vote. But in a summer of growing tension, the biggest test of the resolve of the Wilson Government was still to come. On 12 August, the Apprentice Boys of Derry prepared to march through the city and around its walls in their annual commemoration of the lifting of Catholic King James II's siege of the city in 1689. Chichester-Clark was not minded to ban the parade given that he needed to maintain his image as a unionist strongman, which he never was. To his unionist right wing, a ban would have been seen as a sign of weakness and further capitulation to the civil rights movement that was now seen as the enemy within. The Wilson Government had no such excuse and could have banned the march itself through an order from the Home Secretary, James Callaghan, thereby saving Chichester-Clark the embarrassment and potential political danger of having to do so himself. But no such move was made. 'I'm a libertarian,' Callaghan said. 'I don't like banning marches.' It went ahead and the fuse was lit.

On Tuesday 12 August, before the parade proper began, some Apprentice Boys tossed coins from the city wall into the Bogside below, where 'small knots' of Catholics were congregated.[21] By early afternoon, nails followed by stones had been thrown at the police who had erected barriers to keep the two sides apart. The young Bogsiders' throwing range had extended to the marching Apprentice Boys themselves whose supporters began to throw stones back. By the evening, a full-scale riot was under way. This time when the police pursued the rioters back into the Bogside, they were met by a hail of petrol bombs, many hurled from the roof of the Rossville Flats that guarded the entrance to the area. Its residents were ready. The police were not. The ferocious rioting lasted for three days and became known as the 'Battle of the Bogside'.[22]

In the end the police, who had even resorted to throwing stones back, could not cope and took heavy casualties. They were ill-trained and ill-equipped to deal with what now appeared to be a major insurrection. Police reinforcements were brought in from other parts of the province but they fared no better. Two-thirds of one unit from County Down – forty-three out of fifty-nine officers – were injured. Water cannon and, for the first time in the United Kingdom, CS gas were used but had little effect on the rioters' enthusiasm for the fight. The rioting continued throughout Wednesday 13 August, with the newly elected Westminster MP for Mid Ulster, Bernadette Devlin, urging the Bogsiders on and helping them to break up paving stones for ammunition.[23] One of the young men in the heat of battle was a young republican called Martin McGuinness who was to become one of the IRA's most senior figures and, astonishingly, more than thirty years later, Minister for Education in a devolved Stormont Government.

With the rioting into its third day, Thursday 14 August, and the situation critical, the Stormont Government implemented hastily drawn-up plans to call in British troops to aid the civil power and relieve the exhausted and demoralized police. By late afternoon, the 1st Battalion, The Prince of Wales's Own Regiment of Yorkshire marched into Derry. They had been brought in from Belfast to the outskirts of Derry the previous month because of the deteriorating situation in the city. The battalion was a constituent part of the province's garrison known as 39 Brigade. Its C company was commanded by Major David who had to act swiftly when the order suddenly came to deploy.

> I was actually wearing desert boots at the time because the company
> commanders had spent the day going backwards and forwards into
> Derry in civilian clothes to monitor the situation. When I got back
> from one of the recces, we suddenly got the order to deploy. I dashed

into the Officers' Mess to change but didn't have time to put my boots on. We drove in to cheers, presumably from the Protestants because they thought we were going to sort out the Catholics. It was during the parade that the aggro really started. We took over from the 'B' Specials. They looked like pirates with hankies over their faces.

The hope was that the arrival of British troops would calm things down and the situation would then return to what passed as normality. But it was not to be. The significance of the deployment of the army was not lost on Frank Cooper, then a civil servant at the MOD. 'There was a fear that you were going into an unknown mire and that you didn't know what was there,' he told me. 'You didn't know what was going to happen to you when you were there and how you got out at the other side of the bog. But I think people were persuaded that something had to be done.' At 5 p.m. on Thursday 14 August 1969, reluctantly and belatedly, the 'Brits' touched the Tar Baby. The repercussions were monumental.

Chapter Two

Honeymoon

August 1969–October 1969

Brian was a young Lance-Corporal in the Prince of Wales's Own Regiment when he drove into Derry with Support Company that Thursday afternoon. He had until recently been a full Corporal but had lost a stripe after he had been 'busted' for losing one of his prisoners whilst on night duty in the guard room back in England before the battalion had been deployed to Northern Ireland. Support Company's entry into the heart of Derry was somewhat delayed when a smoke grenade accidentally fell off one of the Land-rovers as they were driving over the Craigavon bridge across the River Foyle that separates the Protestant Waterside from the Catholic Bogside and the Creggan estate that rises above it. Brian was shocked when he first saw the state of the police. 'They were tired and dejected. They'd been at it for three solid days and nights. I think with the limited resources they had, they had done a pretty good job. The force was too great against them at the time and it was obvious that they needed back-up. They probably resented the fact that we'd had to help them.'

Support Company took up position on the section of the ancient city walls by Bishop's Gate that afforded a grandstand view of the Bogside below, littered with the debris of three days of rioting and the smouldering remains of burned-out buildings and cars. 'We didn't exactly know what to expect. We were clapped and cheered. We looked down and people were waving at us and being very friendly towards us. They were even wolf whistling. They were shouting, "We're glad to see you. Thanks for coming. Thanks for saving us." I felt quite elated about it. We were doing a good job, doing something that we'd been trained to do. Then they started to shout up the walls, "Are you hungry?" "Yes." So we sent down a rope and they tied baskets onto it and put fish and chips and flasks of coffee in them. It was wonderful. This was obviously the honeymoon period. They had no reason to fear us. As far as they were concerned, we were there to stop them being subjected to bashings by the police.'

By that Thursday evening, the rioting in Derry had died down. To Brian and his mates, it was mission accomplished. 'We thought, This is it. The end of the Troubles. If only we'd known.' But by that time what was happening in Belfast made Derry look like a side-show. There had been fierce rioting the previous evening along the interface known as the 'Orange–Green' line that separates the Protestant Shankill Road from the Catholic Falls Road on one side and the Catholic Ardoyne on the other. The circumstances that gave rise to it were not as simple as both sides now like to make out. Both maintain they did not start it. Republicans insist that nationalists were subjected to an unprovoked attack by loyalists. Loyalists maintain they were simply responding to attacks by nationalists and the IRA. The truth probably lies somewhere in between. The already tense atmosphere that Wednesday evening was heightened by a television broadcast by the Irish Prime Minister, Jack Lynch, who said his Government could 'no longer stand by' and was sending field hospitals to the border. To the fury of unionists, he also raised the constitutional spectre.

> Recognizing, however, that the reunification of the national territory can provide the only permanent solution for the problem, it is our intention to request the British Government to enter into early negotiations with the Irish Government to review the present constitutional position of the Six Counties of Northern Ireland.[1]

The message was inflammatory, fuelling the emotions already felt by both sides. Nationalists thought that the deployment of the Irish army to the border meant that the Fifth Cavalry was coming. Loyalists thought that doomsday was at hand. The British Government thought that the normally mild-mannered Taoiseach had lost his head.

The situation was already tense because of developments earlier that day. Republicans in Derry had asked their comrades in other parts of the province to take the heat off them by fomenting disturbances elsewhere designed to stretch the RUC even more. However, the Northern Ireland Civil Rights Association decided to exclude Belfast from such diversionary tactics on the grounds that they would be likely to intensify the sectarian tensions already simmering there. But some Belfast republicans disagreed and organized marches that Wednesday evening to Springfield Road and Hastings Street police stations off the Falls Road, protesting 'police brutality' in Derry. Lynch's words spurred the crowd on. Stones, missiles and some petrol bombs were thrown. The targets were the police, not loyalists on the Shankill Road. The police believed they were facing serious attack and, mindful of what was happening to their fellow officers in Derry, mobilized some of their Commer armoured personnel carriers

(APCs) to disperse the rioters. The APCs were known as 'Mothballs' because they had been in storage and were designed for use along the border, not urban riot control.[2] As the Commers drove the crowds back, five shots, believed to have come from the IRA's guns, were fired at one of them and a hand grenade was hurled in its direction. Half a dozen further shots then rang out. At this stage, there is no evidence that the police returned fire. It was the first shooting in Belfast that week. Whilst these confrontations with the police became increasingly serious, loyalists were assembling missiles and petrol bombs on their side of the Orange–Green line, out of sight of the Catholic crowds along the Falls Road and the streets running off it.

In the early hours of Thursday morning, 14 August, Dr Paisley had a meeting with the Northern Ireland Prime Minister, James Chichester-Clark, and offered him the use of a Protestant force should the British Government only agree to send in the army on terms which were unacceptable to unionists.[3] Chichester-Clark had been summoned to London the previous week and warned by the Home Secretary, James Callaghan, that if he requested troops, there might be constitutional strings attached. The Stormont Government had no doubt that this meant their parliament might be suspended or abolished and Direct Rule imposed from Westminster.[4] Such a move was the unionists' nightmare, entailing the loss of all they held dear and the end of the institution by which they had maintained their grip on the province for almost fifty years. Chichester-Clark declined Paisley's offer of assistance.

By the evening, the scenes along Belfast's sectarian interface had become decidedly ugly and a handful of IRA men had laid their hands on the few guns that had been stashed away after previous campaigns and gone into action. The organization that had renounced physical force at the beginning of the decade was in no position to fulfil its traditional role in Belfast as the defender of the nationalist community and had to do the best it could with what few men and weapons it had. The IRA was unprepared because defence was not IRA policy. Its Dublin-based Chief of Staff, Cathal Goulding, believed that defending Catholics from Protestant attack was a sectarian act and counterproductive since the aim of the reconstituted Republican Movement was to bring the two working-class communities together and not drive them further apart.[5] In the two highly charged days and nights of Thursday 14 and Friday 15 August, veterans of the IRA's recent border campaign, 'Operation Harvest', like Billy McKee, Joe Cahill and John Kelly, who had long disagreed with the Goulding line and remained wedded to the IRA's traditional weapon of physical force, did what they could to defend their community from what they saw as an RUC and loyalist onslaught.

On Thursday night, Hastings Street police station came under further missile and petrol bomb attack from the nationalist crowd, triggering a new phase in the violence. Hitherto, most of the fighting had been between nationalists and the police but now the rioting became sectarian as some of the nationalist crowd spilled over into the Protestant end of the streets that ran from the Shankill to the Falls. The loyalists were ready. Vicious street fighting erupted. There were clashes too along other parts of the Orange–Green line. Again, the IRA opened fire and the police returned it. Shortly after midnight, shots were fired at a group of policemen and Protestant civilians standing on a corner. One of them hit 26-year-old Herbert Roy in the chest, killing him almost immediately. Three policemen received gunshot wounds. Less than half an hour later, the police deployed three Shorland armoured cars equipped with .30 mm Browning machine guns capable of firing 500 rounds a minute. As the Shorlands roared into action, they were pelted with stones and petrol bombs. A tracer bullet from one of the Brownings came through two walls and killed a nine-year-old Catholic boy, Patrick Rooney, as he lay in his bed in Divis Flats. Ironically his father was a former British soldier who had served for three years with the British army in Cyprus.[6] In the violence that continued throughout Friday 15 August, five more people were shot dead, four Catholics and one Protestant. Three of the Catholics were killed by RUC bullets. As the shooting intensified through the night, loyalist mobs invaded the Catholic ends of the streets they shared in common and torched their houses. In Conway Street, forty-eight homes were burned to the ground. In Bombay Street, 60 per cent of houses were consumed by flames. Dramatic television pictures of the time show flames leaping out of windows and roofs and people salvaging what they could from their homes. That night entered nationalist folklore as the loyalist 'pogrom', ethnic cleansing in the United Kingdom.

By dawn on Friday morning, the local police commanders decided that the situation was out of control and they would have to ask for the intervention of the British army. They were 'satisfied that the night's events had been the work of the IRA' and informed their superiors that they had intelligence of an imminent armed incursion by the IRA from the South.[7] The intelligence was fanciful. There is no doubt that the IRA was involved but what few veterans there were only came onto the scene once the rioting had become serious and the police had deployed their armoured vehicles. The IRA's most notable engagement, which also entered re-publican folklore, was the defence of St Comgall's Roman Catholic school which had come under loyalist petrol bomb attack.

The demand for troops was passed on to the RUC's Inspector-General (the Chief Constable), who in turn prepared a written request for the

Stormont Home Affairs Minister. The Northern Ireland Cabinet met at midday and at 12.25 p.m. on Friday 15 August, Chichester-Clark made a formal petition for military aid to the Home Secretary, James Callaghan, in London. He submitted this, the second request in two days, with increasing foreboding. 'I thought that initially it would probably blow over,' he told me, 'but when we had a sort of "second calling" of the troops into Belfast, I was beginning to wonder just a little bit where we were really going and whether we would really be able to solve all the problems.'[8] Callaghan had cut his holiday short and returned to the Home Office in the wake of the Lynch broadcast after his civil servants had warned him that the situation was getting critical.

Callaghan, like his Labour Cabinet colleagues, had been extremely reluctant to become directly involved and later admitted to a woeful ignorance of Northern Ireland. 'I never do believe, frankly, that anybody from this side of the water understands Ireland,' he said, 'and I've never flattered myself that I understand the situation fully. I think very few people do. Certainly we didn't have enough understanding of it at the time.' Callaghan also made it clear that there was no enthusiasm for deployment.

> I don't think anybody wanted to send troops in. That was the last thing we wanted to do. We held off until the last possible moment, until we were being begged by the Catholics of Northern Ireland to send them in. What an irony of history, that it was they who begged us, and I understand why. Their lives were in danger and we had to respond, especially as the police seemed to be exhausted and quite incapable of controlling the situation.[9]

At 3.10 p.m. that Friday afternoon, the United Kingdom Government authorized the deployment of British soldiers on the streets on Belfast in aid of the civil power that was the Stormont Government. Three hours later, around 250 soldiers from the 1st Royal Regiment of Wales marched onto the Falls Road and set up their headquarters in Springfield Road police station. This was a truly momentous decision since it entailed sending troops from England to reinforce the limited manpower available on the ground in the province. Among the first to arrive as members of the army's emergency 'Spearhead' battalion were soldiers from The Light Infantry. So unprepared were they that they had to buy maps of Belfast from a filling station on their way into the city from Aldergrove airport. One of their officers, Major Keith, had been in the province on exercise exactly a year before. 'Then all was peace and light,' he told me. 'There were no problems at all. But to arrive back in August 1969 to find the whole place on fire and to sense all the enmity and bigotry was pretty frightening.' His experience going into Belfast was not unlike Major David's going into Derry. 'The Protestants cheered you on because they thought you were coming in to finish off the Catholics. Then when you crossed the divide, the Catholics *did* think you'd come to finish them off. It took us a long time to persuade them that we were actually there to stop the fighting. When they realized that it was true, they actually got down on their knees and prayed. It was quite extraordinary. They were convinced that if we hadn't gone in that night, a huge number of them would have been burned out and probably killed by the next morning. It was very difficult to get through to both sides exactly what our role was.'[10]

To many of the soldiers who arrived, internal security such as this was not a new departure. A huge body of experience had been built up over the years which the army had no doubt would stand them in good stead when soldiers suddenly found themselves keeping the peace in a corner of the United Kingdom. In the late sixties, Jamie was on the threshold of a military career that, thirty years later, was to see him as a senior officer in Northern Ireland.

The army's experience in 1969 was a complete mixture – a combination of internal security and counter-revolutionary warfare which had been developed after the Second World War in the context of the withdrawal from empire. It covered Brunei, the Far East, Aden, Kenya, Cyprus, a whole host of colonial-type campaigns. We had to deal with the revolutionary organizations that were coming to government and internal security situations for which tactics and, to a certain extent, doctrine had been developed over the years.

Do you think that the army realized that it was dealing with a similar situation when it was deployed in Northern Ireland?

I don't think we probably saw it as a counter-revolutionary warfare situation, far from it. I think probably the first year or so it was very much an internal security situation in support of the police. I think everyone was pretty amazed at finding themselves on the streets of the United Kingdom.

For many of the soldiers who arrived in Northern Ireland in the summer and autumn of 1969, their most recent operation was in the British colony of Aden. It marked the final stage of Britain's surrender of empire as pink gradually faded from the globe. The Government set 1968 as the deadline for withdrawal from Aden and did so well in advance. The Union Jack was finally lowered on 30 November 1967 but only after two years of bloodshed and civil unrest as two rival liberation movements, the National

Liberation Front (NLF) and the Front for the Liberation of South Yemen (FLOSY), not only fought British soldiers but each other to seize power in the political vacuum that the British would leave.[11]

Aden added to the army's experience in dealing with both rioters and 'terrorists' in built-up urban areas. At one stage, the NLF turned to selective assassination and, taking the bloody approach of Michael Collins, tracked down and shot the entire operational body of the Aden Police Special Branch. Their corpses were left on the ground.[12] The Crater district, a hot, dusty and inhospitable warren of streets and alleys, was the West Belfast of Aden and the seat of resistance to the British army. Like their future counterparts along the Falls Road, its inhabitants perfected the techniques of rioting and the army its techniques of response. The most dramatic was the curfew, the most common was the deployment of the 'banner men'. When rioting became dangerous, the platoon commander would normally shout through a loudspeaker 'Banner men out!' and they would then march forward and unfurl their banner on which was written in Arabic the words 'Stop or we will open fire'. At that point, the rioters were supposed to disperse. If they didn't, the threat would be carried out. George, who later became a corporal in The Gloucestershire Regiment in West Belfast, knew the Aden drill well.

> If there was a riot situation, you used to have a hollow square with platoon headquarters in the middle and your riflemen on the corners. You'd advance towards the crowd and then stop and someone would go out in front of the crowd and put down a piece of white tape, maybe twenty feet away or whatever. Then you'd have an Arabic-speaking person who would shout out in Arabic, 'If you cross the white line, we will fire.' And that's what they did. Or they'd pick the ringleader out and say in Arabic and English, 'This is an unlawful assembly. Disperse or we'll open fire.' If they didn't, then the man in charge, the sergeant-major, would say, 'The man in the white turban, directly in the middle,' and we all knew who he was. 'Fire!' and someone would drop him. The boss had already told the guy he was going to do it. And that's what would happen. And then they'd all disappear.

'The man in the white turban', more colloquially known as 'the bugger in the red shirt', became part of army folk-lore. But the tactic did not always work out as planned. The Parachute Regiment thought better of it. When their predecessors, The Royal Anglians, tried it three weeks before the Paras arrived, they were hand-grenaded four times. In the early days in Belfast, the banner men came into their own again and during at least one riot unfurled their banner to find the order still written in Arabic.[13]

George knew that dealing with rioters and insurgents in a distant colony was very different from tackling sectarian violence in Northern Ireland. In Aden, George enjoyed a freedom he felt he was denied in Northern Ireland, not least because in the colony soldiers were not bound by the Yellow Card that came to be issued to every soldier in the province. It stipulated that lawfully they could only open fire if there was a threat to life, and that a warning must always be given unless doing so would increase the risk.[14]

> We weren't governed by the same rules that we were in Ireland. The lads over there could be a lot rougher, a lot harder because we never had the newspapers there and we never had the Press there or anyone else who could actually see what we were doing. It made a lot of difference because you were given a freer hand right across the board, from commanding officers right down to the corporals in charge of the men on the ground. You could just be a lot harder, a lot tougher and a lot more ruthless.

When George marched into a still-smouldering Belfast in August 1969, the last thing he expected was another Aden. Most soldiers saw their intervention in simple terms: to stop Catholics being burned out by Protestants. The reception they received was ecstatic. 'We were treated as saviours,' George said. 'There were tears and they were very thankful because we had stopped quite a lot of houses being burned, not all of them because we got there too late. The Protestants were baying at us and they weren't very pleased to start off with but when they realized that we were fair and firm to both sides, then it all settled down.' I asked George how long he thought he would be there for. 'I thought that was it. Clean the mess up, let people re-build their houses and get out. We thought it was a quick nip-in and nip-out job. We didn't realize we were going to be there for thirty-odd years.'

The 1st Battalion of the Parachute Regiment had been on standby for several weekends and finally went into Belfast in the small hours of Monday 13 October 1969. It was the first of the Regiment's many tours that were to be marked by controversy, the most contentious of which was 'Bloody Sunday'. In the years that followed, they supplied many of the recruits for the army's Special Forces, 14 Intelligence Company and the SAS, that were to play such a vital role in the intensifying conflict. 'Jim' was in the car on a Sunday afternoon driving back from East Anglia and listening to Alan Freeman and 'Top of the Pops' ('Je t'aime . . . moi non plus' by Jane Birkin and Serge Gainsbourg was number one) when he heard that his unit was being sent to Northern Ireland. The standby was over.

The soldiers knew a little more about the situation than they did before the army was deployed. 'It had been in the news,' 'Jim' told me. 'We knew there were operations going on over there. There were troubles and riots.' Jim's battalion took up positions along the Falls Road and received the same kind of hero's welcome from the nationalists that soldiers from other regiments had received when they marched into Belfast a few weeks earlier. By this time, 'Jim' and his mates had some idea of the geography of Belfast and did not have to buy their maps at filling stations. 'They were very glad to see us. We came as their saviours, as their protectors. They were clearly worried about what was going on and they welcomed us with open arms and with endless cups of tea and biscuits.' 'Jim' was stationed in an observation post (OP) on top of a building and therefore denied the luxury of 'scoff' back at the mess, but the locals ensured that he did not go hungry. 'Jim' and his mates used the same emergency plan that Brian and the Prince of Wales's Own had done atop Derry city walls. 'We had a basket with a piece of string attached to it and we used to lower it down with some money in it for the kids and they used to go off and get fish and chips. Then we'd haul the basket back up again and that's how we would eat for most of the time. They used to resupply us.' 'Jim' had no idea that many of the young boys who filled his basket and his stomach would be shooting at him in a few years' time.

The OP was located in the heart of the area that had seen some of the fiercest rioting and burning only a few short weeks before. 'This was the place where a police armoured car had gone up and down the road with machine-guns blazing. A young soldier on leave in fact had been killed right opposite the position I was in.[15] There were machine-gun bullets in the primary school. Opposite me there was a row of houses which had been burned down. Clearly, the place was in turmoil.' The more 'Jim' heard about the history of the Troubles, the more he realized, unlike George, that the army was not going to be home by Christmas.

By the time the Paras arrived, the Wilson Government had introduced a series of measures via Westminster and Stormont that it hoped would bring an end to what the Home Secretary, Jim Callaghan, referred to during a visit to the province as 'this nonsense in the streets'.[16] The local-government franchise that had disadvantaged nationalists was to be abolished, a Community Relations bill was introduced and a New Deal for Ulster was announced in a package that included aid for development, jobs and housing. Within less than a month of the deployment of British troops, most of the grievances that had fuelled the civil rights movement had been addressed. But it was too late to stuff the genie back in the bottle. Looking

back, the most glaring omission that Westminster made was not to abolish
or suspend the Stormont parliament and bring in Direct Rule from
Westminster. If any political excuse was needed, the deployment of the
army provided it. If Westminster was supplying troops because the Northern Ireland Government could not cope, why should it not go the whole
way and take over the Government itself? But that was not the way that the
Labour Cabinet was thinking. Callaghan believed in being realistic.

> You have to do things as they become politically possible. Not only
> would it have become politically impossible at that time to have
> abandoned Stormont because public opinion wouldn't have been
> ready for it, but we would not have been in a position to handle the
> situation. It was far better that the Northern Ireland Government
> should handle it themselves, provided they accepted the basic
> principles of human dignity, human liberty and civil rights, and they
> introduced the reforms that we wanted to see. It was much better
> than that the British should try to do it. I've always adhered to the
> view that it will be the people of Ireland themselves who will
> eventually solve the Irish Question, not Westminster and not
> Britain.[17]

Whitehall mandarins were of like mind, aware too of the potentially
seismic repercussions that acting against Stormont would provoke on the
unionist side. Ian Burns, who by the late 1980s had became one of the early
advocates of engaging the IRA in dialogue, had no doubt as a Private
Secretary at the Home Office in 1969 that such a radical step would have
been unwise.

> There was no intrinsic reason to believe that a government, properly
> authorized in Northern Ireland, could not deliver the proper agenda
> for change. I can't pretend to see into Ministers' minds as they were
> in 1969, but I'd be surprised if they didn't feel that the right thing to
> do was to get the duly elected government to change its policies and
> to deliver the changes. To sweep it out of the way and create a new
> machinery of government would have been an extra problem rather
> than a way of solving problems.

To unionists, the most controversial and wounding reforms the Labour
Government introduced were the disbanding of their beloved 'B' Specials
and a proposal to disarm the RUC so it could become an unarmed, civilian
police force like those throughout the rest of the United Kingdom. The
recommendations were made by committee under the chairmanship of

Lord Hunt, the conqueror of Everest. Reforming the RUC was an even bigger mountain to climb. He recognized the need to do so but in a way that would not jeopardize security. He admitted that 'although the threat of terrorist attack may not be great, the fear of them is very real, and public anxiety will not be allayed unless precautions are taken and seen to be taken'.[18]

The Westminster Government hoped that the 'B' Specials replacement would allay unionist anxieties. The force was to be known as the Ulster Defence Regiment (UDR), a locally recruited part-time force under the command of the British army. But far from calming these anxieties, the publication of the Hunt Report on Friday 19 October 1969 caused an unprecedented riot on the Protestant Shankill Road, fuelled by loyalists who saw the axing of the 'B' Specials as capitulation to nationalist demands. That evening crowds roamed the Shankill shouting 'Paisley is our leader' and jeering at the police. The following day, the process of disarming the RUC began, a visible sign to already angry loyalists that Hunt's recommendations were for real and Westminster was not bluffing. The Shankill erupted with loyalist crowds shouting at the soldiers who had been brought in to contain the disturbances, 'Englishmen, go home, you are not needed here. We want the "B" Specials.'[19] Few soldiers had any sympathy for the 'B' Men or shed any tears for their demise.

The loyalist mob tried to make its way to the Catholic Unity Flats, the notorious sectarian flashpoint at the bottom of the Shankill Road, but found the police and soldiers of The Light Infantry blocking their way. Major Keith, who regarded the 'B' Specials as 'thugs', had barely seen anything like it before. 'There were thousands and thousands of them and most of them had been at the Guinness or Bushmills, so they were in a right old fit state. By 11 o'clock that night, the noise and the numbers of them were absolutely terrifying.' Hundreds of petrol bombs lit up the night. Major Keith recorded that during the riot, as in peace-keeping operations in Aden and the former colonies, the opposition lost 'the man in the red shirt'. 'He actually existed and was wounded whilst in the act of throwing a petrol bomb,' he wrote.[20] In the increasingly violent confrontation, the loyalist Ulster Volunteer Force (UVF) brought out its guns and shot dead a 29-year-old policeman, Constable Victor Arbuckle, who was married with two children. He was the first RUC officer to be killed in current conflict, ironically shot dead by loyalists protesting at the disarming of the Royal Ulster Constabulary. No wonder outsiders were bemused.

That night, the army had its first taste of a gun battle in Belfast. Fourteen soldiers, three policemen and twenty civilians received gunshot wounds.[21] The so-called 'Battle of the Shankill' raged for almost two days and nights. According to Major Keith, his men stationed in the neighbouring Catholic

Ardoyne said that the Catholics cheered every time they heard shots, 'because they thought we were having a go at the Protestants'. In the fifty-two hours that Major Keith spent on the Shankill, he calculated that his men had fired 68 rounds of 7.62 mm ammunition, 394 CS gas cartridges and 52 smoke grenades. They, in turn, had been on the receiving end of 'a thousand rounds of assorted calibres, a couple of hundred petrol bombs and half the pavement of the Shankill!' He said he was not sorry to hand over to the 1st Battalion, The Parachute Regiment, so he and his men could return 'to our well-ordered areas and our beds'.[22] The Paras, who had just arrived, had the job of cleaning up.

A couple of days after the riot, Ardoyne Catholics invited Major Keith round to their illegal drinking den, made him an honorary member of their Shamrock Club and presented him with a large shillelagh as the Saviour of Ardoyne. When he arrived back for his next tour in Belfast in 1971, he thought he would pop into the Shamrock Club again to see how everyone was. 'I thought it would be rather nice to go back, say I was a life member, have a drink and see old friends.' But the Major got a reception he had not expected. 'I went back with an escort and we were quickly told by an old well-wisher that we were no longer welcome there and that one's life membership had been withdrawn. There were some very hard men in the pub and it was suggested that it would be probably better if we left.' The mood had changed and not just at the Shamrock Club. 'You could smell the atmosphere had changed completely. There was no chance of stopping on the corner for a cup of tea where you might get a bullet between the shoulder blades.' Soldiers were no longer saviours but, to many nationalists, the forces of an occupying army. The honeymoon was over.

Chapter Three

Divorce

December 1969–July 1970

The soldiers of the 1st Battalion, The Parachute Regiment who came into Belfast and swept up the embers of the Shankill riot had the same experience as Major Keith and his men. They remember being hailed as heroes by the Catholics after seemingly helping to put down the Protestants on the Shankill Road. To Catholics, the army was their saviour in August and their champion in October. Dave, a lance-corporal in the battalion, remembers arriving there 'not having a clue about Northern Ireland' and finding the Catholics so friendly. 'Everyone shook our hand and said, "Nice to see ya",' he told me. 'They'd come round to where we were staying and drop off a crate of beer and magazines and all kinds of stuff. I felt very good that I was doing something but not understanding what was going on.' Dave and his mate used to patrol the area alone, greeting everybody. There was never any sign of aggression or suggestion that they should not be there. A regular stop on their round was a little corner shop where they used to buy soft drinks and sweets and odds and ends. The shop was open all hours and, even when it was closed, they could knock on the door and the shopkeeper would open up and get whatever they wanted. 'He must have thought it was Christmas. We had nothing else to do, really. It was nice to feel appreciated.'

Dave started taking out a girl from the Falls Road whilst some of his mates dated girls from the Shankill. They all used to meet up, Catholic and Protestant girls with their soldier boyfriends, in discos. There was no hassle. The bitterness of the Shankill riot seemed to have been forgotten. Some soldiers married into Falls Road families whose sons later became prominent members of the IRA. It was quite acceptable in those days and there was no shame in a Catholic girl marrying a British soldier. The battalion left Belfast in February 1970 and Dave was sorry to go. 'The girls were sad and the people we'd met were sad too. In those few months, we'd become good friends. I think the crime rate actually went down because we were on the streets. It was a sad day. I was really looking forward to going back again.' One of Dave's mates graphically echoed his feelings.

> It was a day of great sadness. I was leaving friends, people we knew. Leaving the girls behind was probably the saddest thing of all. They all lined up to wave goodbye. It was like the Wailing Wall of Jerusalem. I remember a hit at the time – 'Leaving on a Jet Plane'. You know, the lines about 'packing my bags and hating to go and don't know when I'll be back again'. We were singing our heads off and the girls were waving and throwing their knickers at us. God bless 'em! And they were all shouting 'We'll wait for you!'[1]

When Dave returned for his second tour in September 1970, he went back to the corner shop to say hello to the shopkeeper and his wife and got the same shock as Major Keith did when he ventured back to the Shamrock Club. 'They didn't want to know us. They were scared that we went into their shop. They tried to be polite but basically we were shunned at the door. I felt disappointed and hurt.' Dave tried again and called in on an old lady who used to provide him and his mate with sausages and bacon every morning between half five and six. 'When we went back to see her, she opened the door, looked at us and you could see there was something wrong. She didn't want to know us. She told us to go away. We weren't what we were to her any more.' Dave's mates in the 1st Battalion, The Parachute Regiment had similar experiences when they returned for their second tour from September 1970 until May 1972. Old friends were friends no more. Mick, who had been treated like a son by a lady who gave him and his men the key to her house for rest and refreshments, was shocked when he saw her again during a riot. 'There she was amidst the whistles and spitting and the dustbin lids! I don't know whether she was a combatant or a rioter or whether she was there just to be seen going along with the crowd. That's what I'd like to believe anyway. I want to remember her as I knew her because she was such a good woman.'

The reasons for the turnaround are complex and the result of forces over which few had any control. Although the arrival of the army did calm the situation and at one stage soldiers really did have reason to think they might be home by Christmas, the sectarian tensions that had led to the deployment of the army still burned hot beneath the surface. After the bloody confrontations in the frontline areas of Belfast and Derry in August 1969, the hatred both communities felt for each other intensified. The re-emergence of the IRA simply added to the potent mixture. Had one of the great 'what ifs' of history happened, with Westminster introducing Direct Rule and assuming total responsibility for security, the situation might have been contained and the thirty-year 'war' might never have got off the ground. The problem was that although the General Officer Commanding Northern Ireland (GOC), General Sir Ian Freeland, was nominally in charge of the army, it was deployed to carry out the wishes of the Stormont Government. The unionist Government continued to pursue its own law and order agenda that consisted of trying to nip the emerging IRA in the bud and cracking down hard on the community from which it came. The result was disaster.

After the so-called 'pogrom' in Belfast in August 1969, the graffiti 'IRA – I Ran Away' had appeared on walls and the seeds were sown for the split in the organization out of which the Provisional IRA, the 'Provos', were born. The veteran republican Joe Cahill had resigned from the IRA in 1964 in protest against its Marxist direction but reported back following the 'pogrom'. He was given a hard time when he tried to organize a defence group in Belfast's nationalist Ballymurphy estate. 'I was told to get out,' he told me. 'I wasn't wanted. I was a member of the IRA. The IRA had deserted them.'

Historically, the group of dissidents or IRA traditionalists like Joe Cahill became the nucleus of what evolved into the Provisional IRA. Gradually they won over the doubters like the Ardoyne's Martin Meehan who had joined the IRA a couple of years before and described the experience of being sworn in as 'like joining the priesthood'.[2] At the time the Provisionals were being formed, there was no master plan to drive the 'Brits' out of the North. The grouping came together primarily with the object of making sure that if loyalists were to attack the nationalist areas of Belfast again, the IRA would be ready, trained and equipped to defend them. Nevertheless, given the historical credentials of Cahill and the veterans of the IRA's last border campaign, the prospect of getting rid of the 'Brits' and fulfilling Patrick Pearse's dream of 1916 was always a gleam in their eye. Billy McKee, who, along with Cahill, was another founder of the 'Provos', told Martin Meehan as much when he tried to persuade him to come over to the dissidents' side. 'McKee outlined what his plans were,' Meehan told me. 'He guaranteed first and foremost that the nationalist areas would be defended at all costs and that what happened in August 1969 would never happen again. He didn't indicate that there was going to be an immediate offensive against the British army. He said, "These things take time. People have to be trained. People have to be motivated. People have to be equipped. All this won't just happen overnight." But the intention was there and it sounded good to me.'[3] Meehan promptly switched sides.

It was only a matter of time before the divisions in the Republican Movement – the IRA and Sinn Fein – were formalized. The IRA split at an Extraordinary Army Convention secretly held at an isolated country village in the middle of Ireland on 28 December 1969. The pivotal figure at the Convention was Seán MacStiofáin, a prominent Southerner who had previously supported the Marxist faction under Cathal Goulding. (MacStiofáin, like many IRA veterans, had spent most of the 1950s in gaol but in his case in England in Pentonville prison. Goulding was locked up with him too after both men were sentenced following an abortive raid in 1953 on the armoury of Felsted public school in Essex. Ironically, he was actually born in England of an Irish mother and his real name was John Stevenson, a fact he did not care to be reminded about. His background probably made him an even more fervent Irish republican.) The acute differences and tensions within the IRA pained MacStiofáin and it is said that he broke down and cried at the December Convention at the prospect of a formalized split. Ostensibly the rift was ideological because Goulding and the Marxist faction wanted to change the IRA's constitution so that it would recognize the Dublin parliament, Dail Eireann, and authorize Sinn Fein to contest elections in the South and, if elected, take up its seats. To the traditionalists, such a fundamental theological departure was anathema since Dail Eireann recognized partition. But there was another underlying and even more emotional reason for the split. The IRA in Belfast had been humiliated during the loyalist 'pogrom' of August 1969 when it left the nationalist enclaves undefended because Goulding and the Marxists had abandoned their guns. The traditionalists did not want that to happen again. MacStiofáin agreed with this viewpoint and said so. He left the venue and, sustaining himself with cold chicken, drove straight to Belfast to address the dissidents who had refused to attend the Convention. He knew that he could count on the support of the majority of the IRA units in the city. Having listened to MacStiofáin, the dissidents then set up their own Army Convention and 'Provisional' military structures. The Convention elected an Army Executive which in turn selected an Army Council with Macstiofáin as Chief of Staff.[4] Thus the Provisional IRA (PIRA) was born.

A fortnight later, on 11 January 1970, Sinn Fein also split at its conference held at Dublin's Intercontinental Hotel. The political split was formalized after Seán MacStiofáin went to the microphone and announced that he was giving his allegiance to the 'Provisional' IRA Army Council. In the outcry that followed, the President of Sinn Fein, Ruairi O'Bradaigh, recognizing that the dissident faction (which he supported) would not be able to win the necessary two-thirds majority to carry the day, jumped up and said it was time to leave. 'We had to fight our way out,' he told me. 'It was all very, very tense and very highly charged. So we made our way to another venue and elected a caretaker Sinn Fein Executive to carry on and reorganize the country.'[5] The historic split in the Republican Movement was now complete with two opposing factions of the IRA and Sinn Fein, the 'Provisionals' and the 'Officials' (the name given to those who remained loyal to Cathal Goulding and the existing IRA leadership).

Few 'Brits' had any idea of what was going on in the dark corners of the IRA as rival republicans struggled for supremacy. Nor, perhaps, would it have been of any great concern, as the IRA was not then deemed to be a problem. British politicians and civil servants were far more concerned to ensure that the promised reforms were being implemented by the Stormont Government. To this end, the Wilson Government appointed a United Kingdom Representative whose job it was to see that the reform programme was carried out and to ensure that there was no backsliding. His office was just down the corridor from the Northern Ireland Prime Minister's office at Stormont. Its first occupant was Oliver Wright, who had previously been Harold Wilson's Private Secretary. He took up residence on 26 August 1969 having just returned from being Ambassador to Denmark. Wright, famous for his vivid turn of phrase, was surprised when he got the call. 'I was on leave having just got back and I was up a ladder with a bucket of Flash wiping the orgies of my tenants off the walls when the Foreign Office telephoned and said, "We want you to go to Northern Ireland." I said, "How long for?" They said, "Oh, two or three months. You should be home by Christmas." ' Wright laughed. He knew he would not have an easy ride and feared that Britain's commitment might be open-ended. 'Basically, my job was to superintend the redressal of grievances. I had to draw up a list and then tick them off. I reckoned that we were doing all right. I may be totally misguided, of course. I'm an Englishman and how can an Englishman be expected to understand Ireland? But we were making progress. I'm quite sure that as time went on, the Catholic community saw the British Government as their friend, trying its best to ensure that Stormont introduced the reforms that they, the Catholic community, wanted. And we did.'[6]

Oliver Wright was thrown in at the deep end. The day after he arrived, he found himself escorting the Home Secretary, Jim Callaghan, on a whirlwind tour of the trouble spots. As a former Foreign Office diplomat, Wright was used to officials pressing words and ideas on the Foreign Secretary who listened sagely and then decided what to do. Life with Jim Callaghan at the Home Office was different. At Wright's first office meeting, everyone sat around in silence waiting for the Home Secretary to speak. 'The Home Secretary may have had an idea in the back of his mind, in which case he was keeping it to himself. He didn't speak until he arrived at Aldergrove airport. I had done a sort of John the Baptist for him, preparing the way. I went to meet him and the whole world's television cameras were waiting. I don't know if he knew in advance what he was going to say but if anybody had a politician's instinct, it was Mr Callaghan. He suddenly said, "I haven't come here with a solution to your problems. I have come here to help you find solutions to your problems."' There was a great gasp from everybody. "Oh, the man's a genius!" Suddenly Jim Callaghan was enormously popular. Wright took him on a tour of the Falls and Shankill. 'The people of the Falls were pressing cups of tea on everyone. They were touching the hem of his garment, so grateful were they that the British army had put themselves between them and the majority community. He was the Messiah at that time.'

Callaghan went on to visit Derry the following day accompanied by Ian Burns from the Home Secretary's private office. Burns had gone ahead as Callaghan's advance man to make sure that the Home Secretary's safety was assured 'since his car had been trampled over by an overweight Paddy Devlin [a famous nationalist politician]' during his tour of the Falls. Similar brushes with politicians – overweight or not – and their over-enthusiastic supporters had to be avoided. Burns met the young John Hume who assured him that there would be no trouble and that his master would be well looked after and welcomed. Callaghan, who had to be seen to be even-handed, also visited the unionist areas of the city where Burns remembers he was received 'loyally and respectfully'. But the scenes in the Bogside were unrestrained. 'It was an eye-opening experience,' Burns recalls. 'It was a wild, enthusiastic reception. It's the sort of thing that one had only seen before with the Beatles and I had never experienced anything like this before at first hand.' The crowd was shouting 'Let me touch him!' and 'Help us, Jim!' and so great was the crush and so powerful the emotion that the Home Secretary had to seek refuge in a Bogside terrace house.[7] Callaghan, ever the great populist and presser of the flesh, was in his element and suddenly appeared at the upstairs window to address the crowd. His message was the same: the British Government does not have a solution to your problems but will help you find one. It was more than enough for the crowd who cheered him on. Callaghan promised to return to Northern Ireland and did so six weeks later to keep up the pressure on Stormont in carrying out its reform programme and to assure both communities that the Government was determined to ensure fair play.

By the time of Callaghan's second visit in October 1969, the army had built what became ironically known as 'the peace line' along the sectarian interface between the Shankill and the Falls. Its purpose was to keep the two sides apart and prevent the incursions that had led to the violent clashes the previous August. The army's strategy was for the peace line to go up and the barricades that had sprung up to come down. It was erected like an Irish Berlin Wall but not all the barricades were dismantled since nationalists argued that they needed them for their own protection. Few 'Brits' knew that behind them the Provisional IRA was beginning to organize, often under the guise of Citizens' Defence Committees, many of which simply became an IRA front. At the time there was nothing surprising or contradictory in that since defence was the Provisionals' prime purpose. Certainly at the time the army did not regard the IRA as an enemy but more as an ally in defending nationalists from loyalist attack. In the months ahead, in the still relatively relaxed atmosphere, communication gradually developed between army officers and IRA leaders on the other side of the barricades. To the IRA at that time, loyalists were the enemy, not British soldiers. Dialogue was also a good way of gathering intelligence which later paid off. By February 1970, three of the eight extra army units that had been deployed to deal with the emergency were withdrawn and sent home. The 'Brits' may have thought it was all over but it was only just beginning.

Behind the barricades, the IRA was preparing not to drive out the British but to defend the nationalist population as the 1970 Protestant marching season approached. Parades by the Orange Order and the Apprentice Boys of Derry, as recent history had all too clearly shown, were the traditional recipe for sectarian confrontation. Loyalists saw marches as an assertion of their history and identity. Catholics found them triumphalist and deeply offensive since most celebrated Protestant victories over their Catholic enemies. Each parade had its traditional route, hallowed over the years, and any attempt to change it provoked vigorous protest from the loyalists who insisted that they had the right to march the Queen's Highway without hindrance. Any deviation ordered by the authorities was seen as capitulation to Catholics. Many of these routes passed close by or actually through nationalist areas and the refusal to accept re-routing could readily cloak the desire to cause maximum offence to their enemies. The exchange of missiles and sectarian abuse became a dangerous part of the ritual as nationalist crowds refused to be humiliated and deafened by the warlike thunder of Lambeg drums.[8] In such confrontations, both sides were fuelled by sectarian hatreds that had become even more implacable in the wake of August 1969. No amount of mollification by British politicians and the British army could make them go away. The 'Brits' became prisoners of the problem that they had created by plantation and partition. Marching dragged the army in.

The first confrontations came in Easter week 1970 and they came on both sides. In Derry on Sunday 29 March, following the annual Commemoration of the 1916 Easter Rising, a crowd attacked RUC headquarters in the city centre and tried to storm its gates. The army may not have been the enemy but to most of the 5,000 nationalists who marched that day, the RUC most certainly was. Twelve soldiers were injured in the clashes and the army sealed off the Bogside when rioting broke out. On Easter Monday, there were clashes when loyalists attacked a republican parade in Armagh that had been under the surveillance of 600 troops and 500 police.

Easter Tuesday, however, was the real turning point. It was traditionally one group of junior Orangemen's big day out at the seaside at Bangor, a day that began early in the morning on their home turf of the loyalist New Barnsley estate that stands at the top of the Springfield Road opposite republican Ballymurphy. Ballymurphy's residents did not welcome having their morning disturbed by the sound of the young Orangemen's flutes and drums playing what Catholics regarded as offensive sectarian tunes, especially as loyalists had attacked the republican parade in Armagh the day before. It did not need a prophet to foretell trouble when the juniors returned home that evening.

As a precaution, the army deployed seventy Scots Guards to the Ballymurphy estate in anticipation of trouble. They were not sure what to do in the event of a riot other than keep the two sides apart. Sure enough the Ballymurphy residents were waiting to welcome the young Orangemen home with a barrage of bricks and bottles hurled from behind the line the Scots Guards had formed. A full-scale riot ensued that lasted for two hours with confused soldiers standing in the middle. The following day the army, probably with Stormont's encouragement, decided on a show of force in the expectation that the Protestants of New Barnsley and the Catholics of Ballymurphy would pick up where they had left off the previous evening. A full battalion was deployed to Ballymurphy to show that this time the army meant business and would not tolerate such behaviour. The troops arrived with a squadron of four-wheeled Humber one-ton armoured cars with barbed-wire coils on their bumpers. Each soldier carried an SLR (self-loading rifle), riot shield and short, stubby Greener gun that fired CS gas grenades.[9] They must have been a formidable and unaccustomed sight to the tightly knit community of Ballymurphy, accustomed to seeing the army as their friend. Furthermore, the decision to deploy Scottish soldiers, many of whom would have had natural Protestant sympathies, was bound to antagonize the Catholic residents who would see them as the protectors of the 'Orangies' of New Barnsley on the other side of the Springfield Road.

That evening, the residents of Ballymurphy redirected their missiles and animosities from their old enemy to the new. The British army was now the target. The troops, under orders to take no nonsense, did not stand there offering themselves as targets and doing nothing. When baton charges failed to scatter the increasingly fired-up crowd now armed with petrol bombs, the soldiers fired canisters of CS gas into its midst. If anything was designed to weld a crowd into one it was being drowned in a cloud of throat-choking, stomach-wrenching, eye-watering gas. The rioting continued for a second night, with the Catholic crowd now radicalized and united. As the army pushed it back into the estate, loyalists followed the soldiers, tearing down an Irish Tricolour and confirming the rioters' conviction that the army was on the Protestant side. Significantly, the newly formed Provisional IRA did not come out to take on the army and defend its people because it was not ready.

In the two nights of intense fighting, thirty-eight soldiers were injured. The following day at a press conference, the army's GOC, General Sir Ian Freeland, announced a new, 'get tough' military policy, warning that petrol bombers 'are liable to be shot dead in the street if, after a warning, they persist'.[10] Jim Callaghan's response to the controversy that followed was simple: 'Don't go out with a petrol bomb.'[11]

In the wake of the rioting, several Protestant families left the New Barnsley estate and sought refuge in Protestant strongholds elsewhere in the city away from the sectarian interface of the upper Springfield Road. It was the beginning of a huge shift in population that was said to be the biggest displacement of peoples since the end of the Second World War, defining ever more sharply the sectarian divisions of the city. Areas in which Catholics and Protestants lived together were to become a thing of the past. Territory was everything and many of the confrontations in the years ahead revolved around the holding or seizing of it. The Ballymurphy riots of Easter 1970 could be described as the starting point of the 'war'. The Provisional IRA now had an enemy and the beginning of support from sections of the nationalist community for driving the 'Brits' from Northern Ireland.

The Provisionals may not have been ready at Easter when the sounds of Protestant flutes and drums began, but they were by the end of June when the serious Orange marching began. By this time there had been a British general election on 18 June 1970 which the Conservatives had won. In the Northern Ireland constituencies, Ian Paisley and Bernadette Devlin had both been elected to Westminster; in Ms Devlin's case, re-elected after her victory in the Mid-Ulster by-election in April the previous year. Edward Heath entered Downing Street as Harold Wilson left. Wilson, having largely ignored Northern Ireland through most of the sixties, had been forced to react to events to halt the slide into anarchy triggered by the force of history and his own Government's neglect. By the time he acted, the moment had passed. Heath's Cabinet inherited a problem that it too did not know how to solve. The Conservative Defence Minister, Lord Carrington, told me several years later that he was new in office when the subsequent crisis hit him and did not know a great deal about Northern Ireland. On the face of it, it seemed simply a problem of law and order. If that could be restored, the Government probably reasoned, the reform programme would have the desired effect and in time the situation would settle down, although Ministers were not naïve enough to believe that Catholics and Protestants would live together happily ever after.

The new Government's learning curve was steep. A week after Heath's victory, there was an ominous warning in Derry that the IRA was gearing up for a new campaign. On 26 June, three middle-aged IRA men who were leading republicans in the city, Thomas McCool, Joseph Coyle and Thomas Carlin, died in a premature explosion whilst making up a bomb in a council house on the nationalist Creggan estate. McCool's two daughters, aged nine and four, were upstairs in bed and died in the subsequent blaze.[12] In Belfast the IRA were getting ready too, now with guns, many of them retrieved from dumps where they had been left after previous campaigns, in particular south of the border. At that time, the word 'decommissioning' had never been heard.

Saturday 27 June 1970 was the day when the Provisional IRA first went into action 'in defence' of their community. Tension had already been building as it was the first big day of the serious Protestant marching season that begins with a series of parades that are warm-ups for the grand finale in Belfast on 12 July. That morning the city echoed to the sound of loyalist bands as Orange Lodges all over the city got ready for the parade. The main march was scheduled to go from the assembly point on the Shankill onto the Springfield Road – where the army had taken on the Ballymurphy rioters that Easter – and past the Clonard area and the charred ruins of Bombay Street burned out by loyalists in 1969. The route was bound to stoke the tension, skirting as it did the scene of the loyalist 'pogrom' the previous summer, but neither Chichester-Clark nor the new Conservative Government was minded to ban or re-direct the parade. For Chichester-Clark to have done so would have undermined his position, and for the Government to have overruled him would have meant destabilizing Chichester-Clark. The last thing Edward Heath wanted was to see his Northern Ireland Prime Minister toppled at this delicate moment. Heath had only been in office a week and losing a Prime Minister would not have been a very good start. The new Home Secretary, Reginald Maudling, who found it tiresome to deal with such implacable enemies, chose the lesser of two evils and did not intervene.

As a result 5,000 Orangemen marched past the Clonard with an unsurprising result. Nationalists broke up lumps of road metal from a nearby building site and hurled them at the Orangemen who, like the band of the *Titanic*, played on.[13] The rioting quickly spread to Ballymurphy further up the Springfield Road and the army fired CS gas canisters into the estate as it had done before. Later that afternoon, another Orange parade sparked even greater violence as it marched down the Crumlin Road, the interface between the Shankill and Ardoyne, and past the burned-out houses in Hooker Street that had been torched by loyalist mobs the previous August. Missiles were exchanged between the two opposing crowds but now for the first time the Provisional IRA brought out its guns. Three Protestants were shot dead, Alexander Gould (18), William Kincaid (28) and Daniel Loughlins (32). Martin Meehan, by now a senior Provisional IRA leader in Ardoyne at the time, claimed that the loyalists fired first. 'The IRA had proved beyond a shadow of a doubt what they said they were going to do [defend the people], they had done it,' he told me. 'As a result, the whole broad spectrum of the nationalist people actually supported what the IRA was doing. Every man, woman and child came out and supported us in any way possible. I never saw support like it in my life. It was unbelievable.'[14]

Even allowing for Meehan's hyberbole, there is no doubt that that day marked a turning point for the fledgling Provisional IRA, and not just in Ardoyne. Later that evening, the IRA went into action again across the River Lagan in the Protestant stronghold of East Belfast in defence of the 6,000 nationalists who lived in the small nationalist enclave of Short Strand surrounded by 60,000 loyalists. Again, the circumstances in which a gun battle arose are disputed. It is said that tempers rose when a Tricolour was flown as an Orange band returned home along the Newtownards Road, the spine of loyalist East Belfast, dominated by the great cranes of the Harland and Wolff shipyard. Nationalists say loyalists then attacked them and loyalists say it was the other way round. The outcome is not in dispute. St Matthew's Roman Catholic Church that stands on the edge of Short Strand and the Newtownards Road became the focus of the battle as it came under loyalist petrol bomb attack. Billy McKee and a handful of Provisionals from West Belfast crossed the Lagan river to join local auxiliaries in defending their people and their church. The army had sent a token force across to try to stop the fighting but did not have the resources to deploy enough troops as by now there was rioting all over Belfast and the army was stretched to the limit. The GOC, General Sir Ian Freeland, dispatched a platoon to Short Strand but it is said it was prevented from getting down the Newtownards Road by a loyalist mob.[15]

For whatever reason, the soldiers did not or were not able to intervene, once again fuelling Catholics' perception that the army was on the Protestants' side. The shooting around the church lasted for five hours and, according to McKee, the Provisionals fired 800 rounds. McKee said he knew because the IRA quartermaster subsequently told him.[16] McKee was badly wounded and one of the local auxiliaries, Henry McIlhone, was shot dead. 'All I heard was a clump, like a wet log hitting the ground,' McKee told me. 'It was like a big tree falling. I knew he was hit when he went down. He never said a word. He was hit in the throat. He was taken to hospital but he died that night.'[17] The Provisionals killed two Protestants, Robert Neill (38) and Robert McCurrie (34). 'It was the Provisionals' first battle,' said McKee. The defence of St Matthew's became an IRA legend and Billy McKee a folk hero. Now, the Provisionals claimed, when loyalists attacked nationalist areas, the IRA were there to defend them and they had five notches on their guns to prove it.

The cost of that weekend was high. Six people were dead, five of them killed by the IRA. It was the worst weekend of violence that Belfast had seen. The city had seemed to be in flames with the fire services, called to more than a hundred blazes, as over-stretched as the army. With a scorecard that said IRA five, loyalists one, it was not surprising that Protestant blood was up, with unionists demanding to know why the army had not been able to cope. The province's Security Committee, whose core was the GOC, the Chief Constable, Stormont Ministers and the UK Representative, met on the Monday morning to survey the wreckage. They agreed on one thing: Northern Ireland was back to Square One. Ronald Burroughs, the UK Representative who had succeeded Oliver Wright and who had tried in vain to persuade Reginald Maudling to re-route the main march away from the highly sensitive Catholic areas, described the Home Secretary's inaction as 'the greatest single mistake I have ever seen'.[18]

The following day, Maudling paid his first visit to the province for meetings with the province's Security Committee, Chichester-Clark's Cabinet, nationalist political leaders, churchmen and trade unionists. The army was not impressed. One officer at its Lisburn headquarters described Maudling's response to what he had seen and heard. 'He sat in my office with his head in his hands and said, "Oh, these bloody people! How are you going to deal with them?" "Well," I said, "Home Secretary, we are not going to deal with them. It's you – your lot who have to deal with them. We have got to have a policy." But we never did have a policy. That was the problem.'[19] Maudling returned to the security and certainty of home the following day. His despair was clear on the flight back. 'For God's sake, bring me a large Scotch,' he is reported to have said. 'What a bloody awful country.'[20]

To unionists, the weekend had been a disaster because the army had not been tough enough. The Provisional IRA had flexed its muscles, killed five Protestants, and got away with it. At St Matthew's Church, the unionist nightmare had come true and there had been no 'B' Specials to banish it.

The pressure on Chichester-Clark from the right-wingers in his Cabinet was intense. Although the army was under the control of the GOC, constitutionally it was there in support of the civil power and therefore could be used at the civil power's request. So far the army had simply reacted to events. Now Stormont wanted it to take the initiative and show that it meant business. Lawlessness and the IRA would not be tolerated. A show of force was needed and at the earliest opportunity. The policy was endorsed by the newly elected Conservative Government.

The opportunity for a show of strength came sooner than most had anticipated. As the following weekend approached, Maudling told the Westminster parliament, to cheers from both sides of the House, that the rule of law and not the rule of the gun would be maintained.[21] He gave that assurance on Friday 3 July 1970. A few hours later an arms find in the Lower Falls Road set in motion a chain of events that was to drive many Catholics in the nationalist heartlands of Belfast into the waiting arms of both the Provisional and Official IRA.

Around tea-time soldiers of the Royal Scots sealed off Balkan Street following a tip-off that there were arms in one of the houses. They found half a dozen pistols, an old German Schmeisser sub-machine gun and some explosives and ammunition. An angry crowd gathered, and as soldiers tried to withdraw and get back into their armoured personnel carriers, one of them reversed into 36-year-old Charles O'Neill and killed him. It was subsequently referred to by an army officer as 'a traffic accident'.[22] O'Neill had once served with the RAF. Local reports said he had been trying to warn the army that the area was hostile and it would not be wise to go further.[23] A riot began and, when the Royal Scots feared their retreat was being cut off, reinforcements were sent in to rescue them. In turn the rescuers too became besieged and fired CS gas to clear the way. As evidenced in the recent Ballymurphy riots, CS affected far more people than those against whom it was directed, floating into houses in the warren of narrow terraced streets that was the Lower Falls. Barely an hour after the arms find in Balkan Street, a full-scale confrontation developed with the crowds hurling petrol bombs and nail bombs at the confused and surrounded soldiers. More reinforcements were sent in to rescue the rescuers and chaos was the end result. The Official IRA, whose fiefdom was in the Lower Falls, saw this as an invasion and opened fire against the soldiers, some of whom had just got off the ferry from Liverpool.[24] The Provisionals, not to be outgunned or outflanked by their rivals, also joined in. The army was going to get tough and provide the show of force unionists had been demanding since the humiliations of the previous weekend. This time there was to be no repetition of the fiasco of St Matthew's Church.

The army returned fire and in the gun battles that followed shot dead four civilians, none of whom was a member of the IRA. Eighteen soldiers were wounded, thirteen from gunshot wounds and five from grenade splinters.[25]

To restore order out of the chaos, General Freeland now employed the military tactic used in Aden to control the recalcitrant residents of the Crater district: the curfew. Three thousand soldiers were sent in to impose it over a wide area of the Falls. The curfew began just after 10 p.m. on Friday evening and was not lifted until 9 a.m. on Sunday morning. For almost thirty-five hours, residents were confined to their houses, except for a couple of hours around Saturday tea-time when the curfew was lifted so people could buy basic necessities. With the streets clear, the army used the opportunity to conduct house-to-house searches. Television pictures of the time show the damage that was done as rooms were taken apart in the search for arms. Around sixty houses were believed to have been affected by the soldiers' unbridled enthusiasm in rooting out weapons.[26] Marie Moore, who later became a prominent Sinn Fein figure, told me what she saw in the aftermath of the army's searches.

> Some of the houses I had seen were totally wrecked. Holy statues were smashed on the floor. Family portraits and pictures were smashed. Furniture was ripped and overturned. Windows were broken and doors off the hinges. Some of the people who'd been beaten were still lying there, bloody and bruised.[27]

There is no reason to believe that the account is unduly exaggerated.

When the curfew was lifted, an army of women marched into the area, pushing prams loaded with bread, milk and other essential supplies. Marie Moore was one of them. According to republican legend, they returned with the prams full of the arms belonging to the Official IRA that the army had not uncovered. Gerry Adams says they ended up in the hands of the 'Provos'.[28]

From the military point of view, however, the curfew and the search were successful, producing a not inconsiderable haul of 100 firearms, 100 home-made bombs, 250 lbs of explosives and 21,000 rounds of ammunition. Stormont and unionist politicians were delighted: the army had got to grips with the IRA, clipped its wings and taught its community a lesson. To add insult to injury, two members of the Stormont cabinet were given a conducted tour of the subjugated Falls by the army.[29] One soldier, clearly out of step with the prevailing military view, told me it was like 'the British Raj on a tiger hunt'. Such a triumphalist display might not have seemed out of place in Crater but was insensitively inappropriate in part of the United Kingdom. The damage was done and was never repaired. The previous Sunday, one young officer, 'Jonathan', had marched his men, unarmed, to a church service on the Falls Road. He could never do it again. He looked back on the curfew with sadness and regret. 'It was absolutely clear that this was a turning point,' he said. 'It was felt at the time, militarily, that the best way to prevent any further bloodshed was to seal the place off, search the place thoroughly, remove all the weapons and ammunition and then get back to normal living.'[30] But it was not to be. The divorce between the army and the section of the nationalist community it had come in to protect was complete. Unwittingly the 'Brits' had handed the IRA an issue that it could exploit to justify its actions against soldiers no longer depicted as saviours but as the 'forces of occupation'. Bullets and bombs replaced tea and cakes.

Chapter Four

To the Brink

September 1970–March 1971

By the summer of 1970, the Provisional IRA had no doubt that things were going its way. The tougher the army got, the more recruits it gained. Before taking the oath, each one had been made fully aware of the possible consequences of being sworn in – gaol or death. They were known as 'Volunteers' because that is what they were. There was never any pressure to join and all those who offered their services were carefully vetted. But as yet, following the split at the turn of the year, the Provisionals did not regard themselves as being on a proper constitutional footing. The organization had been set up on an *ad hoc* basis following the bitter internal divisions that had prompted the traditionalists to part company with the Marxists. However bizarre it may seem to outsiders accustomed to dismiss the IRA as a murderous bunch of cowboys, the organization has a disciplined structure with a fastidious regard for its own constitutional proprieties. Now the Provisionals, so called because they were only intended to be temporary, had to formalize their existence by calling a new Army Convention in which representatives from all over the country would elect and give their allegiance to a new Army Executive and Army Council. The Convention took place in September 1970 when delegates repudiated the claim of the 'Officials' to be the true heirs of the men of 1916. Seán MacStiofáin was now officially confirmed as the Provisional IRA's Chief of Staff. Technically, they were no longer the 'Provisionals', although the name and the nickname, the 'Provos', stuck. More than thirty years later, the security forces, with their fondness for acronyms, still refer to them as PIRA, the Provisional IRA. The new Army Council then issued its first statement, setting out its policy objectives.

The Convention decided to continue and intensify the provision of defensive measures for the people of the Six Counties. It re-affirmed that British rule is not acceptable in Ireland under any circumstances and that every effort must be made to bring about its downfall.[1]

The following month, on 25 October 1970, Provisional Sinn Fein held its own special conference and brought itself into line with its military wing. The caretaker Executive went out of office and a new one was duly elected with Ruairi O'Bradaigh as its President. The Provisional IRA and Provisional Sinn Fein were now officially in business and ready to take on the 'Brits'.

The Provisional IRA's statement coincided with the arrival in the province of the soldier who was to become top of republicans' hate list, the 'Brit' they saw as the architect of the 'dirty tricks' that they believe have always been used against them. His name was Brigadier Frank Kitson of the Royal Green Jackets, the guru of British counter-insurgency policy who is still demonized today. As ever, the reality does not bear out the myth. When he set foot in the province, he already had considerable experience of counter-insurgency operations. In the 1950s he had fought Mau Mau gangs in Kenya, Communist insurgents in Malaya, and had been involved as a staff officer in planning an operation against rebel tribesmen in Oman; in the 1960s he had taken part in two peace-keeping operations on the strife-torn island of Cyprus where he experienced the communal tensions of a divided community at first hand; and in 1969, as Belfast blazed, he was on sabbatical at University College, Oxford, writing his seminal thesis on counter-insurgency and peace-keeping. Two years later, whilst Kitson was still serving in Northern Ireland, it was published as a book, *Low Intensity Operations*, which became required reading for all IRA strategists.

Kitson's philosophy for countering insurgents was based on two cardinal principles: the need to acquire, analyse and act on intelligence and to win the support of the people on whom the enemy relies. To his superiors, his appointment in September 1970 as commander of the army's 39 Brigade that covers the Belfast area seemed to be a perfect match of the man and the moment. A week before Kitson arrived to take over command, he visited the province to look at a house and is said to have been surprised to learn that the GOC and the Chief Constable were talking of getting the army out by Christmas. The Chief Constable was Sir Arthur Young, the former City of London Police Commissioner, whom Jim Callaghan had appointed in the wake of the Hunt Report to restore confidence in the RUC. Unionists, unhappy at his measured approach, dubbed him 'Mr Softly, Softly' after a famous television series. Sir Arthur, like Kitson, had fought terrorists in Malaya. However much Kitson may have had his head down at Oxford, he would have known that the situation was getting worse not better and that the notion that the soldiers would soon be going home was not only totally unrealistic but ludicrous. Nor, judging by what he had written in his thesis, would he have approved of the methods the army had been using to try to restore order. Flooding areas with CS gas which affected everyone from a baby to a granny was not Kitson's way of going about things. It was not the best way of winning 'hearts and minds'. Nor did he believe that it was effective as it did not stop the rioting which often put a third of a platoon out of action.

Although when Kitson first arrived, the problem was primarily one of civil disorder, it soon became clear that it might escalate way beyond stones and bottles. The names 'Provisional' and 'Official' IRA were recognized by Kitson and his battalion commanders but they knew them better as the 'Brádaigh group' and the 'Goulding group', the former associated with Frank Card and the latter with Jim Sullivan. But neither 'group' was deemed to constitute any serious threat at this stage and Kitson encouraged his local army commanders to maintain contact with both of them, discussing day-to-day problems like children throwing stones. Kitson himself met Sullivan in his capacity as a member of the Belfast Central Citizens' Defence Committee whereas in fact he was also the Official IRA's adjutant in Belfast. Such dialogue was also a useful means of gathering intelligence and weighing up the calibre and intent of those who held sway within their communities. Kitson had no illusion as to who they were but was not yet thinking of the IRA as an insurgent organization although he undoubtedly saw its potential to become one unless measures were put in place to stop it. Hindsight suggests that the Provisional IRA's statement of September 1970 about bringing about 'the downfall of British rule' should have been seen as an ominous warning but, at the time, military intelligence officers probably thought it was little more that bravado. The IRA may have killed five Protestants in one weekend in June but it had not yet turned its guns against the British army. Nor was there any indication that it was about to do so whatever its private intentions were. The army was still fairly relaxed about the IRA although the days were over when soldiers drinking in Falls Road pubs would find that their ammunition and the occasional weapon had suddenly been spirited away.

Having analysed the situation he inherited, Kitson devised a civil and military plan for Belfast. On the civil front, he recognized that the priority was to try to win back the support of the local population that the army had lost through its actions in Ballymurphy and the Lower Falls. Kitson knew that turning things around would be difficult but not impossible. He began by introducing Divisional Action Committees on which the local RUC Divisional Commander, usually a Superintendent, would sit along with the commanding officer of the local army battalion. To ensure a degree of military continuity, a Major from the Brigade reserve battalion would join them as this battalion was there for two years whereas local battalion commanders were there for only four short months. The Committee would sit and discuss local problems from mending street lights smashed during the rioting to the frequency of army patrols. The RUC's Assistant Chief Constable for Belfast, Sam Bradley, was co-sponsor of the idea. Kitson's chief complaint was that there were no civil representatives on the Committees and he tried hard to rectify the omission but with little success as the IRA dissuaded well-intentioned locals from getting involved. The IRA was not in the business of helping the 'Brits' restore order and start winning back hearts and minds. Despite the lack of this crucial ingredient, the Divisional Action Committees looked good on paper and went some way towards the system used in places like Kenya and Malaya, but Belfast was different. Whatever nationalists felt about the army after the Falls Road curfew, they still saw loyalists as the main enemy and any attempt to introduce a degree of normality into Catholic areas risked being disrupted by their next march or what nationalists saw as the next provocation. 'The Prods were an endless nuisance, prancing around with their bands and annoying everyone,' one frustrated army officer told me. The other factor that began to work against Kitson's civil initiative was the IRA itself which saw his Divisional Committees as a 'Brit'-run power base in opposition to its own. Sabotaging them became one of the IRA's goals consistent with its declaration that 'British rule is not acceptable in Ireland under any circumstances'.

On the military front, Kitson's priority was to put the gathering, sharing and analysis of intelligence on a proper basis. He inherited a system whereby RUC Special Branch officers collected information on the ground, primarily through a longstanding and somewhat dusty network of informers, then passed it to RUC Headquarters who in turn passed it to the army's Headquarters Northern Ireland (HQNI) at Lisburn who then passed it down to its Brigades and thence to its local battalion commanders in the field. Kitson wanted to short-circuit the whole process and have intelligence passed directly from Special Branch on the ground to the local battalion intelligence officers with whom they often shared the same quarters and canteen. This would not only be more efficient but, in theory, would reduce the amount of intelligence that was filtered out along the way and *not* passed on by the RUC to the army. The sharing and co-ordination of intelligence between the army and the police was to remain a constant source of friction for at least the next twenty years and the IRA was the beneficiary. Because intelligence was power, the RUC was not disposed to share it, and at this time the army had very little of its own. This conflict inevitably led to frustration on the part of military intelligence officers and the soldiers whom they had to support. Many felt they were only getting crumbs from the Special Branch table. Soldiers were there for four months and wanted tangible successes to take home in the form of a 'contact', whether it be a shoot-out with the IRA, the interception of a bomb, the discovery of weapons or the arrest of a known 'player'. Peter, a young officer in the Welsh Guards who first came to Belfast in August 1969, knew the frustrations at first hand.

> Soldiers needed to be able to go away feeling they'd done a good job. They needed to justify their training and for this they needed a reasonably quick return. In other words, it took you roughly four weeks to get to know your area. Then you probably had a reasonably productive six weeks in the middle of your tour looking after your area and really getting to know it well and being able to make some inroads given reasonable information. After that there was inevitably a slight sort of feeling, 'Well we're going to go home in a month and we must end on a high note, but let's make sure that we don't end up with too many tears.'

Most soldiers ended their short tours without ever having fired a shot or made an arrest, although most would have been on the receiving end of stones, petrol bombs and colourful abuse. Given the increasing pressure troops came under as the IRA flexed its muscles, there was even greater resentment that Special Branch seemed to be keeping its intelligence to itself. After all, the police and army were supposed to be singing from the same hymn sheet. Peter had no doubt why the RUC had not given out copies.

> Relations with Special Branch were nothing like as close or as good as I suspect that they should have been at battalion level on the streets. We had a uniformed police officer with each battalion who was there to provide straight liaison with the RUC and, we thought, some intelligence. But we were never the recipients of any intelligence and we were very, very rarely the recipients of any visits from the Special Branch. They played their cards pretty close to their chest, I think understandably as they were fearful of compromising their longer-term investment.

The army's frustrations grew even stronger when the IRA started shooting British soldiers and policemen. By the end of 1970, although soldiers had been wounded, none had been killed. The RUC, however, was less fortunate. Two police constables, Samuel Donaldson (23) and Robert Millar (26), had been killed on 11 August near Crossmaglen in South

Armagh. A booby-trap bomb was triggered as they tried the door of a stolen car, exploding 20 lbs of gelignite. They were the first members of the RUC to be killed by the IRA in the current conflict. At the time, Crossmaglen, although staunchly nationalist, was not the IRA stronghold it was later to become. Local people sent wreaths to the policemen's homes, something that would not happen in the years ahead.[2] Less than a fortnight before constables Donaldson and Millar were killed, the army had shot dead an alleged petrol bomber, Daniel O'Hagan (19), during a riot in Belfast. Gerry Adams later wrote that the death of O'Hagan made it seem that 'we were heading inexorably towards war'.[3] The IRA maintained that at this stage its actions were purely in response to the way it claimed the army was treating its community.

As the weeks went by and the New Year dawned, the army and the IRA kept up the pressure on each other whilst, remarkably, still carrying on the dialogue across the barricades that Kitson and Major-General Anthony Farrar-Hockley, his Commander Land Forces, had authorized and encouraged, not least to gather intelligence. On 5 February 1971, following an army cordon-and-search operation in the Clonard that provoked serious rioting, Farrar-Hockley went on television and controversially named some of those he believed to be leaders of the Provisional IRA in Belfast, stung by the jibe of some unionists that the army did not even know who the IRA were. Farrar-Hockley had previously met and talked with some of them personally when they presented themselves as members of street committees wishing to discuss local issues with the army. They always denied involvement with the IRA and claimed they were members of local defence organizations (which they also were). Farrar-Hockley told me what happened. 'With the press and television cameras there, I said, "I now ask the following whether they are members of the IRA and operating in the interests of that organization or not".' He then listed the names: Billy McKee, Frank Card, Leo Martin and Liam and Kevin Hannaway.[4] 'That night they all went into hiding thinking they were about to be arrested, which was the sort of effect we wanted. We wanted to show them that we knew who they were and what they were up to and we wanted to warn them off as far as we possibly could.' Farrar-Hockley's 'naming and shaming' also caused the IRA acute embarrassment as its Volunteers did not know that their leaders were involved in dialogue with the 'Brits'. These prominent Provisionals had also been a useful conduit for the army to get certain messages across. 'Sometimes, when we wanted to release a warning or a bit of advice, we let it go down through these channels,' said Farrar-Hockley. 'We were very much feeling our way then. The fact must not be overlooked that we were not in there to set strategy with a clearly defined set of tactics. Although our tactics were reasonably well defined, the strategy certainly was not. We had to adapt to the situation as it grew. After all, the IRA was not reacting to a long-term strategy.' But that was about to change.

The day after Farrar-Hockley's television bombshell, the real shooting war began. On 6 February 1971, during a riot in Ardoyne following disturbances elsewhere, the army shot dead a local republican, Bernard 'Barney' Watt (28). They said he'd been a petrol bomber but there was no forensic evidence to support the claim. The IRA brought out its guns as the rioting spread and lost one of its Staff Officers, James Saunders (21), to a bullet from an army sniper. In the course of these exchanges and as rioting engulfed the nearby New Lodge area, the IRA shot dead twenty-year-old Gunner Robert Curtis from Newcastle. He had been married for a year and his wife was expecting their first child. His unit had just finished a six-week tour along the border and had returned to Belfast for a rest. The men were just taking their kit off the troop ship where they were billeted in Belfast harbour when they were suddenly rushed to the riot. Norman was standing next to Gunner Curtis when he was hit.

> The crowd was in front of us, throwing bricks, bottles, and petrol bombs. Then all of a sudden the crowd parted and this chap just popped out with a machine gun and just opened up. There were sparks everywhere. Bullets were just ricocheting all over the place and that's when 'Geordie' Curtis got hit. He was standing right next door to me. He just gave a slight scream and then he was on the floor. The bullet must have come up the street, bounced off it and hit him. It was deflected onto his chest and killed him instantly.
>
> Six of our soldiers were shot that night. One dead. Our first night in Belfast. We were told they would give us a welcome party, or a going away party. So we sort of expected it. But we didn't expect to be shot at. Nobody told us they were using weapons. Nobody trained us for that.[5]

At first, Norman and his colleagues did not know that Gunner Curtis was dead since there was little blood. It was only when a cigarette was placed in his mouth and it refused to glow that they realized that life had gone.[6]

Gunner Curtis was the first soldier to die on duty in Ireland since 1921. 'It was the turning point,' Joe Cahill told me, 'defence was out of the window.'[7] (Cahill was now a senior figure in the Provisional IRA's Belfast Brigade.) The following day, Chichester-Clark went on television to declare that 'Northern Ireland is at war with the Irish Republican Army Provisionals.'[8]

The IRA's next killing was cold, calculated and precise in a way that the random shooting of Gunner Curtis was not. Three young Scottish soldiers from the Royal Highland Fusiliers, Dougald McCaughey (23) and two brothers, John and Joseph McCaig, aged 17 and 18 years respectively, were having an off-duty drink at Mooney's Bar in the centre of Belfast. They were wearing civilian clothes. In those days, despite the rioting, off-duty soldiers could still come and go as they wished in the bars, clubs and discos of Belfast. Out of uniform and off-duty, they were not thought to be targets. A former soldier approached them, chatted them up and asked if they'd like to come to a party. Two other men were with him. What the three young Scottish 'squaddies' did not know was that the friendly former soldier was the leader of an IRA group from Ardoyne.

Well plied with drink, McCaughey and the McCaig brothers were driven to a lonely mountain road just outside Belfast where they stopped to relieve themselves. As they did so, they were shot through the back of the head and their bodies left by the roadside. One of them is said to have been propped up with a half-empty beer glass still in his hand.[9] The horrific killings, the cowardly manner in which they were carried out, and the fact that two of the victims were only 17 and 18 years old, sent shock waves through the province and the rest of the United Kingdom. People knew that Northern Ireland was brutal but never imagined it was as brutal as this. Both the Provisional and the Official IRA issued statements maintaining that none of their units was involved.[10] The Provisionals' statement was carefully worded since, although the killings were carried out by members of the IRA, it seems that those responsible were not authorized to do so. It is certainly highly unlikely that Billy McKee, by then the commander of the Provisional IRA's Belfast Brigade, would have given the go-ahead for such an operation. He would have regarded it as unsoldierly and contrary to the principles of republicanism. 'Paul', then a young Special Branch officer, was familiar with the names and history of the suspected killers. The former British soldier who had enticed the three young men to their deaths came from Ardoyne and had applied to join the SAS but was deemed to be temperamentally unsuitable. According to 'Paul', the man was a psychopath who had killed a civilian in controversial circumstances during the army's anti-terrorist campaign against EOKA in Cyprus. He believes that the Ardoyne IRA did know that he had been in the British army but were not aware of his controversial history. Special Branch was not surprised he was prepared to kill as a way of getting his own back on the army. 'Paul' has no doubt that, had the government introduced internment without trial immediately after the killings, it would have been widely supported, not least by the nationalist community, ashamed to think that such barbarity had been conducted in its name.

The revulsion was unbelievable. People within the republican community weren't ready for that. You must bear in mind that the vast majority of nationalists and the vast majority of those who down the years would have supported the republican cause, weren't all ready for a campaign against the 'Brits', against the RUC and against the system. In fact, that was a real turning point, the point at which the IRA themselves thought that internment would have been introduced. Indeed the thinkers in the movement at that time felt that the government would have got away with it then and there wouldn't have been the difficulties there were when it eventually came in.

The pressure on Chichester-Clark now became intolerable. To unionists, the man who succeeded Terence O'Neill with a mission to restore order to the streets had presided over a catastrophe, culminating in horrific murder. There were demands for tougher security, for the army to stop pussy-footing around and, above all, for the introduction of internment without trial which had dealt the IRA a blow in its 1956–62 border campaign from which it had never recovered. It had worked at that time because the Irish Government had introduced it simultaneously, which meant that IRA men on both sides of the border had nowhere to hide. The beauty of internment to its implementers was that there was no need for evidence. But the chances of the Irish Government obliging the 'Brits' a second time round were zero given how the actions of the British army were perceived in the South. Dublin was not about to do what it saw as Stormont's dirty work for it.

On 16 March 1971, Chichester-Clark flew to London for discussions on the security situation with Prime Minister Heath, Home Secretary Maudling, Defence Secretary Carrington and the new GOC Northern Ireland, Lieutenant-General Harry Tuzo. He asked for 3,000 more troops and returned to face an increasingly disgruntled Stormont Cabinet with an offer of less than half that figure, which would have brought the army's total strength in the province to just under 10,000 men. It was not enough. Nor were there the promises of any new military initiatives to curb the IRA and restore some semblance of law and order to the province. Two days after Chichester-Clark's return to Northern Ireland, when it became clear that Downing Street had given him very little, 3,000 loyalists marched on Stormont demanding action from their Government including internment, the return of the 'B' Specials, the re-arming of the RUC and, presumably, Chichester-Clark's head. Northern Ireland's Prime Minister knew he had little option other than to resign. Heath tried to discourage him, knowing that the political upheaval was more likely to stir things up than calm them down, but on 20 March 1971, Chichester-Clark resigned because he saw 'no other way of bringing home to all concerned the realities of the present constitutional, political and security situation'.[11]

He was succeeded by Brian Faulkner, a tough, no-nonsense unionist hardliner with an astute and determined political brain. Faulkner was not a 'toff' and member of the landed gentry like his predecessors, Captain O'Neill and Major Chichester-Clark, but a self-made man who had made his money in the family shirt-making business. Faulkner, who had played his political cards deftly over the years since he first became a Stormont MP in 1949, finally achieved his ambition and became Prime Minister of Northern Ireland, defeating his rival, William Craig, an even harder hardliner, by twenty-six votes to four. Minutes after the result was announced, Faulkner made a statement from notes he had jotted down on the back of an envelope the night before in anticipation of victory.

'Obviously the kernel of our immediate problem is the law and order situation,' he said. 'Let me say right away that what we need on this front are not new principles, but practical results on the ground in the elimination not only of terrorism, but of riots and disorder.'[12]

You could almost hear the cheers from the Ulster Unionist Party's rank and file. To them, Faulkner's credentials were impeccable, which is why he had been elected. As Minister for Home Affairs in 1959, he had been successful in countering the IRA's border campaign and knew that internment worked. He soon began to lobby for it, convinced that what had broken the IRA before would do so again. Faulkner had no idea how wrong he could be.

Chapter Five

Crackdown

August 1971–November 1971

Gavin had his first taste of Northern Ireland in 1966 as a young Captain with the Queen's Regiment in the days when the garrison was known to the army as 'Sleepy Hollow' because nothing ever happened there. If you wanted real action, you hoped for a posting to Aden. If you wanted a fun time with minimum stress and lots of country pursuits, Northern Ireland was the place to be. At that time, the IRA was 'a joke'. The battalion's tour was so quiet that it was sent off to British Guyana for nine months for the independence celebrations. When Gavin returned on 6 February 1971, the place was unrecognizable. It was the day Gunner Robert Curtis was shot dead by the IRA. 'I realized in ten seconds it was a totally different situation,' he told me. 'There were soldiers on the docks with weapons which would never have been seen before. They were all over Belfast and there was protective security everywhere. The situation was getting serious. It wasn't "Sleepy Hollow" any more.'

By now a Major, Gavin arrived to take up a desk job for a two-year posting at Headquarters Northern Ireland as the General Service Officer responsible for plans. He had bribed his wife with a dishwasher and brought his family with him. Scarcely were his feet under the desk when the Chief of Staff, Brigadier Marston Tickell, told him 'we're thinking about internment' and asked for his views. The legislation already existed under Section 11 of the Northern Ireland Special Powers Act that stipulated that any person could be arrested and detained if suspected of acting 'in a manner prejudicial to the preservation of the peace or maintenance of law and order'.[1] The net could be cast as widely as the authorities wished since all that was required was suspicion not evidence.

Gavin started to 'brush up' on the practicalities. To his surprise all he found in the archive was a page and half of notes, the bare bones of a plan. Following the killing of the three Scottish soldiers, the need to do something became even more pressing and bare bones were clearly not enough. The notes suggested that a good place to lock people up was the Isle of Man, an obvious choice as it was near to Northern Ireland and it would be a location from which the internees would find it difficult to escape, unless they were exceedingly good swimmers. Gavin was a little concerned about this, realizing that the Special Powers Act only applied to Northern Ireland and therefore the moment the internees set foot on Manx soil, they would be free. He discussed the proposal with the MOD's Civil Adviser who sat in the next door office and they concluded that the Isle of Man did not seem such a bright idea.

Gavin realized that his superiors would be unlikely to thank him for this novel suggestion and started to look round for something else. He chatted to some of the army's logistical experts and discovered that there might be a location at an old army depot used to store army Land-rovers, trailers and trucks, known in the jargon as 'B' vehicles. ('A' vehicles were tanks, etc.) It was situated just outside Belfast at a place known as 'Long Kesh' and was so old that some of the Second World War-type Nissen huts were still there. Gavin thought he had hit the jackpot and reckoned that with three days' notice of internment, army sappers could put up wires and whatever was required to keep Long Kesh's new inmates in.

The plan was secretly approved and now all that it needed was a name. No army plan was complete without one. Gavin got in touch with the MOD in London and was sent a list of approved code names. 'Most of them were awful, dreadful names. I do recall one was called "Sludge" but that wouldn't lend any sense of occasion to either soldiers or citizens or history. But one stood out as being a little clearer and more understandable, Demetrius. Being a Greek word, I thought this might actually help to cover the plan a little, so we called it "Operation Demetrius". It was better than "Sludge".'

Intelligence was critical to the success of internment and most of that was in the hands of RUC Special Branch. 'Paul', one of its officers involved in the operation, admitted it was less than perfect. The problem was that many of the files were based on individuals from the 'old' IRA who had been involved in the failed border campaign which 'Paul' himself had helped counter. As the IRA ceased to be involved in violence after it had given the order to dump arms on 5 February 1962,[2] the requirement for Special Branch to keep on its toes was less pressing. When the IRA split in the wake of the upheavals of August 1969, a whole new generation rushed to join the Provisionals, and Special Branch was caught on the hop. Identifying and cultivating a whole new range of informants could not be done overnight, and in the climate of the time, new recruits to the IRA were not rushing to betray their new comrades or the nationalist community to the 'Brits'. Special Branch faced an uphill task. 'Paul' admits the shortcomings. 'We knew what their structure was and who the leaders were in most areas, people like Billy McKee and Joe Cahill. We knew their ORBAT, their Order of Battle, and what their "battalions" were, as they were very much geographically organized. But we wouldn't have known exactly the layout of the "company" units within each "battalion" and we wouldn't have known the individual members of the units. At ground level, the information was patchy.'

Ground level was the vital area in which intelligence was urgently needed since it was the 'Provos' who were planting the bombs and pulling the triggers.

When Farrar-Hockley examined the contents of the Special Branch files in preparation for 'Operation Demetrius', he was not overly impressed. 'It became apparent to us that though the records had been excellent up to the 1950s, after the "triumph" of that period which brought the IRA's campaign effectively to an end, there had been very little updating of information. There were some excellent people in Special Branch and there were some not so excellent people. The excellent people were working hard on getting an up-to-date record of everything and the others were doing it when it suited them.' He also knew that the chances of enlisting the support of the Dublin Government for 'Operation Demetrius' were remote if the attitude of its police force, the Garda Siochana, was anything to go by. 'Our relations with the Irish police were poor. They wanted us to tell them everything but when we asked for things, they sucked their teeth.'

Dublin's co-operation was the prerequisite of success and it was a non-starter. As 'Paul' recognized, 'They didn't really have any reason to intern at that time from their point of view. One couldn't envisage how they could do it. It would have been very, very difficult for them.' He acknowledged that the operation was always going to be 'risky', but in the scales of judgment, the political pressures to go ahead outweighed the advice of those who counselled caution. In the end it came down to a stark choice: the British Government had to give Faulkner what he wanted and his party and constituents demanded, or risk losing another Northern Ireland Prime Minister only a few months after losing the last. Three resignations in two years were hardly likely to increase confidence in Stormont. Politically, the 'Brits' were still pushing their fingers in the dyke and trying to keep Northern Ireland at arm's length.

In April 1971, the month after Faulkner became Prime Minister, the army and the RUC held a secret security meeting in Belfast to discuss how intelligence should be obtained from those arrested under the Special Powers Act if internment were introduced.[3] The methods traditionally used by the army to extract information from enemy suspects when countering insurgents in the colonies were known as the 'Five Techniques'. They consisted of making the suspect stand against a wall with arms spread-eagled for hours at a time; placing hoods over their heads to produce sensory deprivation; subjecting them to a continuous high-pitched noise known as 'white noise' to disorientate them, and depriving them of sleep and food. They had been used as a counter-insurgency weapon in Palestine, Malaya, Kenya, Cyprus, the British Cameroons, Brunei, British Guiana, Aden, Borneo and, most recently in 1970–1, in the Persian Gulf.[4] Their origin lay in the accounts that British soldiers gave of how they had been interrogated by the North Koreans during the Korean War. British military intelligence used the techniques not only to interrogate suspects but to train its own soldiers in how to resist interrogation. Remarkably, these practices had never been written down in any army directive, order, training manual or syllabus and there were no guidelines in existence to govern their use.[5] They became part of an oral tradition taught at purpose-built interrogation centres in England.

Because these methods had been part of the army's interrogation training for almost two decades and were never subject to any political approval, Ministers almost certainly knew nothing about them and therefore were not in a position to authorize them or otherwise.[6] No doubt military intelligence chiefs thought that since they had been in use for years and proved highly effective, there was no reason to question their use in Northern Ireland. There is no indication that the fact ever occurred to them that the province was part of the United Kingdom and not some far-flung outpost of Empire.

The English Intelligence Centre, a secret army establishment then situated at Maresfield at the edge of the Ashdown Forest in Sussex, was the storehouse of intelligence principles and practice where 'in-depth' interrogation and the Five Techniques were taught.[7] In April 1971, the month that echoed to the sound of 38 explosions signalling that the IRA was stepping up its bombing campaign, army officers from the English Intelligence Centre went to Belfast for the secret security seminar in which they explained to their RUC colleagues how the strict rules under which policemen had traditionally conducted interrogations could be relaxed. I understand that despite what has been reported, the Five Techniques were not actually taught. The plan was for RUC Special Branch officers to carry out the actual interrogations with military intelligence officers from the Centre present in the control room throughout them.[8] The Five Techniques themselves were administered by military intelligence officers with some assistance from uniformed policemen. All the army and police now required from the Government was the green light for internment. As the security situation deteriorated through the spring and early summer, the question was not *whether* internment would be introduced but *when*.

By the beginning of August 1971, ten soldiers and five policemen had been killed but the statistic does not reflect the anarchy that unionists believed the IRA was causing. Since the beginning of the year, there had been over 300 explosions, 320 shooting incidents and over 600 people treated in hospital for injuries.[9] Faulkner had persuaded the British Government of the need for internment, and once that was done, the operation was almost a *fait accompli*. The military, however, and some members of Special Branch remained sceptical, given the shortcomings of the available intelligence. Although the IRA leaders were known (Farrar-Hockley's accusatory finger having driven several into hiding), for internment to be successful, the targeted suspects had to be sleeping peacefully in their beds when the army came calling, totally oblivious to the fact or timing of the internment swoop.

It was a fond hope. 'Operation Demetrius' was to be carried out by the army not the police. The RUC were to supply the suspects' names and addresses and 3,000 troops were going to ring their bells or knock on – or kick in – their doors. The army being the army, meticulous plans had to be laid and the operation rehearsed as thoroughly and clandestinely as possible. Although this did not involve soldiers tip-toeing through the night and making phantom knocks on doors, it did entail a degree of unaccustomed movement. The IRA, who had expected internment to be introduced five months ago when the three Scottish soldiers were killed, knew it was only a matter of time and were watching the army's every move.

And its moves were hardly subtle. On 23 and 28 July the army mounted a number of extensive search operations, arresting about 90 suspects,[10] with the Home Secretary, Reginald Maudling, declaring that a state of 'open war' now existed between the IRA and the British army, Questioned about the possibility of internment, Maudling said, not surprisingly, that no advance notice would be given.[11] 'Paul' was astonished that the army made its intentions so obvious. 'They went through a series of dry runs as it were. The leaders of the Provisionals were all old-time IRA personnel and they watched all the signs and were able to analyse them. They knew exactly what was happening and almost down to the day. Hence all the leaders were not rounded up.'

Brendan Hughes, who was to become the IRA's Belfast Brigade commander, had seen all the warning signs. At the time of internment he was a senior member of 'D' company of the Provisionals 2nd Battalion that covered the Lower Falls. Because of his swarthy complexion, he was known as 'Darkie'. Like most of his associates in the IRA leadership, he did not need telling that the swoop was coming. 'The military operations carried out by the IRA were increasing daily and everyone was talking about the possibility of internment,' he told me. 'Ten days before it came in, the British army swamped a lot of areas in West Belfast and to us it looked like an information-gathering operation.'

At 4.15 a.m. on Monday 9 August, 3,000 troops swooped on nationalist areas throughout the province. The deafening sound of dustbin lids echoed round Belfast as women warned their menfolk that the army was coming and internment was in. Three hundred and forty-two republican suspects were arrested and, critically, not one Protestant. There were no Protestant names on the Special Branch lists despite the fact that the loyalist Ulster Volunteer Force had been active, although not on a scale comparable with the IRA. Farrar-Hockley offers a simple explanation. 'It was a reflection of the fact that at many levels and in many branches in those days within the Royal Ulster Constabulary there were people who were partial to one extent or another, in many cases, to a considerable extent. I hasten to say that that was not true at the top level.' In other words, many rank-and-file members of the RUC saw themselves as being on the same side as the Protestants.

Internment, as nationalists justifiably pointed out, was entirely one-sided. Any credible claim the 'Brits' still had to being even-handed was shattered in the small hours of that morning. Unionists were jubilant at the sight of scores of suspected terrorists being marched off to the Long Kesh internment camp that was now ready and waiting. The problem was that most of those arrested were the wrong people (105 suspects were released within two days)[12] and the IRA's leaders had gone. To many of the soldiers who carried it out, the whole operation was a fiasco. Brian, the Lieutenant-Colonel who commanded the 1st Battalion, The Gloucestershire Regiment, did not mince his words:

> It was a complete disaster. It turned a large number of the nationalist population, who at that time had been firmly on our side and very sensibly so, against us. To my simple mind, as a regimental soldier, it was lunacy. What it did was put a few people inside who probably didn't matter very much and it didn't intern the people who did matter. It also meant that what little information we were getting at that time just totally dried up. The nationalist population didn't trust the security forces any more and, to my mind, in any internal security operation – and that's what Northern Ireland was – hearts and minds are the most important part of it. And internment destroyed it.

Kitson himself supported the theory of internment on the grounds that it took bad men who could not be charged off the streets but he believed that it had to be carried out with extreme care and precision. Clearly the way it was conducted in August 1971 would not have met those criteria. He is said to have been amazed at the timing and at the impractical and ridiculous way in which it was carried out. At the time of the operation, Kitson himself was on holiday and appears to have been given an assurance that nothing would happen until he was back in the province. For whatever reason, perhaps because of the intense political pressure from Stormont, any assurance that may have been given was not kept. Kitson and his senior officers resented being asked to dance to the unionist tune when it risked undermining what they were trying to do. Alienating the whole nationalist community by taking away their fathers and sons in the small hours of the morning and locking them up without charge did not fit in with Kitson's strategy.

Sir Robert Andrew, who later became Permanent Under Secretary at the Northern Ireland Office, was Private Secretary to the Defence Secretary, Lord Carrington, at the time of internment. He has no doubt that it was political pressure from Brian Faulkner and the Stormont Government that persuaded a reluctant British Government and army to act in the draconian way that it did.

> I think most people in Whitehall who were involved had grave doubts about it. Possibly if the British Government had been in direct control, as we were of course a little bit later on, it wouldn't have happened. The biggest problem was what do you do with these people once you've arrested them. By definition, you haven't got evidence which would stand up in a court of law so you can't bring them to trial. You either have to keep them inside indefinitely, which would be the subject of much criticism, or eventually you have to let them go as they had to do in the end. So I think the policy was a failure.

But there was a plan within a plan, known only to a tiny handful of people, which was to cause even greater political embarrassment to the Government and alienate the nationalist community even more. The lessons of April's secret security seminar were put into practice. Eleven IRA suspects were singled out for special in-depth interrogation at secret centres within British army bases. Even thirty years after the event, it is extraordinarily difficult to pin down who was responsible for making the decision and then carrying it out. Those I spoke to either said they did not know it was happening or, if they did, they were not responsible for it. The buck is passed with alacrity. It is not surprising as the way suspects were treated during 'in-depth' interrogation in the wake of internment remains, for the

'Brits', one of the most politically embarrassing episodes in the whole of the conflict.

The eleven specially selected detainees became colloquially known as the 'guinea pigs' and were subjected to the Five Techniques. The only sustenance they received during their ordeal was a chunk of bread and a pint of water every six hours.[13] They were made to stand against the wall for a total of 245 hours, with each period lasting between four and six hours.[14] There were, however, rules laid down by the Government in a general Directive as to what was and was not permissible during interrogation. 'Violence to life and person, in particular mutilation, cruel treatment and torture' were prohibited, as were 'outrages upon personal dignity, in particular humiliating and degrading treatment'. On paper that all sounds liberal and humane but the application of those principles was called into question by the qualification that followed. 'The precise application of these general rules is inevitably to some extent a matter of judgement on the part of those immediately responsible for the operations in question.'[15] It was tantamount to giving interrogators carte blanche to interpret the rules as they saw fit. Given the increasingly savage nature of the IRA's campaign, it is not surprising that the interpretation was generous. To the 'Brits' in the violent summer of 1971, the end clearly justified the means.

Farrar-Hockley, who was himself a prisoner of war in North Korea, does not subscribe to the view that internment was a disaster and counter-productive. He and the GOC, Sir Harry Tuzo, had originally been in favour of selective internment: picking up certain individuals on whom there was good intelligence, interning them for anything between six weeks and six months, and then letting them out and taking in a fresh batch of suspects. He believes the idea was rejected 'for political reasons'. Although he draws the line at the use of some methods, he makes no apology for subjecting the enemy suspects to rigorous interrogation. 'The IRA call themselves soldiers and say they're carrying out warfare so they must be prepared to be frightened if they're captured and interrogated.' He also refutes the allegation that no intelligence was gained and that every-thing about internment was bad. 'The dozen or so people who were taken, and not by any means the most junior in the ranks of the IRA, were described by those who were carrying out interrogations as "singing like canaries". It's something I've seen in other operational situations across the world. People were shaken and shocked out of their environment and for one reason or another they begin talking and can't be stopped. So in that sense a lot of very good information, though of course of relatively short-term value, was obtained.'

Liam Shannon, a Belfast republican, was subjected to the Five Tech-niques two months after internment. He was arrested by an army foot

patrol at about 10 p.m. on the evening of 9 October 1971 as he was
walking home with his wife. He was taken to Springfield Road police
station and then to Girdwood Park, the Territorial Army centre that was
used as the Belfast Regional Holding Centre for the detainees. He was
eventually driven to Palace Barracks, Holywood, just outside the city,
where he was kept for 48 hours. There he says he received 'continual
beatings'. He was then taken back to Belfast to Crumlin Road gaol where
he was marched into the Governor's office and given 'a removal order'
which Shannon interpreted to mean that he could be removed at any time
to a place where his presence may thought to be 'in the interests of justice'.
He was then put into a helicopter and taken away for in-depth interrogation.

The helicopter landed at what Shannon thought was some kind of
military installation. He was examined by 'a man in a white coat' whom he
assumed to be a doctor and then given an outsize boiler suit to put on. He
told the doctor that he had already been quite badly beaten since his arrest
and showed him the bruising on his back and legs. After this 'two athletic
looking chaps in jeans, T-shirts and trainers' came into the room and made
him stand spread-eagled against a wall with a hood on his head. They
would almost certainly have been soldiers as the army did the softening-up
whilst the RUC carried out the interrogations. I asked Shannon how long
he had been made to stand in this position.

> With this type of interrogation, you just start to go off your head.
> Time means nothing. The tiredness was greater than anything else. I
> collapsed several times because I couldn't stand it any longer. I was
> bundled against the wall again. I received a few slaps. I tried to
> remonstrate with the people but to no avail. The hood was tied
> tightly and securely round my neck. It was like a canvas bag and the
> strings were tied round the epaulettes [of the boiler suit]. Then they
> started the Five Techniques. The 'white noise' I can only describe to
> be like compressed air or steam hissing from a pipe. The degree varied
> from time to time. Sometimes it was soft and at other times it got very
> loud, almost ear-piercing. It was terrible. You completely lost it
> altogether.

Shannon says that the only time the hood was removed was for the actual
interrogations which he described as being like 'something you see in films
about the KGB'.

> This massive bright light was shone in your face. The hood was
> pulled off and there was this person behind a desk. You were sitting

on a chair, you couldn't move, this bright light was cutting the eyes out of you. They then fired questions and allegations at you.

What sort of questions did they ask?

Was I in the IRA? Who did I know in the IRA? What did I do? Did I know where guns or bombs were? All these questions were just spat at you.

Shannon said it was impossible to tell who his interrogators were as the lights were so dazzling when the hood was off. I asked him about their accents. He remembers that some were English and others were Irish. The hood was then put back on and he was made to stand against the wall again. The process was repeated for what Shannon says was seven days.

At the end, I was completely disorientated. I didn't know where I was or how long I'd been there or anything else. The first thing I remember was them bringing me back into a room and removing the hood up to my nose. I was given a plastic cup of water and a slice of dry bread. That was it for the seven days. I had grown a beard within seven days inside this hood. Whether it was the heat or what I don't know. That was my condition. The water was fantastic to drink.

Shannon says he had nothing to tell them. He was then interned. Five years later, he was awarded £25,000 compensation for his ordeal. 'It wasn't near what it should have been, for what they put us through,' he said ruefully. 'No amount of money could ever compensate for that.'

The Heath Government established an inquiry under the Ombudsman, Sir Edmund Compton, on 31 August 1971, which carried out its mission with remarkable speed given the political furore the allegations had caused. The Government had already started attacking the BBC for its reporting, which Lord Carrington described as falling 'below the standard of fairness and accuracy which we are entitled to expect'.[16] The enquiry team visited Northern Ireland over the period 1 September–26 October, which means that Liam Shannon was probably being interrogated at the very time Sir Edmund and his colleagues were conducting their investigation. Cynics would say that there was no let-up in the use of the Five Techniques even though an enquiry was being conducted because the interrogators and those in authority above them knew they had nothing to fear. Fortunately for the Government, when the report was published on 16 November 1971, Compton concluded that there had not been torture or 'physical brutality as we understand the term'. Nevertheless, he observed that there had been 'a measure of ill-treatment'.[17]

The day that the Compton report was published, the Government announced a further inquiry by three Privy Counsellors under Lord Parker of Waddington to consider whether these interrogation techniques required amendment. The other Privy Counsellors were Lord Gardiner and Mr John Boyd-Carpenter. The Committee's deliberations were equally swift and published in its report less than three months later, on 9 February 1972. It concluded that the use of the Five Techniques on eleven suspects in August 1971 after internment, and on a further two in October (one of whom would almost certainly have been Liam Shannon), had produced new information 'as a direct result'. In other words, the Five Techniques had worked, bearing out Farrar-Hockley's conviction that internment was not a waste of time and that internees 'sang like canaries'. These were the 'results' listed by the Parker Committee.

1 The identification of a further 700 members of both IRA factions and their positions in the organizations.
2 Over 40 sheets giving details of the organization and structure of IRA units.
3 Details of possible IRA operations; arms caches; safe houses; communications and supply routes, including those across the border and locations of wanted persons.
4 Details of morale, operational directives, propaganda techniques, relations with other organizations and future plans.
5 The discovery of individual responsibility for about 85 incidents recorded on police files which had previously remained unexplained.[18]

Lord Parker and Mr Boyd-Carpenter, the majority on the Committee, concluded that the methods could be justified only 'in cases where it is considered vitally necessary to obtain information'. Lord Gardiner, however, in his minority submission vehemently opposed his colleagues' view and penned a damning report of such force that the Government could not ignore it. Gardiner concluded that the procedures were illegal in domestic and possibly international law. The memorable words of his last paragraph could have echoed down the following twenty-five years as a reminder to the 'Brits' of their responsibilities.

The blame for this sorry story, if blame there be, must lie with those who, many years ago, decided that in emergency conditions in Colonial-type situations we should abandon our legal, well-tried and highly successful wartime interrogation methods and replace them by procedures which were secret, illegal, not morally justifiable and alien to the traditions of what I believe still to be the greatest democracy in the world.[19]

Ironically, Lord Gardiner wrote those words on 31 January 1972, the day after 'Bloody Sunday'.

The Prime Minister, Edward Heath, announced on the day that the Parker report was published that the Five Techniques would not be used again. I asked Sir Robert Andrew if he had been surprised by the political storm.

One was aware that methods of this sort had been used in places like Aden and it only became clear, certainly to me and I think to most other people in the Ministry of Defence, at a fairly late stage exactly what was being done in interrogation centres in Northern Ireland. I think in justification for these methods it has to be remembered that there was a desperate need to get intelligence and that it was thought, and rightly so, that lives depended on getting it. If, by using techniques which I think most people felt fell short of torture as normally defined, these methods would give intelligence which would save lives then arguably there was a case for using them. I think the so-called 'Five Techniques' were not in the same category as torture as usually understood, such as applying electrodes to tender parts of the body and things of that sort. But they were clearly inhuman methods and I think once it was recognized at what one might call a political level – that's senior civil servants in Whitehall and of course Ministers – that these methods were in fact being used, they were quickly stopped.

Was it not a case of not being able to use techniques within the United Kingdom that had been widely used in other theatres previously?

Well, when you do the things in the United Kingdom they are viewed rather differently from elsewhere.

The repercussions rumbled on for most of the decade. The Irish Government was not satisfied and took the British Government to the European Commission of Human Rights in Strasbourg which, on 2 September 1976, found Britain guilty of breaching the European Convention on Human Rights 'in the form not only of inhuman and degrading treatment but also of torture'.[20] But this was not the end of the story. The case then went to the higher body, the European Court of Human Rights, which, to the Government's intense relief, dropped the acutely embarrassing 'torture' element of the Commission's verdict and ruled on 18 January 1978 that

Britain was only guilty of the lesser charge of 'inhuman and degrading treatment'.[21] It was no consolation to those like Liam Shannon who had been on the receiving end. Interrogation and other controversies were to continue to haunt the Government as the conflict unfolded. The crack-down by the 'Brits' against the IRA had only just begun.

Chapter Six

Aftermath

August 1971–November 1971

However many lives the 'Brits' say internment and 'in-depth' interrogation may have saved, there is no denying that after its introduction the death toll soared. In the following week, twenty people died, sixteen of them shot dead by the British army and two by the IRA.[1] It was almost as many as had died in the previous six months. Only two of the army's victims were members of the IRA. Most were shot during gun battles and riots as Belfast and the nationalist areas around the province erupted. The city and the province had never witnessed scenes like it before. In North Belfast, where nationalist and loyalist areas met, over 200 Protestant homes in the Farringdon Gardens area went up in flames; their inhabitants, fleeing as a result of intimidation and fear, literally scorched the earth to leave nothing behind for the Catholic 'tenants' who would then move in.[2]

That night, with Belfast seemingly ablaze, soldiers from the 3rd Battalion, The Royal Green Jackets, were flown in, among them Jamie, then a young Second-Lieutenant. He had joined what he thought at the time was still a very colonial army 'full of end of empire experiences'. But that was to change. Jamie was about to experience the first of nine tours in Northern Ireland, the last one as a senior officer nearly thirty years later. Two of the tours were for two years. As the Green Jackets flew over Liverpool the day after internment, Jamie could see the glow on the far-distant horizon that got stronger the closer they came to Belfast. As they approached the coast, he could actually see the flames and as they came into land over the city, he could make out details on the ground. 'It seemed to me whole streets were burning. You could see roads that had been blocked and barricaded. You could see fires, from bonfires, burning cars and burning houses. I was shocked. I realized for the first time the size of the problem and the size of the devastation.'

On landing at Aldergrove airport, the Green Jackets drove into Belfast city centre in completely unprotected four-ton trucks because that was all that was to hand at the time. The streets were deserted. Everywhere buildings were smouldering or still burning. Shop fronts were smashed and the roads were littered with rubble and glass. There were burned-out cars used to form barricades, tossed aside like toys as the army tried to clear a way through the debris. It was a scene of utter devastation. Jamie could hardly believe his eyes. 'You were seeing scenes on the streets of the United Kingdom that you tend to associate with the Middle East, with the Lebanon and Beirut. I was amazed. I was only nineteen at the time and I realized that all this was happening in a city of the United Kingdom. You were passing red telephone boxes and red letter boxes and there were double-decker buses lying around the place, and black taxis too. Suddenly seeing them in this setting was quite a shock.'

Jamie's reaction was not unlike that of the Hull bus driver Tom, whom I took to Belfast during Easter 1972. Jamie had just returned from a United Nations tour and meeting Northern Ireland face-to-face and becoming aware of the political landscape in which it had existed, was a profound cultural setback. 'We'd just been upholding human rights and suddenly to come back to a part of one's own country and find that those human rights had not been available to a sizeable percentage of the population was a shock to us. We were gob-smacked that part of the United Kingdom hadn't had "one man, one vote".'

But that was in the past. Jamie and his men were more concerned about the present and staying alive in the mayhem that internment unleashed. They were, he says, 'pretty bloody days'. Every time he took his men out on patrol they were either shot at, blast-bombed or petrol-bombed. Every night there would be at least one 'contact' with the enemy as the army's casualties mounted day by day. Jamie admitted the military response was tough and alienated those sections of the nationalist community that bore the brunt of it.

> I think probably the way we conducted our operations in those days would in fact have strengthened the support that the IRA got in the local communities, certainly. The way we operated was pretty blanket and all-encompassing. I don't think we differentiated nearly enough between those who were true terrorists and those who were normal members of the population, and I think that we paid very little regard to the impact that our operations would have on the majority of the population.

With Kitson commanding the army's 39 Brigade in Belfast, there was to be no nonsense. When republican barricades went up, they were immediately taken down, giving the IRA no chance to seal off and make them 'no-go' areas. The notion that there could be sections of the United Kingdom into which the army could not venture was anathema to Kitson. As far as he was concerned, there was no part of the realm in which the Queen's writ did not run, at least in the Belfast area that he controlled. Two of his toughest barricade-busters were 1st Battalion, The Parachute Regiment, stationed in Belfast on their two-year tour, and The Royal Green Jackets. 'If violence appeared or if roads were blocked, we would clear them at the earliest possible opportunity,' Jamie said. 'We were determined not to allow no-go areas and permit the IRA, as part of its counter-revolutionary warfare strategy, to set up its own areas of administration and control its own areas. We dealt with any such attempts in a pro-active and hard manner.'

The Adjutant of 1 Para confirmed what Jamie said. 'Those barricades would be defended by the IRA and their supporters. We would be going in to restore law and order to remove the so-called "no-go" areas and we'd be resisted. It's not a situation in which half-hearted measures are going to be successful. If they were half-hearted, you'd be taking inordinate risks with the lives of your own soldiers. Belfast was run in a no-nonsense way.'

The Parachute Regiment's Support Company that was to play a crucial role on 'Bloody Sunday' was never far away. It became colloquially known as 'Kitson's Private Army'. Support Company, consisting of the Mortar, Machine Gun and Anti-Tank platoons, was the Battalion's hard edge and made up of some of the Battalion's most experienced and toughest men, many of them veterans of Aden. 'We were very experienced and very highly motivated,' the Mortar Platoon's Sergeant, 'Phil', told me. 'When barricades went up in Belfast, they came down *very* quickly. The whole training of the Parachute Regiment is built on aggression and speed and you can't afford to hang around. This gets through to the blokes and they get very hard-minded about their work. They know what they're doing and they're good at it. I don't think there was a better Battalion at that time in the world, never mind the British army, in terms of internal security. They'd seen it all in Belfast.'

The men of 1 Para idolized their commanding officer, Lieutenant-Colonel Derek Wilford, who had taken over the Battalion in Belfast in June 1971, nine months into its two-year tour. He, in turn, idolized his men. Wilford is a man of many talents. He is an accomplished painter and lover of the Classics who intrigued his men by reading the Roman poet Virgil's war epic, *The Aeneid*, in the original Latin. And, like its eponymous hero, Aeneas, Wilford was a man with a mission. He was as tough as the men he led, having served with the SAS in the Middle East, and could not afford to be otherwise. His mission was to combat terrorism from whatever side it came and ensure that his men stayed alive in the process.

In my view, this was a war. If people are shooting at you, they're shooting not to wound you but to kill you. Therefore we had to behave accordingly. We blacked our faces, we took our berets off, or at least the badges from them, and put camouflage nets over our heads. We always wore our flak jackets and when we moved on the streets, we moved as if we were moving against a well-armed, well-trained army. Now that might have been a compliment to the IRA but it wasn't really. It was a compliment to my soldiers. I wanted my men to stay alive and I actually said to them, 'You will not get killed.' That was really my coda throughout my period of command.[3]

His men took everything in. One who did not and lit up a cigarette was shot by a sniper in Ballymurphy and paralysed for life. Wilford recognized that his Battalion was not liked by the nationalists but 1 Para was not in the business of currying favour. 'No, we weren't popular,' he admits. 'I think that was due to the attitude I instilled in myself and my soldiers. I know it's a much over-used word, but we were being professional.' That is not the word those on the receiving end would have used. Complaints about the Battalion rained in as they took down barricades and put down riots. 'Our philosophy was that a guy can't throw a stone if he's running away from you and therefore we used to get stuck into them,' said 'Phil'.[4]

Most of the Paras loved every minute. To Mick of 1 Para, those days were idyllic. It was what he had joined the Parachute Regiment for. 'We had a legitimate fight almost every day and every night. We had as much beer as we could take and we had all the women we could handle. It was absolutely brilliant. A soldier's dream.'[5] And they kept their sense of humour to wind up the enemy even more. One told me of how he used to put on a Pinocchio nose during a riot and stand there with his thumbs in his ears waving at the crowd.

Northern Ireland may have been a soldier's dream for the Paras but by the end of 1971, with 124 civilians, 44 soldiers and 14 policemen dead in addition to millions of pounds' worth of damage, it was becoming a security and political nightmare for the British Government. The army, however, still believed it could win. 'I think we thought that we could defeat the IRA in 1971,' said Jamie. 'We thought that our success rate, both in terms of arrests and with people being interned, would ultimately force the IRA to realize that continued violence was no longer worthwhile. I think we underestimated the support that the IRA had from the local population and I think we probably overestimated our own capabilities.'

But however confident the army, the Government was getting worried not just because of the intolerable bloodshed that had stained the year but because Britain's international reputation had been severely tarnished by internment and the Five Techniques. Of particular concern was the damage done in America, sections of whose Irish community helped supply the IRA with large amounts of money and guns. The controversy over the methods Britain felt she had been forced to take because of IRA violence only made the supplies of both flow faster as lurid headlines in Irish–American papers seemed to confirm republican propaganda that Northern Ireland was under the British jackboot. As the situation deteriorated, no amount of commuting across the Atlantic by Government Ministers and officials could convince Irish America that it was otherwise.

At last Ireland had become an issue in the House of Commons and one on which the British public could no longer turn its back, with soldiers coming home in coffins. On 25 November 1971, the leader of the Labour Party, Harold Wilson, now in opposition, set out a long-term fifteen-point plan before the House of Commons to help Britain extricate itself from the mess that his own Government had helped create by ignoring the warning signs in the sixties. Having just returned from Northern Ireland, where he visited the Long Kesh internment camp, Wilson recognized that the situation was now so serious that the problem required new thinking. At the heart of his proposals was a recognition that nationalists' aspiration for a united Ireland was not only legitimate but had to be the long-term solution, although, critically, he stressed it required unionist consent. On the matter of how that consent could be won, Wilson was vague. His critics believed that his words could only give encouragement and support to the IRA.

> I believe that the situation has now gone so far that it is impossible to conceive of an effective long-term solution in which the agenda at least does not include consideration of, and is not in some way directed to finding a means of achieving the aspirations envisaged half a century ago, of progress towards a united Ireland . . . A substantial term of years will be required before any concept of unification could become a reality, but the dream must be there. If men of moderation have nothing to hope for, men of violence will have something to shoot for.[6]

Wilson envisaged a time-scale of fifteen years. The unionist response was 'never'. Four months later, he was involved in secret talks with the IRA.

Whitehall's mandarins may not have agreed with Wilson's central thesis but they recognized that something would have to be done and new thinking was required. By the autumn of 1971, there was fresh input when a new face arrived at the UK Representative's Office at Stormont which by now had become almost like an Embassy of the United Kingdom within the borders of the United Kingdom itself. The new occupant was a Foreign Office Diplomat, Howard Smith, who later went on to become Director General of the Security Service, MI5. Smith, who was becoming increasingly overwhelmed by the amount of work required to keep abreast of events on the ground and the doings of Faulkner's Government, decided he needed a deputy. He knew the man he wanted, a Foreign Office colleague by the name of Frank Steele who worked for the Secret Intelligence Service, MI6. Smith had heard that Steele was at home on leave awaiting his next posting and hoped that he might be enticed to join him in the province.

Steele had about as much knowledge of Northern Ireland as most 'Brits' had who had never been there. At his personnel interview he was asked what he knew about the place. Did he, for example, know anything about Faulkner? the panel asked. Steele, who had just read a piece in *The Times* referring to Padraic Faulkner, the Irish Education Minister, thought he would 'show off' and impress his interlocutors with his knowledge. It was pointed out to him, no doubt politely, that the Faulkner they had in mind was Brian Faulkner, the Prime Minister of Northern Ireland. Steele described the panel's reaction. 'Of course, in typical personnel way, they said I'd clearly got an untrammelled mind and would be unbiased and therefore just the person to be sent there.'

Frank Steele and his MI6 successor, Michael Oatley, were to play crucial roles in the years ahead in effecting the secret dialogue with the IRA that continued on and off for over two decades. There were rumours, given Steele's MI6 credentials, that he had been sent over by the Prime Minister, Edward Heath, to establish secret links with the IRA but he told me that nothing could be further than the truth. 'HMG didn't want a line of communication with the IRA,' he said. 'HMG wanted to beat the IRA.' Steele was not impressed by the way the 'Brits' were going about it.

When Steele arrived in Northern Ireland, the situation was bleak. The reforms had not stopped the violence nor prevented thousands of Catholics from giving their support to the IRA. The army may have thought it was winning the war with an increasing number of arrests and seizures of weapons and explosives but its efforts seemed to have had only a marginal impact on the IRA. Most worrying of all for Steele and his boss, Howard Smith, and the other officials around them, was the perception that the 'Brits' had lent their army to Stormont to carry out the Protestants' bidding. It was a perception held not just in the nationalist community but in the world at large, in particular across the Atlantic. 'It was assumed this was with the blessing of the British Government, which it certainly wasn't, and so indirectly we got blamed for activities that we in fact were critical of.'

It became clear towards the end of 1971 that the answer was to do what the Wilson Government had fatally failed to do in August 1969, and that was to suspend the Stormont parliament and introduce Direct Rule from Westminster. The 'Brits' and not the 'Prods' would then be running the province. Steele dismissed the traditional arguments against Direct Rule that had always been wheeled out before: that there would be uproar in Ulster and Protestants would never wear it; that they would see it as the first step on the road to a united Ireland; that officials could never persuade Ministers; and that there would be convulsions in the Conservative and Unionist Party, whose name clearly indicated the umbilical link between the two. Still he harboured doubts, given the huge risks involved in taking a step that would turn fifty years of history on its head. Steele was finally reassured, however, that it would be politically possible when he was having a drink one evening with a senior official from the Northern Ireland civil service and Philip Woodfield, the civil servant from the Home Office with special responsibility for Northern Ireland. The conversation inevitably let to a discussion about what to do next. The eminent Northern Ireland civil servant stunned his companions when he told them that Westminster would have to bring in Direct Rule. It was music to Steele's ears. 'When a senior Northern Ireland civil servant with years of working for a unionist Government, who was himself a "Prod" and a unionist, says this, then you start sitting up and taking notice,' he said. Direct Rule seemed the only way forward, and by far the best way of making a fresh start. The problem was when to do it.

Chapter Seven

'Bloody Sunday' – The Build-up

August 1971–January 1972

Although Kitson's Belfast battalions and 1 Para seemed to have Belfast under control in the sense that it had been made robustly clear that the IRA would not be allowed to establish 'no-go' areas anywhere in the city, the situation seventy miles away in Derry was very different. Here, in what was known as 'Free Derry', barricades had become an established feature on the shattered landscape and remained firmly in place. By the end of 1971, there were twenty-nine of them, sixteen of which were impassable even to the army's one-ton armoured vehicles.[1] Both the Provisional and the Official IRA flourished behind them, flaunting themselves for the media by staging roadblocks with masked men and guns. Unionists were outraged as the IRA cocked a snook at the Queen in a part of Her Kingdom where Her writ did not run. Local businessmen, most of them unionists, who owned the shops and offices in the city centre also grew increasingly angry as the daily tea-time confrontation between the local hooligans and the army grew ever closer to their premises. The rendezvous for the afternoon ritual, at the point where William Street runs down from the Creggan into the city centre, was known as 'aggro corner'. Shops were also being fire-bombed with small incendiary devices concealed in bags and carried by junior IRA foot soldiers who easily evaded army detection and planted them in places likely to cause maximum destruction. The army was convinced that shoppers from the Bogside and Creggan estates often connived in the process. Derry's mainly Protestant business community calculated that the rioting and disorder had already caused £4 million worth of damage and now, as it came ever closer to the commercial heart of the city, they feared it would soon cost much more. Lieutenant-Colonel Wilford and his men in Belfast saw the tea-time ritual on the television and watched in horror.

I wasn't pleased at all that British soldiers could line up behind plastic shields and just stand there and let people throw rocks at them and do nothing whatsover about it. We thought it was a peculiar way for soldiers to behave. They just stood there in the road like Aunt Sallies and never went forward. It was quite horrifying. I actually said publicly that my soldiers were not going to act as Aunt Sallies. Ever! We did not carry shields. We did not wear cricket pads. As far as I was concerned, it was not a game of cricket that we were indulging in.[2]

To Wilford's disgust, he found there was actually a demarcation line between the army that was protecting the city centre and the 'Derry Young Hooligans', the DYH in army shorthand, who made their tea-time sorties from Free Derry. It was literally a series of big, black dots on the military map of the city and was known as 'the containment line'. When Wilford's Adjutant first set eyes on it, he was appalled. There were no maps in Belfast with big, black dots. 'On one side of the line were the nationalist areas where people did what they wanted. The line said, "We stop them here." The map was a clear statement of that philosophy.'

The army had pursued a policy of containment since internment in the hope that, after the supposed removal of republican troublemakers from the streets, things would quieten down and the 'moderate' nationalists represented in Derry by John Hume and the SDLP would prevail. The situation was delicately poised. Hume and his colleagues had maintained their support within the nationalist community in the city by withdrawing from the Stormont parliament after the army had shot dead two local young men, Seamus Cusack (28) and Desmond Beattie (19), on 8 July 1971 during rioting in the Bogside.[3] In conflicting accounts that were to become all too familiar in the years ahead, the army said they were gunmen and local people said they were not. For Hume to have acted otherwise would have destroyed his credibility and jeopardized his power base. The army says the situation 'changed overnight' and dates the beginning of the IRA's campaign in Derry from that point. Prior to that, it regarded the IRA in the city as 'quiescent'.[4]

A month later, on 10 August, the day after internment, an IRA sniper on the Creggan estate shot dead Bombardier Paul Challenor (22) of the Royal Horse Artillery. He was the IRA's first army 'kill' in Derry. His wife had given birth to their first child a month earlier. His mother sent a bitter open letter via her local paper to the people of Northern Ireland. 'You say you are all Christians,' she wrote. 'For God's sake start acting like Christians. I wish you could see the grief that my son's death has caused in my house and in his wife's home.'[5] Her words would have echoed the feelings of many people in England.

Ten days after the killing of Bombardier Challenor, the GOC, Lieutenant-General Sir Harry Tuzo, and his Commander Land Forces,

Northern Ireland, Major-General Robert Ford, visited Derry with the UK Representative at Stormont, Howard Smith. It was a high-powered 'Brit' military and political delegation to review the situation in the city and see if they could prevent it becoming like Belfast where the IRA was doing most of its killing. They met a group of local 'moderate' nationalists opposed to violence, and agreed to lower the military profile in the city in the hope that 'moderate opinion would win the day'. There were to be no routine army patrols in the Bogside and Creggan and no military action unless the army was attacked or soldiers had to make arrests or carry out searches. There was a tacit understanding that this period of 'détente' would last about a month. In fact it lasted until mid-November. But its expectations were not fulfilled. In the five months between the killing of Cusack and Beattie and mid-December 1971, the army in Derry lost 7 soldiers and suffered 15 casualties; it had 1,932 rounds fired at it by the IRA and fired 364 rounds in return; it faced 180 nail bombs and had to deal with 211 explosions.[6]

Clearly 'détente' was not working and, according to Major-General Ford, it had only 'enabled the extremists to increase their hold on the Catholic community and to recruit and train more volunteers'. On 14 December 1971, Ford wrote a remarkable memorandum, marked 'Secret', to his boss, Lieutenant-General Tuzo. He copied it to nine other senior military personnel in the province, including the army's Director of Intelligence, so that the military hierarchy was left in no doubt about his feelings. It was the bleakest of assessments of the situation in Derry at the end of 1971 and provides a chillingly authentic insight into the British military mind at this vital juncture in the conflict. He wrote: 'At present neither the RUC nor the military have control of the Bogside and Creggan areas, law and order are not being effectively maintained and the Security Forces now face an entirely hostile Catholic community numbering 33,000 in these two areas alone.'[7]

Ford calculated that the opposition consisted of around 500 'hooligans', with a hard core of around 250, and 100 IRA men, around 40 of whom were active gunmen. He said it had become almost impossible for the army to achieve the element of surprise as there were now 'sentries and searchlights on all major obstructions during hours of darkness and an efficient alarm system of sirens, hooters and car horns'. Ford's assessment was correct: the IRA had not been idle during the period of 'détente'.

Given that the likelihood of 'moderate' nationalists overcoming this 'extremist and revolutionary element' was zero, Ford concluded that military action was required 'to establish control and stability and enable the political situation to evolve'. He outlined three options. The first was to revert to the previous policy of containment but with a more offensive attitude. This meant keeping fingers crossed that somehow the moderates *would* prevail and normality would at some stage be restored. There were, however, considerable disadvantages to this not quite so 'softly, softly' approach. It would encourage the IRA, sap army morale and anger Stormont and the local Protestants. But above all, it would not restore law and order but simply continue the stalemate.

The second option, now that an extra Battalion was available, was a tougher approach, involving 'arrest, search and barricade-clearance operations interspersed with fighting patrols'. Its advantages were that it broke the stalemate, put pressure on the gunmen, improved morale and 'mollified the local Protestant hard-liners'. Its disadvantages were that it did not restore law and order since the army would have no *permanent* presence in the Bogside and Creggan which were still dominated by the IRA; but above all, given the ineffectiveness of baton rounds and the problems caused by CS gas, it made the use of 'ball ammunition', i.e., bullets, 'more likely' in situations where a few soldiers are 'assaulted by organized mobs numbered in hundreds. This in turn raises the question of opening fire on "unarmed" mobs, whose strength lies not in fire-power, but in numbers and brick power.' Ford had no illusions about the mood of the Bogside and Creggan. 'There are indications that the hate, fear and distrust felt by the Catholic community for the security forces is deeper now than at any time during the current campaign.'

The third option was draconian and would have been welcomed by local Protestants and those in the military who wanted to get stuck in and show the IRA who was really in control. This envisaged a military thrust across the 'containment line', penetration of the hostile areas and the establishment of a permanent army presence with sufficient numbers to ensure the rapid restoration of law and order in the Bogside and Creggan. The advantages were self-evident, with the bonus that in due course the population might come to regard the army as 'the lesser of two evils and co-operate in the destruction of the IRA'. The disadvantages, however, were frightening and, in the light of what was to happen, uncannily prophetic. 'The risk of casualties is high and apart from gunmen or bombers, so-called unarmed rioters, possibly teenagers, are certain to be shot in the initial phases. Much will be made of the invasion of Derry and the slaughter of the innocent.' Because of the huge risks involved, Ford emphasized that the decision to go for this third option would have to be an 'entirely political one'. In his view, although it was 'the correct military solution to the problem of restoring law and order in Londonderry, the drawbacks are so serious that it should not be implemented in the present circumstances'. It is important to note that Ford ruled it out. A week later, Lieutenant-General Tuzo said that he was quietly confident of defeating the IRA.[8]

Ford's controversial assessment concluded with his personal recommendation that, despite all its shortcomings, the first option, suitably beefed-up, was the most sensible course, if not the most militarily desirable. He called it 'course 1½'. This meant that the stalemate would continue and no one would be happy except the IRA. The assessment would have come as no surprise to Prime Minister Heath, who had received a similar briefing in October, outlining almost identical options, from General Sir Michael Carver, the Chief of the General Staff of the army at the Ministry of Defence in London. Carver informed Heath that 'it may become imperative to go into the Bogside and root out the terrorists and the hooligans' but warned that 'the timing, political implications and local reaction to such an operation would have to be carefully judged'.[9]

On 23 December, Heath paid a surprise ten-hour visit to Northern Ireland and in his Christmas message, broadcast on local television, assured the people of Northern Ireland of Britain's determination to end the violence.[10] In his Christmas message, Brian Faulkner echoed Heath by giving 'a guarantee that there will be no let-up whatsoever in the drive that is under way to combat the terrorists'. Thus by the end of 1971, there is no doubt that the army was at least contemplating draconian measures to restore law and order in Derry and the governments at Westminster and Stormont knew of them. On 29 December, another soldier, Richard Ham (20), a gunner from the Royal Artillery, was shot dead by an IRA sniper whilst on foot patrol in Derry. His mother had offered to buy him out of the army several times, but he had refused.[11]

Ford visited Derry again on 7 January 1972 and reported back to Tuzo in an even more pessimistic memo marked 'PERSONAL AND CONFIDENTIAL'. He had met Brigadier Andrew MacLellan, the Commander of 8 Brigade that covers the Derry area, Lieutenant-Colonel James Ferguson, the Commanding Officer of the 22nd Light Air Defence Regiment, Royal Artillery, which covered the Bogside, and Chief Superintendent Frank Lagan, the senior RUC officer in charge of the city. Lagan was a Catholic and as such nearly unique in the upper echelons of the almost exclusively Protestant force. Lagan and the generals did not always see eye-to-eye. Lagan knew Derry and its people like the back of his hand. The generals knew their maps.

Ford was 'disturbed' by the attitude he encountered at the meeting.[12] They told him that there had been no let-up in the daily 'yobbo' activity and, more worryingly, 'The Front' of teenage arsonists was pushing further forward and even more streets and shops would 'go up' unless there was a change in military policy. Ford was not pleased to hear from his commanders that no foot or vehicle patrols were operating around the entrance to the Bogside lest they present themselves as targets for snipers from the

Rossville Flats, the huge blocks that dominate the entrance to the Bogside. He was told that even if soldiers made sorties in the army's armoured personnel carriers (APCs), they ran the risk of being surrounded by 'yobbos', forced to dismount, and becoming sitting ducks for snipers once again. Clearly the first 'option' that Ford had favoured a few weeks earlier did not appear to be working.

Ford also met the city centre traders who clearly gave him an earful in terms of 'the usual pessimistic message'. Under the circumstances, there was no reason for the message to be otherwise. He tried to soothe them 'with the usual encouraging talk about the province as a whole' but seems to have made little headway. He came away with their message ringing in his ears. '. . . they want as a minimum the Rossville Flats cleared (5,000 people live in them and a soldier has never entered them in the history of Londonderry) and ideally the Creggan and Bogside occupied. They also wanted curfews and shooting on sight.'

Ford told Tuzo that it was clear from his visit to Derry that although the situation was difficult, it could be dealt with 'using normal I.S. [Internal Security] methods and equipment'. There was one problem, however, that he feared might not be susceptible to normal I.S. methods, at least not those used in the United Kingdom. He then wrote the following extra-ordinary two paragraphs. The first, in a startling admission, outlined the day-to-day reality the army faced.

> However, the Londonderry situation is further complicated by one additional ingredient. This is the Derry Young Hooligans (DYH). Gangs of tough teenage youths permanently unemployed, have developed sophisticated tactics of brick and stone throwing, destruction and arson. Under cover of snipers from nearby buildings, they operate just beyond the hard core areas and extend the radius of anarchy by degrees into additional streets and areas. Against the DYH – described by the People's Democracy [a left-wing student civil rights organization] as 'Brave fighters in the Republican cause' – the army in Londonderry is for the moment virtually incapable. This incapacity undermines our ability to deal with the gunmen and bombers and threatens what is left of law and order on the West Bank of the River Foyle.

The second paragraph dealt with the extreme and potentially explosive way of dealing with the Derry Young Hooligans.

> Attempts to close with the DYH bring the troops into the killing zone of the snipers. As I understand it, the commander of a body of

troops called out to restore law and order has a duty to use minimum force but also he has a duty to restore law and order. We have fulfilled the first duty but are failing in the second. *I am coming to the conclusion that the minimum force necessary to achieve a restoration of law and order is to shoot selected ring leaders amongst the DYH, after clear warnings have been issued.* [Author's emphasis]

Ford also suggested that consideration should be given to using less lethal ammunition to minimize the danger to those being aimed at. He said such an approach would be reverting to the Internal Security methods 'found successful on many occasions overseas'. He concluded with the startling observation that he was 'convinced that our duty to restore law and order requires us to consider this step.' (He later made it clear that it was not an instruction to kill and pointed out that 'shoot' and 'kill' were obviously different words.) Ford wrote his memo to Tuzo as the Northern Ireland Civil Rights Association (NICRA) was considering an anti-internment march in Derry from the Creggan to the Guildhall Square on Sunday afternoon, 16 January. He asked Brigadier MacLellan for a plan in case the march took place, 'taking into account the likelihood of some form of battle', and sent the army's Director of Intelligence to Derry to make an assessment of the possible strength of the march and its real intentions. His senior commanders had already told him that, however good NICRA's intentions, 'the DYH backed up by the gunmen will undoubtedly take over control at an early stage'. Amongst the Battalions Ford notified was 1 Para. The scene was set for 'Bloody Sunday'.

Since the summer of 1971, all marches had been declared illegal by the Stormont Government as a quid pro quo for internment. The Heath Government hoped that by banning the parades the temperature in the highly volatile summer season would be lowered. But in the charged climate of the time, banning marches did not mean they would not go ahead. A ban might even be an added incentive. On 11 January, five days before the proposed NICRA march, the Cabinet's Northern Ireland Policy Committee, known as GEN 47, met in London to consider, presumably amongst other issues, the situation in Derry. Certainly there is no hint of imminent crisis in the minutes of the meeting. 'A military operation to re-impose law and order in Londonderry might *in time* [author's emphasis] become inevitable, but should not be undertaken while there still remained some prospect of a successful political initiative.'[13] In GEN 47, hope sprang eternal. The wording suggests that the Cabinet had accepted General Ford's first option. There is no indication that Ministers were aware of his alarming memo to Lieutenant-General

Tuzo written only four days before GEN 47 met. Either Ministers were being kept in the dark or they were not sufficiently concerned to find out what the military thinking *really* was. Ministers had not been aware of the Five Techniques. Perhaps a plausible explanation is that Ford's memorandum was merely contemplating the worst-case scenario. We do not know what Tuzo's reaction was.

In the event, NICRA postponed the anti-internment march contemplated for 16 January but its Derry supporters were not to be denied the opportunity to make their point. On Saturday 22 January, around 3,000 people, mainly from the Derry area, marched to the new internment camp that had just opened at Magilligan Point, a headland about twenty miles from Derry on the eastern shore of Lough Foyle, which had been used as a weekend training base for the Territorial Army.

The mood was relaxed and friendly. The commanding officer of the Second Battalion, The Royal Green Jackets who had the responsibility of guarding the camp offered the marchers tea and buns if they followed an agreed route.[14] The marchers, however, declined and made their way onto the long, sandy beach only to find their way barred by coils of barbed wire that stretched along the strand but stopped short of the sea as it was a very low tide. Behind stood not only the Green Jackets but 1 Para's C company (around a hundred soldiers) who had been brought in from Belfast in case of trouble. The Battalion's commanding officer, Lieutenant-Colonel Wilford, was not with them at the time and the Paras were under Green Jacket command. Their Adjutant, however, was there and he feared 'the security of the Internment Centre could be breached'.

The protesters, seeing the gap between the wire and the water and with the internment camp in their sights, made for the opening to find their progress blocked. A fierce battle on the beach ensued, with baton-wielding Paras at the forefront backed by a hail of 'rubber bullets' – the black, hard baton rounds that can be lethal if fired at close quarters.

The violent confrontation was captured by the television cameras and the image was clear: peaceful demonstrators being clubbed to the ground by brutal paratroopers. John Hume was present and looked on in horror but his pleas for calm went unheeded. One paratrooper was subsequently disciplined for repeatedly beating a marcher on the ground. When the Green Jackets told the Paras that they had been too hard, a Para officer replied that if they had not, there would have been 2,000 demonstrators in their internment camp.

The protesters returned to Derry, bloodied and bruised but determined to march again. The following Tuesday, the Derry branch of NICRA issued a statement calling on its supporters to gather for a huge anti-internment march in the city the following Sunday, 30 January 1972. It was to start at Bishop's Field in the Creggan at 2 p.m. and make its way to the Guildhall Square in the city centre. Stormont, in consultation with the Joint Security Committee, had just extended the ban on marches for another year. The same day, to add to the tension, Paisleyites in Derry issued a rallying call. 'We call upon all the loyalists of Derry for their support at this time,' they said. 'The Queen's writ must run in every part of the city and the law must be administered fairly to all sections of the community.'[15]

On Thursday morning, 27 January, the temperature was raised even higher when the IRA ambushed and shot dead two policemen in their patrol car near the Creggan, Sergeant Peter Gilgunn (26) and Constable David Montgomery (20). They were the first members of the RUC to be killed in the city since the outbreak of violence. Sergeant Gilgunn was a Catholic.[16] That afternoon, the IRA sent a message to the Paras by exploding two bombs inside the perimenter fence of Palace Barracks, Holywood, where the First Battalion was based. The same day in London, GEN 47 met to discuss Sunday's NICRA march. Former Prime Minister Heath recollected that 'the possibility of using firearms was not discussed and no specific political authority was sought or given for the use of firearms'.[17]

At Army Headquarters at Lisburn that Thursday morning there had already been a meeting of the Director of Operations Committee ('D. Ops') which assembled every Thursday at 10 a.m. It was run by the GOC, Lieutenant-General Tuzo, and consisted of the Chief Constable, an Assistant Chief Constable, the Head of RUC Special Branch, the Head of Army Intelligence and the UK Representative. The Secretary to the Committee was Gavin, the young Major in army planning who had first suggested Long Kesh as a suitable place for an internment camp. He gave me his recollection of the meeting's agenda that morning.

I believe that there was some discussion about how to handle this march – where to allow it to proceed and where to encourage it to stop or redirect it. The Chief Constable gave his views and I believe that there was a plan in principle. The idea was that the march should be prevented from getting to the centre of Londonderry and it was left to local military and police commanders to work out those sort of general arrangements.

Was there any plan to take on the IRA that day? Any discussion about it?

Oh no, no, no, not at all. Not at all. This was one of several marches that was probably discussed at the time and there was no intention to use this march to make a military or security force point.

Not at all. And indeed the people round the room, they wouldn't have discussed that. That would not be an issue.

But might they have discussed it elsewhere, privately?

I can't say, but I doubt it. I very much doubt it. This is not something that would have been encouraged at all. In hindsight very obviously not. There's no way that those sort of people at that level were considering anything other than containment and avoiding casualties and keeping things played down as much as possible.

The military plan was to prevent the illegal march from reaching its destination in the Guildhall Square by stopping it at the bottom of William Street and diverting it along Rossville Street past the flats and into the Bogside where the marchers could hold their rally at 'Free Derry' corner. Barricades manned by the Green Jackets were to be placed across the approaches to the Guildhall Square and the city centre. The army knew that at this point, barring a miracle, there would be a riot and the Derry Young Hooligans would go into action, no doubt fired up by the television images of Paras beating up Catholics at Magilligan the weekend before. It seemed a perfect opportunity to confront the DYH and take the firm action against them that Derry's Protestant business community had long been demanding. Major-General Ford, it is believed with the approval of higher authority, had ordered 1 Para to be brought in from Belfast to 'scoop up' the rioters. Ministers in London were informed of the plan and gave it their approval. The operation, therefore, had political sanction at the highest level, which is not surprising given the sensitivity of the operation and the climate of the time.[18]

When army commanders in Derry were notified that 1 Para was to be given this 'scoop-up' role, they were not happy. The Paras knew Belfast but had never served in Derry. The Colonel of the Royal Anglians protested to Brigadier MacLellan and argued that his men, who knew the city, should do the 'scooping up' and that if the Paras were to be used, they should be manning the barricades, not chasing rioters. Another senior officer in Derry, who thought the plan to use the Paras was 'mad', told me that he rang up MacLellan and said that he 'must not allow the Paras into Derry'. MacLellan replied that he had his orders.

Chief Superintendent Lagan was not only against the use of the Paras but opposed to diverting the march. He argued that in terms of keeping the peace, it would be far better to let the demonstrators through to the Guildhall Square as the consequences would be far less than stopping the march at the bottom of William Street with the inevitable confrontation with the 'hooligans'. Once the marchers were inside the relatively narrow confines of the Guildhall Square, Lagan argued, they could be photographed and, if necessary, action taken against them later for participating in an illegal march.

Furthermore, Lagan knew from his intelligence reports and through his own personal contacts in the Bogside and Creggan that neither wing of the IRA had any intention of taking on the army that day because of the risk to civilians, and they had been prevailed upon by local community leaders to take their weapons out of the Bogside and store them in the Creggan estate. Dr Raymond McClean, a Derry general practitioner, was one of those who made the plea, fearing the consequences of any possible IRA action. 'We said we would like to have a massive demonstration against internment,' he told me. 'The message came back that if we wanted the demonstration, the IRA would leave that day to us and leave us alone. They weren't using us. We believed what they said.'[19]

Nevertheless, despite Lagan's intimate knowledge of Derry and its Catholic community, his advice was ignored. He contacted the Chief Constable, Sir Graham Shillington, but there was nothing Sir Graham could do. The march was to be stopped and the rioters 'scooped up'. It was seen as a political decision taken way above the heads of Lagan and MacLellan. The plan was put in place and code-named 'Operation Forecast'. The forecast was grim.

On Friday afternoon, 28 January, MacLellan held his final briefing at Ebrington Barracks in Derry for his commanders, including Lieutenant-Colonel Derek Wilford, the commanding officer of 1 Para. The 8 Infantry Brigade Operation Order no 2/72, classified 'Secret' and written by Mac-Lellan the previous day, was discussed line by line. It stressed that the march should be dealt with in as low a key as possible for as long as possible, and if the march were contained peacefully within the Bogside and Creggan areas, then no action should be taken against it.[20] The army was only to respond if the marchers tried to breach the security barriers blocking the route to the city centre or used violence against the security forces. Under those circumstances, water cannon and baton rounds were to be used, and, as a last resort if troops were about to be overrun, CS gas. The section of the Operation Order that applied to 1 Para was headed 'Hooliganism'.

> An arrest force is to be held centrally behind the check points and launched in a 'scoop-up' operation to arrest as many hooligans and rioters as possible . . . This operation will only be launched either in whole or in part on the orders of the Brigade Commander . . . It is expected that the arrest operation will be conducted on foot.[21]

The plan was to wait until the hooligans had become separated from the march and then scoop them up as quickly as possible. The plan did not envisage the army getting sucked into the Bogside. In all the secret security and political minutes and memoranda that were subsequently uncovered and revealed in connection with 'Bloody Sunday', there is no suggestion of any 'secret' plan for the army to draw out the IRA, take on its gunmen and then take over the Bogside and Creggan.[22] As one senior officer closely involved told me, 'I can think of better ways of thumping the IRA than doing it with all the media in the world watching and thousands on the streets.' To date, although no evidence has been found of any 'smoking gun' that would indicate a plan to entrap the IRA, Major-General Ford's memorandum to Lieutenant-General Tuzo of 7 January 1972, in which he concludes 'the minimum force necessary to achieve a restoration of law and order is to shoot selected ring leaders amongst the DYH', is a gun that may not be smoking but might be seen as dangerously loaded.

Lieutenant-Colonel Wilford remembers asking MacLellan at the Brigade briefing what would happen if the IRA started shooting.

I got really what was a very sparse reply to the effect that, 'Oh well, we'll deal with that when it comes.' It's my greatest regret that I didn't pursue that question and say, 'What do you want us to do if we're shot at?'

But why didn't you pursue the question, given its critical importance?

We were the Belfast Battalion. There we behaved in a recognized way. It was never necessary to ask that question. I asked it there in Derry because we were on new ground. But when I got the reply that I did, I accepted that we'd deal with it when it comes, assuming that there'd be specific orders. But I regret now, of course, that I didn't pursue it.

So if shooting did break out, how were your men trained to react?

If someone starts shooting at you, you can behave in a variety of ways. You can run away – which, of course, on the whole soldiers don't. You could take cover behind your shields and just sit in an area until it all passed over. Or you could do what my Battalion was trained to do – move forward, seek out the enemy and engage them.[23]

Most of Wilford's men probably relished the thought of going into Derry and scooping up its 'Young Hooligans'. They too, like their commanding officer, had watched television pictures of the daily ritual at 'aggro corner' and were appalled that the rioters were allowed to get away with it. They knew that Kitson would never have tolerated it in Belfast and saw no reason why it should be tolerated in Derry. 'It had got totally out of control,' Support Company's Sergeant-Major told me. 'I think it was about time somebody went across there and did something about it – somebody with a bit more "go" than the resident Battalions in London-derry. It was time it was stopped.'[24] Although the men of Support Company, which was to be in the front line of the arrest operation, had no personal knowledge of Derry and the Bogside area in which they would be operating, they had been well briefed on its geography and on what to expect. They were certainly familiar with the black dots on the map, the 'containment line' they knew they would have to breach. When Wilford briefed his men, he left them in no doubt what might be in store.

> I pointed out they were going into a situation that was totally alien to them. The Bogside was a 'no-go' area and the army was peripheral. In the arrest operation, we were likely to step over the 'containment line' which would then take us into territory which had previously been declared 'no-go'. That was potentially very, very dangerous because the IRA for the first time would be faced with something they had not come up against. This was bound to make them behave aggressively.[25]

The soldiers of Support Company, who were detailed to cross the line in their armoured personnel carriers and 'de-bus' in the vicinity of the nine-storey-high Rossville Flats, knew what they were likely to face. The Company Sergeant-Major vividly remembers what his men were told to expect.

> The one thing that stuck in my mind was the fact that we were warned about sniper fire, possibly from the Rossville Flats. Sniper fire is very, very accurate and pinpointed. It's feared by soldiers. A sniper can fire through a window from ten feet inside a bedroom and you can't see him at all. It's something to be very, very wary of. The majority of soldiers up to that period killed in Belfast and Derry had been killed by very, very accurate sniper fire and none of the people in my Company wanted to be killed by a sniper.[26]

What the soldiers were not told was that, of the nearly 2,000 shots fired at the army in Derry over the preceding three months, only nine came from Rossville Flats.[27] The Paras were conditioned to expect the worst.

Chapter Eight

'Bloody Sunday' – The Killing Zone

30 January 1972

The morning of Sunday 30 January dawned clear and bright, a perfect day for a march. A huge crowd assembled at about 2 p.m. at Bishop's Field, an area of well-trodden grass by the shops atop the Creggan. The organizers estimated the numbers to be around 20,000. The security forces' estimate was a good deal less, but still one that recognized that a huge number had turned out, many no doubt galvanized by the scenes at Magilligan the previous weekend. There was a carnival atmosphere in the late January cold sunshine. It was so relaxed that Dr Raymond McClean decided to leave his first aid kit at home rather than lug it around on the march. He also believed that the atmosphere was likely to stay relaxed after both wings of the IRA had agreed to take their weapons out of the Bogside. IRA members were present but as stewards on the march, minus masks and guns, which was common practice. As the procession led by a coal lorry wound its way from Bishop's Field around the Creggan and Bogside and finally towards the city centre, the Green Jackets manning the barricades received the news from Army Headquarters in Lisburn that one of their officers, Major Robin Alers-Hankey, had just died in hospital in London. He had been shot in the stomach four months earlier by a sniper in Derry as he deployed his troops to protect firemen fighting a blaze.[1]

It was nearly an hour before the march finally got under way, which was not unusual for an event of this size. By 3.30 p.m. it was moving down William Street towards the Green Jackets who were manning barricade 14 that blocked the entrance to the Guildhall Square. The stewards, not seeking a confrontation with the army, diverted most of the march right along Rossville Street and towards 'Free Derry' corner where the rally was due to be addressed by Bernadette Devlin and the Labour life peer Lord Fenner Brockway, a veteran campaigner on Northern Ireland civil rights issues. But, as predicted, the Derry Young Hooligans, and some older ones too, broke away from the main body of the march to get within, literally, spitting range of the Green Jackets at barricade 14. The soldiers then came under attack from a hail of missiles.

Meanwhile, with the riot gathering momentum, stragglers at the end of the march were still making their way down William Street and past the Paras who had taken up position by the Presbyterian church where they had been doing a 'recce' over a high wall. Two soldiers were positioned on top of an oil tank to do so. 'Phil', the sergeant of the Mortar Platoon, told me that initially the plan was for his armoured vehicle 'to punch a hole through the wall so that we got onto open ground and got behind the crowd if it was required'. Abuse, bottles and bricks were hurled at them too. By now it was clear to the marchers, seeing the soldiers' red berets, that the Paras had been deployed, which probably gave added impetus to their throwing power with memories of Magilligan still fresh in their minds. The Paras responded by firing baton rounds.

The precise sequence of events in what happened next, just before 4 p.m., is confused but of critical importance since it was probably the incident that triggered 'Bloody Sunday'. What is beyond doubt is that both the IRA and the paratroopers opened fire. The IRA fired one round and the soldiers fired five.[2] The critical question is, who fired first? According to the Major who was Support Company's commander, at 'about 3.55 p.m.' a single shot rang out from Columbcille Court, the flats on the other side of William Street, directly opposite the Presbyterian church. The high-velocity round hit a drainpipe running down the side of the church. It did no damage, except to the drainpipe, but its significance was immense. It told the Paras that what they had heard at their briefing was true. 'Phil' has no doubt that *was* the first shot, fired at the two soldiers on top of the oil tank. Lieutenant-Colonel Wilford heard the sound in his command post nearby. 'That shot was aimed at us, sir,' his Adjutant informed him. Wilford was not surprised and knew the implications. 'Its significance was that there was at least one weapon on the other side. And if there was one, then there were probably others.' The shot is believed to have been fired by a member of the Official IRA. The gunman is said to have been confronted by the Provisionals and told in no uncertain terms to get out of the area.[3] Around the same time, just before 4 p.m., two members of Support Company's Machine Gun Platoon in the vicinity of the church fired five shots at rioters they said they believed were nail-bombers. The rounds hit a fifteen-year-old schoolboy, Damien Donaghy, in the thigh, and 59-year-old John Johnston in the leg and left shoulder. Donaghy survived but Johnston died over three months later. Neither was a nail-bomber. Johnston was not actually on the march but on his way to see a friend in Glenfada Park, the low three-storey block of maisonettes opposite Rossville Flats.[4] Donaghy was simply retrieving a rubber bullet.[5]

By this time, the rioting at barricade 14 had become even more intense and the army had brought in water cannon in the hope of dousing the rioters' spirits. Wilford, eagerly awaiting the order from MacLellan to move in for the 'scoop up', thought the scene was 'a bloody shambles' with soldiers playing their accustomed role as 'Aunt Sallies'. The Lieutenant-Colonel was becoming impatient lest the optimum time to strike was being lost, and the commanders of Support and C Companies, who were to make up the snatch squads, were growing impatient too. According to the Brigade log, Wilford finally got the green light at 4.07 p.m. but with the specific instruction in 'Serial 159' that he was 'not to conduct running battle down Rossville Street'.[6] Clearly MacLellan wanted to keep the problem within bounds. C Company was to advance through barricade 14 and up Chamberlain Street and Support Company through barricade 12 and up Rossville Street. Barricade 12 was located in a side street just below the Presbyterian church. Together the two Companies were to form a pincer movement to cut off the rioters and perhaps trap many of them in the extensive courtyard of Rossville Flats.

Wilford gave the command, 'Move! Move! Move!' and Major-General Ford, who was watching close by, purely as an observer of the implementation of MacLellan's plan, wished them well and apparently urged them on with the words, 'Go on, One Para. Go and get them and good luck!'[7] Suddenly pent-up tensions were released as Support Company leapt into their armoured personal carriers (known as 'pigs') and prepared to roar after the DYH. The Company Sergeant-Major (CSM) told me he was concerned when he saw one of his men cocking his weapon as he jumped into the vehicle in front. 'I earmarked him and thought, "When I get back, I'll kick his arse, because cocking a weapon like that is contrary to orders." But I could understand it. The guy was probably tensed up in view of the briefing we'd had.'[8]

Support Company's 'pigs' screamed into the courtyard/car park area of Rossville Flats and fanned out to hem in the fleeing crowd. Chief Superintendent Lagan, who was in MacLellan's office when Serial 159 was given, had no doubt it signified a strictly limited operation and the Paras, by roaring into the Bogside, were exceeding the order 'not to conduct running battle'. The containment line had not just been breached, it had been smashed.

'Phil' was in the second 'pig' behind his Platoon commander's vehicle which hooked left into the crowd. 'Phil' ordered his driver to go past it and then swing left into the crowd as well. 'But we went a little bit further than I'd actually intended and ended up in the car park area of Rossville Flats. We de-bussed there,' he told me. 'By that time, we'd trapped 100 to 150 of the crowd in that area and they were streaming past us. We then went in to make arrests.' 'Phil' says he got hold of one man and, 'after a bit of tussle', dragged him towards the back of the 'pig'. It was at this point that he says he heard shots coming from the area of the Flats. 'Three or four weapons,' he said. 'I've got no doubt in my mind there was a multiple of weapons firing. It was the highest concentration of fire I'd personally heard in Northern Ireland. I'd heard one or two gunmen firing before but this was a quick sort of burst, maybe twenty to thirty rounds from various weapons. There was a strike on the ground between us and the wall which was to my left.' 'Phil' threw the man he had just arrested to his Lance-Corporal, moved to the front of the 'pig', took up position by its left bumper and started looking for targets.

> The weapons were ready cocked. We were ready to go. As far as I'm concerned, we were under fire. It changed from an ordinary 'scoop-up' arrest operation to 'hey, someone's trying to kill me! Let's find out who it is and do the job back.' And that is very much the attitude you'll get from the Parachute Regiment soldier. He doesn't go for cover. He doesn't crawl around on the ground. He looks for targets. We looked for them, started identifying them and started dropping them – shooting them. The first one I saw was in the car park with a pistol, within 50 metres, and I've no doubt whatsoever the man was armed.
>
> **Couldn't it have been a piece of wood he was holding, or a rock or something?**
>
> Why should it be kicking? There was a definite jerk as the trigger was pulled. There was a definite movement of the man firing a weapon at me.
>
> **Wasn't it risky opening fire when there were so many civilians milling around?**
>
> You've got to be joking when you ask a question like that. Someone is trying to kill you. What do you say? 'Well, I'm very sorry. I won't fire back. I'll let someone else just keep shooting at me.' My job was to stop that, to put them down. And that's what we did.
>
> **Did you hit him?**
>
> I'm positive I did. The first round missed, I'll give you that, but the second two didn't. Once I knew he was down, I was then looking for other targets.[9]

In all, 'Phil' fired eight rounds that day, each one, he says, an aimed shot. The second target he says he identified was a man on the first-floor veranda at the junction where two blocks of Rossville Flats meet at an angle. 'I'm clearly convinced that it was a shot by a shoulder-held weapon, not a pistol, and he was firing down into the area where we were. Again, I'd seen the flash of the weapon being fired. I fired three rounds at him. He went down and I'm sure I hit him as well.' He says he then fired two more rounds, making eight in all, into a tunnel of the Flats where he says the same type of weapon was firing back. 'Phil' does not know whether he hit that particular 'gunman' or not, but that was where he put his last two rounds. 'We returned fire and we won the day,' he told me. 'We were hitting them or making them go to ground. They were not hitting us.'

As with the earlier shooting of Damien Donaghy and John Johnston, the question of who fired first in the Rossville Flats area is central to unravelling the true story of what actually happened on the ground. The first person to die in the courtyard of Rossville Flats was seventeen-year-old Jack 'Jackie' Duddy. Four others – Margaret Deery (37), Michael Bridge (25), Michael Bradley (22) and Patrick McDaid (24) – were wounded. Duddy was hit by a single shot in the chest. Father Edward Daly, later Bishop Daly, came to his aid, having seen him running away from the soldiers. Dr Daly and other eye-witnesses had no doubt whatsoever that he was unarmed. Bishop Daly later told me that he was certain that the paratroopers did *not* come under fire. 'I am satisfied in my own mind from the behaviour of the soldiers themselves that they were not being fired at. I'm quite satisfied too that every individual was picked and targeted. But even if there were shots, I do not think that what the Paras did was justified. I believe it was murder.'[10] One of the lasting images of 'Bloody Sunday' is that of a stooping Father Daly, waving a white blood-stained handkerchief as a flag of truce, leading the knot of men carrying Duddy's body. He had already administered the last rites. Bishop Daly confirmed that he *did* see one gunman with a pistol, but only *after* the Paras had started firing.

The other twelve victims of 'Bloody Sunday' died elsewhere. Two men, Pat Doherty (31) and Bernard 'Barney' McGuigan (41), were shot dead on the other side of Rossville Flats. McGuigan was hit in the head as he crawled to the aid of the dying Doherty who had been shot through the buttock with the bullet exiting through his chest. Two others – Daniel McGowan (37) and Patrick Campbell (53) – were wounded in the area.[11] Six men, most of them teenagers – Hugh Gilmore (17), Kevin McElhinney (17), Michael Kelly (17), John Young (17), William Nash (19) and Michael McDaid (20) – were killed in the vicinity of a rubble barricade placed across Rossville Street between the Flats and the maisonettes of Glenfada Park. It has been suggested that McDaid, Nash and Young could have been shot by one or more of the army snipers who were in place on the city walls and who did open fire. These soldiers were not Paras but members of 22 Light Air Detachment and 1st Battalion, The Royal Anglians who were positioned on the walls or in derelict buildings nearby as observers and snipers.[12] Four men – James Wray (22), Gerald Donaghy (17), Gerald McKinney (35) and William McKinney (26) – were shot in Glenfada Park where many had sought shelter after the intensive shooting around the barricade on Rossville Street and elsewhere. In addition, a number of people were shot and wounded – Joseph Friel (20), Michael Quinn (17), Daniel Gillespie (31), Paddy O'Donnell (41) and Joseph Mahon (16).

In the half hour following Lieutenant-Colonel Wilford's command to 'Move! Move! Move!' Support Company had fired 108 rounds and made thirty of the fifty-four arrests.[13] The Paras had overwhelmed the area. 'Quite honestly, I owned the Bogside in military terms,' Wilford told me. 'I occupied it.'[14] Having got so far, his men were ready for the order to carry on up into the Creggan, sweep away the barricades and end 'Free Derry' and the no-go area once and for all. Nothing would have given Wilford and 1 Para more pleasure than to re-establish the Queen's writ. But it was not to be. 'Phil' was left frustrated and bemused.

> The feeling was, 'Look, this has started. We've got to keep moving. Let's roll. We're ready.' We'd won, shall we say, the fire-fight for want of a better word. Now we were ready to move forward. Somebody, somewhere said, 'No. Stand still.' Then it was, 'Right, back out.' Support Company wasn't happy with that. There was obviously trouble in the Bogside that day. Why not stop the trouble completely? I think the no-go area would have gone that day. I don't understand why it was stopped.

In effect, the Paras had carried out the first stage of Option 3 recorded in Ford's memorandum to Tuzo of 14 December 1971. It was the option Ford rejected because, as he wrote, 'the risk of casualties is high and apart from gunmen and bombers, so-called unarmed rioters, possibly teenagers, are certain to be shot in the initial phases. Much will be made of the invasion of Derry and the slaughter of the innocent.' Ford's analysis was a nightmare come true. Wilford's men had shot dead thirteen people. Eye-witnesses insisted that none of them or any of the injured was armed or carrying nail-bombs or any other offensive weapon. At the inquests, the Coroner, Major Hubert O'Neill, did not hide his feelings.

> This Sunday became known as 'Bloody Sunday' and bloody it was. It was quite unnecessary. It strikes me that the army ran amok that day and shot without thinking what they were doing. They were shooting innocent people. These people may have been taking part

in a march that was banned but that does not justify the troops coming in and firing live rounds indiscriminately. I would say without hesitation that it was sheer, unadulterated murder.[15]

To this day, the Paras assert they only targeted gunmen and nail-bombers and insist that they were fired on first. 'Phil' described the atmosphere when they returned to their temporary base at Drumahoe. 'The mood between the blokes was, not elation, but at the same time, it was a job well done. Don't forget if somebody's firing at you and you fire back and you kill him, you've stopped him killing you. You're not going to tell me that's not a job well done.' I asked him if he had any regrets. 'My only regret is that I was put in a position where I had to defend myself on the streets of Britain. If it happened again tomorrow in the same set of circumstances, I would do exactly the same thing and I would think my men would do exactly the same thing with me.' Did the deaths rest on his conscience? 'No, not in the slightest.' 'Phil' blamed NICRA for organizing an illegal march and putting 'innocent civilians into an area where they could be killed' and the IRA for putting 'gunmen into the crowd to take on the British army'.

The question of whether or not there were other gunmen in the Bogside who opened fire on the Paras – apart from the Official who fired the single shot that hit the drainpipe by the Presbyterian church and the man with the pistol seen by Father Daly – still remains unclear. I understand that the Official IRA did leave some weapons behind in the area for 'defensive' purposes. The most that former Officials I spoke to would admit was that 'there was always the possibility that somebody had a small-arm and used it on their own initiative'. They told me that their Standing Orders had just been changed, permitting weapons to be fired only 'in defence and retaliation'. 'Offensive' operations were ruled out. The smashing of the containment line by a phalanx of armoured vehicles and the apparent invasion of the Bogside by the Paras may have been more than enough in the Officials' eyes to warrant the use of weapons in both 'defence and retaliation'.[16] But whatever the uncertainty about the role of both wings of the IRA at the beginning of 'Bloody Sunday', there is no doubt that once the shooting started and it became clear that people were being killed, both the Official and the Provisional IRA came down from the Creggan with weapons in the boots of cars and opened fire. That seems to have happened some time after 4.30 p.m. when most of the shooting was over.[17]

But not every Para shared the gung-ho attitude of 'Phil'. In a remarkable interview I conducted for the BBC documentary, 'Remember Bloody Sunday', transmitted on its twentieth anniversary, the Company Sergeant-Major of Support Company admitted with astonishing candour reservations about what happened. He was still serving at the time of the interview. When his men returned to Drumahoe and were accounting for each round they had fired, he noticed that one had actually fired two more rounds than had been issued to him.

I said, 'What the hell were you doing?' And he said, 'I was firing at the enemy. I was firing at gunmen.'
Did you believe him?
I didn't know what to think at the time.
Did you believe him?
No. Knowing the soldier as I do know him, I don't believe he was firing at gunmen.
Did you see any gunmen?
No.
Did you see any weapons?
No.
Did you see any nail-bombers?
No.
Do you believe, all these years on, that all the dead were gunmen and bombers?
No, not at all. I feel in my own heart that a lot of these people were innocent. I feel very guilty about the subsequent effect of that day [i.e. the number of mates he lost as a result of a strengthened IRA]. I think it was badly handled. By everybody. By me, the Platoon sergeants, the individual soldiers and our superiors. There was control from above prior to the deployment. It was contained. But after the deployment, it became quite chaotic.[18]

After the interview was shown, I received several letters from people in Derry saying how much they appreciated his honesty and courage in breaking what they saw as the 'party line'. Where requested, I passed the letters on to him. Lieutenant-Colonel Wilford, too, had regrets about the effect of that day, and it was clear it had had a profound personal impact on him. After 'Bloody Sunday', Derek Wilford became an army officer with a brilliant future behind him. He had been hoping to follow in Kitson's academic footsteps and go to Oxford to write a thesis but the opportunity never materialized. He retired from the army in 1981, a disillusioned man, and returned to painting on canvas after a series of MOD desk jobs which had taken him from Whitehall to Nigeria. 'There has to be a scapegoat and I was the one,' he said. 'I'm not bitter about it. The only good thing about being a scapegoat is that you protect other people. I adored my soldiers and

I protected them because I believed they were right.' I asked if he was still protecting them. 'I suppose so,' he said.

In 1998, as part of the confidence-building measures on the republican side that were necessary to bring the Republican Movement into the peace process, Prime Minister Tony Blair announced a further inquiry into the events of 'Bloody Sunday' in an attempt to get at the truth. The previous inquiry conducted by the Lord Chief Justice of England, Lord Widgery, in 1972 in the immediate aftermath of the shootings and published barely three months afterwards, was dismissed by nationalists as a 'whitewash' and a cover-up because his report largely exonerated the soldiers. When Prime Minister Heath met Lord Widgery at Downing Street the day after 'Bloody Sunday', he advised him that 'it had to be remembered that we are in Northern Ireland fighting not only a military war but a propaganda war'.[19] Although at one stage Widgery admitted that some soldiers' firing 'bordered on the reckless',[20] his broad conclusions were pro-Para.

> Civilian, as well as army, evidence made it clear that there was a substantial number of civilians in the area who were armed with firearms. I would not be surprised if in the relevant half hour as many rounds were fired at the troops as were fired by them. The soldiers escaped injury by reason of their field-craft and training . . . in general the accounts given by the soldiers of the circumstances in which they fired and the reasons why they did so were, in my opinion, truthful.[21]

To the bereaved families of Derry, the hurt caused by the Widgery Report further compounded that caused by the killing of their loved ones. Since then they have fought for what they see as 'justice'. On 29 January 1998, Tony Blair told the House of Commons that there would be a new, full-scale judicial inquiry into 'Bloody Sunday', chaired by an English Law Lord, Lord Saville of Newdigate, accompanied by two Commonwealth appeal court judges, Sir Edward Somers from New Zealand and William Hoyt from Canada. No expense was spared, witnesses were given immunity from prosecution, and all Government and army records, secret and otherwise, were to be revealed. The timescale was open-ended. The purpose, the Prime Minister concluded, 'is simply to establish the truth and to close this painful chapter once and for all . . . I believe that it is in everyone's interest that the truth be established and told.'[22]

After two years of gathering evidence at a cost of £15 million, the inquiry's formal hearings began on 27 March 2000 in the historic surroundings of

Derry's Guildhall, ironically the marchers' original destination on 'Bloody Sunday'. Twenty-eight years later, they got there. It is estimated that, unlike Widgery's twenty-one-day hearings and report delivered in less than three months after the event, the Saville Inquiry could last up to four years and cost up to £100 million pounds, with senior counsels' fees running at around £1,500 a day and their juniors' at £750.[23] It often seems that there are more lawyers in the Guildhall than spectators, and there are plenty of those. If any truly independent body can get at the truth of what happened on 'Bloody Sunday', it seems that Lord Saville and his colleagues have a good chance of doing so. In his opening address, the Tribunal's counsel, Christopher Clarke QC, set out the Inquiry's position.

> What happened – whatever the truth of the matter – was a tragedy, the pain of which has endured down the passage of years. The Tribunal's task is to discover as far as humanly possible in the circumstances, the truth, pure and simple, painful or unacceptable to whoever that truth may be.[24]

Certainly, by the time the formal hearings began, it appeared that the Tribunal was going to let nothing stand in its way, and that included threatening journalists, including myself, with legal action for refusing to reveal the names of their sources. Whether the Tribunal delivers the 'justice' the families are looking for, remains to be seen.

By the summer of the year 2000, there had been two dramatic developments in the Inquiry. One of Lord Saville's two judicial colleagues, Sir Edward Somers, resigned 'for personal reasons' and 'after much soul-searching'. It was thought that the long and arduous journey from New Zealand to Derry was proving too much for the 72-year-old judge. Sir Edward's place on the bench was taken by the Honourable John Toohey, a former Australian High Court judge.[25]

The second development was even more dramatic. On 18 August 2000, it was revealed that the Inquiry had negotiated financial terms under which a key Para witness, known as 'Private 027', would give evidence. He was tantamount to a 'whistleblower'. The Company Sergeant-Major of Support Company had been startlingly honest when he first suggested in his television interview that all was not well but Private 027 had gone much further. To guarantee his personal safety, the Government agreed to pay him the following out of public funds: £1,400 a month in lieu of earnings for twelve months or until such time as the Inquiry no longer required his services; a 'loan' of £20,000 at a commercial rate of interest towards buying at house; £6,000 to buy a car; £100 a month to buy life insurance; and all travel costs incurred in co-operating with the Inquiry. In return for this, Private 027 agreed to make a statement and give oral evidence to the Inquiry. The Tribunal said that his evidence was likely to be 'of the utmost importance'.[26]

Private 027 was a radio operator with the Anti-Tank Platoon on 'Bloody Sunday' and had clearly been deeply troubled by what happened. He kept a diary at the time which in 1975 he formulated into a statement, apparently for his own personal use and not intended for publication. When his written recollections eventually came to light in an article in the Dublin newspaper *Sunday Business Post* on 16 March 1997, they created a sensation. He described an informal briefing on the eve of 'Bloody Sunday' when the Lieutenant in charge of Private 027's section (just over half a dozen soldiers) came in and told them they were going into Derry the following day.

> As I looked at my friends I could see that after all the abuse and nights without sleep [in Belfast], frustrations and tensions, this is what they had been waiting for. We were all in high spirits and when our Officer said, 'Let's teach these buggers a lesson. We want some kills tomorrow,' to the mentality of the blokes to whom he was speaking, this was tantamount to an order — i.e. an exoneration of all responsibility.

He went on to describe being deployed into the Bogside and his horror at what he saw happening as he took up position along a low garden wall in Kells Walk opposite a rubble barricade and a crowd of demonstrators.

> At this point approximately a 100 yards short of the crowd, [a Corporal in the section] went into the kneeling position and fired at the centre of the crowd . . . [Another soldier] immediately jumped down beside him and also opened fire . . . Just beyond the wall on the pavement [a third soldier] also commenced firing. Looking at the centre of the barricade, I saw two bodies fall. I raised my rifle and aimed but on tracking across the people in front of me, could . . . see no one with a weapon, so I lowered my rifle . . . I remember thinking looking at my friends . . . do they know something I don't know? What are they firing at?

He then described pursuing the fleeing crowd into Glenfada Park.

> A group of some 40 civilians were there running in an effort to get away. [Another soldier] fired from the hip at a range of 20 yards. The

bullet passed through one man and into another and they both fell, one dead and one wounded . . . [Private 027 then describes the killing of the wounded man and the shooting of two other men.] A Catholic priest ran across to the bodies shouting about giving the last rites. He was clubbed down with rifle butts . . . I probably naïvely as I think now was filled with an overwhelming desire that the truth should be known . . . I remember thinking illogically as it turned out that no one would ever know about it.

He said that 'several of the blokes' had fired their own personal supply of 'dum dum' bullets, with the tips filed down to cause even greater destruction to whatever or whomever they hit. He also said that when the shooting was over and they were parked in their vehicle by Rossville Flats, a 'civilian' (presumably army) got in and said, 'You will need some public relations work around here after this.' 'We all laughed, feeling very pleased with ourselves.' Private 027's final dramatic allegation was that his statement to the Widgery Tribunal was falsified and 'bore no relation to fact'. He said he had originally 'rattled off' everything he had seen and heard and had done, only omitting soldiers' names and the manner in which people had been shot. Apart from that, he said he had told the truth.

Then to my utter surprise, one of these doddering gentlemen [presumably taking witness statements for the Widgery Tribunal] said, 'You make it sound as if shots were being fired at the crowd. We can't have that, can we?' And then proceeded to tear up my statement. He left the room and returned ten minutes later with another statement which bore no relation to fact and was told with a smile that this is the statement I would use when going on the stand.

Private 027 said he was appalled. 'What a situation. The Lord Chief Justice of Great Britain, the symbol of all moral standings and justice, having his minions suppress and twist evidence, with or without his knowledge. Who can tell? I was amazed.'

His astonishing allegations became public as a result of a letter he wrote anonymously to the Belfast *Newsletter* around the time of the twenty-fifth anniversary of 'Bloody Sunday' when John Hume was demanding a public inquiry into the killings. He wrote:

1 Para, true to its Regimental ethos, went into the Bogside as though it were the opening clash of a rugby match . . . In the tension of the moment, a few hot heads opened fire with no justification. This

sanctioned similar behaviour by others almost as a knee-jerk reaction to the gunfire . . .

The Widgery Report stated that the firing of some soldiers 'bordered on the reckless' but it is not the appropriate word for the gunning down of unarmed civilians, some of whom were shot at a range of 20 feet. It was shameful behaviour which in no way can be condoned . . . The thought that so much suffering and turmoil over so many years largely stems from the mindless actions of a handful of cowboys is a tragedy indeed.

Following his letter, ITV's *Channel Four News* tracked the author down and interviewed him. Dublin's *Sunday Business Post* subsequently passed on his 1975 statement to the Dublin Government who used it as powerful evidence in its submission to the British Government that there was a strong case to re-investigate what happened on 'Bloody Sunday'. As a result, the Saville Inquiry was born. The Inquiry finally located Private 027 and reached the financial deal under which he would give written and oral evidence. Some felt that the evidence might be tainted because it was being given as a result of a financial incentive but the Inquiry was prepared to live with that, so critical did it believe his evidence to be. After the deal was done, Private 027 made a long statement that confirmed much of what he had written in his 1975 summary, with a few minor changes and clarifications. Significantly, he is understood to have pointed out that the remark made by the Lieutenant on the eve of going into Derry about wanting 'some kills' was in the context of a general conversation not a formal briefing and referred to a likely encounter with IRA gunmen. However sensational his revelations continued to be, there was no suggestion in his statement to the Saville Inquiry that there were orders from on high to go into Derry and kill civilians. In other words, it did not provide any evidence of a state conspiracy.

In thirty years of conflict, Northern Ireland has seen many watersheds, but, because of its momentous repercussions, 'Bloody Sunday' remains the biggest watershed of all and is the pivotal event of the thirty-year 'war' against the IRA. Besides giving the Provisional IRA a boost in support and recruits it had never dreamed of when it was formed barely two years before, it also gave, in its eyes, its Volunteers an even greater moral authority to kill. The impact on the 'Brits' was equally momentous. Frank Steele, who was with the UK Representative, Howard Smith, on 'Bloody Sunday' waiting for the reports of the march to come in, was horrified when they did. 'We just found it very difficult to believe when three, then five and then seven deaths came in,' he told me. 'I think when we got to seven, Howard and I looked at each other and said, "Right. That means Direct Rule." Of course, when it got to thirteen, Direct Rule was inevitable.' On 28 March 1972, almost two months to the day after 'Bloody Sunday', the Stormont parliament was suspended and Direct Rule from Westminster was introduced. Britain could no longer say it was not her problem. The day was a profound watershed too for the army. Jamie, the young officer who had flown into Belfast as the city burned after internment, had no doubts about the military significance of 'Bloody Sunday'.

> I suspect for the majority of soldiers at my level in those days, it was the realization that probably we were not going to win by just a military solution alone. Indeed at that time we thought we were still winning. But certainly I think with the outcry of 'Bloody Sunday', with the deaths of so many civilians, and the international storm of protest that that caused, we realized, I think, that a solution by military means alone was no longer possible, even if it was desirable in the first instance.

That meant that if the security forces could not effectively counter the IRA in conventional military terms, they would have to find other means of doing so. 'Bloody Sunday' was the turning point.

Chapter Nine

The 'Funny People'

March 1972

To Northern Ireland's Prime Minister, Brian Faulkner, Direct Rule was a savage blow and the final implementation of what unionists had been desperately hoping to avoid since 1969. It meant the loss of their Stormont parliament and the end of the political and ethnic hegemony they had enjoyed in the province for fifty years. In the immediate aftermath of 'Bloody Sunday', many unionists were 'cock a hoop' that the 'Brits' had finally got tough. 'I know it's a horrible thing to say,' Frank Steele remarked, 'but although it did us the most enormous harm with the Catholic community, it did us quite a lot of good with the more bloody-minded of the Protestant community. The only good thing that came out of it was that it enabled Direct Rule to be brought in.' At the time, few unionists envisaged that 'Bloody Sunday' would signal the end of all they had clung to.

When the enormity of what had happened dawned in nationalist areas all over the province, the rush to join the IRA was so great that people had to be turned away. Most were young and eager to get revenge rather than embrace republican ideology. Awash with recruits and with money now pouring in from America, both wings of the IRA made it brutally clear that the 'Brits' were not going to get away with what they had done. On 22 February 1972, the Official IRA planted a bomb near the Officers' Mess at the Headquarters of the Parachute Regiment in Aldershot, killing not a single soldier but five women working in the kitchen, a gardener and a Catholic army padre. It was the first IRA attack in England since the 1940s. The Officials made much of the target but were not too keen to dwell on the victims. Five dinner ladies and a gardener hardly represented a blow against the might of the state. Three days later, they almost succeeded in assassinating John Taylor, the Stormont Minister for Home Affairs, as he got into his car in Armagh.[1]

The Provisionals too exacted their revenge, killing ten soldiers, one policeman and five civilians in a bloody six-week period after 'Bloody Sunday'. Two of the civilians, both women, died in a horrific bomb blast on 4 March 1972 at the Abercorn Restaurant in the centre of Belfast at tea-time on a busy Saturday. More than a hundred people were injured.[2]

A week later, on 11 March, the Provisionals began a three-day cease-fire, in part a reaction to public outrage at the Abercorn atrocity, in part because they felt they were winning and the 'Brits' might be ready to talk. In Dublin, the Provisional leadership declared that for the cease-fire to last, the British would have to withdraw their forces, give an amnesty to their prisoners and abolish Stormont.[3] At this stage, Heath was in no mood to talk since to have done so would have been seen as a sign of weakness and caused ructions in the Conservative and Unionist Party at Westminster but the Leader of the Opposition, Harold Wilson, felt otherwise. He had already told the House of Commons the previous November that in the long term he believed the solution was a united Ireland. Wilson told Heath that he proposed to hold secret talks with the IRA and Heath raised no objections. At least it was a way of finding out at first hand what the IRA leaders were like and if there was a way of persuading them to stop, without, of course, granting them their demands. To the IRA, Wilson was probably a preferred interlocutor anyway given his public stance on Ireland. If its leaders could not talk to the Government itself, the Leader of the Opposition was the next best thing.

On 13 March, the final day of the IRA's cease-fire, Wilson and Labour's shadow Northern Ireland spokesman, Merlyn Rees, flew to Dublin for a clandestine meeting with three of the Provisional IRA's top leaders, two from the North and one from the South: Joe Cahill, the IRA's Belfast Brigade Commander, John Kelly, a Northerner on the IRA's General Headquarters Staff (GHQ), and David O'Connell, a Dubliner and the leading political strategist on the IRA's Army Council. It was the first ever contact between British politicians and the Provisionals. The meeting took place in Phoenix Park at the house of Dr John O'Connell, one of the intermediaries who had made the encounter possible.

It lasted from dusk until midnight, the cease-fire deadline, but the two sides remained poles apart and Wilson had no authority to speak for the British Government. The Provisionals had probably been more encouraged than was justified by Wilson's remarks to the House of Commons in support of a united Ireland. John Kelly, however, remembers Wilson asking a pointed question.

> He puffed on his pipe in the way that he did and asked what the Republican Movement's intention would be towards a bombing campaign on the British mainland, in the event of there being no

resolution to the conflict. We gave him a non-committal answer and said we didn't know and that it was not for us to answer that question.[4]

As midnight approached, Wilson tried to persuade the IRA to extend its deadline but to no avail. At 12.00 p.m. Kelly looked at his watch and said, 'It's too late. The cease-fire's over. It's started again.' The meeting was at an end. There was nothing else to say. 'Well, that's it then,' said Wilson. 'Off we go.'

The following day, the Provisionals exploded a 200-lb bomb in the centre of Belfast, the largest in the city to date. But there was far worse to come. On 20 March 1972, Belfast was shattered by the effect of what was probably the IRA's first car-bomb. Two hundred pounds of explosives packed in a vehicle exploded in Donegall Street, rocking Belfast city centre and killing seven people and injuring 150. There was a telephone warning but it gave the wrong location for the bomb, with the result that people were shepherded from the street where it was not, into the street where it was. Two of the dead, Ernest McAllister (38) and Bernard O'Neill (36), were respectively Protestant and Catholic policemen who had been escorting the crowd to what they thought was a place of safety. Three of the five civilians killed were dustbin men whose lorry was parked near the car bomb. The other two were pensioners.[5]

Two days later, Faulkner was summoned to Downing Street. The 'Brits' had finally decided to bite the bullet. When he walked into Heath's study at 11 a.m. on 22 March, he was surprised to see the large figure of William 'Willie' Whitelaw. He had no idea that facing him was the man who was about to take over as the British Government's first Secretary of State for Northern Ireland. Without ceremony, Faulkner was told that his Government was being stripped of its security powers and that, henceforth, these would rest in the hands of British Ministers. He protested that without responsibility for law and order, Stormont would have no credibility and therefore he would have no option other than to resign. Faulkner had no choice and Heath knew it. Northern Ireland's last Prime Minister was handed the loaded gun. Faulkner and his Cabinet were finished. 'I was shaken and horrified, and felt completely betrayed,' he later said.[6]

Stormont's suspension was all the more galling since it was one of the demands the Provisional IRA had made in its cease-fire statement. Heath announced that Direct Rule was to be 'a fresh start' but to unionists it was the beginning of the road towards a united Ireland into which they believed the British Government was now bent on driving them. The IRA was jubilant. The British had delivered at least one of its three demands. If they kept up the pressure, they were confident that the 'Brits' would deliver the other two: troop withdrawal and amnesty. The Provisionals had no doubt they had brought Stormont down, and their slogan, 'Victory '72', reflected the mood. They really believed that victory was just around the corner. Martin Meehan, one of their senior commanders in Ardoyne, was confident that the slogan was true. Sinn Fein barely got a look in. It was the IRA that made the running.

> Politics was a dirty word in those days. We actually believed we could drive the British army into the sea. It was raw determination, a gut feeling that if we kept up the pressure, we could do it. All the signs were that we were on the road and we had moved mountains.[7]

The mountain of Stormont had hitherto been immovable.

Heath's 'fresh start' meant clearing the decks at Stormont Castle, the administrative hub from which the province had been run since partition, in preparation for the army of civil servants from Whitehall who were to arrive with the new Northern Ireland Secretary of State, Willie Whitelaw, to run the new Northern Ireland Office (NIO). Stormont Castle is a baronial, grey stone pile with architecture of Disneyland gothic. As the *ancien régime* moved out, the new rulers moved in. The familiar political faces that had been part of the fabric of Stormont Castle were banished but the officials of the Northern Ireland civil service stayed on and were amalgamated into the NIO. The 'Brits' needed officials who knew their way around, as most of the mainly English newcomers were woefully ignorant of the province, its people and its manners.

One of those who stayed on was a young woman called Joan Young. Joan was a loyal and faithful unionist who had worked for the Stormont Government from 1963 and latterly for Sir Harold Black, the Secretary of the Northern Ireland Cabinet. Joan had seen it all from civil rights to 'Bloody Sunday'. She had watched two Prime Ministers, Terence O'Neill and James Chichester-Clark, come and go and now she was seeing the third, Brian Faulkner, going. She observed the new breed of English civil servants looking round the offices, checking out who would go where. Joan had had to sketch out a floor plan since she knew the layout of the building and the new arrivals did not. When they breezed into the former Cabinet Secretary's office, a post that was no more, she winced as they blithely said 'that will do for so-and-so'.

'They had little or no regard for this person who was a very senior Northern Ireland civil servant,' she told me. 'He was God in many ways and a genuinely very, very nice man. I felt bad for him because I thought he had been demeaned in a way by these people coming in.' Joan was admittedly concerned 'perhaps selfishly' for her own future but was relieved to find that there was an opening for her in the new Secretary of State's Private Office alongside two English civil servants. 'They wanted "a voice",' she said with just a hint of sarcasm, 'a Northern Ireland voice to give a feeling of continuity.' Joan's beautifully articulated unionist tones softened the edge of Direct Rule. 'My Northern Ireland voice helped, there's no doubt about it. There would have been people who telephoned in those days and asked for me because they felt they could communicate better with a Northern Ireland person.'

But whatever the façade, there was no hiding the fact that the 'Brits' were now the masters ruling the Northern Ireland natives. Joan bitterly resented it. She resented their voices, their attitude and, above all, their manners. Until Stormont was made ready for its new rulers, the influx of civil servants from the motherland was accommodated in considerable style at the Culloden Hotel, nestling in some splendour along the 'Gold Coast' that fringes the shores of Belfast Lough. For years, the Culloden was *the* place to be and be seen. On special occasions, Joan and her friends would get dressed up and go there to dine.

> The Culloden was, for Northern Irish people, a very special place to go. You went there for a twenty-first birthday party or an engagement party, something very special. And I can still recall quite vividly being taken there for dinner on one occasion, some months after Direct Rule, and being disgusted and quite seriously offended by the attitude of the English civil servants living there. They came down into the dining-room, which they treated very much as their own living-room, casually dressed. It was upsetting to go into the Culloden in your long skirt, having made quite an effort to get yourself dressed up, and to be confronted by these tables of people in casual sweaters and jeans and, on many occasions, perhaps reading at the table. They were not really giving any attention at all to the local people who were there for special occasions and that upset me as well. They just didn't treat the place the way *we* would have liked.

Joan admits that some of the senior English civil servants, like Philip Woodfield who had moved from the Home Office to become Deputy Secretary at the NIO, were perfect gentlemen, as were senior officials with whom she subsequently worked, like Frank Cooper and Brian Cubbon. It was the middle- and lower-ranking English officials that she could not stand. But most upsetting of all was the attitude she detected among some of the 'Brits' for whom Northern Ireland had become like a colonial outpost. On one occasion, Joan was having lunch at the Culloden in a group of sixteen people. She was the only Northern Irish person there. At some point there was a brief moment of silence as people paused for breath or took stock of the various conversations going on around the table.

> Suddenly this silence was interrupted by a very English voice saying, 'Oh, the trouble with the Irish is that they're genetically inferior to the English.' Everyone was paralysed momentarily and then they all frantically tried to engage me in conversation. It sort of passed over and after lunch, the person concerned came to me and apologized. But I didn't really want an apology. I mean, he was saying what he thought and he wouldn't have apologized had I not been Northern Irish and in the party. And I didn't know how many other people in the restaurant in the Culloden heard him saying it to whom he did not apologize.

The loud, offending voice that froze the lunch party belonged to an army officer commanding a battalion in Northern Ireland. Joan declined to say who he was but implied that his apology was purely a formality. 'He never gave me any evidence to think that he had learned from it in his subsequent behaviour,' she said.

Civil servants were not the only Englishmen to move into Stormont Castle. Other shadowy figures slipped through its grand entrance hall and disappeared into the woodwork. They were the 'spooks' of MI6, MI5 and Military Intelligence. Joan used to call them the 'funny people'. 'Although I knew, they didn't realize that anybody knew who they were.' The 'funny people' were the nucleus of the new intelligence cell under the direction of a senior MI6 officer that was designed to put intelligence-gathering and analysis on a proper footing to counter the ever-increasing threat from the IRA.

When Direct Rule was introduced, Peter was treading the streets of Belfast and looking forward to going home at the end of a grinding four-month tour. He had just been promoted to Lieutenant-Colonel and thought his next posting would be to teach at Sandhurst and was surprised when he was told he was going to go to Stormont Castle to be the Military Assistant to the MI6 officer who was to be the first Director and Controller of Intelligence (DCI) in the province. Nor was he to have much of a break before joining the team. He was told to find himself a house in Northern Ireland, put on plain clothes and meet 'this very high-priced chap' on the steps of Stormont Castle the following week.

> He was going to come in and assume this job which, at that stage, frankly, was badly needed. There was a sense drawn, I think, by

reference to the Malayan campaign[8] that what you really needed was an overall intelligence co-ordinator, and that was what we were put in to do. We were, of course, also put in to provide the Secretary of State with the political information which he required to be able to carry out his role.

This 'political' information was also being provided by the new DCI's MI6 colleague, Frank Steele, who was now based at an outpost of the NIO at 'Laneside', a house down a leafy lane along the 'Gold Coast'. Together, the British intelligence agencies now hoped to get a grip on things. Although there was liaison with the RUC's Special Branch, there was no Special Branch officer on the team. What became known euphemistically as the 'liaison staff' consisted entirely of 'true Brits'. When the new 'top team' was first shown its quarters in the Castle, they were not quite as expected. Peter and his colleagues were taken up a tower by one of the Castle's staff, known as 'blue-bottles', who threw open the door in an expansive gesture and indicated that this was the DCI's office. Peter was a little taken aback. 'There were no boards on the floor at all, just bare joists. We all roared with laughter, came back down the steps and said, 'We think you'd better get a cheap carpenter up there to nail some floorboards down and then we'll think of occupying it.'

The 'spooks' in the turret and top floor of the Castle over which they spread, kept themselves to themselves and their workings restricted to a tight circle of people, all of them 'Brits'. Highly sensitive intelligence information was marked with the classification 'UK Eyes Only'. 'English Eyes Only' would have been more appropriate. 'Northern Irish Eyes' were strictly out of the loop. To Joan working downstairs as Assistant Private Secretary in the Secretary of State's office, this new classification came as a surprise. She first became aware of it a couple of days into her new job when one of the 'funny people' came into Whitelaw's office and handed her an envelope for the Secretary of State marked 'UK Eyes Only'. Joan was alone at the time as the two English officials were elsewhere. She did not take any particular notice of the classification and reached for her letter opener since part of her job was to open the Secretary of State's post. The emissary from above hit the roof.

To say he had an apoplectic fit is not an overstatement. He really nearly lost it. He said, 'No, you cannot open that!' And I said, 'Why not? We open everything for the Secretary of State in this office,' and I held onto the envelope. He said, 'No, no, you can't. It says "U.K. Eyes Only".' I said, 'Excuse me, I live in the United Kingdom. It's Great Britain and Northern Ireland but it *is* the United Kingdom. I live here and I am a civil servant and I have been vetted. I have never given anybody cause to think that I would tell anything.' But he said, 'No, you cannot. This is something just for the Secretary of State.' In fact, a colleague and I, after a particularly hurtful day, looking through the bottom of an empty bottle of gin, decided that probably we only had to buy the *Irish News* [the nationalist daily paper] and read it the next morning to find out what was going on. In fact I was really personally very hurt by it all, the thought that there I was, working, and working jolly hard and giving total commitment and loyalty to that office and, yet, there was still this feeling amongst the English civil servants that here was someone who couldn't be totally trusted.

The House of Commons passed the legislation formalizing Direct Rule on 30 March 1972 but, far from curbing the violence, the constitutional change added a new and sinister dimension to it. 1972 was the bloodiest year of the 'troubles', with 496 deaths, 106 of which were brutal sectarian killings carried out by the loyalist paramilitaries of UVF and the recently formed Ulster Defence Association (UDA).[9] Direct Rule did for them what 'Bloody Sunday' had done for the IRA. Recruits poured in. The loyalist paramilitaries saw the suspension of Stormont as a victory for the IRA and were determined to hit back against the organization that seemed to be making all the running and forcing the British Government to bend to its will. They did so not by killing IRA members, who were difficult to identify and locate, but by attacking the community from which the IRA came, the theory being that by killing innocent Catholics, the community would put pressure on the IRA to stop. In fact, the reverse was the case since the Provisionals had initially come into being to defend nationalists from loyalist attack. But despite the loyalist 'offensive' against the nationalist community, it was still the Provisional IRA that was responsible for nearly half (234) of the 496 deaths.

After Direct Rule, the 'Brits' faced what they had always feared and tried to avoid, a terrorist war on two fronts. In what now became a steep learning curve, they were rapidly realizing that a concession to one side produced a swift and often bloody reaction from the other. They also realized that the key to ending the spiral of violence was to get the IRA to stop. If they stopped, the 'Brits' calculated, the loyalists would stop too: as long, that is, as the Government did not seem to be giving the IRA more of what it wanted in the desire to make it stop. Such was the British conundrum. Although in some quarters there was a military view that the IRA could still be defeated, it was not a view shared by Frank Steele of MI6 and the 'funny people' in the tower. 'Some of the army thought they could be beaten, others of us thought they could not be beaten by military means and that it would require political means to beat them.' The 'Brits' knew what they had to achieve. The question was how to do it.

Chapter Ten

Talking to the Enemy

May 1972–July 1972

By the early summer of 1972, there was increasing pressure on the IRA from within its own community, not necessarily because of what republicans called the 'loyalist death squads', but because people were fed up with the violence that made normal life impossible. The turning point came on 21 May when the Official IRA shot dead a young nineteen-year-old soldier, William Best, of the Royal Irish Rangers who was serving with the British army in Germany. Ranger Best's death was different. He came from Derry's Creggan estate and had arrived home on leave on Monday 15 May. He had never served in Northern Ireland. The following Saturday evening, he left the house to make a telephone call and never returned. His body was found on waste ground near William Street early on Sunday morning. He had been shot through the head. Many of the nationalist community in the Bogside and Creggan were outraged that a teenager and one of their own, albeit serving in the British army, had been so brutally murdered, and murdered in their name. Four days after Ranger Best's body was found, the Official IRA declared a cease-fire in recognition that there was 'an overwhelming desire of the great majority of all people of the North . . . for an end to military actions by all sides'.[1] By this time, the conflict had claimed 328 lives, including 81 soldiers and 22 policemen, since 1969.

With the Official IRA's cease-fire in place, which lasted indefinitely as they re-embarked on the political path they had pursued through the sixties before the split, the 'Brits' now only had one IRA to fight. The spotlight was now on the Provisionals, who, besides feeling community pressure, were also anxious to test the water and see if the 'Brits' were willing to talk. They believed they were winning and wished to take advantage of what they regarded as their position of strength. The young Martin McGuinness, who had become commander of the IRA's Derry Brigade after 'Bloody Sunday', went to Dublin with the veteran Derry republican, Sean Keenan, to see the IRA's Chief of Staff, Seán MacStiofáin. Whilst the IRA's Derry Brigade was carrying out a devastating commercial bombing campaign in the city centre that cost millions of pounds but no lives, McGuinness thought it worth sounding out the 'Brits'. MacStiofáin agreed there was nothing to lose and, heavily disguised with a wig and false moustache, travelled to Derry to give an audacious press conference on 13 June 1972. He was flanked by Martin McGuinness, the Army Council's David O'Connell and the hardline commander of the Belfast Brigade, Seamus Twomey.

MacStiofáin announced that the IRA was prepared to declare a truce and invited Mr Whitelaw to come to 'Free Derry' or 'elsewhere' to meet the Provisional leadership and talk peace. He assured the Secretary of State that he would be guaranteed 'safe conduct'. To the Provisionals, 'peace' meant withdrawing troops from nationalist areas, ending internment, giving amnesty to its prisoners and men 'on the run' and granting the Irish people, North and South, the right to decide their own future without British interference, known as 'self-determination'. If Mr Whitelaw accepted the offer within forty-eight hours, MacStiofáin said, the IRA would call a cease-fire for seven days, on condition that the British army ended arrests, raids and 'harassment' of the civilian population.

Not surprisingly, Mr Whitelaw declined the invitation and said he could not respond to 'an ultimatum from terrorists'.[2] But his officials, in particular Frank Steele, were not so dismissive. They were interested in the prospect of meeting the IRA and testing them out. The 'Brits' however had far more to lose than the IRA. Unionists were still incensed at the loss of their Stormont parliament, and the loyalist paramilitaries were still seething at the continued existence of the IRA's 'no-go' areas and the apparent impunity within which its gunmen and bombers seemed to operate. The UDA had even set up 'no-go' areas of its own, challenging the army to take them down, which the army did. The UDA then argued that if the army could take down loyalist barricades, why could it not take down the IRA's? The Government hardly needed reminding that if word leaked out that there were secret talks with the IRA, the impact on unionists and the loyalist paramilitaries might well be catastrophic. But Steele thought the risk was worth taking and felt no compunction at talking to the 'men of violence'. To the 'Brits', who had engaged in dialogue with the former 'terrorist' leader Jomo Kenyatta in Kenya – and others elsewhere – such an activity was nothing new.

The day of the Provisionals' press conference in Derry, there was a growing crisis in Belfast's Crumlin Road gaol where the IRA's former Belfast commander, Billy McKee, was on hunger strike with other republican prisoners and now rumoured to be dead. Buses and lorries were hi-jacked and burned in nationalist areas of the city. McKee had been arrested on 15 April 1971 along with Frank Card, one of the Provisionals 'named and shamed' by Farrar-Hockley the year before. He had begun refusing food in the hope of forcing the Government to grant IRA prisoners 'political status' in recognition that they were not common criminals but 'prisoners of war'. A week after the Provisionals' press conference, the hunger strike was resolved after thirty days, almost certainly as part of the 'confidence-building' measures prior to HMG secretly pursuing MacStiofáin's offer of talks. According to McKee, the settlement was negotiated by David O'Connell. 'We thought it was part of the peace process that was going on at that time,' he told me. In effect, the Government capitulated, giving McKee and *all* prisoners, both republican *and* loyalists, what amounted to political status in everything but name. Prisoners were allowed to wear their own clothes, which to them was always the most symbolic and important issue, and to have extra visits and parcels. The Government called it 'special category status' but McKee was not bothered about the name. 'It was exactly our demands they gave us. Every one of them,' he said. 'They didn't say it was political status, but we weren't worrying.' The decision to grant 'special category status' was to have momentous consequences for the 'Brits' in the years ahead. To the IRA, Whitelaw had shown good faith by resolving the issue that could have destroyed the tentative moves now being made towards some kind of dialogue.

The British also gave in on the other issue that was a prerequisite of progress. The Provisionals had insisted that if there was to be a meeting with Whitelaw, they should be allowed to choose their own delegation. They demanded that one of its members be the young Gerry Adams. The problem was that Adams was in Long Kesh and would have to be released from internment. The Government agreed and Adams, to his surprise, was set free. He had just come off a fourteen-day hunger strike in solidarity with Billy McKee. Whitelaw was finally persuaded, not least by Paddy Devlin from Belfast and John Hume from Derry, that the 'Provos' were serious and the risk should be taken. It was now a question of arranging the logistics.

The still-dazed Adams, who had originally thought his release was a leg-pull, was met outside the gates of Long Kesh by Dolours and Marion Price, who were to become notorious on their own account as part of the team that bombed London the following year.[3] He was told there were to be talks with the 'Brits' and he was to be involved. He was driven by Paddy Devlin to Derry on 20 June and then taken to a large country house near the Donegal border for a secret meeting to arrange the logistics for the IRA's meeting with Whitelaw. (The British had provided Adams with a special pass to get through the army checkpoints.) There he joined David O'Connell who was to make up the IRA's two-man mini-delegation. Their British opposite numbers were Frank Steele and Philip Woodfield. The only time on the journey that Steele became nervous was when Woodfield swore he had misread the map and they ended up across the border in Donegal, which, as Steele said, could have 'put us at terrible risk'. They had considered arming themselves in advance of the meeting but decided it was not a good idea as the IRA's intention was to have talks with Whitelaw not kidnap his emissaries.

The first ever meeting between the IRA and British Government officials (Wilson had met them as Leader of the Opposition) was polite and formal. Steele could not remember whether he shook hands but said he would have had no objection because 'one's shaken hands with some fairly unpleasant characters over the years'. Steele was amused by the formalities. 'They wanted to represent themselves as an army and not a bunch of terrorists so we all had to have letters of authority. They had them and we had them signed by a Minister or "Willie". I thought at the time it was simply ridiculous, I mean what else were the four of us doing there? We obviously hadn't just wandered in off the street for a chat. We were obviously representing HMG and the IRA.' Details of an IRA cease-fire were discussed and a telephone 'hot-line' was agreed between Steele in Belfast and O'Connell in Dublin. Steele also passed on the army's message that the IRA should remember to 'de-boob' all its booby-traps in case one went off and inadvertently brought the cease-fire to an end. Steele and Woodfield agreed that IRA Volunteers would be allowed to walk about freely without being lifted, as long as they did not engage in criminal acts like burglary. If they did, they said, they would be arrested. As the meeting broke up, Steele was dying to ask Adams a question. He knew him to be 'a senior member of the Belfast Brigade having been commander of his area, Ballymurphy' but also regarded him as a person with 'a terrific future ahead because of his qualities'.

> I said, 'You don't want to spend the rest of your life on the run from us British. What do you want to do?' He said, 'I want to go to university and get a degree.' I said, 'Well, we're not stopping you. All you've got to do is to renounce violence and you can go to university and get a degree.' And he grinned and said, 'No, I've got to get rid of you British first!'

On 22 June 1972, two days after the meeting, the IRA announced that it would suspend offensive operations from midnight on 26 June. But that did not mean that the IRA scaled down its campaign. In the intervening four days it killed five soldiers and one policeman.

At midnight on 26 June, the IRA's guns fell silent as agreed. The cease-fire held, although it was a tense time. The 'hot-line' between Steele and O'Connell glowed to make sure there were no misunderstandings that could jeopardize the cessation and, therefore, the planned meeting with Whitelaw. Finally, after the agreed interval, the day finally dawned for the historic meeting between the Secretary of State for Northern Ireland and what was tantamount to the IRA's Army Council. Steele must have heaved a sigh of relief as Whitelaw, not surprisingly, had had wobbles about the meeting.

At 8 a.m. on the morning of Friday 7 July 1972, Steele made his way to the agreed rendezvous in open country to the north-west of Derry near the border with Donegal. He was in a mini-bus with brown paper taped over its windows, driven by an army Captain in civilian clothes. 'He was very taciturn and obviously disapproved of the whole proceedings.' This time there was no map-reading error. Steele arrived on time but there was no sign of the IRA delegation. He waited and waited, fearful that the whole enterprise was about to fall apart.

Then suddenly 'up drove a car at a rate of knots, simply bulging with IRA'. Its occupants explained that they had started off in two cars but one had broken down. There were six of them, all IRA and not one Sinn Fein: Seán MacStiofáin and David O'Connell from Dublin; Gerry Adams, Seamus Twomey and his second-in-command, Ivor Bell, from Belfast; and Martin McGuinness from Derry. They all got into the mini-van to a 'look of utter disgust on the army officer's face' and made off for the field where a helicopter was scheduled to pick them up and take them to Aldergrove airport.

At Aldergrove, Steele and the six IRA leaders boarded an RAF Andover, with an Air Force 'meeter and greeter' standing to attention and saluting the delegation 'with his jaw hanging open'. They were flown to RAF Benson in Oxfordshire where they were met by a Special Branch driver and taken to London via Henley-on-Thames, where they stopped off so the IRA could telephone their Dublin-based legal adviser, Miles Shevlin, to give him the location of the meeting. They had demanded an independent witness and Shevlin was he. The talks were to be held in Chelsea at the exclusive Cheyne Walk residence of one of Whitelaw's junior ministers, Paul Channon.

Realizing the delegation might be hungry, Steele went into a grocer's shop in Henley to buy a bag of apples. He returned to the car and passed them to the IRA men sitting in the back but they were in no hurry to take a bite. 'I thought, My God, they think they're drugged! So I took one of them at random and took a great bite out of it and then handed the bag to the Special Branch driver so he could have one. I then handed it over to the back. I think they were satisfied. It was typical of their conspiracy theories. We wanted talks. We didn't want to drug them.'

Not surprisingly, the meeting lacked warmth. Despite all his reservations, Whitelaw conducted himself as the gentleman he was. He had learned how to pronounce MacStiofáin's name correctly, which impressed the Chief of Staff, and went round the six IRA men shaking each by the hand. Adams noted that Whitelaw's was 'quite sweaty'. Whitelaw obviously concealed his distaste for shaking the hands of the leaders of an organization responsible for the deaths of nearly 100 soldiers but did so knowing that British governments had talked to 'terrorists' before and would probably do so again. Drinks were offered but declined, perhaps out of fear that they, unlike the apples, might be 'spiked'. After a few words of welcome that must have stuck in Whitelaw's throat, the two sides got down to business. The British side consisted of Whitelaw, Channon, Woodfield and Steele. Steele was startled when MacStiofáin began by reading out the IRA's demands: self-determination for all the people of Ireland; a British government declaration that it would withdraw all British forces from Irish soil by 1 January 1975; an end to internment; and an amnesty for all 'political prisoners, internees, detainees and wanted persons'. Steele was appalled.

> It was far worse than I thought it was going to be. I did at least think they'd say, 'Well, we're all in a very difficult situation. Fighting each other is getting us nowhere so let's see what we can do by talking and if it doesn't work OK we'll go back to fighting.' But there was nothing like that. MacStiofáin behaved like the representative of an army that had fought the British to a standstill, Montgomery at Lüneberg Heath telling the German Generals what they should and shouldn't do if they wanted peace. He was in cloud-cuckoo-land.

Because the British did not want the cease-fire to end, Whitelaw made polite noises about having to refer matters to his Cabinet colleagues and the meeting was brought to a close. A cloud of depression descended on the British delegation as they realized that the IRA was making impossible demands that no British Government could accept. MacStiofáin and his colleagues were absolutists with no concept of the Government's obligations to the Protestant majority in the North and the constitutional position of the province.

Gerry Adams, apparently, said very little at the meeting. Steele was convinced that the experience of that day made Adams realize that 'armed struggle' alone was not enough to achieve the republican goal and the IRA would have to have a *political* dimension to what it was doing. Adams was to spend the rest of the century developing it. Twenty-five years later, on 10 December 1997, Gerry Adams and Martin McGuinness walked into Downing Street to shake hands with the British Prime Minister, Tony Blair. By then over 3,500 people had died in the continuing conflict. Sadly, Frank Steele never lived to see that historic day as he died from a terminal illness shortly before it happened. Nor did he see Martin McGuinness becoming Minister for Education. I remember visiting Frank shortly before he died. 'Peter,' he said, 'when you next see Martin McGuinness, give him my congratulations on becoming a statesman.' I passed on the message.

The IRA delegation arrived back from their historic away-day to London on Friday evening, 7 July. It was clear from the meeting that the 'Brits' were not ready to give and it was only a matter of time before the cease-fire ended. It did so two days later on Sunday 9 July in Andersonstown's Lenadoon Avenue in a confrontation between the army and a republican crowd, with Seamus Twomey at its head. I was there at the time and had little doubt the ending of the cease-fire was orchestrated by the IRA who were on standby at the top end of Lenadoon Avenue with guns at the ready. The issue revolved around the re-housing of Catholic families intimidated out of loyalist areas at the height of the marching season.

MacStiofáin had decided to 'intensify' the IRA's campaign. The result was 'Bloody Friday', 21 July, the day the IRA planted twenty-two bombs in Belfast, killing nine people – five Protestants, two Catholics and two soldiers. Seven were killed at the crowded Oxford Street bus station in the city centre. Warnings were given but they were inadequate and imprecise. The carnage was horrendous, with television pictures showing young policemen sweeping body parts like black jelly into plastic bags. Like the photographs of the dead on 'Bloody Sunday', the images were never forgotten.

Joan Young caught one of the last buses out of Oxford Street bus station before the bomb went off. She was in the Secretary of State's office in Stormont Castle when she heard the explosions tearing Belfast apart.

> I think it was three or four a.m. the following morning before we got out of the office. There were high-level discussions going on. Lord Carrington had flown in. There were lots of people around. The GOC was in the office with the Secretary of State. There were endless meetings. I was manning the telephones with other colleagues and we were getting telephone calls from mothers whose children hadn't come home. The man who ran the morgue in Belfast rang and, crying down the phone, demanded that 'Willie' Whitelaw come down to the morgue and see the bodies. It was a very, very emotional time to be working in Stormont, to be Northern Irish and

to feel all the pain. It was difficult. This was my community. This was where I lived.

'Bloody Friday' was the IRA's nadir, at least for a good many years. It was an operation that went hopelessly and tragically wrong for which the IRA paid the price, although it still retained a hard-core of support that was sufficient to maintain its operations. To many nationalists, 'Bloody Friday' cancelled out 'Bloody Sunday' although the IRA was at pains to differentiate between the two, alleging that the former was a mistake and the latter was not. But 'Bloody Friday' gave the army the chance it had been waiting for to implement its plan to end the IRA's no-go areas. The plan had been in existence for some time and was not just dreamed up in the wake of 'Bloody Friday'. The question always had been when to implement it and, with 'Bloody Sunday' in mind, how to do so with the minimum risk. 'Bloody Friday' offered the perfect opportunity. It was thought that few beyond the IRA's most dedicated supporters would complain if the army went in and destroyed the protected nests that were harbouring members of the organization responsible for such carnage. No doubt this was one of the options being discussed in the Secretary of State's office whilst Joan and her colleagues were manning the phones next door.

The plan was code-named 'Motorman' by Gavin, the army planning officer who had picked out Long Kesh as the internment camp the previous year. 'It had a ring about it and did give some impression of the army in control, of the army "motoring", doing something positive rather than reacting,' he said. ' "Bloody Friday" was a grievous and sad high point in that it probably stiffened resolve to sort things out. There was no question that this could go on in the manner that it was.' The plan went to Whitelaw and, ten days after 'Bloody Friday', on 31 July 1972, 12,000 soldiers with bulldozers and tanks smashed their way into the 'no-go' areas of Belfast and Derry in the biggest military operation since Suez. At last the 'Brits' felt they were taking the initiative and were getting on top. The IRA offered no resistance, not wishing to have a shoot-out with hundreds of soldiers. In Derry, after 'Bloody Sunday' the most sensitive area of all, they piled their arms into vehicles and simply melted across the border. In Belfast, they simply left the area. With great convoys of trucks, bulldozers and soldiers rumbling across Northern Ireland, there was no chance of the army creeping up on the IRA. The whole operation was orchestrated by both sides through intermediaries as neither side wanted a showdown with 'Bloody Sunday' and 'Bloody Friday' still fresh in their minds.

To Gavin, 'Motorman' was in military terms the turning point of the campaign. 'It had to be done to put a stop to chaos and anarchy and violence, and to try and allow time for the situation to settle down and sort things out.' Until this time, the 'Brits' had been fighting a counter-insurgency campaign, that is one directed not only against the 'terrorists' but against the community that supports their insurgency. From the summer of 1972, it became a counter-terrorist campaign, now focused almost exclusively on the 'terrorists' themselves. The problem was how to identify them, infiltrate them and stop them. The covert agencies of British intelligence were about to come into their own.

Chapter Eleven

Piratical Ventures

Late 1972

Although fighting an undercover war was nothing new to the 'Brits', it was never something they had expected to do within the borders of their own country. Most recently the SAS had carried out covert operations in Aden and had infiltrated the notorious Crater district disguised as Arabs to seek out the gunmen who had been accounting for far too many of the local Special Branch officers. They were known as the 'Keeni-Meeni' men, Swahili for 'snake in the grass'.[1] The technique, as the origin of the nickname suggests, was pioneered in the forests of Kenya during the Mau Mau emergency of the early 1950s by Frank Kitson who was then a young Major attached to the Special Branch of the Kenya Police as a Military Intelligence Officer.

Kitson realized that in order to engage the terrorist enemy, you first had to find out *who* he was and then *where* he was and the best way of doing this was to induce someone from the enemy camp to change sides and show you. The inducement, as in Northern Ireland, might take many forms, from paying money, to letting them off or convincing them that they were on the wrong side. Once a person had been identified and won over, Kitson's men would 'black up', dress in Mau Mau rags and follow the defector to the enemy camp in the forest. Exact information could then be passed to the army or, in certain circumstances, the enemy could be attacked on the spot. It was simple, dangerous and effective. These undercover units were known as 'counter gangs' and featured in Kitson's first book.[2] By 1972, the army was applying similar techniques in Northern Ireland in increasingly controversial circumstances. What undercover soldiers might have got away with in the dense jungles of Kenya, the barren wastes of Oman or the dusty alleyways of Aden, was not 'acceptable' on the streets of Belfast when the 'natives' were British citizens.

The army used these methods in Northern Ireland because they had worked before, because the situation lent itself to them and because it had to take the initiative, given the paucity of the intelligence being passed on by Special Branch. IRA suspects were arrested, 'screened', and where possible 'turned', either by money or by having potential and often relatively minor charges dropped. To those who used them, such methods were legal and seemed justifiable in the face of an increasingly vicious and unscrupulous enemy. Few had any doubt that the end justified the means. Army intelligence did not need many defectors to try to turn the tables. In those days, because the IRA was structured along British military lines with Brigades, Battalions and Companies, a well-placed defector would know most of the IRA men in his area. Half a dozen dedicated 'turned terrorists' would do, and that was roughly the number employed. They became known as the 'Freds' and were housed in army quarters at Palace Barracks, Holywood, and looked after by a woman from the Women's Royal Army Corps (WRAC).

The idea of recruiting and using the 'Freds' came from 39 Brigade in Belfast, was approved by HQNI, and became 'operational' around November 1971. Gradually, the 'Freds' helped army intelligence piece together the IRA's 'ORBAT', its 'Order of Battle'. Surprisingly, no one seemed to know what the word 'Freds' stood for. I guessed it was an acronym for something like 'Friendly Republican Enemy Defectors'. I mentioned this interpretation to those who knew of their existence and was met with a smile and a negative shake of the head. I was told it was ingenious but not correct. The 'Freds', it seems, was simply a way the army referred to 'those guys at Palace Barracks'. They would travel round republican areas in Belfast in armoured cars, identifying IRA men and women through small slits in the side of the vehicle. The army would then know who to watch, who to follow, who to stop and search and who to arrest.

The information that came in from the spying trips of the 'Freds', along with other sources, was then fed to a covert unit known as the Mobile Reconnaissance Force (MRF) that had been set up by HQNI a few months earlier in the escalating violence of the midsummer of 1971. As the MRF's activities became increasingly controversial, its acronym became interpreted as the Military Reconnaissance Force and then, by republicans and others, as the Military Reaction Force. The MRF's origins lay in the army's bomb squad, previously set up by HQNI, that had tried to curtail the IRA's increasing attacks on the city centre and elsewhere by driving around in plain clothes in unmarked cars. But the MRF had more men, more cars and a broader brief. Initially, its personnel had no special training and no officers out on the ground with them. To the IRA, the MRF, whatever its initials stood for, was a British undercover murder gang.

Inevitably, the recruiting of the 'Freds' and the establishment of the

MRF were laid at Brigadier Kitson's door because they appeared to be based on the 'counter gangs' he had used so effectively in Kenya, and Kitson was, at the time of their establishment and until April 1972, the commander of 39 Brigade in Belfast. Although the MRF was not actually Kitson's brainchild, he certainly encouraged its use as it was consistent with the techniques he had developed in Kenya. Many soldiers on the ground, frustrated at the way the IRA appeared to be running rings round them, wanted to see more senior officers with Kitson's qualities and attitudes running operations in Northern Ireland. 'Alan', of 1 Para, who had cleared more barricades in Belfast than he cared to remember, saw Kitson and his no-nonsense approach as the answer to countering the IRA.

'Alan' had been on duty in Belfast on 20 March 1972 when the IRA exploded the car bomb in Donegall Street that killed seven people including two policemen and two pensioners. 'I was seeing things I hoped I would never see,' he told me. 'If ever there was a defining moment for me, that was it,' he said, reliving the experience with tears in his eyes. 'It made me realize the kind of people we were fighting. I began to wonder how they slept at night and it seemed that they didn't really have a problem doing so. That's what changed me, I think, that they really didn't care about who they killed.' But 'Alan's' revulsion and horror also took on a more tangible form. 'If ever there was a point when I wanted to catch and kill those responsible, that was it. I wanted to sort out the terrorists once and for all. A terrorist who drives a bomb into a street should be as likely to be shot for that crime as someone with a gun who is pointing it at me or my comrade. And I wanted to hit the people who told that man to do what he did on that day.'

'Alan' was aware that besides the 'green' army that conducted endless uniformed patrols around republican and loyalist areas, there was another side to soldiering in Northern Ireland. They were 'guys in flares with long hair' who used to wander in and out of military bases, keeping themselves to themselves. 'Alan' did not know who they were or what they did until one day at the time of 'Operation Motorman' he was asked if he would like to join them. The approach was made by the commander of the MRF in Belfast whom 'Alan' knew because he was an officer in the Parachute Regiment. 'He said, "Would you like to join me?" and I said, "Yes" because I knew what he was doing was OK.' At least, 'Alan' assumed it was OK because the secret organization he was joining was operating with the blessing of HQNI. He said the MRF's role was 'defensive' and, in certain circumstances, 'offensive'.

But what 'Alan' did not know was what the MRF had been up to in the months between 'Bloody Sunday' and 'Operation Motorman' that had given the organization such notoriety in republican circles. On 12 May

1972, the day the Government announced that there would be no disciplinary action against the soldiers involved in 'Bloody Sunday',[3] an MRF unit operating in the Andersonstown area approached a trestle table stretched across the road with a red warning light. It was an unauthorized checkpoint being operated by members of the Catholic Ex-Servicemen's Association (CESA), vetting all cars entering the area and probably on the look out for suspicious vehicles which might contain loyalist gunmen or plain-clothes 'Brits'. In this case, it was the latter. The MRF car stopped and then reversed. One of the undercover unit opened fire from the car with a sub-machine gun and killed Patrick McVeigh (44), an ex-service-man who lived close by. Four others were wounded. As ever in such controversial shootings, there were conflicting accounts. The MRF sol-diers said they had been fired on by six men armed with rifles and revolvers. Local eye-witnesses insisted there were no weapons involved on the CESA side and that McVeigh was not even manning the checkpoint: he had just wandered over to have a chat with friends. At the inquest in December 1972, the Coroner heard that neither McVeigh nor the four wounded men had fired weapons. The soldiers were never prosecuted.[4]

The following month, the MRF was in hot water again in the same general area. On 22 June, the day the IRA announced they would be calling a cease-fire as a prelude to the Whitelaw talks, an MRF unit opened fire from its car on a group of men standing at a bus terminal in Andersonstown's Glen Road. Three black-taxi drivers – Hugh Kenny, Joseph Smith and James Patrick Murray – were wounded. A fourth person, Thomas Shaw, was injured by a ricochet. This time the car was stopped by an RUC patrol and its occupants were arrested. Inside was a Thompson sub-machine gun, for years the IRA's favourite weapon before the Armalite rifles started flooding in from America. One of the two plain-clothes soldiers arrested was an officer in the Parachute Regiment, Captain James McGregor. The other soldier was Sergeant Clive Graham Williams, Williams who fired the Thompson, was charged with attempted murder and subsequently acquitted on 26 June 1973. He said they had come under fire and he had responded. McGregor had been cleared the previous month when the charge of possession of the Thompson was withdrawn after it was shown to have been legally held.[5] It had apparently been used by the military for training purposes. Although the court was convinced, republicans were not.

At HQNI there was a realization that this was the kind of publicity that the army could do without, since it appeared to confirm republican propaganda that the MRF was a 'Brit' undercover hit-squad with a licence to kill. The fact that both of these incidents occurred *after* Kitson had left Northern Ireland did not deter the IRA from laying such operations at his door. As Secretary to the Director of Operations Committee (D. Ops), Gavin was aware of the ripples such ventures caused.

> There was some concern about some of their activities vis-à-vis the law and the way they were operating. We did get the information that things weren't quite right in the MRF and that the results were affecting the rest of the army potentially adversely.
> **But you didn't expect to find soldiers, including an officer, in a car with an IRA Thompson sub-machine gun shooting at Catholics, did you?**
> I wouldn't have anticipated that, no. I would anticipate that the army needed to get involved in some of these grey areas and that we shouldn't fight shy of being involved in that sort of activity, but only under very careful control and with the proper authorities behind it.

But even the questions raised by the discovery of an IRA weapon in the hands of the MRF were not enough to curb its activities. Clearly military intelligence calculated that the potential gains far outweighed the risks.

The MRF also relied on intelligence provided by the regular 'green' army battalions. On 27 September 1972, a month after he joined, 'Alan' saw how that intelligence was used. The Green Jackets, 'who had done a good job in getting the locals to talk', had information that an IRA ambush was to take place in West Belfast and the MRF was tasked to stop it. Again, the circumstances were controversial. The army said that a plain-clothes surveillance patrol came under fire and the soldiers responded. In their statements, the soldiers said they were shot at five times and returned fire with a Sterling sub-machine gun and Browning 9 mm pistol. According to the army version, two men were hit, one of whom, Daniel Rooney (19), died soon afterwards in the nearby Royal Victoria Hospital. Although the Green Jackets claimed that Rooney was a known gunman, there was no IRA funeral nor was his name placed on the IRA's roll of honour. Again, local people said he was totally innocent and was simply chatting to a friend when he was shot from a passing car. At the inquest held in December 1973, the court was told that lead tests on Rooney's clothing gave no indication that he had been firing a weapon.[4]

But although the IRA tended to attribute all undercover operations to the MRF and Kitson, military intelligence was running other intelligence operations that did not always involve the MRF. As a planner Gavin had nothing to do with intelligence-gathering, but his position as Secretary to the 'D. Ops' committee meant that he was privy to what was going on when such matters were discussed at the highest level at Army Head-quarters. He knew, for example, that, as one of its covert intelligence-gathering operations, the army was monitoring the 'Gemini' massage parlour at 397, Antrim Road. Apparently IRA men or their associates from nearby Ardoyne would come in for a bit of relaxation and, in the intimacy of the parlour, would say things they would not repeat outside. What they did not know was that the army was upstairs, watching and listening. Gavin, a man of probity and strict moral principle, thought 'Gemini' was fair game. 'One thought, well, if that's what is useful to gain intelligence, then so be it. I wasn't shocked to hear about it as some people might be. Get on and do it, but under the proper arrangements.' It appears that these covert operations were being backed up by undercover soldiers based in premises in College Square in Belfast's university area. Peter and the 'funny people' in the tower at Stormont Castle also knew what was going on, although they were not the instigators of it. The MRF and enterprises such as the massage parlour were operations they inherited and had no wish to stop as long as they were producing results. With Stormont suspended and Direct Rule now imposed, the 'Brits' wanted to squeeze the IRA in every way possible, in the belief it would improve the climate for a political solution. But Peter knew how risky such operations were.

> There was a slightly 'piratical' atmosphere prevailing at the time. There were gaps to be filled and there was no point in sitting back in an ivory tower of any sort and not doing something about it. Some of these slightly piratical ventures failed, some had to be modified and led to very good things. But the idea was you had actually to go out there and do something because clearly intelligence wasn't working as it should have been. You had to make the overtures yourself. The military were carrying out these kind of ventures on their own, in itself a kind of piracy I suppose, but it was only because they themselves felt that there were gaps to be plugged.

The most contentious and dangerous 'piratical' venture of all was a bogus laundry service run by military intelligence. It was called the Four Square laundry and its van drove around republican areas collecting and returning washing to its clients. Everything was thoroughly washed, neatly pressed and delivered back to its owners. The laundry itself was carried out by a genuine laundry service that presumably had no idea who its client really was. The Four Square laundry's prices must have been highly competitive as not many people living in these generally depressed republican areas could afford such luxury. But what its customers did not know was that Four Square did other things besides washing. When the clothes were returned they had been forensically tested for traces of explosives and firearms. The woman who went round knocking on doors, offering the laundry's services and collecting and delivering the washing, belonged to the Women's Royal Army Corps and came from Northern Ireland so her accent would not arouse suspicion. Farrar-Hockley was one of Four Square's great champions.

> I supported it whole-heartedly and it went on far longer than anyone expected. It was extremely efficient and the prices were right and the goods were right when they were returned. It enabled us to operate in republican areas right in front of the eyes of all those who lived there without people saying, '*Watch out, there's an RUC patrol or there's an army patrol.*' There was no sign of any of those things. And so one had a look-in at what was going on, in particular in areas where you knew that weapons might be moved or explosives planted or people having meetings. We could watch all this by simply looking out of the van windows. It was a little observation post going round on wheels with nobody cottoning on to the fact that it was picking up a very useful flow of information.

By the autumn of 1972, the IRA had become increasingly concerned about where the MRF and military intelligence were getting their information from. Brendan Hughes, who was then a senior figure in 'D' Company of the IRA's Second Battalion in Belfast, was well aware of how vulnerable the organization was to penetration. Paranoia about informers or 'touts' within its ranks has always been endemic in the IRA, to the extent that a procedure for dealing with informers was clearly set out in its 'Standing Orders'. The suspect is 'tried' before an IRA 'court' and, if found guilty, 'executed' – usually by means of a bullet in the back of the head. The body is invariably found hooded and bound by the side of the road, sometimes covered with a black bin-liner.

Hughes became concerned when one of his men failed to turn up for the daily meeting at the 'call house' where members of 'D' Company routinely assembled to be given their orders. 'The Company would have been doing five or six operations a day,' Hughes told me. 'They would rob a bank in the morning, put a sniper out in the afternoon, put a "float" [a roving ambush] out that night, put a bomb in the town. There was a whole series of operations taking place and every day the Volunteers would have had to report in. So within twenty-four to forty-eight hours it was obvious that one of the people were missing.'

The absentee was Seamus Wright (25). Hughes described him as 'a quiet, unassuming character and a good Volunteer'. Hughes had never had any reason to doubt his loyalty. Wright had recently married a young woman from a staunch republican family from Leeson Street in the heart of 'D' Company's area, although Hughes says that Wright's new bride was not involved in the IRA. Wright had been arrested on 5 February 1972 and interrogated at Palace Barracks, which at the time was notorious for the brutal methods that were alleged to have been used to extract information from suspects.[7] The chances are that he was 'turned' then and given the choice of going to gaol, being interned, or joining the 'Freds' and working for the MRF. He appears to have chosen the latter and was installed and trained in the 'Freds' quarters at Palace Barracks. At some stage, Wright went to England, almost certainly under army protection, perhaps when his handlers thought that things might be getting too hot. Whilst he was away, he phoned his wife and said he wanted to see her. Mrs Wright consulted Hughes who said she should go and tell Seamus to come back. A week or so later, she returned without her husband. She told Hughes that Seamus had told her that he had broken under interrogation and wanted to come home but was frightened to do so. She said she met him 'in a house with two soldiers'. The IRA then told Mrs Wright, who still had a means of communicating with her husband, that under the circumstances he was free to come home. With this assurance, Wright finally did so and returned to their house in the Kashmir Road. The following is based on Hughes's account of what happened.

The next day, he was arrested by his former comrades in 'D' Company and began to talk. 'I think he wanted to clear the sheet and get the military personnel off his back,' said Hughes. 'I think that's the reason why he gave up the information.' Wright apparently mentioned a laundry van with a secret compartment above the driver that concealed a soldier with an SLR rifle. Shortly afterwards, the IRA 'arrested' two other 'Volunteers' who were also suspected of working for the 'Freds'. One of them, Kevin McKee, was from the Second Battalion's 'B' Company based in Ballymurphy. The other person's name is not known.

It soon became clear that Wright's revelations had implications far beyond 'D' Company's patch, and others would have to be called in to continue the questioning. It was the nightmare every informer dreaded, arrest and interrogation by the IRA's feared internal security squad, the 'Unknowns'. The 'Unknowns' worked to the Belfast Brigade with a roving brief to cover all the IRA's three Battalions in the city, rooting out suspected 'touts' and getting as much information from them as they could. No doubt their methods would not withstand scrutiny. Wright and McKee, and possibly the third man, were taken across the border and the 'Unknowns' set about their work. Wright apparently told all that he knew, about being trained in a compound at Palace Barracks with the 'Freds', about the activities of the MRF and, crucially, about the Four

Square laundry. The interrogation of McKee and the third person apparently confirmed and amplified the picture.

Gradually, the Belfast Brigade pieced things together. Hughes, who had been 'devastated' when he found out that there had been an informer in 'D' Company's midst, was then debriefed on what Wright and the others had revealed under interrogation. He was even more astonished and shocked. 'We had no idea that British intelligence was running a laundry service and massage parlour,' he told me. 'Obviously people at that period would have been watching out, gathering intelligence, watching for suspicious cars and so forth but until this information came in, no one suspected the Four Square laundry team were military personnel.' Hughes was all for hitting the laundry van as soon as possible before the 'Brits' discovered it had been rumbled and closed it down, but another senior IRA figure, who subsequently became a prominent Sinn Fein politician, argued that the IRA should bide its time so all three targets – the laundry, the massage parlour and back-up team in College Square – should be attacked at the same time. Hughes was finally persuaded that this was the better plan and that the IRA should bide its time. 'The idea was to wipe out the whole intelligence set-up and to try and deal a blow to British military intelligence,' he said.

The combined operation was planned for 2 October 1972 and master-minded by the Belfast Brigade. The IRA's Third Battalion was to attack the massage parlour and the Second Battalion was to take out College Square and the Four Square laundry. The plan was to intercept the van during its rounds in the republican Twinbrook estate, kill the driver and riddle the area above the cab that was believed to conceal the soldier doing surveillance. Four Volunteers were chosen, one to drive the car and three to do the shooting, armed with a Thompson sub-machine gun, an M1 carbine and a pistol. The original plan had been to ambush the van when it stopped by the parade of shops in Juniper Park to buy some fish and chips, which the IRA had established was part of the laundry crew's routine. It was, however, aborted when one of the IRA unit decided it was too risky. 'There were too many kids swarming around,' he told me. So the van was attacked further up the street. The gunmen got out of the car and 'sprayed the whole 'heap', with the Thompson raking the top of the van, 'although we had no proof there was anyone there'. One of the gunmen was hit by a ricochet and 'did some squealing but was not seriously hurt'.

There was no soldier concealed above the cab but the driver, Sapper Edward Stuart of the Royal Engineers, was hit five times and killed. The woman from the WRAC was collecting and delivering laundry at the time and took refuge inside the house. According to Hughes, the occupants thought loyalists were attacking the van and kept the woman safe. A year later, she received the Military Medal, the first member of the Women's Royal Army Corps to receive the award.[8]

About an hour later, the same IRA unit attacked College Square. They headed upstairs but there was no one there. The only shot fired was an accidental discharge.

A unit from the IRA's Third Battalion attacked the Gemini massage parlour, which they had also been watching, and made for the room upstairs from where they believed the army had been carrying out surveillance on the clientele below. They claimed they hit three under-cover soldiers, two men and a woman whom they believed to be the daughter of a senior army officer. However, no casualties were ever admitted.

Although two of the three operations were largely unsuccessful, the IRA maximized the propaganda potential of its attack on the Four Square laundry and its 'unmasking' of the army's undercover operations. Brendan Hughes, who was familiar with what happened that day, was delighted with the outcome. 'It was a great morale booster for the IRA and for the people that were involved. They believed it would be a massive blow against the British military machine.' Hughes was dismissive of the way in which the 'Brits' had handled the Four Square laundry. 'It was very amateurish. The very fact that the British army knew, or should have known, that two of their operatives were in enemy-controlled territory, should have cancelled the operation right away. To me it was a very, very amateurish and very badly run military operation.'

But Sapper Edward Stuart was not the only victim. At some stage, only the IRA knows when, the 'two operatives' Seamus Wright and Kevin McKee were 'executed' by the IRA. Although never forgotten by their families, their names caught the public's attention again in 1999 when, as part of the Good Friday Agreement, the IRA agreed to help the authorities trace the bodies of nine people it had killed. They became known as the 'disappeared'. Some bodies were found but those of Wright and McKee were not amongst them.

Some weeks after the Four Square laundry was ambushed, a 'very honest' army NCO came to see Gavin at Army Headquarters with the profits made by the operation. He asked him what to do with the money as the laundry was no longer in business. Gavin was slightly embarrassed. 'It certainly wasn't designed to be profit-making,' he said. 'So we arranged for the proceeds to go to a suitable charity and that was the end of that. It was a sort of loose end that hadn't been tied up.'

The end of the Four Square laundry marked the end of the MRF. Soon afterwards, the organization was disbanded. Viewing its demise from the tower that housed the 'funny people' at Stormont Castle, Peter saw it as an inevitable part of the learning curve. 'The Four Square laundry partly worked and partly failed with disastrous consequences,' he said. 'It was a major factor in realizing that things could no longer go on this way. It's rather like the first parachute. Somebody has got to have the notion of a parachute, jump out of an aeroplane and be killed before somebody says, "Well, I think we've got to design a better parachute."' After the disaster of the Four Square laundry, military intelligence set about designing it. There were to be no more 'piratical ventures'.

Chapter Twelve

A Better Parachute

Early 1973

Brian, the Colonel of the 1st Battalion, The Gloucestershire Regiment, returned to Belfast with his men at the beginning of 1973. He was a colourful commander, patriotic, extrovert and larger than life, and his men thought the world of him. Headquarters for the Battalion's tour was the disused Albert Street mill in the heart of the IRA stronghold of the Lower Falls and in the shadow of the notorious Divis Flats. To the Gloucesters, the mill was a sand-bagged fortress in the middle of the 'reservation'. The 'reservation' was Indian country. Out there were the men of Brendan Hughes's 'D' Company of the IRA's Second Battalion that covered the Gloucesters' patch. Inside Albert Street mill, the soldiers felt reasonably secure, barricaded in tiny rooms with a little red light and three bunks. The windows had been shot out months ago and the sandbags, three or four deep, came right up to the top, leaving only a sliver of natural light to pierce the gloom inside. Once a soldier ventured outside the fortress and set foot in the 'reservation', he never knew if he was going to return. George, one of Colonel Brian's men, had no love for the people beyond Albert Street mill. The feeling was mutual.

> It was a battleground. I don't care what anybody says, we were at war and against an enemy that was good. The snipers were always out there, waiting for us and for the opportunity to have a 'bang'. You could feel the hatred. It was like an animal, like something from Hell. And we hated them too with the kind of hatred I never thought could get into me because I'm quite a nice bloke. You could feel the fear. It was a place where they were going to kill you. You knew that some of us weren't going to come out alive, that we were going to die in those gutters and die in those derelicts and inside those Flats. You try to keep this out of your mind but it's always there. Every time you went out on patrol, you'd put one up the spout, suck in the

old breath and gee each other up, you know, 'Come on lads! Everything's going to be fine!' And you'd go and touch a little talisman, whatever you had. I had a cross and chain and I used to touch that and say, 'Look after me and look after the lads.'

Colonel Brian knew what he was in Albert Street mill to do. 'I had a very simple mission statement from 39 Brigade and that was to destroy the IRA in my area,' he told me. 'As a Battalion commander, that was meat and drink to me and that's what we got on to do. It meant capturing or killing everybody who was killing and maiming innocent people in my area.' Besides relishing his 'mission statement', the Colonel also had a wicked sense of humour and took full advantage of the mill's giant chimney that could be seen for miles around.

So that we could make sure that the locals were aware of what was going on in their area, we got hold of the highest ladder available in Northern Ireland, you know, one of those gantries that put television cameras up to very high heights. Then we stencilled our back-badge[1] at the top and put the scoreboard on it. For instance, Gloucesters 2, IRA 0. We used to update it regularly so that we could keep them up to date on what was going on. The locals used to go bananas and many, many, many were the requests we used to have to get this thing taken down but, sadly, when we got these requests, we could never get hold of the ladder!

Despite such light relief, the Gloucesters' tour was overshadowed by the loss of two of its young soldiers, Christopher Brady (21) and Geoffrey Breakwell (20). The loss was all the more keenly felt because Colonel Brian's Battalion was so close. They died on 17 July 1973 when an IRA booby-trap bomb exploded in Divis Flats whilst their section was examining a suspicious-looking rolled-up mattress. Two other members of the patrol were seriously injured. George was a member of the stretcher party swiftly dispatched to the scene. The sight was horrendous. I asked him how he felt about the Flats and the people in them, having just lost two of his mates and seen two more seriously injured. 'We wanted to go in and tear the place down, basically. We wanted to go in and just pay them back but the Colonel knew what was going to happen and he kept us out. Then he put another Company in the Flats with orders to keep us out for 24 hours at least.'

Three weeks later, at 2 a.m. one morning, when George was patrolling Divis Flats, he heard that those suspected of planting the bomb were being detained. He went running down to another floor of the Flats where his mate, 'Butch', was located and to his astonishment, three 'kids' aged fifteen, sixteen and seventeen were being held. 'We arrested them immediately and took them back to base. The Colonel came out to see us and he was very pleased. He said, "You haven't touched them, have you?" I said, "No, they've not been touched."'

I asked George if he had been tempted. 'We wanted to throw them off the balcony of the Flats, you know, that's the first thing that comes into your mind,' he said. 'But you just don't do that. We knew that if we touched them in any way, they'd get away with it. They'd get some smart-arse lawyer with no scruples and he would get them off, even though two of our men had been killed and two others badly wounded. So, fair do's, my lads didn't touch them.'

When the case came to court, the murder charges were dropped and the defence offered guilty pleas for causing an explosion.[2] Because the accused were juveniles, the sentences were relatively light. The seventeen-year-old was sentenced to four years. He was alleged to have cleared the area before the bomb went off to make sure none of *his* people were hurt. The sixteen-year-old juvenile, who was said to have triggered the bomb and who could not be named because of his age, was sentenced to be detained at an institution for five years. The fifteen-year-old was cleared of all charges. The 'kids' had been caught just before the Battalion's tour ended.

At their trial, the accused claimed they had made confessions after being ill-treated by detectives during their interrogation but the judge, Mr Justice Kelly, ruled that their statements were admissible as evidence. Such allegations were common and invariably dismissed by the authorities as IRA propaganda but there is no doubt that some were often based on fact. Although it is rare to hear policemen admit what they did, soldiers tend to be more open. For George and those who served in hard republican areas, it was a matter of survival.

If we caught them with a rifle, we'd give them a good hiding, basically. Oh yes, you know, it did happen because they were going to kill us and it was the law of the jungle.

What was a good hiding?

A good thumping, basically, you know.

That wouldn't endear you to the local population.

We didn't need endearing to that lot, mate. There was no nice people in that area. You know, people don't understand how much they hated us.

On one occasion during an incident in the Lower Falls involving George and his section, a notorious IRA gunman from 'D' Company was shot in the leg.

> He was hit in the thigh and the blokes trod on the wound just to try and get information out of the guy. He was a tough bloke and there was no way he would have bent or anything. You could have probably cut his legs off and he wouldn't have said anything. It's what happened in those areas. You lost a lot of humanity in there, you lost a lot of your decency. Some of the things I did then, I'm not ashamed of doing really but I do wish I hadn't done them sometimes, you know.

Soldiers who did the questioning in the army's interrogation centres at the time did not wear kid gloves. They were desperate for information. On 'a bad night' after some incident or other, about eighty suspects, usually between the ages of sixteen and twenty-five, could be hauled in. 'It kept the little bastards off the streets,' an army officer of the time told me. Once inside, they were given 'a pretty hard time'. The words were a euphemism. Army intelligence knew who was in the IRA but not necessarily who pulled the trigger. Soldiers would put on ski-masks and hold a gun to suspects' heads. Others were made to crawl over broken glass. Years later, the officer recognized that such methods were counter-productive. Many of his contemporaries came to share his view. 'We got information and thought we were doing the right thing but we weren't. We were turning those on the periphery of the IRA into the IRA or at least into their active supporters. In those early days, we failed to appreciate the difference between Borneo and Belfast. We'd learned the lessons but they hadn't been transposed properly. By this time we'd done sufficient damage to keep the IRA going for the next ten years.'

Colonel Brian had more subtle ways of gathering intelligence and knew what to look for when trying to recruit an agent, like the barman sleeping with the wife of an internee. 'With the right questions, he can be extremely useful to you.' Or the priest walking along with a slightly stiff leg who has a rifle strapped under his cassock. 'You might chat to him and make one or two points and in the confessional box a few weeks later you might get pieces of information that you might not otherwise have got.' I asked him if these cases really happened. 'Of course they did,' he said roaring with laughter. 'You don't get intelligence by sitting on your backside and doing nothing. My job was to destroy the IRA in my area. The Gloucestershire Regiment have been energetically engaged in destroying the Queen's enemies for upwards of three hundred years and we didn't see any reason why we should stop now. And we didn't. The whole Battalion got stuck into it and they were marvellous.'

Brian used his initiative and was probably more enterprising than most in finding ingenious ways of picking up information. One evening he was sitting in the operations room 'putting the world to rights' when his signaller, who was browsing through an American security magazine, suddenly said, 'Cor! Look at this! Here's a bug that you can stick in the back of a television set and you can hear what they're saying in the room. And it's got a range of a mile and half!' He passed the magazine over to the Colonel who was equally impressed and said, 'Let's buy one!' It arrived in a small package ten days later, two inches by two inches with a little receiver tuned to the frequency of the bug. Brian knew of a nearby house where the IRA held some of its meetings, the only problem now was how to get it into the back of the television set in the target house. Again, the Colonel's ingenuity triumphed: three Gloucesters with Irish accents and white overalls bluffed their way into the house as TV repair men and installed the bug.

A few days later, the Gloucesters noticed known IRA men going into the house and immediately informed the Colonel. The receiver was switched on and 'we heard things of enormous interest'. At some stage they picked up a vital piece of information about a car bomb the IRA intended to plant in the city centre. The car that was to be used, invariably a Ford Cortina, was noted and the information passed up the army's chain of command so that appropriate action could be taken. The following morning it was stopped by soldiers from the Royal Artillery Regiment who told the surprised and nervous occupants that there had been a bomb warning and they were going to cordon off the area. Would they mind staying in the car whilst they did so? Not wishing for a premature meeting with their Maker, the youths owned up to the bomb and told the soldiers how to defuse it.

Later, the Colonel was asked by his superiors how he had obtained the vital information and 'in all innocence' he told them. The result was 'an interview without coffee' with the new GOC, General Sir Frank King, who had taken over from Lieutenant-General Tuzo in February 1973. King gave Brian a memorable dressing-down, saying that such operations were off-limits unless properly authorized. The bug was removed and the Colonel was summoned back to see the GOC. General King asked if his order had been carried out. Brian said it had. 'Fine,' King said, 'now let's go and have a drink and you can tell me all about it.'

Brian's encounter with the GOC was a warning that the days of 'piratical ventures' were over. There were to be no more MRF 'cowboy' operations, no more Four Square laundries and no more unauthorized freelance operations by enterprising local Battalions. From now on, covert activities were to be strictly controlled and monitored. Nothing was left to chance and proper systems were put in place. Lessons had been learned. The Four Square laundry, for example, had no back-up team. If it had, although it may not have been able to prevent the ambush, it would probably have stood a good chance of intercepting the IRA unit as it made its getaway. Those who had been involved in such operations had had no special training or special selection course. 'Alan' had been recruited into the MRF simply because its commanding officer knew him as a fellow Para and thought he was the right kind of soldier for the job.

The change in intelligence-gathering came around the beginning of 1973. The army knew that it had special needs if it was effectively to combat the IRA and the loyalist paramilitaries who were now posing a serious threat with their random sectarian killings. The RUC's Special Branch operated on a long-term basis, recruiting and cultivating informers and agents with the ranks of both enemies but the army needed more immediate information if it was to thwart the murderous attacks.

After much discussion and an agreed assessment of what was needed, the army established a new covert unit designed to revolutionize intelligence-gathering. It was to be so secret that even those involved in it did not know each other's real names. It was originally known as '14 Intelligence and Security Company' or '14 Int. and Sy' but its name was soon abbreviated to just '14 Intelligence Company'. Its members were known as 'operators' because they 'operated' out on the ground in the enemy's heartlands. To the hand-picked élite selected to join, '14 Int.' soon became known as the 'Det' because its operations were based on 'Detachments' to each of the army's three Brigades in Northern Ireland. North 'Det' was based in Derry and covered the 8 Brigade area in the west of the province; South 'Det' was based in Armagh and covered the 3 Brigade area that includes the border and South Armagh; and East 'Det' was based in Belfast and covered the 39 Brigade area. The men and women of the 'Det' were to play a vital role in the conflict, the crucial importance of which was never recognized by those outside the tight inner circle of the intelligence community because its operations were so secret. Whereas the Special Air Service (SAS) played a vital and often spectacular role in the conflict, it tended to do so at relatively infrequent intervals that invariably attracted a blaze of publicity. In contrast, the 'Det' ground away at the IRA and its loyalist counterparts day after day under their very noses. Their achievements could never be publicized nor their critical contribution recognized since to do so would jeopardize their work. On the numerous occasions in which operators shot dead IRA men, republicans invariably laid the killings at the door of the SAS. The army did nothing to disabuse them. To some extent the personnel were interchangeable. SAS 'troopers' joined 14 Intelligence Company and 'Det' operators joined the SAS.

14 Intelligence Company's mission was to infiltrate republican and loyalist areas and become part of the landscape in order to watch and track the enemy. They had to do so without attracting suspicion. They dressed like the locals and acted like locals but, wherever possible, avoided opening their mouths. Grunts not words were the preferred and safer option. It was intelligence-gathering of the most sophisticated and dangerous kind, requiring extraordinary physical and mental courage, limitless patience and superhuman feats of memory. In terms of results, a single 'operator' was said to be worth a Company of a hundred regular soldiers. As the years went by and the intelligence services' technical expertise became more sophisticated, the 'Det' became an even more lethal weapon in the counter-terrorist armoury of the 'Brits' and played a huge part in the war of attrition against the IRA. They bugged or 'jarked' terrorist weapons by secretly removing them from their 'hides' and then replacing them, having inserted a tiny beacon inside that emitted a signal so their move-ments could be tracked. Consignments of explosives were monitored in the same way. Through their specialized training in Methods of Entry (MOE), operators could break into premises undetected so the Security Service, MI5, could plant its 'technical devices' or bugs. A credit card was a favourite tool to 'card' locks: 'Your Flexible Friend', the operators called it. In the turret at Stormont Castle, Peter saw the 'Det' being born and watched it flourish as the years went by. 14 Intelligence Company was 'the better parachute'.

> They were a remarkable gang of men and women. I have nothing but the highest admiration for them. I think it requires a coolness and a dedication and a strength of nerve which actually is quite remark-able. They really did have to have nerves of steel. To go into a known republican shop and actually buy packets of cigarettes over the counter so that you can see who is in there and eyeball them, takes a lot of doing. And there were a lot of people who did that sort of thing. They were very brave, very brave. I think 14 Intelligence Company were actually pivotal and they will prove to have been one of the most significant weapons in the battle against that kind of urban terrorism.

'Alan' was one of 14 Intelligence Company's first recruits. It was, he said, a natural progression from the MRF, the difference being that the 'Det' was properly trained and had a clearly defined purpose.

> For the first time I believe there was a political will to gain intelligence that wasn't simply source-generated. There was a re-

quirement for hard intelligence which was real and which was current. 14 Intelligence Company was set up to provide the surveillance that would generate the positive intelligence that would support – or not – source information. It was vital in the war against terrorism.

Most of the training of the 'Det' was carried out by army intelligence officers and the SAS until operators became sufficiently experienced to do it themselves. Members of all three services – army, navy and air force – were eligible although most came from the army. In 1973, 'Alan' was one of 300 accepted for selection, of whom only seventeen finally made it to Northern Ireland. The selection process began at 'Camp One' at the secret location in England. In the early days, few recruits had much idea of what they were being selected for, and those undergoing assessment knew better than to ask questions. The role of the 'Det' was later euphemistically referred to as 'special duties'. The process of weeding people out began immediately. 'Alan' told me what happened. 'Before we arrived, we were told to bring nothing that was attributable, nothing that had badges of rank or unit or anything like that. The very first morning after our arrival, everything was searched, and any diary freaks or address book freaks immediately had a question mark placed over them.'

For many officers, Camp One was a culture shock. One complained that there was no sherry in the evening. Many dropped out, 'binned' themselves, because they could not take it. The instructors wore people down to the point of exhaustion, gave them precious little sleep, and then tested their mental powers when their brains were as dead as their bodies. After a day of strenuous exercise and the promise of a good night's sleep, candidates would be turfed out of bed at 3 a.m. and made to run round a field carrying a telegraph pole until they almost dropped. It was not 'Alan's' idea of a joke. In the middle of another night, 'Alan's' sleep was shattered again.

A thunder flash, a sort of training grenade, was dropped down the chimney into this old pot boiler stove which then blew bits of the stove and bits of coke all over the room. Then you had to get to a rendezvous [RV] point in the dark, totally disorientated. You weren't allowed to put the lights on and you had to get yourself out of your bed, out through the window, or wherever, and get to the RV where you were then given somewhere else to go.

On that particular night, 'Alan' was told to go to the gym. The moment he entered, he knew what was in store. In the middle a set of benches had been arranged in a square. It was a makeshift boxing ring and 'Alan', being a Para, knew they were going to 'mill'. 'Milling' involved knocking the hell out of your opponent for two minutes with no holds barred. That night, 'Alan' faced a soldier he had served with before and whom he regarded as one of his mates, a Light Infantryman called Richard 'Dusty' Miller. 'Dusty' was the Battalion boxing champion. 'My nose was already broken, so it wasn't a big problem,' 'Alan' said. 'He battered the lights out of me but at the end of two minutes, we were big mates again.' I asked 'Alan' what the point of this was. 'To show you could control your aggression, that you could turn it on and turn it off,' he said. 'I think it's a sign of true comradeship that you could batter seven lights out of each other and still walk away with your arm round the guy's shoulder.' Intense comradeship bound the 'Det' together.

The mental tests were equally demanding. They too would be applied in the middle of the night, even after a 'milling'. Candidates would undergo a version of 'Kim's Game' in which they were shown one article after another, from 'a pencil and a piece of string, to a Biro and a cuddly toy'. Sometimes there were as many as seventy. They had to remember them all and then write them down on a piece of paper. Out on the ground in Northern Ireland, operators would have to notice and record dozens of items which they simply had to remember and they could not afford to get them wrong. 'Alan' admitted there were other things he would rather have been doing but it stood him in good stead later in the province when the only technical aids he had were 'two eyeballs, two hands and two feet'. But there was one exercise that remained indelibly etched on every operator's mind that was as painful as 'milling' but in a different way. Again they were roused in the early hours of the morning and this time taken to a building in which there was a projector and a screen. There they were shown what all without exception admitted was the most boring film they had ever seen. It was a black-and-white film, probably made in the 1950s, about a hill tribe in Borneo who made everything out of bamboo. The bleary-eyed audience had to remember each item for a test at the end, after which they never wanted to hear about or see a bamboo ever again. It was too much for some, as one operator observed. 'You'd look around and there were several "noddy-dogs" around the place. A few people just gave up and put their head on the desk and went to sleep. Those people were "binned".'

At the end of the three weeks, those who had not already been 'binned' or given up through sheer exhaustion were then told if they had passed selection. 'Alan' was one of the handful who did. These chosen few went on to the second phase at Camp Two in Wales. There operators spent an equally exhausting and testing six months or so, including a fortnight at the army's intelligence school at Ashford, being taught all the skills they would require in Northern Ireland: surveillance techniques on foot and in cars; a range of driving skills that would equip them to be stunt drivers in a Hollywood movie; covert photography; the importance of body language and how to dress and act in a way that would not attract attention; training and familiarization with a whole range of weapons, including the enemy's; and, most important of all, Close Quarter Battle (CQB) skills that would help them survive a shoot-out if 'clocked' and confronted by the IRA. Much of this training was carried out by the SAS whose offensive skills gave operators the confidence they needed. But the most controversial part of the training, for which people had to volunteer, were exercises in which they were taught how to resist interrogation if captured by the IRA. This was vitally important as the possibility of it happening was real given the kind of missions undertaken in the heart of hostile areas. The SAS was involved in the interrogations and a doctor was always on standby. However realistic the treatment, it could never mirror the reality of an interrogation by the IRA's 'Unknowns'.

Later, when women joined the 'Det' and gave its operations a whole new dimension, they too volunteered for the exercise to prove they were as good as the men. For the women operators we met, it was a horrific experience that none ever forgot and would never wish to repeat. All are remarkable women. They asked for and received no special treatment. 'Anna' never forgot the experience.

A bag was put over my head, and then I was thrown onto a concrete floor in a very cold location. I was hosed down in cold water and my clothes were taken off me. While this was happening, the bag was still over my head and I couldn't see what was happening. I was kicked, punched and abused by both men and women, judging by their voices. I was stripped and when the clothes came off my body, they were sarcastic about how I appeared. They put overalls on me and then soaked me again with cold water.

Did you crack?

I did at the end. I told them my correct name. I just wanted to get out of there. I was just at my limits of endurance. It just got to a point where I didn't care if I lived or died.

But 'Anna' still passed, became a fully fledged operator and went to Northern Ireland.

When I first heard 'Mary' describe what she went through, I found it difficult to believe her account until I heard others confirm it. Astonishingly, she was subjected to some of the Five Techniques that the Government had banned in 1972. When I raised this in the appropriate quarters, I was told it was different because in this instance, the 'guinea-pigs' were army volunteers not IRA suspects. 'Mary' was deprived of sleep and food and hooded 'with a hessian sack or something'. She had her boots taken off her to increase the sense of isolation. She was then placed in a variety of 'stress positions' including being spread-eagled against a wall with arms and legs apart, supported only by her fingers, 'like in an American movie search position'. She was also subjected to 'white noise' similar to that experienced by IRA suspects after internment in 1971. 'It's like having a badly tuned radio playing constantly, for hours and hours, really loud. So your senses were deprived. You were physically deprived. You didn't know where you were, what's going to happen to you next and what you were in for.'

I asked 'Mary' if she was ill-treated.

We weren't ill-treated as such because there was always a team monitoring us and there was a medical officer on hand but we were roughed up a bit, beaten up a little bit. Just bundled about and a couple of kicks and punches. Just general abuse really.

But you're a woman.

So? I wanted to be part of Special Forces. It didn't matter if I was young, old, black, white, or a woman. It didn't matter. I wanted to be part of that group and part of that was undergoing the inter-rogation. What you must remember is that if ever we were captured by the IRA or any of the splinter groups, or by any terrorist organization, then they would undoubtedly play with us in the form of interrogation before they would kill us. So you had to be equipped for those instances and that training was part of it.

There were around 120 people on the course with 'Mary' at Camp Two. Only twelve made it and she was one of them. She said she survived through 'inner strength, an instinct for survival and pride. Pride has a lot to do with it. *You will not fail. You will not go back to your old unit.*' She was too exhausted and drained to feel elation at the end. 'It was more of "Oh God, this is it. Here we go. I've passed the course but now it's a reality check. I'm going on to the streets of Northern Ireland. I hope I'll be able to cope." It's not something to celebrate because you've passed a course. Now it's time to put the training into action.' 'Mary', like 'Alan' and all 'Det' operators, lived on a knife-edge. Despite the training, not all operators survived.

Chapter Thirteen

Success

March 1973–May 1974

14 Intelligence Company could not act on its own. It had to be guided. 'Targets' had to be identified before they could be followed; premises had to be pointed out before they could be put under surveillance or 'technically attacked'; and weapons hides had to be located before their contents could be 'jarked'. The 'Det's' guide in all this was the RUC's Special Branch, a unit as secretive and self-contained as '14 Int.' with the risks often just as high. The 'Branch' cultivated, recruited and handled informers or 'sources', from those on the periphery of the republican and loyalist paramilitary organizations to those close to the top. Special Branch's investment was long term. The skill of its officers was to identify someone in the early days who clearly had the potential to rise within the organization, recruit him or her and then stick with them as they penetrated the higher levels of whatever group they belonged to. Prime targets were those in the IRA's 'Quartermaster's' Department because they knew where the weapons were and, at least until the late 1970s when the IRA reorganized, who was using them.

As with the 'Det', the human price was high. Marriages were destroyed because the job came first, and lives were lost because the nature of their work meant that Special Branch officers were often dangerously exposed. Unlike 'Det' operators, some of their faces became familiar in republican areas as sources could not be recruited and handled by remote control. The cases of Seamus Wright and Kevin McKee who fingered the Four Square laundry show that the IRA could always 'turn' sources back again, although their subsequent chances of survival were thin. From time to time, as the inroads made by Special Branch took their toll, the IRA offered amnesties with a promise that informers would be allowed to live if they told all. They would then often be paraded before Sinn Fein press conferences to extract the maximum propaganda advantage and invariably allowed to live *pour encourager les autres*. There was a difference between a

Volunteer coming forward and making a confession and one extracted by the IRA's 'Unknowns'.

'Mike' joined Special Branch in July 1971, a month before internment, and spent a lifetime in it, becoming one of its most experienced and successful agent-handlers. 'We joined a service to give of our best and suddenly we found we were fighting a war,' he told me. 'I ran the arse off my trousers for years.' 'Mike' went to West Belfast in 1972 and was based there through most of the 1970s and into the 1980s, working alongside many of the army officers already mentioned. All spoke highly of him and said 'Mike' knew everything. After years of experience, he acquired an encyclopaedic knowledge of just about every family in the area, its relations, its history and, above all, its IRA connections. Unlike many regular soldiers who viewed 'touts' with almost as much contempt as the IRA, 'Mike' had great respect for his sources. 'It was our function in those days to infiltrate these organizations and the only way to do that was to get people to talk to you,' he said. 'We didn't pull any punches. We told them the facts, what they were doing, how we expected them to do it and the risks they would run. We told them what we would do to look after them and, in truth, our life was in their hands as much as theirs was in ours.' Often agent and handler became very close, sharing a common danger and common purpose. One agent 'Mike' handled rose to an extremely high level within the IRA until, to keep him alive, he was finally 'exfiltrated' and resettled outside Northern Ireland with the help of the Security Service, MI5, who assist in such matters. But given their importance, no source was turned away, whatever the value of the information he or she might bring. 'Mike' knew that every scrap of information helped with the big picture.

> As far as I was concerned, this was a war, and we had to gain the best intelligence we could. Sources are the lifeblood of intelligence and it all stems from there. You're fighting against a secret organization that wants to keep its secrets and you want them to impart those secrets to you. Terrorist organizations don't advertise their working parts so it's up to us to penetrate them.

But why would anyone risk becoming an informer when exposure meant death?

> It's a very complex question to which I've never been able to find out the answer. But when you're working with these people, or talking to these people, there is some trigger that will decide whether they're doing the right thing or the wrong thing. Pure greed is one of the

lesser attractions about it. The monetary incentives aren't huge. We're talking 1970s here. It could be anything from £5 to £500. It depends on the status of the individual. If you give somebody who's used to having a few shillings in his pocket, fifty quid, it soon becomes obvious that there's something wrong.

Did they get bonuses?

For particularly good information relating to finds of weapons or explosives or to the arrest and charging of terrorists, yes, there were inducements.

'Mike' agreed that money was important but it was far from being the only motivation.

Spite and grudges against a particular person or organization all play their part, as does the feeling that the group they represent is not doing the right thing, like killing innocent civilians or children. Then there's the 'James Bond' element where some people get a real buzz out of being involved, the feeling that they're actually doing something and they can see the result. It's things like that. I couldn't possibly explain the complexities of it but the bottom line is, it works.

The critical step was recruiting an agent or informer. It was rather like fishing: for most of the time, the fish never took the bait, but then suddenly one did and that made all the effort worthwhile. There were certainly plenty of fish in 'Mike's' West Belfast pond. Catching them required skill, patience, courage and nerve.

It's no use lying, saying you're a travelling salesman who can make them a lot of money selling blinds. You have to be up front about it and you have to tell them who you are, what you are, and that they may be able to help you. You wouldn't walk up to somebody in the street and say, 'Excuse me, I'm Jo Bloggs from the RUC. Will you work for me?' You've got to do your homework, you've got to know who you're talking to. You've got to know where he's coming from, what his background is and what his associations are. You do it anywhere you can have a chat with them, where you can explain your point of view, convincing them that perhaps they're on the wrong side. It may be their own feeling of self-importance. You help them feel that they are going to become an important part of a larger organization and can have a huge input in it.

Sometimes 'Mike' would make a direct approach on the street. Most knew he was from the 'Branch' or the police. So what happened then?

> Stunned silence sometimes! On other occasions, a lot of verbal abuse. Some would tell you to go away. Others would ignore you and walk past or sometimes listen and walk off. Then maybe one out of twenty, thirty or forty would make a phone call.

'Mike' never lost a source but came close to death himself. He knew that any weakness could be exploited and any opportunity seized. When Special Branch received anonymous letters detailing the IRA activities of 'Theresa', a member of 'Cumann na mBan' (the women's section of the Republican Movement), 'Mike', who was nothing if not direct, got in touch with her and indicated that he had something she might be interested in. Some time later, 'Theresa' rang and arranged to see him. They met in one of the dozens of cafés in Belfast city centre. 'Mike' explained that he had a collection of letters which he assumed she would not like to fall into the wrong hands. 'You give me an arms dump,' he said, 'and I'll give you one of the letters.' Presumably the others were being held for further trading. It might be blackmail but to 'Mike' the end justified the means. He knew that if 'Theresa' took the bait, she was hooked and there would be more finds and high-grade information to come. Even when the letters ran out, 'Theresa', once compromised, would have no escape. If she became unco-operative, 'Mike' or one of his Special Branch partners could always drop the hint to her IRA associates that 'Theresa' was not as loyal to the cause as she might seem.

To complete the transaction, 'Theresa' agreed to meet 'Mike' at 2 p.m. on Sunday afternoon in the casualty department of the Royal Victoria Hospital (RVH) in the heart of the Falls Road. 'Mike' had done his homework. There were two telephone boxes at the RVH and his plan was to have 'Theresa' ring him from one and give him the location of an arms 'dump'. He would then have his colleagues confirm the accuracy of the information and, if it checked out, he would then give 'Theresa' one of the letters. He had no intention of handing over an original but had arranged for one of his female colleagues to make a hand-written copy. But 'Theresa' had clearly weighed up the risks of each course of action. Becoming a 'tout' would mean certain death if she was ever found out and the IRA had no scruples of putting a bullet in the back of a woman's head as well as a man's. Coming clean with the IRA about how she had been compromised, though uncomfortable, would at least preserve her life and might even enhance her own standing within the organization were she able to deliver a dead Special Branch man.

On Sunday afternoon, 'Mike' went to the RVH as agreed, unaware that he was going to almost certain death, although he knew the risk was always there. As luck would have it, one of his Special Branch colleagues was also at the hospital but purely in a private capacity. His daughter had fallen off a horse and he was taking her to the casualty department for treatment. On the way in, he noticed two well-known IRA 'hit-men' stalking the hospital and immediately rang Special Branch and alerted 'Mike's' boss. 'Mike' got the warning just in time. He never got the arms dump and 'Theresa' never got her letter. But 'Mike' got to live. I asked him if he feared death. 'None of us could have done the job if we had,' he said. 'I think if you're on your knees and it's your last thirty seconds, of course you fear death. But on a day-to-day basis, no. It's like being hit by a bus or falling in a river, it's never going to happen to me. Unfortunately it happened to too many.' Two of 'Mike's' colleagues were shot dead in the same area around the RVH within a few hundred yards of each other in the space of a few months. I asked him what he felt he had achieved. 'Personally, a pension,' he said. 'Collectively, taking into account all that we and the other intelligence agencies did, the achievements are too great to enumerate. Together we saved thousands of lives and people will never know.'

Although there were rivalries and jealousies at senior level between army intelligence and Special Branch, at the operational level relationships between 'Det' operators and Special Branch officers like 'Mike' were excellent. 14 Intelligence Company was formed around the beginning of 1973 at a time when the IRA had already suffered a series of devastating blows to its leadership on both sides of the border, not least as a result of the clearance of the 'no-go' areas in 'Operation Motorman' the previous summer and much-improved co-operation with the Irish police, the Garda Síochana. Since then, 200 IRA 'officers' had been arrested, including key leaders like Seán MacStiofáin, Martin McGuinness, Martin Meehan and John Kelly. Billy McKee, still in gaol and now enjoying 'special category' status, admitted the IRA was in crisis and agreed that it was now time for the IRA to start bombing England. 'Our people were suffering,' he told me. 'The English people were telling us that they knew nothing about the situation. It's time they were made to find out what was going on here and not brush it under the carpet.'[1]

On 8 March 1973, the Provisional IRA planted its first bombs in London with strict orders, given the lessons of 'Bloody Friday', to avoid civilian casualties. 'I agreed with the strategy,' McKee said, 'but I didn't agree with bombing civilians and pubs that were full of people.' An hour's warning was given, with details of the cars containing the bombs, their registration numbers and their locations in London. Scotland Yard immediately gave the order to 'Close England' to make sure the bombers did not escape. The Metropolitan Police were on standby having already received intelligence, presumably from RUC Special Branch, that London was going to be bombed that day. Two car bombs were defused and two others exploded, one of them at the Army Recruiting Centre in Whitehall and the other at the Old Bailey. The police had not been able to clear the area around the Old Bailey in time and 180 people were injured. One of them later died of a heart attack. Shortly afterwards, members of the IRA's bombing team were arrested at Heathrow as they prepared to return to Belfast on a scheduled flight. They were tried and sentenced in London on 14 November 1973. Eight of them received life sentences. The escape plans for future IRA operations in England were to become far more sophisticated. Among those arrested and sentenced were the Price sisters, Dolours and Marion, who had met Gerry Adams when he was released from internment to meet the British, and Gerry Kelly who subsequently escaped from prison, ran guns in Europe, and became a senior member of the Sinn Fein leadership years later.[2]

But the Provisionals' propaganda coup in bombing England was soon offset by a series of dramatic setbacks driven by British and Irish intelligence. The 'Brits' now regarded the Irish as being more 'onside' in the 'war' against the IRA. On 28 March, barely three weeks after the London bombs, the Irish navy arrested Joe Cahill off the coast of County Waterford on board a Cyprus-registered boat, the *Claudia*. It was brimful of weapons from Libya destined for Cahill's colleagues in the North. In the hold were 250 rifles, 240 small arms and a quantity of anti-tank mines and explosives.[3] The consignment was believed to have been tracked by British intelligence. Cahill later admitted the interception of the *Claudia* was a disaster for the Provisionals' campaign.

By the summer of 1973, it had become increasingly clear to the 'Provos' that the 'Brits' had got their act together. But an even bigger blow was to come that struck at the heart of the IRA in Belfast, which remained the epicentre of the 'war'. If the IRA was to succeed in getting rid of the 'Brits' – which was still its professed aim – they had to win there. Special Branch and 14 Intelligence Company, now forged in a new partnership, were determined to prevent that happening as they put pressure on the organization at every level. This culminated in spectacular success when the army swooped and arrested twenty-three known IRA Volunteers and thirteen known IRA Officers. But they were not the main targets, as members of the IRA's rank and file could easily be replaced. The 'Brits' knew that the key to crippling the IRA was to hit the leadership of the Belfast Brigade in the hope that, if they cut off its head, the terrorist body would die. British intelligence believed that two of the Brigade's most senior members at the time were Brendan Hughes and Gerry Adams, who was reported to have risen through the ranks of the IRA in Ballymurphy to become one of the IRA's key strategists and most prominent commanders in the city. Although Adams has always denied being a member of the IRA, the 'Brits' never had any doubt about it. Adams, Hughes and other members of the Brigade Staff were placed under close 'Det' surveillance. Their movements were monitored and meeting places identified. The plan was not to pick them off one by one, which would have alerted the others, but to net them all in one decisive swoop. It was meticulously planned and executed. For the first time, the 'Det' really came into its own. The date of the operation, 25 June 1973, was a milestone in its history.

That day, Adams and Hughes had arranged to meet other members of the Brigade Staff in a house on the busy Falls Road. It had already been staked out by the 'Det'. The arrest operation was only to be triggered once Adams and Hughes were inside. 'Alan' was a member of the 'Det' team charged with triggering the signal for the army to move in. He was in the most vulnerable position, sitting in a car on the other side of the road fifty yards from the house, pretending to be an insurance salesman.

He watched most of the Brigade staff go inside except Gerry Adams who, to 'Alan's' horror, came across and sat on the bonnet of his car. 'I was nervous, very nervous,' he said. Whatever he felt, he knew he must not show it and carried on flicking through his papers lying on the empty passenger seat beside him.

To his relief, Adams gave him a little wave and 'Alan' waved back, knowing that the Fianna, the junior IRA, who were keeping a look out for 'Brits' whilst the Brigade staff held its meeting, would not be suspicious. To them and to Adams, the stranger in the car parked in the road across from the house was just someone going about his business. 'It was brilliant', he said, 'because the wave gave me a clean bill of health. I knew too that if I'd have been "clocked", Adams would not have been around and certainly would not have sat on the car bonnet. Yes, I was worried but not to the extent that I thought I had to do a quick reverse.' Adams then got off the bonnet, walked across the road and went into the house.

Immediately, there was a request to trigger the operation but 'Alan' wanted to wait a little longer as he had just seen Ivor Bell, who was believed by the intelligence agencies to be the Belfast Brigade commander, 'stick his head out of the front door of the Royal Victoria Hospital' in a way that suggested he knew something was wrong. He then turned round and promptly disappeared. The operation was triggered and the 'green' army swooped, arresting Adams, Hughes and another senior Provisional, Tom Cahill (Joe Cahill's brother). Before the arrest, Hughes had been uneasy at the sight of a 'dodgy' car in the area and had climbed over the back wall of the house and asked a couple of local republicans to check it out. They came back and said it was OK as they had seen two people get into the vehicle and drive away. It was not 'Alan's' car. Hughes remembers vividly what happened next.

> Within seconds, the house was surrounded. The British army kicked the door in and arrested us. There was a lot of shouting and bawling as soldiers do in a situation like that. They didn't know what to expect. But they certainly knew that I was there and they knew who I was as soon as they came into the house. So it was a matter of putting your hands up and surrendering. They were quite enthusiastic about the whole thing. They knew who'd they'd got.

Adams and Hughes were taken round the corner to Springfield Road RUC station for questioning where they say they were badly beaten by men in plain clothes. Hughes said they put a gun to his head, cocked it and told him he was going to get killed and dumped in a loyalist area so loyalists would be blamed for his death. They then put his fingers on a desk and beat them with a toffee hammer 'until they swelled up'. As I listened to Hughes describe what happened, I tended to believe him. 'I've no reason to tell lies,' he said. 'Possibly if I'd been shot or killed by one of these soldiers, I would have no reason to complain. I'm not crying or complaining about it. I'm just telling what happened to me.' Adams, too, says that he was severely ill-treated.

The 'Brits' were jubilant. 'There was a general feeling of euphoria amongst politicians and senior army officers,' 'Alan' said. 'Amongst ourselves it was just a culmination of an operation that had been going on for a long time which we could have sprung at any moment.' The Secretary of State invited 'Alan' and the other operators involved for a celebratory drink. 'Certainly "Willie" Whitelaw seemed very pleased. He came and gave us a pep talk and brought a fairly large quantity of champagne with him, which went down well. He said that we were probably worth three or four Battalions to him.'

Hughes, Adams and the others were shipped off to the compounds or 'cages' of Long Kesh and interned. But 'Alan's' elation was soon tempered by the killing of a friend and colleague two months later. The victim was Richard 'Dusty' Miller with whom 'Alan' had 'milled' during selection. It was believed to be the 'Det's' first loss. An IRA gunman had shot him on 25 August opposite the Royal Victoria Hospital. He died from his injuries three weeks later. 'Alan' was close by on duty with him at the time of the shooting.

> The vehicle that he was using on that particular day was a very old vehicle that we'd taken over from the MRF. It had been compro-

mised in the past and I think that the Brigade staff of the IRA were monitoring our radio net and had broken our code. The operation had obviously taken them some time to plan. They hijacked a car at the end of the motorway, which was about two minutes' driving time from the RVH, and got the gunman into it. The last thing I can remember 'Dusty' saying on the net was 'It's an orange Audi.' They drove by and shot him with an Armalite.

Brendan Hughes did not remain in captivity for long. On 8 December 1973, he escaped wedged in a mattress like the meat in a sausage roll. The mattress was left out along with the rest of the compound's rubbish to await collection by the Long Kesh refuse truck. Mattress and Hughes were dumped on the back and the unsuspecting rubbish collectors drove Hughes to freedom. The escape, which would have done credit to Mr Toad in *The Wind in the Willows*, caused the prison authorities and the 'Brits' huge embarrassment. Once outside the prison, Hughes hitched a lift to the border town of Newry and took a taxi across the border to Dundalk from where he was driven to Dublin. Hughes had no wish to languish there squandering his freedom and was anxious to get back to the 'war'. The problem was that with his dark hair, moustache and swarthy complexion, which had earned him the nickname 'Darkie', Hughes was just about the most easily recognizable IRA figure in the North. He had a face that was made for a 'Wanted' poster. So he dyed his hair, shaved off his moustache and assumed a completely new identity. He became 'Arthur McAllister', a travelling toy salesman. (There had been a real Arthur McAllister who had died when he was a baby and would have been about Hughes's age.)

Hughes, a.k.a. McAllister, returned to Belfast and moved upmarket from the Lower Falls to a house near an exclusive detached villa in Myrtlefield Park, a leafy suburb off the fashionable Malone Road. In fact, the villa became the headquarters of the re-organized Belfast Brigade of which Ivor Bell, who had escaped arrest with Hughes and Adams, was believed to be the commander. Bell remained at liberty for another seven months before he was finally arrested on 23 February 1974 and sent to join his comrades in Long Kesh. But he remained inside for an even shorter period of time than Brendan Hughes and escaped less than two months later, on 15 April, having changed places with a prisoner going out on parole to get married. But Bell was re-arrested a fortnight later, on 28 April, as a result of 'Det' surveillance.

With Bell back inside Long Kesh, Brendan Hughes is believed to have taken over command of the Belfast Brigade, directing operations from its new 'des. res.' in Myrtlefield Park. Hughes and the Belfast Brigade were confident that the IRA was one step ahead, despite the re-arrest of Bell.

Astonishingly, the IRA was now eavesdropping on secret conversations between military intelligence and Special Branch. It was ironic as MI5 had only just published a report on the IRA's ability to penetrate the security forces' communications, which concluded that the communications were secure. They were not.

Hughes outsmarted the 'Brits'. He had set up a 'special personnel squad' of republican-minded technical experts to penetrate the communications of the 'Brits'. One of those who volunteered his services was a friendly telephone engineer who was installing a new back-up telephone exchange at the army's Lisburn Headquarters. 'Tom' was not a member of the IRA but supported its cause, having apparently become a sympathizer when he saw the army shoot dead a stone-thrower in Andersonstown, two days after internment.

Because he lived in the republican stronghold of West Belfast, 'Tom' had given a false address which, surprisingly, the army had not rumbled. It gave him full security clearance which meant that 'Tom' could come and go as he wished at Army Headquarters. Initially, it seems, he tried to tap the GOC's phone but decided that it was too difficult and, through a combination of looking at the internal telephone directory and trial and error, he finally tapped the telephone line that led to the desk of the army's intelligence cell, 'G2 Int.'. The tap itself was not particularly sophisticated and consisted of a voice-activated tape-recorder attached to the telephone line. Apparently the bug remained in place for several months. 'Tom' then delivered the tapes to Brendan Hughes at Myrtlefield Park. But at first there was a problem. 'You couldn't understand them,' said Hughes. 'It sounded like Mickey Mouse.' But, ever resourceful, 'Tom' solved the problem by 'borrowing' a de-scrambling device from a room at Army Headquarters and adding it to the growing tape collection in Myrtlefield Park. Mickey Mouse then disappeared.

But what Hughes did not know was that Special Branch and the 'Det' were now hot on his trail and had been staking out Myrtlefield Park for several weeks, having received intelligence that it harboured an arms dump as well as Hughes. Finally, on 10 May 1974, Special Branch moved in. 'Arthur McAllister's' days as a toy salesman were over. Hughes has never forgotten the day. 'They came to the door and they knew right away who I was. I was protesting about the fact that they were raiding this house when the Special Branch man turned round to me and said, "Come on, Brendan, you've had a good enough run." They were quite friendly this time.'[4] The Special Branch man was 'Paul'. He remembers it equally vividly too. 'I think initially he made some derogatory comment that I don't remember but then he quickly changed and said, "I suppose it's a fair cop." I said wasn't he happy that we'd allowed him to have a reasonable run and I remarked that he shouldn't be complaining. He did congratulate Special Branch on the operation, which I thought was a bit ironic.' Had the operation been delayed a few more minutes, 'Paul' would also have netted 'Tom' who was on his way to Myrtlefield Park but had apparently stopped off en route for a sandwich.

When the security forces turned the house inside-out, they found four rifles, a sub-machine gun, two pistols and more than 3,600 rounds of ammunition. Fleet Street, as it then was, had a field day. 'Pin-stripe Provo chief seized at £50,000 HQ', triumphed the *Daily Telegraph*. The Press also made much of the fact that documents were found which they referred to as the IRA's 'Doomsday Plan' to take out loyalist areas in the event of civil war. According to Hughes the documents were nothing of the kind but a plan to defend nationalist areas and avoid a repetition of August 1969. But what was tightly concealed from the media was the most sensitive discovery of all – the tapes and the de-scrambling device that 'Paul' and his colleagues had found hidden away inside the house. 'IRA Bugs "Brits"' was not a headline that HQNI wanted to read. The army's spin doctors did their stuff.

Hughes was arrested and interrogated. Optimistically, 'Mike', the Special Branch handler, tried to 'turn' him. 'I explained that he was in a great position to help us put an end to what was going on,' he said. 'But it fell on stony ground.' What did Hughes reply? I asked. 'Absolutely nothing.'

Hughes remembers it too. 'He said I could have a suitcase full of money if I came over.' How big was the suitcase? I asked. 'I never said a word,' Hughes smiled. 'I never even answered.' He was duly sentenced and sent off to Long Kesh, leaving others to fight the 'war' the IRA now feared it might be losing.

Hughes's arrest took place on 10 May 1974, a time of great tension as loyalists were building up to a massive strike in opposition to the political structures Whitelaw and the British and Irish Governments had put in place in the hope of finding a political solution to end the conflict.

By this time, the Unionist Party had split. The former Prime Minister, Brian Faulkner, who had pressed HMG for internment and been devastated by the subsequent suspension of Stormont, had realized that if there was to be peace, an accommodation would have to be reached with John Hume and the nationalist SDLP. On 21 November 1973, he had agreed to set up an Executive in which for the first time unionists would share power with nationalist politicians. Sinn Fein did not figure in the political equation at this stage and did not do so until more than a quarter of a century later.[5] A few weeks later, on 9 December, the British and Irish

Governments, meeting in conference at the Civil Service College at Sunningdale in Berkshire, agreed to set up an 'Irish Dimension' to the new political structures. At its heart was to be a Council of Ireland consisting of Ministers from Dublin and the new power-sharing Executive in the North. Faulkner was in a unionist minority in accepting the new institutions and was faced with massive opposition from all shades of Protestant opinion in the province. Most loyalists saw what became known as the 'Sunningdale Agreement' as a sell-out to Dublin and a prelude to a united Ireland.

The Executive came into being on 1 January 1974 and as it did so, Direct Rule from Westminster ended. The first sign for the 'Brits' that big trouble was in store came with the result of the Westminster General Election on 28 February, which had become known as the 'Who Rules Britain?' election in the wake of the crippling coal-miners' strike. Labour was returned to power although without a working majority. The good news for Harold Wilson was that he was back in Downing Street: the bad news was that a showdown was clearly on its way in the province. When Wilson walked out of Number Ten in June 1970, the situation seemed containable: when he returned four years later, it had reached crisis proportions. To the unionist majority in Nothern Ireland the election had been a referendum on Sunningdale and power-sharing. Unionist politicians opposed to the new political structures and to Brian Faulkner, whom they regarded as a traitor, united under the banner of the United Ulster Unionist Council (UUUC) whose leading light was Ian Paisley, and won a resounding victory, taking eleven of the twelve Westminster seats. Their spectacular success sent a clear message to Harold Wilson and his new Northern Ireland Secretary, Merlyn Rees, with whom he had secretly met the IRA at the house in Phoenix Park, Dublin, in 1972. On his first visit to Belfast, Rees was taken aback by the intensity of loyalist opposition to Sunningdale and power-sharing. 'They saw it as the supreme sell-out, the supreme betrayal,' he told me. 'Brian Faulkner came to see me and told me in so many words that he couldn't carry the Unionist Party with him. He said, "I cannot carry it. I have lost my reason to be. I'm beaten, over-whelmed by the vote against my sort of unionism or the unionism I'm trying to carry out." '[6]

However, it was not Paisley and Faulkner's opponents who brought the new political edifice crashing down but the working-class Protestants who ran the province's economy and public utilities. They had come together under the banner of the Ulster Workers' Council (UWC) and, on 14 May, four days after Brendan Hughes's arrest, the UWC announced it was calling a province-wide strike in opposition to the new political structures. As their opening shot, the strike leaders declared that the province's electricity supply would be reduced from 725 megawatts to 400. Few in the province had ever heard of the UWC and most took its declaration as a joke. It was not. Weeks of planning had gone into the organization of the strike in consultation with the loyalist paramilitaries of the UDA and UVF. At first, the UWC's call to Protestants in the province to join the strike was ignored. Most went to work as usual only to find their routes blocked by barricades manned by loyalist paramilitaries in masks, some of whom wielded clubs. There was widespread intimidation in other ways, too, without which the strike would probably never have got under way. The port of Larne was sealed off. Soon attitudes changed as people realized that the UWC was serious and, backed by paramilitary muscle, could deliver what it promised. Support grew as the power-station workers gradually ran down their generators and the province slowly and dramatically ground to a halt. Seventy-five per cent of the power was cut in Derry and 60 per cent throughout the province as a whole. The giant Harland and Wolff shipyard fell silent after workers inclined to ignore the strike were warned that they might find their cars burned out in the car park.

The army did move in to remove the barricades, but paramilitaries manning them simply disappeared only to return once the soldiers had gone. The UWC strategy was to avoid any violent confrontation with the forces of law and order which might erode the broad base of support they were seeking beyond the Protestant working class. Two thousand extra troops were flown in to deal with the emergency and help run the power stations but there was a limit to what they could do. After a few days it became clear that the UWC was effectively running the province and not the 'Brits' – and certainly not Brian Faulkner and his power-sharing Executive. On 25 May, the eleventh day of the strike, Harold Wilson went on television and made a monumentally insensitive broadcast which far from weakening the strike, only strengthened support for it.

> British parents, British taxpayers have seen their sons vilified and spat upon and murdered. They have seen their taxes poured out almost without regard for cost – over £300 million this year – going into Northern Ireland. They see property being destroyed by evil violence and are asked to pick up the bill for rebuilding it. Yet people who benefit from this now viciously defy Westminster, purporting to act as though they were an elected government, spending their lives sponging on Westminster and British democracy and then systematically assault democratic methods. Who do these people think they are?[7]

Wilson's message would have played well in the living rooms of England but was disastrous in the Protestant parlours of Northern Ireland. The word 'spongers' was hugely offensive to the deeply ingrained Protestant work ethic. Furthermore, it wasn't loyalists who were spitting on British soldiers and murdering them, but republicans and the IRA. It was hardly the 'Brits'' finest hour. One of the UWC leaders, Glen Barr, was ecstatic as he watched the Prime Ministerial broadcast to the nation. 'I thought, Great stuff! This is fantastic!' he told me. 'We'll make him an honourary member of the UDA after this. I think that was the best thing that happened to us. After that, we couldn't go wrong.' Meryln Rees had advised against the sentiments that Wilson intended to express but his advice was ignored. I asked Rees why the Government had not used its authority and ordered the army to confront the strikers and restore order to the paralysed province.

> I didn't let them win. They were going to win anyway. We couldn't do a Prague. You can't put down a popular rising by killing people. We're not Russia. The [Protestant] police were on the brink of not carrying out their duties and the middle classes were on the strikers' side. This wasn't just an industrial dispute. This was the Protestant people of Northern Ireland rising up against Sunningdale and it could not be shot down.

Rees described it as 'lancing the boil' of a political initiative that he believed was never going to work in the teeth of opposition from the Protestant majority in the province. The lesson was not lost on his successors.

The GOC at the time, Lieutenant-General Sir Frank King, agreed with the Secretary of State. 'Certainly if you get a very large section of the population which is bent on a particular course, then it is a difficult thing to stop them,' he told me shortly after the strike was over. 'You can't go round shooting people because they want to do a certain thing.'[8] The last thing the army wanted to do was to face a 'war' on two fronts, with the IRA on one side and the loyalist paramilitaries on the other.

On 28 May, three days after Wilson's broadcast, Brian Faulkner and the Executive resigned and Direct Rule was re-introduced. Sunningdale and power-sharing were almost a quarter of a century ahead of their time. The humiliating collapse of the political solution that the 'Brits' had hoped would finally bring peace played straight into the hands of the Provisionals, who cited it as proof that the only solution was not an internal settlement but a British withdrawal. With the strike over and the political initiative in ruins, the IRA's strategy was to carry on bombing and shooting and keep up the pressure. The problem for the IRA was that the 'Brits' intended to keep up the pressure too.

Chapter Fourteen

Changing the Course of History

May 1973–November 1974

In May 1973, Frank Steele, the MI6 officer who had played such a critical role in facilitating the Cheyne Walk meeting between Whitelaw and the IRA leadership, left Northern Ireland, certain in the knowledge that there was a long haul ahead. 'I don't think either community had suffered enough to make peace an absolute imperative,' he said wearily, 'and so we settled down to twenty-five years of waste and murder.' His replacement was another MI6 officer, Michael Oatley, whose influence on events at critical moments over the following two decades was to prove crucial, although he had no idea of what lay in store when he moved into Frank Steele's quarters at Laneside, the house along the shores of Belfast Lough. Laneside was more than just a roof over the head for the 'Brits' who lived there. It was also the sounding board for the murderous politics of the province. Here Oatley worked alongside James Allan, a senior Foreign Office diplomat who had been sent to Northern Ireland as Whitelaw's Political Adviser. Oatley posed as his Deputy. At Laneside, Allan hosted many secret meetings with the province's politicians and representatives of the paramilitary organizations on both sides in an attempt to bring the warring factions together. His ear was finely tuned to any change in entrenched positions that might make peace possible. Much of the groundwork that led to the Sunningdale Agreement of 9 December 1973 was done in Laneside's secluded rooms, well away from the public gaze. So sensitive were the secret negotiations that the 'Brits' heaved sighs of relief at the beginning of every meeting when all the heads were counted and none was found to be missing. There was genuine fear that some of those present might be targets for gunmen who felt that the politicians were going too far. Allan was well respected as a man of integrity, and even some of the toughest loyalist paramilitaries came to like and trust him. Oatley's public position as Allan's Deputy gave him convenient cover for his real mission, which was to develop covert contacts with, and channels of influence to, the IRA.

Oatley used Laneside as a base for forays into the most troubled areas of the province, and his official position as a passport to anyone at the grassroots level who was prepared to accept the possibility of at least some measure of good faith in British Government intentions. Under Allan's management, Laneside continued as the venue for informal soundings with legitimate politicians of all shades and eventually for the secret inter-party talks conducted by Frank Cooper which led to Sunningdale.

Oatley had much in common with Steele: he was unorthodox, charming and willing to try anything, and, like Steele, he admitted he was starting from scratch. 'I knew absolutely nothing about Northern Ireland,' he told me, 'and I was, in that sense, typical of most of the people who went to help the Secretary of State to deal with this new problem.' Oatley had never expected to go to the province any more than Steele had. He was stuck in London at the time at the end of a home tour, and had been promised 'some exciting posting' by the Secret Intelligence Service's Personnel Department which, in the end, failed to materialize. Oatley was anxious to get back into the field and, with friends in the military in Northern Ireland, he thought that the province might be the kind of 'exciting posting' he was looking for. Although it was not exactly the foreign field in which he and his colleagues had long been accustomed to serve, it was unlike any other part of the United Kingdom and a theatre in which he thought he might be able to exercise his particular talents. He also knew that with Frank Steele leaving, a post was coming free. 'Obviously it was the most urgent problem facing the British Government at that stage and I thought that it was a situation in which intelligence would not be a matter of simply reporting on situations but trying to influence them,' he said. And so Michael Oatley packed his bags and went off to Northern Ireland for what was to be an eventful two-year stint.

When he arrived he found 'an engaging group of amateurs led by a marvellously charismatic figure, "Willie" Whitelaw, trying to grapple with a maze of problems which they didn't understand at all.' Such was the nature of Direct Rule in its infancy. Whitelaw's team would sit around discussing the myriad problems that arose on an almost daily basis, agree a Ministerial statement on a particular issue and then have to withdraw it when they realized it was inoperable. In the end, there were occasions when the team thought it better to say nothing rather than be caught on a hook from which the new administration found it difficult to escape. In a light-hearted moment one of them devised a Direct Rule crest and shield, prominently featuring three hooks. It would no doubt accompany the motto Frank Steele had suggested, 'It seemed like a good idea at the time.'

When Oatley first arrived and established his political bearings, he was surprised that no one in the team, civil or military, was giving much thought to understanding the nature and motivation of the IRA leadership and its followers. Not surprisingly, the IRA's continuing campaign had hardened attitudes and the natural inclination of the security forces, especially the army, was to identify their enemy in stark terms. Oatley suspected the analysis was not quite as straightforward as they would have it appear. His wide-ranging brief from MI6 gave him the opportunity to test it. Of all the members of Whitelaw's entourage Oatley was the one most free of specific responsibilities. His instructions were to make himself useful in whatever way he thought best. At an early stage he decided to apply his energies to filling in the picture of what lay behind the IRA campaign and to seeing whether something could be done to influence it.

Oatley soon became very conscious of loss of life, particularly of the number of young British soldiers who were being killed in a situation of virtual stalemate. One weekend he picked up the *Sunday Times* colour supplement with photographs of all those killed. By the end of 1973, there were 211 of them, in addition to 39 members of the UDR and 44 policemen. Oatley knew that although the IRA, both Provisional and Official, was responsible for just about every one of those deaths, loyalist violence was casting its own increasingly bloody shadow over the statistics. In the same period, the UDA and the UVF and their related organizations had killed 240 people, the vast majority innocent Catholics and most them killed in the period 1972–3.[1]

Nevertheless he calculated that if the Provisional IRA could be per-suaded to stop killing (the Official IRA remained on cease-fire), the loyalist paramilitaries might be persuaded to do the same on the basis that their violence was a reaction to IRA violence. He reasoned that the key to reducing the death toll must lie in the minds of republican leaders. Oatley knew what he had to do. 'If I was going to spend two years or longer in Northern Ireland, I ought perhaps to try to concentrate on seeing whether my particular skills and background could enable me to find a way to influence the leadership of the IRA or to make some kind of contact through which they could be influenced.' The question was how to do it. While his colleagues battled to contain the situation, Oatley was free to explore. 'I was trying to understand what was going on in the grass roots areas where the violence was actually taking place,' he said. Frank Steele had done the same, and had left him some exceptional guides as well as a range of contacts in both communities and a reputation for using the Secretary of State's authority to bring solutions to immediate practical problems. There might be an argument between the local community and a Battalion commander over the intensity of military patrolling, or the failure of housing officers to attend to repairs, or the need to support a youth centre which might keep young people away from violence. Both men found that people in areas of social deprivation on either side of the sectarian divide had been equally badly served during the years of devolved government. When Oatley first arrived in the province, he believed, like most of his colleagues and contemporaries, that the IRA was the cause of the problem and not the symptom of it. The longer he spent in republican areas, the more he realized the reality was far more complex than that and was surprised at what he found.

> The quality of the young people joining the IRA was very impressive and you could go to a street in the Creggan and find that everybody's favourite son had joined the IRA. However much their mothers might disapprove of what they were doing or be frightened by it, that was what happened. From this I came to deduce that if so many young people were going to do this, then there must be social and political reasons more complex than I had understood propelling them in that direction. I thought that the quality of the leadership of the organization was probably quite interesting and would be worth studying.

Six months into his tour, how to get through to the IRA leadership became one of Oatley's main preoccupations. The problem was that he could only study it from afar. The revelation of Whitelaw's meeting with the IRA at Cheyne Walk had caused the Secretary of State great embarrassment, and that, added to the IRA's carnage of 'Bloody Friday', had resulted in a ban on any Government representatives talking to or approaching the IRA. Oatley was well aware of the injunction from his political masters but realized that, unless some way could be found of prevailing upon the leadership of the Republican Movement, the violence could continue indefinitely, however successful the security forces and the intelligence services might be at containing the IRA. Oatley was fortunate, however, in that the Permanent Under Secretary at the Northern Ireland Office, Frank Cooper, came to the province at roughly the same time as Oatley and was a man of formidable strength and independence of mind. He too arrived in ignorance and, apart from the violence with which he was now familiar, was astonished at the social conditions he found.

Cooper had been brought up in and around Manchester during the depression of the 1930s and thought that, nearly forty years later, Belfast did not seem much different. Although Cooper might have disagreed with Oatley's analysis of the IRA itself, he was at least as willing to take risks in the hope of developing a solution.

> I didn't think the IRA could absolutely be beaten because there had to be a political settlement of one kind or another at the end of

whatever period it took to achieve it. In the meanwhile, I thought it could be contained. My own view is that if you're dealing with a terrorist organization, at some remove you always ought to have a dialogue going because the basic problem about terrorism is that it's very difficult to snuff out. You've got, in the end, to find some way of stopping terrorism. We can't go around shooting everybody we think is a terrorist, which is certainly one possible way of doing it. Nobody in this country would have stood for that. We are, after all, a parliamentary democracy, and we did behave throughout as such, which is a very, very important point. But if a political situation made it possible, one should never discount the need to have a dialogue, although one should be extremely careful and extremely clear about what you were trying to do if you did.

Cooper himself had never been overly optimistic that Sunningdale and its political linkages would work. He thought the arrangements were 'very, very clever indeed but too clever by three-quarters' and admitted that he had not realized just how fractured a society Northern Ireland was. Cooper recognized that Sunningdale, with its carefully balanced give-and-take, was simply too sophisticated a solution for the divided citizenry and politicians of the province to take. As with most other British politicians, he realized that political progress could not be made if the majority of Protestant opinion was deeply opposed to it. The UWC strike could not have brought the point home in a clearer and more dramatic way.

Fortunately for both Cooper and Oatley, the new Northern Ireland Secretary, Merlyn Rees, was also flexible and imaginative in his political approach to the problem. He once rationalized the Labour Government's lack of decisive action in countering the strike as if it were a calculated, strategic political act, which it was not. Certainly, with the UWC strike over, Rees and Cooper believed that they could start again with a clean slate. Again, both realized that for the violence to stop, the republicans and loyalists responsible for it would have to be brought into the political process. Controversially, with that in mind, Rees legalized Sinn Fein and the UVF. (The UDA had never been proscribed.) The order was passed at Westminster without debate on 14 May 1974, four days after the arrest of Brendan Hughes in Myrtlefield Park and a fortnight before the collapse of the power-sharing Executive.[2]

But, at this stage, legalization did nothing to blunt either side's campaign. Three days later, on Friday 17 May 1974, the UVF exploded three car bombs without warning in the centre of Dublin and one car bomb in Monaghan. The Dublin bombs killed twenty-six civilians and injured 140, most of them going home in the Friday afternoon rush hour and looking forward to the weekend. Twenty of those killed were women and two of them were baby girls aged five months and seventeen months, one of whom was decapitated. The Monaghan bomb killed a further seven civilians and injured twenty more. The final death toll of thirty-three was the biggest loss of life in a single day in the whole of the conflict.[3] It was the UVF's own 'Bloody Friday'.

To the triumvirate of Oatley, Cooper and Rees, the horror of the Dublin and Monaghan bombs and the shock of the successful UWC strike made a political solution even more imperative, however difficult it might be to achieve it. The IRA had also been causing mayhem in 1974, notably in England where it could operate with much greater freedom than in Belfast, where it was being increasingly hemmed in by the activities of Special Branch and the 'Det'. On 4 February 1974, an IRA bomb exploded on a coach travelling along the M62 in Yorkshire carrying military personnel from Manchester to Catterick army camp near the Scottish border. The 50-lb bomb, concealed in the boot, killed nine soldiers, one woman and two children, aged five and two. The attack also had other implications for the 'Brits' because Judith Ward, the person convicted and sentenced to thirty years for planting the bomb, was later proved to have been the victim of a miscarriage of justice. She had always maintained her innocence and the IRA denied she had ever been one of its members. The Court of Appeal finally quashed her conviction in 1992 on the grounds that it had been unsafe. In delivering its verdict, the Court criticized the forensic scientists involved in the case analysis.[4]

Having legalized Sinn Fein and the UVF, Rees's strategy was to hold elections for a Constitutional Convention after a decent interval had elapsed in which the bitterness and memory of the strike had subsided, and to encourage all the parties, including those that represented the paramilitaries on both sides, to participate. The Convention, under an eminent chairman, would then work out its own home-grown solution to the problem, free from 'Brit' interference. On paper it looked fine and if it took place in a climate free from violence and one in which there was also the prospect of an end to internment, then there was a glimmer of hope that it might stand some chance of success. Rees hinted that, given 'a genuine and sustained cessation of violence', anything might follow. This phrase was to become a mantra which, as Rees said, 'could have been emblazoned in neon lights over Stormont Castle'.[5]

Getting the IRA to declare a cease-fire was a critical part of the process. As Oatley knew from his predecessor, cease-fires of any duration and meaning had to be carefully negotiated and could not be done in a vacuum. That is why Frank Steele and Philip Woodfield had held their secret meeting with Gerry Adams and David O'Connell as a prelude to the IRA's 1972 cease-fire and the talks at Cheyne Walk. The problem for Oatley and for Cooper, too, was that there was still a strict injunction in place about talking to the IRA, although both the Prime Minister, Harold Wilson, and the Northern Ireland Secretary, Merlyn Rees, had done so when they were in opposition. Now, however, the political situation was precarious because Wilson was leading a minority Government after the February General Election had left him without an overall working majority. Labour won 301 seats, the Conservatives 296 and the Liberals 14. The Liberals, therefore, held the balance of power. Wilson was gambling on going to the country again as soon as the situation seemed favourable and the last thing he wanted was a potentially damaging political storm over the Government's secret contacts with the IRA. As Billy McKee had anticipated, bombs in England had concentrated the mainland mind in a way that bombs in Belfast had not. Oatley and Cooper knew the tightrope they were walking as Oatley began to put out feelers to the IRA. At first, Rees was not in the 'loop' and probably involved only on a 'need-to-know' basis, although he knew Michael Oatley and his general brief.

Oatley developed first two and later three secret channels to the IRA leadership. One was through an English businessman based in Northern Ireland who, Oatley says, approached him to sound out the possibility of a conversation, however vague, with David O'Connell, the most politically inclined member of the IRA's Army Council. As a result, Oatley 'made various noises' but they did not get very far. The second involved a former Commander of the Provisional IRA's Belfast Brigade. However, it was felt that these two channels were merely a convenient cover for the third, and by far the most important contact. This was a person in Derry who had a line to Ruairi O'Bradaigh, the President of Sinn Fein. (I will simply refer to him as the Contact as his true identity has been one of the most carefully guarded secrets of the current Troubles.) O'Connell and O'Bradaigh were the Republican Movement's foremost political thinkers. The Contact had originally met Frank Steele whilst Steele was taking the political temperature in Derry and, although he himself was not a member of the IRA, he appeared to have a good understanding and appreciation of its thinking, which was not surprising in such a small and tightly knit community. In fact, he was the person who had mediated between the army and the IRA to ensure that 'Operation Motorman' did not become a second 'Bloody Sunday' and had personally encouraged the IRA's removal of its weapons from the 'no-go' areas in Derry before 'Motorman' got under way. Steele suggested that Oatley should maintain the link with him. Over the years, the Contact made superhuman efforts with Oatley and others, often at great personal cost and danger to himself, to develop initiatives to end the conflict. He was trusted by both the British and the IRA leadership and few in the history of the past thirty years have fought harder, more devotedly or with more imagination to bring peace to the province.

The problem for Oatley, given the strictures under which he operated, was how to begin and then conduct a dialogue with the IRA leadership without doing so directly. If at some stage there were to be negotiations, the ground had to be prepared. Perhaps Oatley took his inspiration from the ancient black and white film that had bored 'Det' recruits rigid.

> The person in Derry and I constructed a situation where we had, in effect, a hollow bamboo 'pipe' leading from me, held by him and winding up at the other end with Ruairi O'Bradaigh. It existed with O'Bradaigh's agreement but down which neither of us was saying anything. What we were in fact able to do was to blow gently down the 'pipe' and the person at the other end would be able to feel the draught and blow back. So we knew that we were there. This seemed to me to be not much more than a slight bending of the Secretary of State's rules. So I went to my boss, Frank Cooper, and said, 'Look, I haven't really stepped very far out of line. I've got this bamboo "pipe" and I haven't said anything down it yet but I know that if I do say anything, it will be heard at the other end. And in any case, it's quite a nice "pipe" so can we, perhaps, put a bit of material down it to see if we can develop a relationship?'

Cooper agreed.

> So then, over the next few months we found very, very minor things to talk about down this 'pipe' and it developed into an exercise which enabled O'Bradaigh and, to some extent, O'Connell to feel that they were in contact with a part of the British Government which might, at some stage, help them to move in a political direction.

All the indications were that the Provisionals were interested in going down that road. O'Bradaigh believed that the UWC strike marked a watershed. 'It threw British policy totally into the melting pot. It swept the decks clean,' he told me. 'It was back to the drawing board. The word coming through was that every solution was up for consideration.'[6] That was certainly the message that O'Bradaigh believed he was getting down the 'pipe' from Oatley via the Contact in Derry. What precisely it meant was as yet unclear but it was enough to encourage O'Bradaigh and O'Connell, the Provisionals' 'doves', to want to find out more. Some of their more militaristic colleagues in the IRA leadership, the 'hawks', were sceptical about the enterprise but agreed that the process of exploration should be allowed to go ahead.

Both 'hawks' and 'doves' realized that although the IRA was nowhere near the brink of defeat, its operations, particularly those in Belfast, were being severely curtailed by the increasingly successful activities of the 'Det', Special Branch and other agencies. In the three months following the end of the strike – June, July and August 1974 – the IRA killed nine soldiers, only three of them in Belfast, each shot by a sniper. A policeman was also shot dead in the city and two others were killed elsewhere. In September 1974, no soldier or policeman died anywhere in the province. The 'Brits', at least those at the sharp end out on the ground, believed they were winning the 'war'. 'Alan' of the 'Det', who had helped trigger the arrest of Hughes and Adams, had no doubt that this was the case.

> Our operations, combined with the political will behind them and the much, much more professional 'green' army had, between them, brought the IRA to its knees. I am convinced that we could have changed the course of history had the political will remained there. IRA activity could have been stopped completely in the two cities. It probably wouldn't have stopped punishment beatings or knee-cappings but we could certainly have stopped major bombing operations and shoots against the security forces in Belfast and in Londonderry too. It was not the case in the border area.

'Paul' of Special Branch, who had arrested Brendan Hughes at Myrtlefield Park, held a more sophisticated view of what 'winning' actually meant.

> It was my assessment at the time that we had them. We had them really at that point where we wanted them. Those at the very top of the organization were fully aware that they didn't have any room to manoeuvre and little room to carry on a campaign for much longer. I think many of the IRA leaders at that time, not all of them but many, thought that there was a fair chance that the campaign would come to an end within a fairly short period of time. I don't think any of them, at that point, felt it was going to go on for another twenty years.
> **Did you think you had won?**
> Yes. At that time all of us, I think, within the Special Branch and associated departments and within the army intelligence set-up that was operating with us [i.e. 14 Intelligence Company] would be fairly certain that we had. But 'winning' wasn't really part of the strategy. It was getting them into a position to call the campaign off.

Even Brendan Hughes did not dispute the analysis. For a former IRA commander of his standing to make such an admission is remarkable. The IRA rarely publicly admits its setbacks and tends to dismiss such comments as 'Brit' propaganda designed to undermine morale. Hughes's assessment of the state of the IRA at the time carries both weight and authority.

> I think for the first time since the early 1970s, the police and the military machine were actually working and the IRA was under severe pressure. When they raided the house in Myrtlefield Park, I certainly saw a great deal of confidence and a great deal of cockiness there. And the tabloid papers in England were involved in this as well in a psychological type of way, saying that the IRA was being defeated, 'dumps' were being found, there were well-placed informers and the military machine was getting on top.

When I asked him if he thought the IRA was losing, he said he thought that it was. Billy McKee confirmed Hughes's analysis. When he came out of gaol on 4 September 1974, four months after Hughes went in, he was appalled at the condition of the Belfast IRA he returned to. 'It was in a very poor state, a very poor state indeed,' he told me. 'There were only a handful of men in each area and weaponry was very poor.' With Brendan Hughes, Ivor Bell and Gerry Adams all locked up, McKee became commander of the Belfast Brigade once again.

But if the IRA was going to talk, it intended to do so from a position of strength and planned to strike where it hit the enemy hardest and generated the biggest headlines – in England. Although no doubt the decision was made on tactical grounds, the pressure the IRA was under on its own home ground probably reinforced it. The IRA intended to show the 'Brits' it was far from down and out, and in the autumn of 1974, it did so to horrendous effect. Its offensive began at the height of the British General Election campaign through which Harold Wilson was hoping to win the overall majority that had eluded him the previous February. Ireland was not an election issue, it seldom was in British elections, but the 'Provos' intended to make it one. On 5 October, the IRA struck at what they claimed were 'military' targets: two pubs in Guildford, the Horse and Groom and the Seven Stars, that were frequented by off-duty soldiers from nearby training camps. Four soldiers, who were sitting in an alcove where a nitroglycerine bomb had been placed, were killed in the blast.[7] Two of them were women. A civilian also died and fifty-four people were injured.

Five days later Wilson retained the tenancy of Downing Street with the overall majority he had been looking for, although it was only three. In Northern Ireland anti-Sunningdale unionists swept the board, and the new party in favour of compromise formed by Brian Faulkner, the Unionist Party of Northern Ireland (UPNI), attracted only 3 per cent of the vote. The omens for agreement on Rees's planned Constitutional Convention did not look good.

With a still potentially unstable Government in power at Westminster with a knife-edge majority, the IRA kept up the pressure in England. On 7 November, it bombed the King's Arms pub in Woolwich, killing a soldier and fatally wounding a part-time barman who later died from his injuries. Twenty-six people, including five soldiers, were injured.[8] The same day, it killed two soldiers in Northern Ireland in a landmine attack near Stewartstown.

Three men – Gerard Conlon, Paul Hill and Patrick Armstrong – and a woman, Carole Richardson, were arrested, interrogated, tried and gaoled for the Guildford and Woolwich bombs. They became known as the 'Guildford Four'. Fourteen years later, the Court of Appeal ordered their release on the grounds that the confessions extracted during interrogation by the police were fabricated. Paul Hill was implicated in another case and remained in prison for another five years until his conviction for Guildford and Woolwich was also quashed. A further seven people who had also been arrested and sentenced for making the Guildford bombs were finally released in 1991 after they, too, had been cleared by the Court of Appeal. They were known as the 'Maguire Seven' after the family name and had been convicted on unreliable forensic evidence. One of them, a brother-in-law, Patrick Giuseppe Conlon, died in gaol and never tasted freedom.[9]

But the most shocking IRA attack of all, not only in 1974 but any time, came two weeks after Woolwich on 21 November when bombs exploded at two pubs in Birmingham, the Mulberry Bush and the Tavern in the Town. A warning was given but only minutes before the bombs ripped through the pubs, killing twenty-one people and injuring 182. The nation was shocked and outraged at slaughter on such a scale, and a tide of anti-Irish feeling came dangerously close to sweeping the country. The Irish community in England was as appalled as its English neighbours and horrified at what was being done in its name. Birmingham, like 'Bloody Friday', was almost certainly a catastrophic mistake that made a mockery of the IRA's claim to attack only military targets and not civilians.

Two days later the IRA issued a statement in Dublin. 'It has never been and is not the policy of the IRA to bomb non-military targets without giving adequate warning to ensure the safety of civilians,' it said as it disclaimed involvement in Birmingham. Try as they might, the Provisional IRA could not hide its responsibility for the carnage. Billy McKee, now commanding the Belfast Brigade, was genuinely shocked by Birmingham. He had not been aware of the specific operation as the 'mainland' campaign was planned in Dublin by the IRA's 'England' department. McKee had supported bombing across the water but had always insisted that civilian casualties must be avoided at all costs. 'I was shocked over the civilian loss of life,' he told me. 'I never approved of civilian loss of life. I didn't mind our own people and the 'Brits', the security forces, going down but I didn't agree with ordinary civilian people losing their lives. At the time there was no report coming in to us about who was responsible [for Birmingham] and I think it was about a month later that I found out that it was our own people who had carried it out.' I then asked him directly, 'Who bombed Birmingham?' 'The IRA,' he said.

A few hours after the bombs exploded, five men were arrested as they were about to board the Heysham–Belfast ferry and a sixth man was arrested in Birmingham. They became known as the 'Birmingham Six'. Three days later they were charged in connection with the explosions. I asked Billy McKee if the six men arrested were involved with the bombs. 'No,' he said.

> The people who were arrested were completely innocent people. Completely innocent. Some of them weren't even known to the IRA. When their names came out, nobody seemed to know them, except an odd person from Belfast. They might have bought fund-raising tickets or something like that for prisoners' dependants. I think one of them even said he wasn't a republican. I don't know if any of them were republicans or not.

The Birmingham Six – William Power, Hugh Callaghan, Patrick Joseph Hill, Robert Gerald Hunter, Noel Richard McIlkenny and John Walker – were interrogated, found guilty of murder in front of Mr Justice Bridge and sentenced to life imprisonment. The finding was based on forensic evidence and confessions made during interrogation. As they were sentenced on 15 August 1975, there were no defiant shouts of 'Up the IRA' or clenched-fist salutes, as was common when members of the IRA were sent down. The Six went to serve their life sentences in silence.[10] They were finally released on 14 March 1991 (following their second appeal in three years after serving sixteen years in gaol), when it was decided that the evidence against them was unsafe. New tests on police documents had suggested that the police may have forged their notes and given false evidence. There had also been claims of ill-treatment during interrogation. It was the third case in eighteen months in which Irish people had been victims of miscarriages of justice.[11]

The wrongful convictions of the Birmingham Six, the Guildford Four (quashed 1989), the Maguire Seven (quashed 1991) and Judith Ward (quashed 1992) were an indelible stain on a system of justice that had long been regarded as one of the finest in the world. It brought to mind Lord Gardiner's damning conclusion at the end of his minority report on the use of the Five Techniques in 1971 when he stated that the practices were 'alien to the traditions of what I believe still to be the greatest democracy in the world'. This string of wrongful convictions might merit a similar sentiment. The fact that they happened was probably a reflection of the understandable hysteria of the time caused by the wave of IRA bombs in 1974 and the pressure on the authorities to produce swift results. There is no doubt that in an attempt to bring the guilty to justice some of the rules were bent as they had been before in relation to Northern Ireland and would soon be again.

Four days after the Birmingham bombings, as the public demanded action, Harold Wilson's new Labour Government introduced the Prevention of Terrorism Act (PTA), under which suspects could be held without charge and interrogated for up to seven days, and 'exclusion orders' could be served on individuals suspected of terrorist connections, expelling them from mainland Britain and preventing them from returning. Introducing the legislation in the House of Commons, the Home Secretary, Roy Jenkins, made no apology. 'These powers are draconian,' he said. 'In combination they are unprecedented in peacetime. I believe they are fully justified to meet the clear and present danger.'[12] However draconian the Act may have been, the Metropolitan Police Special Branch (MPSB) regarded it as an essential weapon in their anti-terrorist armoury. 'Without it, we would have had one arm up our back,' one of its senior officers told me. 'Exclusion Orders played a significant role in the 1970s and 1980s because they took out of our system those whom intelligence indicated were terrorists. It gave us the power to detain and question people on suspicion and at ports of entry, which were the vital pinch-points. It also gave Special Branch officers stationed there the potential to recognize and turn sources.' To the police and Roy Jenkins, a reputedly liberal Home Secretary, the attenuation of personal freedom was justified by the end of defeating terrorism. By the mid-seventies, the 'war' in Ireland had caused mayhem in England, infected the criminal justice system and jeopardized the civil rights that British citizens could no longer take for granted.

Chapter Fifteen

Structures of Disengagement

December 1974–December 1975

On 10 December 1974, a fortnight after the Birmingham bombs, an extraordinary secret meeting took place between eight Protestant clergy-men mainly from the North and prominent figures in the leadership of the Republican Movement, including three senior IRA men who, on 31 October 1973, had made a dramatic escape from Dublin's Mountjoy gaol in a helicopter. The meeting took place in Smyth's Hotel in the village of Feakle in County Clare. One of the architects of the encounter was the Reverend William Arlow, Assistant Secretary of the Irish Council of Churches, who wanted to convince the IRA that its campaign was counter-productive because every killing made it less likely than ever that Protestants would one day agree to join a united Ireland.

The Reverend Arlow and his colleagues had some hard men, and one very hard woman, to convince. At the talks, the Sinn Fein wing of the Republican Movement was represented by its President, Ruairi O'Bra-daigh, its vice-President, Maire Drumm, who was to be shot dead by loyalists in 1976, and Seamus Loughran, Sinn Fein's Belfast organizer. The IRA's wing was represented by Billy McKee, David O'Connell and the three helicopter escapees from Mountjoy gaol, J.B. O'Hagan, Seamus Twomey and Kevin Mallon, all of whom were still on the run. The clergymen were surprised at how civilized and polite their interlocutors turned out to be, as McKee remembered. 'I think they were expecting men coming in with trenchcoats and rifles over their shoulders and bayonets by their sides. But it wasn't like that. It was a very cordial meeting and very, very good.' The feeling was reciprocated by Dr Arthur Butler, the Church of Ireland Bishop of Connor. 'We were all most impressed by their attitude, with their fair-mindedness, and we were so pleased to find that they were talking seriously and deeply and with great conviction and had listened very carefully to what we had to say,' he said.[1]

The clergymen had prepared a document to which they hoped to get the IRA's agreement and then present it to HMG as a basis for a settlement and an end to the violence.

The meeting came to a rather abrupt end, however, when the Irish Special Branch arrived armed with sub-machine guns, hoping to arrest Twomey, Mallon and O'Hagan. The Branchmen stormed the hotel and found McKee and O'Bradaigh comparing notes downstairs. When asked where the 'others' were, they replied, 'Upstairs.' The raiders dashed up to find a group of Protestant clergymen who were also comparing notes. Their quarries, who had received a tip-off, had already gone, this time using a less dramatic form of transport. The Branchmen left Smyth's Hotel embarrassed and empty-handed.[2]

Michael Oatley regarded Feakle as a side-show and distraction from the enterprise upon which he and Frank Cooper were embarked, although the fact that the Feakle meeting subsequently became public would help draw the sting should it ever be revealed the Government was undertaking its own secret dialogue with the IRA.

At this stage, the existence of Oatley's bamboo 'pipe' down which the signals were being sent was known to only a small handful of people and was certainly not known to the Government at large. Its own response to Guildford, Woolwich and Birmingham had been security force pressure, not seeking out the possibility of talks with the organization responsible for the outrages. Oatley admitted there was a 'grotesque' contradiction in the IRA's position. 'I think one of the things I'd come to understand at a fairly early stage was that the continuation of a violent campaign was not inconsistent with a willingness to consider political options,' he said. As Christmas 1974 approached, Oatley was hopeful that the New Year might produce more positive soundings from Provisional representatives with whom he was not directly in contact. 'The sorts of noises we'd been hearing over the previous weeks suggested that the communication, which had been at a very low level, could perhaps become really significant and that we had an opportunity to do something really important. So everybody packed their bags and went off to London feeling that we were probably all right for a week.'

Oatley had been informed via the 'pipe' that the IRA would declare a Christmas cease-fire, this time to create a climate in which a more meaningful dialogue might be pursued. On 20 December 1974 the IRA announced it was ordering 'a suspensions of operations' to last from midnight on 22 December until midnight on Thursday 2 January 1975 in order to give the British Government an opportunity 'to consider the proposals for a permanent cease-fire'.[3] The efforts of all those involved in the process, not least the Contact himself, finally seemed to be bearing fruit. The Feakle clergy had no doubt played their part too in helping to crystallize the IRA leadership's thinking. On the day the cease-fire was due to begin, the IRA endeavoured to make it clear it was entering talks from a position of strength, as was now customary, by opening fire on two police stations and exploding six bombs in Northern Ireland and by hurling a bomb from a car at the London home of former Prime Minister Edward Heath.[4] Heath was not at home and only a few windows were shattered. At midnight, the IRA's guns and bombs fell silent. The IRA now waited for a reciprocal response from the 'Brits' and apparently expected it to come within the hour. When it did not materialize, the IRA felt it might be being conned and started threatening to go back to 'war' unless there was some response from the 'Brits'.

Late on Christmas Eve, Oatley received an urgent call from the Contact, who had a habit of ringing in the middle of the night, with a warning that the situation was breaking down and the IRA was getting restless. He told Oatley that he needed to do something quickly to hold the position. Oatley took advice, probably from Frank Cooper, and got agreement that he could 'say something encouraging about the sort of talks that would take place' (he cannot remember the precise formula used). The Contact made a note of the conversation.

On Christmas Day morning, Ruairi O'Bradaigh was surprised to see a car pull up outside his house in Roscommon and from it emerge the Contact after a long drive from Derry. He gave O'Bradaigh a message in the form of a letter he had drafted after the late-night telephone call to Oatley. According to O'Bradaigh, the letter said that the British wished to meet the Republican Movement to devise 'structures of British withdrawal from Ireland' – or 'structures of disengagement from Ireland' (he told me that he could not remember the exact words). There was no doubt, however, in his mind what the thrust of the message was. I asked Oatley if he had been as specific as this in his telephone conversation with the Contact on Christmas Eve night. As ever, he chose his words with care.

> I always made it clear that the Government's ability to consider withdrawing from Northern Ireland was entirely dependent upon the will of the majority in Northern Ireland and that there was no question of a unilateral withdrawal of Crown Rule in Northern Ireland as a result of any conversations which might take place with the Republican Movement. But when asked what I was prepared to discuss, I said I am prepared to discuss anything you like. Whatever phrase was communicated to O'Bradaigh, it was nothing like a suggestion that the British Government was about to abandon the province to the embrace of the South.

But the phrase 'structures of disengagement from Ireland' or 'withdrawal from Ireland' is neatly ambiguous, isn't it? It can mean one thing to them and something entirely different to you.

Well, I think that was the nature of our dialogue and I think that the ambiguity was recognized by both sides so that each could make what it wanted from it. Ambiguous phrases were very much the currency we were involved in.

But O'Bradaigh did not see any ambiguity in the communication. He immediately contacted the IRA's Army Council (time was of the essence as the cease-fire had only a week left to run). The IRA leadership agreed to meet on 31 December 1974 to discuss the dramatic development and decided that the Contact should be there to authenticate himself and the message he had brought from the 'Brits'. Billy McKee, who now also had a seat on the Army Council, was present at the meeting. At the time, British intelligence appeared to be unaware of how quickly McKee had been re-inserted in the IRA's command structure. But they certainly believed he was a person of some integrity who, although a 'hawk' in military matters, was a potential 'dove' in the political field and therefore one with whom business might be done as he appeared to straddle both camps.

On New Year's Eve, with only three days of the cease-fire left, the Contact arrived at the meeting in Dublin. O'Bradaigh vouched for the Contact's integrity and assured the obsessively secretive Army Council that he could be trusted. McKee remembers the encounter. 'He had a message that the British wanted to meet us and we asked him what was on the agenda. He said, "Withdrawal" and we said we were interested.' The Contact said the man who wanted to talk was called Oatley and the only person he wanted to meet was Billy McKee. McKee was instinctively suspicious. The IRA had never heard of Oatley but assumed, correctly, that he was some kind of 'spook' although it would not have known of his precise connection with MI6. Twomey, who was chairing the meeting as Chief of Staff, asked McKee if he was willing to go and meet him. McKee had reservations, suspecting he might be walking into a British intelligence trap. 'I said, "I'm not going to meet any British agent on my own. I want a witness there to hear what's going on. Twomey agreed and it was decided that I should go with another man.' The 'witness' deputed to accompany McKee was a senior IRA commander in Derry who was also a member of the IRA's GHQ staff and a close colleague of Martin McGuinness with whom he had been in gaol in the South.

Oatley's 'message', ambiguous or otherwise, had the desired effect and the IRA extended its cease-fire for another two weeks until 16 January 1975. Unionists were getting extremely nervous, suspecting that this would not have happened unless some sort of deal was being done. Loyalist paranoia, never far from the surface, began to intensify.

On 7 January, McKee and his GHQ colleague travelled to Derry for exploratory talks with Oatley at a secret location set up by the Contact. When Oatley arrived and saw the senior IRA man accompanying McKee, he considered calling off the meeting. 'I didn't want to meet anybody who looked like a publicly recognized terrorist and cause potential embarrassment to the Secretary of State,' he said. In the end, the Contact persuaded Oatley to stay, knowing that if the meeting fell apart, the whole enterprise might fall apart too.

McKee insists that Oatley mentioned 'withdrawal' at the meeting.

> I asked him what was on the agenda and he said 'Withdrawal' and he said that he needed our help.
> **Are you sure he said 'Withdrawal'?**
> Oh, he said 'Withdrawal' all right. 'Withdrawal' was used during the whole negotiations with Oatley and others. They said that's what they wanted and they needed the IRA to help them so that there wouldn't be a bloodbath. They said they wanted us to meet the loyalists and we said that could be arranged all right. I can tell you, if they hadn't mentioned withdrawal, there'd have been no cease-fire and no truce at that time.

Oatley would dispute that he ever said anything as specific as that, maintaining that by agreeing to an 'open' agenda, nothing could be ruled out, including 'withdrawal'. It was a clever and politically defensible form of words.

During further meetings in which O'Bradaigh took part in his capacity as President of Sinn Fein, and Oatley was joined by his Laneside colleague, James Allan, an indefinite cease-fire was negotiated. The IRA announced on 9 February 1975 that it would begin the following day and called it a 'bi-lateral truce'. According to Frank Cooper, O'Bradaigh described the enterprise 'as the most exciting thing that had ever happened to him. There is no doubt at all that they were delighted to be involved in what they saw as a political dialogue.' According to the Republican Movement's secret minutes of the negotiations, to which I was finally given access as a result of republicans I knew in the South, the British agreed to the truce on consideration of a list of points, all predicated on 'a genuine and sustained cessation of violence'.[5] The most important were:

- If there is a genuine and sustained cessation of violence and hostilities, the army would gradually be reduced to peace-time levels and withdrawn to barracks.
- Discussion will continue between officials and representatives of Provisional Sinn Fein and will include the aim of securing a permanent peace.
- Once violence has come to a complete end, the rate of release will be speeded up with a view to releasing all detainees.

They did not give the IRA all it wanted but they seemed to contain a big enough hint. Certainly they were sufficient to merit an indefinite cease-fire. At the last minute, there was a problem over allowing two dozen IRA men to carry weapons for their personal protection but Cooper agreed to let them do so if that was all that stood between the two sides. He was not going to let the prospect of peace founder on twenty-four permits.

For republicans, the most tangible evidence of the truce was a series of 'incident centres' established across the province and manned by Sinn Fein to avoid the kind of confrontation that had brought the 1972 cease-fire to an end. Each one contained a 'hot-line', initially to Laneside where Oatley and Allan were based and subsequently to Stormont Castle, manned twenty-four hours a day by officials who had direct access to the Secretary of State. Historically, the incident centres gave Sinn Fein a political base and prominence within the nationalist community which the party had never enjoyed before. The rise of Sinn Fein and its growing influence over the next twenty-five years can be traced from this point.

There was movement on prisoners too. On 18 March 1975, the Price sisters, convicted for the Provisional IRA's first London bombings in 1973, were transferred from England to Armagh gaol. Two more London bombers, Gerry Kelly and Hugh Feeney, were later transferred from England to Long Kesh, which had now become officially known as the Maze Prison. (Long Kesh had too many bad historical associations for the 'Brits' when they were trying to feel their way towards peace.) Kelly joined Gerry Adams in 'Cage 11' along with other prominent republican prisoners.

Inside the Maze, Adams and his colleagues watched with scepticism as they saw the IRA outside being drawn into a dialogue with the 'Brits' out of which, they believed (perhaps with a liberal dose of hindsight), no good could come. They knew that once Volunteers were stood down and remained inactive during an indefinite cease-fire, the initiative would lie with the 'Brits'. Again with hindsight, and with some justification, they felt the Republican Movement was being led into a trap and the Dublin leadership, most notably O'Connell and O'Bradaigh, were too blind to see it. Martin McGuinness, who had been released from Portlaoise prison in the Republic on 13 November 1974, having served his second sentence for IRA membership, which he admitted,[6] was never directly involved in the negotiations and therefore was not tainted by them.

Increasingly, as the months went by, the indefinite cease-fire became meaningless as the loyalist paramilitaries lashed out with unbridled ferocity to force the IRA to retaliate and thus precipitate an end to the truce. Loyalists, seeing the incident centres in operation with Sinn Fein having direct access to Ministers, had no doubt that a deal had been done. In 1975, the UVF and the UDA killed 120 Catholics, the vast majority innocent civilians. The UVF was responsible for 100 of those deaths.[7] Among its most horrific attacks were the bombing of the Strand Bar in Belfast on 12 April in which six Catholics, including three women, died; the massacre of the Miami Showband on 31 July in which three Catholics who were members of Ireland's most popular band were killed; and the gunning-down of four Catholics during a robbery on 2 October at Casey's wholesale wine and spirits warehouse on the edge of the Shankill and the Falls. One of the gunmen was Lennie Murphy who was soon to become notorious as the leader of the so-called 'Shankill Butchers' who tortured and carved up their Catholic victims with butchers' knives before finally putting them out of their agonies. Over the years, eleven members of Murphy's gang murdered nineteen people, clearly taking pleasure in rituals whose horror defies the imagination, even by Belfast standards.[8]

Despite the cease-fire, the IRA hit back in kind, not least because it felt it had to in order to maintain its own credibility as the 'defender' of its community. In retaliation for the Miami Showband, the IRA bombed the Bayardo Bar on the Shankill Road on 13 August 1975, killing four civilians and one UVF man. It was seen as a purely sectarian attack. Another attack followed a couple of weeks later on 1 September, when masked gunmen walked into the Tullyvallen Orange Hall near Newtownhamilton in South Armagh and sprayed it with machine-guns, killing four members of the Guiding Star Temperance Orange Lodge. Responsibility was claimed by a group calling itself the South Armagh Republican Action Force, a flag of convenience for the South Armagh Provisional IRA.

Towards the end of the year, however, events in London made utter nonsense of the 'truce', which by this time was little more than a name anyway. An IRA Active Service Unit (ASU) had been in place in England for many months and had brought back to the streets of the capital the kind of fear that had not been seen for almost a year. Workers went to their offices, fearful that they might be blown up on the way. Commuters shunned the Underground, suspecting it might be the next target for the bombers. Women refused to go shopping in the West End in case they never returned. And the intelligence services did not know who the IRA cell was or where it was. Its security had been kept very tight.

After lying low for the first half of 1975 as the secret talks between the Republican Movement and the British stumbled on, the ASU resumed its attacks once it became clear that the 'Brits' had no intention of delivering what the IRA wanted. On 29 August, its members booby-trapped a bomb in Kensington which killed an army bomb-disposal expert, Captain Roger Goad, as he attempted to de-activate the device. On 5 September, they bombed Park Lane's Hilton Hotel, killing two people. There had been a twenty-minute warning but no indication as to where the bomb had been placed.[9] On 22 September, they bombed the Portman Hotel off Oxford Street. The following month, they changed tack by targeting prominent people for 'assassination' on the grounds that the offensive was directed against the British 'establishment'. On 23 October 1975, they returned to Kensington where they planned to kill the Conservative MP Sir Hugh Fraser by leaving a bomb under his car. The bomb exploded prematurely and killed an internationally renowned cancer specialist, Professor Gordon Hamilton-Fairley, as he was walking his dog near his home in Campden Hill Square.[10] They then turned their attention to attacking prestigious restaurants. On 28 October, they bombed Lockets in Westminster, a favourite dining place for Members of Parliament, and on 18 November, they threw a bomb packed with miniature ball-bearings through the window of Walton's restaurant in Chelsea, killing two diners.

By this time, London was on the verge of panic and its restaurants were virtually empty. Ross McWhirter, a founder of the *Guinness Book of Records* and a founder-member of a right-wing group known as the National Association for Freedom, offered a £50,000 reward for the capture of the bombers. On 27 November, members of the unit staked out his house, waited for his wife to come home and forced her to ring the bell at gunpoint. When her husband came to the door, they shot him dead. One of the gunmen is later alleged to have told the police that they killed him because 'He thought it was the Wild West. He put a price on our head.'[11] By now the ASU was acting as if *it* was in the Wild West, driving round London, bombing hotels and restaurants without getting caught. There was no 'Det' to put them under surveillance or RUC Special Branch informers to give the police leads. All members of the ASU came from the Irish Republic and were therefore difficult to trace. Unlike in Belfast, the intelligence services in London were working virtually blind.

But on 6 December 1975, the ASU's luck finally ran out. The Metropolitan Police, now under huge pressure to produce results, flooded the West End with mobile patrols in the hope that the bombers would strike again and get caught in the police net. It was known as 'Operation Combo' and the gamble paid off. Four members of the ASU stole a car and raked Scott's restaurant in Mayfair with gunfire. It was their second attack on the premises, an indication of how brazen they had become. The police gave chase and ran the gunmen to ground in Balcombe Street where they had abandoned the car and taken refuge in flat 22B, holding its occupants, John and Sheila Matthews, hostage.

After an epic six-day siege that hooked the nation, the quartet finally surrendered. The four men, who became known as the 'Balcombe Street Gang', were Harry Duggan, Martin O'Connell, Edward Butler and Hugh Doherty. Although luck on the part of the police and carelessness on the part of the IRA had led to their capture, it was a carefully directed Metropolitan Police operation that ensured their apprehension without any shots being fired or harm being done to the hostages – a crucial benefit in a propaganda war that made great use of 'martyrs'.

The four were tried and sentenced at the Old Bailey on 10 February 1977 and received forty-seven terms of life-imprisonment. The judge, Mr Justice Cantley, described them as 'criminals who called themselves soldiers' and recommended that each serve not less than thirty years.[12] During their interrogation, some of the 'gang' said that they were responsible for the Guildford and Woolwich bombs and that those convicted for them were innocent. Their evidence was discounted.

In a controversial postscript, the Balcombe Street Gang did not serve their thirty years. On 23 April 1998, a fortnight after the Good Friday Agreement, the four were transferred to Portlaoise prison in the Republic after serving twenty-two years in English gaols. The following month, to tumultuous applause, they made a dramatic appearance on the platform at a special Sinn Fein conference in Dublin called to ratify the change in the party's constitution that would enable Sinn Fein candidates to take their seats in the new Northern Ireland Assembly. I was in the hall at the time and remember being deafened by the sound of stamping feet, wild applause and triumphant cheering as the four men stood there beaming, with clenched fists in the air. It was as if they had won a great victory. In the eyes of their ecstatic supporters, they had, and had come home as heroes. I wondered how the families of their victims felt. Shortly afterwards, the Irish Government announced that they would soon be released to honour the spirit of the Good Friday Agreement.

The bloody trial of death and destruction left by the ASU towards the end of 1975 dispelled any notion that the IRA's indefinite cease-fire was still intact. The Provisionals felt they had been strung along by the 'Brits' for long enough and were no longer prepared to play politics to the enemy's agenda. They had already dealt a blow to the Government's hopes earlier in the year by boycotting the elections for Rees's Constitutional Convention held on 1 May, declaring the Convention meaningless as it encompassed only six of Ireland's thirty-two counties. Time and again in the ongoing secret talks they had pressed the British to deliver on 'structures of disengagement' but no concrete assurance had been forthcoming. Oatley never saw the process through because, in March 1975, he left Northern Ireland to take up an MI6 posting in Hong Kong. Others took over from him. As a farewell gesture, the two sides exchanged parting gifts. Oatley presented the Provisionals' representatives with gold Cross pens and they gave him a Long Kesh harp. Even if Oatley had stayed on, it is unlikely that things would have been different. According to the Republican Movement's minutes, which I have no reason to believe are other than reasonably accurate, the closest the British came to fulfilling the IRA's expectations was at a formal meeting on 2 April 1975 between Ó'Brádaigh and McKee and James Allan and one of Oatley's successors. The minutes begin with the British trying to soothe Ó'Brádaigh and McKee who were becoming increasingly concerned at the lack of progress on the key issues.

The acceptability of the Republican Movement as a respectable movement has greatly increased. It is now viewed as a serious political movement which should be listened to. This is an enormous gain. It would be lost if the Republican Movement goes back to war. There is no magic way forward. This is an extremely historic moment. It may never happen again for a long time. The alternative to going back to war is to accept a rate of progress which is slow but will increase as it goes along.

If on the other hand the Republican Movement helps the Government to create circumstances out of which the *structures of disengagement* [author's emphasis] can naturally grow, the pace quickens immensely once the groundwork is laid. The only way to develop is to get the groundwork right. HMG cannot say they are leaving Ireland because the reaction would prevent that happening. They cannot make a stark, definitive statement . . . If one looks at events . . . *The tendency is towards eventual British disengagement . . . but [it] will stop if the Republican Movement goes back to war.*[13] [Author's emphasis]

The British were counselling patience and continued to do so as the meetings petered out against the increasingly violent backdrop of tit-for-tat sectarian killings and the Balcombe Street Gang's killing spree in London. The reference in the minutes to the 'historic moment' that might not happen again for a long time proved prophetic. The 'truce' gradually fell apart to the sound of gunfire and bombs. It was to be more than a quarter of a century before the 'Brits' and the IRA tried to change the course of history again.

Chapter Sixteen

Enter the SAS

January 1976–May 1976

The horrific tit-for-tat sectarian killings that had stained the closing months of 1975 were but a prelude for the even greater horrors of the first few days of 1976. I was in South Armagh at the time and vividly remember the fear that gripped both communities as killers from both sides pulled the triggers of raw sectarian hatred. The loyalist UVF from mid-Ulster struck first in a co-ordinated attack that left six members of two Catholic families dead. None had any paramilitary connections.

The UVF's first target was the Reavey family who lived in a small cottage in the village of Whitecross in South Armagh. It stood on its own away from the main village and surrounded by fields. On Sunday evening, 4 January, Mrs Reavey and her husband had gone to visit a relative, leaving three of her sons at home, Anthony (17), Brian (22) and John Martin (25). There were no undue concerns about security and the key was left in the door as was still customary in areas where there had been no trouble. Just after 6 o'clock, as the boys were watching television, at least four masked gunmen walked in and opened fire. John Martin was killed immediately and Brian seconds later as he tried to make for the bedroom. Anthony got to the bedroom and, terrified, crawled under the bed where the gunmen shot him and left him for dead. He recovered but died in hospital less than a month later when he suffered a relapse from the gunshot wounds. Forty-three spent cartridges were found amongst the pools of blood. Later that evening, a deeply shocked Mr Reavey went on television and made a plea. 'He said he didn't want any retaliation and didn't want anybody to suffer the way we had suffered,' Mrs Reavey told me. 'He didn't want anybody shot in retaliation for our sons. He said he would forgive them and made us kneel down that night and pray for the ones who killed them. He said it was worse for them than it was for us because they had to live with what they'd done, killing three innocent young men.'

I was making a film for Thames Television's *This Week* programme at the time and went to the Reaveys' cottage the night of the wake. I remember army helicopters raking the night sky and the fields below with powerful searchlights, probably more to show a security force presence that to deter the UVF. I had never been to an Irish wake before and found it difficult at first to come to terms with seeing John Martin and Brian immaculately laid out in their coffins, powdered and lifeless and bordered by dozens of mass cards. There were no tears as family friends filed past to pay their respects before being served with tea and sandwiches by Mr and Mrs Reavey. The order and calm seemed unreal after the unimaginable ordeal the family had been through. I met Mrs Reavey again twenty-four years later. Remarkably she seemed little changed although the pain and the memory of that night were still there. 'The years have been hell,' she said. 'I think of the boys all the time but I'll soon be coming to the end of my days. I hope that the ones that shot them will be found out before I die. Nobody was ever arrested for the killing of them and we never heard who did it.' Robin Jackson, the UVF commander from Mid-Ulster who is believed to have planned and ordered these killings and many more, is now dead. He was known as 'The Jackal' and died of cancer in 1998, a few weeks after the Good Friday Agreement was signed.

Ten minutes after the Reavey brothers were shot, another Catholic family, the O'Dowds, were having a post New Year sing-song around the piano at their home in a village near Gilford fifteen miles away.[1] In an obviously co-ordinated attack, another group of UVF gunmen burst in and sprayed the room with automatic weapons, killing three members of the family.

The twin killings in one small corner of the province were to have an even bloodier climax twenty-four hours after the Reavey brothers and the O'Dowd family were gunned down by the UVF. Around tea-time on 5 January 1976, a dozen workers were being driven home in a minibus to the village of Bessbrook from the Glenanne textile factory in which they worked. It was a wet, dark, miserable evening. The driver and ten of the workmen were Protestants and one was a Catholic. The bus took the same route every day and on this occasion the passengers were not surprised to see a man in army uniform with a red light step out into the road and wave the bus down at a place called Kingsmills: given that they were only a couple of miles from Whitecross, where the Reaveys had been shot the night before, everyone on board fully expected army patrols to be thick on the ground that night. All were ordered out of the bus and made to stand spread-eagled against the side.

Alan Black was one of the passengers. 'We thought the van was going to be searched, which is the most natural thing in the world,' he told me. 'We had nothing to hide so no one was worried.' Nevertheless, Alan was a little surprised that the driver had not been asked for his licence. As he got out of the bus, Alan saw a dozen men in combat jackets lined up in the road. They were carrying automatic weapons and their faces were blackened with 'cam' (camouflage) cream. He was even more surprised at what he heard next. The man who had stopped the bus then barked, 'Who is the Catholic?' Alan thought this a bit strange, as it was not the kind of question British soldiers normally asked. Suddenly fearing that they had not been stopped by the army but by *loyalist* terrorists bent on killing their Catholic workmate, two of the Protestants standing next to him put their hands on top of his to stop him moving out.

However, the men were not loyalists but members of the South Armagh IRA, and it was clear that they already knew who the only Catholic on the bus was. The man who did all the talking grabbed him by the shoulder and ordered him to run off down the road. One of the gunmen made sure that he did. Then, with the eleven Protestants lined up against the side of the minibus, the man issued a single command. 'Right!' Automatic fire ripped the evening air for about ten seconds, although to Alan it seemed an awful lot longer. 'The gunfire was deafening, like something you have in your worst nightmare,' he recalled. 'I could not believe it the first time I was hit. I could not believe it was happening. It was total unreality. But the pain was real enough.' Then there was absolute silence, the only noise being the metallic sounds of guns being re-loaded. The IRA then opened fire again to make sure that all eleven Protestants were dead and no witness survived.

Miraculously Alan Black did although he was shot eighteen times. 'When the shooting stopped, there was not a sound. There was just dead silence. There was not a word, not a noise, nothing. I watched them walk off down the road. They were wearing Doc Marten boots.' Alan lay there, with the rain trickling down his face, in unbelievable pain, convinced that he was going to die and putting his fingers in the bullet holes to try to stop the blood coming out. Eventually a schoolteacher arrived on the scene and started to say a prayer for the dead. Ambulances and the police soon followed. Alan was rushed to hospital and made a remarkable recovery, although he is still haunted by the memory of that dreadful night. To this day, he cannot understand why it happened.

It was calculated. That's what made it so hard to take. Ten lads that would not harm a fly and just wiped out. They didn't mean to leave anyone alive. How do you reason with people that would go out and do that? They knew when they were putting on their uniforms, when they were blacking out their faces, when they were hijacking the van that was used to transport them out here, they knew what they were going to do. How can they live with themselves? I just don't know.

I remember watching the funerals. The drizzle never stopped. It was as if the sky was weeping too. The massacre was claimed by the South Armagh Republican Action Force, the group responsible for the slaughter at the Tullyvallen Orange Hall. In fact it was the South Armagh IRA, allegedly acting without the authority of the IRA leadership. After Kingsmills, the tit-for-tat killings in South Armagh stopped.

Two days later, on 7 January 1976, Harold Wilson announced he was sending in the SAS for the purpose of 'patrolling and surveillance'. Such a public announcement was unprecedented as the Regiment's operations are normally shrouded in secrecy. In the wake of the sectarian bloodletting and the public outrage it caused, Wilson had to be seen to be doing something, and sending in the SAS in a blaze of publicity gave the impression of a firm Government, prepared to hit back at the IRA.

Initially, some members of 14 Intelligence Company were not impressed. 'They were about as much use as tits on a goldfish,' one of them told me. Only a handful were deployed to South Armagh, primarily to put the 'frighteners' on the IRA which, under the circumstances, seemed a not unreasonable thing to do. Few men were available as most of the Regiment were still involved in fighting rebel tribesmen, known as *adoo*, in strategically important Oman, although the operation was brought to a successful end in September that year, thus releasing more of its 'troopers' for service in the province. It was not as if the SAS had not set foot there before. Members of D Squadron, 22 SAS, were deployed with the regular army in 1969 and a handful had been present ever since attached to other regiments.[2] Apparently the decision to deploy the SAS was not warmly greeted in every quarter of the Regiment, one of whose members at the time told me, 'No bugger wanted to go. It wasn't an attractive job and the vast majority didn't want to get involved in Northern Ireland. We may be daft but we're not stupid.'

Operating in 'Bandit Country', as South Armagh had become known, was very different from fighting in Oman and winning the hearts and minds of the tribesmen as the SAS had so successfully done, thus turning the tide of the campaign. In fiercely republican villages like Crossmaglen there were few hearts and minds to be won. Even more difficult was the fact that, unlike in faraway places, the enemy could not be followed to its safe havens over the border in what was known as 'hot pursuit'. The Irish Republic was a sovereign state and jealously guarded its territorial integrity although it knew that the IRA was operating from the border counties of Monaghan and Louth adjacent to South Armagh. To the SAS the border was a line on a map that was as big a challenge as the IRA. Inevitably, shortly after its deployment, the Regiment was involved in a series of controversies.

The first occurred on 12 March 1976 and involved Sean McKenna (23), whose father had been one of the eleven detainees subjected to the Five Techniques immediately after internment in 1971. The young McKenna was living in a small, two-roomed cottage a couple of hundred yards over the border near Edentubber. The SAS had no doubt that he was a senior commander in the IRA and better out of circulation. He had already been acquitted of murder at two separate trials in the previous four years.[3]

McKenna thought he was safe but he was not. According to his own account, he was asleep in bed in the early hours of the morning when two men came in through the window, made their way through the kitchen and kicked down his bedroom door against which he had wedged a chair.[4] Both were wearing civilian clothes. One of them put a 9 mm Browning pistol to his head and told him not to move. A flashlight was then shone in his face to make sure the intruders had the right man. McKenna was then told to get out of bed slowly and put on his clothes. One of the men gave him a choice: to come quietly or resist and be shot. He was then taken across several fields and across the border where he says three soldiers in uniform were waiting. One of them sent a message over the radio, 'We have our friend.' The SAS men then handed him over with the instruction to shoot him if he made a wrong move. McKenna was then formally arrested and taken to the village of Bessbrook in South Armagh in whose disused mill the SAS, the regular army and the RUC were based. He was interviewed there by the RUC and made statements that resulted in his being sentenced to a total of 303 years for offences ranging from attempted murder to bombings, possession of firearms and explosives and membership of the IRA. According to one SAS source involved in the operation, 'He was sure he was going to be shot when he was told to get dressed and go outside. He couldn't stop talking and gave away everything he knew without having been asked a single question. When he was handed over to the RUC he was genuinely astonished and delighted to see them.'[5]

The army, of course, never admitted that McKenna had been lifted from across the border or that the SAS had been involved. Instead they issued a cover story saying that he had been found, drunk and incapable, staggering along the Northern side of the border. Whatever the exact truth, one of the IRA's most wanted men in South Armagh was now safely locked up in the Maze prison. As far as the authorities were concerned, the end justified the means. After the Kingsmills minibus massacre, few would have argued.

McKenna later came within hours of death on the IRA's first hunger strike in 1980.

A month later, on 15 April 1976, the SAS lifted another IRA man they had been watching, Peter Cleary (26), a 'Staff Officer' with the 1st Battalion of the South Armagh PIRA who was 'on the run' across the border. Cleary was about to get married to his girlfriend and surveillance revealed that he made regular visits to see her at the house where she was staying a few hundred yards on the Northern side of the border. That evening, he was spotted making one of his visits, having left his car a few hundred yards away in the Republic. Around 10 o'clock, he was watching the television news about an IRA attack on a helicopter in Crossmaglen when the SAS arrested him in a situation of some confusion. Their presence had already been revealed when a neighbour, alerted by the barking of dogs, shone a torch into a ditch and illuminated two soldiers, one of whom then fired a warning shot.[6] Helicopters were called up from Bessbrook, and Cleary was taken outside to await their arrival. According to the SAS soldier who was left to guard him, Cleary attacked him and tried to escape. The soldier shot him three times and said he had no chance to issue a warning.[7] (Witnesses later said that Cleary had been beaten up by the SAS before he was shot.) Bessbrook was then radioed and told to have a body bag ready on the landing strip.

The following day, HQNI issued a statement that said that Cleary, who was wanted for questioning by the police in connection with several serious crimes in the area, had tried to escape and 'assaulted the soldier guarding him and in the ensuing struggle was shot dead'.[8] Word was put about, presumably by the authorities and duly reflected in the English press, that Cleary had been wanted for questioning in connection with the Tullyvallen and Kingsmills massacres as well as a 300-lb landmine attack a fortnight earlier that killed three soldiers of the Royal Scots Regiment near Cleary's home in Beleek.[9] At his wake, Peter Cleary lay in his coffin, dressed in his wedding suit. The IRA refuted the SAS account of what happened and claimed that Cleary had been picked out for selective, cold-blooded assassination. Whatever the truth, there is no doubt that the kidnapping of McKenna and the killing of Cleary within months of the Regiment's deployment sent a clear message to the IRA. The SAS meant business.

But D Squadron's operations in the border area suffered a severe setback and embarrassing blow late at night on 5 May 1976. Two SAS soldiers in plain clothes, one in an overcoat and green shirt, the other in a brown jersey and white shirt, were arrested at a checkpoint manned by the Garda and the Irish army about half a mile on the Irish side of the border. They were driving a Triumph Toledo with an Armagh registration. One was an

Englishman and the other one of several Fijians serving with the Regiment. In their car was a Sterling sub-machine gun, a Browning pistol and
eighty-two rounds of ammunition. A large map marked with certain
houses on the Irish side of the border was also apparently found in their
possession. Around three and a half hours later, six other SAS men, four in
plain clothes and two in army uniform, in a Hillman Avenger and Vauxhall
Victor, were also arrested by the Irish police at the same checkpoint.
Between them they were carrying three Sterling sub-machine guns, two
Browning automatic pistols, a pump-action shotgun and 222 rounds of
ammunition.[10]

The British presented the incident as a 'map-reading error'. The whole
incident had elements of farce about it and gave the Regiment's reputation
a severe knock. The troopers of D Squadron might be deadly marksmen
but clearly left a lot to be desired when it came to orienteering.

Precisely what the first SAS car was doing across the border has never
been convincingly explained by the authorities, but I understand that the
first pair of SAS men were going to pick up or relieve two of their
colleagues who were manning a Covert Observation Post (COP) *on the
Irish side of the border*. When they did not return, the six others were sent out
to find them. The eight SAS men were arrested and charged under Section
30 of the Republic's Offences Against the State Act. One of those detained
is alleged to have said, 'Let us go back. If the roles were reversed, we would
let you back. We are doing the one bloody job.'[11]

Although British officials can smile today when you mention the SAS's
map-reading shortcomings, there was little amusement at the time as it
became a major diplomatic incident between the British and Irish Governments. There was great embarrassment at Stormont Castle where a new
Permanent Under Secretary, Brian Cubbon, had just been installed at the
Northern Ireland Office in succession to Frank Cooper. 'I could never
understand the "map-reading error" ', he told me. The eight SAS men
were released on bail of £40,000, guaranteed by the British Embassy in
Dublin, and returned to stand trial on 7 March the following year. Cubbon
was phlegmatic. 'My own view was that we'd just got to put our hands up
for this one and if the Irish wanted to go through a trial with damage
limitation, then we had to make the best of it. It was a bad episode and it
was an affront to Irish sovereignty.'

At their trial, the SAS men were acquitted of the charge of taking
weapons into the Republic with intent to endanger life, which could have
carried a penalty of twenty years in gaol. They were admonished and fined
£100 each for taking weapons into the Republic without firearms
certificates. The Garda then handed the weapons back to the British
army.[12] It was hardly a glorious page in the Regiment's history. The

apparent reluctance of many of its troopers to become involved in the conflict seemed to be justified by events. SAS involvement in Northern Ireland did not have an auspicious beginning. To the IRA, the initials now meant 'Special Assassination Squad'.

Chapter Seventeen

Piling on the Pressure

July 1976–March 1979

By the time Sean McKenna was arrested, convicted and gaoled, there was a new regime inside the Maze prison. Merlyn Rees had announced an end to internment on 5 December 1975 and the last internees were released. 'If all I have is a footnote in history saying, "Merlyn Rees ended internment", that will satisfy me,' he told me.[1] Since it was introduced in 1971, 1,981 suspects had been locked up without trial, only 107 of whom were loyalists.[2] But the compounds in which they had lived out their existence (whose Nissen huts, barbed wire and watchtowers seemed to confirm the inmates' insistence that they were prisoners of war) were not emptied. Those prisoners left behind were not internees but men who had been convicted and sentenced through the courts. They lived on in the compounds, enjoying the privileges of the special category status that Billy McKee and his colleagues on hunger strike had extracted from 'Willie' Whitelaw in 1972. They had weekly visits, letters and parcels, did not have to do prison work and, crucially, were allowed to wear their own clothes and mix freely with each other. Prisoners saw this as 'political status' and a recognition by the Government that they were 'political' prisoners. They had always believed that when the 'war' was over, they would all be released, despite the fact that successive British Governments swore this would never happen. They could not really do anything else. Ministers and senior officials who presided over this anomaly and saw the IRA turning the incarceration of its men to huge propaganda advantage, were determined to bring an end to special category status and treat prisoners as the criminals they believed they were. Frank Cooper had never believed the IRA was ever anything other than a bunch of criminals, whatever its protestations to the contrary.

There may have been some truth in the original IRA ethic, if you like to bestow that word upon it, but it increasingly got totally clouded, became corrupted, became criminal in every sense of the word. It was run for profit in many cases on both sides of the divide. Don't you tell me it's not criminal, it *was* criminal. Whenever you have murders on a large scale against innocent people going about their normal, daily, lawful business, those responsible have got to be made subject to the criminal law and dealt with as criminals.

To find a way of ending the contradiction between the way the Government viewed its prisoners and the way it treated them, Cooper and Rees pressed the former Lord Chancellor, Lord Gardiner, into Government service again. In his report he concluded that 'terrorists who break the law are not heroes but criminals; not the pioneers of political change but its direst enemies . . . the development of a "prisoner of war" mentality among prisoners with social approval and the hope of an amnesty, lends tacit support to violence and dishonesty . . . they are more likely to emerge with an increased commitment to terrorism than as reformed citizens.'[3] He recommended that, as a matter of urgency, the Government should start work on building new cell blocks in which prisoners could be locked up and treated as criminals as they were throughout the rest of the United Kingdom. The building programme began and, before their releases, the last internees recalled seeing new structures rising beyond the wires of their compounds. They were the new 'H Blocks', so called because their wings made an H shape. Although neither the 'Brits' nor the IRA knew it at the time, the H Blocks were to herald a new phase in the 'war' of which the repercussions were to be immense.

In 1976, the Government embarked on a totally new policy as advocated in the Gardiner report. It became known as 'criminalization'. Six years into the conflict, the 'Brits' realized that hostilities were likely to go on for a very long time since, despite its setbacks on the military front before the 'truce', and on the political front during it, the IRA showed no signs of giving in or, as the secret talks had indicated, making the compromises necessary for peace. The IRA remained absolutist in its aims and in its means of achieving them.

That did not mean that all the IRA leadership was confident of eventual victory, although it could never admit it since to do so would shatter morale and play into the hands of the enemy. Billy McKee remembers a conversation with Seamus Twomey in early 1976 when they discussed calling off the campaign. 'Things weren't going well and it was getting very rough,' he told me. 'We were short of money, short of arms and men were getting arrested. Things were getting a bit critical and we made plans about what way it would finish. I said to Seamus, "If we do ever have to call it off, no matter what happens, one thing we can always say is that we got rid of Stormont."'[4]

But the IRA did not need to cover what might well have been its failure with the fig-leaf of the abolition of Stormont. 'We got another kiss of life,' McKee added. 'Criminalization' was the 'kiss'. The policy that was designed to bring the IRA to its knees, however long the process might take, gave republicans their life-line, although few realized it at the time.

To the fury of the Provisionals, the Government abolished special category status, depriving *all* prisoners not only of the freedom to run their own lives with their own command structure, military training and parades, but of the visible manifestation that they were different from 'ordinary' prisoners. From 1976 onwards, all those sentenced for crimes committed *after* 1 March 1976 were to be locked up in the cells of the H Blocks and no longer accorded special category status. For the 'Brits' the new policy was designed not only to put the 'terrorists' behind bars but to change the perception of the conflict and undermine the IRA's depiction of it as a war of liberation to complete the unfinished business of 1921 and get the British army and state out of Ireland for ever. To the mortification of many army officers who felt that their wings were being clipped, the RUC was to become the lead agency in the 'war against terrorism'. Suspects on both sides were to be arrested and interrogated by the police, brought before the courts and sentenced by due process of law, just like 'ordinary' criminals. The army, the theory went, would gradually retire to the wings and let the RUC get on with the job, with policemen replacing soldiers on the streets. The policy became known as 'Ulsterization'. This did not mean diminishing the role of 14 Intelligence Company whose importance was, if anything, increased. With the SAS now in place and the 'Det' becoming more sophisticated with the use of the latest surveillance technology, the 'Brits' were not going to let down their guard. Nor were the IRA. Despite the realistic private assessments of Twomey and McKee, the 'Provos' had no intention of winding down their campaign. By the end of 1976, the IRA had killed 12 soldiers, 16 members of the UDR and 24 policemen in the course of the year.[5]

By the early summer of 1976, there had been both diplomatic and political changes. On 16 March, Harold Wilson had stunned the country by announcing that he was standing down as Prime Minister, for reasons that have never been fully understood. The Press immediately sniffed some great scandal on the horizon but were disappointed when none materialized. The truth may well have been that, as Wilson suggested, he had had a long run and it was time for someone else to take over whilst he retired to his beloved Scilly Isles. As well as all the vicissitudes of domestic politics, Ireland too had taken its toll with its seemingly unending catalogue of killing and the stubborn refusal of its politicians to reach agreement. Wilson's successor as Prime Minister on 5 April 1976 was Jim Callaghan, who, like Wilson, was no stranger to Ireland. But now glad-handing visits to the Bogside were out.

There were diplomatic changes in Dublin, too. The British Embassy had a new Ambassador, Christopher Ewart-Biggs, who gave the local press corps great copy. With his black eye-patch, designed to cover the loss of an eye during the battle of El Alamein in World War Two, double-barrelled name and aristocratic bearing and vowels, Ewart-Biggs was a colourful character anxious to dispel the view widely held by the Dublin media that he was straight out of P.G. Wodehouse. Within days of becoming Ambassador, he had had a meeting with the Gardai to discuss his security. He got the impression there was no great sense of urgency although they agreed he was a possible target for the IRA. 'They are not very re-assuring,' he wrote in his diary. 'They do not seem to have given much thought to the scenario of attack. They thought for some reason that an attack on the car was unlikely – "It hasn't happened yet".'[6] The Ambassador asked to be kept informed if there was any change in the Gardai's assessment of risk. None apparently came.

Nine days later, on 21 July 1976, Ewart-Biggs was being driven to the British Embassy from his official residence in Sandyford, County Dublin, shortly before 10 o'clock in the morning. He was scheduled to meet the Irish Foreign Minister, Garrett FitzGerald. With him in the armour-plated Jaguar were Brian Cubbon, the NIO's new Permanent Under Secretary, Judith Cook, his Private Secretary,[7] and Brian O'Driscoll, the driver. Two hundred yards beyond the gates, the IRA triggered a command wire to detonate a 200-lb bomb hidden in a culvert. The Jaguar was hurled into the air, killing the Ambassador and Ms Cook.[8] The driver and Brian Cubbon survived, although badly injured. It was a moment the new Permanent Under Secretary never forgot.

> It was quite horrific. The explosion was enormous. The car turned over on its left-hand side. Christopher Ewart-Biggs and Judith Cook were killed instantly. I was very fortunate indeed. The next thing I knew was that I was on some table somewhere with arc lights peering down at me, with a surgeon cutting up my suit in order to get at me more easily. The Gardai claim that when they fished me out of the car I said, 'Would you please tell the Irish Foreign Minister that we may be a little late for our appointment?'

The bombers were never caught. The Ambassador's widow, Jane Ewart-Biggs, channelled her grief into working for peace and established a literary memorial prize in her husband's name. She was made a Labour life peer in 1981 and died in 1992, before the peace that she had worked so tirelessly for had become a reality.

On 10 September 1976, unionist spirits were lifted when the new Prime Minister, Jim Callaghan, announced his Cabinet re-shuffle. Roy Mason, the tough, straight-talking former Yorkshire miner and MP for Barnsley, was moved from being Secretary of State for Defence to being Secretary of State for Northern Ireland. At first Mason was less than enthusiastic because he regarded the MOD as his natural home.[9] The NIO was unfamiliar territory, as it was for all Secretaries of State who entered Stormont Castle. To unionists, Roy Mason was an answer to their prayers, a man who, unlike his predecessors, would never contemplate having dealings with the IRA. Mason believed the IRA was to be beaten not talked to.

Unlike the slightly dishevelled but famously affable Rees, Mason was always formal, business-like and never off duty. 'He didn't like to meet anyone he hadn't met before,' one of his officials told me. 'He would never sit around in braces and always wore a tie. And he always liked people on time.' He was happiest when he was with the military, which reminded him of his golden days at the Ministry of Defence. He felt he spoke their language and they spoke his. He found the company of unionist politicians congenial, too, but was never really comfortable in that of nationalist politicians like the gregarious and expansive Gerry Fitt and Paddy Devlin. (His Labour successor many years later, 'Mo' Mowlam, was just the opposite. She could not stand many of the unionists and was most at home with the SDLP.) Mason loved the media's attention. One of his officials described him as being 'switched on by the cameras, like being jerked into action by electricity'. Appearing on television, invariably on his terms under the skilful direction of the NIO's legendary media adviser, David Gilliland, not only appealed to his vanity but enabled him to get his uncompromising message across with sound-bites that made unionists jump for joy and nationalists tear their hair out. To Mason the IRA *was* the problem, not the symptom of it.

The new Secretary of State had no time for political initiatives and new-fangled Constitutional Conventions and no time for secret talks with representatives of those he called 'gangster mobs'. One of his first acts was to close down Laneside which had been home to Frank Steele and Michael Oatley. His priority was security and jobs, both of which, he recognized, were interdependent. Now, he decided, 'it was time to take the war to the enemy'.[10] Mason was a huge fan of the SAS and, having sent them to Northern Ireland in the first place when he was Defence Secretary, he was keen to use their capabilities to the full, not only by increasing their numbers but by extending their operational role to the rest of the province. His aim was to put enormous pressure on the IRA, applied by Special Branch, the 'Det' and the SAS. The IRA could no longer attack with impunity. One of Mason's officials told me that one SAS officer wanted to squeeze even harder and attack the IRA's havens over the border. 'When are you buggers going to let us send Tornadoes into Dundalk?' the official claimed the officer said.

Mason took a black-and-white view of the conflict. Those who were not with him were against him, foreshadowing similar views expressed with equal, if not even greater, force by Callaghan's Conservative successor as Prime Minister, Margaret Thatcher. The sentiment applied to the media, too. Mason did not make any secret of his views, especially on the BBC's coverage of the conflict. Early in January 1977, he told its Governors what he felt during a private dinner at the Culloden Hotel. 'There was no point in mincing words,' he said. 'I suggested that by giving publicity to the IRA, television was making things easier for terrorism and worsening the plight of the province. By filming Provisional gangs in secret and flashing pictures all around the world, the BBC was effectively encouraging violence and undermining democracy. What it was doing was irresponsible if not disloyal.'[11]

Mason's outspoken attack on the BBC became known as the 'Second Battle of Culloden'. He did not regret a word he said and hoped that the media in general, and television in particular, 'would at last wake up to the dangers of being exploited by murderers'.[12] His attack was directed at people like myself and some of my colleagues who tried to depict the nature of the conflict as it was and not as the Government would like the world to see it. In the process, to Mason's displeasure, we exposed practices employed to defeat 'terrorism' that were questionable in a liberal democracy, in particular in relation to the interrogation of terrorist suspects by the RUC. Ironically, eight days before Roy Mason became Secretary of State in September 1976, the European Commission on Human Rights (ECHR) delivered its verdict on the use of the Five Techniques in 1971, declaring that they constituted not only 'inhuman and degrading treatment' but 'torture'.[13] I was therefore surprised, when working in the province in the early summer of 1977, barely a year after the ECHR's verdict, to hear so many reports of suspects being ill-treated whilst being detained for questioning at the RUC's euphemistically named 'Holding Centre' at Castlereagh in Belfast.[14]

Castlereagh and its sister operation at Gough Barracks, Armagh, which were in fact special interrogation centres, were beginning to have spectacular results in getting statements of admission from suspects that were sufficient to convict them before the non-jury 'Diplock' courts (named after Lord Diplock, who in 1972 headed a Commission that recommended that trial by jury for terrorist offences should be abolished in Northern Ireland as juries and witnesses were subject to widespread intimidation by paramilitaries from both sides). The Castlereagh interrogation centre was able to operate as successfully as it did because the Government changed the law on the admissibility of confessions. Again this was done on the recommendation of Lord Diplock who believed that terrorist suspects were getting away with their crimes because the test for the admissibility of any confession was that it had been made on an entirely *voluntary* basis. Accordingly, to make it easier to get convictions, the Government changed the law so that confessions could be accepted as evidence provided the Diplock judge was convinced that they had not been obtained as a result of 'torture, inhuman or degrading treatment'. This critical change in the legal definition gave RUC interrogators a latitude they had not previously enjoyed. In one landmark case, 'a certain roughness of treatment' was not ruled out as a means of getting a suspect to confess. The temptation by interrogators to overstep the mark to get results was great, and the temptation was not always resisted. Castlereagh now became the engine room of the Government's 'criminalization' policy, churning out the confessions that put scores of IRA men (and loyalists) behind bars.

The results soon became evident as more and more paramilitary suspects were carried along what republicans called the 'conveyor belt' that took them from interrogation at Castlereagh to trial by the non-jury Diplock courts, to incarceration in the H Blocks and no special category status. By the summer of 1977, the RUC, having been buffeted and criticized for so many years, now felt it was getting on top. 'Tails were up, the scent was clear and we were heading for home,' I have a note of one of its senior officers telling me in 1979. 'Terrorists were vomiting confessions all over the place.' He said that when detectives were debriefed after interrogations, it was 'like emptying buckets'.[15] Once a suspect started talking, there was no telling where he would stop. Detectives called it 'laxity of tongue control'. Crimes going back years were now being cleared up. In 1977, 1,308 suspects were charged with terrorist offences, almost a thousand of them by members of the four Regional Crime Squads that the new Chief Constable, Kenneth Newman, had set up to cover the province.[16]

Newman, who had arrived in Northern Ireland on 1 May 1976 to implement the new policy of police primacy, was Roy Mason's soul mate. Both shared an undisguised contempt for the 'terrorists', regardless of the side from which they came. Both were determined to beat them. Neither had any time for defeatist talk. Like Mason, Newman was an Englishman, but of the more reserved and clinical type. He came to Northern Ireland after distinguished service with the Metropolitan Police and was determined to make the RUC the most effective anti-terrorist police force in the world. In that he and subsequent Chief Constables – Hermon, Annesley and Flanagan – succeeded. From the outset, Newman made

his objectives clear to the people of Northern Ireland. 'Terrorism continues
to bring death and destruction,' he said. 'I will not be satisfied until the
shooting and the whole squalid catalogue of criminality is brought to a
finish. Our purpose is to put behind bars those criminals who up to now
have perhaps regarded themselves as being beyond the reach of the law.'[17]
Newman and Mason both spoke the same language. Castlereagh became
the most potent weapon of the 'Brits' against the IRA. Mason graphically
described the inroads the security forces were making.

> We are squeezing the terrorists like rolling up a toothpaste tube. We
> are squeezing them out of their safe havens. We are squeezing them
> away from their money supplies. We are squeezing them out of
> society and into prison.[18]

A secret document found by the Irish police during the search of a flat
outside Dublin where Seamus Twomey had been staying prior to his arrest
on 3 December 1977, confirmed the damage that the interrogation centres
at Castlereagh and Gough Barracks, filled by the Emergency Provisions
and Prevention of Terrorism Acts, were inflicting on the IRA. 'The three-
and seven-day detention orders are breaking Volunteers and it is the
Republican Army's fault for not indoctrinating Volunteers with the
psychological strength to resist interrogation . . . [this factor] is contributing to our defeat.'[19] It could not have been put blunter than that.

By this time, 'Mike', Special Branch's experienced agent-handler, was
based with the Regional Crime Squad at Castlereagh. The interrogation
centre was not only a means of getting convictions but the perfect
environment for 'turning' suspects and recruiting agents. It was certainly
more effective and less dangerous than walking up to someone in the street.
'Obviously it was an intimidating place to be for any of the people arrested
there,' he said. 'The intelligence we had was very specific in relation to all
the people arrested. Those who were being interviewed by the Regional
Crime Squads were not just pulled out of a hat. They were people on which
there was good intelligence that they had been involved or were on the
periphery of serious terrorist criminal offences. So, it was an ideal place and
we did recruit from there, yes.' 'Mike' was delighted with Newman and
Mason's approach and the support both gave to those at the sharp end.

> To my mind, it showed a willingness to actually defeat the problem
> of terrorism as opposed to appease it or deal with it in any other way.
> Roy Mason encouraged the work that was being done and on many
> occasions spoke to lads that were involved and congratulated them.
> He showed a positive interest and we felt, on a personal basis, that we

were actually achieving something. We were arresting, interviewing and charging people for terrorist crimes. They went to court and were convicted and to my mind this was the only way to deal with it. We were fighting a war, but it seemed up until then that only one side was fighting a war. We were now being much more positive about it. We were going after them, and it was working.

And what effect did that have on the IRA?

I think it brought them to their knees at that particular period. Reports that I had knowledge of certainly said they were in disarray.

Were you concerned that some of the methods used at Castlereagh in, as you say, fighting that war, were methods that shouldn't have been used, that some people were ill-treated?

It's alleged that people were ill-treated and I can't deny in the light of events [i.e. subsequent inquiries] that some people were abused. But the bottom line was, we were dealing with murderers, we were dealing with people who were quite prepared to shoot and kill innocent civilians. I accepted as a policeman, and soldiers accepted it too, that we were 'legitimate' targets for terrorists. That was part of the job. But we were arresting and charging and convicting people who were putting bombs in shops, and killing innocent civilians, killing children. I've sat across the table from people who I know have murdered colleagues of mine and we've had to look into the eyes of people that we know are murderers and killers. I had no compunction about making them uncomfortable. But it's your job and you just get on with it.

How did you make them uncomfortable?

Oh, through interviews, through long interviews, through letting them know how we felt about them in no uncertain terms. But there certainly was no institutionalized ill-treatment of prisoners.

That did not mean that it did not happen: 'institutionalized' was the key word.

By the late summer of 1977, I had no doubt that there were grounds for many of the allegations of ill-treatment that I had heard, having spoken to many – both republicans and loyalists – who had been interrogated and released, either because they had not made admissions or because there was no other evidence against them. In addition to descriptions of general beating and of suspects being made to stand in various stress positions as practised after internment in 1971 and replicated in the 'Det' anti-interrogation training, a clear pattern of abuse seemed to emerge with descriptions of fingers being bent backwards over the wrist and ears being banged with cupped hands. It was always possible these were carefully rehearsed and fabricated stories, but somehow I doubted it.

Even more critically, I had spoken to Dr 'Bertie' Irwin, the police surgeon who examined prisoners in Belfast after interrogation at Castlereagh, and to Dr Denis Elliott, the Senior Medical Officer who examined them at Gough Barracks. Irwin and Elliot were both remarkable and courageous men. Neither had any sympathy for the IRA or the UVF and the UDA. But their concern about the pattern of injuries they were seeing ultimately ensured the treatment of suspects became a political issue once again and not something that was simply brushed aside as 'terrorist propaganda'. At the Northern Ireland Office, the Permanent Under Secretary, Brian Cubbon, now recovered from the injuries he had received when Christopher Ewart-Biggs's car was bombed, was also becoming aware of the potential problems. 'I think we became conscious of the pressure on the RUC officers to deliver results,' he told me. 'I was concerned at what was being said. I was concerned at some of the rumours. I was particularly concerned at some of the medical evidence. Kenneth Newman knew about the rumours and what was said and gave assurances that he'd no reason to think that there was widespread malpractice happening.' 'Widespread', like 'institutionalized', was a convenient piece of casuistry. I had never believed the ill-treatment was widespread in the sense that it had been authorized from on high but I had no doubt it was happening on a sufficient scale to merit further investigation. The authorities argued that the injuries Irwin and Elliott had drawn attention to were self-inflicted.

In October 1977, I made a programme for Thames Television's *This Week* called 'Inhuman and Degrading Treatment' that examined ten cases in which there was strong medical evidence of ill-treatment. It was one of several controversial programmes I had made that summer, each one dealing with aspects of government security policy. In August, a *This Week* programme on the Queen's Jubilee visit to Belfast called 'In Friendship and Forgiveness' was banned by ITV's regulatory body, the Independent Broadcasting Authority (IBA), because it showed, amongst other things, masked IRA men manning a checkpoint. A few weeks later, in a programme about conditions inside the Maze prison called 'Life Behind the Wire', the Secretary of the Prison Officers Association (POA), Desmond Irvine, gave a brave interview and was then shot dead by the IRA.[20] After 'Inhuman and Degrading Treatment', the NIO launched an unprecedented personal attack.

It is significant that the producers and reporter of this programme have produced three programmes in quick succession which have concentrated on presenting the blackest possible picture of events in Northern Ireland. After the last programme on prisons, a prison officer who appeared on the programme was murdered, and last night's programme may well place police officers, who deserve all support, at even further risk. That is not what one expects of responsible commentators.[21]

Roy Mason charged the programme with being 'irresponsible and insensitive' and 'riddled with unsubstantiated allegations'.[22] The IBA felt the heat and told *This Week* to lay off Northern Ireland for a while and suggested it might find another reporter to cover it. *This Week* did give the issue a break but did not replace its reporter.

In the wake of the intense controversy surrounding Castlereagh, Amnesty International sent a team to Northern Ireland at the end of November 1977 to investigate the allegations. Mason facilitated their visit although he had no doubt why the issue had gathered such momentum. 'We were without question hurting the IRA and hindering its ability to conduct operations. The reports I saw daily established that; so it didn't surprise me that the terrorists were squealing. Still, it was disappointing to see their complaints taken so seriously, when by definition any evidence from the IRA had to be tainted.'[23]

Amnesty sent its report to Mason on 2 May 1978. After its investigation of seventy-eight cases of alleged ill-treatment, its conclusion was damning.

Amnesty International believes that maltreatment of suspected terrorists by the RUC has taken place with sufficient frequency to warrant the establishment of a public inquiry to investigate it.[24]

Mason consoled himself with the observation that 'At least none of Amnesty's findings amounted to outright torture.'[25]

The Government had given the Amnesty team every facility and was taken aback at the result. The report was dynamite and difficult to dismiss. The NIO sat on it for over a month, no doubt working out how it was going to deal with it. It was finally leaked and, having got hold of a copy, we planned a follow-up programme for *This Week* that vindicated the claims of maltreatment made in 'Inhuman and Degrading Treatment' the previous October. Again, the IBA intervened and the programme was banned on the grounds that the contents of the Amnesty report should not be discussed until it was presented to parliament and made public. Thames Television planned to transmit an alternative programme in the *This Week* slot but members of the television technicians' union, with the support of the National Union of Journalists, blanked the screen. The viewing figures were surprisingly good. I noted in my diary 'Blank screen ensued and rumpus'.

And still the controversy was not over. Amnesty's demand for a public inquiry was out of the question and Mason appointed Judge Harry Bennett QC, an English Crown Court judge, to head a Committee significantly *not* to investigate the allegations but to examine procedures and ways of improving the system. The Government was not going to grace the issue by appointing a Lord Gardiner or Lord Diplock. 'The fact that Bennett was a circuit court judge was a measure of how much importance they attached to it,' one civil servant of the time told me. The Committee was also circumscribed by its specific remit. Its report was finally published on 16 March 1979. Judge Bennett had strayed, however gingerly, outside his remit. Under the circumstances, he could hardly have done otherwise. He concluded that there had been 'cases in which injuries, whatever their precise cause, were not self-inflicted and were sustained in police custody.'[26] When Mason studied their conclusions – and he had plenty of time to do so – he had to admit that 'some of the allegations against the RUC seemed to gain weight'.[27] As a result of Bennett's recommendations, closed-circuit television was installed in the interrogation rooms, and suspects were given improved access to solicitors and doctors. With rare exceptions, allegations of physical ill-treatment at Castlereagh ceased. A disturbing chapter had ended. The 'Brits' had come very close to defeating the IRA but 'criminalization', and the methods used to enforce it, had provided IRA prisoners in the H Blocks of the Maze with the weapon to fight back.

On 28 March 1979, less than a fortnight after the Bennett report was published, the Labour Government fell, brought down on a vote of no confidence. It had been living on a knife-edge for months. Ironically, Castlereagh was the issue that brought it down. On their hair-line mathematics, the party whips calculated that they needed two votes to survive and both of them rested in the hands of Northern Irish MPs. One was Frank Maguire, an Irish republican and the Independent MP for Tyrone and Fermanagh, who, as an abstentionist, seldom came to Westminster. The other was Gerry Fitt, the SDLP member for West Belfast. Whenever he did turn up at Westminister, Maguire was as unpredictable in his voting as Fitt was reliable. On this occasion, having had his arm twisted to attend, he abstained. The Government's survival now depended on Fitt. In an impassioned speech to the House, he explained how he had reached his decisions on the way he would cast his deciding vote. 'I made up my mind when I read the Bennett report on police brutality in Northern Ireland,' he said. 'When the true story emerges of what has been happening in the interrogation centres, the people in the United Kingdom will receive it with shock, horror and resentment. That is why I take this stand.' Fitt abstained too and the Government fell, losing the vote of confidence by 311 votes to 310.[28] Castlereagh had returned to haunt its defenders.

Chapter Eighteen

Shootings and Stakeouts

1978

Whilst Castlereagh was squeezing the IRA on the inside, the 'Det' and the SAS were doing the same on the outside.

If 'Jim' had nine lives in the 'Det', he had used most of them up by the end of his second tour in 1978. He was a crack shot who had taken out IRA gunmen with a record-breaking anti-sniper unit before joining 14 Intelligence Company. He was clinical and professional in everything that he did and was matter-of-fact about the IRA. 'I don't love and I don't hate them,' he told me. 'As individuals, some of them were very good; some of them were very bad as terrorists. We often used to talk and say that if we had been brought up in those areas at those times, then maybe we would have joined the IRA in the same way as they did. So there's a certain amount of sympathy but I personally don't have any sympathy for extremists. People that come over here and plant bombs in crowded shopping centres on a Saturday afternoon are the scum of the earth.' 'Jim' believed that 'terrorists' should be given no quarter. He also loved life in the 'Det'. 'There was a sense of adventure and it was a highly professional operation, a high level of modern-day soldiering,' he told me. 'It was what was required and I felt I was doing something towards ending the "Troubles" in Northern Ireland.'

As IRA leaders attended meetings in the 'safe' university area of Belfast, 'Jim' kept watch from adjacent premises purchased by the army for surveillance purposes. Were the meetings bugged? 'Well, it would be foolish *not* to bug the meetings of the Belfast Brigade Staff,' he said. (At some stage 'Det' operators were apparently living in one of the houses where the Brigade Staff were meeting and regularly changed the audio tapes.) As part of his training, 'Jim' had been trained in 'Methods of Entry' (MOE) and had become expert at it, paving the way for MI5 officers to plant the listening devices, or simply going through whatever documents and material he could find. 'We would break in, log what was there and then Special Branch would decide what to do with it. It was quite a desperate situation and desperate measures were needed. But everything was within the law and authorized by the Government.'

Just as 'Jim's' fellow operator 'Alan' was tasked to keep tabs on Brendan Hughes, so 'Jim' was later directed to keep under observation another senior member of the Belfast Brigade Staff who went on to become one of the Republican Movement's well-known public figures. (I will refer to him as 'Liam'.) Special Branch had pointed 'Liam' out and detailed his activities within the Belfast IRA. 'Jim' then started to follow him round, knowing that if he got too close or was seen too often, he would be 'pinged' and possibly 'finished'. 'Jim' suspected he had been 'pinged' when 'Liam' and another member of the Belfast Brigade Staff followed him into a shop where he had gone to buy a paper. 'Some leading terrorists, who we were monitoring, started monitoring me.' 'Jim' returned to his car, locked the door, took the safety catch off the Browning concealed under his leg, and eased his finger round the trigger. It was a Friday afternoon and rush hour on the Falls Road meant traffic was crawling along at a snail's pace. The two senior IRA men came over and 'Liam' started banging on the roof calling 'Jim' 'a British bastard' and other things. 'Jim' made a gesture indicating that he did not know what the man was talking about and wondered whether he should shoot him before it was too late, but drew back because he says it would not have been within the directives of the Yellow Card (the military Rules of Engagement in Northern Ireland): 'Liam' was not armed and at that moment was not a direct threat to 'Jim's' life.

What concerned 'Jim' however, was the sight of the other IRA man beckoning to a known gunman across the road. He knew his chances of escape were remote once shooting started and, seeing his chance, hit the accelerator and roared off into a gap in the traffic.

Fortunately, he escaped. 'I knew I had to play it right to get out of it,' he said. 'I was a very lucky man.' Special Branch finally caught up with 'Liam' and he went to gaol. I saw him a few years after his release and asked him if he remembered 'pinging' the 'Brit' and banging on the roof of his car. He smiled as the memory came back but did not want to be named and quoted as by then he had endeavoured to put his past behind him. He asked what had happened to the soldier. I said that, like 'Liam', he was still alive and retired.

With his cover blown, 'Jim' was no use as an operator in Belfast. He returned to England and became an instructor alongside the SAS, training future 'Det' operators. By 1978, he was back in Northern Ireland but this time attached to North 'Det' which monitored the extensive area covered by the army's 8 Brigade, most of it in the north-west of the province, including, most important of all, Derry City itself. Here 'Jim' would not be recognized. His second tour took place at a time of considerable tension after an IRA incendiary bomb planted on 17 February 1978 incinerated twelve Protestants dining at the La Mon country house hotel outside Belfast. The nine-minute warning was inadequate and the bomb appears to have gone off prematurely, igniting a huge fire-ball that consumed those in the restaurant. It was a 'mistake' and the IRA apologized for it.[1] Nine days later, unionist demands for action were satisfied when the SAS ambushed and killed a member of the IRA's East Tyrone Brigade, Paul Duffy (23), as he was moving explosives from a derelict house near Lough Neagh.

'Jim' arrived in North 'Det' to take the place of another operator, Lance-Corporal David Jones (23) of the Parachute Regiment, who had been killed by the IRA on 17 March 1978 in confused and dramatic circumstances. Corporal Jones, known as 'Jay', and another operator whom I will refer to as 'John' had been staking out a farmhouse near the Glenshane Pass in South Derry which was being used by the unit commanded by South Derry's most notorious IRA commander, Francis Hughes. The 'Det' and Special Branch believed they were on the point of putting an end to his violent career. As one IRA commander later said, 'He was the sort of man who would shoot up a few policemen on his way to a meeting to plan our next attack on the police.'[2] On 8 April 1977, Hughes and his colleagues, one of whom was suspected to have been the equally notorious Dominic McGlinchey, were believed to have shot dead two members of an RUC Special Patrol Group when they tried to stop their Volkswagen car.[3] Shortly afterwards, police posters went up all over the province featuring Francis Hughes, the most wanted man in the North.

The area around the derelict building that 'Jay' and 'John' were watching had been placed out of bounds by the army because of the special operation in progress. The two operators were therefore surprised to see men looming out of the shadows dressed like soldiers. Thinking they were probably UDR men who had wandered into the area by mistake, 'John' issued a challenge.

The 'soldiers' were Francis Hughes and members of his unit returning from a patrol. Hughes opened fire and a fierce but brief gun-battle ensued. 'John' opened up with his Sterling sub-machine gun, hitting Hughes who carried on firing. Both soldiers were wounded. 'Jay' did not survive but 'John' did. One 'Det' operator later told me that in the light of what happened to 'Jay', in future shouting warnings in an out of bounds area was out. 'We all knew there was no room to f*** around and issue a challenge,' he said. He also pointed out that all shootings involving the 'Det' had always been 'clean'.

Hughes managed to crawl away and hide before the 'Det's' back-up
team and the Quick Reaction Force (QRF) arrived. Shortly afterwards,
Geoffrey, a corporal from the Gloucesters who was part of the QRF, found
Hughes after following a trail of blood across a field. As was clear on
meeting him, it was an encounter Geoffrey never forgot.

I saw this guy with peroxide blond hair. At first I thought he was
SAS. There he was sitting down by a big clump of bushes. He was
wearing a plain green combat jacket. I asked him who he was and he
said nothing. We then cocked our rifles and he said, 'Don't shoot,
you've got me.' He said his name was Seamus Laverty. Then an
RUC guy came up and said, 'Do you know who you've got there?
They've done a bad job with the peroxide hair!' I said to my mate,
'Christ, we've got the bastard!' We knew what he'd done. Hughes
said, 'I've no problem with you lot, it's those black bastards [RUC]
that we hate.' It was a bit like being soldier to soldier, although I
don't consider them soldiers. We were heroes. The Sergeant-Major
said, 'For the rest of your lives you'll never buy a drink in the
Company bar!'

Hughes is said to have shouted, 'Up the Provos!' as he was carried away.[4]
When he was fully recovered and deemed fit for interrogation, he was
taken to Castlereagh and interviewed by the RUC's top detectives. He said
nothing apart from a string of expletives. Statements were not necessary as
there was enough other evidence to convict him. He was finally sentenced
to life imprisonment and sent to join the other IRA prisoners in the H
Blocks, where, on 12 May 1981, he died after fifty-nine days on hunger
strike.

'Jim' took 'Jay's' place in North 'Det' and was glad to be back on the
ground. It was not long before he came face to face with the IRA again.
One Saturday afternoon on 10 June 1978, his unit got a phone call from
Special Branch saying they had intelligence that there was going to be a
bombing in the town and the 'Det' was tasked to go into Derry to see if
there were any 'players' on the ground. 'Jim' set out with his partner, 'Mal',
to have a look round the Bogside. They were in separate cars but always
close together. Meanwhile, two other operators were checking out the
Creggan. Given that it was a Saturday afternoon and the Bogside was busy
with shoppers going back and forth to the city centre, no one was likely to
give 'Jim' and 'Mal' a second look. As 'Jim' was driving by Rossville Flats,
he was suddenly stopped. 'The IRA had a system then of hijacking cars to
use in bombings and they assumed I was a prime target for a hijack, as a
relatively young, single bloke in a car on my own. Two gunmen emerged

from the corner of a street and flagged me down, drew their guns and tried to get me out of the car. Unfortunately the gunmen that day took on the wrong people.'

'Jim' pretended he did not know what the hijackers were on about and played for time until he saw 'Mal' about fifteen yards behind him in the driver's mirror. He knew he had a split-second advantage as the hijacker's gun, a 'Star' 9 mm pistol, had the hammer forward in the half-cock position. 'Jim's' Browning was in his waistband. It was a situation that both men had spent weeks training for with the SAS back in England. 'Mal' leapt out of his car and fired two shots at each of the gunmen. He missed one, who ran away, and hit the other in the leg. With the wounded IRA man sitting on the ground, 'Jim' got out of the car and finished him off with four bullets through the chest. But why kill him, I asked, if he was wounded already? 'He had to go down. He had a gun in his hand and was still a threat. That was the only way. It was an instant, split-second decision.' 'Jim' said he could have fired at the other gunman who was running away, confident that he would have hit him, but decided it was too risky with so many people around. 'One doesn't know what bullets may do after they've passed right through a body.' He picked up the 'Star' pistol and showed it to the astonished and terrified crowd of busy shoppers, to prove that his victim was armed.

The whole encounter was over in seconds. There was a stunned silence and then pandemonium. 'We were out of it within five or ten seconds of the shooting. Another ten seconds and we wouldn't have made it. They'd have ripped us to pieces.' Shortly after the shooting, the rioting started. 'The IRA didn't like it so they went into Derry and trashed it.' The dead man was Denis Heaney (21). The previous month he had been arrested along with his accomplice for an attempted hijacking and detained at Strand Road RUC station for three days, during which time he alleged that he had been beaten up by the police and presented with a statement that he refused to sign. At that time his family did not know that he had joined the IRA.[5] When neither 'Jim' nor 'Mal' was prosecuted for murder, Heaney's family brought a civil action for damages against the MOD but without success. The judge ruled that Heaney had been armed and the force used had been 'reasonable' under the circumstances. At the trial the family were convinced they were denied justice, claiming that he was shot in the back and pointing out that there were no witnesses to testify that he had a gun in his hand. Although a crowd of people watched the shooting, no one was prepared to testify against the IRA. It was 'Jim's' second lucky escape.

By this time, a new batch of operators had arrived in North 'Det' fresh from training. 'Some didn't just look the part,' 'Jim' remembers. 'Some had had their hair cut and looked like "squaddies".' On 11 August 1978, four operators were tracking IRA weapons round the Creggan acting on intelligence that some were to be used to kill a member of the security forces. The 'Det' may have already taken the precaution of secretly lifting them from their hide and doctoring some of the ammunition by removing most of the powder so the bullets would not go very far or do much damage if they hit their target. (Operators had no hesitation in de-activating guns should the opportunity arise. At one stage there seems to have been talk of rigging ammunition so it exploded in the gunman's face but this was ruled out as a step too far.) At the same time one or more of the weapons may have been 'jarked'.

One of 'Jim's' partners on the operation was a new arrival, a Scots Guardsman called Alan Swift. 'Jim' knew the Creggan intimately whereas Alan, having just been assigned to North 'Det', did not know it as well. They were both in separate cars and 'Jim' kept checking on the radio 'net' that Alan was all right. Another operator in a helicopter was tracking the operation from above. On several occasions Alan told 'Jim' he was not sure where he was and, to 'Jim's' consternation, he was not giving the correct call signs. At 3.30 p.m. 'Jim' heard forty to fifty shots being fired in two to three bursts from several automatic weapons, almost certainly those that had been concealed in the 'hide'. He was around 400 yards away from Alan at the time. He immediately checked with the other two operators on the radio and they had not been attacked. There was no reply from Alan.

'Jim' drove to Alan's location and saw the sight he had feared the worst. 'Alan was half in and half out of the car and a load of kids were dragging stuff out. Instead of doing the murder that they were going to do, they "sussed" out Alan and shot him instead. They were just after killing any "Brits" and we were fair game.' I pointed out that it was equally hazardous for the IRA. 'It's not as dangerous,' he said. 'They could make lots and lots of errors and they're not necessarily dead. If they get "sussed" out by their opposition, they get a nice cup of tea and a warm friendly bed for the next fifteen years. But if we got captured by them, we knew exactly what they were going to do to us. Make one error and you're dead.'

In 1978, after Roy Mason had extended the role of the SAS from South Armagh to the whole of the province, the Regiment became very busy. On 21 June, it ambushed an IRA ASU from its 3rd Battalion as it was about to fire-bomb a post office depot on the Ballysillan Road in North Belfast. Five SAS troopers had staked out the premises and around mid-night opened fire, killing three members of the unit, Denis Brown (28), William Mailey (31) and James Mulvenna (28). No guns were found. The

SAS said they had issued a challenge. The bombs were not unlike that used in the La Mon inferno four months earlier.

There was Special Branch intelligence that four IRA men were to be involved in the operation, as a result of which the SAS shot dead a fourth person, William Hanna (27). This was a mistake. Hanna was a Protestant, not an IRA man, and was simply passing by. The fourth member of the unit escaped. For the first time, as part of 'Ulsterization', undercover RUC officers were also directly involved in an SAS ambush. It was a taste of things to come.[6] In all, 111 shots were fired at the IRA unit, 22 of them by one RUC officer. The SDLP demanded an inquiry into the shootings, claiming it was part of a 'shooting without question' policy by the army.[7] The phrase was soon honed to 'shoot to kill'. Roy Mason said there was no need for any investigative inquiry. But the controversy over the SAS's 'mistake' was nothing compared with the furore caused by the Regiment's next killing only three weeks later.

Dunloy is a staunchly republican village in North Antrim on the side of a hill overlooking the vast rolling amphitheatre bordered by the Corkey Mountains and the Glens of Antrim beyond. On the evening of 10 July 1978, a sixteen-year-old schoolboy, John Boyle, was in the ancient village graveyard looking at a faded Boyle family headstone, one of many that lurch out of the overgrown grass, making it the sort of place one would not like to be alone in at night. Some youngsters were in the graveyard too and John noticed that they appeared to have found something under one of the many fallen headstones. When he went over, they ran away. Curious to see what they had found, John looked under the stone and saw a bundle and other material pushed underneath. It was clear that it had not been there for long. He did not attempt to examine the find further but went home to tell his father, Cornelius ('Con') Boyle, about his discovery. Con then went back to the graveyard with his son to have a look for himself. 'I think it was a jacket wrapped up and probably tied in a bundle and a plastic parcel the size of a half-stone bag of groceries,' he told me. 'There was something behind that too. When I saw the bulky thing, I thought it was a bomb.' Con, like John, never touched anything.

The Boyles, whom I first met in the late 1970s, are a God-fearing Catholic family with no republican connections. When they got home around 8 o'clock that evening, Con rang an RUC police constable whom he knew from the constable's time in Dunloy and who was now a detective in Ballymoney RUC station a few miles away. Con told him it was something that ought to be looked into and said that if he would care to come to Dunloy, Con would take him to the exact spot. The detective

British troops deployed in Londonderry, 1969.

'Bloody Sunday', 1972. Father Edward Daly, with bloodstained handkerchief, escorts the dying Jack Duddy, shot by British paratroopers.

Peter. Former military
intelligence officer, 1972.

Lt-Gen. Sir Anthony Farrar-
Hockley. Commander Land Forces
Northern Ireland (1970-1).

Donegall Street, Belfast, minutes after the IRA bomb exploded in 1972,
killing seven people and injuring 150.

William 'Willie' Whitelaw, the first Northern Ireland Secretary (1972-4).

Roy Mason, Northern Ireland Secretary (1976-9), with British troops.

Lt-Col. Brian of the
Gloucestershire Regiment.

George of the
Gloucestershire Regiment.

Michael Oatley,
former MI6 officer.

IRA leader Francis Hughes. He was the 'Most Wanted Man' at the time of his arrest in 1978. He died on hunger strike in 1981.

John Boyle. He was shot dead by the SAS during a stake-out in Dunloy graveyard, 1978.

'Jim' as a member of 14 Intelligence Company, late 1970s.

The wreckage of the IRA's attack on the Parachute Regiment convoy at Warrenpoint, 1979. Eighteen soldiers died, the army's heaviest loss in a single day in the current conflict.

Prime Minister Margaret Thatcher visiting British soldiers in Northern Ireland.

Stuart of the Parachute Regiment, a survivor of Warrenpoint, in army quarters in Northern Ireland.

John Stalker, Deputy Chief Constable of Greater Manchester police, removed from his RUC inquiry, 1986.

Sir Colin Sampson, Chief Constable of West Yorkshire police who took over John Stalker's RUC inquiry, 1986.

The old German rifles, without ammunition, found in the hayshed where Michael Tighe was killed by an RUC anti-terrorist unit, 1982.

Wreckage of the police patrol car blown up by an IRA bomb on the Kinnego embankment, 1982. Three RUC officers died. The explosives had been stored in the hayshed and removed without the knowledge of the intelligence services.

The Grand Hotel, Brighton, bombed by the IRA during the Conservative
Party conference, 1984. Four members of the Conservative Party were killed.
Mrs Thatcher narrowly escaped death.

The British and Irish
Prime Ministers,
Margaret Thatcher
and Dr Garret
FitzGerald, sign the
Anglo-Irish Agreement
at Hillsborough Castle
in 1985.

Member of the IRA East Tyrone Brigade active service unit shot dead by the SAS at Loughgall, 1987.

'Frank' of the 'Det', early 1980s.

The cake baked for the SAS and the 'Det' after the SAS shot dead IRA man, William Price, at Ardboe, 1984.

above Brian Nelson. British army agent of the Force Research Unit (FRU).

left Solicitor Pat Finucane, who was gunned down by loyalists of the UFF at his home, 1989.

RUC Chief Constable, Sir Hugh Annesley (right) and John Stevens, Deputy Chief Constable of Cambridgeshire police, with the first Stevens Report, commissioned (1989) following allegations of collusion between loyalist paramilitaries and the security forces.

Aftermath of the IRA mortar attack on Downing Street, 1991. The mortars were fired from a van in Whitehall, which can be seen in flames in the photograph.

Peter Brooke, Northern Ireland Secretary (1989-92).

Prime Minister John Major (right) and Sir Patrick Mayhew, Northern Ireland Secretary (1993-7) at Hillsborough Castle.

Sir Kenneth Stowe, Permanent Under-Secretary of State Northern Ireland Office (1979-81).

Sir Robert Andrew, Permanent Under-Secretary of State Northern Ireland Office (1984-8).

Ian Burns, Deputy Under-Secretary of State Northern Ireland Office (1987-90)

Commander John Grieve, head of Scotland Yard's anti-terrorist squad at the scene of the Docklands bomb, February 1996.

Above: James McArdle, the 'triple thumbprint man', who drove the Docklands bomb to Barking on the outskirts of London.

Above left: An artist's impression of the lorry and trailer carrying the Docklands bomb.

Below left: The waste ground in Barking, where the lorry carrying the bomb was parked before the explosion, and where a copy of *Truck and Driver* magazine that provided the vital thumbprint clue was found.

David Trimble and Gerry Adams during the Good Friday Agreement negotiations, 1998.

British and Irish Prime Ministers, Tony Blair and Bertie Ahern, 1998.

Mo Mowlam, Northern Ireland Secretary (1997-9).

Senator George Mitchell.

The Northern Ireland Executive: (*clockwise from right*) David Trimble MP (UUP), First Minister; Seamus Mallon MP (SDLP), Deputy First Minister; Brid Rodgers (SDLP), Minister of Agriculture; Mark Durkan (SDLP), Minister of Finance; Dr Sean Farren (SDLP), Minister of Higher and Further Education; Sam Foster (UUP), Minister of the Environment; Sir Reg Empey (UUP), Minister of Enterprise, Trade and Investment; Michael McGimpsey (UUP), Minister of Culture; Bairbre de Brún (Sinn Fein), Minister of Health; Martin McGuinness MP (Sinn Fein), Minister of Education; John Semple, Head of Northern Ireland Civil Service.

Peter Mandelson, Northern Ireland Secretary (1999-2001).

Gerry Adams and Martin McGuinness on their historic first visit to No.10 Downing Street, 1997.

Gunner Robert Curtis. The first British soldier to be killed by the IRA (1972) in the current conflict.

Lance-Bombardier Stephen Restorick. To date (January 2001) the last British soldier to be killed by the IRA (1997) in the current conflict.

thanked him, declined the offer and said he would be in touch. For a
Catholic in a republican area to inform the police about a possible IRA
'hide' required considerable courage. 'There was no trouble around here at
the time and I didn't want any,' Con said. 'I didn't want to see any
policeman hurt so I thought this was the best thing to do.'

Con heard no further word from the policeman that night. He left home
the following morning about 9 a.m. to visit a neighbour in a farm about
half a mile from the graveyard. John had left home earlier that morning to
help his brother, Hugh, with the hay in the field close by the graveyard.
When Con arrived, the neighbour asked him if he had heard the shots.
Whilst the two men were talking, the neighbour's mother came out of the
house and told Con that his wife had just telephoned to tell him not to go
near the graveyard.

Con realized the message came from the police. But it was too late. John
was dead, shot three times by two members of a four-man SAS team who
were lying in wait in the graveyard, obviously waiting for the IRA to come
to retrieve the contents of the hide. Con went straight to the spot to find
Hugh lying face-down on the ground being guarded by a soldier with a
gun. Two other soldiers promptly stopped him. 'They said that the other
bastard was lying in there, dead. It had to be John. I wasn't allowed to
speak. I told them that I had warned the police about it but they told me to
"shut up", poked me with a gun and told me to keep quiet.'

It is impossible to know what made John return to the graveyard.
Perhaps it was out of curiosity to see if the 'hide' was still there. In an
unprecedented move, two of the four SAS men, Sergeant Alan Bohan and
Corporal Ron Temperley, were charged with the murder of John Boyle.
The court heard that they thought he was a terrorist returning to the 'hide'
which in fact contained a rifle. They said that Boyle removed the weapon
from under the headstone and turned towards them as if to shoot. Bohan
and Temperley said they thought their lives were in danger and fired three
shots, killing John instantly. They were less than twenty feet away. The
judge, the Lord Chief Justice, Lord Lowry, returned a verdict of not guilty
but described one of the soldiers as 'an untrustworthy witness, eager to
make unmeritorious points'[8] and described the operation as 'a badly
planned and bungled exercise'.[9] Despite the fact that Con Boyle had
done his civic duty at considerable risk to himself and his son, the family
never received any apology from the SAS, the army, or the RUC.
Although bitterness is an emotion foreign to the family, time has not
eased the loss. 'John's killing was a waste,' says Con. 'I could see no reason
why they couldn't have arrested him. It would have been easy. As time
went on and you watched what was happening around, the SAS didn't
arrest very many.'

The SAS were to kill one more person in 1978. This time it was in Derry at an IRA weapons 'hide' at 2 Maureen Avenue, an unoccupied house that was being renovated in the Brandywell area of the Bogside. The premises had been under surveillance by the 'Det' for some weeks, during which time it was established that some IRA equipment was being stored in one of the bedrooms in a wardrobe-type cupboard with a single latch lock. At this stage, it was not thought that weapons were inside. The house was then kept under close observation. When there were suspicions that the IRA was planning a 'hit' and the 'hide' would be involved, three SAS men secretly broke in well after midnight and took up position in the loft above the bedroom containing the 'wardrobe'. At 1 a.m. on 23 November they began 'eyes-on' surveillance on the 'hide' below them. Their orders were monitor all movement in and out of the house and to challenge and apprehend anyone seen handling weapons or explosives. Their instructions were to open fire only if necessary and then only in accordance with the Yellow Card.[10] With innocent workmen there during the day, the risk of compromise was great.

Just before 10 p.m. the following evening, two men entered the house and went into the bedroom. From their O.P. in the loft, the SAS heard 'dragging noises'. When the nocturnal visitors had left, the SAS team examined the wardrobe and found that it now contained 'illegal weapons and ammunition'.[11] The SAS did not challenge the two men as it was decided, again presumably on Special Branch information, that they were of lesser importance and not worth challenging as this would have 'blown' the carefully planned operation to catch one of the main 'players' who would be associated with the team chosen to carry out the 'hit'.

Around 9.30 p.m. on 24 November, by which time the SAS had been in place for about 44 hours, Patrick Duffy (50), a member of the IRA's Derry Brigade, entered the house. He was unarmed at the time.[12] He went into the bedroom and was shot dead by the SAS. At the inquest, the soldiers said that he had 'opened the wardrobe, leant inside and relocked it'. They then said they challenged Duffy with the warning, 'Don't move! Security Forces!' They then opened fire with their Sterling and Ingram sub-machine guns, hitting Duffy a dozen times. They said he reacted as if he was about to use a weapon and they feared their lives were in danger.

When the shooting happened, 'Jim' recollects being outside the house although he says he did not hear any shots and only became aware of them through the radio traffic. But whatever happened, he was convinced that the SAS 'would have worked within the rules of the Yellow Card'. In describing the complementary roles of 14 Intelligence Company and the

SAS, one 'Det' operator said, 'We lick 'em. They stick 'em.' That may have been the case in the bedroom of 2 Maureen Avenue.

The Bishop of Derry, Dr Edward Daly, who had been a crucial eye-witness on 'Bloody Sunday', was uncompromising in his criticism of the SAS and the policy he believed it was pursuing at the time. 'Members of the British Army here seem to be able to act outside the law, with immunity from the law,' he said. 'The shooting dead of a person merely because he enters a house or a place where illegally held guns or explosives are stored is quite unjustifiable. This policy gives soldiers the power to act as judge, jury and executioner.'[13] Bishop Daly also believed that 'shoot to kill' only encouraged more young people to join the IRA.

It was to be five more years before the SAS made another 'kill' in Northern Ireland. Clearly, lessons had been learned.

Chapter Nineteen

Double Disaster

27 August 1979

Towards the end of 1978, as 'Jim' and the 'Det' were monitoring the arms cache in the wardrobe in the unoccupied house in Derry, Brigadier James Glover of the army's Defence Intelligence Staff was preparing one of the most insightful and prescient papers on the IRA ever to emerge from the MOD. On completion it was entitled *Future Terrorist Trends*, marked 'Secret' and dated 2 November 1978. How it was leaked or lost and came into the public domain has never been convincingly established.[1] In it he wrote, 'The terrorists are already aware of their own vulnerability to Security Force intelligence operators [the 'Det'] and will increasingly seek to eliminate those involved.' In the previous eighteen months, the IRA had 'eliminated' two operators, Corporals Paul Harman and Alan Swift, and shot dead Corporal David 'Jay' Jones. It had also 'executed' 14 Intelligence Company's most publicly famous member, Captain Robert Nairac, the Grenadier Guard who was working in South Armagh as an SAS Liaison Officer (SASLO). Nairac, a Roman Catholic educated at Ampleforth College and Oxford, was a maverick (his hero was T. E. Lawrence, 'Lawrence of Arabia') and used to pose as a republican, singing rebel songs in the bars of 'Bandit Country'. Such bravado would have been contrary to all his 'Det' training. He sang his last song on Saturday evening, 14 May 1977, at the Three Steps Inn at Drumintee, a few miles from the border, and was never seen by his colleagues again. Astonishingly and against all 'Det' custom and practice, he had no back-up partner with him. Nairac had aroused suspicion, was abducted by the IRA after a struggle, taken across the border, interrogated and shot. It is said he didn't give his interrogators a scrap of information. His body was never found and is believed to have been disposed of in an animal feed processing plant. Captain Nairac was awarded a posthumous George Cross. In the same eighteen month period, the 'Det' had played its part both directly and probably indirectly in 'eliminating' one member of the INLA, Colm McNutt, and five IRA men, Paul Duffy, Denis Heaney, Denis Brown, William Mailey and James Mulvenna. The score card for that year and a half's deadly undercover war was 'Brits' 6 – IRA 4. Three weeks after Glover's report was finished, Patrick Duffy was shot dead by the SAS near the wardrobe, bringing the 'score' of the 'Brits' to seven.

But Glover's observation was not the reason for the significance of his report. Its purpose was to review the state of the IRA as the end of the first decade of hostilities approached. Glover knew that the widely held perception of the enemy did not match the reality. (One civil servant of the time confessed to me that he used to think the IRA were simply 'petty criminals running black taxis' and said he felt guilty for not taking them more seriously.) Glover thought it was time that his superiors and presumably their political masters woke up to the fact and recognized that if the IRA's strategy was to fight 'the long war', the 'Brits' had to dig in for it too. Glover predicated his report on looking at least five years ahead. He recognized that the IRA had changed and the tactical and strategic response of the 'Brits' would have to be modified accordingly.

The main change in the IRA was structural. As its leadership had admitted a year earlier in the GHQ report seized after Seamus Twomey's arrest, Castlereagh was 'breaking Volunteers' and 'contributing to our defeat': therefore there was an urgent need for 'reorganisation and remotivation and the building of a new Irish Republican Army'. The basis of the reorganization to equip the 'new' IRA for 'long-term armed struggle' was to be 'cells' of four Volunteers.[2] This cellular structure would replace the old ORBAT (Order of Battle) of Brigades, Battalions and Companies which had been so deeply penetrated by British intelligence. In theory, members of each cell would know the identity of each other but not of those outside it. Glover (later General Sir James) told me he had no doubt where the impetus for change came from in preparation for a campaign of attrition that the IRA called the 'long war'.

It was really Gerry Adams, and his cohort Ivor Bell, languishing in the Maze Prison who set out to do a really deep study of the classic terrorist movement and it was they between them who drew up a new blueprint for the IRA. The new cellular structure demanded far less people, was more professional, required a lower level of popular support and was more difficult to penetrate. Rather like the Chinese, the IRA had a totally different sense of timing to that which we had had. We had tended not unnaturally to look one or two years ahead and the IRA at this stage were preparing to look five to ten years ahead.

Controversially, in his report Glover challenged the prevalent perception of the enemy.

> Our evidence of the calibre of rank-and-file terrorists does not support the view that they are merely mindless hooligans drawn from the unemployed and unemployable. PIRA [the Provisional IRA] now trains and uses its members with some care. The Active Service Units (ASUs) are for the most part manned by terrorists tempered by up to ten years of operational experience . . . the expertise of the ASUs will grow and they will continue to be PIRA's prime offensive arm . . . PIRA . . . will still be able to attract enough people with leadership talent, good education and manual skills to enhance their all-round professionalism.[3]

Glover believed that the IRA was no longer an almost exclusively working-class organization based on the depressed housing estates of Belfast and Derry but one that had now drawn well-educated recruits from the middle classes attracted by the ideology of republicanism. He described it as a 'sea change in the IRA'. As a result the Republican Movement now had a 'far stronger intellectual and professional base' which posed an even greater long-term threat for the 'Brits'. He left the army's top brass in no doubt that the IRA had not only a sufficient number of high-calibre and well-motivated recruits available to prosecute its 'long war' but the necessary weaponry and technical expertise to do so. 'PIRA strategy', he wrote, 'is based on the premise that a campaign of attrition, with its attendant costs in both lives and money, will eventually persuade HMG to withdraw from Northern Ireland.' Hitherto, as Glover recognized, the IRA had not mounted sustained attacks on prominent figures, but he warned that this was now likely to change, with PIRA staging 'a few spectacular attacks to indicate that their normal lower posture stems from restraint rather than weakness'.

Future Terrorist Trends was greeted with less than universal enthusiasm within the MOD. 'It didn't find all that much favour,' he told me. 'Perhaps underneath it all, everyone realized that this was the likely way in which things were going to go but at the time it hadn't really been paraded in front of them in such an overt, and, I hope, persuasive way.'

Glover's warning about IRA 'spectaculars' was grimly prophetic although not even he could have anticipated how cataclysmic they were to be. On one day the following summer, 27 August 1979, the IRA struck two devastating blows against the 'Brits' in the space of a few hours. I remember the day vividly, just as millions will never forget where they were when they heard that John F. Kennedy had been shot. I was at home writing *Beating the*

Terrorists? when I turned on the radio and heard that Earl Mountbatten, the Queen's cousin and the last Viceroy who oversaw the ending of British rule in India, had been blown up by the IRA at his holiday home at Mullaghmore, County Sligo, in the Irish Republic. The IRA had planted a 50-lb bomb under the deck of his fishing boat, *Shadow V*, which was detonated from the shore by radio control just after the boat had put to sea. Three others died with him: his fourteen-year-old grandson, Nicholas Knatchbull; his daughter's mother-in-law, 82-year-old Lady Brabourne, and fifteen-year-old Paul Maxwell from Enniskillen, who was working with the boat as a summer job. The 79-year-old Earl Mountbatten, who had spent holidays in the pretty coastal village every summer for the past thirty years, had sought advice from the Cabinet Office in the early seventies about his safety. The Foreign Office (presumably MI6), the Home Office (presumably MI5) and the MOD (presumably Defence Intelligence) were all consulted and Mountbatten was told in a memo that, although no visit to Ireland could be regarded as risk-free, nevertheless 'all feel that the risk is one that can reasonably be taken'.[4]

Brigadier Glover was in a helicopter flying from Derry through the mists to Army Headquarters at Lisburn when the Mullaghmore bomb went off. When he heard the news he was shocked. He had warned of high-profile targets and of the IRA's growing sophistication with remote-control bombs but even that had not prepared him for this. He then heard news that doubled his astonishment. Hours after Mullaghmore there had been two massive explosions near Warrenpoint, close to the border with the Republic. Although Glover would not have known the details at the time, the explosions left eighteen soldiers dead, sixteen of them members of the 2nd Battalion, The Parachute Regiment. It was the Parachute Regiment's biggest loss since Arnhem in World War Two.

The ambush was carefully planned and there was no intelligence to alert the army or Special Branch to it. A convoy of paratroopers were driving from their base at Ballykinler in County Down to relieve the Queen's Own Highlanders in Newry who were about to return home after their tour of duty. The convoy consisted of two four-ton trucks, preceded by a Land-rover. One of the passengers in the Land-rover was Stuart, a signaller. He had initially intended to travel in one of the trucks but because the radio signals came and went along the route to Newry, he was told he was needed in the lead vehicle. Stuart remembers it being a stunningly beautiful day as they drove along the dual carriageway alongside Carlingford Lough, the stretch of water that marks the border between Northern Ireland and the Republic. 'It was just lovely,' he told me, 'and it made me think, you know, isn't it a shame that there's so much hatred and so many nasty things going on in this country when it's got so much to offer.' Stuart's Land-rover passed a hay lorry parked in a lay-by and 'didn't give it a second thought'. The first truck drove past it and, just as the second truck was doing the same, there was a huge explosion and the hay lorry went up in the air. Stuart watched in horror as the second truck was thrown 100 feet in the air and then landed on the central reservation of the dual carriageway. Eight hundred pounds of explosives had been concealed amongst the bales of straw.

> The hay lorry and the second truck just disappeared together. There was smoke, debris and straw all over the place. We immediately turned round our Land-rover and went back to the seat of the explosion to render what assistance we could. There were bodies and bits of bodies everywhere and there was ammunition exploding in some people's pouches. We were putting some people out who were on fire and we were just checking to see if anybody was alive. By some miracle, two of the soldiers were just still alive but the other six were killed. I never felt an anger like it. It just didn't seem fair that a bunch of really good mates, each one a thoroughly professional soldier, should die in such a way in such a cowardly attack. They were just helpless. They were just sat in a truck.

The rest of the convoy ran for cover as their training had taught them to do and took shelter by the Gate Lodge of the nearby Narrow Water Castle. As they did so, they came under fire from the IRA unit on the other side of Carlingford Lough from where the bomb had been detonated. The Paras returned fire and in the process killed an English tourist, Michael Hudson (29), who was bird-watching on an island opposite the castle.[5]

What the soldiers did not know was that the IRA had planted a second 800-lb bomb by the Gate Lodge, anticipating that the soldiers would make the practised moves that they did. But in order to create the maximum carnage, the IRA were waiting until reinforcements arrived. Immediately the first bomb had gone off, the Paras had radioed the Queen's Own Highlanders in Newry for help and were now expecting the arrival of a QRF with medical assistance. Roughly twenty minutes later, a Gazelle helicopter landed in a field behind the Gate Lodge. The rest of the QRF arrived in army vehicles. Casualties from the first bomb were loaded on board the Gazelle and, as it was taking off, a second explosion shattered the afternoon sunshine, killing twelve more soldiers, including the commanding officer of the Queen's Own Highlanders, Lieutenant-Colonel David Blair (40), and his wireless operator, Lance-Corporal Victor McCleod (24).

In the space of barely half an hour, the IRA had killed eighteen soldiers, sixteen of them members of the Parachute Regiment. It was the army's biggest loss of life in a single day in the whole of the conflict. Stuart and

Glover both agreed on the significance of what became known as 'Warrenpoint'. 'From the IRA's point of view it was the most successful operation they've ever carried out,' said Stuart, 'and what better target from their point of view than the Parachute Regiment. The IRA would see this as revenge for Bloody Sunday.' To Glover, his prophecy about an IRA 'spectacular' had come doubly true. 'It was arguably, I think, the most successful and certainly one of the best planned IRA attacks of the whole campaign,' he told me. 'It was almost inevitable that at some stage they were going to succeed because we'd failed to interdict them. So the event itself was not a surprise but the nature of it was. It was ghastly.'

No one was ever convicted for Warrenpoint. From intelligence reports, the army had a good idea who the bombers were but convictions need evidence or witnesses and both were in short supply. I asked Stuart if he and his colleagues who survived knew who the bombers were. He said they had absolutely no doubt. One of the main suspects was Brendan Burns, who remained a highly active member of the South Armagh IRA for most of the next decade. He had originally been stopped by the Gardai when he was driving away from the scene with another man on a motor bike but was released when there was no evidence against him. 'He was a very capable bomber and probably responsible for the death of quite a large number of soldiers in South Armagh,' said Stuart. But the activities of one of the IRA's top bombers came to a swift end on 29 February 1988, when Brendan Burns (30) was finally blown up by his own bomb which detonated prematurely when he was moving it just outside Crossmaglen. The Paras were ecstatic when they heard the news.

The army believed that, had it been allowed to fly its helicopters across the border in hot pursuit of the bombers (given that they remained in place for some time after the first explosion), it would probably have caught them. But 'hot pursuit' was not permitted by an Irish Government that in 1977 had put eight SAS men on trial for merely 'straying' across it. Downing Street was furious that it appeared to have had such scant co-operation from its counterparts in Dublin and, not least, from the Irish police.

By this time Number Ten had a new occupant, Margaret Thatcher, who was to become the IRA's most implacable enemy. Her triumph in the General Election of 3 May 1979 had been overshadowed by the death of the Conservatives' Shadow Northern Ireland Secretary, Airey Neave, at the opening of the election campaign. He was one of Mrs Thatcher's closest personal friends and had organized her successful campaign for the Conservative Party leadership. He had been driving out of the House of Commons underground car park on 30 March when an INLA bomb, triggered by a mercury tilt switch, exploded under his car as it drove over a ramp. He died almost instantly. In opposition, he had argued for giving the army a freer hand, increasing the use of the SAS and giving terrorists longer prison sentences.

Mrs Thatcher was at Chequers when she heard about Mountbatten and Warrenpoint. She was shattered by the news. 'Words are always inadequate to condemn this kind of outrage,' she wrote. 'I decided immediately I must go to Northern Ireland to show the army, police and civilians that I understood the scale of the tragedy and to demonstrate our determination to resist terrorism.' Mrs Thatcher flew to Northern Ireland, visited the casualties in hospital and was helicoptered to the army's fortress in Crossmaglen to show solidarity with those she regarded as her 'boys'. Her presence had an electrifying effect on the army whose morale had every reason to be rock-bottom after the disaster. The officer who took over from Lieutenant-Colonel David Blair, who was killed at Warrenpoint, was one of those who met her in Crossmaglen.

> She came in out of the sky in her helicopter with blue dresses and coats and scarves flapping in every direction. She really was like a blue tornado and it was good to see her. It was just marvellous the way she arrived and greeted everybody and took a real interest in what was going on. She gave us some very strong words of encouragement and explained in no uncertain terms how determined she was to defeat terrorism as best she possibly could.

The NIO's Permanent Under Secretary, Sir Brian Cubbon, was also present at one of the briefings given to the Prime Minister and remembers a dramatic gesture made by one of the senior officers.

> It was the first time that I had met Mrs Thatcher and I was very impressed with the patient way in which she received the briefing about what had happened. I think it was a Brigadier who made quite a dramatic presentation about Warrenpoint. The culmination of it was to throw down on the floor of the conference room the epaulets of the officer who had been killed at Warrenpoint, saying that was all that was left of him. Again I was impressed with her. She took that in her stride.

Mrs Thatcher visited both the police and the army and their respective commanders in the province, Sir Kenneth Newman and the GOC, Lieutenant-General Sir Timothy Creasey. Creasey and Newman did not see eye to eye and the tangible friction between them filtered down to the middle and lower ranks in each organization with the result that – perhaps with the notable exception of Special Branch and the 'Det' – no love was lost between them. Although Creasey had little choice other than to go along with police primacy, he embraced it less than whole-heartedly. 'He had a simple view of the problem,' one of those who dealt with him told me. 'He divided the problem into the "good guys" and "bad guys". He believed the "good guys" should be given medals and the "bad guys" put up against a wall and shot.' Creasey, who had commanded the Sultan of Oman's forces, was a man of action who, as GOC, did not subscribe to the view that the IRA could *not* be beaten. He was enthusiastic about the use of the SAS and it was no coincidence that the Regiment became so active whilst he was GOC. He is said to have 'erupted' when the eight SAS troopers were arrested for crossing the border. Creasey's strong views were shared by some of his senior officers. A civil servant told me how he had stood next to one of Creasey's commanders, who was looking at the 'Rogues' Gallery' (a photomontage of IRA 'players'). 'Give me the word and I'll take them out,' the official told me he said.

In contrast, Newman was a cerebral Chief Constable, dedicated to systems and structures and the modernization of the RUC, convinced that the police, not the army, would finally turn the conflict around. The clashes between Creasey and Newman were bound to happen. Sir John Hermon, who succeded Sir Kenneth as Chief Constable in 1980, described relations between the two as 'strained'.[6] That was probably putting it euphemistically. According to one of the civil servants at Stormont, Creasey was 'unbearable', so much so that he, although a lower-ranking official, had to deal with the GOC as his more senior colleague could not. When Mrs Thatcher visited the two camps, who were supposed to be fighting the same enemy rather than each other, each told the Prime Minister its side of the story. Sir Kenneth Stowe, who succeeded Sir Brian Cubbon as Permanent Under Secretary shortly after Warrenpoint, was amazed at the bad blood he found between the two arms of the security forces when he first went over to Northern Ireland. But he understood what caused it.

> I think the basis of their mutual difficulty was the criminalization policy which meant that every crime, every murder, every shooting had to be addressed as a crime with the police in the lead. It could not be addressed as a terrorist operation which required a counter-terrorist response [by the army]. Another element was that the intelligence-gathering of the RUC and of the army was not, I suspect, effectively shared. That is my suspicion but I think it's probably well-founded.

In what sense?

They weren't talking to each other when they should have been talking to each other. That was the problem.

Mrs Thatcher and her advisers decided that something had to be done. The army wanted the Government to appoint a military supremo, as General Templer had been in Malaya, to co-ordinate the drive against the IRA but this was rejected out of hand as it would have meant turning back the clock, stabbing police primacy in the back and giving the army the upper hand once again. A compromise was reached and probably brokered by Sir Frank Cooper who was now Permanent Under Secretary (the senior civil servant) at the Ministry of Defence. It was decided that there should be a supremo but he should not be a military man. Cooper said he probably had a dozen potential names in his pocket and, in the end, Sir Maurice Oldfield, the head of MI6 from 1965 to 1977, came out on top. At the time, Sir Maurice, who is thought to have been the model for John Le Carré's George Smiley, was a fellow of All Souls College, Oxford. He was consequently plucked from the dreaming spires and thrust into the strife-torn world of Northern Ireland as its Chief Intelligence Co-ordinator. His office was a few yards away from Sir Kenneth Stowe's and the two men had regular discussions. 'He was supposed to ensure that the combined resources of intelligence-gathering of the police and of the army and their subsequent operations were effectively integrated,' Sir Kenneth said. 'He was totally committed to engaging with the senior people on both sides and actively engaged in trying to get them to work together and working out systems that would ensure greater, more effective collaboration than had always been achieved in the past.'

When I asked Sir Kenneth what Sir Maurice had achieved, he said it was 'difficult to say' beyond getting the police and the army to work together better, which was his primary task. To Sir James Glover, Oldfield was 'a referee, a catalyst, a Solomon who got us together to produce a solution based on logic rather than emotion'.[7] But to Sir John Hermon, who became the RUC Chief Constable on 1 January 1980, he was superfluous. 'I must say, I paid scant attention to him,' Sir John told me. 'Quite frankly, I didn't consider his role was necessary or that it contributed very much. He very quickly became superficial. Not because of his inabilities or anything else, but because he wasn't needed.'[8] Hermon felt this way not least because he got on very well with Creasey's successor as GOC, Lieutenant-General Sir Richard Lawson. The two were as close together as their predecessors had been far apart.

But the shadow of Warrenpoint that Oldfield had been recruited to dispel was soon eclipsed by a crisis that was to have even more lasting repercussions for the 'Brits': the Hunger Strike.

Chapter Twenty

The Iron Lady and the Iron Men

March 1976–October 1981

There were two great watersheds for the 'Brits' during the thirty-year 'war'. One was 'Bloody Sunday' in 1972, the other was the IRA hunger strike of 1981. Both had profound repercussions for British policy and the course of the conflict. In *Future Terrorist Trends* Brigadier Glover had warned that 'an isolated incident such as "Bloody Sunday" can radically alter support for violence'. Like so much of his report, that too was prophetic.

The origins of the hunger strike lay in Merlyn Rees's decision to abolish special category status for all prisoners convicted of terrorist offences committed after 1 March 1976 and send them to the newly constructed H Blocks of the Maze prison where they would be locked up in cells like common criminals. The first IRA prisoner to be convicted under the new regime was a nineteen-year-old IRA man from West Belfast called Kieran Nugent who had been arrested in May 1976 and found guilty of possessing weapons and hijacking a car. When he entered the Maze, he was ordered to put on a prison uniform and refused on the grounds that he was not a criminal but a political prisoner. Nugent stayed unclothed for his first day in the H Blocks but on the second day prison officers gave him a blanket so he would not have to walk round the exercise yard naked. 'If they want me to wear a uniform,' he said, 'they'll have to nail it to my back.' He spent the rest of his three-year sentence wearing the blanket.[1] In the ensuing weeks and months, other IRA prisoners followed his example, forming the nucleus of what became known as the 'blanket' protest. One of those who came close on Nugent's heels was Gerard Hodgkins who was gaoled in December 1976 for a firearm and bombing offence as well as IRA membership. He told me what happened when he entered the prison.

The prison officer said, 'Right, you're here to do your time. You can do it the hard way or the easy way. If you take my advice, you'll get

them uniforms on you now. If not, strip.' So you stripped there and
then whilst you were being ridiculed and jeered at by the screws
[prison officers].[2]

In those early days, the 'blanket' protest attracted no great attention outside
republican ranks, as Hodgkins was the first to admit. The handful of
'blanket men', as they became known, felt a profound sense of isolation.
Nevertheless, Hodgkins was convinced that the prisoners would win and
do so very quickly. 'Believe it or not, you were hoping against hope that
we'd get political status,' he said. 'Being honest about it, within a few
months, we really believed we'd get it.'[3] For years it was a vain hope. The
prisoners had little else to keep them going until, over the months and
years, the handful became hundreds. Solidarity, shared hardship and
deprivation forged a bond that became ever stronger in the face of the
'Brit' enemy. By 1978 there were nearly 300 'blanket men' – or 'non-
conforming prisoners' as the authorities called them – in the H Blocks of
the Maze. Nevertheless, despite the numbers and the attempts of their
supporters outside to generate sympathy for the prisoners, the issue failed to
take off. The La Mon inferno in February 1978 had reinforced Roy
Mason's determination not to make any concessions. He made it clear that
there would be 'no change in our policy of treating jailed terrorists as
anything but common criminals. No amnesty. No concessions to prisoners.' To grant special category status once more would, he said, 'undermine
our effort to defeat the IRA and the loyalist gangs'.[4]

But the situation was about to change, due to the arrival in the H Blocks
of the former commander of the IRA's Belfast Brigade, Brendan Hughes.
Originally Hughes had been serving his sentence in the compounds
following his arrest at Myrtlefield Park in 1974, but three years later he
was involved in a fracas with a prison officer that led to a five-year sentence
for assault. As the offence was committed after 1 March 1976, Hughes was
despatched to the H Blocks where he was given a hero's welcome by his
comrades. Naturally, he refused to wear prison uniform. 'It didn't matter
whether it had arrows on it or Mickey Mouse,' he told me, 'it was still the
prison uniform.'[5] Hughes promptly became the IRA prisoners' Officer
Commanding (OC) and set about trying to turn the tables on the 'Brits'
and the 'screws', who were seen as their representatives on the wings.
Initially, Hughes thought that the prisoners should abandon the blanket
protest and should set about sabotaging the prison system from within. His
suggestion was howled down by the 'blanket men' who saw it as
capitulation. The prisoners' new OC then had to think again, and in
March 1978 the so-called 'dirty' protest was born (republicans insisted on
calling it the 'no-wash' protest on the grounds that it sounded more

dignified). Again, as with the 'blanket' protest, it is difficult to say to what extent it was planned or was simply a reaction to circumstances and events. The tension between the prisoners and their guards had almost reached breaking point because the IRA had started to kill prison officers to show solidarity with their comrades inside and to retaliate for the brutality the prisoners said they repeatedly suffered at the hands of the 'screws'. By the start of the 'dirty' protest, four prison officers had been shot dead. Prisoners complained that, whenever they left their cells to wash, they were beaten and humiliated, and so they refused to leave their cells to wash and slop out their chamber pots. Hughes then ordered them to daub their excreta on the walls to get rid of it. 'Other people were suggesting that we smear excreta on ourselves,' he told me, 'but it was a step I wasn't prepared to take.' Even smearing it on the walls was bad enough, as Gerard Hodgkins told me.

> I just smeared it on the wall. I ripped off a lump of the mattress to do
> it with. You were going against your whole socialization of how you
> had been brought up. You were going against everything you'd ever
> learned about basic hygiene and manners and stuff like that. I lived
> like this from 1978 to 1981 . . . You were literally waking up in the
> morning and there were maggots in the bed with you. It just gets to
> the stage where you just brush them off . . . I think the human spirit
> can become accustomed to any environment.[6]

Mason, who was fully aware of the Provisionals' propaganda expertise after the experience of Castlereagh, realized that they now had a potent weapon. 'From their point of view, it was a brilliant stroke,' he admitted. 'Now in their desperation to be noticed, they'd hit the jackpot and at last started to believe that they might actually win.'[7] Suddenly, the issue caught fire. The media had never been particularly interested in men wrapped in blankets but cells covered in shit was a different matter. As Mason admitted, the images of Christ-like figures with long hair and even longer beards were undeniably powerful. 'But despite the adverse publicity, I couldn't give way,' he said. 'To do so would give the IRA its biggest victory in years. It would appal the law-abiding majority in Northern Ireland. It would dismay the security forces. It would mean the abandonment of the policy of police primacy and the rule of law. It would in the end lead to more death and misery.'[8] The Secretary of State's counter-offensive was statistical: he pointed out that of the 300 prisoners fouling their cells, 74 had been convicted of murder or attempted murder, 80 of firearms offences and 82 of crimes involving explosives.[9] But four months into the protest, he realized that what he had thought containable (though embarrassing) was now almost beyond control, following a visit to the H Blocks on 31 July 1978 by the Roman Catholic Primate of All Ireland, Cardinal Tomas O'Fiaich. O'Fiaich met the prisoners, saw their conditions and was horrified. When he left the Maze, he issued a statement that made Government Ministers hold their heads in a mixture of anger and despair.

> One would hardly allow an animal to remain in such conditions, let alone a human being. The nearest approach to it I have seen was the spectacle of hundreds of homeless people living in sewer pipes in the slums of Calcutta. The stench and filth in some cells, with the remains of rotten food and human excreta scattered around the walls, was absolutely unbelievable . . . I was unable to speak for fear of vomiting.[10]

Mason was shell-shocked and furious. 'He seemed to be undermining the legitimacy of our entire struggle against terrorism,' he said. 'In fact his words could have been written by Sinn Fein. I was appalled that such a prominent churchman could appear so indulgent towards gangsters who had caused such pain to so many innocent people over the years, including members of his own flock.'[11]

The 'dirty' protest dragged on with neither side prepared to move lest it be interpreted as a sign of weakness. Mason, true to his nature and word, made no concessions and left office in May 1979 when Mrs Thatcher and the Conservative Government inherited the problem. Like Roy Mason, she saw the protest in simple black and white terms. 'They were keen to establish . . . that their crimes were "political", thus giving the perpetrators a kind of respectability, even nobility. This we could not allow,' she wrote.[12] Inside the stinking cells, morale was sky-high due to the slaughter being inflicted on the 'Brits' by their comrades outside. It was 'us hitting back at what they were doing to us,' said Brendan Hughes. 'Certainly there was nobody going to cry over Mountbatten or the soldiers getting killed.'[13] But the assassination of Lord Mountbatten and the carnage at Warrenpoint were hardly likely to make the new Prime Minister any more amenable to the prisoners' demands for 'political' status, and by the beginning of 1980 the prisoners were starting to get anxious at the lack of any breakthrough and issued a set of Five Demands in the hope of convincing the world that their claims were not unreasonable:

1 The right not to wear prison uniform.
2 The right not to do prison work.
3 The right to associate freely with other prisoners.

4 The right to a weekly visit, letter and parcel and the right to organize educational and recreational pursuits.

5 Full restoration of remission lost through the protest.[14]

Tactically, the purpose of the 'Five Demands' was to create a broader base of support: it allowed people to feel they were in favour of the prisoners' right to live in civilized conditions without necessarily being in favour of the IRA. It was a subtle but fundamental change in presentation, liberating support from those who would normally have withheld it in fear of appearing pro-IRA (to this end, the words 'political status' were deliberately kept out of the document). Although Mrs Thatcher pointed out that conditions in the Maze were among the best in any prison anywhere, this had little effect. In Autumn 1980, after all attempts at mediation had failed, the prisoners decided to use their weapon of last resort, the hunger strike. They chose to do so despite the opposition of the IRA leadership outside the gaol who feared that a hunger strike would dilute the 'armed struggle' and divert resources from it. Perhaps even more significantly, they also believed that the hunger strikers would be unlikely to win. In the end, the Army Council had to go along with it since to have forbidden it in the face of the prisoners' determination to go ahead would have risked splitting the Republican Movement. The notion that the Army Council manipulated the hunger strike and encouraged the prisoners to put their lives on the line is simply not true.

By now there were around 500 prisoners protesting. Hughes asked for volunteers and 170 came forward. In the end, seven were chosen who represented geographically the whole of Northern Ireland. Hughes himself, as the prisoners' OC, was to lead it and represent Belfast. Joining him were Tommy McKearney from Tyrone, Raymond McCartney from Derry City, Leo Green from Lurgan, Thomas McFeeley from County Derry and Sean McKenna (kidnapped from over the border by the SAS) from South Armagh. The seventh person was John Nixon, the Irish National Liberation Army (INLA) OC in the H Blocks, one of 34 INLA prisoners who were also on the protest. Nixon's place as OC was taken by Patsy O'Hara from Derry.[15] Hughes's place as the Provisionals' OC was taken by Bobby Sands.

It had been decided that all seven prisoners should start their hunger strike together which meant it was only as strong as its weakest link. This proved to be a mistake because all prisoners would approach death at roughly the same time which meant that the 'Brits' only had to stand firm for a relatively short period of time. The prisoners' other mistake was to underestimate their opponent. 'If we had known anything about Thatcher and her personality, perhaps we mayn't have embarked on the hunger strike at that stage,' Hughes admitted.[16] The prisoners' ignorance of the character of the new Prime Minister was the result of not having read a newspaper, seen a television or heard a radio since the protest began. The only news they received was from their families when they came on visits, for which the prisoners agreed to put on prison clothes. Mrs Thatcher had no illusions about the real purpose of the 'Five Demands'.

> The IRA and the prisoners were determined to gain control of the prison and had a well-thought-out strategy for doing this by whittling away at the prison regime. The purpose of the privileges they claimed was not to improve prisoners' conditions but to take power away from the prison authorities . . . The IRA were pursuing with calculated ruthlessness a psychological war alongside their campaign of violence: they had to be resisted at both levels.[17]

The fast to the death began on 27 October 1980. In the days running up to the start date, the Government had tried to reach a compromise by announcing that it was scrapping prison uniform in favour of 'civilian-type' clothing but this was not enough for the prisoners. The Government had granted only half a demand. There were four and half others still to be met. Again, Mrs Thatcher made it clear that the Government would not give in. 'There can be no political justification for murder,' she said. 'The Government will never concede political status to the hunger strikers or to any others convicted of criminal offences in the province.'[18] Twelve days into the hunger strike, the seven prisoners were moved to a separate part of the H Blocks which had previously been set aside as a hospital wing in case an epidemic broke out from the filth in the cells. Priests and lawyers now became the sole intermediaries, most notably Father Brendan Meagher, a priest from Dundalk, who was to become the main mediator between the prisoners and the Northern Ireland Office. His code-name was 'the Angel'. The NIO was in a quandary as to what more it could do without appearing to bend to the prisoners' will. Its Permanent Under Secretary, Sir Kenneth Stowe, knew he did not have many options.

> My reaction was, I suspect, the same as everybody else's, what do we do now? One knew that forced-feeding was out, therefore, if the hunger strike continued, these people would die. Then we would have more martyrs, and Northern Ireland is not a place to grow martyrs if you can avoid it. Therefore we were very anxious to try to find some way of enabling the hunger strikers to get off the hook.

Mrs Thatcher was equally opposed to forced-feeding, which she described as 'a degrading and dangerous practice which I could not support'.[19]

The NIO set up its own emergency hunger strike committee consisting of Sir Kenneth; the GOC; the Chief Constable; and Humphrey Atkins, the Conservative Secretary of State who had succeeded Roy Mason. 'There was a continuous discussion taking place about how we can find a way out of this,' Sir Kenneth recalled. 'We spent many hours just kicking this around, asking, How can we find a solution? We were all aware that if it went on, there would be new martyrs and new killings to avenge the martyrs. So the stakes were very high. We began to explore whether the rules regarding prison dress could, in any way, be adapted in a UK context so that some of the steam could be taken out of this issue.'

Then, at a crucial moment, with some of the hunger strikers now in a critical condition, a *deus ex machina* emerged in the person of Michael Oatley, the MI6 officer who had kept his 'bamboo pipe' in working order since he had helped negotiate the IRA 'truce' in 1975, despite Roy Mason's forbidding undercover negotiations and any contact, direct or indirect, with the IRA by any British official following the resumption of violence. Oatley had decided to ignore these instructions. Without seeking permission or advising either his own Service or the NIO, he remained in touch with his friend in Derry, the Contact, and agreed with him that the IRA's leadership should be told that a secret channel of communication to the British Government, represented by himself, remained in place for use when needed. This situation was maintained and tested from 1975 to 1991, during which time Oatley became known to the IRA as the 'Mountain Climber'.

> This was a personal decision. I merely allowed the situation to develop over the next year or two where some members of the Provisional IRA leadership were aware that the 'pipe' was still there and that I was at the other end of it. From my own point of view I think that people on the IRA side thought I had come out of it as a reasonably reliable person with whom they could deal and I, for my part, had been quite clearly convinced that people on the other side were able to keep secrets. So I didn't think I was running any serious risk politically for the Government in letting the IRA know that there was still a point of contact if they should ever need it and it would operate wherever I happened to be in the world.

Oatley knew he was taking a risk: had Roy Mason found out that Oatley's 'pipe' was still 'live', he would have been 'severely reprimanded'. Ironically, the IRA leadership, as well as the British Government, wanted to find a way out, not least because there was growing pressure from the nationalist community to do so. In Derry, the Contact was well aware of the mood and, as crisis point approached, with Sean McKenna now close to death, he activated Oatley's 'pipe' and rang him in the middle of the night, as was his wont, suggesting that an acceptable compromise could be worked out, given the IRA's desire to resolve the impasse. 'We spent two or three hours discussing it in veiled language over the phone,' Oatley said. 'It seemed that one might be able to develop a formula with, no doubt, some ambiguities in it, which would be a gesture by the British Government to the demands of the hunger strikers.'

The following morning, 18 December, Oatley went to see Sir Kenneth Stowe at the Northern Ireland Office in London, which had already been considering ways of amending the prison regime. Sir Kenneth met Oatley in his room at about 9 a.m. and remembers Oatley explaining the IRA's position. 'It was, in effect, "Is there a way out, is there something that can be done?" At which point our thoughts about adapting the prison regime in order to find an escape hatch for the hunger strikers began to become highly relevant and we then started talking to see whether we could achieve something along those lines.' During their discussion Stowe remembers Oatley getting the Contact on the telephone to make sure that the compromise they were working on would be acceptable to the IRA and the prisoners. 'Michael Oatley was able to discuss this, standing beside me, with his Contact in Northern Ireland, and through that process the arrangement was put in place.' Oatley and Stowe then produced a revised version of the prison rules which Sir Kenneth described as 'a face-saving formula', now satisfied that it would be acceptable. Oatley described it as 'fairly open-ended and in some ways ambiguous', covering 'parcels and visits and clothing and so forth' without being too specific in any area. Ambiguity had been one of the notable features of the phrase 'structures of disengagement' which the British had used to entice the IRA into the 'truce' of 1975. I asked him if the formula allowed prisoners to wear their own clothes since that was the issue that lay at the heart of the 'blanket' and 'dirty' protests and the hunger strike. He said he could not quite remember but thought 'it left that sort of question rather open'. Stowe then had discussions with Ministers without Oatley being present 'in a few very crowded hours', since he could not move without their approval. Nor, even more crucially, could he move without Mrs Thatcher's. The Prime Minister, whose Principal Private Secretary Sir Kenneth had been, was consulted and gave her approval.

It was agreed that the formula would be conveyed to the IRA leadership and the hunger strikers themselves via Oatley and their intermediary Father Meagher, and not through the official prison channels. Had it gone the formal route, the Government's backstage negotiations would almost certainly have been leaked, destroying both the Government's credibility and the initiative to end the hunger strike, which was approaching its fifty-third day with Sean McKenna ever closer to death, Stowe knew that 'We had to act speedily if we were going to resolve this situation before we had a martyr.'

With Prime Ministerial approval, Stowe told Oatley to use his NIO official car and get the document to Northern Ireland before it was too late. Oatley was then driven to Heathrow at high speed along the hard shoulder of the M4 motorway.

Oatley met Father Meagher at Belfast's Aldergrove airport in the evening. The Arrivals area was already empty and a bizarre situation developed with the arrival of several Special Branch officers who had suspected that something was afoot, tailing Father Meagher. There were probably also a few IRA men around to make sure they were not being taken for a ride by the 'Brits'. The formalities were kept to a bare minimum. Oatley gave the document to Father Meagher as arranged and left the airport. The priest first took the document to representatives of the IRA leadership convened at a safe house on the Falls Road. They were dismayed at what they read. In their eyes the document was too vague and gave none of the guarantees they required. As they were studying its thirty-plus pages, a Sinn Fein member, Tom Hartley, came rushing into the room with the news that the hunger strike was over. Brendan Hughes, having been assured in advance of the contents of the document, had called the hunger strike off in order to save Sean McKenna's life. The news was received with huge relief at the NIO. Stowe immediately rang the Secretary of State, Humphrey Atkins, to tell him it was all over. Hughes had taken a gamble which he believed was vindicated when Father Meagher brought the document into the hospital wing accompanied by the prisoners' OC, Bobby Sands.[20] 'By that stage I'd been on hunger strike for fifty-three days so I couldn't read the document so I asked Bobby and Father Brendan what they thought. They believed that we had a settlement. The euphoria was fantastic that night in the prison hospital.'

Whatever its shortcomings, the document was all the prisoners had. There was a feeling they had been outmanoeuvred by the 'Brits'. Sands said it was so wide open, he could drive a bus through it.[21] Mrs Thatcher believed the Government had won. 'The IRA claimed [that they had called the strike off] because we had made concessions, but this was wholly false. By making the claim they sought to excuse their defeat, to discredit us, and to prepare the ground for further protests when the non-existent concessions failed to materialize.'[22] It was only a matter of time before the agreement negotiated between the Contact, Oatley and Stowe fell apart. Relatives brought the prisoners' own clothes into the gaol, expecting them to be handed over immediately so they could put them on. But the clothes never reached the wings. The settlement only worked with the combined goodwill of both the prisoners and the prison authorities, but, after four years of confrontation in the H Blocks and the deaths of prison officers, there was precious little of that around. It seems the regime dug in its heels and was in no hurry to give the prisoners what they believed they now had a right to expect. Brendan Hughes, recovering from his fifty-three days without food, feared the worst.

> A few days later it became obvious that something wasn't right. It needed the co-operation of the prison authorities to implement the agreement and Bobby [Sands] became increasingly frustrated at the sabotaging of this agreement by the prison administration. They just didn't want this to work and they really went out of their way to make sure it did not work.

It was only a matter of time before the prisoners picked up the gauntlet again. Despite the spirit of the document Oatley had brought, the prisoners never got their own clothes.

There was a tragic inevitability to what happened next. Plans were laid for a second hunger strike, this time to be led by Bobby Sands. Now there was to be no compromise. It was victory or nothing. The Army Council was even less enthusiastic than before but had no choice other than to support its prisoners. Nor this time was there any Michael Oatley on the spot (who had been posted to South Africa) to help avert the headlong rush to disaster. The Provisional Army Council (PAC) made it clear to the prisoners that although it had tempered its operations during the first hunger strike so as not to alienate public support, it now reserved the right to return to full-scale operations against the 'Brits'. The PAC was true to its word: during the seven months of the 1981 strike, the IRA killed 13 policemen, 8 soldiers, 5 members of the UDR and 5 civilians. In total during the period, sixty-one people died, more than half of whom were civilians as the loyalist paramilitaries too unleashed their gunmen.[23] This time, unlike the previous occasion, the strike was to be staggered, with prisoners joining at regular intervals so that if one died, another would take his place in the spotlight, in the hope that negotiations would take place in the short interval before the next death came. It was agreed that Bobby Sands would be first, then Francis Hughes from County Derry (who had survived the shoot-out with the 'Det' in 1978), Raymond McCreesh from South Armagh, and Patsy O'Hara, the INLA prisoners' OC from Derry. If they all fasted to the death, there were plenty of other volunteers. It was to become a titanic struggle between the Iron Lady and the Iron Men. Neither Mrs Thatcher nor the prisoners had any intention of giving in.

The second hunger strike began on 1 March 1981, the fifth anniversary of the ending of special category status. I asked Sir Kenneth Stowe if he thought Bobby Sands would go through with it.

> I feared he would and he did. That was what we were fearful of when we dealt with the first hunger strike. Yes, we did believe that they had the resolution to go through with this and that men would die. That was why we tried to avert it and did so on the first hunger strike. But having averted it once, I could well see that there was very, very little that anybody could do to avert it a second time. There was no room for compromise and none was sought.

From the outset Mrs Thatcher made her position clear. 'We are not prepared to consider special category status for certain groups of people serving sentences for crime. Crime is crime. It is not political.'[24] The Prime Minister meant it and stuck to it.

At first the second hunger strike failed to attract the support that had been generated by the first. On the Sunday before Sands embarked on his fast, 3,500 people turned out in West Belfast in a rally to support him. It was not a bad crowd but nothing like the 10,000 or so who had marched four months earlier. It seemed like we all had been here before. I must confess to feeling the same, not convinced that, second time around, the hunger strike would end in death. I thought it would go to the brink once again and then another compromise would be reached. We were all wrong. Few of us reckoned with the fierce determination of the hunger strikers and the steely resolve of Mrs Thatcher.

Then, suddenly, five days after Sands first refused food, there was an accident of history that was to transform the hunger strike and the future of the Republican Movement. It was neither planned nor foreseen. On 5 March 1981, Frank Maguire, the Independent republican MP for Fermanagh–South Tyrone, died. (It was Maguire's abstention that had contributed to the fall of the Callaghan government in the crucial vote of confidence two years earlier.) In an inspired stroke of political opportunism, the Republican Movement decided to run Bobby Sands as a candidate in the by-election. After a combination of gentle persuasion and some heavy political arm-twisting, other nationalist candidates agreed to stand down to give Sands a clear run against his unionist opponent, the Fermanagh farmer Harry West, who had briefly held the seat in 1974.

The election was held on 9 April 1981, the fortieth day of Sands's hunger strike. The result was cataclysmic. In a straight fight, Sands, the 'H Block–Armagh' candidate, beat West by almost 1,500 votes. The turn-out was an astonishing 86.9 per cent.[25] An IRA prisoner and hunger striker had been elected to Westminster, confounding the legion of British politicians down the years who had repeatedly claimed that the IRA was a minority terrorist group whose support was based on intimidation and fear. Although the circumstances in which Sands was elected were unique and he did not stand as an IRA or even a Sinn Fein candidate, which would have put many people off, his victory came as a profound shock to the British and gave the Republican Movement a political impetus it had never dreamed of. 'This was a beginning of a time of troubles,' Mrs Thatcher wrote. 'There was some suggestion, to which even some of my advisers gave credence, that the IRA were contemplating ending their terrorist campaign and seeking power through the ballot box. I never believed this.'[26] In the short term, Mrs Thatcher was right. Long term, it was a different matter. Gerry Adams and those around him who had long argued that 'armed struggle' was never an end in itself but only a means to it, saw the election of Sands as proof that, properly harnessed, there was a vast reservoir of political support that could lead the Republican Movement on to the next phase of its 'struggle' against the 'Brits'. The increasing success that Sinn Fein was to enjoy through the next two decades had its seeds in Sands's historic victory. Hitherto Sinn Fein had been very much the junior partner in the Republican Movement, now it began to stand on equal footing with the IRA. Mrs Thatcher added a grim and prophetic postscript to Sands's death. 'It was possible to admire the courage of Sands and the other hunger strikers . . . but not to sympathize with their murderous cause,' she wrote. 'From this time forward I became the IRA's top target for assassination.'[27]

On 5 May 1981, almost a month after his election to Westminster, Bobby Sands MP died on the sixty-sixth day of his hunger strike. About 100,000 people came to his funeral – not all of them republicans – who came to pay tribute to the IRA man who, as they saw it, had laid down his life for his cause. In the last entry of his prison diary Sands wrote, 'They won't break me because the desire for freedom, and the freedom of the Irish people, is in my heart.'[28] Mrs Thatcher was unmoved. 'Mr Sands was a convicted criminal,' she said. 'He chose to take his own life. It was a choice his organization did not allow to many of its victims.'[29] The 'Brits' did not break Bobby Sands nor the nine hunger strikers who followed his example. Francis Hughes died on 12 May on the fifty-ninth day of his hunger strike; Raymond McCreesh and Patsy O'Hara (INLA) on 21 May on their sixty-first day; Joe McDonnell on 8 July on his sixty-first day; Martin Hurson on 13 July on his forty-sixth day; Kevin Lynch (INLA) on 1 August on his seventy-first day; Kieran Doherty on 2 August on his seventy-third day, less than two months after he had been elected *in absentia* to the Irish Parliament; Thomas McElwee on 8 August on his sixty-second day, and Michael Devine (INLA) on 20 August on his sixtieth day.

As the procession of coffins emerged from the Maze, the prisoners wondered how many more of their comrades Mrs Thatcher would let die, and the 'Brits' wondered how many more were prepared to. Neither side could afford to give in. After four hunger strikers had been buried with full IRA military honours, Mrs Thatcher famously poured scorn on the IRA. 'Faced with the failure of their discredited campaign, the men of violence have chosen in recent months to play what may well be their last card.'[30] The Prime Minister was wrong on two counts. The IRA was neither instigator nor manipulator of the hunger strike and the card 'the men of violence' played turned out to be an ace, although few at the time had any idea how decisive it would be. As the summer drew on, with ten men dead, the hunger strike finally collapsed as families, who had the legal right to intervention, began taking their sons off the strike because they believed the prisoners were dying for nothing in the face of Mrs Thatcher's unshakeable resolution. Despite repeated attempts at mediation, ranging from the Pope's personal emissary to the Irish Commission for Justice and Peace, no compromise could be brokered. The hunger strikers themselves were caught. For them to have accepted anything less than the 'Five Demands' that Bobby Sands had been prepared to die for would have been a betrayal of his sacrifice.

The hunger strike was finally and formally called off on 3 October 1981 after it had become clear that there was nothing more to be gained by men dying. A grim reality had also become clear: the more men died, the less media attention they got. In a macabre way, deaths in the Maze and IRA funerals had almost become routine. James Prior, who succeeded Humphrey Atkins as Northern Ireland Secretary on 13 September 1981, finally drew a line under it. He told me he had been sent to the province because Mrs Thatcher 'wanted to get rid of me from London and wanted me out of the way'. He had never wanted to go to a post that was regarded as a bed of nails, but he was determined to do what he could to make a new beginning. 'I saw the hunger strike as a great obstacle to making progress on anything else,' he said, 'and I didn't think I could make political progress with the hunger strike still in operation and therefore I wanted it ended.'[31] Shortly after the prisoners called off their fast, the Government made concessions on clothing, free association and loss of remission. Mrs Thatcher described the outcome as 'a significant defeat for the IRA'.[32]

In the short term, the ending of the hunger strike was seen as a victory for the Iron Lady but ultimately it was a victory for the Iron Men. Within a few years, with minimum fanfare, the prisoners got all that they wanted. When almost a decade later I spent several weeks inside the H Blocks during the summer of 1990 making a BBC documentary, 'Enemies Within', republican and loyalist prisoners were running their wings just like the compounds, wearing their own clothes and mixing freely together with little interference from the prison officers. They even went on to have telephones installed on the wings. The prison authorities, who had seen fifteen of their officers and a deputy-governor killed by the IRA – most of them during the 'dirty' protest – had no wish to trigger another confrontation nor to lose any more of their men. For their part, IRA prisoners had no wish to play the hunger strike card again and lose more of their comrades. Both sides had learned their lessons. Both sides had decided that accommodation, not confrontation, was the way forward. It was a remarkable turnaround.

Given all that had happened and all that was to come, would it not have been better for the 'Brits' to have let the prisoners wear their own clothes? Sir Kenneth Stowe who, with Michael Oatley and the Contact, skilfully negotiated an end to the first hunger strike, made a remarkably frank admission. 'Probably, yes,' he said. 'But once the stakes are raised on both sides, it becomes very difficult. It developed its own emotional language that made it harder and harder for anyone to take a rational view on what should be done.' The agonizing deaths of the ten hunger strikers re-invigorated the IRA and provided Sinn Fein with the launch-pad for its remarkable political rise over the next two decades. In the year 2000, when Martin McGuinness became Minister for Education in the new Government of Northern Ireland, many republicans (but by no means all of them) decided that Bobby Sands and his comrades had not died in vain.

Chapter Twenty-One

'Firepower, Speed and Aggression'

Autumn 1982

After the series of controversial killings by the SAS in 1978, the brakes were put on the Regiment. Although the SAS carried on operating in the province, it did not kill anyone for another five years. The RUC now did the shooting. Nevertheless, the 'shoot to kill' allegations did not die away. The focus of them simply moved from the army to the police. In a sense, such controversy was inevitable once a decision had been made that the RUC should set up its own versions of the 'Det' and the SAS. The long-term strategic thinking was for the police to take over the army's role, and if this were to happen, it was recognized that the RUC would have to develop its own specialist covert units.

The RUC's equivalent of the 'Det' became known as 'E4A' (the letter 'E' being the code to signify 'Special Branch' in the RUC's structure). One of those involved in setting up the new unit was 'Paul', the Special Branch officer who told Brendan Hughes that he had had a good run for his money when he arrested him at Myrtlefield Park in 1974. Although it was an entirely new departure for the RUC and was a direct response to the terrorist threat, such covert units were already being used by other mainland police forces, like the Metropolitan Police, and forces in other parts of the world, primarily against organized crime and drug traffickers. 'Paul' and his colleagues clocked up many miles studying how it was done outside the United Kingdom. 'Paul' also exchanged ideas with the Garda Siochána who were thinking along the same lines. This was possible because, unlike in times past, the Garda and the RUC now had 'a good working relationship'.

Undercover E4A operators were trained at the SAS main base in Hereford and other locations by experienced 'Det' and SAS instructors. For policemen, selection and training was almost as rigorous as it was for soldiers. They were about to run the same risks and therefore could not be expected to be any less prepared. 'Paul' recognized that his new recruits initially had an advantage: the IRA knew about the 'Det' but not about E4A. 'They were looking so much in one direction that they were ignoring Special Branch which gave us a breather over those years,' he said. 'We learned too from the "Det's" evolutionary mistakes.' He described the new E4A operators as 'absolutely fantastic, very brave and very effective'. All were Special Branch officers. They were also trained to use the technical resources of the 'Det': 'cameras, lenses and covert photography'.

The RUC's equivalent of the SAS was known as Headquarters Mobile Support Unit (HMSU) and also made up of Special Branch officers. Its officers underwent the same rigorous training as their E4A colleagues, in particular being instructed by the SAS on how to confront armed terrorists with 'firepower, speed and aggression'. Acting on intelligence from their Special Branch colleagues, MI5 and military intelligence agents, these new undercover police units working alongside the 'Det' and the SAS were designed to be the cutting edge in the covert response of the 'Brits' to the IRA's renewed offensive in the wake of the hunger strike.

As 'Paul' recognized, the clear lessons of the mistakes of 1978 – epitomized by the SAS killing of young John Boyle in the graveyard – had been learned. In future such complex anti-terrorist operations had to be carefully co-ordinated to avoid the fatal errors of the past. 'The problems that had developed showed that the police had to play a controlling part in the decision-making process, in the planning and execution of the operations right to the end,' he said. The result was the establishment of Tasking and Co-ordinating Groups (TCGs), under the control of the RUC, and based on the three 'Det' areas that covered the whole of the province, TCG Belfast, TCG South and TCG North. Co-ordination was the key. During the critical stage of any operation, the TCG office would be packed with the representatives from Special Branch, E4A, the HMSU, 'Det', military intelligence, SAS and MI5 – with all eyes fixed on huge blow-up maps on the wall around which players (the 'Brits' and the IRA or their loyalist equivalents) were moved around like pieces in a giant, real-time game.

In the autumn of 1982, the TCG and its operational arm on the ground, the HMSU, were involved in three shooting incidents that were to become amongst the most controversial in the conflict. Six men died at the hands of the HMSU in confrontations that would previously have been the preserve of the SAS, and provoked republican and nationalist allegations of 'RUC death squads'. In one incident at Mullacreevie Park in Armagh, two members of the INLA, Seamus Grew (31) and Roddie Carroll (22), were shot dead. Neither was armed. In another at Tullygally Road East outside Lurgan, three IRA men, Eugene Toman (21), Sean Burns (21) and Gervaise McKerr (31), were killed. Again, none of them was armed. In the third incident at Ballynerry Road North, again near Lurgan, a seventeen-year-old youth, Michael Tighe, was shot dead in a hayshed where some old rifles were found without ammunition. Tighe was not involved in the IRA. The 'hayshed' shooting became the most controversial of the three incidents and its repercussions echoed through the decade. All were subsequently investigated by the Deputy Chief Constable of Greater Manchester, John Stalker, and gave rise to what became widely known as the Stalker 'Shoot to Kill' inquiry.[1]

As Chief Constable Hermon noted, compared with the bloody years that preceded it, 1982 had been 'relatively peaceful' in Northern Ireland.[2] It was otherwise in England where the IRA had learned from the experience of its intermittent mainland campaign that, in terms of impact, one bomb in London was worth a dozen in Belfast. In the summer of 1982, it planted two in the nation's capital. On 20 July, the IRA almost replicated its 'success' at Warrenpoint with remote-control bombs that killed four Guardsmen of the Household Cavalry in Hyde Park *en route* to ceremonial duties in Whitehall and seven Royal Green Jackets bandsmen who were giving a lunchtime concert in Regent's Park. Whereas the names of the victims tend to be forgotten except by their families and loved ones, the name of Sefton, the horse that fought to survive the terrible carnage, lived on in the public mind, the recipient of thousands of messages and gifts, almost as a symbol of defiance against the IRA.[3]

However, as Hermon went on to record, by the autumn of 1982, the IRA and the INLA were 'hell-bent on stepping up their activities' in the province in intense 'terrorist competition'.[4] Between September and the beginning of December, the IRA killed six RUC officers, one former policeman, three soldiers, one former UDR man, one civilian and Lenny Murphy, the leader of the UVF's notorious 'Shankill Butchers'. In the same period, the INLA out-killed its IRA rival by accounting for the deaths of thirteen soldiers, two policemen and ten civilians. The INLA's greater death toll was the result of one incident on 7 December when eleven soldiers, most of them from The Cheshire Regiment, and six civilians were killed in a bomb attack on the Droppin Well Bar, a pub in Ballykelly near Derry used by many off-duty army personnel. The INLA had strategically placed a small 5-lb bomb under a support pillar which brought the ceiling of the function room crashing down on the crowded dance floor during a disco. With seventeen people dead, the Droppin Well bomb caused one of the highest death tolls in the conflict.[5]

As the killings escalated during those bloody autumn months, demands for the 'Brits' to make a decisive military response mounted. The prime target for the intelligence services and their operational arms was the INLA gunman Dominic 'Mad Dog' McGlinchey, who since his days with Francis

Hughes in South Derry had been expelled from the Provisionals for 'indiscipline' and defected to the INLA. He later admitted to having killed thirty people. 'I like to get in close to minimize the risk for myself,' he said.[6] McGlinchey was alleged to have ordered the Droppin Well bombing and became the most wanted man in Ireland, as his former Provisional associate Francis Hughes had once been. Because McGlinchey was based across the border and only came North for a 'hit', it was difficult to keep him under surveillance, so the 'Det' did the next best thing and latched on to an INLA associate, Seamus Grew, who was already being watched.

Grew, from a staunchly republican family, had decided to take up arms – like hundreds of other young men – in the wake of 'Bloody Sunday'. 'For him, it was the deciding day,' said his brother, Aidan, who has himself spent seventeen years in gaol. 'I remember he was very frustrated at being able to do nothing about it, the fact that people could come over from another country and shoot our people and just leave without being prosecuted.' The Grews were already a target. In 1976, loyalist paramilitaries bombed the family home, almost killing the six children.

In November 1982 Seamus Grew was arrested and questioned by the RUC about the killing of two police reservists, Constable Ronnie Irwin (24) and Constable Snowden Corkey (40), as they stood at the security gates in Markethill. They were cut down with 45 rounds from automatic weapons. Grew was released without charge. 'If the RUC couldn't put him through the courts, then the obvious answer was to shoot him dead,' said his brother Aidan bitterly.

Putting Seamus Grew under surveillance had not been easy. 'He was a switched-on kid,' one of the operators who tracked him said. 'We had an O.P. in a hedgerow about forty yards from his house and it was very hairy. We stuck with him for months and followed him for three or four days every week. Whenever he stopped at a roadblock, he was very polite and passive and never batted an eyelid.' But Special Branch also had a well-placed informer who could lead them to McGlinchey via Grew. His name was George Poyntz (57) and he was connected with a bar in Castleblaney in County Monaghan, three miles from the border. Poyntz was a former chairman of Castleblaney Sinn Fein and had good contacts with the INLA.[7] When Special Branch received intelligence that there was a plan for Seamus Grew to cross the border on 12 December 1982, less than a week after the Droppin Well bomb, and pick up McGlinchey from the bar associated with Poyntz for a 'shoot' in the North, TCG South based at Gough Barracks, Armagh, arranged for the 'Det' to intensify its 'tail' on Grew. Contrary to general belief, E4A was not involved in the 'eyes on' surveillance operation because it was thought that it was not yet sufficiently experienced to operate in hostile border areas.

As Grew and one of his associates, Roddie Carroll, crossed the border with Grew at the wheel of his Austin Allegro, the 'Det' notified TCG via the 'Det' 'ops' officer that the operation had begun as the intelligence had indicated. 'Det' operators in several unmarked cars then followed Grew and Carroll across the border and into the Republic using a complex pattern of surveillance manoeuvres to avoid arousing suspicion. Grew made the rendezvous with McGlinchey at the bar as arranged but when McGlinchey realized that Grew was using his own car, he 'went ape' at what he saw as Grew's carelessness and ordered him to go back across the border and return with a vehicle that was not known to the security forces. Grew and Carroll set off to get another car from the North. The 'Det' immediately radioed their base and told the 'ops' officer to notify TCG South that, although the Allegro was on its way back across the border, McGlinchey was *not* on board, the understanding being that the 'Det' would wait and then carry on with the operation, tracking the 'new' car once McGlinchey was inside.

For whatever reason, TCG either did not receive the message or did not interpret it correctly or decided to ignore it. What the police said then happened and what actually did happen are two entirely different things and bear little relation to each other except for the fact that Grew and Carroll both ended up dead. The following is the true account. By now it was a cold, icy December night and the road surfaces were slippery. In its efforts to stay with the 'follow' (the Allegro), one of the 'Det' cars skidded and crashed on the Keady Road just outside Armagh. The pursuers knew they had to keep the Allegro in their sights in order to track the 'new' car that would pick up McGlinchey. The operators could not hang around in Castleblaney watching their main quarry – who might well move on from the bar – since officially they were not allowed to carry out surveillance in the South. They were not even supposed to be there since such an incursion into a sovereign state was politically highly sensitive. The other 'Det' operators did not lose Grew and Carroll and followed them until they turned into Mullacreevie Park in Armagh, the republican estate where Grew lived. There, to their surprise (given their assumption that TCG South had been notified that McGlinchey was not on board), they saw an HMSU roadblock. The fact that it was there at the entrance to a republican estate was not unusual and they assumed that Grew would politely talk his way through it as he had done so many times before. Instead they watched in horror as a Special Branch officer, Constable John Robinson, approached the Allegro and started shooting when Grew opened the door. The 'Det' operators were 'raging', knowing that the real target, Dominic McGlinchey, was not in the car and that they had lost the opportunity to confront him when he crossed the border. Months of work had been wasted and the operators knew that McGlinchey would kill again. They actually felt for Constable Robinson whom they believed might have been given 'duff' information by TCG South about McGlinchey being on board.

The story the police told at the instigation of senior Special Branch officers at TCG South was largely fabrication, conveniently built around the 'Det' car crash on the icy road. The following is the complex lie they wove. It was a mixture of tragedy and farce. They said that the plan had been to establish a vehicle check point (VCP) on the Keady Road to intercept the Allegro as it came across the border. There had been a crash involving an army surveillance car and Constable Robinson, who was involved in setting up the VCP, also skidded and ran into them. In the confusion, Grew and Carroll drove by, followed by an E4A car driven by a Special Branch Inspector from Armagh who was already tailing the Allegro. The Inspector stopped, picked up Robinson and one of his colleagues and set off in pursuit. Robinson, having been given no information to the contrary, assumed that McGlinchey *was* on board and had every reason to believe, as the HMSU's briefing had indicated, that he would be armed and likely to resist arrest.[8] (This was almost certainly true.) Just as Grew and Carroll were about to enter Mullacreevie Park, Constable Robinson (as he said in court) drew level, made a sign for the Allegro to stop and watched as the Inspector forced it into the verge. According to Robinson's account, the car started revving and the front passenger door was flung open. As the Allegro broke free from the kerb, the door slammed shut again. 'As the door shut, there was a loud bang,' Robinson said. 'I believed I had been shot at. I immediately opened fire . . . because I believed my life was in danger.'[9] Robinson shot Grew and Carroll dead with several rounds from his Smith and Wesson pistol. Neither was armed.

This cover story was invented by Special Branch the following day to protect the sensitivity of the operation and the crucial source for it, George Poyntz. It was designed for the consumption of the CID who would as a matter of routine be investigating the shooting and taking statements from the officers involved. The public explanation was straightforward. It simply said that Grew and Carroll had driven into a routine police check point and the shooting was the result of a purely chance encounter. It was nothing of the kind. Constable Robinson and his HMSU colleagues were informed by their Special Branch superiors at TCG South that they were covered by the Official Secrets Act and therefore the cover story was legitimate to protect vital intelligence systems. It was only when Robinson was charged with the murder of Seamus Grew that some, but not all, of the true story came out. The involvement of the 'Det' and the fury of its operators was never revealed. In court, Robinson admitted the fabrication and said that he had been instructed to tell the cover story by his senior officers. The judge, Mr Justice McDermott, acquitted him with the observation that policemen 'are not required to be "supermen" and one does not use jewellers' scales to measure what is reasonable in the circumstances'.[10] It was during the trial that the court learned from the cross-examination of the RUC's Deputy Chief Constable, Michael McAtamney, that HMSU officers were trained to 'neutralize a dangerous target' with 'firepower, speed and aggression'.[11] George Poyntz was a lucky man too and was swiftly spirited away by his Special Branch handlers to be given a new identity and new life elsewhere. He never returned to the bar in Castle-blaney. Dominic McGlinchey was finally shot dead on 10 February 1994 as a result of the many, bloody internal feuds that eventually tore the INLA apart.

The other two incidents that John Stalker investigated involved an agent of a much higher order, located within the ranks of the IRA itself. Although it was not widely known at the time, both incidents were linked, which is one of the reasons why they were so sensitive. I understand the agent had originally been recruited by the army, taken over by Special Branch and then put on MI5's payroll. I will refer to him as the Mole.

The Mole was a superlative source of information. By the late summer of 1982, he had already proved his worth by identifying the IRA's explosives supply route from Dundalk. On 20 August, officers from the HMSU swooped and, in the guise of a routine checkpoint, stopped a hay lorry on the main Banbridge–Gilford road, having let the IRA 'scout' car drive on ahead. When the hay bales were removed as part of the 'routine' search, the police officers found sixty plastic sacks of home-made ex-plosives (HME) – 'blowie' – manufactured from chemical fertilizer. They also found detonators and fuse wire. The RUC announced that it was 'one of the biggest, if not *the* biggest, explosives finds during thirteen years of violence'.[12] The Mole would have been given a bonus for his efforts.

A few weeks later, around the end of September, he gave his handlers another tip-off about another huge consignment of 'blowie' coming from the South, along with information about the place where it was going to be stored – a hayshed located just off Ballynerry Road North outside Lurgan. This time TCG South chose to let the explosives 'run' in the hope of catching a unit from the IRA's North Armagh Brigade red-handed. E4A kept the consignment under surveillance until it reached the hayshed. At this stage, E4A wanted to mount a Static Observation Post (SOP) close by so they would have what they regarded as the best form of surveillance of all, the human eye – 'Mk 1 Eyeball'. However, it was decided that this was too dangerous given the hayshed's proximity to the road and the cottage where its owner lived. There were also concerns about the SOP being sniffed out by republican-minded dogs, which had happened before. (It appears that the 'Det' was never consulted about 'eyes-on' surveillance because Special Branch wanted to run the operation itself. 'Det' operators later said they could have carried it out with no great problem as they had done so in far more difficult situations.) TCG South therefore decided that the hayshed should be placed under 'technical' surveillance, in other words MI5 should install a listening device inside the hayshed itself. This, it was thought, would be a fool-proof way of monitoring the explosives without any risk to undercover personnel.

One night in October, an MI5 technical officer and a specialist technician from another branch of the 'Det' based at HQNI Belfast entered the breeze-block and corrugated-iron hayshed where the 1,000 pounds of 'blowie' was now concealed in sacks under the hay bales. The Security Service officer carefully planted a listening device – expertly crafted to fit in with its surroundings – in one of the rafters of the roof and started reciting 'Humpty Dumpty' and 'Mary had a Little Lamb' to check that the signal was being received at the listening post some distance away. As back-up, the 'Det' expert from Headquarters set up his own 'technical trigger', designed to send a signal when the IRA removed the hay bales to get to the explosives. The listening post, located in a Portakabin some distance away, was manned by an RUC officer and regular soldiers from the army's 2 SCT unit, the Special Collation Team that worked closely with MI5's technical operations. The team recorded on tape any sounds or voices that were emitted from MI5's device. By this time, there were similar operations in place all over the province, primarily designed to gather intelligence. The tapes would then be transcribed by a group of women police officers (known to the more macho 'Det' operators as the 'Hen Shed') and then routinely destroyed once the intelligence had been gleaned. The hayshed and the explosives remained under technical surveillance for several weeks.

TCG South believed that the 'blowie' was to be used to pull off an IRA 'spectacular' and was anxious to ensure that no unnecessary risk was taken by RUC and army personnel. Therefore when the van that had taken the explosives to the hayshed was spotted in the vicinity of the neighbouring Kinnego embankment, the area was placed out of bounds. Normal policing went on as far as possible so as not to arouse suspicion, since the IRA would become wary at any change in regular policing patterns.

On 27 October 1982, the RUC received a telephone call from a farmer about the theft of a battery from a farmer's tractor in the vicinity of Kinnego. The call was orchestrated by the IRA and the 'theft' was pure fabrication. A check was made to see if police could investigate and Special Branch enquired if MI5's 'bug' had registered any movement in the hayshed. When Special Branch had been assured that all was well and the explosives were undisturbed, the uniformed police were authorized to investigate the report of the theft. Three RUC officers, Sergeant Sean Quinn (37) and Constables Alan McCloy (34) and Paul Hamilton (26), then got into their armoured Cortina and headed for the Kinnego embankment. At 2.19 p.m. their vehicle was blown seventy feet in the air by a 1,000-lb bomb, leaving a giant crater forty feet wide and fifteen feet deep. The RUC officers died instantly.

Unknown to Special Branch, MI5 and TCG South, all the explosives had been removed from the hayshed. MI5's listening device was not working properly and had failed to register any movement or voices. There had, however, been a signal from the 'Det' technician's trigger on the hay bales but it had been dismissed by the 2 SCT monitors as something like a dog chasing a chicken as there had been no corroboration by MI5's 'bug'. Had there been 'Mk1 Eyeball' surveillance on the hayshed by E4A or the 'Det', the three policemen would not have died. Removing 1,000 lbs of explosives was not something that the IRA could have done in five minutes. That night, the handlers of the Mole are thought to have met the agent and demanded to know who was responsible. The Mole named two people, Sean Burns (21) and Eugene Toman (21), both IRA men 'on the run'. They were immediately placed under E4A surveillance. At one stage, an E4A officer actually got so close to them and their IRA accomplice, Gervaise McKerr (31), that he lit one of their cigarettes. The 'Det' regarded this as unnecessary bravado.

A fortnight later, the Mole told his handlers that the men he had named were planning to kill an off-duty member of the security forces. On the evening of 11 November, Toman, Burns and McKerr drove off in a Ford Escort for what TCG South believed to be the murder bid. In the now-familiar pattern, the HMSU had been instructed to set up a 'routine' vehicle checkpoint to intercept the IRA car. With McKerr at the wheel, the Escort drove through the VCP and a high-speed car chase ensued, with the HMSU officers firing at the car in front. The Escort crashed, more shots were fired by the Special Branch officers and Toman, Burns and McKerr were killed. None of them was armed (though the HMSU officers maintained they opened fire first). The police had fired 109 bullets. Immediately there were allegations of 'shoot to kill' as a cover story was devised, once more featuring a 'routine' VCP. The three HMSU officers who did the shooting were subsequently prosecuted for murder and acquitted. In his judgment on 5 June 1984, Lord Justice Gibson heightened the controversy by saying the officers were 'absolutely blame-less' and commended them for bringing three IRA men 'to the final court of justice'.[13] To republicans and nationalists alike, the verdict and the judge's unfortunately chosen words indicated that there was a 'shoot to kill' policy underwritten by the highest levels of the judiciary. Three years later, on 25 April 1987, the IRA took its revenge by killing Lord Justice Gibson (74) and his wife, Cecily (67), in a carefully planned landmine attack as the couple were crossing the border on their way home from holiday.

But the hayshed story was far from over. When the covert units carried out their search in the wake of the Kinnego explosion, they found that three old German Mauser rifles, without ammunition, had been left behind. It was assumed, therefore, that the IRA would return at some stage to collect them. MI5 installed a second device and the 'Det' technical expert re-set his trigger, this time under the weapons. The 2 SCT unit then waited with tape recorders at the ready and the HMSU on standby. On 24 November 1982, a fortnight after Toman, Burns and McKerr had been brought 'to the final court of justice', there were sounds of movement in the hayshed. This time, MI5's bug was working. The HMSU moved in and shot dead seventeen-year-old Michael Tighe, who had no IRA connections, and seriously wounded his friend, nineteen-year-old Martin McCauley. Again, senior Special Branch officers at TCG South invented a cover story, with HMSU officers saying they were conducting a 'routine' anti-terrorist patrol when they noticed a gunman moving to the hayshed from the nearby cottage.[14] McCauley was charged with possession of the weapons and found guilty and given a two-year sentence suspended for three years. The members of the HMSU were never charged. At his trial, McCauley said that he had been asked to keep an eye on the cottage whilst the owner was away and he had entered the hayshed with Michael Tighe out of curiosity when he saw 'a metal object rising from the top of the hay'. He then said they went inside and found the three rifles. He claimed that the police opened fire without warning and then discussed finishing him off on the ground. The HMSU told a different story. They said that when they heard the sound of a rifle being cocked and 'muffled voices', they shouted, 'Police. Throw out your weapons.' They said they then repeated the warning and were confronted by two men pointing rifles whereupon they opened fire. The critical question is, who was telling the truth?

By December 1982, with five 'terrorists' and one innocent teenager dead, the 'shoot to kill' furore had not only refused to die down but intensified. Throughout the following year, nationalist demands for a Government inquiry grew. In the end the pressure became politically irresistible. In May 1984, John Stalker, the Deputy Chief Constable of Greater Manchester, was appointed to head what became unofficially known as the 'shoot to kill' inquiry to get at the truth of what had happened and to unravel the circumstances in which six men had been killed and cover stories invented. But of all the incidents, it was the shooting at the hayshed that came to absorb the attention of Stalker and his team. It was only six months into the investigation that they discovered – to Stalker's astonishment – that the hayshed had been bugged by MI5. For months the team pushed to find out more, in the face of objections and obstructions from Special Branch, until finally they established that not one but forty-two tapes had been made while the hayshed was under surveillance. Tape 42, Stalker concluded, must therefore contain the answer to the vital question: *Was* a warning given?

Stalker now felt he was searching for possible evidence of murder. He spent the next eighteen months trying to get access to Tape 42 and was thwarted at every turn. He was finally told that it had been destroyed, although a transcript existed. The transcript, it transpired, was vague and inconclusive and concluded with a phrase along the lines of 'nothing more of security interest'.

What Stalker and his team did not know was that a cassette copy of the tape did exist as a result of an extraordinary sequence of events. One of the 2 SCT soldiers monitoring the device at the time of the shooting had made his own personal copy of the master tape, presumably as a macabre souvenir of the shooting. (Soldiers had a habit of collecting such memorabilia, usually in the form of souvenir photographs of IRA dead bodies. But a killing on tape was unique.) A few days later MI5 found out about the cassette and ordered it to be handed over. The order was obeyed and the cassette copy of Tape 42 was given to the Security Service in Northern Ireland. It was then stored in a secure place in the province, a time bomb ticking away. When Stalker appeared on the scene, there were fears in MI5 circles that the bomb was going to explode. One of the senior MI5 officers stationed in the province ordered one of his MI5 colleagues to destroy it. He did so. The vital evidence was gone. By this time, several other members of the Security Service had heard the tape, in addition to members of 2 SCT. The vast majority heard no warning.

In a dramatic turn of events, John Stalker was removed from his inquiry in controversial circumstances in May 1986 just as he believed he was about to find out exactly what was on the tape, which would establish whether a warning *was* given. The reason given for his sudden removal was his association with a Manchester businessman, Kevin Taylor.[15] But most of the public, and Stalker himself, thought he had been removed from his inquiry because he was getting too close to the truth. In his report, Stalker had already concluded that there had been no 'shoot to kill' policy but the fact was generally lost in the welter of speculation and conspiracy theories generated by his removal.

The dramatic dénouement of the mystery of the missing tape finally came when Sir Colin Sampson, the Chief Constable of West Yorkshire, took over Stalker's inquiry and his team on 6 June 1986 and began to piece the rest of the picture together. Sir Colin brought with him his colleague from the West Yorkshire Police, Assistant Chief Constable Donald Shaw, who was in charge of the Force's Complaints and Discipline branch. Almost a year later, Sampson delivered his report, built on the groundwork of Stalker's team, to the Director of Public Prosecutions in Northern Ireland, Sir Barry Shaw. Neither the Sampson Report nor the Stalker Report was ever made public since both contained highly sensitive intelligence material that went to the heart of national security. Sampson, however, did recommend that police officers should be prosecuted for conspiracy to pervert the course of justice for fabricating the series of cover stories. It is not generally known that he also recommended that MI5 officers should face the same charge for destroying the copy of the tape. Far from covering up what happened, Sampson and his team were prepared to have it exposed in open court. If there had been a 'Brit' conspiracy to get rid of Stalker (which I do not believe), then appointing Colin Sampson as his successor, in the expectation that he would collude in a cover-up, was a major mistake. This is one of the main reasons why the conspiracy theory does not hold water.

Sir Barry Shaw concluded that there was sufficient evidence to warrant the prosecutions of both the police officers *and* the MI5 officers. It was now for the courts to decide. The Thatcher Government was in a quandary. Because Stalker and Sampson and their teams had done their jobs thoroughly and got to the bottom of what had happened, not to proceed with prosecutions would confirm the widely held suspicion that there had been a conspiracy and cover-up. To go ahead and have MI5 officers in the dock – albeit incognito – being cross-examined about the destruction of the copy of Tape 42 would have been political dynamite. The Security Service had not yet taken its first tentative steps out of the shadows and the prospect of its officers facing cross-examination on any issue, let alone this one, would have been unthinkable in Whitehall.

Under the circumstances, the Attorney-General, Sir Patrick Mayhew (later Lord Mayhew), told the House of Commons in January 1988 that there would be no prosecutions 'in the public interest' since national security was involved. Members of Parliament were under the impression that the issue revolved solely around RUC officers since the fact that they told cover stories had already been revealed. They had no idea it involved MI5 and the destruction of vital evidence of what happened when Michael Tighe was shot dead by the HMSU.

When I asked Lord Mayhew about the prosecution of Security Service officers, he was reluctant to be drawn. All he would say was, 'A lot of intelligence matters would have been brought out that would have been very deleterious to the intelligence operation that was essential in the circumstances of the time.' Sir Robert Andrew, who was by then Permanent Under Secretary at the Northern Ireland Office and had to deal with this explosive issue, was more forthright. He told me that he had only found out that a cassette copy of the tape had been made and then destroyed when he read the Sampson Report.

> This, if true, was most unfortunate. It was a very difficult one. There was an argument for saying that prosecutions should have been brought to clear the air and to demonstrate that the Government was not covering up illegal activities. On the other hand, there was a fear that if police officers and, even more so, officers from the Security Service were put in the dock and had to answer questions on oath, intelligence-gathering methods and the identity of individuals would have become known and prejudiced the effectiveness of intelligence-gathering operations. This is why the Secretary of State, Tom King, judged on balance that a prosecution was undesirable.

Sir Robert, who was present at some of these discussions between King and Mayhew, confirms that the decision not to prosecute was made on political grounds. He was clearly uneasy at the decision. I tried to draw him on his personal view. 'It was very difficult,' he said. 'I saw it as a finely balanced case. I don't think I would want to go further than that.'

After the HMSU's display of 'firepower, speed and aggression' in the three controversial confrontations in the autumn of 1982, it was decided that the SAS were, after all, the best exponents of these attributes. Whatever the consequences, SAS men were expected to display them. Policemen were not.

Chapter Twenty-Two

Group Activity

December 1983–April 1986

By the mid-1980s, the SAS and the 'Det' had become known as the 'Group'. Its undercover soldiers not only worked together but lived together when an operation was under way. Between 1983 and 1992, the 'Group' shot dead one member of the INLA and thirty-five members of the IRA, including many of the Provisionals' most seasoned operatives. The SAS killed twenty-eight of them and the 'Det' killed eight. By this time, except where operational circumstances required, the SAS was no longer permanently co-located in the three 'Det' areas but based at Aldergrove as a resource that the TCGs could draw on when necessary. The SAS was now not only centralized but its soldiers were stationed in the province for twelve-month tours of duty instead of six.

After the intense controversy that engulfed the HMSU in the wake of the six killings in the autumn of 1982, the SAS came into its own once again: not that it had been idle during the preceding four years, it just had not been killing 'terrorists'. All that was to change. Significantly, the vast majority were killed in rural areas. There were to be no more shoot-outs in built-up city streets. But although the SAS got most of the 'kills', for often that could be the culmination of its operational role, the groundwork of the 'Det' and other agencies with which it worked lay behind every one. 14 Intelligence Company was now a highly experienced, highly trained and highly effective counter-terrorist force. The introduction of women had transformed it, giving its operators greater flexibility and cover.

Through the mid-eighties and early nineties, 'Anna' and 'Mary' were closely involved in several of the operations of the 'Group' although not necessarily together, and they sat alongside the SAS at TCG briefings prior to a likely 'contact' with the IRA. They assert categorically that, although it has almost become enshrined as fact in nationalist and republican folk memory, there was no 'shoot to kill' policy. They say the SAS were never instructed to bring the IRA back dead not alive. The Yellow Card rules applied.

Although there may not have been a 'shoot to kill' policy in the sense that the SAS were instructed to bring back dead bodies, none the less, when soldiers did open fire, they were instructed to shoot to kill not to wound. Lord Mayhew, who as Sir Patrick Mayhew was Northern Ireland Secretary between 1992 and 1997, put it graphically. 'If you do shoot, then you don't shoot to tickle, you don't shoot to miss, you do shoot to kill,' he told me. 'This thing about "shoot to kill", as though it's sort of self-evidently wicked, is absolutely wrong. It's nonsense. You don't shoot to do other than kill in the circumstances where the law permits you to shoot.'

'Anna' and 'Mary' were involved in operations that drew on a variety of intelligence data: 'jarking'; information from agents; MI5 listening devices planted in the homes of key IRA 'players', sometimes as they were under construction, as a long-term intelligence investment; 'Mk 1 Eyeball' surveillance on the ground and, later, from hidden video cameras transmitting live, colour pictures that would even indicate the colour of the household rubber gloves an IRA member might be wearing.

When some or all of these ingredients came together, ensuring minimum risk to the SAS and maximum surprise to the IRA, an operation would be triggered. Such were the circumstances in place on Sunday 4 December 1983 when three men from the Coalisland unit of the IRA's East Tyrone Brigade, Brian Campbell (19) and Colm McGirr (22) and a third person, went to retrieve two weapons from a cache hidden in a patch of brambles in a heavily overgrown field.[1] One was an Armalite with a magazine fitted and the other a shotgun. Two black hoods and gloves were also part of the cache. One of the weapons, perhaps the Armalite, had been 'jarked' by the 'Det' and tracked for some time. It had already been used in four killings and eighteen other shootings.[2] McGirr and Campbell were 'bad boys', one 'Det' operator told me. TCG South had a choice, either to 'lift' the weapons or 'do something'. It chose the latter and the SAS staked out the field. According to the account of the soldiers involved, a car drove up and McGirr and Campbell got out and went to the cache, leaving the third man, the driver, in the car. McGirr retrieved the weapons and handed the Armalite to Campbell whilst he held onto the shotgun. One of the SAS men said that as he shouted 'Halt! Security Forces!' the two IRA men turned with their guns. 'I then thought that my life was in immediate danger, and fearing for my life and that of my comrades, I opened fire.'[3] McGirr and Campbell were both shot dead by the SAS soldier and other members of the team. McGirr was hit thirteen times and Campbell twice. The driver managed to escape, although he was badly wounded by shots the SAS fired at the vehicle. He is believed to have been taken across the border where he survived, although he has never fully recovered from his injuries. The car was later found, covered in blood.

The survivor subsequently said that when McGirr and Campbell were shot, 'neither was armed nor were they at any time challenged to stop. Those who carried out these killings . . . had every opportunity to stop and detain us all . . . but they chose to open fire without any warning.'[4] One of the 'Group' involved in the operation assured me that a warning *was* given. He also said that the third man survived as a 'cabbage'.

Just over six months later, the SAS struck another blow at the IRA's East Tyrone Brigade. There was intelligence that an ASU was to carry out an incendiary bomb attack on a kitchen fittings factory in the Ardboe area along the shores of Lough Neagh on 13 July 1984 to mark the third anniversary of the death of the hunger striker Martin Hurson, who came from the East Tyrone village of Cappagh. Eight SAS soldiers took part in the ambush. According to their account, they had the area around the factory under surveillance when, through the night sights of their rifles, they saw men coming towards them, one of whom seemed to be wearing a hood. When the nearest IRA man was about thirty metres away, one of the soldiers said he issued a challenge, 'Halt! Hands up!' In his statement the soldier said, 'This man raised his hands up very fast. I believed he was going to shoot me so I fired one aimed shot at the centre of his body. I heard him scream.'

The man who fell was William Price (28) from Ardboe. He was subsequently hit with three other bullets, including one to the head which killed him. His sister, who later examined the body, said his head was blown apart like the shell of an egg.[5] Two pistols were found by and near the body. Two other members of the ASU, Raymond Francis O'Neill and Thomas McQuillan, were arrested by the SAS. It was evidence that the SAS could and did make arrests in appropriate circumstances. They were subsequently convicted and sentenced to nine years.

There was a macabre postscript to the killing. When members of the SAS and the 'Det' operators returned to base, having put three IRA men out of circulation, one of them for ever, there were celebrations in the bar as invariably happened when the 'Group' celebrated an IRA 'kill'. (They argued that if the IRA celebrated the death of a soldier or policeman, why should the 'Brits' not do the same?)

For the killing of William Price, a cake was baked, iced and decorated in the shape of a cross. It bore the inscription '*R.I.P. PRICE. ARDBOE*'. I understand it was not the first or the last of its kind. It brought to mind the ancient custom of a tribe eating its enemy. When I visited William Price's parents – simple country folk who apparently had no idea that their son had joined the IRA – and told them about the cake, they expressed no surprise.

The final operation by the 'Group' before the 'spectaculars' that were to mark the rest of the decade was almost the settling of an old score. The victim was Seamus McElwaine, an IRA commander who had been arrested by the SAS in 1981 and sentenced to life imprisonment. He had been part of a mass break-out from the Maze in 1983 and had become active along the Fermanagh border once again, going backwards and forwards from his 'billet' in County Monaghan. The SAS, however, finally brought his second run to an end on 26 April 1986. McElwaine and another IRA commander, Sean Lynch, were attending to a culvert bomb, unaware that the firing point was under surveillance. Both IRA men were armed and wearing combat gear. The SAS opened fire, killing McElwaine and wounding Lynch who, like Francis Hughes after his fire-fight with the 'Det' in 1978, crawled away to hide. Again like Hughes, Lynch was discovered by the 'green' army and the RUC, given medical attention and survived. He was duly tried, sentenced to twenty-five years and sent to the Maze where he subsequently became the prisoners' OC. The judge said Lynch was not a soldier but a criminal. Republicans accused the SAS of finishing off the wounded McElwaine whilst he lay harmless on the ground. At the funeral, Martin McGuinness, who gave the graveside oration, described him as 'an Irish freedom fighter murdered by British terrorists'.[6]

All the shooting incidents in which the 'Det' were involved happened in the first half of the decade. All the operators came from North 'Det'. Given the circumstances of some of the shootings, it was not surprising that they were put down to the SAS. At one point it appeared that the 'Det' was assuming its offensive role. In two confrontations, two and a half months apart, the operators of North 'Det' shot dead five armed IRA men on 'active service'. Several operators told me that at this period TCG North preferred to use the 'Det' in circumstances where the SAS would normally have been deployed. The first incident took place on 6 December 1984 and involved William Fleming (19) and Daniel Doherty (23) from the Creggan who had recently served a four-year sentence in the Republic for possession of explosives and IRA membership.[7] Two of Fleming's brothers were in prison and a cousin had drowned in the River Bannagh only four days earlier whilst trying to escape after a gun-battle between the IRA and the SAS. When there was intelligence that the IRA were planning to kill a part-time member of the security forces who worked at Derry's Gransha psychiatric hospital, the 'Det' placed Fleming and Doherty under surveillance and, on the day of the planned operation, tracked the motorcycle on which they were to carry out the attack.

Just before 8 a.m., the time of a shift change, the two IRA men entered the hospital grounds with Doherty driving and Fleming on the pillion. Both were armed.[8] The 'Det' was ready. One of the operators in an unmarked car said he saw a motor bike coming towards him and the pillion rider was armed with a gun. He said he shouted an order to stop at which point the pillion passenger 'raised the handgun and pointed it towards me'. The operator rammed the bike, knocking Fleming to the ground. The operator said Fleming then pointed a gun at him and he shot him twice with two bursts of three rounds.[9] Although the bike had been rammed, Doherty managed to ride on to be faced with another operator from the 'Det' team. The soldier opened fire at Doherty 'because I feared for my life'. The bike finally crashed, throwing off the dying or dead Doherty who had also been hit by a burst of fire from another operator. In all, the 'Det' team fired fifty-nine rounds at the two men. A forensic examination showed that six shots had been fired at Doherty whilst he was on the ground.[10] Both men had wounds to the head. Unionists were jubilant at the operation. Gregory Campbell, a local politician from Ian Paisley's Democratic Unionist Party, put their thoughts into words. 'I am delighted that the two IRA men were intercepted and executed by the undercover army squad. The only way the IRA will be dealt with is when they are executed. They deal in death and must be dealt with by death.'[11] Nationalists were horrified and asked why, if there had been intelligence on the operation, Fleming and Doherty could not have been arrested instead of being killed. At their funeral, Martin McGuinness said that only the freedom fighters of the IRA could bring Britain to the negotiating table. Elsewhere, Gerry Adams said the British 'do not want to take prisoners. They only want dead bodies.'[12]

Just over two months later, on 23 February 1985, three operators from North 'Det' shot dead three more IRA men, Charles Breslin (20), Michael Devine (22) and his brother, David Devine (16). Breslin and Michael Devine were regarded as 'serious players'. The shootings took place near the Head of the Town district in Strabane, a small border town fifteen miles south of Derry. Special Branch had received intelligence that an IRA unit was going to attack a police vehicle with an improvised armour-piercing grenade launcher and then shoot any surviving RUC officers as they tried to escape. The IRA scheduled the attack for 4 a.m., the time when the police vehicle was expected to drive by, presumably on its routine patrol. But in the early hours of that morning, the vehicle did not come. Breslin and the Devine brothers and two other IRA men waited to launch the attack and, when there was a 'no show', they decided to call off the operation and return their weapons to the 'hide' in a nearby field. The ASU then split up with Breslin and the Devines heading back to the field.

What they did not know was that the 'Det' had the 'hide' under surveillance. One or more of the weapons may have been 'jarked'. It appears the three IRA men almost stumbled upon the 'Det' when they were only a few yards away from their O.P. According to one of the soldiers who opened fire, he told his two colleagues to 'watch out', at which point 'all three gunmen swung their rifles towards us'. 'I knew then we were in a contact situation and that the lives of myself and my colleagues were in immediate danger,' the soldier said.[13]

The three operators fired a total of 117 rounds from two HK 53 rifles and a Browning pistol at the IRA men, killing all three. The rifles Breslin and the Devines were carrying – two Belgian FNs and a mini-Ruger – were found at the scene. The three IRA men had not had a chance to fire them. Ballistic tests proved that they had been fired before in four separate attempted murders and one actual murder.[14] At Breslin's funeral, Gerry Adams said he had been shot by 'a British terrorist SAS gang'. The action of the operators involved showed that they had learned the lesson from their former colleagues in North 'Det' during the exchange between 'Jay' and 'John' and Francis Hughes in 1978 in which 'Jay' had been killed after issuing a challenge.

In the first four years of the decade in which the gloves appeared to have been taken off, 'Group' activity accounted for twelve IRA men and one member of the INLA.[15] More bodies were to follow.

Chapter Twenty-Three

The Political Front

May 1980–November 1985

Through most of the 1980s, the 'Brits' had almost despaired of finding an internal political solution in Northern Ireland that might bring an end to the conflict which by the beginning of the decade had claimed well over 2,000 lives, almost 600 of them were soldiers and policemen.[1] Given that there were precious few signs that unionists were prepared to reach a realistic political accommodation with the nationalist SDLP, the 'Brits' felt they were banging their heads against a brick wall. Nevertheless, they realized that politics could not be allowed to die, not least because they saw Sinn Fein making significant political gains in the wake of the hunger strike. Accordingly, British political strategy through most of the decade ran on twin tracks: to try to stem the rise of Sinn Fein, and to bring the Dublin Government into the political equation in order to boost the constitutional nationalists of the SDLP. The 'Brits' had no intention of giving in and capitulating to IRA violence. A new context had to be explored in which the political deadlock might gradually be broken. For most of the decade, this context certainly did not include Sinn Fein. They were to be marginalized not encouraged. On the threshold of the decade, the NIO's Permanent Under Secretary, Sir Kenneth Stowe, who had been instrumental in ending the first hunger strike, wrestled with the problem and decided a new, more imaginative approach had to be tried.

> In dealing with all these issues in Northern Ireland, one was in a perpetual state of exploration. Will this help, can we make some ground here, can we open up a subject in this way? Can we see a way of just inching our way forward? What was clear to me was that we could not address our concerns solely in a dialogue between London and Belfast. It was unreal to suppose that we could achieve a stable society in Northern Ireland and one with an economic future without the collaboration of the Republic. Therefore we wanted

to create an axis between London and Dublin as well. The Irish Government also wished to create it, as it could not have been done only from one side. Whatever one attempted in Northern Ireland, sooner or later you would hit a veto somewhere. What we wanted to do was to broaden the ground of debate, to create a wider context, remembering always that we were now addressing another partner in Europe. It's to do with looking at the overall relationship of two member states within it, each of whom has a profound interest in the stability of Northern Ireland.

Sir Kenneth set the political compass for the course that almost two decades later was to lead to the Good Friday Agreement. Certainly he did not foresee where it would lead at the time and simply plotted the direction with his fingers crossed, secure in the knowledge that it had to be an improvement on the political atrophy in the North. He knew that a start had to be made with the two Prime Ministers who had both come to power in 1979, Mrs Thatcher in London and Charles Haughey in Dublin. It was appropriate that Downing Street should play host for the inaugural meeting, held on 21 May 1980. Nevertheless, the Prime Minister was mindful that unionists might get the wrong idea when they discovered she had been dining with the Taoiseach who ten years earlier had been involved in the gun-running scandal that engulfed the Irish government.[2] With this in mind, Mrs Thatcher told the House of Commons on the eve of the meeting that 'the future of the constitutional affairs of Northern Ireland is a matter for the people of Northern Ireland, this government and this Parliament and no one else.'[3] It seemed like Haughey was being given his marching orders before he even crossed the threshhold of Number Ten.

The following day, the Taoiseach arrived bearing the gifts of a Georgian silver teapot, which was much appreciated by the British Prime Minister who was not averse to flattery and charm. They lunched in the small dining room at Number Ten and Sir Kenneth was well pleased with the result. 'It was a significant step forward in a new relationship,' he said. 'The exchanges were courteous and formal. I think they were only too well aware of their own standing and what lay behind them, so they were very cautious.' Unionists were behind Mrs Thatcher and republicans in his Fianna Fail party behind Charles Haughey. 'There was no personal animosity, neither do I recall there being any personal warmth. This was very, very high-level political business and they were two very accomplished politicians at work. That seemed to me to be the essence of their relationship.' The post-prandial communiqué referred to a 'unique relationship' between the two countries and promised closer political co-operation.[4] There was self-interest on both sides. Thatcher wanted tougher security from Dublin and more speedy extradition of IRA suspects from the South whilst Haughey, true to the tradition of his party and family (his father had been commander of the IRA's Northern division),[5] wanted the 'Brits' out of the North, although not at the point of a gun.

Later that year, on 8 December 1980, in the shadow of the first hunger strike, Haughey reciprocated his new-found friend's hospitality by entertaining the highest-powered British delegation ever to visit the Irish Republic in the splendour of Dublin Castle, once the seat of British power in Ireland. The meeting was officially part of the European bi-laterals between member governments. The delegation consisted of Mrs Thatcher, Defence Secretary, Lord Carrington, Home Secretary, Geoffrey Howe, and Northern Ireland Secretary, Humphrey Atkins. The resultant communiqué became a political landmark: the British and Irish Governments agreed to set up special study groups to examine 'the totality of relationships within these islands'.[6]

Despite the impression an over-eager Haughey tried to create, however, the constitutional position of Northern Ireland was not discussed. There were predictable roars of 'betrayal' from Ian Paisley and profound dismay amongst unionists. But Stowe was encouraged. 'The points in that communiqué were significant and have remained significant, although they were not able to be exploited very quickly.' At the time, Sir Kenneth could have had no idea of just how significant they were to be, given the way the politics were to unfold. 'If you roll the clock on nearly twenty years, that is pretty well what the Good Friday agreement has achieved,' he said. 'But we had no expectation then that it would ever get that far. We could hope, but it was no more than a very, very early stage in identifying that the relationship between London and Dublin could be of crucial importance in resolving the problems of Northern Ireland and to mutual benefit.'

Even as the two Prime Ministers met, events were coming to a head in the Maze prison whose repercussions were in the long term to change the shape of Northern Ireland's political landscape. The ending of the first hunger strike led to the impasse over prisoners wearing their own clothes which in turn led to the second hunger strike and the election of Bobby Sands to Westminster. It was proof to the Provisionals that politics worked. Nor was Sands's election the aberration the sceptics portrayed it to be. When Sands died and the parliamentary seat became vacant again, Sinn Fein's Owen Carron, who had been Sands's election agent, contested the by-election as an 'Anti-H Block Proxy Political Prisoner' candidate and won, increasing Sands's vote by 786 on an increased turnout of 88.6 per cent.[7]

Two months later during Sinn Fein's Ard Fheis (annual conference) at the Mansion House in Dublin, Danny Morrison took the platform to assure the party faithful and the sceptics in the Republican Movement that politics did not mean that the IRA's 'armed struggle' was about to take second place. Morrison will go down in the history of the Republican Movement's 'struggle' for many reasons but he will be best remembered for coining the phrase the 'Armalite and Ballot Box'. Contrary to the belief that the concept and the wording of it had been carefully discussed beforehand with Adams and McGuinness and the leadership of the Republican Movement, it was a purely 'off-the-cuff' remark that Morrison thought up minutes before he rose to his feet. When the words were uttered, McGuinness, who was sitting beside Morrison on the platform, looked up and said, 'What the fuck's going on?' Morrison seemed to be making up policy on the hoof. In fact, the phraseology was not as neat as history would have it. His actual words were, 'Who here really believes we can win the war through the ballot box? But will anyone here object if, with a ballot paper in one hand and the Armalite in the other, we take power in Ireland?'[8] However, the actual words came out, they did encapsulate the policy that the Republican Movement was to follow for most of the next two decades until the IRA's second cease-fire, following Tony Blair's election in 1997. The notion that Provisionals could move towards their goal of a united Ireland by pursuing a twin strategy of violence and politics convinced most of the doubters who by this time had realized that, were the 'Brits' to leave Ireland, it wouldn't be at the point of a gun. The 'long war' was now to be fought on two fronts.

A year after Morrison's exhortation, the strategy passed its first test when, on 20 October 1982, Sinn Fein's triumvirate of Adams, McGuinness and Morrison all won seats in the election to the Assembly set up by Secretary of State, James Prior, in which he held out the promise of 'rolling devolution'. The theory was that the more responsible its elected members turned out to be, the more powers Westminster would devolve. But it never worked out that way and the Assembly was finally dissolved in 1986. The elections were the first that Sinn Fein had contested on a province-wide basis since the outbreak of the conflict in 1969. The party won five of the seventy-eight seats with 10.1 per cent of the vote. The SDLP, Sinn Fein's rival for the nationalist vote, took 18.8 per cent.[9] A week later, the IRA exploded the 1,000-lb bomb that killed the three policemen on the Kinnego embankment. Armalite and Ballot Box were marching hand in bloody hand. But Sinn Fein's most spectacular electoral success came at the Westminster General Election on 9 June 1983 when Gerry Adams contested the safe nationalist West Belfast seat and won, beating the incumbent, Gerry Fitt (formerly SDLP but now running as an Independent candidate), and the SDLP's Dr Joe Hendron. The nationalist vote was split, giving Adams a famous victory with a majority of 5,445 votes over

Hendron who came second. The contest was bitterly fought with Adams's nationalist rivals presenting the issue as a choice between violence and democracy. Province-wide, Sinn Fein won 13.4 per cent of the vote while the SDLP won 17.9 per cent.[10] The writing was now on the walls of Belfast and Derry and James Prior did not like what he saw.

> I think my reaction was almost one of despair that they were going to elect someone whom we considered to be a terrorist and who was not going to play any part at Westminster. I had no doubts at all that he belonged to the Provisional IRA. I think he encapsulated the Armalite and Ballot Box completely. What a waste the whole thing was.[11]

Five months later, on 13 November 1983, the new MP for West Belfast was elected as President of Sinn Fein, ousting Ruairi O'Bradaigh who had led the political wing of the Republican Movement since 1970. It was not only a clear indication that the Northerners were now in charge but an early sign of the split that was to come three years later when O'Bradaigh, David O'Connell and the dissidents who supported them walked out of the Sinn Fein Ard Fheis to form Republican Sinn Fein (RSF). The issue that tore the Movement apart was its new leadership's determination to change Sinn Fein's constitution so its members could take seats in Dail Eireann, the Irish Parliament. This was anathema to the traditionalists and the ways were parted with a degree of bad blood. At least there was no real blood on the floor. Supporters of the dissidents subsequently set up the Continuity IRA (CIRA), claiming that it alone had the right to claim the IRA's historic mantle since the Provisional IRA had sold out. In his first Presidential address, two months after thirty-eight IRA prisoners made their dramatic mass break-out from the Maze, Adams reassured delegates of the primacy of the IRA's military campaign.

> Armed struggle is a necessary and morally correct form of resistance in the Six Counties against a Government whose presence is rejected by the vast majority of the Irish people . . . There are those who tell us that the British Government will not be moved by armed struggle. As has been said before, the history of Ireland and of British colonial involvement throughout the world tells us that they will not be moved by anything else. I am glad therefore to pay tribute to the freedom fighters – the men and women Volunteers of the IRA.[12]

On 18 December 1983, the 'freedom fighters' took their campaign to London once again, killing three policemen (including a WPC) and three civilians in a car bomb attack outside Harrods when Knightsbridge was crowded with Christmas shoppers. The police had been called to the scene minutes before the blast. A hundred people were injured, including fourteen members of the Metropolitan Police. With three dead civilians and so many injured, the IRA said the attack had not been authorized by the Army Council.[13] It was not what the new President of Sinn Fein had had in mind.

A year later, the IRA struck the most devastating blow in its history when it almost wiped out Mrs Thatcher and most of her Cabinet as they gathered at the Grand Hotel in Brighton for the Conservative Party's annual conference. At 2.45 a.m. on 16 October 1984, a 20-lb bomb strategically placed behind a bath panel in Room 629 exploded, collapsing four floors in the centre of the building like a house of cards. The bomb had been triggered by a sophisticated electronic timing device, similar to those found in video recorders.[14] It had been set about a month earlier and timed to explode when the Prime Minister and members of her Cabinet were asleep. Five members of the Conservative Party were killed, including Sir Anthony Berry MP (59) and Roberta Wakeham (54), the wife of John Wakeham, the Tory Chief Whip. More than thirty people were injured, many of them seriously, including Margaret Tebbit, the wife of the Industry Secretary, Norman Tebbit, who was himself dug out of the rubble after a four-hour rescue operation by firemen.[15] Mrs Thatcher, whose bathroom was badly damaged by the explosion, miraculously survived. In defiance of the IRA and its works, the Prime Minister insisted it was business as usual and addressed the conference as planned. She received an eight-minute standing ovation.

Many months before the conference I had talked to a senior Provisional. He was surrounded by young lieutenants who showed respect for the man who was clearly regarded as their military leader. At some stage, Mrs Thatcher's name inevitably came into the conversation. The person looked me straight in the eye and said she was going to pay. This was a time when memories of the hunger strike were fading – at least for the British – and I naïvely asked, 'For what?' 'You'll see,' he said. Brighton was no doubt what he meant.

In the wake of the devastation and death, the IRA issued a chilling statement.

Mrs Thatcher will now realize that Britain cannot occupy our country and torture our prisoners and shoot our people in their own streets and get away with it. Today we were unlucky, but remember we only have to be lucky once. You will have to be lucky always. Give Ireland peace and there will be no more war.[16]

A criminal investigation on an unparalleled scale immediately got under way. Almost 4,000 dustbins of debris were removed for forensic examination, 38,000 records were logged and 6,000 statements taken. More than 800 inquiries were made in fifty countries as detectives tried to trace guests on the Grand Hotel's list.[17] In particular, police inquiries focused on the previous occupants of Room 629. In an astonishing piece of detective work, all were traced, except one man who had signed the registration card as 'Roy Walsh' and booked into the hotel with another man a month earlier. 'Roy Walsh' was the name of a member of the IRA unit who had bombed the Old Bailey and other London targets in 1973. On the registration card the police found a palm print and a finger print which they eventually matched with those on record of a teenager convicted for theft in England many years before.

The prints belonged to Patrick Magee, a Belfast man whose family had moved to Norwich when he was four years old and whose grandfather had been in the IRA in the 1920s. Magee left school at thirteen, got into trouble with the authorities and police, and eventually returned to Belfast in 1971 and joined the IRA.[18] After a complex surveillance operation, he was arrested on 24 June 1985 in a Glasgow flat along with an IRA unit that had been planning to explode bombs with delayed timers at several English seaside resorts. Arrested with Magee in the raid were Peter Sherry, a former Sinn Fein by-election candidate who had met up with Magee at Carlisle railway station when Magee had been under surveillance; Gerard McDonnell, another Maze escaper; and two women, Martina Anderson, a former Derry beauty queen, and Ella O'Dwyer, from a respectable middle-class family in the Irish Republic with no republican connections.[19] On 11 June 1986, all five were sentenced for conspiring to cause explosions in England. Magee was the only one convicted for the Brighton bomb. The judge sentenced him to life imprisonment with the recommendation that he served a minimum of thirty-five years. In fact, he became the 277th paramilitary prisoner to be released under the terms of the Good Friday Agreement, having served fourteen years of his sentence. On 22 June 1999, the 'Brits'' most notorious prisoner, and now a graduate of the Open University, walked free from the Maze prison as Dr Patrick Magee Phd, BA (first class hons).[20]

Far from making the Government more amenable to engaging in dialogue with the Republican Movement, the outrage of Brighton made it even more determined to hit back on both the military and political fronts. Mrs Thatcher, the Iron Lady of the hunger strike, was in no mood to do business with members of an organization that had just killed five of her friends and colleagues and tried to kill her. Four months after the Brighton bombing, on 28 February 1985, her determination was reinforced when an IRA mortar bomb hit the canteen of Newry RUC station, killing nine police officers as they were eating their evening meal or relaxing. Newry was the RUC's Warrenpoint, the Force's biggest loss in a single day in the whole of the conflict. Despite the setbacks inflicted by the SAS, the IRA was still a force to be reckoned with.

If the SAS and the 'Det' were spiking some of the IRA's Armalites, the Anglo-Irish Agreement (AIA) was designed to spoil Sinn Fein's Ballot Box. It was signed by Mrs Thatcher and the Irish Prime Minister, Dr Garret FitzGerald, at Hillsborough Castle, County Down, on 15 November 1985, nine months after the IRA's lethal mortar attack. From the point of view of the 'Brits', it was designed primarily to do two things: to arrest the apparently inexorable rise of Sinn Fein (in May its candidates won fifty-nine seats in the district council elections – which it contested for the first time – with 11.8 per cent of the first-preference votes);[21] and to enlist more support from Dublin for more stringent security measures against the IRA who, despite Mrs Thatcher's discussions with Charles Haughey at the beginning of the decade, were still using the Republic as a haven and operational base with apparent impunity. The discussions that led up to the signing of the Agreement were conducted in the utmost secrecy by a joint Anglo-Irish working party led by the Cabinet Secretary, Sir Robert Armstrong, and his Irish opposite number, Dermot Nally. Mrs Thatcher instructed Sir Robert Andrew, the NIO Permanent Under Secretary, not to mention a word in Belfast since a leak could torpedo the whole endeavour. Being his Prime Minister's obedient servant but also feeling loyalty to his Northern Irish officials in Belfast who were out of the loop, Sir Robert observed the letter of the Prime Minister's instruction. 'I told the Head of the Northern Ireland Civil Service in strict confidence in *London*,' he said, 'because I wanted his reactions.' Being a unionist from hat to handbag, Mrs Thatcher was never wholly enthusiastic about the Agreement anyway and was only finally persuaded of its merits by Sir Robert Armstrong. He regarded getting the Prime Minister to put pen to paper at Hillsborough as the greatest achievement of his governmental career.

The first that people outside this tight circle of Whitehall mandarins saw of the Agreement was when it was signed at Hillsborough Castle on 15 November 1985. From the outset, both Governments agreed in Article 1 that 'any change in the status of Northern Ireland would only come about with the consent of the people of Northern Ireland'. They recognized too that 'the present wish of a majority of the people of Northern Ireland is for no change in the status of Northern Ireland'.[22] These were the twin pillars of what became known as the principle of 'consent' and were to underpin all political developments for the next fifteen years.

Dublin was now to have a direct say in Northern Irish affairs through the establishment of a Permanent Representative's office at Maryfield outside Belfast and regular meetings of what became known as the Anglo-Irish Conference, at which British and Irish Ministers could co-ordinate policy and discuss contentious issues and matters of mutual interest, not least security policy. The Conference, as set out in Article 4, was to provide a framework 'for the accommodation of the rights and identities of the two traditions' and for 'peace, stability and prosperity throughout the island of Ireland by promoting reconciliation, respect for human rights, co-operation against terrorism and the development of economic, social and cultural co-operation'. To Mrs Thatcher, Article 9 on cross-border co-operation on security was crucial, setting out mechanisms for co-ordinating 'threat assessments, exchange of information, liaison structures, technical co-operation, training of personnel and operational resources'.

Nationalists and the SDLP were jubilant at what they saw as the provision of a voice – albeit through Dublin – they had long lacked. Despite the 'guarantee' underpinning the whole Agreement that a majority would not be coerced into constitutional change against its will, unionists were outraged and saw it as the latest and most perfidious betrayal by the 'Brits'. Thousands of loyalists took to the streets to protest, most memorably at a huge rally outside Belfast City Hall, where Paisley roared one word three times to a crowd of around 100,000. 'Never! Never! Never!' Street protests turned to violence, policemen were attacked and their houses burned. There was even the bizarre sight of one 'loyalist' hitting a member of the *Royal* Ulster Constabulary over the head with a Union Jack. It seemed like the long prophesied Protestant backlash had finally arrived. Mrs Thatcher and the Chief Constable, Sir John Hermon, stood firm. This time the 'Brits' were not going to cave in as they did over the 1974 UWC strike. Looking back on that turbulent time, Sir Robert Andrew provided a rare insight into the way officials were thinking and Mrs Thatcher's response to their thoughts. In the run-up to the Agreement, Sir Robert and other senior officials were at Number 10 discussing Northern Ireland with Mrs Thatcher.

> We were looking at the various options, from a united Ireland, to redrawing the boundary, to the full integration of Northern Ireland in the United Kingdom and all the other possibilities. At one point the Prime Minister said, 'Well, where shall we be in a hundred years' time?' And I and another very senior official, without collusion, said, 'Well, probably a united Ireland, Prime Minister.' To which the Prime Minister said rather forcefully, 'Never! Never!'

In the light of his remark, I asked Sir Robert Andrew to elaborate on his view about the likelihood or inevitability of a united Ireland at some stage in the future.

> The demographic trend is moving towards an eventual Catholic majority in Northern Ireland. Of course you can't be certain that all Catholics would vote in favour of a united Ireland. You just can't tell; but even if 51 per cent voted in favour of a united Ireland you'd still have 49 per cent who were opposed to it. So I think the thing to do is that somehow, between now and the time when there might perhaps be a vote in favour of a united Ireland, which the British Government has pledged to respect, one has got to try to make sure that if that transition were to come about, it would do so in a peaceful way rather than in a non-peaceful way.

Arguably, this is what the long-term political strategy of the 'Brits' is all about. But the first step was to end the violence by making it clear to the IRA that they were not going to win, at least not through 'armed struggle'. The 'Group' – the SAS and the 'Det' – were the most powerful instruments in making sure the message hit home.

Chapter Twenty-Four

Loughgall

8 May 1987

The nightmare for any handler was to find his source turning up on an IRA operation that the SAS were about to ambush. The risk of this happening was perilously high since the source might actually be part of the ASU that was the target of the 'Group'. Although every precaution was taken to avoid this, there was no guarantee that it would be successful on every occasion. Calling in sick could easily arouse suspicion in an organization whose habitual paranoia about informers had intensified in the mid to late 1980s as more and more operations were intercepted or thwarted. Under such circumstances, sources would face a dreadful dilemma. To participate might mean death at the hands of the SAS. Not to do so might mean death at the hands of the IRA. Often the TCG chose to sidestep the dilemma by aborting the operation if a handler learned from the source that he had to take part. Sources were too valuable to be sacrificed and the suspicion that one had died whilst on active service for both sides was hardly good for recruitment and morale. 'Mary' knew the frustrations when a 'job' was called off, sometimes after weeks of painstaking investment and discomfort.

On one particular occasion we'd done a job and it went on for ten weeks. We were in an army base along the border and we'd been living like rats in the attic. The conditions were really bad. The 'troop' [the SAS] were there and the 'Det' and the police and all the different authorities were there for this massive job. The 'troop' had 'eyes-on', the heli-surveillance had gone mobile and it was all happening. That one ended abruptly because the informer was part of the team. Now, after sitting in this army barracks for ten weeks and when all of these organizations had all been revved up for the job, it was total devastation at the end of it. It was the closest myself and the 'troop' members I was with had got to mutiny. It was really bad, you know. What can you do after such a build-up? It's like telling a child he's getting a bike for Christmas and when Christmas Day comes, he gets a bag of cinders. It's a real let-down at the end of the day.

How close were you getting to intercepting your targets?

Well, seconds away. The troop had 'eyes-on'. The helicopter was airborne. We were seconds away from the scene. They cut it really fine.

What would have happened if the operation hadn't been called off?

Well, on that particular one, there would have been a dead informer.

Was the informer armed?

All of the terrorists on that job were armed.

'Mary' said she and the 'Group' would not ask why an operation was called off. There was no point. They would know in their bones. 'It's source protection. A lot of jobs ended like that.' And although Special Branch would be upset if a source was shot dead, to most of the 'Group', who did not 'run' sources, a dead agent would simply be another dead terrorist. 'Mary' was matter-of-fact. 'They were terrorists performing a terrorist act.'

There were occasions when a Special Branch source was involved in an operation without being the source of the intelligence for it. But the most tragic situation of all is when an informant is involved in an operation for which he has provided vital intelligence and which, for whatever reason, has not been called off. This is what happened during the most spectacular SAS ambush of all, on 8 May 1987, when a heavily armed eight-man ASU from the IRA's East Tyrone Brigade was wiped out whilst attacking Loughgall RUC station in County Armagh. The informant was part of the ASU and gunned down in the hail of 600 bullets fired by the SAS from a variety of weapons including Heckler and Koch G3 rifles and General Purpose Machine Guns (GPMGs). The SAS outnumbered the IRA by three to one. Amongst the bullet-riddled bodies left in the road and inside the blue Toyota Hiace van in which the ASU had been travelling were some of the IRA's most wanted men. They included Patrick Kelly, the leader of the ASU and commander of the East Tyrone Brigade; Jim Lynagh, known as the 'Executioner' and based in Monaghan where he had been a Sinn Fein councillor, and Padraig McKearney, another Maze escapee. The other members of the ASU were Gerard O'Callaghan (29), Tony Gormley (25), Eugene Kelly (25), Seamus Donnelly (19), and Declan Arthurs (21). One of the eight was the informer. The latter four were from the Cappagh area of East Tyrone and had all joined the IRA in the wake of the death of the Cappagh hunger striker, Martin Hurson.[1] Amelia Arthurs, Declan's mother, remains bitter about the way her son died. 'He was mowed down,' she told me. 'He could have been taken prisoner. They knew that the "boys" were coming and they lay in wait. The SAS never gave them a chance. Declan died for his country and I'm very proud of him. He was caught up in a war and he died.'[2]

By the time of Loughgall, the 'Provos' had entered a new phase of their 'war' against the 'Brits', on the military as well as the political front. Although the IRA had never been short of arms, given the steady stream from America and elsewhere, it had always lacked the heavy weaponry it believed was necessary if it was to deal the 'Brits' a decisive blow and change the face of the 'war'. By the mid-1980s, that weaponry had arrived in the shape of an arsenal of 136 tons, courtesy of Mrs Thatcher's sworn enemy, Colonel Gaddafi of Libya. The vast tonnage was made up of four shipments brought ashore on the County Wicklow coast south of Dublin between August 1985 and October 1986. A converted fishing boat, the *Kula*, landed three consignments of seven, ten and fourteen tons, respectively, whilst the fourth consignment of 105 tons was brought in on board a boat called the *Villa*, which was twice the size of the *Kula*. Astonishingly, all these shipments were transferred to the shore by Zodiac inflatable dingies and then taken to underground bunkers prepared in advance across Ireland without detection by either British or Irish intelligence. More than a decade later, these great 'dumps' of Libyan arms became central to the issue of IRA decommissioning.

Gaddafi's munificence gave the IRA the capacity to fight an even longer 'war'. The consignments included heavy-duty machine guns, surface-to-air missiles, AK 47 assault rifles, Semtex high explosive and vast quantities of ammunition. The 'Brits', however, were not caught napping a fifth time when, on 1 November 1987, a freighter called the *Eksund*, carrying a further 150 tons of Libyan arms, was seized off the French coast by French customs authorities. Although British intelligence insists it was a 'chance' seizure and a stroke of good luck, it probably owed as much to 'chance' as did the HMSU checkpoints that dominated the era of 'firepower, speed and aggression'.

An attack such as that planned on Loughgall police station was nothing new. Strategically, the IRA had determined to create 'liberated' zones – as the Vietcong had done in South Vietnam – in the border and contiguous areas in which there would be no effective security force presence. The Maze escaper Padraig McKearney was thought to have been one of the architects of the strategy, which was also designed to remove what the IRA saw as the unionists' 'second border' or second line of defence.

Not only were security force bases attacked but civil contractors brought in to repair them were also targeted and killed. One of the IRA weapons recovered at Loughgall was believed to have been used only a few weeks earlier in the killing of Harold Henry (52) whose family firm, Henry Brothers, carried out work for the security forces. Five masked men came to his home on 21 April 1987, demanded the keys to his car and then stood him against a wall and shot him four times in the head. The IRA said, 'such people are a more prime target than the foot soldier or the RUC constable because of the crucial function they perform'.[3] The fact was that they were also 'soft' targets. The IRA found it increasingly difficult to kill soldiers and police because of their improved body armour. As a rule builders wear donkey jackets not flak jackets.

The IRA's new strategy began with the devastating mortar attack on Newry RUC station on 28 February 1985 in which nine police officers died. It was followed by a gun and bomb attack (believed to have been led by McKearney) on Ballygawley RUC station on 7 December 1985, in which the IRA shot dead two police constables, George Gilliland (34) and William Clements (52), before planting a 100-lb beer-keg bomb that destroyed the station. The IRA took the hand-guns from the dead constables, one of which is believed to have been used in the killing of Harold Henry and subsequently at Loughgall.

The following summer, on 11 August 1986, the IRA attacked the RUC station in the tiny village of The Birches along the southern shore of Lough Neagh. It was unmanned at the time. On this occasion, the East Tyrone Brigade used a new delivery system, a JCB digger with a 200-lb bomb placed in the bucket. The JCB crashed through the perimeter fence, the bomb exploded and the station was reduced to rubble. The attack was so successful that the IRA decided to use the tactic again at Loughgall. But this time, TCG South knew the IRA was coming.

The 'Group' was already on high alert in the spring of 1987 after the IRA had killed Lord Justice Gibson, the controversial judge who had commended the HMSU for bringing three unarmed IRA men to 'the final court of justice'. The headlines of the British tabloids echoed the national mood: 'Unleash SAS on the killer squads', demanded the *Daily Mail*. 'SAS set to swoop – undercover army is briefed for battle', revealed the *Daily Mirror*. The Northern Ireland Secretary, Tom King, visited Killeen, the scene of the explosion, and knew he not only had to talk tough but act it. 'It was obviously my duty after that appalling outrage to give reassurance to the law-abiding people of Northern Ireland that they would be protected from being terrorized and murdered in that way,' he told me. 'We were conscious that we were facing an enhanced threat and we took enhanced measures to meet them.'[4] The 'Group' was ready.

Loughgall police station, which was only open for four hours a day and manned by a token force, was hardly Fort Knox. The IRA clearly thought they could pull off Ballygawley and The Birches again.

Uncharacteristically, it put together a large eight-man ASU armed to the teeth and led by some of its most experienced operatives. It was known as the 'A Team'.

'Eyes-on' and technical surveillance with a listening device had been going on for weeks, with premises being bugged by MI5 and the 'Det'. Critically, there was also intelligence from the Special Branch agent who was part of the ASU. Cornering the 'A Team' was a highly complex operation involving all the police, army and intelligence resources at TCG South's disposal – MI5, Special Branch, E4A, the 'Det' and the SAS. The operation was put in place on Thursday 7 May 1987, the day before the IRA's attack. Three Special Branch officers from the HMSU volunteered to remain inside the station as decoys to give the appearance of normality when the IRA did its 'recce'. 'Matt' was one of them. He and two Special Branch colleagues entered the station with some of the SAS as darkness fell on the Thursday evening. They made sandwiches and cracked jokes to lighten the tedium of waiting, knowing the station was going to be attacked but not aware at that stage of the precise details. 'I knew there was danger. Every tasking we were on was a danger. But I took it in my stride, followed my orders and was quite happy to do so,' 'Matt' told me. But 'Matt' did know some of the IRA 'players' who were likely to be involved. 'We were briefed on personalities at various times. We just knew they were a lethal unit and ruthless outfit of PIRA.'

Whilst 'Matt' and his HMSU colleagues waited inside the station, 'Anna' and her partner were part of the 'Det' surveillance cordon covering a wide area around the approach roads on the look out for the approach of the A Team. All 'Anna' knew was that Loughgall police station was to be attacked by a heavily armed IRA unit which, presumably, would be travelling to the target in some vehicle. The vehicle was, in fact, a blue Toyota Hiace van that had been hijacked in nearby Dungannon that afternoon. Anna and her partner scoured the country lanes three or four miles from Loughall village in the hope of being able to give the TCG early warning that the IRA was on its way.

Suddenly, they spotted a van. At first they thought it was simply stuck behind a slow-moving vehicle but when they saw that the vehicle in front was a JCB digger and the driver of the van was in blue overalls – the clothing often worn by the IRA on operations – they immediately put The Birches and Loughgall together. 'You suddenly realize that it's a previous MO [*modus operandi*] used by the East Tyrone Brigade,' 'Anna' said. 'It was like a replay. But this time we were on top of it and we knew what was happening. So we passed on the information and pulled off.'

The intelligence of the imminent arrival of the ASU was passed on to TCG South and the SAS got ready outside the station and the HMSU inside. I asked the Chief Constable, Sir John Hermon, why the unit could not have been arrested before it reached Loughgall. He said it was never a realistic option. 'People see every movement. I cannot see that putting up roadblocks is going to help. You know the way the IRA work. They've got vehicles going ahead, people looking at the scene and radioing back. In operational terms it doesn't make sense, unless you're 100 per cent certain that it would work.'[5] Yet roadblocks had been used in anticipation of stopping Toman, Burns, and McKerr and Grew and Carroll in the shootings that John Stalker investigated. In the case of Loughgall, either it was deemed too risky to take on an exceptionally large number of heavily armed IRA men, or the plan was to lure them into the SAS ambush and teach the IRA a lesson they would never forget. Perhaps it was a combination of both.

The JCB, with the 200-lb bomb raised high in the bucket, rumbled past the RUC station accompanied by the blue Toyota van. Both then turned and headed back in the direction whence they had come. Suddenly, the JCB revved, headed for the perimeter fence and crashed through it as the van drew up outside, disgorging Patrick Kelly and some of his comrades who sprayed the station with their assault rifles. The SAS almost certainly opened up the moment Kelly started firing. Everything seemed to happen at once in a deafening crescendo of noise. 'Matt', who had taken up position by the window at the front of the station, was only about ten metres from the JCB when it came to a halt. He turned and ran, amidst the gunfire, with one word on his mind.

> Bomb! I just thought of The Birches and Ballygawley. The next minute there was an almighty bang. I was hit in the face, knocked to the ground and buried. I thought, *I'm dead*, simple as that. But the fact I was still thinking made me realize I was still alive. I found myself buried at the corner of the station, in rubble, inhaling dust and in darkness. A colleague grabbed my belt and we pushed our way through to the rear of the station, completely covered in dust and rubble. Our green uniforms were now grey. I saw the light of a window at the back and just went for it. I don't know where I got the strength from but I just pushed myself out through it. Colleagues helped us out and gave us first aid.

'Matt' and his colleagues survived but the IRA did not. They died in a thunderous barrage of fire put down by the SAS's GPMGs and Heckler and Kochs. The van was riddled like a sieve. The photographs taken at the

scene are gruesome. Forensic tests carried out on the IRA weapons
retrieved were linked to eight murders and thirty-three shootings.[6]
Although the world did not know it, one of the bodies was that of the
informer who had provided his handlers with intelligence on the attack.
Special Branch officers waiting at TCG South are said not to have been
pleased. In the wake of the biggest loss the IRA had suffered since 1921
(when it lost a dozen of its men at the hands of Black and Tans)[7] the IRA's
internal security unit left no stone unturned nor interrogation undone to
find the informer. They did not succeed. Recovering in hospital, 'Matt'
had no sympathy for the dead.

> I hate to see anybody being killed, but they were there to kill us. If
> we hadn't been there, the police officers in the station would have
> been annihilated. These guys were responsible for lots and lots of
> deaths in that area and other parts of the province. Dead terrorists are
> better than dead policemen.

When the 'Group' got back to base, 'There was a huge party and it probably
went on for over twenty-four hours,' 'Anna' said. 'A lot of beer was drunk.
We were jubilant, there's no two ways about it. We thought it was a job
well done. It sent shock waves through the terrorist world that we were back
on top. It was a huge blow for the IRA and a big victory for the security
forces, a "coup" if you like. We'd really sort of put them on the back foot
again. We were really on top of the intelligence game at that point.' And
how did she feel about eight dead IRA men? 'They're all volunteers and
actively engaged against the British army. They're at war, as they would
describe it. My attitude is that if you live by the sword you die by the sword.
We were just happy at the end of the day to be alive ourselves.' The
Permanent Under Secretary, Sir Robert Andrew, was well pleased too.

> My personal first reaction was really one of some satisfaction that we
> had 'won one', as it were, in this continual conflict and that it was a
> victory for the forces of law and order. I would think it was a salutary
> message. I think it demonstrated to the IRA that the other side could
> play it rough and that they could not with impunity carry out the sort
> of attack which had been planned and which fortunately we gained
> intelligence about. I hope it sent a message that the British Govern-
> ment was resolute and was going to fight them. It may also have
> contributed to a view in the IRA and Sinn Fein that they weren't
> going to get their way by terrorism, and that perhaps a political
> solution was something which they ought to be putting more
> emphasis on.

But eight IRA men were not the only deaths that day. An innocent civilian, Anthony Hughes (36), was also shot dead by the SAS, and his brother, Oliver, was wounded and scarred for life. They had been returning home from work through Loughgall village and were a few hundreds yards from the police station when the SAS, perhaps thinking they were an IRA 'scout' car or part of the ASU, opened fire on their white Citroën. Forty shots were fired at the car. No warning was given. Anthony was wearing blue overalls, which may be one reason why the SAS mistook him for part of the IRA unit. Oliver was hit twelve times in the body and twice in the head. He told me of his brother's dying breath. 'He gave a bit of a shout, "Oliver, Oliver, help me!" Those were the last few words he said.' Sir Ronnie Flanagan, who later became the RUC Chief Constable, described it as 'an unspeakable tragedy' and blamed the IRA not the SAS for his death. But the culpable party was TCG South who had not cordoned off the area to prevent any 'innocent' vehicles straying into the area. 'I think it was very unjust,' said Oliver. 'They could have had a checkpoint and stopped us from going in there and told us about the danger. But they didn't.' Had they done so, they would have risked scaring off the IRA. Anthony and Oliver Hughes paid the price. Oliver was awarded substantial compensation but, like Con Boyle who lost his son, John, in the SAS ambush in the graveyard in 1978, he never received an apology from the MOD or RUC.

At Jim Lynagh's funeral, Gerry Adams said that Loughgall would become a 'tombstone for British policy in Ireland and a bloody milestone in the struggle for freedom, justice and peace'. He described the 'executions' of Lynagh and his seven comrades as 'the pound of flesh demanded by the British colonial murder machine'.[8] 'Anna' was convinced that the disaster at Loughgall would act as a powerful deterrent to the IRA. 'I don't think volunteers were particularly willing to "volunteer" for missions after that because obviously they didn't want to die or be captured,' she said. But 'Anna' was wrong.

Chapter Twenty-Five

Death in the Afternoon: Gibraltar

6 March 1988

Ireland-watchers always knew that the IRA would no more let Loughgall go unavenged than they had the hunger strike. If the Brighton bomb was the response to ten men dead, what blow would be struck to settle the score of eight IRA men riddled with SAS bullets? But time erased the thought for all those outside the Republican Movement. If it took three years before the IRA almost wiped out Mrs Thatcher and her Cabinet, the Provisionals were in no hurry to take vengeance for Loughgall. In the 'long war', the IRA reasoned, time was on its side. Success, although never guaranteed, was most likely to come from the careful identification of the target, meticulous planning and painstaking selection of an ASU. Lough-gall sent the IRA the message not only that the 'Brits' could 'play it rough', as Sir Robert Andrew bluntly put it, but also that they knew the IRA's plans. Accordingly a decision was made to hit the 'Brits' overseas, at a place and time when they were least expecting it and at a location likely to be free of their prying cameras and eyes. British bases in Germany were too obvious a target and already on alert following an IRA bomb attack two months before Loughgall on a British army base at Rheindalen in which thirty-one people were injured.[1] The IRA looked south to Gibraltar.

I remember driving down the M6 on Sunday 6 March 1988 after a short family holiday in Scotland. I had decided to take a break after completing a film for BBC *Panorama* called 'The Long War' in which I analysed Loughgall, the arms shipments from Libya and the IRA's long-term strategy. As we approached the Lake District with a long journey still ahead, there was a news flash on the radio. There had been a confrontation involving the security forces in Gibraltar and three people were dead. I cannot remember whether the IRA was even mentioned at that stage. The details were very sketchy and did not come much clearer as we drove on through the evening. It was only the following morning that things gradually began to emerge. The early news bulletins told us that the

IRA was involved and there had been a bomb. The calm voice of the news reader, Peter Donaldson, gave some of the still-hazy facts. 'It's now known that the three people shot and killed by the security forces in Gibraltar yesterday were members of the Provisional IRA. It's thought they were challenged while trying to leave Gibraltar after planting a huge car bomb in the centre.'[2] We were then told that the target had been a military band and the army's prompt action had saved many lives. Not knowing the full facts, I thought that what had happened was probably a confrontation like Loughgall, albeit on a smaller scale and much further from home. I assumed the SAS had intercepted an armed IRA ASU as they had done at Loughgall police station ten months earlier. Shortly afterwards, the Minister for the Armed Forces, Ian Stewart, went on the *Today* programme to reveal that a car bomb had been found and defused. That morning's newspapers all carried varying accounts of the same story. There was mention of a shoot-out with armed members of the IRA. ITN reported that 'a fierce gun-battle broke out' and that 'Army explosives experts used a robot to defuse the bomb'.[3] By this time, the IRA had issued a statement saying that three of its members, two men and a woman, had been killed whilst on 'active service'.

Through the fog of 'war', what had happened seemed dramatic but, like Loughgall, it also seemed pretty clear-cut: an armed engagement in the 'war' the IRA always insisted it was. But as the hours went by, the picture gradually changed as the truth began to emerge. There had been *no* bomb and the three IRA members were *not* armed. The Foreign Secretary, Sir Geoffrey Howe, made a statement to the House of Commons that for the first time provided the facts and the Government's interpretation of them, most notably that a warning had been given.

> On their way to the border, they [the three IRA members] were challenged by the security forces. When challenged, they made movements which led the military personnel, operating in support of the Gibraltar police, to conclude that their own lives and the lives of others were under threat. In the light of this response, they were shot. Those killed were subsequently found not to have been carrying arms.[4]

It seemed like a replay of the 1982 shootings in County Armagh that John Stalker had investigated – dead terrorists and no guns. Clearly there had been good intelligence on the ASU but it had not been good enough. At least, that was the benign interpretation. The malign version was that British intelligence knew what the putative bombers were up to and had been authorized by the Prime Minister and her Cabinet to take 'executive action' and finish the IRA off before they could plant and detonate their bomb.

Whatever the case, there was unlikely to be much public sympathy for those whose organization had, only four months earlier on 8 November 1987, exploded a bomb in Enniskillen on Remembrance Sunday, causing wholesale slaughter in an IRA atrocity whose enormity ranked alongside 'Bloody Friday', La Mon and Birmingham. The IRA's intention had been to detonate the bomb and kill members of the security forces as they carried out a security sweep before the service but it exploded prematurely killing eleven bystanders and injuring more than sixty others. The most poignant memory was of one of the injured, Gordon Wilson, as he comforted his dying daughter, Marie. Both were trapped under six feet of rubble. 'Daddy, I love you very much,' she said. They were the last words she uttered. The IRA expressed 'deep regret' but the day came to haunt it and perhaps marked the beginning of the IRA's road to peace.

After Enniskillen, most of the British public probably thought that the three dead IRA members in Gibraltar got no more than they deserved, armed or not. However, once the story of a gun-battle and bomb had been relayed by Government and media, whether 'spun' by design or trans- mitted in ignorance, it became fixed in the public's mind. However, the unadorned and 'unspun' facts are as follows. The three dead IRA members were Mairead Farrell (31), a former IRA prisoner in Armagh gaol from a respectable middle-class family in Andersonstown who, after her release, became a student at Queen's University, Belfast;[5] Sean Savage (23), who had spent a brief period in gaol in 1982 on the word of a 'supergrass' before the charges against him were dropped;[6] and Danny McCann (30), a former IRA prisoner who had also been 'fingered' by a supergrass. McCann and Savage are also believed to have been the gunmen who shot dead two Special Branch officers on 26 August 1987, as they sat in the Liverpool Bar by the ferry in the Belfast docks. Neither had any compunction about 'shooting to kill'.[7]

The Gibraltar ASU had been carefully selected to carry out an operation to bomb the Royal Anglian regimental band at the ceremonial Changing of the Guard on the Rock. At least two other IRA members were also involved but were never captured or killed. One of them was a woman operating under the false identity of 'Mary Parkin'. The other was a man travelling under the pseudonym 'John Oakes'. Both, like other members of the ASU, were experienced in counter-surveillance techniques and, although observed, succeeded in giving there MI5 'watchers' the slip, thus evading the 'Brits'' tightly-drawn net..

The IRA had been planning the operation for months and the 'Brits' had been watching them in Belfast and Spain where the Spanish authorities were alerted and asked for their co-operation. They duly obliged. British intelligence code-named its counter measures 'Operation Flavius' after the Roman Emperor, who put down a rebellion and established peace.[8] The 'Brits' hoped to do the same. The Belfast end of the operation was based on Special Branch information.[9] From the early stages, the intelligence services kept tabs on the operation, as at Loughgall, without necessarily knowing the fine detail of the IRA's plans. One or more members of the ASU was spotted at Spain's Malaga airport, roughly seventy kilometres from Gibraltar, on 5 November 1987, four months before the planned attack.[10]

On 19 February 1988 the various intelligence agencies and their surveillance teams set up their operational headquarters in Gibraltar's Rock Hotel,[11] where they waited, watched and planned, keeping in touch via London with their counterparts in Spain. The SAS are thought to have moved onto the Rock a week later as the IRA made its final preparations for the attack. The intelligence indications were that it would be carried out during the Changing of the Guard ceremony on Tuesday 8 March and that the huge car bomb driven in from the Spanish mainland would be triggered by remote control. The tactical leader of the SAS team now in place briefed his men that 'at least one of the three terrorists, if not more, would in all probability be armed . . . and there was a strong likelihood that at least one, if not more, of the three terrorists would be carrying a "button job" device [to detonate the bomb from a distance]'.[12]

The commander of the SAS team was also given 'Top Secret Rules of Engagement' for 'Operation Flavius'. He was told that his objective was 'to assist the civil power [the police] to *arrest* members of the IRA, but subject to the overriding requirement to do all in your power to protect the lives and safety of members of the public *and of the security forces* [author's emphasis in both cases]'. The SAS claimed that the order to arrest was nothing new as the ratio between arrests and kills over the preceding decade in Northern Ireland had been three to one.[13] Crucially the directive contained a specific paragraph on 'Firing without a Warning'. It said: 'You and your men may fire without a warning if the giving of a warning or any delay in firing could lead to death or injury to you or them [the SAS team] or any other person, or if the giving of a warning is clearly impracticable.'[14] The Rules of Engagement, which were based on the Yellow Card, appeared to give the SAS *carte blanche*.

The ASU flew into Malaga airport on Friday, 4 March, four days before the scheduled attack. Savage and McCann arrived via Paris and Farrell via Brussels. The two men booked into the Hotel Escandinavia in Torremolinos that night under false names. Farrell joined them and apparently shared their room.[15] By this time, MI5 is believed to have provided the

Spanish authorities with full details of their unwelcome guests. On Saturday, the ASU hired two Ford Fiestas, one red and one white. The red Fiesta left Marbella to pick up the explosives, while the white Fiesta was left in the basement of the Sun car park in Marbella. When the explosives (140 lbs) arrived, they were transferred to the white Fiesta and left in the car park.[16] There they remained until they were finally discovered by the Spanish authorities the day after the SAS shot three members of the ASU dead.

The IRA also hired a third car that Saturday, a white Renault 5 that was to be driven to Gibraltar and left in a parking space close to where the Changing of the Guard ceremony was due to take place. It was thought the intention was to leave it there until the white Fiesta with the explosives inside arrived some time before the ceremony was due to begin. The Renault and the white Fiesta would then change places.

Sometime after the explosives had been safely delivered and transferred to the white Fiesta, Savage, McCann and Farrell left for Gibraltar, with Savage in the Renault and McCann and Farrell in the red Fiesta. None of them knew that they were under Spanish surveillance as they drove along the Spanish coast to Gibraltar, and under British surveillance once they entered the British dependency. McCann and Farrell left the red Fiesta at La Linea on the Spanish side of the border and walked into Gibraltar on foot. Savage, driving the Renault, was allowed into the colony without being searched.

One of the key questions is *why was Savage not stopped and arrested if he was under surveillance and the British suspected the car might be full of explosives?* Arguably, the IRA ASU at Loughgall was not stopped on its way to the police station because it was fully armed and would no doubt have put up a deadly fight. Sean Savage was a lone man in a car who could have been surrounded by plain-clothes SAS men and taken by surprise, increasing still further the Regiment's ratio of arrests to kills. According to the British, Savage parked the white Renault 5 at 12.50 p.m. that Sunday afternoon.[17] Savage and the parked Renault were subsequently 'clocked' by MI5 'watchers'. A specialist soldier was ordered to carry out a visual inspection of the vehicle, obviously without attracting too much attention. He reported back that, in his view, 'the car was a suspect car bomb. The most distinctive thing about it was that there was an old aerial placed centrally on the roof of a relatively new car.'[18] One would have thought that if it *was* a car bomb, there would have been a noticeable weight on the rear axle. Photographs taken of the car at the time give no such indication.

By this time, Savage had been joined by Farrell and McCann and the three were walking back towards the border along Winston Churchill Avenue. At 3.40 p.m. the Gibraltar Police Commissioner, Joseph Luis

Canapa, passed control of 'Operation Flavius' to the SAS. Minutes later, Farrell, Savage and McCann were dead. The three had been chatting in the sunshine near a Shell petrol station and then had split up, with McCann and Farrell walking off in the direction of the border whilst Savage went the other way. McCann suddenly looked round and made eye-contact with one of the SAS soldiers. At the subsequent inquest the soldier said, 'He had a smile on his face . . . We looked directly at each other. The smile went off McCann's face . . . almost as if McCann had a realization actually who I was, or I was a threat to him.'[19] The soldier said he intended to shout a warning but was not sure whether it ever came out as things moved so swiftly. 'The events took over the warning,' he said. 'The look on McCann's face, the alertness, the awareness . . . then all of a sudden his right arm, right elbow, actually moved across the front of his body. At that stage, I thought McCann was definitely going to go for the "button" [to detonate the bomb by radio-control].' He fired one round at McCann, then a second round at Farrell as, he said, she was grabbing at her shoulder bag. He then fired a third round at McCann. The second SAS soldier also opened fire, hitting both with seven rounds. 'I perceived McCann as a threat to me and Gibraltar and my comrades,' he said.

As soon as Savage, walking off in the other direction, heard the first shot, he swung round to be confronted by two other members of the SAS team. One of them told the inquest that as he shouted a warning, 'Stop, police! Get down. Hands above head. Stay still!' Savage 'went down with his right arm to the area of his pocket, adopting CQB or Close Quarter Battle stance.' The soldier opened fire and carried on firing 'until I was sure he had gone down and was no longer a threat [capable] of initiating that device'. His partner did the same, firing nine rounds in quick succession into his body, two of which were aimed at his head. In two brief and bloody minutes, the SAS gave the IRA three more celebrated martyrs to join Bobby Sands.

But the killing was not over. Ten days later, as Farrell, Savage and McCann were being buried in Belfast's Milltown Cemetery with full IRA honours, a lone loyalist gunman, Michael Stone of the Ulster Freedom Fighters (UFF), attacked the mourners with a handgun and grenades. Those gathered around the graveside could hardly believe their eyes. Gerry Adams called out for calm as the crowd dived for cover behind the headstones. Stone tried to make his escape on foot along the M1 motorway that ran along the bottom of Milltown Cemetery but was overpowered by pursuing republicans. Only the swift intervention of the RUC prevented Stone from being beaten to death amidst screams of 'Get the Orange bastard!'[20] He had killed two civilians, Thomas McErlean (20) and John Murray (26), and one IRA man, Caoimhin MacBrádaigh (30), who was pursuing Stone when he was killed. Stone was subsequently given life sentences for six murders and became a loyalist folk hero.

When I later met Stone in the Maze prison, he told me his attack was retaliation for the IRA's Enniskillen bomb four months earlier. He said it was symbolic: the IRA had attacked a British cenotaph and he was taking revenge by attacking the IRA equivalent, the hallowed republican plot in Milltown Cemetery where the IRA's martyrs are buried. His targets, Stone said, were Adams and McGuinness. Stone was released from the Maze prison in July 2000 under the Good Friday Agreement, having served just over twelve years of his sentence.

But not even Stone's murderous rampage was the end of the spiral of death triggered by Gibraltar. Three days later, one of his victims, Caoimhin MacBrádaigh, was being given an IRA funeral when two army Corporals in a VW Passat ran into the cortège as it made its way along Andersonstown Road to Milltown Cemetery. The soldiers were definitely *not* 'Det' operators carrying out surveillance but army signallers who, bizarre and unwise though it may seem, had apparently stopped to watch the funeral out of curiosity. The Passat was immediately surrounded, and one of the signallers pulled out his Browning and fired a warning shot in the air. One 'Det' operator told me that if any member of the 'Group' had been involved, under those circumstances they would have shot to kill not to warn. He also stressed that no member of Special Forces would ever have put themselves in that position.

The mourners and IRA stewards, thinking it was a replay of Michael Stone's attack, dragged the corporals out of the car, bundled them into a black taxi and drove them off to be 'executed' by the IRA. It was one of the most dramatic and harrowing images of the conflict as television cameras captured the frenetic crowd surrounding their vehicle and the army's 'heli-tele' in the sky recorded the moment of 'execution'. Corporal Derek Wood (24) and Corporal David Howes (23) were stripped and savagely beaten before meeting terrifying and lonely deaths. Wood was shot twice in the head and four times in the chest and stabbed four times in the back of the neck. Howes was shot five times, once in the head and four times in the body.[21] One of the most poignant images of the conflict is the photograph of the Redemptorist priest, Father Alec Reid, administering the last rites over the corporals' bleeding and battered bodies.

The horrific pictures confirmed the majority of the British public in its view that republicans were savages. Little account was taken of the circumstances in which it had happened and the trail of death from Gibraltar to Milltown Cemetery that had preceded it, intimately involving members of the West Belfast community. In a statement that evening, the IRA claimed responsibility for the 'execution' of 'two SAS members who launched an attack on the funeral cortège of our comrade'.[22] The IRA got it wrong. Mrs Thatcher was waiting on the tarmac with the families as the Royal Air Force brought the two coffins back home to England, each draped in a Union Jack. The IRA gunmen who pulled the triggers were never charged. There was no evidence against them and no one was prepared to identify who they were.

There was one more element to be added to this maelstrom of controversy. Thames Television's *This Week* programme under its Editor, Roger Bolton, investigated Gibraltar in an edition called 'Death on the Rock' produced by Chris Oxley and reported by Julian Manyon. Mrs Thatcher and her Government were furious and demanded that the programme be stopped on the grounds that it was being transmitted before the inquest and would prejudice the outcome. Thames and the IBA both stood firm in the face of an attack by Government on broadcasters of unprecedented ferocity even by Northern Ireland standards. The intensity of the onslaught was fuelled above all by Manyon's interview with an eye-witness, Carmen Proetta, who said that McCann and Farrell had been shot 'with their hands up'.[23] 'Death on the Rock' did not affect the inquest. On 30 September 1988, the jury concluded by a majority verdict of nine to two that the three members of the ASU had been 'lawfully killed', thus apparently vindicating the Government's position. But it was not until seven years later, on 22 September 1995, that the European Court of Human Rights, to which the families had taken their case, had the final word on whether the killings were a breach of Article 2 of the European Convention on Human Rights that safeguards the right to life. The Court ruled by ten votes to nine that the killings were unnecessary and that Farrell, Savage and McCann could have been arrested. That was the bad news for the 'Brits'. The good news was that it ruled that those involved had *not* been operating a 'shoot to kill' policy.[24] By the time the European Court delivered its verdict, the SAS had shot dead a further twelve IRA men. This time, all of them were armed.

Chapter Twenty-Six

Collusion: Brian Nelson

1983–January 1992

'Collusion' is one of the emotive slogans in the Provisionals' propaganda armoury deployed to discredit and undermine the 'Brits'' campaign against them. But to republicans, 'collusion' – like 'shoot to kill' – is more than propaganda, it is a cardinal article of belief. They are convinced that collusion is institutionalized and that the 'Brits' not only set up the loyalist paramilitaries in the early 1970s but continually used them as surrogates to carry out the state's murderous work. They believe the loyalist 'death squads' are simply the 'Brits' in another guise, orchestrated from on high.

Undoubtedly during the thirty-year 'war' collusion did exist – to suggest otherwise would be naïve – and it was not surprising given that there were some members of the RUC and, above all of the UDR who believed the loyalist paramilitaries were fighting on the same side against the same enemy. There were even cases where police officers and UDR soldiers were also members of loyalist paramilitary organizations. Constable William McCaughey, for example, was not only a member of an RUC special unit but a member of the UVF. In 1980 he was convicted of the murder of a Catholic shopkeeper in the village of Ahoghill in 1977 and sentenced to life imprisonment along with another RUC officer, Sergeant John Weir, who was also convicted of involvement in the murder. Neither was the trigger puller. McCaughey told me that he carried out this and other terrorist crimes in the belief that he was defending Ulster. Four other police officers, who were colleagues of McCaughey, were also convicted of serious offences committed in 1978. One was found guilty of kidnapping a Catholic priest and three others of the bombing of a Catholic bar in South Armagh where they erroneously believed a notorious terrorist was drinking. McCaughey was also involved with them on both occasions. The four policemen were given suspended sentences. In delivering his verdict, the Lord Chief Justice, Lord Lowry, said that all the accused had acted under the same powerful motives that something more than ordinary police work was needed to rid the country of the pestilence that was destroying it. He described the disgraced police officers as 'misguided, wrong-headed, but above all, unfortunate men'. It is significant that all six policemen were brought to justice: an unlikely outcome if collusion was state-approved.

Most examples of collusion were not as blatant as that but took the form of some police officers and UDR soldiers passing on intelligence material to the loyalist paramilitaries or their associates (who might be neighbours in the staunchly loyalist estates where many members of the almost exclusively Protestant local security forces lived). One loyalist gunman told me that at one stage his unit had so many intelligence documents, they didn't know where to put them.

Although in my view collusion was not institutionalized or approved at the highest level of Government, the case of Brian Nelson does raise disturbing questions about how far up the intelligence chain collusion went.

Nelson was a former loyalist paramilitary who was recruited as an agent by the army's most secret intelligence wing (believed to have been established in 1979), euphemistically known as the 'Force Research Unit' or the FRU for short. The 'research' involved was the identification and recruitment of potential republican and loyalist agents prepared to defect and work for army intelligence. Its motto was 'Fishers of Men' and its crest depicted a man in a loin-cloth with a trident and net. The existence of the FRU, for years a closely guarded secret, only became publicly known due to an astonishing court appearance in 1992, in which Brian Nelson pleaded guilty to conspiracy to murder. He had risen to become the head of intelligence for the loyalist Ulster Freedom Fighters (UFF), the 'killer' wing of the Ulster Defence Association (UDA). The allegation against Nelson was that he was used by the FRU to target IRA suspects and get the loyalist 'death squads' to eliminate them, thus doing the dirty work of the 'Brits' for them.

The FRU favoured the direct approach, as one of its handlers I met clearly indicated. At one stage 'Geoff' said that he was running seven sources at the same time, both republicans and loyalists. He pointed out that the FRU had a great advantage over Special Branch in that they had more money to offer informants. 'Whatever I needed to recruit a source, I could get, in cash,' he told me. 'If I had wanted £250,000, I could have had it.' When I expressed incredulity, he explained this would not have been a lump sum. 'Maybe the quarter of a million wouldn't have been in a suitcase,' he said, 'but I could have been okayed that amount of money over a period of three or five years or whatever. What price is a life? The army flies helicopters every day in Northern Ireland and that costs thousands of pounds. A quarter of a million isn't a lot of money in those terms.' As every Special Branch and FRU agent-handler knew, a top-grade source was a priceless long-term investment.

'Geoff' had ingenious ways of confronting a potential source, like on one occasion 'accidentally' bumping his car, inevitably forcing the annoyed driver to get out and meet 'Geoff' face to face. On one such occasion, 'Geoff' told his target he wanted a word with him, took him round to the boot of his car, opened it and showed him a briefcase. He flicked it open and inside was £25,000 in cash. 'That's for half an hour of your time,' he said. 'What took you so long?' came the answer. In this particular case, although £50,000 was a good hourly rate, the potential source declined to sign up. 'Geoff' was philosophical about it.

He knew his job was dangerous and could never be valued in terms of money but only in the number of lives saved. That was his reward. Like his Special Branch counterparts, he lived with death every day and accepted it as an occupational hazard, but he never expected that as a 'Fisher of Men' he would become caught in the net that entangled Brian Nelson. 'Geoff' had no idea what lay ahead when he was first introduced to Nelson at the beginning of 1987 as the loyalist paramilitaries of the UFF and UVF intensified their campaign of terror. 'He seemed quite a nice person. A family man,' he said. 'He told me he hated violence and he didn't agree with the way in which loyalists were carrying out their attacks. He saw himself as the spear-point in the thrust against terrorism.'

Before Nelson became a FRU agent, he had led a chequered life. He was brought up on the loyalist Shankill Road and then, like many of his contemporaries, joined the British army. He enjoyed a less than glorious military career and was discharged. In 1972 he joined the UDA and was subsequently sentenced to seven years for kidnapping. On his release, he returned to the UDA, which by then had spawned the UFF, most of whose targets were innocent Catholics. In 1983, he offered his services to the FRU. He said he was sick of violence and had had enough. With remarkable speed he rose to become the UDA's Senior Intelligence Officer for West Belfast, feeding vital intelligence to his FRU handlers. After two years, he decided to quit and went to work in Germany, taking his wife and children with him. Whilst he was away making a good living as a roof tiler, loyalist killings dramatically increased from four in 1985 to fifteen in 1986. Again, most of the victims were innocent Catholics. Strategically, the UFF and UVF calculated that if they killed enough Catholics, pressure from the terrorized nationalist community would finally force the IRA to stop.

As the loyalist 'death squads' cut their murderous swathe through 1986, a new commander took over the FRU. He became known as Colonel 'J' and had been decorated with the Queen's Gallantry Medal (QGM) for his previous service with the unit between 1979 and 1982. (In 2001, he was believed to be still serving, although in a different capacity.) 'In January 1987 we were reviewing our current agent coverage and we identified a gap in our coverage of the loyalist paramilitaries,' he said. 'We examined the case of Brian Nelson and decided that we should try and re-recruit him.'[1] Accordingly, at the beginning of 1987, in the teeth of opposition from MI5 who believed the loyalist paramilitaries were sufficiently covered, the FRU decided to bring Nelson back from Germany and re-infiltrate him inside the UFF. Colonel 'J' ordered the move. MI5 felt that Nelson should be left where he was and not brought back to muddy the waters. The FRU got its way. Nelson was persuaded to return to his old haunts on the Shankill Road, given a code number, Agent 6137, and instructed to pick up where he left off.

'Geoff' was a fan of Nelson. 'He was a soldier not a "tout",' he said. 'He saw himself as part of a team.' Colonel 'J' claimed that although Nelson provided the UFF with much of the information its gunmen required, he was not really in a position to know who was going to be involved in the attacks, when they would actually take place or how the planning was done. In some cases, he said, Nelson might find out, in others he would not. Every time a handler met Nelson, invariably around once a week, a record of the encounter would be compiled in what was known as a Military Intelligence Source Report (MISR, pronounced 'miser'). Overall, Colonel 'J' calculated that the FRU produced 730 MISRs on its dealings with Nelson, involving threats to 217 individuals.[2] He described such information as of 'life-saving potential'. Colonel 'J' also pointed out that senior Special Branch officers at RUC Headquarters and Regional level as well as senior MI5 officers knew of Nelson and his work for the FRU.

When Nelson was brought back from Germany, 'Geoff' became his co-handler and was responsible for his resettlement in Belfast. 'We brought his family back into this dangerous job, paid the deposit on a house and car and set him up in a taxi firm. Initially we paid him a salary of £200 a week, rising as time went on, to do this job specifically for us. He was also paid generous bonuses on a regular basis. At the time there was a lack of information coming in from the loyalist side and we needed someone to give us that information. They were just killing people and they didn't care who they were. To me Brian Nelson was a patriot doing an extraordinary job.' Again, with surprising rapidity, Nelson rose to become the UFF's Senior Intelligence Officer, this time not just for Belfast but for the whole of the province. His remit from the FRU was to encourage the UFF to redirect its 'death squads' from innocent Catholics to suspected republican terrorists. The FRU was pleased with the results, as the MISRs clearly indicate. One dated 3 May 1988 reports, '6137 wants the UDA only to attack legitimate targets and not innocent Catholics. Since 6137 took up his position as intelligence officer, the targeting has developed and become more professional.'[3] Nelson's 'professionalism' was not always apparent. A week after that MISR was written, he gave a UFF gunman an incorrect address with the result that the 'wrong' man, Terence McDaid (29), was shot dead instead of the 'target', his brother Declan. Nelson had carried out 'eyes-on' surveillance of Declan McDaid but identified the wrong address in the electoral register.

The FRU assisted Nelson to be more 'professional' in his targeting by helping him to compile the intelligence to carry out such operations. 'Geoff' showed him how to organize the material and make presentations that would impress his paramilitary bosses. 'We suggested that he collate all the information and we taught him the rudimentary system of compiling "P" [Personality] cards and photographs.' Nelson used to bring 'Geoff' and the other handlers intelligence material that the UFF had gathered from other sources, mainly from the RUC and UDR, usually packed into a large kitbag. The documents would then be copied and returned since Nelson could not afford to attract suspicion by having to explain that some of the material had gone missing. In the end, to facilitate the process and minimize the risk to their agent, the FRU suggested that Nelson put everything on computer. (The UDA, not the FRU, had provided it on the basis that it would streamline the UFF's operation.) From then on, Nelson could bring his handlers the data on floppy disk without arousing suspicion.

In theory, the FRU's purpose in encouraging Nelson to focus the UDA's targeting on IRA suspects was to save lives, not only the lives of innocent Catholics but the lives of republicans too. That was certainly 'Geoff's' understanding, the theory being that once Nelson informed his handlers that an attack was due to take place, the target could be warned or appropriate steps taken by TCG Belfast to prevent it.

This is how the chain was supposed to work. Nelson would warn 'Geoff' and then 'Geoff' would warn his FRU superiors who would then inform Colonel 'J'. TCG Belfast would then be brought into the picture and decide what, if any, action to take. On many occasions the system worked as intended, most notably when Nelson told 'Geoff' of a planned assassination attempt on Gerry Adams.

Adams had already survived one assassination attempt by the UFF on 14 April 1984 when he was attacked by gunmen as he left Belfast Magistrates Court on the second day of his trial for a minor public order offence.[4] The gunmen fired twenty shots and hit Adams with four of them. Adams was rushed to the nearby Royal Victoria Hospital, given emergency surgery and survived. I subsequently interviewed one of his UFF attackers, John Gregg, in the Maze prison. His only regret, he said, was that he had not succeeded in killing him. Adams is alleged by some to have survived because the bullets had been 'doctored' by the 'Det', thus negating their lethal impact.

Having failed to kill Adams once, the UFF was determined to try again. In early 1987, Nelson rang 'Geoff' and said he needed to see him urgently as the UFF was planning to kill the Sinn Fein President near Corporation Buildings in the centre of Belfast. 'Geoff' explained what the plan was and how it would work. 'The UFF knew that this time he was in an armoured vehicle with two or three minders. The plan was to use a Libyan-type limpet mine with a short fuse and magnet, have a pillion rider clamp it on the roof and accelerate away.' Adams and his minders would have been burned to a cinder.

'Geoff' passed the intelligence upwards and Belfast TCG placed the loyalist who had the mine under surveillance. The location of the limpet mine was identified and the army then conducted a 'rummage' search of the general area, looking into dustbins, hedgerows, derelict buildings and everything. 'And lo and behold,' said 'Geoff', 'there was a grip with the device in it! The mine was seized, the plan was aborted and Gerry Adams lives.' Nelson's involvement was never suspected as he was several removes from the discovery. The fact that Adams is alive today illustrates that the system worked. Many other lives were saved too. But many were not. The theory and practice were fine when used as intended. But that was not always the case. There were times when Nelson did not tell his handlers everything, and even when he did and the information went 'upstairs', it was not always acted upon. The brutal UFF killing of one republican, which took place after 'Geoff' had ceased to handle Nelson, is a chilling illustration.

Just after 4 a.m. on the morning of 23 September 1988, Teresa Slane and her husband, Gerard, were awakened by sounds outside the bedroom window of their house off Belfast's Falls Road. Gerard, who'd just bought a new Nissan Sunny, got up to check that joyriders, who were the plague of the area, were not about to make off with it. He returned to bed and told Teresa it was probably only an army patrol checking the registration. A few minutes later, four masked UFF gunmen smashed in the door with a sledgehammer and rushed upstairs to find their target.

The UFF later claimed that Gerard Slane had been involved in the killing of a prominent UDA man, William Quee, a fortnight earlier. Quee was gunned down by the Irish People's Liberation Army (IPLO), a tiny splinter group that had parted company with the INLA after a feud in 1986. An RUC detective said there was nothing to suggest that Slane had been involved in the killing.

Gerard tried to fight the intruders off on the stairs with a step ladder but was gunned down in the process. He was shot four times in the head. His final words were, 'Teresa, it's the "Orangies"!' When she rushed out onto the landing, she saw her husband lying dead. 'He was completely covered in blood. I actually saw a pin-hole in the side of his head and blood coming out through his nose and mouth. Blood was all over the wall.'

Nelson had provided the killers with the vital intelligence that had enabled the 'hit' to go ahead. He had found Slane's address, checked it in the electoral register, got hold of a photograph and made out a 'P' card on him. 'Brian Nelson may not have pulled the trigger,' Teresa told me, 'but to me he was as guilty of my husband's murder as the actual murderers themselves.' But in the case of Gerard Slane, Nelson had done his job. He had warned one of 'Geoff's' successors on two occasions that Slane was being targeted, initially ten days before the attack took place and then the day before the attack itself.

For whatever reason, the intelligence from Nelson was not acted upon. Teresa had no warning visit from the RUC and no attempt was made to thwart the attack. 'My husband might have been here today were it not for the RUC,' she says bitterly. But there's no evidence that the RUC ever knew about it. So what happened to the information? Did it get beyond the FRU? Was it sanitized somewhere up the chain? Did it ever get to the TCG? Was a decision taken to let the killers go ahead? Or was the information simply not precise enough?

Those who came to know Nelson said he had a passionate hatred for the IRA and a 'psychopathic tendency'. This may have inclined him to act on his own as well as with the encouragement of the FRU. 'Geoff' claims Nelson did much of the intelligence work himself and had to do so to maintain his own credibility with the UFF. 'He constantly asked me for information, to check out a car number plate or an address. As a rule I used to say to him, "It's better that you collect this information yourself because you have to be seen to be doing this job. You can't just disappear and come back with it in a day or two."' 'Geoff' was aware that people would get suspicious and his agent's life was on the line every day. But did 'Geoff' personally ever supply him with information? 'No, not directly. But if he said, "Is that so-and-so's registration?" I would say to him, "You don't have that wrong."' If that was the case, I asked, and the car owner was killed, weren't he and the FRU complicit in murder? 'Geoff' was matter-of-fact. 'Well, it's a fine line you walk,' he said. I pointed out that in the end Nelson went to gaol for conspiracies to murder. 'Yes,' he replied, 'at our request.' Encouraged by him and his colleagues? 'Yes.' And by the FRU? 'Yes.' And by British intelligence? 'Yes.' 'Geoff' was astonishingly candid:

I'm ashamed of it. He strayed outside the law at our behest. We instructed him to carry on his job of targeting these people. There were certain risks but it was loosely seen by my hierarchy that if he carried out an action and then reported it, it would negate his guilt. In other words he was doing his job under our direction and once he'd informed us of what he had done, it would not be illegal. Brian believed, not that he was bullet proof, but that he had protection from us and that what he was doing, he was doing at our request and therefore he had immunity. And he didn't.

Nelson's role as a FRU agent came to light in the wake of the UFF's killing of a Catholic from Rathfriland, County Down, called Loughlin Maginn (28) on 25 August 1989. Maginn had never been charged or convicted of any terrorist offence. The UFF insisted he was an IRA intelligence officer, and what is more, said they could prove it. The UDA subsequently produced copies of confidential security force material containing information on suspected terrorists. Details of Maginn were included. The classified details were thought to have come from a UDR base in County Down. To republicans and nationalists it was evidence of what they had always maintained, that the loyalist 'death squads' were the puppets of British intelligence.

On 14 September 1989, in response to the huge outcry that followed the killing of Maginn and revelation of the classified intelligence material, Sir John Hermon's successor as RUC Chief Constable, Sir Hugh Annesley, appointed the Deputy Chief Constable of Cambridgeshire, John Stevens, to investigate the theft and leaking of the security force intelligence documents. Eleven years later, when Mr Stevens became Sir John Stevens, Commissioner of the Metropolitan Police, the now widened investigation was still going on as Sir John and his team of detectives continued to piece together the elaborate jigsaw of alleged collusion between the FRU and the loyalist paramilitaries.

In his initial inquiry, Stevens made numerous arrests as a result of which members of the old UDA/UFF leadership were gaoled, leaving the way open for Johnny 'Mad Dog' Adair and his associates to take over the UFF's 'C' Company on the Shankill Road. Four months into the inquiry, as the trail led the Stevens team ever closer to Nelson, whose fingerprints were on many of the intelligence documents, a mysterious fire broke out on 10 January 1990 at the office of the Northern Ireland Police Authority in Carrickfergus where the team was based. The fire broke out on the very day that Nelson was due to be arrested. That same day he fled to England to escape arrest. The events seemed to be too coincidental to be an accident. When the team discovered the blaze, they found that the fire alarms were not working and the telephone lines were dead.[5] The obvious suspicions were aroused – that the FRU were involved in the fire. But Nelson's freedom was short-lived. He was quickly arrested by Stevens' team. From early on, he had been under strict instructions that were he ever to be arrested, he was to say nothing to the police about his involvement with the FRU. Under the circumstances, he had little choice and gave the team the name of his handler as everything began to come out.

When Nelson was arrested, the intake of breath from FRU's 'Office' at HQNI must almost have been audible. What would happen when he appeared in court? What would his fate be? Would he 'sing' and if so to what tune? Nelson appeared in court on 20 January 1992 accused of possessing details on republicans that would be of use to terrorists.[6] At first it was thought he was just another UDA/UFF member caught in the net until the sensational news broke that he was not only the UFF's intelligence chief but a British agent. The only jaws that did not drop were those of republicans who had insisted all along that the 'Brits' were hand in glove with the loyalist killers. Colonel 'J' gave evidence anonymously, and Nelson pleaded guilty to five charges of conspiracy to murder, thus sparing the army and the FRU the embarrassment of a potentially explosive cross-examination. These charges reflected only a fraction of Nelson's activities. The army's records together with Nelson's own notes are said to indicate that Nelson was involved in at least fifteen murders, fifteen attempted murders and sixty-two conspiracies to murder during the two years when he was handled by the FRU.[7] Nelson was sentenced to ten years. He served half of his sentence, was released in 1997 and given a new identity outside Northern Ireland.

'Geoff' had always assumed that the 'Brits' would look after Nelson and was astonished and dismayed when he went down for simply carrying out his orders from the FRU. At least that's how 'Geoff' saw it.

> He saved, in my estimation, dozens of lives. He was essential to the war effort and gave us an insight into the loyalist organizations we never had in the past. He was the jewel in the crown. I'm ashamed at the way he's been treated by the Establishment who used him and guided him and put him in that position. He was hung out to dry. I was disgusted. I promised Brian that the Establishment would look after him and it didn't. It let him down and I'm ashamed of that.

Towards the end of his time as handler, 'Geoff' did become concerned at the way Nelson was behaving. Not surprisingly, given his perilous position, he was under intense psychological pressure. The pressure was physical too. In August 1988, Nelson was taken to a house on the outskirts of Lisburn and subjected to a violent interrogation by the UFF in which he was 'assaulted, brutalized', and thrown into 'physical convulsions on the floor' when he was stabbed on the back of the neck with an electric cattle-prod.[8] Remarkably the interrogation was *not* because the UFF suspected that Nelson was working for the 'Brits' but because they suspected he was leaking information to the IRA. In 'Geoff's' view, Nelson was also getting reckless. 'He would take unnecessary chances. For example, he would sit on the Falls Road licking an ice-cream, targeting what he believed to be top Provisional IRA members, with no back-up whatsoever. He was becoming careless and I could see that he was getting into this targeting very deeply.' 'Geoff' put his concerns in writing and sent a report to his superiors, recommending that Nelson should be stood down for a while. His report was ignored. 'I was told that he was too important and that he had to stay in place because the information coming in was so important,' he said. Nelson stayed put and became involved in even more controversial killings, which, many years later, were to have sensational repercussions. By the year 2000, with the Inquiry now more than a decade old, Sir John Stevens had entrusted day-to-day operational command of the investigation to one of his Deputy Assistant Commissioners, Hugh Orde, with orders to leave no stone unturned. Mr Orde and the Stevens team carried out the Metropolitan Police Commissioner's instruction, finally getting access to the FRU's top secret records (including the book that recorded all intelligence passed on to Special Branch) and getting ever closer to the truth of what happened. The MOD's nerves were jangling at the prospect of what might be revealed, so much so that injunctions were issued against the *Sunday Times* and the *Sunday People* newspapers who sought to tell their readers what the FRU was alleged to have done in their name. The most potentially explosive allegation of all was that the FRU had guided Brian Nelson to direct the UFF to kill a 66-year-old veteran Ballymurphy republican, Francisco Notarantonio, who was shot dead as he lay in his bed on 9 October 1987. Notarantonio had been involved in the IRA in the 1940s and interned in the 1970s but he had long ceased to be active. It was alleged that the unwitting UFF had been inadvertently directed to do so in order to divert their attention from the person believed to have been the FRU's top agent within the IRA, code-named 'Steak Knife', whom they planned to kill. 'Steak Knife' was a priceless asset for the 'Brits' and is alleged to have worked for British intelligence for many years at a rate of £75,000 per annum, reportedly paid through a secret bank account in Gibraltar.[9] Astonishingly, it alleged that when the FRU found out from Nelson that the UFF were planning to shoot 'Steak Knife' (without either Nelson or the UFF having any idea that he was working for British intelligence), the FRU gave Nelson the name of Notarantonio as a substitute target to protect their top agent. The scenario seems more suited to a Tom Clancy thriller but in Northern Ireland fiction and fact sometimes mingle – hence, no doubt, the injunctions against newspapers. If the remarkable allegation proves to be fact not fantasy, Hugh Orde and the Stevens team were on the brink of breaking one of the most explosive stories of the Troubles.

Almost equally sensitive was the killing of the solicitor Pat Finucane, who represented Bobby Sands during his hunger strike and acted for many republicans over the years. Two of his brothers, Dermot and Seamus, were senior members of the IRA. A third brother, John, died in a car crash whilst on IRA 'active service' in 1972.[10] Pat was gunned down by masked UFF gunmen whilst he was having supper with his family on 12 February 1989. A week before, a MISR indicated '6137 initiates most of the targeting. Of late, 6137 has been more organized and he is currently running an operation against selected republican targets.'[11] The loyalists smashed in the door with a sledgehammer and shot Pat Finucane fourteen times in front of his wife, Geraldine, and their three children. They left him bleeding to death on the kitchen floor.[12] Nelson had helped provide the intelligence that led to the attack by supplying the killers with a photograph of Pat Finucane leaving Crumlin Road Courthouse with one of his republican clients. He handed it over three days before Finucane was shot. Nelson maintained that he assumed the client was the target not his solicitor.[13]

The killing of Pat Finucane and Francisco Notarantonio and the allegations of collusion that swirl round them remain the most sensitive of all the matters still under investigation by the Stevens Inquiry more than a decade after its inception. Sir John and his team remained determined to get to the bottom of what happened, not just in these two cases but in the others in which Brian Nelson was involved. John Stalker plunged into the murky world of covert operations in Northern Ireland and lived to rue the day. The Commissioner of the Metropolitan Police had no intention of letting the same thing happen to him. The can of worms labelled 'Brian Nelson' that he opened all those years ago still has to be closed. At the time of writing, the dénouement has yet to come.

Chapter Twenty-Seven

Turning the Screw

June 1988–February 1992

Although the IRA's four shipments from Libya contained a few spectacular additions to its armoury like SAM 7 surface-to-air missiles,[1] the most lethal donation from Colonel Gaddafi was a large quantity of Semtex high explosive. This could be used on its own to devastating effect or as a booster for the IRA's huge fertilizer-based bombs. Nineteen eighty-eight was the year of Semtex and there was little the 'Brits' could do to counter it beyond warning the security forces to be vigilant and look under their cars before they got in. Twelve people died that year when Semtex booby-trap bombs exploded under their vehicles.[2] Although the SAS operations at Loughgall and Gibraltar were severe setbacks for the IRA, as was the Remembrance Day bomb at Enniskillen, none of them blunted its offensive. Largely due to Semtex, thirty-four soldiers died in 1988, more than in any other year since 1982.[3] Fourteen of the victims died in two bombings. In the first, on 15 June, six were killed as they returned to their barracks in an unmarked van after taking part in a charity 'fun run' in Lisburn to raise funds for the YMCA. The IRA had placed 7.5 lbs of Semtex under their vehicle which exploded when the van stopped at traffic lights. It was thought that the IRA had planted the bomb whilst the soldiers were running.[4]

The second incident, two months later, was even more traumatic. Soldiers from The Light Infantry Regiment, with only six months of their two-year tour of duty to go, were returning from leave and on their way back to their base at Omagh, having been collected by coach from Aldergrove airport. For whatever reason, the driver chose to take a particular stretch of the A5 trunk road, known locally as 'bomb alley', that the army had been told to avoid as there was intelligence of 'a threat' along it. As the coach bypassed the village of Ballygawley, the IRA detonated a 25- to 30-lb Semtex bomb by command wire. The coach was hurled into the air and crashed on its side. The result was devastating.

Eight young soldiers, all between eighteen and twenty-one years old, were killed, most of them instantaneously. Twenty-seven were injured.

One of the IRA suspects was Gerard Harte (29), who was believed to be the commander of the IRA in mid-Tyrone. Ten days later, he was dead, along with his brother, Martin (22), and another IRA man, Brian Mullin (25). All were killed in an SAS ambush not far from the spot where the eight young soldiers had died. The operation against this particular ASU had been planned for some time and was not put in place as a direct result of the Ballygawley bomb. The three had been under 'Det' surveillance and an MI5 'bug' had been planted in one of their houses.[5] TCG South had established that the unit planned to kill a UDR man who drove an easily recognized lorry around the area, calling at coal depots and visiting the joint RUC/army barracks in Carrickmore and the UDR barracks in Omagh.[6] A carefully planned ambush was set up. An SAS soldier, bearing some resemblance to the driver, took over the wheel of the lorry as a decoy and for a couple of days followed the UDR man's usual route to lure the IRA into a trap. On 30 August, the SAS decoy stopped the vehicle at a pre-arranged spot on a country lane near Drumnakilly, knowing that the IRA was unlikely to ignore such an obvious opportunity for a 'kill'. He acted as if his vehicle had broken down and pretended to be attending to a wheel. The Harte brothers and Mullin drove by in a white Sierra, planning to kill the driver of the truck whom they believed to be the off-duty UDR soldier. They were wearing blue overalls and black masks and armed with two AK 47s and a Webley .38 revolver.

Around a dozen SAS soldiers were lying in wait, some of them manning a heavy machine gun as they had done at Loughgall the previous year. The army said the IRA opened fire first and the SAS returned it as the 'decoy' dived for cover over a wall. A local farmer working in a field a few hundred yards away told a different story. He did not see the shooting but heard the first burst of firing, describing it as loud and rapid, which would suggest the SAS machine gun. But whoever fired first, the ASU was never going to leave the scene alive. The IRA fired sixteen shots. The SAS fired 236. The IRA never stood a chance. The subsequent inquest did not reach any conclusion about who fired first. There is no doubt that the SAS soldier changing the wheel was an *agent provocateur*, and a very brave one at that. Two days later, Mrs Thatcher made her position clear. 'When you are faced with terrorism, you obviously do not let the terrorists know precisely what steps you are taking to counter their terrorism. Nor shall we. But my message to them is this: *Do not doubt our resolve to defeat terrorism.*'[7]

In the face of increasing demands for tougher action after the Bally-gawley bomb, the Government acted on another front too. On 19 October 1988, six weeks after the Drumnakilly ambush, the Home

Secretary, Douglas Hurd, announced restrictions to prevent broadcasters from transmitting the voices of members of organizations involved in 'terrorism' or organizations that were deemed to support it, except when discussing constituency matters or at election time. Although the restrictions were primarily aimed at the IRA and Sinn Fein, they affected other republican organizations and loyalist groups too. Those covered by the restrictions, which became known as 'the broadcasting ban', could be seen but not heard. The 'ban' was introduced on the grounds that the British public found it offensive to hear the words of those who espoused violence. If that was the case, clearly the sight of them on television would be even more offensive but the Government was not going to fall into the trap of actually banning them from the screen as this would have been a propaganda 'own goal', skilfully exploited by Sinn Fein.

Broadcasters were not prepared to take this restriction to their freedom lying down, and used sub-titles and actors' voices to repeat the words of the 'banned' individuals. Some got it down to a fine art, lip-syncing an actor's voice to the real person's lips. One actor, who imitated Gerry Adams to perfection, is said to have made a small fortune. Despite the ridicule the restrictions increasingly attracted, not least from the broadcasters themselves, they did have some effect. In the four months before the 'ban', Sinn Fein had 471 enquiries for interviews. In the four months after, the party had enquiries for only 110.[8]

The 'ban' presented us with almost insuperable difficulties when we made the BBC television documentary 'Enemies Within' in the summer of 1990, when, with the NIO's permission, I interviewed a host of IRA and loyalist paramilitary prisoners inside the Maze. In principle we faced the prospect of wall-to-wall sub-titles or actors' voices; in practice we found what we believed to be a legitimate way round it. After long discussions, we decided that as long as the interviewees were deemed to be speaking in their *personal* capacity and not as spokespersons for their particular 'banned' organizations, we could transmit the sound of their own voices. This we did with one or two exceptions, the most notable being the IRA's 'food spokesman' who, in discussion with the prison's cooks, was complaining about the size of the sausage rolls. We subtitled his words, 'the thing about the sausage rolls, they're getting smaller' as he was speaking in an official capacity on behalf of the IRA. I understand that following the programme, his reign as IRA 'food spokesman' came to an abrupt end.

The restrictions were finally removed, after nearly six years, on 16 September 1994, just over a fortnight after the IRA announced its historic cease-fire. Lord Mayhew, who as Sir Patrick Mayhew was both Attorney-General (1987–92) and Northern Ireland Secretary (1992–7) whilst the 'ban' was in operation, was not convinced, with hindsight, that it had been effective. 'It came after a series of hideous outrages by the IRA and there was a very great need to be seen to be doing something about it,' he told me. 'I don't think it actually served very much purpose but I wholly understood why it was introduced.' It was Sir Patrick who finally put an end to it.

As they continued to pile on the pressure, Special Branch and the 'Group' were far more effective than any broadcasting restrictions in countering the IRA. The 'ban' was cosmetic whereas the impact of the intelligence services was real and increasingly worrying to the IRA, given the growing sophistication of the technical and electronic surveillance aids now at the disposal of the 'Brits'. By the end of the 1980s, Mrs Thatcher had quietly authorized a huge sum of money (I heard the figure £20 million) to be spent on acquiring and developing the latest technology. The ring of giant watchtowers the military constructed along the border, in particular in South Armagh, was a visible sign that the army could keep an eye on its enemy in both North and South. On top of the towers were cameras with enormous lenses giving the army the ability to monitor 'targets' without the 'targets' necessarily knowing that they were being watched. The watchtowers advertised the fact that the IRA was under surveillance. The 'Det' covert cameras did not. 'Ken' was trained to be one of 14 Intelligence Company's technical surveillance experts, using video cameras that could transmit live, 'real time' television pictures, in colour, of whatever premises or person they were focused on. These live pictures could then be transmitted by microwave link to intelligence monitoring stations up to fifty miles and more away. 'We could watch the daily routine of particular suspects and the buildup of operations,' he told me. 'You could work out what was going to happen or the intelligence services could figure out the type of operation from the type of characters who turned up.'

The 'Det' covert cameras were particularly useful for cross-border surveillance, enabling the 'Brits' to watch what was going on without running the political risk of being physically caught on the wrong side of the line. 'Ken' said in one operation they had been watching 'one of South Armagh's main players' living just across the border in the South for two years.

> With a long lens, we could see into his house, watch him having his breakfast, see what was on the table and who was with him. We knew when he left his house and when he came back. We knew what he was doing in the house and around it. Blokes sat watching him for weeks. And these are live, television pictures, transmitted back to TCG South so they could be watched and acted upon with decisions being made at the highest level very quickly. We could watch him at night too in black and white with infra-red.

Concealing a camera with a giant lens was not easy. It was usually dug into the ground and camouflaged 'using all the skills of nature' to hide it in places so remote that only the 'Det' could get to them. Operators could either stay with the camera or operate it from a distance by remote control which meant that if the camera was compromised, the operator was not. Such close-up surveillance operations on the 'bad guys' were conducted province-wide and against loyalists as well as republicans. 'Ken' worked everywhere from South Armagh to Bangor and Derry. 'I know who they are, who they meet, where they go, when they leave, when they come back, both day and night depending on the type of camera you're watching.' Microphones attached to some cameras could pick up conversations taking place a considerable distance away.

Where appropriate for intimate surveillance close up to the 'target', the 'Det' used tiny cameras with even tinier lenses. But however small, these still had to be camouflaged to blend in with their surroundings. And it was not just the camera itself that had to be concealed. The battery that powered it and the cable to the transmitter all had to be disguised and hidden, using whatever natural material was available. Sometimes the camera would be concealed inside a rock that was an exact replica of a real rock at a particular spot close to the 'target'. The rock would be covertly photographed at night with an infra-red camera and an identical replica made, usually by the operator himself, back at base. It was then replaced at night on the exact spot it had come from but now with a tiny camera inside. 'Ken', like most of the 'Det' operators, loved his work and knew how important it was. 'To think that these operations may well have saved one or two lives is a great achievement,' he said.

It would be naïve to think that the IRA did not know what was going on. They did, and made every effort to counter the increasingly effective surveillance of the 'Brits' by 'executing' informers, electronically 'sweeping' premises and individuals, and uncovering hidden cameras and listening devices in rooms, cars and the countryside. When Brendan Hughes was finally released from the Maze in 1986, he found the 'Brits' were far ahead in their surveillance and intelligence-gathering techniques compared with when he was arrested in 1974 at Myrtlefield Park. The days of the 'Four Square laundry' were long gone. 'British Intelligence learned an awful lot by their war here,' he said.

The listening devices, the undercover operations, the tailing, the cameras, were everywhere. The 'Brits' would leave a car sitting on the street with a small camera looking at a particular house. They just parked the car and put a small camera on the house. It was fitted inside the car aerial and the aerial could be directed by remote control. And they were live pictures. There was no need to leave an undercover operations officer sitting there.

According to Hughes, the 'Brits' left a trail of high-tech equipment littered across the province.

There were loads of cases where they've been caught, where they've actually left cameras looking into the gardens of prominent republicans' houses. All over the country, they were finding them all the time. The houses of prominent active republicans [IRA men] are known to have been bugged with sophisticated devices bolted into the beam of the ceiling which covered the bedrooms, the sitting room and kitchen. I know of two cases where this happened. They go in the middle of the night and install these listening devices or do it during renovation work or even when a house has been searched. You have no control over what is planted so a massive amount of listening equipment has been dropped in Belfast.

What did the technology enable British Intelligence to do?
Effectively to bring the IRA to a standstill where it could move very, very little. I think that's what that technology did and what the intelligence services were able to do. I think they were able to effectively stop the IRA and contain it.

But although the intelligence services may, on 'Ken's' calculation, have been successful 80 per cent of the time, that still left the IRA with a 20 per cent window of opportunity of which they took full advantage. England remained the prime target not only because of the impact of bombs on the mainland but because England was not covered by the surveillance net that now ensnared Northern Ireland. Getting under the wire in an English city in the late 1980s and 1990s was easier than doing so in Belfast or Derry. Military bases across England were particularly vulnerable and their security could not be guaranteed: in Northern Ireland, an army barracks was a fortification, at home it was part of the scenery.

To the regimental bandsmen at the Royal Marines School of Music at Deal in Kent, eating their breakfast and relaxing before the morning rehearsal on 22 September 1989, the 'war' in Northern Ireland seemed a million miles away. Suddenly, at 8.22 a.m., a 50-lb bomb on a timer exploded, killing ten members of the regiment. It was the biggest bomb the IRA had set off in England since Brighton in 1984. Their Commandant General referred to the IRA as 'thugs, extortionists, torturers, murderers and cowards, in fact the scum of the earth'. The mother of the band's alto-sax player said, 'I can never forgive the IRA. All we have to look forward to is the funeral and an empty life. Instead of putting them in prison, which does no good, they should be put up against a wall and shot.'[9] Security at Deal had been the responsibility of a private security firm. As a result, security around all military establishments was tightened.

The IRA also struck again in Europe, where it enjoyed an even greater freedom of movement. On 26 October 1989 two IRA gunmen with automatic weapons opened fire on a car at Wildenrath, in Germany, as it stopped at a petrol station snack bar. The driver, Corporal Maheshkumar Islania, was not a soldier but a member of the Royal Air Force who was a supervisor at the RAF communications centre at Wildenrath. Corporal Islania tried to drive away but was pursued by the gunmen, firing repeatedly. He was not alone in the car. With him was his wife and six-month-old baby daughter, Nivruti Mahesh. She was shot once through the head and became one of the youngest victims to die in the conflict. Her father was hit many times. Her mother, Mrs Smita Islania, survived although in deep shock. She refused to leave her daughter and sat there, wrapped in a blanket, clutching her tiny, lifeless frame.[10]

The German police subsequently issued a warrant for the arrest of Desmond 'Dessie' Grew (37). His brother, Seamus Grew, had been killed with Roddie Carroll by the HMSU in 1982 in one of the shootings that John Stalker investigated. Dessie Grew, like his brother, was originally a member of the INLA but left to join the Provisionals. Like Seamus, Dessie was kept under close surveillance by the 'Det'. 'Mary' was one of the operators on his tail. 'He'd been a terrorist for twenty-odd years,' she told me. 'We all knew his chequered past, how many people he'd killed and how many acts of terrorism he'd been involved in.'

In the autumn of 1990, there was intelligence that Grew was going to collect weapons and kill someone, presumably a member of the security forces, although the intelligence did not specify whom. The weapons, AK 47s, were concealed in an IRA 'hide' in a mushroom shed on a farm just outside Loughgall. The shed had been under surveillance for some time and one of the assault rifles may have been 'jarked' at some stage. There may also have been a listening device. 'Mary' was tasked to be the 'drop-off' driver for the 'troop', the members of the SAS team who were to set up an OP near the shed. The operation had already been going on, round the clock, for about a week. 'Mary' planned to drop the 'troop' off near the location and then lie up in a quiet and secluded position where the van would not be seen from the road. That particular night, 9 October 1990, there was no specific intelligence that Grew was coming and 'Mary' just expected it to be a routine 'drop-off' and to do what she usually did.

As a drop-off driver, your tasks are very simple: to drive them in, pick them up and take them home. I would make a couple of flasks of coffee and I would have some moist baby-wipes because obviously the guys are all 'cammed' up with cream all over their faces. When they came off in the morning, they'd be freezing cold, gagging for a cuppa and wanting to get all this dirt off their face. Maybe I'd have some biscuits or crisps stashed in the vehicle with me, ready to give the guys in the morning.

'Mary' sat in the van in her 'lay-up' position for about three or four hours listening to the radio 'net'. She was about 350 to 400 metres away from the mushroom shed. It was a quiet, dark autumnal night and the air was very still. Suddenly she heard 'Standby, Standby', which meant that something was going to happen. Grew and another man had turned up to collect the weapons. The 'other man' was Martin McCaughey from Cappagh, a former Sinn Fein councillor. She then listened to the commentary from the 'troop' hiding in the bushes, watching Grew and McCaughey's every move.

I was sitting in the van with the doors locked and the windows slightly wound down and just listening. Suddenly there was this thunderous roar of 7.62 fire going down. It's very loud and you feel the jolt. It's not like watching it on TV when you just hear like a crack or a bang. This is 'kerboom', several times, shattering the quietness of the night.

McCaughey and Grew wouldn't have stood much of a chance, would they?

They walked out of that barn carrying AK 47s, walking in the direction of the 'troop' guys. At the end of the day, they were terrorists on a mission and they met their Maker. I didn't feel sad or elated. I didn't feel anything at the terrorists' deaths. They chose to do that. I was just glad that our guys were all right. The terrorists had a clean 'getaway' car as well as the 'operational' car there. And in the clean car was a bottle of whisky. Now why would you have that? Only to celebrate the death of some innocent person they're just going out to murder in cold blood.

Was a warning given?

Yes. A warning is always given. Special Forces, like regular forces, operate under the rules of the Yellow Card. We are governed by the same body of rules as anybody else when it comes to opening fire.

Grew and McCaughey died where they fell, with two AK 47s close by. 'Mary' handed out the coffee and the baby-wipes on the way back to base.

The following year, 'Mary' was involved in an operation in which the intelligence was spot-on. The targets were three members of the IRA's East Tyrone Brigade, Lawrence McNally (38), Pete Ryan (37) and Tony Doris (21). 'They'd been part of a Provisional IRA terror group for years,' 'Mary' said. 'Again, we knew all their history, all the incidents that they'd played a part in and all the deaths they'd been a party to. On this particular occasion they'd planned to go and assassinate a civilian on his way to work. We had information and it was very good.' I understand there was also technical surveillance involved. The intelligence indicated that the IRA's target was to be killed in the heart of the Protestant village of Coagh on the morning of 3 June 1991. A car had been hijacked the previous evening in nearby Moneymore. At least half a dozen agencies were tasked by TCG South to carry out the operation. The planning was meticulous. 'Every job has a very detailed plan which is gone over and over and over again,' 'Mary' said. 'That's one of the reasons why the Special Forces are seen to be as good as they are because it's prior planning and preparation, over and over.'

Early the following morning, the stolen car was tracked both on the ground and from the air on its journey to Coagh. The three IRA men had no idea they were being followed and that an SAS ambush had been prepared in Coagh's main street. Nor did they know that their 'target' was an SAS decoy who, like the driver of the broken-down lorry at Drumnakilly in 1988, bore a passing resemblance to the person the IRA were intending to kill. The SAS soldier was sitting in the car, as the target usually did, as if waiting for his friend to go to work. 'He was a sitting duck, waiting for the terrorists to turn up and take him out.'

At 7.30 a.m., the IRA drove into Coagh high street and, according to 'Mary', were pointing their weapons and about to open fire on the man in the car when the SAS issued a warning and then opened up. The decoy, within inches of his life, leapt out of the vehicle and made for cover. 'He was literally seconds away from being "malleted" by PIRA and he managed to escape at the last minute. Who else is going to do it apart from an SAS man?' The car, riddled with 200 rounds, crashed and burst into flames. 'Mary' had never seen anything like it before. 'There was a massive fireball and smoke, hundreds of feet in the air. It was like watching a James Bond movie.' McNally, Ryan and Doris died in the car. The weapons recovered were forensically examined and shown to have been used in four previous killings. 'Mary' had no sympathy or regrets. Nor had the local Westminster MP for the area, the Reverend William McCrea, a member of Ian Paisley's DUP. 'They have fallen into the pit they planned for others,' he said. 'Justice has now been done.'[11]

Despite 'Mary's' view, shared by her 'Det' colleague 'Anna', that the

'Group' had decimated the IRA's East Tyrone Brigade, killing eight of its members at Loughgall, three at Drumnakilly, two at the mushroom shed, and now three at Coagh, there was no shortage of recruits to take their places. Four more were to die a year later, the SAS's last victims in Northern Ireland. On 16 February 1992, an ASU attacked Coalisland RUC station with a 12.7 mm Russian-made Degtyarev heavy machine gun mounted on the back of a hijacked lorry. It was believed to have been part of one of the Libyan arms shipments. They then drove through the town, an IRA stronghold in East Tyrone, waving an Irish Tricolour. It was suspected they might have been making an IRA propaganda video since there would normally have been no operational reason for them to make such a rash display. Again, there was pin-point intelligence on the IRA's bravado. The lorry drove to the car park of St Patrick's Church at nearby Clonoe where a getaway car was waiting. So too were the SAS.

Four members of the ASU were cut down: Kevin Barry O'Donnell (21), Sean O'Farrell (23), Peter Clancy (19) and Daniel Vincent (20). The previous year, O'Donnell had been acquitted at the Old Bailey in London following a car chase after which two AK 47s were found in the back of his car. In his defence, O'Donnell said he was horrified to find that the IRA had been using his vehicle and claimed he was on his way to dump the weapons at the time.[12] Had the Old Bailey verdict been different, O'Donnell would have still been alive and later eligible for release under the Good Friday Agreement. When he returned to Tyrone, he would immediately have become a target for surveillance, as he returned to his old haunts and picked up again with his old comrades. Kevin Barry O'Donnell had joined the IRA the year after Loughgall. At his funeral, the priest, Father MacLarnon, echoed the feelings of all sides who had suffered so much when he said that it was time for 'the politics of co-operation' to replace 'the politics of confrontation'. His words were prophetic. On the wider political front, outside the killing fields of East Tyrone, things were already moving in that direction.

Chapter Twenty-Eight

The Road to Peace
1988–1992

The long road to peace began with the election of the hunger striker Bobby Sands to Westminster in 1981. The journey was tortuous and bloody. After Sands was buried, over 1,200 more funerals were to follow before the Republican Movement and its former enemies finally signed up to the Good Friday Agreement in 1998.[1] The 'long war' took a long time.

The Provisionals' political thinkers always knew that at some stage the Armalite would have to give way to the Ballot Box. That was the way of 'liberation' movements like Yasser Arafat's Palestine Liberation Organization (PLO) in the Middle East and Nelson Mandela's African National Congress (ANC) in South Africa. The question was when. There were still those in the IRA, however, who believed that the British presence would only end at the point of a gun and that being sucked into a political compromise was walking into a trap designed by the 'Brits' to split and defeat the IRA. They were convinced that although the Ballot Box might be indulged, the Armalite should be grasped firmly in *both* hands as that was the only language British governments understood. They were not prepared to honour the sacrifice of their comrades with anything less than a British withdrawal and the realization of the united Ireland they had fought and died for. The achievement of Gerry Adams, Martin McGuinness and the leadership of the Republican Movement was to travel the road to peace without losing too many of its followers along the way. Peace inevitably involved compromise, and compromise was not a word in every republican lexicon. There were inevitably defections but none that led to the disastrous split that the leadership feared and laboured mightily to avoid.

For their part, the strategy of the 'Brits' was to convince the IRA that they would not be allowed to win. Although in Northern Ireland nothing is straightforward, there is no doubt that the relentless pressure from the intelligence services and their covert arms finally helped bring it home to the IRA that the military victory it believed was attainable in the early 1970s was now no longer possible. The 'Brits' simply knew too much. Nevertheless, it would be wrong to believe that the British *forced* the IRA to the negotiating table. They did not. The IRA was going that way anyway, as its electoral success through the 1980s indicated. What the 'Brits' did, primarily through their covert agencies, was to limit the IRA's options, as the IRA's former Belfast Brigade commander and first hunger strike leader, Brendan Hughes, recognized. When he returned to West Belfast, following his release in 1986, he came to the view that the 'Brits' were causing the IRA major problems because of the number of informers they ran and the sophisticated technology now at their command.

> I think prominent IRA people came to the conclusion that the British military regime could not be defeated, and there had to be negotiations and that was the only way through it. Otherwise, the only alternative was [to carry on] a futile war which I didn't think the leadership were prepared to do.

Hughes was saying publicly and controversially what republicans only whispered, confirming what the 'Brits' themselves believed. Not surprisingly, 'Paul', who had arrested Hughes at Myrtlefield Park in 1974 and whose experience in Special Branch spanned two decades, agreed with his old adversary.

> The IRA didn't change its policy because they had won. They changed their policy because they realized they couldn't win. They recognized that the 'long war' strategy could equally be countered by the security forces and Special Branch, which by now had become a highly sophisticated, efficient and effective organization. They realized that there was no point in their so-called 'war' going on, that their campaign was a waste of time. It had reached an end.

Sir Ronnie Flanagan, who became RUC Chief Constable in 1996 and was knighted in 1998, took a similar view. He had been intimately involved in countering the IRA and the loyalist paramilitaries throughout the 1980s and 1990s in a variety of departments including Special Branch, as a Detective Inspector in 1981 and its Head (HSB) in 1994.[2] He believed the IRA entered negotiations for a whole range of reasons.

> I think, in terms of those who headed the Republican Movement, there was the realization that if they cannot be defeated by military means alone, then neither can they win by military means alone. I

think they came to sense that, 'Yes, we could go on for another twenty-five years engaging in terrorist attacks, but would that actually mean progress towards our ultimate objective?' I think one might wonder that if part of that objective was the reunification of Ireland, did all that violence bring that any closer or did it actually put that day off? I think it was a pragmatic decision that 'yes, we can go on doing this, but will it actually bring closer the achievement of the objective that we are pursuing?' I think they came to the conclusion that the answer to that was 'no'.

In effect, what became known as the 'peace process' developed because of a convergence of interest between the two sides. The 'Brits' too had long reached the conclusion that they could not 'win' in terms of achieving a military victory over the IRA. To do so would have meant using methods that were alien to a liberal democracy. Whatever republicans might think of the *modus operandi* of the 'Brits' (and they would point to collusion and Brian Nelson as examples), the security forces were not in the business of going into republican or loyalist areas and just taking 'terrorists' out, as Mossad and the Israeli Defence Forces were prone to do both at home and abroad.[3]

Having recognized that defeating the IRA was out of the question, the 'Brits' settled in for a war of attrition to wear down and contain it. By the end of the 1980s, a stalemate of sorts had been reached with both sides recognizing the stark choices before them: to carry on shedding more blood or talk. Talking seemed the better option. The problem for the 'Brits' was how to do it without triggering a loyalist explosion in Northern Ireland or a public outcry in England. From the British point of view, there was no blueprint or neatly plotted course on the road to peace. It was almost 'suck it and see'. The objective, however, was clear: to persuade the IRA to abandon the Armalite altogether and embrace the Ballot Box in its entirety. Clearly such a policy would not bear fruit overnight, as the Whitehall mandarins, like republicans, had their own problems, not least with the Prime Minister, Mrs Thatcher. She had set her face against making any concessions to the IRA and there were ten dead hunger strikers to prove it. In fact, the British made a major policy U-turn although it was never admitted as such and certainly never put to Mrs Thatcher in those terms, given that she had once memorably proclaimed that 'the Lady is not for turning'. The U-turn was made on the political front in the context of Sinn Fein, while security policy remained the same: to hit the IRA as hard as possible whenever possible.

The strategic purpose of the 1985 Anglo-Irish Agreement had been to marginalize Sinn Fein and boost their constitutionalist SDLP rivals in the hope that moderate, anti–IRA opinion would prevail. At the first test in the by-elections that took place two months after the Agreement was signed because fifteen unionist MPs had resigned their Westminster seats in protest, the Government's strategy seemed to be working. The SDLP saw its own vote rise by 6 per cent and Sinn Fein's fall by almost as much.[4] But for Sinn Fein, the setback was short-lived. In the 1987 General Election, Gerry Adams held his seat in West Belfast (despite a determined campaign against him by the SDLP) with an increased majority and share of the vote. Although the overall nationalist beneficiary was the SDLP, increasing its share of the vote on the 1983 general election by 3.4 per cent, the high-profile success of Gerry Adams in holding his seat was what grabbed the headlines.[5] For Sinn Fein, that was the critical test. Although overall its vote was down 2 per cent on 1983, it still polled 35 per cent of nationalist voters.[6] Rumours of Sinn Fein's demise were premature.

As far as the British were concerned, the policy U-turn came in 1987 or thereabouts when they saw that Adams's success in 1983 was not just an aberration in the wake of the hunger strike. Ian Burns, who as a private secretary in 1969 had paved the way for Home Secretary James Callaghan's famous visit to Derry, was now Deputy Under Secretary at the Northern Ireland Office, charged with the job of seeing if some form of political rapprochement might be effected. He knew that on the security front, the policy of containment was working.

It was plain that after twenty years there was plenty of evidence that the terrorists could not win and each new incident tended to increase British resolve that they should *not* win. It was also clear that the British Government would never stoop to the sort of measures which the terrorists were using, and that even if they did so, they would be wrong in principle and they would not themselves actually produce a solution. So we had a security situation in which we could certainly contain terrorism. In individual incidents, we could defeat the terrorist; but we could not eradicate terrorism. The question then was, how you go forward from there.

The conclusion we came to, rather a trite one perhaps, in retro-spect, was that terrorism would end when the terrorists decide to end it. That meant trying to show to the terrorists that their existing policy of the Armalite and the Ballot Box was mistaken, and that the Armalite should be put on one side. If the *terrorists* wanted to make progress, they could not do so through a terrorist campaign. But *republicans* could make progress through using the political process. That was the essence of the emerging strategy at the end of the eighties. Republicanism did not have a future through terrorism.

Mrs Thatcher may have been persuaded with some difficulty, not least when, on 30 July 1990, the IRA killed another of her close friends and associates, Ian Gow MP, with a Semtex booby-trap bomb. A staunch supporter of the unionist cause, he had resigned his ministerial post at the Treasury in protest against the Anglo-Irish Agreement. According to his widow, his attitude had been 'bugger the IRA'.[7]

On the other side of the battle lines, the Provisionals too were beginning to shift their ground. Adams, the Republican Movement's most astute political thinker, knew that at some stage the process of talking to the British would have to begin again but this time the political balance would be different. During the secret talks with the British Government in 1972 and 1975, the IRA had no quantifiable political base. They had their supporters in the nationalist community and could not have operated without them but there was no political machine behind the IRA. The incident centres set up as part of the 1975 'truce' gave Sinn Fein its first real toe-hold in the nationalist community and Adams and McGuinness and their politically minded colleagues spent the 1980s in the wake of the hunger strike building upon it. Adams never advocated laying the Armalite aside since to have done so would have been politically suicidal as Sinn Fein drew its strength and mandate from the IRA. He knew, however, that the IRA's role increasingly had to be balanced by Sinn Fein. In a seminal text, *The Politics of Irish Freedom*, written in 1986, Adams put the Provisionals' strategy in context.

> The tactic of armed struggle is of primary importance because it provides a vital cutting edge. Without it, the issue of Ireland would not even be an issue . . . armed struggle has been an agent of bringing about change . . . At the same time there is a realization in republican circles that armed struggle on its own is inadequate and that non-armed forms of political struggle are at least as important . . .[8]

Adams recognized that, by the end of the second decade of the conflict, Sinn Fein was still, as its Gaelic name broadly means, 'ourselves alone'. Although the party was making gains in its electoral support in the North, it had been almost wiped out in the Irish General Election of 19 February 1987, winning no seats and taking less than 2 per cent of the vote. Adams realized that if Sinn Fein was to progress, it would have to embrace others and make alliances with them, most notably the SDLP, the Dublin Government and Irish-America. Republicans would have to start making friends and influencing people instead of repelling them by its association with IRA violence. John Hume, who since his emergence as a leader of the civil rights campaign in the late 1960s had been a passionate opponent of violence, was thinking along similar lines. Father Alec Reid, who had administered the last rites to the two corporals shot dead by the IRA after their Passat ran into Caoimhin MacBrádaigh's funeral cortège, was instrumental in bringing them together. The purpose of the exercise was to try to work out a common front – agreed by the representatives of the physical force and constitutional traditions in Irish nationalism – to put to the British Government.

Adams and Hume and their respective Sinn Fein and SDLP delegations met and talked together throughout 1988 against a backdrop of violence that gave a deadly immediacy to their deliberations. The names that year were a byword for blood on the hands of all sides, 'Brits', loyalists and the IRA: Gibraltar, Michael Stone, Corporals Wood and Howes, Ballygawley and Drumnakilly. Hume knew that if the conflict was to be resolved and peaceful progress made towards Irish unity, the IRA would have to be persuaded to give up the gun, and the Republican Movement would have to be realistic in the demands it made of the 'Brits'. Declarations of intent to withdraw, which had haunted the secret talks in 1972 and 1975, were out. If there was to be a united Ireland, Hume argued, it would have to come about by peaceful means, which meant that the million Protestants in the North would have to be persuaded that it was in their best interests. This would never happen as long as the IRA continued killing. Furthermore, Hume argued, he believed that the British Government would remain neutral in any political process and simply act as facilitator.

Adams may have agreed with some of Hume's analysis, although he was highly sceptical about British 'neutrality', but he knew that to carry the IRA, the Army Council would have to be convinced that ending its campaign would lead to talks with the British and ultimately, in whatever way, to Irish unity. If Adams could not take the IRA with him, the project was doomed. Martin McGuinness, with his impeccable IRA credentials, was his key ally. The fact that the two men have stuck together, close personal friends as well as comrades-in-arms, apparently without jealousy or bitterness, is one of the crucial factors that cemented the Republican Movement to the peace process. Time and again, the word amongst IRA Volunteers and their families during a difficult and testing time for 'active republicans' was, 'If it's good enough for Martin, it's good enough for us.' Not that Gerry was held in any lesser esteem: he was just viewed in a different light.

As the discussions between Hume and Adams and their party representatives ended on 5 September 1988, there was no communiqué of agreement but common ground had been established. The ground was 'self-determination', although there were different interpretations of it. At worst, as far as the 'Brits' were concerned, it was a more sophisticated way of saying 'Brits Out', with *all* the people on the island of Ireland, North and South, voting on their destiny at the same time. At best, it was allowing the Protestant majority in the North, but a minority on the whole island, to have its say and have its verdict respected. This was the foundation on which the peace process was established. Dublin was listening and kept informed, and the 'Brits' were listening too. The peace process was built on two twin pillars: Sinn Fein and the SDLP, and London and Dublin. The challenge was to involve the unionists in the architecture without bringing the whole structure down. It was to take many years.

Three weeks after Hume and Adams had ended their deliberations with an agreement to keep in touch, the Secretary of State, Tom King, made a speech at a lunch hosted by the province's Institute of Directors. In it he planted a critical seed, no doubt at the encouragement of John Hume. He said that Northern Ireland remained part of the United Kingdom 'by the express desire of a significant majority of its people' and that there was '*no secret economic or strategic reason* [author's emphasis], but simply that Northern Ireland's position is based entirely and clearly on the self-determination of the people of Northern Ireland'.[9] This is what Hume had meant by 'neutrality'. In other words, HMG was saying that, contrary to what had become a mantra of republican liturgy, the British presence in Northern Ireland was based on the wishes of the majority of its citizens and not because Britain had any imperialistic or self-interested designs on the province. Having planted the seed, Tom King was not around long to see it grow. When his successor, Peter Brooke, took over on 24 July 1989, the world was already beginning to change and there were signs of the first cracks in the Berlin Wall. 'There was already movement in Eastern Europe, in South Africa and the Middle East and there were people who said that the IRA were beginning to become worried that they were going to be the last unsolved problem,' he told me. To republicans, Brooke was simply another unreconstructed unionist like Tom King but they could not have been more wrong in their assessment. In media interviews he gave on 1 November 1989 to mark his first 100 days at Stormont Castle, the new Secretary of State stunned everybody, not least republicans, by an answer he gave to a question from Derek Henderson of the Press Association. Brooke was asked whether, in the context of a military stalemate, he could ever envisage himself talking to Sinn Fein. The standard answer, practised down the years by successive British Ministers, would have been 'no' on the grounds that democratic Governments do not 'talk to terrorists'. Brooke broke with tradition and said what he genuinely believed.

. . . it is difficult to envisage a military defeat [of the IRA] . . . if, in fact, the terrorists were to decide that the moment had come when they wished to withdraw from their activities, then I think the Government would need to be imaginative in those circumstances as to how that process should be managed . . . Let me remind you of the move towards independence in Cyprus. A British Minister stood up in the House of Commons and used the word 'never'. Within two years there had been a retreat from that word.[10]

Brooke's off-the-cuff remarks caused a storm. Unionists were horrified. Barely a month earlier, the IRA had bombed the Royal Marines School of Music in Deal, killing ten young bandsmen and injuring twenty-two others. Even mentioning the possibility of talking to Sinn Fein, whom unionists did not distinguish from the IRA, was bad enough but to mention the words 'Cyprus' and 'independence' in the same breath was the stuff of which unionist nightmares were made. Brooke rode the storm. 'I gave an honest answer to an honest question,' he said. 'I was arguing that if you reach this kind of impasse, it was sensible to explore other ways of resolving matters.' As the months went by, Brooke was informed by the intelligence services that the debate within the Republican Movement was ongoing. 'In a case like Northern Ireland, like in warfare, the preoccupation is to work out what is going on on the other side of the hill,' he said. 'I had to send a signal that, were that debate to reach a point where they wished to talk rather than engaging in terrorism, then there would be something to talk about from our side of the table.' Brooke sent the signal on 9 November 1990 via the unlikely medium of the British Association of Canned Food Importers and Distributors at the Whitbread Restaurant in London. The assembled guests, whose knowledge of matters Irish was likely to be more agricultural than political, were treated to a seminal discourse on 'The British Presence'. The ideas and language were a development of those first expressed by Tom King.

An Irish Republicanism seen to have finally renounced violence would be able, like other parties, to seek a role in the peaceful political life of the community. In Northern Ireland, it is not the aspiration to a sovereign, united Ireland against which we set our face but its violent expression . . . The British Government has *no selfish strategic or economic interest in Northern Ireland* [author's emphasis: note also there is no comma between the words 'selfish strategic']: our role is to help, enable and encourage. Britain's purpose . . . is not to occupy, oppress or exploit but to ensure democratic debate and free democratic choice.[11]

Brooke was confident that he was sending the right message, having tested the proposition with John Hume. 'The era of NATO and the nuclear deterrent meant that the importance of Ireland in strategic terms to the United Kingdom, which would have been significant over a period of about five hundred years, no longer obtained,' he said. 'With regard to the economic return, the United Kingdom was putting far, far more money into Northern Ireland than into any other part of the Kingdom and there was, by definition, no economic return coming out.'

The IRA made a direct response to the Whitbread speech by declaring a three-day cease-fire over Christmas 1990. The last time it had done so was in the run-up to the secret talks in 1975 when the MI6 officer Michael Oatley had orchestrated the dialogue with the Provisionals via the Contact in Derry. A matter of days later, again at a critical moment in the province's history, Oatley emerged from the shadows once more to play a vital role in re-establishing contact between HMG and the IRA that had been dormant for a decade since his intervention in the first hunger strike in 1980.

Although Oatley had become head of MI6 operations in Europe, he had kept in touch with the Contact, who knew that Oatley was there if ever it was felt his services were needed again. They were not. Mrs Thatcher was not interested in talking to the IRA. According to Oatley, the 'pipe' consequently 'rusted up' during the following decade. Nevertheless, it remained in place. Around the time of the IRA's 1990 Christmas cease-fire, some of the 'rust' was brushed off and messages were exchanged down the pipe once again. The initiative came from Derry not London. Oatley received a message that, in the light of the comments made by Peter Brooke, Martin McGuinness might be interested in sounding out the 'Brits'. Accordingly, Oatley arranged to pay a visit to Derry in January 1991.

By this time, there had been a seismic change on the British political scene when Mrs Thatcher was advised to step down by the Conservative Party in the leadership election and John Major became Prime Minister on 27 November 1990. The fact that he had not suffered the personal agonies of Mrs Thatcher (who had lived though the carnage of more than a decade, in which she had not only weathered the hunger strike and endured the Brighton bomb but lost her close friends Ian Gow and Airey Neave) meant that Major could make a fresh start, unclouded by any sense of personal loss, however keenly he felt the deaths of British soldiers, policemen and civilians. When he moved into Downing Street, one of the first things he did was to make a list of his priorities. Northern Ireland was at the top. He was determined not just to stand in the trenches and recite the familiar mantras 'we never give in to violence' and 'the IRA will never win' because he knew such attitudes would never produce a solution, and a solution was what John Major wanted. 'If what had been happening in Northern Ireland had been happening in Surrey or Sussex or in my constituency, Huntingdon, it would not have been acceptable,' he told me. 'And it wasn't acceptable to me in Northern Ireland.' Major knew that one of the keys to finding a solution was to enlist the support of the Dublin Government in doing so, and the mechanisms were already in place through the Anglo-Irish Agreement. He did not know, however, about Oatley's visit to Derry to meet McGuinness and only found out after it had happened.

Oatley was due to retire in February 1991 and was anxious to make one last effort to see if he could do anything to help resolve the conflict that had occupied him on and off since he first went to the province in 1973. 'I developed a feeling that in my last year in government service I would like to make use of my connections one more time to see if I could have any influence on the situation before I retired,' he told me. 'It seemed to be a pity just to walk away and leave it all as something one simply remembered. So I had conversations about it. It did seem, during 1990 and the early part of 1991, that there might be a mood developing within the Provisional leadership, where a political strategy, as an alternative to violence, might be something that they would consider pursuing.'

The meeting with McGuinness, in the presence of the Contact, lasted several hours. Gerry Adams was supportive of the initiative but not able to attend. 'I'd never met McGuinness before and I was considerably impressed by his intelligence and firmness of manner. I thought him very serious and responsible and I didn't see him as someone who actually enjoyed getting people killed. He was certainly very well informed and had a sophisticated view of what was going on in British political life. I found him a good interlocutor. It was rather like talking to a middle-ranking army officer in one of the tougher regiments like the Paras or the SAS.' Oatley outlined to McGuinness his view of the IRA's position. 'It hadn't really achieved anything for many years in terms of advancing its objectives and, although it had killed a lot of people and continued to give the Government and security forces a hard time, nothing tangible had been achieved.' He then spelt out how he saw HMG's position. 'Clearly the Government was willing to go on for ever, if necessary, with a policy of containment but if the IRA wished to pursue a political course, given a considerable change in political circumstances with the development of the European Union, there might be things the British Government could do to help.'

Oatley concluded that McGuinness was prepared to consider these possibilities in 'a hypothetical and very positive way'. He then returned to London, wrote a report and went to see the new Permanent Under

Secretary at the Northern Ireland Office, John Chilcot, who was to become one of the 'Brit' architects of the peace process. Oatley told Chilcot that the Provisionals had shown some interest in pursuing a political course, 'though perhaps not very quickly', and that that was something that could be 'encouraged or discouraged' according to whatever policy HMG adopted. Oatley had told McGuinness that he had recently retired and could play no further part, but that if the leadership wished to pursue some sort of dialogue, another senior official might be made available to conduct it. Oatley had no authority to make this suggestion and had sought none for attending the meeting. McGuinness said that should the British wish to appoint a successor to Oatley, the Republican Movement was 'morally and tactically obliged not to reject their offer'.[12]

Oatley then retired to watch from the wings, having set in train through the Contact the sequence of events that four years later was to lead to the IRA cease-fire and, ultimately, eight years later, to the Good Friday Agreement. The 'long peace', like the 'long war', took a long time. A successor was appointed, a former MI6 officer who was brought out of retirement and seconded to MI5 to carry on where Oatley had left off. He met the Contact and showed him a letter of authentication from Peter Brooke. Oatley also confirmed his status to the Contact. This person, who was anonymously referred to as the 'British Government Representative' (BGR), was to play a critical and highly controversial role in the years that followed, although initially that role largely consisted of briefings on upcoming speeches and political moves.

No sooner had Oatley left MI6, whose top job had narrowly eluded him, than the IRA sent a more familiar message to the British Government. This time it was directed at its very heart. On 7 February 1991, at the height of the Gulf War, the IRA fired three deadly Mark 10 mortar bombs at Downing Street. It was barely a month after the meeting between Oatley and McGuinness. They had been used to devastating effect in Northern Ireland, most notably in the attack on Newry RUC station in 1985 in which nine police officers had been killed, but had never been used in England before. They were fired from a white Transit van parked opposite Horse Guards Parade, near the Ministry of Defence. One landed in the back garden of Number Ten, almost wiping out the Prime Minister and members of his Cabinet. Two more had landed in St James's Park, just beyond the garden wall. Each bomb weighed around 140 lbs, was over four feet long and carried a payload of 40 lbs of Semtex high explosive. At the time, John Major was presiding over a meeting of the Overseas and Defence Committee, discussing the Gulf War. 'Suddenly there was this tremendous explosion and then an after-shock and then what seemed like a second explosion,' he said. 'Then all the windows came in. At that stage, Tom King, who was sitting directly opposite me, said, "It's a mortar!" He clearly recognized it from his time in both the army and Northern Ireland. And everybody ducked under the table. I thought for a second that it might have been a present from Saddam Hussein but it quickly became apparent it was the IRA.' As the members of the Cabinet Committee emerged from under the table, the Prime Minister announced they had better continue the meeting somewhere else at which point they all went off to the underground bunker beneath Downing Street known as the Cobra Room.[13]

Despite Oatley's discussion with McGuinness only a few weeks before, the IRA's audacious and near-fatal attack did not cause Major, Brooke, Chilcot or Oatley any great surprise since they fully expected the IRA to carry on with, and even intensify, its campaign whilst putting out peace feelers, on the grounds that when and if talks with the British began, the IRA would be doing so from a position of strength. They also knew that McGuinness and Adams had to carry their comrades with them in the enterprise and the best way of doing so was to carry on hitting the 'Brits' and making them count the human and financial cost. Talking and killing were not mutually exclusive.

A year later, on 17 January 1992, the East Tyrone IRA detonated a huge landmine at Teebane crossroads just outside Cookstown. The target was a minibus taking home Protestant workmen who had been working on an army base at Lisanelly, Omagh. Eight workmen were killed. The 500 lbs of home-made explosives left a crater more than six metres wide and one metre deep.[14] It was the IRA's biggest attack on Protestant workers since the Kingsmills massacre in 1976. That same evening, Peter Brooke appeared on Ireland's most popular television chat show, the *Late Show* with Gay Byrne, and, having talked about the horror of Teebane, was inveigled into singing 'My Darling Clementine' in front of the studio audience. Unionists were appalled at the Secretary of State's apparent insensitivity and demanded his resignation. Brooke, realizing the error of judgment, apologized and offered his resignation to the Prime Minister. John Major refused.[15]

Nearly three weeks later, on 5 February 1992, the loyalist UFF took their revenge by walking into Sean Graham's bookmaker's shop on Belfast's Lower Ormeau Road and gunning down five Catholics, including a sixteen-year-old boy and a pensioner. The UFF concluded its statement claiming responsibility with the words 'Remember Teebane'. By the end of 1992, for the first time in the history of the conflict, the loyalist paramilitaries had claimed as many victims in one year as the IRA. Both organizations had killed thirty-four people. Three of the loyalists' victims were members of Sinn Fein, as the UFF and the UVF increasingly targeted known republicans.

The day after the killings at Sean Graham's betting shop, Albert Reynolds, the Irish Finance Minister, succeeded Charles Haughey as leader of Fianna Fail and was ratified as Taoiseach by the Irish parliament. John Major was delighted. As Chancellor of the Exchequer he had worked with Reynolds within the European Union and liked him a lot. Both were deal-makers and there was a natural chemistry between them. Major recorded that relationships between London and Dublin immediately improved. 'He was easy to get on with, naturally cheery and loquacious, and as keen as I was to see real progress in Northern Ireland . . . his commitment was a plus. So was his love of a deal, born of making a fortune selling pet-food and owning dance-halls.'[16] Both Prime Ministers were convinced that, given time and persuasion, a deal was there to be done. The tit-for-tat carnage at Teebane and Sean Graham's simply brought the urgency home. Time was not on the province's side.

Chapter Twenty-Nine

Secret Talks

1992–1993

John Major knew that if he was to make any progress on Ireland he would have to win the next General Election since he was very much regarded as the caretaker Prime Minister whom fate had thrust into Margaret Thatcher's shoes. He was also conscious that his Premiership had to be put to the nation which would bestow on him, or not, the authority to continue. Major called the election for 9 April 1992. The omens did not look good. At the start of the campaign, one of the Downing Street officials asked the Prime Minister's wife, Norma Major, if she had ordered a removal van.[1] He was being realistic not facetious, but there was no need for packing: Major remained in Downing Street with a majority of twenty-one seats, defying most predictions. The Labour pretender, Neil Kinnock, had run a highly professional, super-smooth campaign, orchestrated to the last sound-bite, carefully staged rally and soft-focus-image TV party political broadcast. In contrast, John Major took to his 'soap box', fending off eggs and other unsolicited missiles, to bring his message to the people. The soap box won. Ireland was never an issue in the campaign, nor had it ever been in any British General Election in living memory. There was good news for Major in Northern Ireland, too, with the SDLP vote up 2.4 per cent and the Sinn Fein vote down 1.4 per cent. But best news of all in the province for the Government was that Gerry Adams lost his West Belfast seat to the SDLP candidate, Dr Joe Hendron, not least because Protestants on the Shankill Road, part of the West Belfast parliamentary constituency, cast their votes strategically for Hendron to ensure Adams's defeat. It was not often that loyalists voted for the SDLP.

The day after the election, as the Tories were still rubbing their eyes in partial disbelief and celebrating Major's victory, the Government was given a reminder of what lay ahead when the IRA rocked the City of London with a huge explosion at the Baltic Exchange. Three people were killed in the blast, including a fifteen-year-old schoolgirl, Danielle Carter. The

IRA's warning was inadequate. The bomb caused £800 million worth of damage, eclipsing the £600 million that had been the total cost of the damage in Northern Ireland since the outbreak of the 'Troubles' in 1969. The IRA had welcomed Major to Downing Street with mortars and were now serving him notice on the day after his victory that, although Ireland had not been an election issue, it had not gone away.

Major did not need reminding. With the giant sweep-up operation in the City under way and insurance companies holding their heads in their hands, Major reshaped his Cabinet and summoned his old friend Sir Patrick Mayhew to Downing Street. Mayhew, who had been Attorney-General since 1987, was at home when he got the call and did not know whether he was being summoned for a job or the sack. 'It was a lovely sunny day,' he told me, 'so I picked a camellia that was in flower, stuck it in my button-hole and up I went.' Before the Prime Minister could say anything, Mayhew congratulated him on his 'terrific achievement' of winning the election on his own and said he just wanted to get that out of the way first. Major then offered him the job of Northern Ireland Secretary. 'I'm afraid I didn't say any of the solemn things that people are supposed to say on these occasions,' he said, 'I simply said, "Whoopee!"'

The Baltic Exchange bomb reinforced what the Prime Minister and his officials knew already from the mortar attack on Downing Street: however good intelligence on the IRA might be in the province, it was sadly lacking in London. Major ordered the Home Secretary, Kenneth Clarke, to carry out an urgent review and make recommendations to improve the structure of intelligence-gathering on the mainland. The review was conducted by Ian Burns who had been transferred from the Northern Ireland Office to the Home Office's Police Department. Ever since its origins in 1883 (to combat Irish terrorism), the Metropolitan Police's Special Branch (then known as the Irish Special Branch) had been responsible for countering the IRA. Clearly by the early nineties, with mortar bombs raining down on Downing Street, there was a feeling in high places that Special Branch was not up to the job. MI5, which was gradually emerging from the shadows under its new Director-General, Stella Rimington, was waiting in the wings to take over. Reports of a fierce turf war between the Met's Special Branch and MI5 were probably not exaggerated. The Security Service won and in May 1992 the Home Secretary announced that MI5 would take over as the lead agency in the battle against the IRA. There was dismay in Scotland Yard at what some Special Branch officers saw as a snub but a working relationship was established, bonded in the face of the common enemy.

One of MI5's first acts in its new over-arching role was to visit every police force in the country to carry out an intelligence audit on every IRA suspect on their books. The result was 1,000 names which were then categorized and computerized. It then set about recruiting agents in Great Britain with connections going back to Belfast where most operations started. In Northern Ireland, one in every twenty people approached by MI5 officers with a view to becoming an agent signed up. Recruiting on the mainland was unlikely to prove any easier with an even tighter network of IRA activists.

In Downing Street, policy towards the IRA did not change. The message to the Republican Movement remained the same. Stop the killing and HMG will be prepared to listen. Sir Patrick Mayhew carried on where Peter Brooke had left off and sent the IRA another public message on 16 December 1992 in a keynote speech at Coleraine on 'Culture and Identity'. It did not need decoding.

> Unity cannot be brought nearer, let alone achieved, by dealing out death and destruction. It is not sensible to believe that any British Government will yield to an agenda for Ireland prosecuted by violent means . . . provided it is advocated constitutionally, there can be no proper reason for excluding any political objective from discussion. Certainly not the objective of a united Ireland through broad agreement freely and fairly agreed . . .
>
>   . . . in the event of a genuine and established cessation of violence, the whole range of responses that we have had to make to that violence could, and would, inevitably be looked at afresh . . .[2]

The words could almost have been taken from Merlyn Rees's speaking notes in the run-up to the 1975 IRA cease-fire and the secret talks that followed.

Just over two months later, on 22 February 1993, the IRA made what John Major and Sir Patrick Mayhew considered an astonishing response that added an extra dimension to what Major had thought was possible. The Prime Minister had no doubt it came from the Provisional IRA's Army Council (PAC), routed through Martin McGuinness. Major believed that both McGuinness and Adams were members of the PAC. 'That a settlement could be delivered without them did not seem to me to be credible,' he told me. 'If there was to be an agreement, it had to involve Adams and McGuinness, so great was their authority within their own Movement.'

The response came in the form of a message that MI5 told Major and Mayhew had been sent by Martin McGuinness. The 'message' was transmitted by the Contact to the MI5 officer known as the British Government Representative (BGR), who then transmitted it to his superiors. They then passed it on to Number Ten and the NIO. Major received it late in the afternoon of a 'pretty miserable, dreary, dark day' as dusk was falling. He was working on his own in the Cabinet room when his Private Secretary came in with the 'message'. It was written down as follows.

> The conflict is over but we need your advice on how to bring it to an end. We wish to have an unannounced cease-fire in order to hold dialogue leading to peace. We cannot announce such a move as it will lead to confusion for the Volunteers because the Press will interpret it as surrender. We cannot meet the Secretary of State's public renunciation of violence [as read into his Coleraine speech], but it would be given privately as long as we were sure we were not being tricked.[3]

Major and Mayhew both took advice from the Security Service and were assured that the message was genuine. Major knew he had to take it very seriously. If it was merely a publicity stunt, then the worst that could happen would be egg on the Prime Ministerial face. But if it was real, then there was the possibility of a genuine breakthrough leading to round-table talks and an acceptable settlement to the interminable dispute. Sir Patrick Mayhew was equally up-beat.

> I certainly didn't regard it as a 'white flag'. I was very pleased that it had come and I certainly wasn't expecting it. I wanted to regard it as a recognition that, contrary to the IRA's belief over many years, the British Government was not going to be shoved away from the principle of consent and democracy by violent attacks, whether in Northern Ireland or in the City of London. If it was that, then I wanted to sustain that conversion to politics and abandonment of violence.

When the wording of the 'message' subsequently became public, McGuinness was enraged and denied he had ever said any such thing, let alone in a message. Given its provocative wording about needing 'advice [from the 'Brits'] on how to bring it to an end', McGuinness could do little else. Whatever the interpretation put on it by Mayhew, its wording would suggest surrender and that was the last thing on McGuinness's mind. The intelligence services had put the IRA under great pressure but had certainly not won a military victory. As the IRA rightly pronounced, it was 'undefeated'. The flip side was that it had not won. There was almost certainly a degree of confusion over the 'message'. It may have been that the Contact or, more likely, the BGR was interpreting too liberally McGuinness's general sentiments in the hope of giving the peace process a much-needed impetus at a critical time.

Behind the scenes, events moved quickly.[4] The British responded promptly to the 'message' they had received, assuring McGuinness in a document forwarded by the BGR, via the Contact, that 'all those involved share a responsibility to work to end the conflict'; that there was need for 'a healing process'; that it was essential that 'both sides have a clear and realistic understanding of what it is possible to achieve', and that there was 'no blueprint' but a search for 'an agreed accommodation, not an imposed settlement, arrived at through an inclusive process in which the parties are free agents'. Critically, the Government emphasized that there was no question of accepting any prior objective of 'ending partition'. It accepted, however, that 'the eventual outcome of such a process could be a united Ireland but only on the basis of the consent of the people of Northern Ireland'.[5] In the light of what was to happen a few days later, one sentence in HMG's submission was of paramount importance. It stressed that 'any dialogue could only follow a halt to violent activity', which it accepted 'in the first instance would have to be unannounced'.[6] The document was dated 19 March 1993. When the BGR handed it over to the Contact, he also passed on an oral message recognizing the difficulties involved for both sides and warning 'that all acts of violence hereafter could only enhance those difficulties and risks, quite conceivably to the point when the process would be destroyed'.[7]

The following day, 20 March 1993, the IRA exploded two bombs concealed in litter bins in Warrington, near Liverpool, when the town centre was packed with busy Saturday shoppers. Warnings were given but they were inadequate. Two young boys died in the blasts. One of them, Jonathan Ball, was only three years old. He had been out shopping for a Mother's Day present. Twelve-year-old Tim Parry had been going to buy a pair of football shorts. Jonathan died cradled in a nurse's arms and Tim died in hospital five days later. He had been running away from the first bomb and was caught by the second. Public revulsion was almost on the scale of Enniskillen. Thousands of letters of sympathy poured in, consoling the parents in their grief. A Timothy Parry Trust Fund was established to promote greater understanding between Great Britain and Ireland, North and South, and Tim's parents became tireless campaigners for peace.[8] Jonathan's parents said, 'If these initiatives lead to peace in Ireland, we shall be better able to bear our pain. If not, Jonathan's death is a meaningless blasphemy.'[9] As ever in such circumstances, it was difficult to find words of condemnation that were strong enough. Sir Patrick Mayhew expressed 'disappointment' as well as revulsion. 'Here again they appeared to believe that violence, however disgusting and however random, was going to advance their political thinking,' he said. 'Equally it was important not to be deflected from our political analysis by yet another manifestation of that mistake.' The 'Brits' intended to press on.

Following the Government's message of 19 March, a face-to-face meeting in Derry between the BGR and Martin McGuinness had been scheduled for 23 March, arranged through the auspices of the Contact. The Provisionals expected that the BGR's boss, John Deverell, would also be there. To the IRA, such a meeting would be a breakthrough. It was agreed by the Contact, the BGR and the Provisionals that both sides should be represented by two delegates with McGuinness and Gerry Kelly on the republican side and the BGR and John Deverell on the British side. When the meeting was arranged, neither party had any idea that Warrington would intervene. Neither McGuinness nor Kelly knew the minutiae of the IRA's plans in England.

The meeting almost did not happen. The BGR turned up in Derry at the appointed time and place but Deverell did not. A degree of confusion surrounds what happened. Either Deverell realized that such a meeting would be inappropriate three days after Warrington, given the Government's insistence that dialogue could only follow 'a halt to violent activity', or he had never intended to go anyway, or he knew nothing about it. Such are the unanswered questions that hang over this critical meeting. John Deverell did not live to provide an answer as he was one of twenty-five British intelligence officers who died on 2 June 1994 when their helicopter crashed on the Mull of Kintyre on the way to a counter-terrorism conference.

In the end the Derry meeting only took place at the insistence of the Contact who knew how important it was to maintain his own credibility and the credibility of the peace process. The Contact was present and minutes were taken on the Provisionals' side. When Sinn Fein subsequently published them, they made extraordinary reading. According to Sinn Fein, the BGR said that Mayhew, having tried to 'marginalize and defeat the IRA', had now changed tack, as evidenced by his Coleraine speech, which was 'a significant move': Mayhew was prepared to involve Sinn Fein, not because he liked them, but because he realized that the process 'cannot work without them'. This preamble was, according to the Republican Movement's minutes, then followed by a series of astonishing sentences.

Any settlement not involving all of the people North and South won't work. A North/South settlement that won't frighten unionists. The final solution is union. It is going to happen anyway. The historical train – Europe – determines that. We are committed to Europe. Unionists will have to change. This island will be as one.[10]

On the face of it, it seemed to be the message that the IRA had waited for more than two decades to hear from the 'Brits': that 'the final solution is union' and 'this island will be as one'. I understand that Sinn Fein's account of the meeting is broadly accurate, although the BGR was perhaps not quite as blunt as its record suggests. The minutes concluded by saying that the opportunity for formal meetings between the two sides 'must be grasped' as soon as possible. According to Sinn Fein, the BGR ended by saying that HMG would agree to talks the minute the IRA agreed to an undeclared cessation of violence. This suspension of violence would last for two to three weeks, during which time talks would take place. The BGR had already assured the Provisionals that at these delegation meetings, the British would convince the IRA that 'armed struggle is no longer necessary'.[11]

Sinn Fein assumed, quite naturally, that the BGR was acting on behalf of HMG and was authorized to say what he did. He was, after all, the 'British Government Representative'. Sir Patrick Mayhew did not find out about the meeting until many months later in the autumn of 1993 and was furious when he did. He regarded the meeting as a clear breach of HMG's condition that there would be no face-to-face dialogue until the IRA had agreed to a cessation of violence, albeit unannounced. The Secretary of State had been kept in the dark and was appalled when he found out not only that the BGR had met McGuinness and Kelly but that he was alleged to have said what he did.

If it was true, it would have been dangerously and damagingly outside the remit because of reasons which hardly need explaining. So that was very unfortunate. It may have been an expression of this man's personal views. It was certainly not an expression of the views of the British Government or a fulfilment of anything he'd been authorized to do or say.

One of Mayhew's officials who was involved in the 'back channel' told me that the BGR 'severely damaged' HMG policy by having the face-to-face meeting. 'When news of the secret meeting broke, there was anger, confusion and a feeling that we had been let down,' he said. 'Our whole strategy was to be straight with them [the Provisionals] and build up trust. We were "banging on" about no face-to-face meeting before an IRA cease-fire and they couldn't understand that because they'd already had one. It just made things more difficult.' What really happened at that vital meeting and what was *actually* said remains one of the unresolved mysteries of the secret, backstage manoeuvres that finally led to the IRA's 'cessation' eighteen months later and the subsequent talks between the Government and the Republican Movement.

In the weeks and months that followed the Derry meeting between the BGR, McGuinness and Kelly, the talks about talks ran into the sand. In the view of the 'Brits' they were driven there by the IRA's actions. On 24 April, the IRA launched a devastating attack in the heart of the City of London. This time the target was the NatWest tower in Bishopsgate. The bomb, made up of 1,000 lbs of fertilizer explosives packed into the back of a van, caused even more damage than the IRA bomb at the Baltic Exchange the previous year. The insurance bill was estimated to be more than £1,000 million. Despite the fact that eighteen 'mostly accurate' warnings were given, a *News of the World* photographer, Edward Henty (34), was killed.[12] John Major's reaction was similar to Sir Patrick Mayhew's after Warrington. He was dismayed but not surprised.

> Frankly, we thought it was likely to bring the whole process to an end. And we told them repeatedly that that was the case. They assumed that if they bombed and put pressure on the British at Bishopsgate or with some outrage or other, it would affect our negotiating position to their advantage. In that judgment they were wholly wrong. Every time they did that, they made it harder not easier for any movement to be made towards a settlement. They hardened our attitude, whereas they believed that their actions would soften it. That is a fundamental mistake the IRA have made with successive British governments throughout the last quarter of a century.

The Bishopsgate bomb was followed by a series of huge bombs in the centre of Belfast (20 May), Portadown (22 May) and Magherafelt (23 May), causing millions of pounds' worth of damage. Major decided that enough was enough and, on 17 July 1993, after even more bombs and killings, sent a blunt message to the IRA. It said that a temporary halt to violence was not enough and that 'dialogue leading to an inclusive political process' could only begin 'after we have received the necessary assurance that organized violence had been brought to an end'. Major described this as 'a holding message'. 'I thought it essential to show the Provisionals that these tactics would not wash . . . We were determined to make them realize that terrorism and talking were incompatible . . . [The message] repeated our insistence on a lasting end to violence. It began to seem we were in a blind alley.'[13]

By this time, Major was looking in other directions, too, because he realized that for a settlement to work it had to involve *all* parties. He recognized that the IRA were a critical component but by no means the only one. He also knew that if and when the Army Council declared 'a lasting end to violence', the Republican Movement would have to be realistic in what it thought it could achieve at the negotiating table with all the other parties and in particular with the unionists, assuming, of course, that they could be persuaded to sit in the same room and negotiate with the representatives of the IRA. The Prime Minister's frustration with the IRA's insistence on killing and talking at the same time was understandable. With this attitude ingrained in the republican psyche, there seemed little chance of making significant progress. No wonder Major thought he was in 'a blind alley'. He firmly believed that the Provisionals *were* serious in seeking to end their campaign but felt that their actions were contradictory.

By the summer of 1993, several different dialogues were being conducted at different levels in different places with the common objective of trying to make the peace process work. The British were communicating indirectly with the IRA through the Contact. John Hume was talking to Gerry Adams. John Major was talking to the unionists and to Albert Reynolds in Dublin. And the loyalist paramilitaries, who also recognized that at some stage the killing would have to stop, were talking to the Belfast Presbyterian minister, the Reverend Roy Magee, and Archbishop Robin Eames, the Anglican Archbishop of Armagh and Primate of All Ireland.[14] For the peace process to work, all strands would somehow have to be brought together. It was like juggling plates whilst wearing a blindfold. John Major, through whose fingers at some stage all the threads ran, did not underestimate the task. 'Building a peace in Northern Ireland is like playing multi-dimensional chess,' he said. 'You need everything in place at the right time.'

Gerry Adams and John Hume had resumed in earnest the discussions they had begun in 1988, and on 24 April 1993 set out an agreed position on the elements for a settlement.

1 That an internal settlement [i.e. within Northern Ireland] is not a solution because it obviously does not deal with all the relationships at the heart of the problem.
2 That the Irish people as a whole have a right to national self-determination.
3 That the exercise of self-determination is a matter for agreement between the people of Ireland.
4 That an agreement is only achievable and viable if it can earn and enjoy the allegiance of the different traditions on this island.

Major knew that unionists would not accept this since to them 'self-determination' was a euphemism for 'Brits Out'. Tempering this was one of the main purposes of Major's dialogue with Reynolds. He had to persuade the Taoiseach that the critical factor in establishing a set of principles that would underpin any settlement was republican recognition that unionists must be allowed to give their consent to any agreement. In other words, they could not be coerced. The 'consent' principle was the key to any overall settlement. John Hume had long accepted the principle, and Albert Reynolds accepted it too.[15] Gerry Adams, however, did not because the Republican Movement had always maintained that the unionists' insistence on their right to say 'no' – the unionist 'veto' – had been the stumbling block to the resolution of the Irish problem.

John Major's juggling was made even more difficult by the Westminster arithmetic. As his parliamentary majority became increasingly slender as a result of a string of lost by-elections, the votes of the nine Ulster Unionist MPs under their uncharismatic but politically astute leader, James Molyneaux, became increasingly critical to the Government's survival. On 22 July 1993 Major only survived a critical vote on the Social Chapter of the Maastricht Treaty (which was opposed by the powerful Euro-sceptic wing of his party) because of the support of the Ulster Unionists. Nevertheless, Major insisted that he never let the narrowness of his majority and the consequent importance of unionist votes in the House of Commons affect his decisions on Ireland. He bridles at any suggestion that he might have done. 'That is a piece of propaganda that a proper light on history will show to be utterly false,' he told me. 'I can tell you categorically that at no time was there a deal with the unionist parties that put the survival of the Conservative Government before the peace process. At no time, in any way. I was not prepared to put at risk the process that I had started at the beginning of the 1990s for purely political ends. I was not prepared to do it and I did not.'

By autumn 1993, the situation had seldom looked bleaker as, once again, the province seemed on the brink of the abyss. On Saturday 23 October, two IRA men from Ardoyne, Thomas Begley and Sean Kelly, walked into Frizzell's fish shop on the Shankill Road, carrying a bomb. They were dressed in white coats to give the impression they were making a delivery. Their target was an office of the UDA/UFF located directly above the shop. The IRA believed that Johnny Adair and the command staff of the UFF's 'C' company were meeting there. The bomb had an eleven-second fuse, theoretically enough for the bombers to shout a warning and clear the shop before the explosion. The blast was designed to go directly upwards not outwards.[16] The bomb went off prematurely, collapsing the building and killing Begley and nine Protestants. Fifty-seven people were injured. The room above was empty. The UFF had stopped meeting there when they suspected it was under security force surveillance.

Begley was buried with IRA honours, another martyr to add to the list. Had he wiped out Adair and the UFF leadership, his community would have seen him as a hero. Gerry Adams was one of those who carried his coffin, thus inviting nigh-universal condemnation for associating himself with such an atrocity. But, as the RUC Chief Constable, Sir Hugh Annesley, told me, 'In a pragmatic way, I don't think he had much option.'[17] Not to have done so would have damaged Adams's credibility in his own community and made it even more difficult to bring the Republican Movement along with him and accept the compromises that he knew might be necessary in the search for peace.

Sean Kelly, the other IRA bomber, who was seriously injured but survived, was given nine life sentences. Giving his verdict, the judge said, 'This wanton slaughter of so many innocent people must rank as one of the most outrageous atrocities endured by the people of this province in the last quarter of a century.'[18] Few would have disagreed. Kelly was among the last batch of prisoners to be released under the Good Friday Agreement in the summer of 2000. He said he accepted that he would be a target for the loyalist paramilitaries for the rest of his life. 'Honestly, it was an accident and if I could do anything to change what happened, believe me, I would do it,' he said. 'While we did go out to kill the leadership of the UDA, we never intended for innocent people to die.' He acknowledged he would have to live with what he had done for the rest of his life. 'I am an ordinary guy who got caught up in the conflict.'[19]

The loyalist paramilitaries exacted dreadful revenge. During the week following the bombing of Frizzell's fish shop, the UVF shot dead two Catholics and the UFF two more. But it was to be seven days before the nationalist community felt the full force of the loyalists' terrible revenge. On 30 October 1993, Hallowe'en Eve, UFF gunmen walked into the Rising Sun bar in the village of Greysteel outside Derry, shouted 'Trick or Treat?' and opened fire on the horrified customers with an AK 47 and a Browning pistol. Six Catholics, one of them eighty-one years old, and one Protestant were mown down. The perpetrators were subsequently released under the Good Friday Agreement.

Politicians were by now almost beyond despair. John Hume, who wept at the funeral of the victims, blamed the lack of political progress for creating the vacuum in which such unspeakable horrors flourished. In the House of Commons, two days after Greysteel, Hume attacked Major for not seizing the opportunity, as Hume saw it, of using his deliberations with Gerry Adams as a basis for peace. Stung by Hume's words and the emotion with which they were expressed, Major retaliated with an equally emotional riposte, saying that if Hume was implying that the Government should sit down and talk with Gerry Adams, he would not do it. 'The thought would turn my stomach,' he said. 'I will not talk to people who murder indiscriminately.'[20]

The Contact, like Hume, must have been despondent at the outbreak of events that he too had striven so hard to avoid. He had been out of the country during the dreadful week that had begun on the Shankill and ended at Greysteel. But distance had not blunted the sense of urgency. He immediately got in touch with the BGR and arranged to meet him in London on 2 November on his way back to Derry from abroad. It was the day after the bitter exchange between Hume and Major in the House of Commons. It appears that the Contact left the BGR in no doubt what his feelings were about the way he believed the Government had squandered the opportunity for peace by effectively ending the secret dialogue with the Provisionals. The Contact did not pass on any message to the BGR from McGuinness. McGuinness was therefore astonished when he learned that, after the meeting, the BGR had passed on to the Government the following 'message' purporting to come from 'the leadership of the Provisional Republican Movement'.

> You appear to have rejected the Hume–Adams situation . . . Now we can't even have a dialogue to work out how a total end to violence can come about. We believe that the country could be at the point of no return. In plain language, please tell us as a matter of urgency when you will open dialogue in the event of a total end to hostilities. We believe that if all the documents [i.e. the respective position papers] are put on the table – we have a basis of an understanding.[21]

McGuinness was outraged and felt he had been duped by the BGR and the 'Brits'. He knew the Contact was blameless because the London meeting had been attended by a third party who was a personal friend of McGuinness and had come over from Derry to observe. It appears the BGR fabricated the message on the basis of his conversation with the Contact in London and, no doubt with some embellishment, presented it as a message from McGuinness. With its reference to 'a total end to violence' and 'a total end to hostilities' it contained the words the Government had been waiting months to hear. Perhaps with the best of intentions, the BGR had taken the initiative, as he had done in attending the meeting in Derry with McGuinness and Kelly earlier in the year, in the hope of breaking the dangerous stalemate and pushing the peace process forward. He knew how close the IRA was to calling off the campaign and was probably trying to bridge the gap between the Provisionals and HMG to avoid more Shankills and Greysteels.

The Government, unaware that McGuinness had nothing to do with the message, sent a fulsome reply, saying it was 'of the greatest importance and significance' and offering a meeting for 'exploratory dialogue' within weeks 'following an unequivocal assurance that violence has indeed been brought to a *permanent* end [author's emphasis]'.[22] HMG thought the IRA had finally agreed to end its campaign for good but the IRA had done nothing of the kind. McGuinness sent the Government a message repudiating what had erroneously been presented as the IRA's position by the BGR and pointing out that it had been done entirely on his initiative 'without our authority and knowledge'. This may have been the reason, on top of the unauthorized meeting with McGuinness and Kelly, that the BGR's services were deemed to be no longer required. The BGR had broken the rules again. McGuinness subsequently told me that the Government had 'abused the Contact to destruction' and that the dialogue was now over. John Major probably knew nothing of the dispute over the provenance of the latest 'message' but was sufficiently encouraged by it to make an upbeat speech at the Lord Mayor's Banquet on 15 November in the City of London. 'There may now be a better opportunity for peace in Northern Ireland than for many years,' he said.[23] At the time he did not know just how shaky the foundation was. Despite his optimism, peace was not just around the corner. Things were to get worse before they got better.

A fortnight later, on Sunday 28 November, the Northern Irish journalist Eamonn Mallie delivered a bombshell on the front page of the *Observer* when he revealed that the Government had been involved in secret talks with the IRA. It was the last thing the Government needed at this difficult and sensitive time. The source of the leak of a dialogue that had been kept secret since Michael Oatley first set it up almost three years earlier was never established. The Provisionals themselves, still smarting from what they regarded as the Government's abuse of the Contact and the dishonesty of the BGR, were probably prime suspects. Sir Patrick Mayhew faced the media on what must have been one of the most embarrassing days of his political life. He had been informed of Mallie's story around midnight on Saturday and was characteristically determined to take on the media the following morning. He called a press conference for 11 a.m. at Stormont Castle. He admitted he was nervous. 'There they all were, slavering for blood, a good opportunity to screw this Minister.' Although what Sir Patrick said was technically true – that the Government had not been *negotiating* with the Provisionals – the distinction between that and conducting a dialogue through third parties did not placate the Press. The Secretary of State's conscience was clear, however, as he knew that the meeting between the BGR and McGuinness and Kelly in March had not been authorized by the Government. But Mayhew was more concerned about the reception he would get when he made a statement to the House of Commons.

> I remember saying to my officials when we had a conference on the video link on the day when I was going to make my statement to the House, 'I'm determined to sail through this storm and come out the other side' and that's exactly how I felt. And one of them said, 'Well if you sink, a lot of us will sink with you.' On that rather morose note I climbed into the aeroplane and took off for Westminster. I didn't sink.

Despite his worst fears, Sir Patrick got almost a hero's reception from both sides of the House when he made his statement. It was as if Honourable Members were relieved that the Government was taking such risks for peace. Their anger was reserved for a Government that did not.

The events of these dramatic and traumatic days finally came to a climax on 15 December 1993 when John Major and Albert Reynolds stood shoulder to shoulder in Downing Street and told the world that the two Governments had reached agreement on the principles that would under-pin a settlement. It became known as the 'Downing Street Declaration' (or 'Joint Declaration') and was the result of weeks and many sleepless nights spent hammering out a deal. Reynolds had originally pressed Major to embrace the Hume–Adams dialogue but Major refused on the grounds that it would have been the kiss of death to unionists. Reynolds also tried to get the British Prime Minister to declare that HMG would act as a 'persuader' for Irish unity. Again, this was rejected for the same reasons. Major's priority was to keep the unionists on board, knowing from history and experience their capacity to wreck any settlement. The final document was far less 'green' than Albert Reynolds would have liked but after lengthy horse-trading the Taoiseach felt it was something that he and constitutional nationalists could live with. The tortuous wording of the Declaration, painfully crafted by British and Irish mandarins, gave all sides some, if not all, of what they wanted. Crucially, it gave unionists the guarantee *five times* that nothing would be done against the wishes of a majority of the people of Northern Ireland.

> The Prime Minister, on behalf of the British government, reaffirms . . . that they have no selfish strategic or economic interest in Northern Ireland.
> The role of the British government will be to encourage, facilitate and enable the achievement of . . . agreement . . . They accept that

such agreement may, as of right, take the form of agreed structures for the island as a whole, including a united Ireland achieved by peaceful means on the following basis.

The British government agree that it is for the people of the island of Ireland alone, by agreement between the two parts respectively, to exercise their right of self-determination on the basis of consent, freely and concurrently given, North and South, to bring about a united Ireland, if that is their wish.[24]

With the unionist 'guarantee' that the Provisionals had spent years fighting to destroy so firmly enshrined in the Joint Declaration, it was not surprising that the Republican Movement was not happy, despite the fact that its overall colour was 'green'. The question for the 'Brits' now was how to bring the Provisionals on board and, crucially, to get the IRA to silence its guns and declare that its campaign was over for good. Both Major and Reynolds had no doubt, from intelligence via their contacts, that at some stage the IRA would declare a cease-fire and join the peace process. The question was when.

Chapter Thirty

Getting Rid of the Guns

January 1994–February 1996

The Provisionals were less than enamoured of the Downing Street Declaration but realized they had nowhere else to go if they wanted to journey down the political road. The 'Brits' and the Dublin Government had set the agenda and the principles of the Declaration were set in stone. However hard Sinn Fein tried to chip away at them, the message came back that they were wasting their time. Demands from Gerry Adams for 'clarification' were seen by the British as an attempt to buy time. There was, however, a sophisticated understanding of his position, given the difficulty he and McGuinness faced in holding the Republican Movement together in the face of a Declaration that was clearly not what the IRA had been fighting for. There was increased concern in Provisional circles when, shortly after the Declaration, Sir Patrick Mayhew raised the issue of the 'decommissioning' of terrorist weapons as part of any settlement. Decommissioning was the 'D' word that was to haunt politicians, governments and paramilitaries on all sides for the rest of the century and beyond. (Decommissioning was less emotive than 'disarmament', with its connotations of surrender.) The Declaration had not mentioned the word itself but had stated that 'peace must involve a permanent end to violence' and that dialogue on the way ahead was only open to 'democratically mandated parties which establish a commitment to exclusively peaceful methods'.[1] Adams read the warning signs and knew the damage the issue was likely to do to the Republican Movement and the support he needed to carry the peace project through. 'This is what they want,' he said. 'They want the IRA to stop so that Sinn Fein can have the privilege twelve weeks later, having been properly sanitized and come out of quarantine, to have discussions with senior civil servants on how the IRA can hand over its weapons.'[2] It was an ominous shot across the bows of the 'Brits'.

In political terms, Sinn Fein was clearly swimming against the tide. That was nothing new but now the circumstances were different. An opinion poll conducted in the Irish Republic showed that 97 per cent of the population believed that the IRA should end its campaign at once.[3] Significantly, the Provisionals did not reject the Declaration out of hand, knowing that in the end they would have to come to terms with it and work it to the best of their advantage. Adams's position was strengthened, however, on 29 January 1994 when the Americans granted him a 'limited duration' visa to address a one-day peace conference organized by one of President Bill Clinton's most powerful financial backers, William Flynn. Adams took America by storm. I remember watching television coverage with IRA prisoners in the Maze whilst making a BBC *Panorama* programme on the secret back-channel talks. The prisoners clapped and cheered and were clearly ecstatic at the reception that the man they regarded as their leader was receiving across the Atlantic. But their enthusiasm for the Sinn Fein President was not matched by their enthusiasm for the Declaration. There was even talk of more bombs in London on the grounds that that was still the only lesson the 'Brits' would understand.

Major was furious that Clinton had personally authorized the granting of Adams's visa, against the advice of the US State Department, the Department of Justice, the FBI and the US Embassy in London, all of whom had taken heed of British objections. They had been told that Adams was still a 'terrorist' whose organization had not only not renounced violence but not even given its support to the Downing Street Declaration. Relations between Downing Street and the White House were to deteriorate even further when Adams was granted more visas and given the go-ahead to make fund-raising trips to America. Other Sinn Fein leaders were given visas, too. At one stage, Major did not return Clinton's calls as a sign of his anger at the lack of support he felt he was getting from the American President. 'Here we were, well on the road towards a settlement, and there were principal Sinn Fein figures going to America where they were going to raise more money,' he told me. 'We knew what that money was being used for. It would have been used for arms. So of course we were very peeved. We thought it was a bad signal to give at that time.'

Meanwhile, the IRA carried on killing soldiers and policemen, planting fire-bombs in London's Oxford Street and even mortaring the runway at Heathrow airport. None of this surprised Major and his Cabinet who by now were well used to the Provisionals' tactic of talking and killing at the same time. The Prime Minister knew that the increasingly dangerous stalemate had to be broken and he had to take the initiative. He finally agreed to 'clarify' the specific points of the Declaration that Sinn Fein maintained were unclear and amplified the offer of exploratory dialogue which had been made during the secret talks of the previous year. He now made a formal offer of a meeting within three months of the IRA's announcement of a cessation of violence. Since Adams had already scathingly referred to the twelve-week 'quarantine' period made during the secret talks, this was not in itself significantly new, but now the Prime Minister himself, not the BGR, was making it.[4]

Gradually, the IRA moved towards its cease-fire but in the increasing shadow of violence from the loyalist paramilitaries who also had a cease-fire in mind and were equally determined to call it from a position of strength. Their strategy professed to be to escalate the 'war' in order to bring it to an end. In the months prior to the IRA and loyalist cessations in 1994, the IRA killed nineteen people and the loyalists thirty-seven. For the third year running the UFF and UVF had 'out-killed' the IRA.[5] The UVF headed the list with twenty-five killings, twice as many as its UFF rival. The most notorious attack took place on 18 June 1994 when UVF gunmen opened fire on customers in the Heights bar in the tiny village of Loughinisland, County Down. Most were football fans watching television as Ireland played Italy in the World Cup. Six Catholics were shot dead, including an 87-year-old pensioner, Barney Green. He had put on his best suit for the occasion.[6] The UVF claimed it was retaliation for the INLA's killing of three of its members two days earlier as they were standing talking on the Shankill Road. It seemed like Greysteel all over again. People could not believe that peace was in the air in the midst of such horror. They thought the Downing Street Declaration was supposed to mark the beginning of the end.

On 31 August 1994, amidst rising expectations, the long-awaited announcement of an IRA cease-fire finally came. In its statement the IRA said:

> Recognizing the potential of the current situation and in order to enhance the democratic peace process and underline our commitment to its success, the leadership of Oglaigh na Eireann [the IRA] have decided that as of midnight, Wednesday 31 August, there will be a complete cessation of military operations. All of our units have been instructed accordingly . . .
>
> We believe that an opportunity to create a just and lasting peace has been created . . . We note that the Downing Street Declaration is not a solution, nor was it presented as such by its authors. A solution can only be found as a result of inclusive negotiations.[7]

The predominant mood was not one of jubilation but more of relief that, with luck, the 'war' might be over and Northern Ireland freed from the nightmare it had endured for twenty-five years. There were celebrations in the republican heartlands and emotional words about the sacrifice that IRA

Volunteers had made in the 'struggle' but there was no feeling that the IRA had won: it had held out against the might of the 'Brits', dealt them crushing blows and finally forced them to recognize the legitimacy of the Republican Movement. The IRA was 'undefeated'. The word 'victorious' was notably absent. John Major was pleased but not satisfied. The word 'permanent' was nowhere to be seen in the IRA's statement. That had been one of the issues on which, in the end, the secret talks had foundered. The Prime Minister remained sceptical about the IRA's long-term intentions, given that the magic word was missing. 'I had my doubts,' he told me. 'There was no indication from them that satisfied me that they were really *not* going to return to violence if things didn't go their way.' Nevertheless, all the advice the Prime Minister received from his security advisers suggested that the cessation was genuine and likely to last.

In the end, Major decided to make 'a working assumption' that the cease-fire was meant to last. He could do little else but he still had his doubts. 'It wasn't a conviction in my heart that it was definitely going to be permanent. I didn't believe that it was,' he told me. 'But I believed that we had to roll with that particular tide and see if we could turn what looked like a temporary but welcome cessation into something that was continuous.'

Everyone now waited to see if the second piece of the paramilitary jigsaw would fall into place. Would the loyalists also declare a cease-fire? When I had talked to the leaders of the UDA/UFF and UVF prisoners in the Maze earlier that year, it was quite clear that if the IRA stopped killing, the loyalist paramilitaries would stop too. They had always maintained, to hollow laughter from the Provisionals, that their violence was purely reactive. Six weeks later, the loyalist paramilitaries, under their umbrella organization, the Combined Loyalist Military Command (CLMC), announced their cease-fire. The UFF had killed one Catholic, John O'Hanlon (32), on the day after the IRA's 'cessation' and then stopped. The CLMC's announcement was made by the former UVF commander, 'Gusty' Spence, who almost thirty years earlier had been convicted of one of the first murders of the present conflict. Unlike the IRA, Spence apologized for the grief the loyalist paramilitaries had caused.

By the autumn of 1994, for the first time in a quarter of a century, the future looked bright with the guns on both sides of the paramilitary divide falling silent. But to the Republican Movement, the continuation of their silence depended on the progress made towards the all-party talks they had been led to believe would follow the IRA's cessation. The optimism was infectious. At about this time I talked to a senior British civil servant who had been intimately involved in the peace process almost from its very beginning. When I asked him how long he thought it would be before a final settlement was reached, he said, 'About five years.' It was at least four years more than I had anticipated. His estimate was far better than mine.

The British stuck to their promise of exploratory talks with Sinn Fein when, on 9 December 1994, just over three months after the IRA's cessation, the Sinn Fein delegation drove up to Stormont's Parliament Buildings in black taxis. On a cold, bright sunny morning, I stood with dozens of other journalists and watched history being made as Martin McGuinness and Gerry Kelly, in suits and ties and with briefcases in hand, disappeared through the side entrance of Stormont with the rest of the Sinn Fein delegation. Inside the 'Brits' were waiting. This was a very different Martin McGuinness from the young IRA leader I had first met in Derry in 1972. Now he would be eye-balling his old enemies. One of the British officials across the table who had been working on the peace process for a good many years had no doubt about McGuinness's position. 'We assumed he was on the Army Council when we talked to him,' he told me. 'It wouldn't say much for the Army Council if he wasn't.' In a carefully prepared opening speech, the British official chairing the meeting mentioned arms and the disposing of them and was met with 'stony faces' all round. The British appear to have mentioned the word 'decommissioning' itself towards the end of the meeting. 'Initially it was a way of getting off the "permanency" hook,' one of the officials present told me. 'We got hung up on it and it came to haunt us. At one stage in our discussions, Martin McGuinness said we could sort out the modalities [of decommissioning] in ten minutes and when I said, "OK, let's do it," he danced away.'

Once caught on the decommissioning hook, there was no getting off it. The British claim that although it might not have been specifically mentioned as such, it was always understood that dealing with terrorist weaponry *on both sides* was one of the issues to be addressed once the cease-fires were in place, and all-party talks were the next step. The loyalist paramilitaries were to be involved in them on the same terms as Sinn Fein through the medium of their own political parties, with the UDA/UFF represented by the Ulster Democratic Party (UDP) and the UVF by the Progressive Unionist Party (PUP). The Provisionals insist that the issue of decommissioning was never raised during the secret back-channel exchanges with the British. Michael Oatley believes they are probably right and it was certainly not something he mentioned at his seminal meeting with Martin McGuinness in January 1991. 'It would have been a ridiculous thing to raise,' he told me. 'After all, it was a fundamental tenet that it wouldn't be on offer.' I asked him why it was so illogical to ask the IRA to decommission its arsenal if the IRA was genuinely interested in peace.

The argument for decommissioning has been dishonestly presented from the outset and offers a powerful threat to the peace process. There are three reasons why it is not sensible to press the IRA to decommission at this stage.

The first is that it would have little practical effect in reducing the risk of renewed violence. Weapons will always be available to those in Ireland who have support and the means to pay for them. The IRA has both. The issue is not whether guns are held or can be obtained, it is whether they are to be used.

The second is that it is provocative and makes more difficult the task of those who are leading the Republican Movement to abandon terrorism in favour of politics. Republican Volunteers who joined up to pursue a campaign of violence and who have been persuaded to support instead a political and non-violent strategy are not ready to take this further step and do not want to be asked for it. They see it, rightly, as a call to surrender. The provocative effect is gleefully recognized by politicians who wish to destroy the Belfast Agreement without being held responsible for doing so.

The third is that the pressure is selective. Why put pressure on the IRA, which maintains a disciplined cease-fire, while loyalist groups are equally disinclined to give up their weapons and are clearly prepared to use them? The climate for decommissioning, on either side, is simply not there.

The IRA in its modern form developed as a response – like the introduction of British troops – to the loyalist campaign of ethnic cleansing: the eviction from their homes of thousands of Catholic families in 1969. Every step it takes along the political path surrenders a measure of its capacity for violence. That is progress enough. Why insist on meaningless forms – unless political progress is not what you want?

To the IRA, decommissioning was the issue above all others that was most likely to trigger the split that the leadership was so desperate to avoid. What was critical, the Provisionals countered, was that the guns remained silent and not that they were handed in or destroyed. It was the intention to use them that mattered. The IRA had never decommissioned in its entire history and it had no intention of starting now. As it became clear to the Provisionals that, if they were to be party to a final settlement, concessions would have to be made that were hitherto unthinkable in their ideology, the Republican Movement agreed that whatever else the IRA agreed to, it would never hand over its weapons. Nothing could have been more categoric. When I asked one senior Provisional if there would ever come a time when the IRA might do so, he said, 'Five million years, in the short term.'

Unionists and the British Government saw the issue through entirely different eyes. If the IRA was serious about its cease-fire and about peace, they argued, why did it need its guns? They remain convinced that the IRA insisted on holding on to them because at some stage it intended to use them again. But to John Major, decommissioning was both a political and a security issue. He really *did* believe that if the IRA was serious in giving up violence for good, which he doubted, it had no reason to hang on to its guns. He therefore believed it was critical that the IRA should begin to hand over or destroy some of its weapons *before* it was allowed to take part in all-party talks. This was known as 'prior decommissioning'. The fact that the IRA refused to do so simply confirmed Major's scepticism about the Provisionals' long-term intentions.

> You were asking unionists and others to sit down at a table with people who had an Armalite and a bomb underneath the table which, if the talks got to a sticky phase, they would then take out and use. Was that likely to engender an atmosphere at the talks that would lead to a proper settlement? Now they had the option. Some prior decommissioning. We didn't try and embarrass them. I said at one stage that they could melt down their weapons and build a statue of Eamon de Valera wherever they liked with the product of melting down their weapons. We were trying to get them into talks in a way that other people would talk to them. If 'the conflict is over', as the Provisional Army Council said, what was the need for weapons? What was the need to prevent at least a token destruction of weapons to show that they were genuine?

Politically the issue was crucial for Major. His whole strategy was to ensure that unionists became wedded to the peace process and, once involved, stayed with it. They were now led by David Trimble, who had succeeded James Molyneaux as leader of the Ulster Unionist Party (UUP), following Molyneaux's resignation on 28 August 1995. Trimble defeated the favourite, John Taylor, not least because of the high-profile, hard-line stance he had taken at Drumcree the previous month.[8]

If the Prime Minister was doubtful about the IRA's commitment to a permanent cessation of violence, unionists, whose community had for so long borne the brunt of its campaign, were even more sceptical. Major knew that the chances of getting them into all-party talks involving Sinn Fein were virtually zero unless the IRA moved on 'prior decommission-ing'. But it soon became clear that it was a non-starter: the Provisionals would not accept decommissioning as a prelude to a settlement.

The Government's resolution to stand firm on the issue was confirmed by intelligence reports that indicated that although the IRA was on cease-fire and military *operations* had ceased, military *activities* had not. Sir Patrick Mayhew knew from his intelligence briefings precisely what the IRA was up to during its cease-fire period.

> Governments are not blind and it would be very remiss if, after a campaign of that sort against violence for so long, we had been blind. I think that we knew a lot of what the IRA was doing and what we knew was sufficiently disturbing to prevent us regarding this as a total abjuring of violence. As time went on, unfortunately, we came to know that their preparations were continuing: their targeting of future assassination victims, their development of new weapons, their testing of new weapons, their recruiting of more Volunteers and so forth. We knew that that was going on and it appeared to be increasingly incompatible with the belief that a proper cease-fire was what they had in mind.

There were no more bombings and killings but Volunteers were not inactive. 'Ken', the 'Det' operator who was expert at concealing micro-cameras, confirmed that during the cease-fire period, the 'Det' was still in business.

> We declared a cessation of aggressive operations although covert surveillance still did carry on. We would never have been able to scale that down to non-existent surveillance, due to the untrustworthiness of the IRA. We found out that they were still targeting people, such as policemen and individuals from opposing [loyalist] organizations, and planning operations for the future. So covert operations still had to go ahead.

Nineteen ninety-five was the first year in Northern Ireland for more than a quarter of a century in which no member of the security forces was killed. This is what the IRA meant when it referred to 'a complete cessation of *military* operations'. Violence, however, did not abate completely, as the IRA shot dead six suspected drug dealers, mainly under the flag of convenience Direct Action Against Drugs (DAAD). Paramilitary beatings and knee-cappings also increased in the vacuum of so-called 'peace'. Between the IRA and loyalist cease-fires in 1994 and the end of 1995, the Provisionals carried out 148 'punishment' attacks and the loyalists 75.[9]

As the first anniversary of the IRA cease-fire came and went, there was still no sign of movement towards all-party talks nor indication that the IRA was going to move on decommissioning. The IRA and its Volunteers on the ground became increasingly restless at the lack of progress towards the inclusive dialogue they had been led to believe would follow their cease-fire. The Government stood firm on decommissioning and so did the IRA. Neither side was going to blink first. I remember meeting two senior Provisionals in Dublin towards the end of 1995 on the eve of President Clinton's visit to London and Belfast at the end of November and they were clearly extremely worried at how critical the situation had become. They wondered if the British Government had any idea of the narrowness of the ledge on which they were standing and how difficult it was to keep the IRA on-side, given the lack of political progress. They did not make threats but it was quite clear that the threat was there.

By that time, the Army Council had decided enough was enough and it was imperative to hit the 'Brits' again and hit them where it hurt the most, as close to the City of London as possible, given the 'ring of steel' around the area after the Baltic Exchange and Bishopsgate bombs. Plans were also laid towards the end of 1995 for a series of attacks on the mainland that would follow the after-shock of the 'big boomer' that was designed to mark the end of the cease-fire. By December 1995, the huge bomb that would deliver the IRA's message was already being put together in South Armagh, the area that British intelligence had found most difficult to penetrate. There were no 'Det' cameras in place to monitor bomb-making nor Special Branch or MI5 agents to tip off their handlers. The 'Brits' were aware that something was afoot but did not know what it was nor when or where the IRA would strike.

Meanwhile, John Major and John Bruton, who had succeeded Albert Reynolds as Taoiseach on 15 November 1994, were still trying to break the political deadlock over decommissioning and open the path to all-party talks. They came up with the idea of a 'twin-track' approach in which decommissioning might take place in parallel with talks. To that end an International Body on Arms was established to investigate what might and might not be possible. It consisted of three eminent international states-men: former US Senator George Mitchell, who was Chairman; General John de Chastelain, a former Canadian Chief of the Defence Staff and former Ambassador to Washington; and Harri Holkeri, a former Finnish Prime Minister who was the epitome of neutrality. Their contracts were for six months. Mitchell had no idea he would be there for four years and de Chastelain into the next century.

Major asked the three wise men to report if possible by the end of January 1996 in the hope of commencing all-party talks by the end of February. Major and Bruton kept their fingers crossed that their distin-

guished foreign visitors would sever the Irish Gordian knot. Trimble's
Ulster Unionist Party, which was instinctively deeply hostile to foreign
'meddling' in the province's affairs, in particular when it involved Clinton's
friends, was muted in its response because Senator Mitchell had impressed
its members in his former role as the President's Special Adviser for
Economic Initiatives in Ireland.[10] Mitchell knew his task would not be
easy.

> The Unionists quite rightly wanted some reassurance. They did not
> want to have talks occur in a setting in which the threat of violence or
> the use of violence influenced the negotiations. That's the reason for
> the request for prior decommissioning. It soon became obvious to us,
> very soon into our consultation, that prior decommissioning, how-
> ever desirable, was simply not a practical approach. It wasn't going to
> happen. The British Government wanted prior decommissioning
> and they wanted inclusive negotiations and it became clear that they
> could not have both.[11]

As a compromise, Senator Mitchell and his colleagues worked out a set of
principles to which all participants in all-party talks had to sign up, hoping
that unionists would accept agreement to these 'Mitchell Principles' in
place of actual decommissioning, at least at this stage. They included a
commitment to 'democratic and exclusively peaceful means of resolving
political issues'; the total disarmament of all paramilitary organizations; a
renunciation of the use of force to influence the outcome of all-party
negotiations, and an end to 'punishment' beatings and killings. Sinn Fein
said it accepted them all, thus securing admission to all-party talks without
the IRA making any move on decommissioning. But the International
Body did not rule out decommissioning further down the line. Its report,
delivered on 24 January 1996, concluded:

> . . . there is a clear commitment on the part of those in possession of
> such arms to work constructively to achieve full and verifiable
> decommissioning *as part of the process of all-party negotiations* [author's
> emphasis]; but that commitment does not include decommissioning
> prior to such negotiations . . .[12]

Major was surprised at Mitchell's optimism, which appeared to bear no
relation to any indication that the British Government had received. The
Senator later confided in him that he had stretched the point 'for tactical
reasons' and privately suspected that the IRA was on the point of breaking
its cease-fire.[13] This coincided with the intelligence that Major himself was

receiving and on which he had privately briefed President Clinton at Downing Street. Mitchell's report helped but it was not a magic wand. Major then decided that the only way to get the parties together was to call an election for a Northern Ireland Assembly, which would at least be a starting point for the process of negotiations. Unionists welcomed the prospect but Sinn Fein and the SDLP were bitterly opposed to the idea which they dismissed as a unionist ploy and an attempt to reinstate the Stormont of old.

To the Republican Movement, the Government's decision to go for elections was the last straw. At 6.59 p.m. on Friday 9 February 1996, the huge bomb the IRA had been secretly preparing in South Armagh exploded at South Quay in London's Docklands, in the car park of a building near Canary Wharf. The scene of devastation was shocking, like something out of the Blitz. A coded telephone warning had been given but the evacuation of the area was not complete. Two men, Inan Ul-haq Bashir (29) and John Jeffries (31), who worked in a nearby newspaper kiosk, were killed in the blast. They had been warned by a police officer to leave but they never made it.[14] Shortly before the bomb went off, the IRA issued a statement. 'Instead of embracing the peace process, the British government acted in bad faith with Mr Major and the unionist leaders squandering this unprecedented opportunity to resolve the conflict,' it said. 'The blame for the failure thus far of the Irish peace process lies squarely with John Major and his government.'[15]

The 'Brits' now had to pick up the pieces.

Chapter Thirty-One

Back to the 'War'

February 1996–July 2000

Commander John Grieve, the Metropolitan Police's Director of Intelligence, was looking forward to Friday evening, 9 February 1996. The following Monday, after a weekend of taking it easy, he would take over the hottest job in the 'Met' as Head of the Anti-Terrorist Squad (SO13). He was busy clearing out his filing cabinets and getting ready to move out of his office when one of his colleagues invited him to a wine bar for a farewell drink. He did not have long to savour it. Suddenly his pager went off and there was a message from the Metropolitan Police Commissioner's PA, to call her boss, Sir Paul Condon. At first, Grieve thought his mates were playing a valedictory practical joke but he decided he had better make the call.[1] It was no joke. 'The ceasefire's over and there's a bomb in Docklands,' the Commissioner said. 'What are you going to do about it?' The IRA had given over an hour's warning, not wishing to repeat the tragedies of Enniskillen and La Mon.

Grieve dashed back to New Scotland Yard to confer and remembers hearing the blast, watching the windows shake and seeing a red glow in the sky in the east.[2] It was seven o'clock. When he arrived at Docklands' South Quay, he looked at the devastation and tried to come to terms with the size of the task that lay ahead. 'I suppose you wouldn't be human if you didn't ask yourself, "Gosh! Where do I start?"' he said. In his thirty years as a detective in the 'Met', he had never seen devastation like it before, at least not that he would have to deal with directly. 'I was looking at half a billion pounds' worth of criminal damage, two deaths, seventy Grievous Bodily Harms (GBHs), and three hundred-odd injuries of one kind or another,' he told me. He consoled himself with the fact that he was surrounded by a 'highly experienced team of detectives, trained over the past twenty-five years, who were totally unfazed by the scale of the task.'

Grieve began by triggering the public's response. Over the years during which the IRA had targeted the capital, the 'Met' had developed a strategy known as 'Communities Defeat Terrorism' in which the public's help was enlisted and every scrap of information it provided was sifted and analysed. In Northern Ireland, getting information from *all* sections of the community was not easy when some members of one side supported the IRA, but in London, where the entire community was ranged against those who sought to terrorize it, it was a different story. As Grieve explained, the strategy was to make the environment as hostile as possible for the terrorist to operate in.

I would argue that communities defeat terrorism. Che Guevara and Mao Tse-Tung and all of them tell you the terrorist as the irregular fighter swims in the sea of the population. You poison that sea for them and you make life very difficult. You make it difficult for them to hire houses, make it difficult for them to move about, make their documentation difficult, make it difficult for them to get transportation, make it difficult to get reconnaissance. Closed Circuit Television (CCTV) makes them extraordinarily nervous. You can make this a hostile environment, and that, hopefully, drives them into the democratic process. They decide terrorism's not worth the candle.

Soon Grieve and his team had identified the bomb-truck and traced its route by scrutinizing the videos from motorway cameras. A computer-generated picture of it was widely disseminated through the media and the public was asked to help by ringing a specially dedicated hot-line. The 300th call provided the lead that Grieve's team had been hoping for. 'Your bomb-truck was parked on a piece of wasteland outside my business,' the caller said, 'and there's material still here that they threw off the vehicle.' The bomb-truck had been spotted in River Road, Barking. Police officers on their hands and knees did a finger-tip search of the area and finally came up with a vital clue that put SO13 on the trail of the bombers. Specialist police officers found a thumb-print on a *Truck and Driver* magazine discarded in River Road that matched a thumb-print on an ash tray at a truck stop on the M6 outside Carlisle, which matched a thumb-print on the loading ticket on the Stena Line ferry from Belfast. With the help of the RUC, the prints were meticulously checked against the records of every IRA suspect on file but all enquiries drew a blank. 'We looked everywhere for him,' said Grieve, 'but we had no idea who he was.' He became known as 'The Triple Thumb-print Man'.

The bomb-truck's trail led to South Armagh and Grieve was determined to follow it through. The RUC warned him just how difficult and dangerous it would be to collect the kind of evidence they were looking for. 'One of the things they said to us was, "How many casualties are you

willing to take amongst yourselves, us and the army if you carry out the
kind of search regimes that you carry out in London?"' He was advised
that searching a particular house or premises for several days on end would
entail 'substantial casualties'. Grieve and the RUC worked out a plan that
would enable the team to operate to maximum effect with the minimum
danger under the RUC's careful security control. By this time, the team
knew what they were looking for. 'We became experts in paint chipping,
welding and aluminium extrusion,' Grieve said. He was not prepared to let
the IRA rest untouched in its redoubt. He and his team shared the same
view: that the IRA had come to London to plant a bomb, and now they
were coming to South Armagh to get them. They found the forensic
evidence they were looking for on the farm where the IRA had prepared
the bomb-truck but they failed to get any closer to identifying 'The Triple
Thumb-print Man'. He remained at liberty, unknown and untouched – at
least for the time being.

The Docklands bomb was only the beginning of the IRA's renewed
offensive which had been planned months before. The tactic employed
became known by the security forces and intelligence services on both
sides of the Irish Sea as 'focused terrorism', the objective being to cause as
much disruption as possible without killing or injuring civilians. The IRA
knew that it was vital not to alienate Sinn Fein's growing political support
that was the launch pad for the next phase of the 'struggle'. The IRA had
presented itself as the occupant of the moral high ground by blaming John
Major for insisting on decommissioning and reneging on the promise of
all-party talks following a cessation. To hold that ground, the IRA needed
to be wary of what it did once it returned to 'war'. 'New' Sinn Fein voters
would probably accept IRA attacks on military installations in the North
and economic targets in Great Britain but would not be supportive of
operations that resulted in civilian deaths.

In the run-up to the British General Election of 1 May 1997, which was
to see the landslide victory of Labour's Tony Blair, the IRA gave warnings
of bombs on England's motorway and rail network and at the Aintree
Grand National. The result was chaos with no inconvenience to Sinn
Fein's electorate. The IRA intended to take care, not that that meant its
attacks would be any less devastating. The intelligence services were caught
on the hop, suspecting that the IRA would end its cease-fire but not
knowing when or where. The Docklands ASU got under the wire, not
least because the operation was planned and prepared in South Armagh
which, to the intelligence services, was almost the dark side of the moon.

Nine days after the South Quay bomb, SO13 and MI5, to whom the
'Met's' Anti-Terrorist Squad now worked, had a breakthrough when a
young IRA Volunteer, Edward O'Brien (21), blew himself up with his

own bomb in London's Aldwych. He had boarded a Number 171 double-decker bus carrying a take-away food bag and had been standing by the door of the bus when the bomb exploded, killing him and injuring the bus driver, another passenger and three bystanders. O'Brien, who had been a 'sleeper' in London for two years, was a 'clean skin' who had never come to the attention of British intelligence. Not even his family, who lived in the Irish Republic, in Gorey, County Wexford, knew their son had joined the IRA. The family was strongly anti-republican and issued a statement condemning all paramilitary organizations 'unreservedly' and saying that they wished to have nothing to do with them. When Grieve's men searched O'Brien's flat, they found 15 kg of Semtex, 20 timers, 4 detonators and ammunition for the Walther 9 mm handgun he was carrying when he died.[3] They also found a new list of IRA targets.[4]

But the IRA's next target was not on the list. On 15 June 1996, a 3,500-lb lorry bomb exploded in the centre of Manchester, injuring 200 people and causing damage estimated to be between £100 and £300 million. Again, there was no intelligence that it was coming. Grieve believed it bore all the hallmarks of an impromptu operation designed to have maximum impact with minimum of planning, thereby reducing the risk of the perpetrators being caught during the preparatory stage. 'Manchester said that they'd changed their tactics. When you look at that device, there were fairly strong indications that it was set up and delivered in a fairly short time-scale without doing all the complex, sophisticated things that they did around the Docklands bomb. It looked like "get in and out fairly quickly. Pick up the bomb-truck over here, load it here and deliver it here."' Although the vehicle used in the Manchester bombing was purchased in England, Grieve had little doubt that the bomb itself was made up in South Armagh.

By the early summer of 1996, with Docklands and the centre of Manchester reduced to bomb sites, things did not look good for what Grieve referred to as 'UK Counter-Terrorism PLC'. This was the umbrella anti-IRA front of the 'Brits', embracing Northern Ireland and the mainland and utilizing the resources of RUC Special Branch, the 'Det', the FRU (though its name had been changed after the Brian Nelson controversy), MI5, the 'Met' and Special Branch officers in London and around the country. After Manchester, to the relief of intelligence chiefs, 'UK Counter-Terrorism PLC' came good. The operation was code-named 'Airlines' and involved over 100 police officers and 100 officers from MI5. On 4 July 1996, Dublin-born Donal Gannon (33), one of the IRA's most experienced 'engineers', was spotted in London by CCTV at Tooting Broadway Underground station in South London. Given the way that the intelligence services work, it is unlikely that this was the first sighting or knowledge that Gannon was in town. There was almost certainly prior intelligence, in this case probably from MI5 and possibly MI6 agents in Ireland, that he and other experienced IRA men were on their way.

The IRA had assembled one of the most experienced ASUs in many a. year to carry out one of its most audacious attacks. They planned to shut down London by blowing up six of the main national grid electricity sub-stations encircling the capital at Amersham, Elstree, Waltham Cross, Canterbury, Weybridge and Rayleigh. 'Shutdown' date was planned for 22 July 1996. The operation was based on the IRA's 'S' (for 'Sabotage') plan in which it had hoped to do a similar thing at the outset of its wartime mainland campaign in 1939.

Different agencies used different code-names for Gannon. MI5 called him 'Paradise News' and SO13 called him 'Felt Tip', presumably after he had been watched copying from *The Electricity Supply Handbook* at a public library in Lavender Hill.[5] Gannon was followed to 58 Woodberry Street in Tooting where other members of the ASU were identified, including John Crawley (39), a former US Marine who had been gaoled for gun-running after the *Marita Ann* was seized by the Irish authorities in 1984 off the coast of Kerry with seven tons of American arms on board; and Gerard Hanratty (37), who had been arrested in Germany in connection with the IRA's European campaign. Intensive surveillance also led the 'watchers' to other members of the ASU and a house at 61 Lugard Road in Peckham where thirty-seven large wooden boxes fitted with batteries, electrical circuits, and timer power units (TPUs) were found. The TPUs were being electrically charged in the cellar. The Semtex (estimated to be around 133 kilos) that would have pulled the plug on London's power supply was never found, although the police searched more than 7,000 lock-up garages and similar premises in South London. As a consolation, however, they did find forty stolen vehicles and uncover more than £1 million worth of drugs and stolen property.[6] It is almost certain, given experience in Northern Ireland, that the premises in both Tooting and Peckham had been bugged. On 15 July 1996, a week before 'shutdown', SO13 moved in and arrested eight men believed to be members of the ASU.

When the case came to court in June 1997, one of the accused, Gerard Hanratty, put forward the defence that the reason no explosives had been found was that they did not exist. He claimed from the dock at the Old Bailey that the plan had been to make 'dummy' bombs with icing sugar which, when X-rayed, looked just like Semtex. The theory was, according to Hanratty, that the authorities would then do the IRA's job for it by turning off the electricity supply so bomb-disposal experts could 'defuse' the 'explosives'. He said the IRA had no wish to alienate public opinion at a delicate stage in the peace process 'by massive explosions'.[7] Hanratty's defence did not convince and, at the end of a fifty-six-day trial, six of the eight accused were sentenced to a total of 210 years for conspiring to cause explosions. Hanratty and Crawley were amongst the most senior IRA men ever convicted in England. Prosecuting counsel, Nigel Sweeney QC, told the court that, had the IRA's updated 'S' plan succeeded, it would have been 'the coup of the century for the IRA'.[8] John Grieve knew that 'UK Counter-Terrorism PLC' had struck a powerful blow against its enemy.

> I would have said it was one of the best teams that the IRA ever put together. We thought it was the mainland 'A Team' as every single member of it [of those convicted] was highly skilled with a long track record of commitment. Their downfall on this occasion was that they had to send a team that was willing and able to operate in this hostile environment. So they had to send people who would not betray themselves because of their nervousness and who understood how the world over here operated and could detect surveillance. They were very good at looking behind them. The trial at the Old Bailey heard how they would walk along, looking for evidence of surveillance offices, looking for earpieces in people's ears, looking for microphones, looking for second people in cars. They were very slick but they just weren't as good as the surveillance teams that were behind them.

No sooner had the 'Airlines' arrests been made than MI5 and SO13 were involved in an undercover operation against another IRA ASU based in London. It was code-named 'Tinnitus'. In August 1996, two IRA men, Brian McHugh and Patrick Kelly (not the 'Brighton bomber'), arrived in England to meet three men in London: Michael Phillips who worked as a British Airways engineer at Gatwick; James Murphy, an assistant groundsman at Latymer Upper School in West London; and Diarmuid O'Neill, who had been born in England and had worked in London for a number of years, having been a pupil at the prestigious London Oratory school.[9] The plan was to succeed where the mainland 'A Team' had failed and attack power supplies and other targets in London and the south-east.

As in the 'Airlines' operation, the ASU was put under surveillance and followed for six weeks. A listening device was placed in their base, a flat at 38 Glenthorne Road, Hammersmith. Undercover officers watched O'Neill doing a 'recce' of the power supply to the Channel Tunnel and visit premises in Hornsey where they subsequently discovered ten tons of home-made explosives (ten times the amount used in the Manchester bomb), 2 lbs of Semtex, 3 AK 47s, 2 car booby-trap devices, 2 handguns and 13 timer units. Police described it as a terrorists' 'one-stop shop'. Undercover experts, again using custom and practice pioneered by the 'Det' in Northern Ireland, 'de-activated' the weapons and detonators so that, if they were used, nothing would happen.

But 'Tinnitus' did not end as planned. At 5 a.m. on 23 September 1996, armed police from Scotland Yard's Tactical Firearms Unit, SO19, stormed the Glenthorne Road flat where O'Neill was staying. The room had been searched by undercover officers beforehand and no weapons had been found. The surveillance equipment likewise gave no indication that there were weapons in the flat.[10] Officers from SO19 smashed down the door after the duplicate key had failed to work and swamped the room with CS gas. In the confusion, two of the officers opened fire and shot O'Neill six times. One of them, code-named 'Kilo', said he thought O'Neill's body language 'was aggressive' and, because there was no reply to the shout of 'Show me your hands!', he believed his life was in danger.[11] O'Neill was unarmed when he was shot. He died from his wounds a few hours later in nearby Charing Cross Hospital. Preliminary police reports said he was shot in a gun battle. No weapons were found in the flat. At the trial at the Old Bailey, three of the four accused were convicted on 16 December 1997 and gaoled for sixty-seven years for a plot to launch a bombing campaign in England.[12] Michael Phillips, the British Airways engineer, was acquitted.

Since the ending of its cease-fire in February 1996, the IRA's tactic had been to hit England in the belief that it would force the 'Brits' to honour their pledge of all-party talks and drop the insistence on decommissioning as a prerequisite. But it also resumed its more politically conscious campaign in Northern Ireland, albeit at a less intense level. This may have been because of the IRA's desire not to alienate its growing electoral support or because the activities of British intelligence made it difficult to do otherwise. Perhaps it was a combination of the two. Killing soldiers and policemen, in particular in urban areas like Belfast and Derry, had become increasingly difficult not only because of pre-emptive intelligence but because their body-armour was designed to withstand most of the rounds the IRA could fire at them. Nevertheless the IRA's attacks made up in publicity what they lacked in frequency. On 7 October 1996, in a security breach of massive proportions, two car bombs were driven into Army Headquarters (HQNI) at Lisburn through the 'Pass Holders Only' lane. Warrant Officer James Bradwell (43) was standing thirty feet away when the first bomb went off and then was caught again by the second whilst being treated for his injuries. He died in hospital four days later, never having recovered consciousness. Although he had been in his regiment for nineteen years, it was his first tour in Northern Ireland. He was due to retire in three years' time. Thirty-one other people were injured in the two blasts.[13]

Four months later, on 12 February 1997, the IRA killed a second soldier, 23-year-old Lance-Bombardier Stephen Restorick from Peterborough. He was hit by an IRA sniper's high-velocity bullet whilst manning a checkpoint in the village of Bessbrook in South Armagh. His parents, John and Rita Restorick, were devastated. It was what they had always feared since Stephen first went to Northern Ireland. 'He always wanted to go into the RAF like his father and grandfather but recruitment was cut back and he wasn't interested in the trade he was offered,' Mrs Restorick told me. 'He'd been unemployed for a few months and out of sheer desperation he went and signed on for the army. He knew it was the last thing I wanted him to do, but it was his life and he just saw it as a good career. I'd heard that there was a sniper working in South Armagh, and I always told Steve to keep his head down but there's nothing you can do if you're on a checkpoint. He was just a sitting duck.'

Rita Restorick filled the emptiness left in her life with an endless quest for peace, lobbying everyone from the Prime Minister to the President of Sinn Fein. 'I was driven to do what I could to move the peace process forward,' she wrote. 'I wanted to be a symbol of the hopes of all mothers who wanted an end to the violence. I also wanted English people to take an interest in the suffering that had been allowed to happen in Northern Ireland, instead of only taking notice when the violence crossed over to England . . . I felt that Stephen was with me every step of the way, pushing me on when the situation seemed so bleak, telling me to speak out to stop other young lives like his being thrown away.'[14] Stephen Restorick was the last soldier to die in Northern Ireland before the IRA declared its second cease-fire on 20 July 1997, five months after his death and almost three months after the election of Tony Blair.

Stephen was the ninth victim of an IRA sniper team that had become a republican legend in South Armagh. There were signs by roadsides and country lanes depicting a silhouetted IRA man waving a rifle with the warning, 'Danger! Sniper at Work!' The lethal 'work' was invariably carried out by an American-made Barrett Light 50 sniper rifle, which is five feet long and fires a .5-inch calibre bullet capable of penetrating body armour with ease. One of the trigger-pullers' favourite shooting-positions was from the back of a Mazda hatch-back car behind a hinged armoured plate which was dropped the moment the shot had been fired. The team had killed seven soldiers and two police officers. The first victim was Private Paul Turner (18) who was hit in the chest by a single shot on 28 August 1992 as he stood in Crossmaglen's main square. The death of Stephen Restorick made the army and police even more determined to track down the team and put an end to their killing. Jamie, who was now a senior officer in the army's 3 Brigade area that covers South Armagh and the border, was candid about the threat the sniper posed.

> You never knew where the bullet was coming from. You got virtually no warning. The fact that the sniper was very successful and that when he fired, in the majority of cases you were killed, clearly had a mental and not just a physical impact. Tactically, he was quite difficult to counter. He only had to fire once or twice a year to maintain his reputation as a one-shot killer.

The operation to catch the team was complex and dangerous and embraced all the agencies of British intelligence operating out of TCG South. It lasted for months. 'Ken' was one of the many involved. 'It wasn't just a single operation to catch the sniper, it was a great concerted effort across South Armagh,' he told me. One of 'Ken's' tasks was to monitor what was thought to be the cottage of one of the suspects. It took weeks of planning and reconnaissance to get the tiny camera installed in a location close enough to it. The camera was capable of transmitting live black-and-white pictures of the premises and all those who entered and left. 'Ken's' most alarming moment came when he was doing a 'recce'. He was lying in a ditch, camouflaged from head to foot, when a car with a number of men inside pulled up only feet away from him.

> They parked right in front of the cottage and you have to lie there still for hours and hours, waiting for them to go, just wishing that they would bugger off so you could get your work done. You can't move, you can't look, you can't shift around, you're getting cramps, you're lying in a damp, cold, wet ditch for hours on end waiting for people to go. Then suddenly one of the blokes got out of the car and came towards the ditch. The old heart races then because you think, Oh, no, have they seen us? Have we been clocked? He walked over to the ditch and literally had a pee on me. You lie in there and you just want to jump up and bop him one on the nose, tell him to bugger off because by that time you've just had too much. You just think, Oh, come on, I've got work to do. I've been here hours. I'm cold, wet and I've got absolutely nothing achieved for that particular night – a whole night wasted. And the more times you go back, the more it increases the chances of compromise.

Gradually the net closed around the sniper team. The 'Det' and others had identified a farm complex at Cregganduff Road, two and a half miles outside Crossmaglen, from where they were planning to mount their next 'kill'. It is thought to have been bugged by MI5 assisted by the 'Det'.[15] On Thursday 10 April 1997, a sixteen-man SAS team swooped and arrested the IRA unit after violent scuffles. No shots were fired. The IRA were not carrying weapons at the moment of arrest. The Mazda hatch back, with the firing platform and metal plate ready assembled in the back, was in the barn with them. The Barrett Light 50, with telescopic sight and three rounds in the magazine, was subsequently found concealed in a hidden compartment of a cattle trailer. One of the sniper team's key members, Michael Caraher, tried to run away across the fields but was overtaken and detained. There is little doubt that a decade earlier, he would have been killed along with his colleagues. When I asked one SAS soldier involved in the operation why the members of the ASU had not been shot dead as they were at Loughgall and Gibraltar, he said the arrest of the sniper team was a 'professional' operation in the way that some of the SAS killings in the 1980s were not. With intelligence indicating that another IRA cease-fire was in the offing, the last thing the 'Brits' wanted was a bloodbath that would only make it more difficult for Adams to persuade the IRA to put its guns away again. Jamie was jubilant at the success of the operation.

> We'd suffered so much from the South Armagh sniper team. We'd caught them red-handed. We'd struck the first proper blow, probably for twenty years, against South Armagh PIRA, who'd almost thought they had become invincible. We'd struck right at the heart of their morale and their feeling of invincibility. It was a great feeling for all the members of the army and for the police because we'd worked a long time to achieve this. We'd lost Bombardier Restorick a couple of months before and we really felt that this was one back for him. I think the fact that we had arrested them and not killed them was very important as well because it sent a message that there weren't going to be any martyrs. It must have been a major blow to their confidence. We proved that actually we could take the initiative, that we could pre-empt what they were doing and that we could successfully disrupt their operations.

The significance of the arrests was not lost on the RUC Chief Constable, Sir Ronnie Flanagan, who as Director of Operations in the province was ultimately responsible for the planning and implementation of the bloodless ambush.

I think it was an outstanding and stunningly successful operation. I think for the IRA to be arrested and their weapons seized right in their own back yard where they felt a certain degree of relaxation, brought about a sense of shock on their part. It's an example of the acquisition of high-grade intelligence, proper assessment of that intelligence, and the ultimate exploitation of it.

The arrest of the sniper team was the culmination of intelligence techniques perfected and honed over twenty-five years after disasters like the Four Square laundry.

Shortly after the arrest of the sniper team, Commander John Grieve was at a Bryan Adams rock concert in London when his pager went off. 'It was a message to call my contacts in the RUC urgently, and it was clear even from the pager message that they were very excited about something,' he said. 'They are incredibly elliptical in the way that they talk, even when you're sitting opposite them, let alone when you're talking at the end of a phone. But they left me in no doubt at all that they had had a very considerable success.' One of the sniper team now in RUC custody turned out to be 'The Triple Thumb-print Man' that Grieve and his colleagues had spent the past fourteen months looking for. His name was James McArdle. 'The RUC had just delivered probably one of the greatest operational coups and finest bits of detective work and co-operation that I think I've ever seen,' Grieve said. 'It's a brilliant case.'

In June 1998, McArdle was found guilty at the Old Bailey of delivering the Docklands bomb-truck to England and was sentenced to twenty-five years. He also stood trial in Belfast with the other members of the sniper team, Michael Caraher, Martin Mines and Bernard McGinn. On 19 March 1999, the Lord Chief Justice of Northern Ireland, Sir Robert Carswell, sentenced McArdle, Mines and McGinn to twenty years for possession of rifles and ammunition with intent to endanger life. Caraher was sentenced to twenty-five years for the attempted murder of a policeman. During his interviews with the police, McGinn verbally admitted 'riding shotgun' with an AK 47 when Stephen Restorick was shot. According to the police, he made this admission and others on condition that no official notes of the interview should be taken. On the same understanding, he also verbally admitted mixing the explosives for the Docklands bomb in a shed 200 yards inside the Republic. He said he had done up to twenty 'mixes' over the years, ranging from 200 lbs to ten tons, including two tons for the massive Baltic Exchange bomb of 1992. McGinn received three life sentences for three murders, including that of Stephen Restorick.[16] At the trial, McGinn's counsel argued that his client's alleged admissions should not be accepted as evidence because they had been made in breach of the Codes of Practice governing interviews. The Lord Chief Justice rejected the argument and accepted what the police said were McGinn's admissions. 'McGinn made comprehensive admissions of a string of terrorist offences in his interviews,' he said. '. . . In my opinion the admissions were a reliable account of McGinn's activities with the IRA, revealed to the police because he hoped for gain from making the revelations.' McGinn was heard to laugh as sentence was passed. Rita Restorick was in court to hear the judgment in the knowledge that, under the Good Friday Agreement, those responsible for the killing of her son would be free in a matter of months.

> It's very hard, like it is for all the other victims' families who are having to see this happen. But if we could be sure that this route we're taking works, and there'd be no more killing, then it's something we have to accept. It is very difficult for us, but if it did lead to peace and no other people having to face what we faced, then it would be worth it.

The IRA's South Armagh sniper team were released under the Good Friday Agreement on 28 July 2000, having served sixteen months of their sentences. They were among the last batch of prisoners to exit the Maze. Three months later, Rita Restorick received a profound shock. On 6 October 2000, she learned that the Northern Ireland Court of Appeal had cleared Bernard McGinn of the murder of her son as well as the two other murders of which he had been found guilty. The Appeal Court also cleared him of the explosives offences, including those in connection with the Baltic Exchange and Docklands bombs. The Court ruled that the convictions must be quashed because McGinn had not been properly cautioned by the police before volunteering the information and the interviews had involved substantial breaches of the Code of Practice relating to cautions and the conduct of interviews. Nevertheless, the Court ruled that his convictions stood on the charges of possessing guns and conspiracy to murder for which he had been sentenced to twenty years.[17] To those not involved this might seem academic since McGinn was already a free man, but Rita Restorick was amazed by the ruling and felt totally let down. 'Perhaps when members of the nationalist community say that they have never received justice from the British legal system, I shall now be able to say, "You are not the only ones."'

Chapter Thirty-Two

Out of the Mire

1997–1998

Almost three weeks after the Docklands bomb, John Major and John Bruton announced a date for the commencement of the long-awaited all-party talks. They were to begin on 12 June 1996 and would be preceded by elections to an Assembly from which delegates for the negotiations would be drawn. Coming so soon after the devastation at Docklands, the setting of a date for talks, which was what the IRA had been looking for during its seventeen-month cease-fire, seemed to prove that violence worked. John Major vehemently denied it, as he also denied that his narrow majority at Westminster and the need to keep the support of the Ulster Unionist MPs dictated his Irish policy. Major's aim was to pull off the seemingly impossible and get the Unionists into talks and keep them there with Sinn Fein also at the table. That is why he made decommissioning such an issue: he knew that without it, or at least some assurance that it would happen, the Unionists would never play ball. Major played the long game and the Docklands bomb was the result. He made no apology for his strategy.

There were two ways of getting the unionists into talks. One was a gesture, however slight, from the republican side towards decommissioning or commitments for parallel decommissioning. The other was to have the Assembly, which had previously been discussed with the Irish Government. We needed to get people into talks. That is the point that you must never take out of your mind. Whatever happens, unless *all* the people are in talks, you cannot reach a deal. You cannot reach a deal without the republicans and you cannot reach a deal without the unionists, we've seen that in the history of Northern Ireland time and time again. What I had to do was to facilitate the fact that everybody was prepared to sit down together. Without the actions we took, they would not have done so. *They would not have done so.*

The elections to the Assembly, which was Major's way of locking the unionists into the process, were held on 30 May 1996. A week before, the Ulster Unionists' leader, David Trimble, had insisted that his party wanted to see the IRA produce 'equipment of some sorts' during the weeks in which the opening session of the talks would be held. For his part, Gerry Adams, who said that Sinn Fein supported the 'Mitchell Principles' of non-violence, insisted that decommissioning was not a prerequisite or con-comitant of negotiations.[1] In the elections, Sinn Fein, having prevaricated over a boycott, exceeded all expectations, except perhaps its own, by achieving its best result ever. The party won seventeen seats with 15.5 per cent of the vote. Its rival, the SDLP, won twenty-one seats with 21.4 per cent.[2] The minority loyalist parties representing the UVF and the UDA/ UFF also won seats, as did the Women's Coalition, ensuring that the negotiations would be truly inclusive. All the pieces were now in place, except for the vital one of Sinn Fein, whose ticket of admission was IRA decommissioning in some form or other. It was a ticket the Republican Movement refused to buy, arguing that Sinn Fein's acceptance of the 'Mitchell Principles' was enough. Major and the unionists would not accept this.

The all-party talks opened on schedule on 10 June 1996 under the chairmanship of Senator George Mitchell, whom the Government had persuaded to try to see the enterprise through, but there was no Sinn Fein at the table. Five days later, the IRA gave its reply by bombing Manchester. Despite the IRA's continuing campaign, with its mainland ASUs getting ready to wreak havoc in London and the south-east, Major believed that at some stage the IRA would re-instate its cease-fire and Sinn Fein would enter all-party talks. As 1996 drew to a close and a British General Election approached, there was little sign of this happen-ing. Major admitted 'the logs were pretty well jammed'.[3] Although he made it clear that Ministers would not meet with Sinn Fein again until the IRA declared a 'genuine end to this renewed violence',[4] British officials were authorized to keep in touch with leading members of its party in the hope of releasing the critical log in the jam. It seems there was only one actual face to face meeting in 1996 and that was barely a few weeks after the Docklands bomb. One of the officials present described the attack as 'cathartic' for the IRA. 'They'd re-established their self-respect and sent a message that they couldn't be messed around,' he told me. Both sides recognized that, since the secret contacts in 1993, they had travelled too far down the road not to go on trying to find a way forward. The 'Brits' knew from all their intelligence reports that the IRA was serious in wanting to end its campaign but was prepared to carry on turning the screw with a strategy it called the Tactical Use of Armed

Struggle (TUAS). By this time, Sinn Fein was also using tactics on another front, radicalizing nationalist communities that saw themselves under loyalist siege, most notably at Drumcree, which had now become an annual flashpoint.

It took the British General Election of 1 May 1997 and Tony Blair's landslide victory to make the breakthrough. The Labour leader entered Downing Street with a staggering majority of 179 seats. Major's tiny majority had severely restricted his room for manoeuvre; Blair's gave him virtually *carte blanche* to do what he wanted. Some time before the election, Blair had met some of the British officials involved in the peace process at the Travellers' Club in London, anticipating that he would soon be working with them. They were impressed by the Prime Minister-in-waiting. Blair said that his hands were not tied by any internal party political differences, unlike John Major, who was trapped by an alliance between the Ulster Unionists and the Eurosceptics within the Conservative Party. From the outset, Blair made Northern Ireland a priority, just as Major had done when he entered Number Ten. But Blair could make a fresh start, unencumbered by the baggage collected over years of negotiation.

The General Election had seen Sinn Fein win a record 16.1 per cent of the poll in Northern Ireland and the twin figureheads of the Republican Movement elected to Westminster. Gerry Adams won back the seat in West Belfast and Martin McGuinness won in Mid-Ulster. In accordance with republican principle, neither took his seat in the House of Commons. The new Prime Minister could now negotiate with Sinn Fein's two new MPs, but only after the IRA had re-instated its cease-fire. The new Northern Ireland Secretary was Dr Marjorie 'Mo' Mowlam. To say Mo was unconventional was an understatement. At meetings she would kick off her shoes, put her stockinged feet on the table and apply moisturizer to her face whilst listening and talking. Unionists were taken aback. Nationalists loved her. Mo had no pretensions, airs or graces and was most frequently described, either in admiration or horror, as being 'touchy-feely'. Her predecessor, the patrician Sir Patrick Mayhew, had been neither 'touchy' nor 'feely'. With the need to coax Sinn Fein in from the cold and establish the relationship and trust necessary to encourage the IRA to declare a new cease-fire and proceed down the path of peace, Mo was the right person, in the right place, at the right time. Within days of taking up her post, the new Secretary of State visited Derry and said that decommissioning would not be a block to Sinn Fein's participation in the all-party talks. 'What we want to see first is a cease-fire which is definite in words and deeds so that people know it is serious,' she said. 'When we get that, we will be very keen to see Sinn Fein in the talks process.'[5]

Under Blair's 'New Labour', party policy on Ireland underwent a subtle change of emphasis. When Blair became leader following the sudden death of his predecessor, John Smith, in May 1994, official party policy was a commitment to seek Irish unity by consent and had been such for many years. Blair endorsed it shortly before becoming leader but the realities of leading the party and becoming more closely familiar with the complexities of the Northern Ireland problem led to the side-lining of 'unity' and an emphasis on 'consent'. Blair recognized that a million Protestants could not be forced into a united Ireland against their will. He was by instinct a unionist and had no wish to preside over the break-up of the United Kingdom by encouraging the province to sever its bonds with the mainland. One of his officials told me that Tony Blair was more of a unionist than John Major. Blair believed the solution to the Northern Ireland problem lay in the context of devolution for the constituent parts of the United Kingdom, with elected assemblies for Scotland, Wales and Northern Ireland. Whilst recognizing that any agreed solution in the province would have to have strong nationalist or 'green' elements, involving institutional links with Dublin as outlined in the Downing Street Declaration, Tony Blair, like John Major before him, steadfastly opposed the urgings of John Hume and Gerry Adams that the British Government should be a 'persuader' for Irish unity.

Nationalists were therefore dismayed when, a fortnight after the election, Blair made a speech at the annual Balmoral Agricultural Show in Belfast on 16 May 1997 in which he smoothed unionist feathers ruffled by Mo Mowlam's overtures to Sinn Fein in her visit to Derry the previous week. Within a few weeks of coming to power, 'New Labour' learned the necessity of balancing every step and utterance in treading the tightrope to peace. He assured the predominantly Protestant gathering that his agenda was *not* a united Ireland. 'None of us in this hall today, even the youngest, is likely to see Northern Ireland as anything but a part of the UK,' he said. 'That is the reality, because the consent principle is almost universally accepted.'[6] Unionists heaved a collective sigh of relief, calculating that in Blair's view, if there was to be a united Ireland, it was probably seventy or eighty years away, assuming babies in pushchairs were in the audience. Blair also offered immediate talks between Government officials and Sinn Fein if the IRA instituted a new cease-fire, warning that the 'settlement train' was leaving the station with or without them. Five days later, Sinn Fein had every encouragement to get on board when its electoral rise continued at the District Council elections, with the party winning 74 seats and 16.9 per cent of the vote. Gradually it was closing the gap with its nationalist rival, the SDLP, which won 120 seats with 20.6 per cent.[7]

Unionist scepticism about the IRA's true intentions was increased even more when, on 16 June 1997, two IRA gunmen killed Constable Roland Graham (34) and Reserve Constable David Johnston (30) as they were on foot patrol in Lurgan. Both were shot through the head. Blair immediately banned further contact between his officials and Sinn Fein. Nevertheless the dialogue continued, with both sides recognizing that the best way to avoid further killings was to persuade the IRA to re-instate its 'cessation' of 1994 so Sinn Fein could get on the 'settlement train'. On 9 July, the Government wrote to Martin McGuinness MP saying that Sinn Fein could participate in the all-party talks *without any decommissioning* as long as it adhered to the 'Mitchell Principles'. Unionists were outraged, accusing the Government of buying a cease-fire at any cost. In opposition, Tony Blair had supported John Major in insisting on decommissioning as the *sine qua non* of Sinn Fein's inclusion in talks. Now the condition had been dropped. Blair knew that if a cease-fire was to be won and the all-party talks were to be genuinely inclusive, decommissioning would have to be placed on the back burner. The new Prime Minister soon learned that the realities of Northern Ireland politics dictated that some principles, like deadlines, had to be flexible.

Ten days after the letter had been sent to McGuinness, the IRA announced that it was restoring its 1994 cease-fire with 'a complete cessation of military operations' from midday on 20 July 1997. Its statement said, 'We want a permanent peace and therefore we are prepared to enhance the search for a democratic peace settlement through real and inclusive negotiations.' It stressed that the IRA remained 'committed to ending British rule in Ireland'. There were no celebrations in West Belfast.[8] Blair had already set out a timetable with substantive talks beginning in September and a final settlement envisaged by the following May. Ian Paisley's DUP would have nothing to do with what it regarded as a sell-out and walked out of the talks, never to return. David Trimble, stepping onto a tightrope that was to become ever more frayed the further he progressed along it, agreed to stay in and do business with Sinn Fein, although refusing to address its representatives directly. Trimble was able to persuade his party to back him – although it did so with no great enthusiasm – because the British and Irish Governments had given assurances that decommissioning would be pursued in tandem with all-party talks.

When the talks opened at Government Buildings, Stormont, on 15 September, Tony Blair and Bertie Ahern, who had succeeded John Bruton as Taoiseach on 6 June 1997, issued a statement saying they viewed 'the resolution of the decommissioning issue as an indispensable part of the process of negotiation'.[9] The mechanism for this was to be the establishment of the Independent International Commission on Decommissioning

(IICD), headed by General John de Chastelain, Senator Mitchell's former colleague on the International Body on Arms that had tried to resolve the same problem almost two years earlier. Realizing that the IRA was *not* going to make any move in that direction short of a final settlement – and even then there was no guarantee that it would do so – the British and Irish Governments had little alternative to fudging the issue in the hope that it would either be resolved, or go away as a political settlement and the prospect of a lasting peace appeared on the distant horizon. But however hard the two Governments tried, like Banquo's ghost, it could not be exorcized. The issue was always there at the table.

Meanwhile, the problems for Adams and McGuinness were growing within the Republican Movement. It came as no surprise to the agencies of British intelligence that Sinn Fein's two new Westminster MPs faced some fierce internal opposition to the policies they were pursuing. Since embarking on the peace process, the strategy of the leadership of the Republican Movement had been to draw the Provisionals into the political mainstream without causing a split. With Sinn Fein now in all-party talks designed to end up with a devolved Government in Northern Ireland – albeit with strong cross-border links – and the party signed up to the 'Mitchell Principles', a split within the IRA became inevitable. The problem for the leadership was to minimize its effect. This, through careful lobbying and planning, it skilfully did. Opposition crystallized around the IRA's Quarter Master General (QMG), a powerful figure because of his rank, track record and personal standing. Although his support was limited, those prepared to follow him were experienced, battle-hardened IRA men.[10]

The split, small though it was, finally came after an Extraordinary Army Convention held on 10 October 1997 in the tiny village of Falcarragh in County Donegal. The QMG and his supporters had tabled two motions: that the 'Mitchell Principles' should be rejected and that the IRA's renewed cease-fire should be ended. Both motions were defeated and the QMG – who was apparently bent on engineering a coup – left to form the splinter group that became known as the 'Real' IRA. Its 'political' wing became known as the '32 County Sovereignty Committee'. Its Vice-Chairperson was Bernadette Sands-McKevitt, the sister of the republican icon Bobby Sands. Although the numbers were small, there were now two dissident groups at large as a magnet for disaffected Provisionals. The other was the Continuity IRA (CIRA) that had been formed after the earlier split in 1986. It had already made its presence felt in a series of attacks through 1997, culminating in a 350-lb bomb that exploded outside Markethill RUC station, County Armagh, on 16 September, as Sinn Fein made its historic entry into all-party talks.

The split was a concern for Adams and McGuinness and the Provisionals' leadership but in the event it could have been far worse. I understand that the QMG and his fellow defectors were subsequently door-stepped by senior IRA men and told to keep their hands off the Provisionals' arms dumps if they wanted to carry on breathing. The split, it was thought, was contained, leaving Sinn Fein to maximize the opportunity of being involved in the talks from which it had hitherto been excluded. Tony Blair had met Gerry Adams during one of the sessions in Belfast and was reported to have shaken his hand, but the real sign that the Republican Movement had finally been brought in from the political cold was when Adams and McGuinness and a Sinn Fein delegation walked into Downing Street on 11 December 1997. Six years earlier, the IRA had mortared Number Ten. The last time Sinn Fein had been entertained there by a British Prime Minister was when David Lloyd George met Michael Collins during the Treaty negotiations of 1921. One senior Provisional had told me that they wanted to be 'friends' with the new British Prime Minister. This was the beginning of the process.

Finally, after months of intensive negotiations in Belfast, Dublin and London, during which time both the loyalist UDP and Sinn Fein had been briefly suspended from the talks for breaches of the UDA/UFF and IRA cease-fires, the elusive agreement seemed in sight. It had been touch and go and only the patience of Senator Mitchell and the 'inter-personal' skills of Mo Mowlam had kept the talks on track. The most difficult moment had come at the beginning of January 1998 when UFF prisoners in the Maze, led by Johnny Adair, voted by two to one to withdraw their support from the peace process and had sent out an instruction to their political party, the UDP, to pull out of the talks. Barely a week earlier, between Christmas and New Year 1997, the loyalist paramilitary icon Billy Wright had been shot dead by INLA prisoners in the Maze, triggering a bloody cycle of tit-for-tat killings the like of which had not been seen for several years.[11] To save the process, as she saw it, the Secretary of State went into the Maze for a face-to-face meeting with the leaders of the UFF prisoners, including Johnny Adair and Michael Stone, who in 1988 had attacked the funerals in Milltown cemetery of the three IRA Volunteers shot dead by the SAS in Gibraltar. The loyalist prisoners' concern was that the Government was selling out to the IRA and that the Union was in jeopardy. Mowlam had to convince them that neither was the case. 'It was a very, very difficult and tough time,' she told me.

She convinced the UFF prisoners to stand by the peace process and assured them that the Union was safe. The principle of consent guaranteed it. As one British official involved backstage in the talks told me, 'The problem with the unionists is that they don't realize they've won. Look how clever Gerry Adams is, claiming victory at every stage. If the unionists asked for bacon and eggs, they'd complain if you gave them champagne and caviar!'

Finally, as May 1998 approached and agreement seemed frustratingly just out of reach, Senator Mitchell set a deadline to concentrate the minds of all the parties involved. It was to be midnight on Thursday 9 April 1998, the eve of Good Friday. Tony Blair and Bertie Ahern – realizing that, after not just months but years of negotiation, the talks stood on the brink of success or failure – offered to fly to Belfast, roll up their sleeves and do all within their power to push the parties the last inch of the way. George Mitchell accepted their offer on condition that there was to be no break in the final negotiations, however exhausted the participants. 'We will stay in session until we finish,' he said. Without his patience and personal, political and diplomatic skills, it is unlikely that any consensus would have emerged. Over the long, hard months of negotiation, he won the respect and admiration of all sides.

The historic Agreement was finally reached at 5.30 p.m. on Good Friday afternoon after Senator Mitchell received a telephone call from Trimble confirming that the Ulster Unionists were on board. Mitchell said he felt 'a great sense of relief, gratification and really genuine happiness'. Mo Mowlam said she was 'too tired for elation after such a long, hard slog'.[12] John Major, who with Sir Patrick Mayhew and officials from the NIO and Number Ten had done the vital spadework, sent Tony Blair his congratulations.

Blair, who in his first year as Prime Minister had spent as much time on Northern Ireland as on any other issue in government, said the Agreement gave the people of Northern Ireland the chance to live in peace and to raise their children without fear. 'This isn't the end. Today we have just a sense of the prize that is before us,' he said. 'I hope that the burden of history can at long last start to be lifted from our shoulders.' Addressing the parties who had put their names to the Agreement, he then added a prophetic warning. 'Even now, this will not work unless in your will and your mind you make it work.'[13] None of those involved underestimated the difficulties that lay ahead but perhaps few realized how fine was the margin between success and failure. Ian Paisley, whose party had taken no part in the negotiations and who was, unwisely, being written off yet again as a political dinosaur whose day of extinction had come, warned that the Agreement was capitulation to the IRA and 'the saddest day that Ulster has seen since the founding of the province'.[14] If all parties stuck to both the letter and the spirit of the Agreement, then there was a good chance it would work. If any departed from it, the likelihood was that it would fail.

The Good Friday Agreement was a meticulously worded document that remarkably gave both sides just enough of what they wanted to make the deal possible. Most important of all to unionists, it guaranteed the security of the Union. That, above all, enabled David Trimble and most of his Ulster Unionist Party to go along with it since it was underpinned by the principle of consent. This was the foundation on which it stood, as Tony Blair made absolutely clear.

> At the very heart of it is the principle of consent: that there should be no change to the status of Northern Ireland except with the consent of the people here; that Northern Ireland remains part of the United Kingdom as long as the majority of people here in Northern Ireland wish it to be so . . . This is the chance for Northern Ireland to gain a better future. I don't know if that chance will come again this generation if we turn our back on it now but I do know . . . we've got the chance now to provide the future that our children need.[15]

Unionists knew, too (although they rarely publicly credited the fact to their enemy), that the IRA had made enormous ideological concessions in tacitly accepting the principle of consent and giving Sinn Fein dispensation to participate in a Stormont Assembly and take seats in a new Northern Ireland Cabinet. By doing so, the Republican Movement was effectively accepting partition, at least for the time being, a volte-face that would have been unimaginable only a few years before. Furthermore, as part of the Agreement, republicans and nationalists had to swallow the abolition of Articles Two and Three in the Irish constitution that enshrined the Republic's historic territorial claim to the North. Acceptance of such concessions was a measure of how far the Republican Movement had come to reach an accommodation that it believed would ultimately lead to the united Ireland the IRA had fought for. The strength and the weakness of the Agreement was that it gave both sides reason to believe they would achieve mutually incompatible goals, the guarantee of the Union and a united Ireland.

Unionists had to swallow hard too. There were to be elections to a new Assembly from which an executive would be drawn that reflected proportionally the strength of the various parties in the Assembly. This meant that, should Sinn Fein win sufficient seats, unionists would not only have to share power with the nationalists of the SDLP (although the emotive word 'power-sharing' was never used) but with the political representatives of the IRA. This held out the astonishing prospect of what was tantamount to the IRA in government. The Agreement, like the Downing Street Declaration, also had a powerful Irish dimension which nationalists and republicans saw as a stepping stone to a united Ireland.

There was to be a North–South Ministerial Council and cross-border bodies set up to oversee matters such as Agriculture, Education, Transport, Social Security, Health, Environment and Urban and Rural Development. To reassure unionists, these 'green' institutions were balanced by a 'British–Irish Council' with the purpose of promoting 'the harmonious and mutually beneficial development of the totality of relationships among the peoples of these islands'.[16] It was to be made up of representatives from the British and Irish Governments and the newly elected Welsh and Scottish devolved Assemblies and was designed both institutionally and psychologically to underpin unionists' continuing attachment to the rest of the United Kingdom. The matrix of the Agreement therefore comprised three sets of relationships: cross-community, cross-border and cross-channel. The 'strands' were interlocking and interdependent. It was pointedly described as 'Sunningdale for slow learners'.

But the most controversial aspects of the Agreement had nothing to do with the intricacies of political structures and institutions but concerned three gut issues that every person in Northern Ireland could identify with and felt passionately about. They were the release of prisoners, decommissioning and the reform of the RUC, which the Agreement described as 'an opportunity for a new beginning' for the vexed issue of policing in the province.[17] As far as the British Government was concerned, although it never openly said so, the Agreement was a deal in which the paramilitaries on both sides would agree to give up their arms in return for the release of their prisoners. Although the word 'amnesty' was never used (for that, like 'power-sharing', had emotional connotations), effectively that was what it was. Prisoners belonging to organizations on cease-fire were to be released on licence which could be revoked should they transgress. Making prisoner-releases happen, as long as the respective paramilitary organizations remained on cease-fire, was emotionally charged, not least for the families of their victims, but was administratively quite straightforward once the British Government had given its commitment to enact the appropriate legislation.

Decommissioning was different. The issue that had held up Sinn Fein's participation in all-party talks and led to the Docklands bomb was not resolved by the Agreement, although the British thought and hoped that it was. Whereas the clauses concerning prisoner-releases were specific, those concerning decommissioning were aspirational. At no stage did any paramilitary group, be it the IRA, the UDA/UFF or UVF, give any specific guarantee, either directly or via its political representatives, that it would hand over its weapons. The issue was fudged. Had it not been so, there would have been no Agreement. Certainly, as far as the British were concerned, there was a clear obligation on the part of the paramilitaries to decommission since their political representatives – Sinn Fein, the UDP and PUP – had signed up to *all* the Agreement, including the clauses on decommissioning. The key clause said:

> All participants accordingly reaffirm their commitment to the *total disarmament of all paramilitary organizations*. They also affirm their intention to work constructively and in good faith with the Independent Commission [on Decommissioning], and to use any influence they may have, *to achieve the decommissioning of all paramilitary arms within two years* following endorsement in referendums North and South of the agreement *and in the context of the implementation of the overall settlement*.[18] [Author's emphasis]

This critical clause subsequently became the focus of much splitting of hairs. Sinn Fein argued that it was not the IRA and could not speak for it, and although it would use 'any influence' it might have, it could not force the IRA to decommission. The loyalist paramilitaries, through their political representatives, made it clear that they would only start to decommission once the IRA had begun the process. Unionists accused Sinn Fein of being disingenuous and simply hiding behind excuses. Further clauses in connection with the formation of the Executive stipulated that all Ministers must pledge a 'commitment to non-violence and exclusively peaceful and democratic means and their opposition to any use or threat of force by others for any political purpose . . . those who do not should be excluded or removed from office'.[19] Sinn Fein argued that it had signed up to the 'Mitchell Principles' and that it was committed to non-violence as a democratic political party. Again it claimed it could not speak for the IRA. Decommissioning, or the lack of it, was to dominate political developments in Northern Ireland for the next two years and beyond. It was the rock on which peace would be built or founder.

Chapter Thirty-Three

The Hand of History

May 1998–March 2001

For the time being, the contentious issue of decommissioning was put to one side as parties geared up for the referenda and elections to the Assembly that were the bedrocks of the Good Friday Agreement. The dual referenda, to be held North and South on 22 May 1998, were designed to give the Irish people on both sides of the border the opportunity to ratify what had been agreed on Good Friday. This was seen by the British and Irish Governments as the expression of the collective will of the Irish people in whose name the IRA had claimed the legitimacy of its 'war'. If the vast majority voted for peace, London and Dublin calculated the IRA would be stripped of any such 'moral' authority for its campaign.

To the alarm of the British Government, the 'no' camp, led by a re-invigorated Ian Paisley, made most of the running, seizing on the release of IRA prisoners and the absence of any decommissioning guarantee as well as the more traditional cry of the 'sell-out' of the Union. Trimble campaigned for the 'yes' vote as if his heart was never really in it and only took the stage with John Hume – introduced by the rock superstar Bono of U2 – at Belfast's Waterfront Hall in the dying days of the campaign. Worried that the Agreement might be killed off before it had time to breathe, Tony Blair flew over to pump energy into the 'yes' camp's flagging campaign and to give personal reassurances to unionists' deep concerns, in particular on prisoner-releases and decommissioning. In the glare of the cameras, he put his signature to five personal pledges, including 'Those who use or threaten violence excluded from the Government of Northern Ireland' and 'Prisoners kept in unless violence is given up for good'.[1] There was no reference to decommissioning. On the morning of the referenda, the *Irish News* and the *News Letter*, the main newspapers of the nationalist and unionist communities, respectively, carried an article by the Prime Minister in which he wrote:

Representatives of parties intimately linked to paramilitary groups
can only be in a future Northern Ireland government if it is clear that
there will be no more violence and the threat of violence has gone.
That doesn't just mean decommissioning but all bombing, killings,
beatings, and an end to targeting, recruiting and all the structures of
terrorism.[2]

There was still nothing more specific on decommissioning.

When the results of the referendum in the North were announced, the
'yes' camp just squeezed past the critical 70 per cent mark by 1.2 per cent,
thus narrowly avoiding what would have been seen by the 'no' camp as a
defeat. There was huge relief, not least in Downing Street. Perhaps the
Prime Minister's eleventh-hour intervention had made the difference.
David Trimble was hardly jubilant, perhaps aware of the enormous
problems that lay ahead, both from within his own increasingly divided
party and from an IRA that was likely to remain adamant on no
decommissioning. He said he now wanted to see 'the squalid little terrorist
campaign and the IRA dismantled'.[3] In the light of the result, Gerry Adams
was repeatedly asked if the 'war' was over. He refused to say that it was.

There was never any question of the result of the referendum in the
Republic, despite the decision to erase the territorial claim to the North
from its constitution, but the outcome exceeded all expectations, with 94
per cent of voters saying 'yes' (although on a turnout of only 56 per cent).

With barely time to catch breath, the political parties in the North then
launched straight into the campaign to elect the Assembly, as the poll was
scheduled for 25 June 1998, only four weeks after the referendum. You
could see from the expression on the party leaders' faces that all energies
were practically spent. Despite the danger of voter overkill, 68.8 per cent of
the electorate cast their ballots. (The turnout for the referendum had been a
record 81 per cent, the highest since 1921.)[4] There were even greater sighs
of relief from Downing Street and the 'yes' camp when 75 per cent of the
electorate voted for pro-Agreement candidates. Good Friday had survived
its first two critical tests. The Ulster Unionists became the largest party in
the Assembly with twenty-eight seats, therefore making its leader, David
Trimble, Northern Ireland's first Prime Minister for more than a quarter of
a century. Trimble became 'First Minister' designate. But his majority over
his unionist opponents, led by Paisley's DUP who collectively won
twenty-seven seats, was slender. The party that made the greatest advance
was Sinn Fein, receiving its highest ever percentage of the vote at 17.6 per
cent and winning eighteen seats. Many of these were held by leading
Provisionals who had played prominent roles in the 'war', including Gerry
Adams, Martin McGuinness, Pat Doherty, Gerry Kelly, Mitchel

McLaughlin, Alex Maskey and John Kelly. The UVF's political party, the PUP, also won two seats to be occupied by two of its former 'soldiers', David Ervine and Billy Hutchinson. The UDA/UFF's political party, the UDP, won no seats and was thereby excluded from the political process, and dangerously so.

The next step was the selection of the new Executive, the ten departmental ministers who were to serve under the First Minister, David Trimble, and the Deputy First Minister, Seamus Mallon of the SDLP. The SDLP had become the second largest party with twenty-four seats and 22 per cent of the vote. Sinn Fein was entitled to two ministerial posts in proportion to its representation in the Assembly.

Inevitably, it was not long before the spectre of decommissioning returned to haunt political progress and the formation of the new Government of Northern Ireland. Trimble insisted on 'guns before government', demanding that the IRA must start decommissioning *before* Sinn Fein could enter the Cabinet. Sinn Fein's position was the exact opposite, 'government before guns', suggesting that the IRA might be persuaded to make some move but only when Sinn Fein had taken up the Cabinet seats to which it was entitled. But even then, there was no guarantee. Hopes, however, were briefly raised when Padraig Wilson, the leader of the IRA prisoners in the Maze, said that 'a voluntary decommissioning would be a natural development of the peace process' although he ruled out any prospect of the IRA handing over its weapons to the 'Brits'.[5] For their part, the 'Brits' knew the latter would never happen because the IRA would see it as surrender. Other ways would have to be found to decommission. In the meantime, deadlock replaced hope. Northern Ireland had a new Assembly but no Government. That could only happen once the decommissioning issue had been resolved and power was devolved from Westminster. The euphoria of Good Friday soon began to fade as unionists and republicans returned to their entrenched positions and dug in to see who would cave in first.

Although the IRA and loyalist cease-fires held, the promised new dawn was not violence-free. Once again, the annual stand-off at Drumcree in July triggered rioting across the province as the army erected a wall of steel to prevent the Portadown Orangemen from marching down the nationalist Garvaghy Road. Loyalists' visceral opposition to the Good Friday Agreement, which they saw as capitulation to the IRA, made their anger and their protest all the more incendiary. Had David Trimble, whose previous support for the Portadown Orangemen had been a critical factor in his election as party leader, shown his face on the hill at Drumcree, he would probably have been lynched. Paisley was welcome. Trimble was not. The protest only came to an end following the deaths of the Catholic

Quinn brothers – Richard (11), Mark (10) and Jason (9) – who died on 12 July when their home in Ballymoney was torched by a loyalist petrol bomb. Courageously, the Reverend William Bingham, chaplain of the County Armagh Orange Order, urged his Orange brethren to call off their protest at Drumcree saying 'no road is worth a life'.[6] Despite Tony Blair's insistence on the morning of the referendum that no party with para-military connections (i.e. Sinn Fein) could take its place in Government as long as violence *of any kind* persisted, including so-called paramilitary punishments and beatings, there appeared to be no end to them, inflicted by both republicans and loyalists determined to maintain their grip on their respective communities. The Northern Ireland Civil Rights Bureau, an organization committed to exposing and countering such community violence, calculated that between Good Friday 1998 and summer 1999, there were 61 IRA and 71 loyalist punishment shootings (invariably through the knee) and 152 IRA and 171 loyalist punishment beatings (invariably with baseball bats and iron bars).[7] Despite the cease-fire, in the months that followed Good Friday, the IRA was believed to have been involved in five 'non-political' killings, although it claimed none of them. One was the result of a personal grudge, one was a former IRA 'super-grass',[8] one was a suspected Special Branch informer and two were suspected drug dealers. One British official infelicitously referred to such killings as 'internal housekeeping'. But this intermittent relatively low-level violence (compared, that is, to years gone by) was overshadowed on 15 August 1998 by the carnage of the 'Real' IRA's Omagh bomb. Twenty-nine people were killed and over 300 injured in what became the worst atrocity in Northern Ireland of the conflict. Three hundred pounds of explosives had been placed in the centre of the busy County Tyrone market town on a Saturday afternoon during Omagh's civic festival. Coded warnings were telephoned forty minutes before the bomb went off but the wrong location was given, with the result that the crowd was inadvertently directed towards the bomb rather than away from it. The scenes were horrific and defied description. In a statement the 'Real' IRA apologized and said the attack was directed against 'a commercial target, part of an ongoing campaign against the 'Brits''.[9]

Tony Blair was on holiday in France at the time. 'I can barely express the sense of grief I feel for the victims of this appalling evil act of savagery,' he said. 'But our emotion has got to be not just outrage and determination to bring the perpetrators to justice, but an equal determination that these people will not succeed in returning Northern Ireland to the past. There is a future for Northern Ireland and even amongst the grief and sense of loss of the families, we have to carry on to give the people of Northern Ireland the future they deserve.'[10] David Trimble, who was also on holiday, said the tragedy would never have happened had the IRA decommissioned its weapons. 'Sinn Fein cannot escape responsibility in this bloody atrocity,' he said. Trimble was wrong or misinformed. The Provisional IRA had nothing to do with it and Gerry Adams condemned the attack unreservedly. Just over three weeks later, the 'Real' IRA announced it was suspending all 'military operations'. Despite a massive RUC and Garda investigation, there were great difficulties in assembling the crucial evidence that would bring the bombers to justice. The police said they knew who they were but did not have the evidence to charge them. It may be that, for obvious legal and security reasons, the police kept their counsel, but on 9 October 2000 BBC television's *Panorama* programme controversially named four of the main suspects after a detailed investigation by reporter John Ware and his team.

Omagh strengthened the resolve of all parties involved in the Good Friday Agreement to see it through and make it work, whatever the difficulties. The immediate signs were auspicious. On 2 September Gerry Adams said that Sinn Fein was committed 'to exclusively peaceful and democratic means . . . [and] the violence we have seen must be for all of us now a thing of the past, over and done with and gone'.[11] It was the closest the Sinn Fein President had come to saying the 'war' was over. The same day, Sinn Fein announced that Martin McGuinness would be working with General John de Chastelain's decommissioning body, the IICD. Suddenly things seemed to be moving in the right direction. Four days later, Adams and Trimble held their first ever one-to-one meeting at Stormont to try to resolve their differences. It was the first official encounter between a Unionist and Sinn Fein in over seventy-five years.

By the end of the month, forty-two loyalist and republican prisoners had been released but there was still no agreement on decommissioning. At the Labour Party conference, Trimble reminded the Prime Minister of his commitment to ensure it. 'There has been no movement on the part of the paramilitaries,' he said. 'This is not a precondition. It is an obligation under the Agreement. It must happen if the Agreement is to work . . . Real peace can only be implemented if every part is implemented.'[12] The following month, he re-affirmed his position at his own UUP conference by repeating that Sinn Fein could not take its seats in Government without IRA decommissioning. The ball, according to the First Minister, was in Sinn Fein's court but the IRA had no intention of picking it up. By the end of 1998, the IRA had made it clear on three separate occasions – in April, September and December – that it would not be handing in any guns.[13]

On 18 December 1998, a week after David Trimble and John Hume had been awarded the Nobel Peace Prize, decommissioning finally began. However, it was not the IRA but the Loyalist Volunteer Force (LVF), a splinter group of the UVF formed by the late Billy Wright, that handed in its guns to be cut up and destroyed before the television cameras. Even then, 9 guns, 350 bullets, 2 pipe-bombs and 6 detonators was hardly a terrorist arsenal.[14] The exercise was supervised by General de Chastelain and the IICD. At least it showed that the 'modalities' were in place and the exercise could be done. But there was no sign of the IRA following suit. As the guns were being ground down, agreement was reached at Stormont on the specific responsibilities of the ten-department Executive and six cross-border bodies. But without some resolution of the decommissioning impasse, the Executive only existed on paper.

Sinn Fein's Chairman, Mitchel McLaughlin – probably looking over his shoulder at the 'Real' and Continuity IRA – warned that even a token gesture on decommissioning could destabilize the IRA leadership, with unpredictable consequences. Above all, the Republican Movement feared that any move would trigger a more serious split in its ranks and provide the republican dissidents with a windfall of recruits. That it could not afford. Martin McGuinness, not wishing to close every option, said that decommissioning should be dealt with 'down the road'. He gave no indication how long that road would be. Tony Blair stood by his First Minister, demanding that the IRA should begin handing over its weapons if Sinn Fein was to join the Executive. 'People have got to know if they are sitting down with people who have given up violence for good,' he said.[15] With the arrival of the first anniversary of the Good Friday Agreement, prisoners continued to flow out of the Maze – by this time, 131 republican and 118 loyalists had been released – but there was still no sign of weapons flowing from their organizations' stockpiles. The main loyalist paramilitaries of the UDA/UFF and UVF had indicated to General de Chastelain that they were prepared to decommission in principle but only in response to moves from the IRA. The feeling amongst unionists a year after the Agreement was that they had given everything and got nothing back in return, which gave David Trimble little room for political manoeuvre.

As the spring of 1999 arrived, the British and Irish Governments decided it was time for their personal intervention lest all that had been achieved on Good Friday was lost. They arrived at Hillsborough Castle, rolled up their sleeves again and settled in for another marathon session with the parties who had signed up to the Good Friday Agreement. What emerged became known as the Hillsborough Agreement. There was to be 'a collective act of reconciliation' which would see 'some arms put beyond use on a voluntary basis', to be verified by General John de Chastelain's IICD. Then 'around the time' of this collective act, which would also involve ceremonies of remembrance for all victims of the conflict, the new Northern Ireland Government would be formed, with Sinn Fein taking up its two ministerial posts, and full powers devolved from Westminster. The Agreement would then be fully implemented.[16] But, however fine the time-scale, this compromise still involved 'guns before government' and Sinn Fein rejected it out of hand, describing it as 'a massive change' and 'an unacceptable departure from the commitments given on Good Friday 1998'.

The two Governments tried again, setting an 'absolute' deadline of 30 June for agreement on setting up the Executive, to be followed by the devolution of full powers to the new institutions. The date was not arbitrary. It was four days before the Portadown Orangemen's march from Drumcree parish church on 4 July and a fortnight before powers were due to be devolved to the new Scottish and Welsh assemblies. The two Prime Ministers were anxious to get agreement before the anticipated Drumcree storm broke for the fifth time in five years and smashed everything. As the deadline approached, Tony Blair and Bertie Ahern flew to Belfast for the second time in two months to try to hammer out a compromise on decommissioning that would let Sinn Fein into the Executive without David Trimble losing face. Not all of the First Minister's colleagues were convinced that their leader was prepared to stand firm. 'My job's to rugby tackle Mr Trimble if he walks down the corridor to sign anything,' said one.[17] The deadline, as with Good Friday, came and went. The following day, 1 July, after seventy-five meetings over fifty hours, Tony Blair emerged to make the tantalizing but unexplained declaration that there had been 'seismic shifts in the political landscape of Northern Ireland'. It was assumed that Sinn Fein had given the Prime Minister some assurance on IRA decommissioning: not that it would happen *before* the establishment of the Executive but that it would take place at some agreed time afterwards. This, the two Governments hoped, would enable Trimble and Adams finally to 'jump together'. 'The entire civilized world will not understand if we cannot put this together and make it work,' the Prime Minister said.[18] Sinn Fein's statement which had fuelled the Prime Minister's optimism was significant but hardly 'seismic'. It said:

> . . . we believe that all of us, as participants acting in good faith, could succeed in persuading those with arms to decommission them in accordance with the Agreement. We agree that this should be in the manner set down by the Independent Commission on Decommissioning within the terms of the Good Friday Agreement.[19]

The key word was 'could'. What was meant by 'decommission' was again not specified. The guarantees remained as elusive as ever.

Expectations that a deal had finally been done were raised by the arrival of General John de Chastelain's long-awaited report which said that 'the Sinn Fein statement offers promise that decommissioning by all paramilitary groups may now begin . . . and can be completed in the time prescribed by the Good Friday Agreement'.[20] Following five days of intensive discussions, the British and Irish Governments issued a joint statement known as 'The Way Forward' that had been put to all the parties as a route 'to establish an inclusive Executive and to decommission arms'. It also contained a 'failsafe' clause that said that if the commitments on decommissioning were not met, the Government would 'automatically and with immediate effect' suspend the Executive and the other institutions set up by the Good Friday Agreement.[21] But expectations were dashed yet again when David Trimble and the UUP rejected 'The Way Forward'. As far as Unionists were concerned, it put 'government before guns'. Trimble knew that, had he accepted it, he would have been finished. His party would have eaten him alive. The rank and file were in no mood to compromise, convinced that the 'Brits' were following Sinn Fein's agenda and that republicans were reaping all the benefits of the Agreement and suffering none of the pain. Unionists were in no mood to compromise when less than a fortnight before they had watched the Brighton bomber, Patrick Magee, walk free from the Maze prison.

By now Mo Mowlam had become the target of the UUP's frustration and anger. They believed that she was too close to Sinn Fein and turning a 'Nelsonian' blind eye to the continuing violence as the IRA and the loyalist paramilitaries enforced their grip on their communities. The day Magee was released, Trimble called for the Secretary of State's removal. He believed she had become an obstacle to peace. 'One of the great difficulties we have had in implementing the Agreement has been the widespread lack of confidence in the community, particularly among Ulster Unionists, with regard to what the Secretary of State will do,' he said.[22] But Mo had no wish to go until she had finished the job. 'I want to make sure I do everything I can to make the process work,' she said, 'and I hope I am allowed to stay long enough to do that. I haven't had my fill of Northern Ireland.'[23] Nevertheless, Tony Blair heard what Trimble said.

In September 1999, Unionist morale, already rock-bottom, was dealt a further blow when the independent Commission on policing under the chairmanship of Chris Patten, a former Northern Ireland Minister and last Governor of Hong Kong, published its report and recommendations. What became known as the Patten Report was as much a part of the Good Friday Agreement as decommissioning and every bit as emotive. Positions were as polarized on policing as they were on decommissioning: Sinn Fein wanted the RUC abolished; Unionists, whilst recognizing the need for reform, wanted it left largely untouched. The Report took unionists' breath away. Patten advocated extensive reform that would change the face of policing in Northern Ireland for ever. Its 175 recommendations included:

- A new oath excluding any reference to the Queen.
- A new nineteen-member Policing Board with ten to be drawn proportionally from the new Northern Ireland Assembly members. This meant that Sinn Fein would be entitled to two seats.
- Neighbourhood policing teams. 'Empowered to determine their own local priorities and set their own objectives.' This meant that Sinn Fein and the loyalist paramilitary representatives would have considerable influence.
- Anti-terrorist legislation to be abolished when the security situation permitted.
- 'Holding centres' [i.e. interrogation centres] at Castlereagh, Gough (Armagh) and Strand Road (Londonderry) to be closed.
- An equal number of Protestants and Catholics to be drawn from the pool of candidates qualifying for selection.

But for unionists, the most offensive recommendation of all was the abolition of the name of the RUC which, in their eyes, was tantamount to the abolition of the force itself. For three decades they had regarded it as the bulwark against terrorism and seen over 300 of its officers give their lives in defence of Ulster. The Patten Report seemed shoddy thanks. The Royal Ulster Constabulary was to become The Northern Ireland Police Service. There were also recommendations that the new force should have 'a new badge and symbols' and that the Union Jack should no longer be flown on police stations. David Trimble called the Patten Report 'a gratuitous insult' but the Government expressed its determination to push ahead.[24]

In a last-ditch effort to try to solve the problem of decommissioning, Tony Blair finally persuaded Senator Mitchell to return to the province to see if he could work his magic again. Mitchell was less than overjoyed at the prospect: he was now happily back in America with his young wife and new baby, but, being a man of strong principle, he agreed. He would never have forgiven himself had the Good Friday Agreement collapsed and he had not done all in his power to save it. In September, Mitchell returned to Northern Ireland and began all over again. On 11 October, whilst the Senator was entering his second month closeted with the parties, Tony Blair reshuffled his Cabinet and Mo Mowlam was succeeded by Peter Mandelson as Northern Ireland Secretary. Unionists were jubilant. The appointment was controversial not only because 'Mo' had not wanted to go but because Mandelson had spent the previous ten months in the political wilderness having resigned from the Department of Trade and Industry following the storm over a loan(to buy a house in London's fashionable Notting Hill) from a friend and former Treasury Minister, the controversial Labour millionaire Geoffrey Robinson.[25] Northern Ireland was Mandelson's political rehabilitation. He arrived in the province and made it clear that, if the Mitchell review failed, there was no 'Plan B'.

The review lasted for two and a half months and concluded on 18 November 1999. The critical closing sessions were conducted head to head at the American Ambassador's residence in London away from the distracting notebooks, microphones and cameras of the media. Remarkably, Mitchell achieved the breakthrough. Sinn Fein were to enter the Executive and the IRA would issue a statement as soon as it did so. It was still not 'guns before government' but it was the best deal Tony Blair and David Trimble were likely to get. Both calculated, despite their previous adamantine positions, that the compromise was better than the collapse of the Agreement. On 27 November, the Ulster Unionist Council, the ruling body of the Ulster Unionist Party, endorsed the Mitchell compromise by 480 votes to 349, paving the way for the formation of the Executive and the devolution of powers to it within days.

At the stroke of midnight on 1 December 1999, power was at last devolved. The following day Bertie Ahern signed away Articles Two and Three of the Irish constitution and the new Northern Ireland Executive was finally formed, with Martin McGuinness as Minister for Education and his Sinn Fein colleague, Bairbre de Brun, as Minister for Health. It was, after the Good Friday Agreement, a second historic moment. Tony Blair returned to his favourite metaphor: 'The hand of history is at last lifting the burden of terror and violence and shaping the future of the people of Northern Ireland.' Bertie Ahern was slightly less poetic. 'Every Irish person is entitled to feel a great sense of pride in what we have achieved to bring about a lasting peace.'[26] One felt that, if it were true, they were right. But it was not over yet. As Sinn Fein took up its seats, the IRA issued the promised statement, saying that it had appointed a representative 'to enter into discussions with the IICD'.[27]

Trimble's acceptance of the compromise was, however, conditional. If the IRA had not begun the process of *actual* decommissioning by the beginning of February 2000, two months after the formation of the Executive, he would resign. He had already written and lodged his letter of resignation as a guarantee. He knew by agreeing to the formation of the Executive without decommissioning, he was at the very extremity of the Unionist ledge, with dissident members of his own party already waiting to push him off. As the deadline approached, it looked increasingly likely that Trimble's letter of resignation would have to be produced.

On 31 January 2000, the IICD reported on its discussions with the IRA's representative, alleged to be the veteran Provisional leader Brian Keenan. The IICD's Report did not give much cause for optimism. It said that although the IRA's representative had given an assurance of the IRA's 'unequivocal support for the current political process' and that there was 'no threat' to the process from the IRA, nevertheless 'we have received no information from the IRA as to when decommissioning will start'.[28] Five days later the IRA issued a statement that it had not entered into any agreement to decommission its arms. On Friday 11 February, there was chaos. Trimble was on the brink of resigning, which would have risked collapsing the whole peace process, and the IICD was hurriedly drafting a further statement to reflect last-minute developments from the IRA. Mandelson acted decisively and, in a blaze of controversy, suspended the Executive. Sinn Fein was livid, accusing the 'Brits' of playing the Unionists' game. The contents of the IICD's new Report were published that evening. What it said amazed most people, who wondered why, if the Secretary of State knew its contents, he had suspended the Executive and plunged the province into crisis again. For the first time, there were signs of genuine movement from the IRA.

> The [IRA] representative indicated to us today the context in which the IRA will initiate a comprehensive process *to put arms beyond use, in a manner as to ensure maximum public confidence* [author's emphasis]. The Commission believes that this commitment . . . holds out the real prospect of an agreement which would enable it to fulfil the substance of its mandate.[29]

But by the time its contents had been fully digested, it was too late. The Executive had been suspended. Perhaps Peter Mandelson, who was unlikely to have been taken by surprise by the IICD's latest analysis, judged that even though it indicated progress, it was not enough to stave off Trimble's resignation, and so gambled that after the furore had died down, the pieces could be picked up again.

Mandelson's gamble paid off. After weeks of backstage manoeuvring, on 5 May 2000 the British and Irish Governments issued another Joint Statement. They moved the deadline for the implementation of all aspects of the Good Friday Agreement – which was an elliptical way of saying 'decommissioning' – to June 2001. On the understanding that the parties concerned would take the necessary steps to make that possible, they said the Executive would be restored on 22 May 2000. However, they stressed that the paramilitaries must 'urgently state clearly that they would put their arms completely and verifiably beyond use'. If this happened, the British

Government would take 'further substantial normalization measures by June 2001'.[30] Although it was not specified as such, this was coded language for further troop reductions and the removal of more security force bases in what the 'Brits' called 'normalization' and the Provisionals called 'demilitarization'. The Joint Statement was a series of nods and winks to both sides. The following day, 6 May, in a process of carefully agreed sequencing, the IRA issued a statement saying that it would 'completely and verifiably' put IRA arms 'beyond use'.[31] On this basis, on 27 May David Trimble secured the backing of his party to re-enter the Executive despite no practical evidence of decommissioning. But he had been assured that things were about to happen. A fortnight earlier, the former Finnish President, Martti Ahtisaari, and the former Secretary General of the ANC, Cyril Ramaphosa, had been appointed as independent weapons inspectors. Just over a month later, they were taken secretly by the IRA to 'a number' of arms dumps (probably no more than two), almost certainly in the Irish Republic, which they inspected. In their report to the IICD they said:

> The arms dumps held a substantial amount of military material, including explosives and related equipment, as well as weapons and other materials. We observed that the weapons were safely and adequately stored. We have ensured that the weapons and explosives cannot be used without our detection. We are satisfied with the co-operation extended to us by the IRA to ensure a credible and verifiable inspection. All our requests were satisfactorily met.[32]

At last real progress seemed to be being made. But it was not enough for those in the UUP who wanted to see Trimble fall, believing that he had been hoodwinked by both the 'Brits' and the IRA and was leading Ulster to disaster whilst dancing to the Provisionals' tune. He had already survived one challenge to his leadership by his Westminster colleague, the Reverend Martin Smyth, on 23 March 2000. Trimble won by 57 per cent to 43 per cent. Now others were waiting in the wings. On the security front, there was blood-letting on the loyalist Shankill Road as a long-simmering feud between the UDA/UFF and the UVF erupted in violence and death. The instigator of it was generally assumed to be Johnny Adair, who had been released earlier under the terms of the Good Friday Agreement. Peter Mandelson acted swiftly, revoked Adair's licence, had him arrested and returned to gaol. 'The legislation enables me to act on the basis of my belief that he has or is about to commission acts of terrorism,' he said. 'I received a pretty strong case, very full information from the RUC and I acted on that. He has been pursuing and associating himself very directly with acts of violence.'[33] It was also a warning to all loyalist and republican prisoners who had been released on licence. If they returned to violence, they could be returned to gaol. Mandelson also extended an olive branch to the UDA/UFF's political party, the UDP, who had no representation in the Assembly, which was no doubt part of the frustration in that particular loyalist camp. 'I do what I can to compensate for that, to draw them into the political process all the time,' the Secretary of State added. 'They are people of good quality and integrity.'[34]

The violence on the Shankill Road added fuel to Trimble's unionist opponents who charged that the Good Friday Agreement had not brought peace. The reckoning, they declared, was at hand. The test came shortly afterwards in the form of the South Antrim by-election on 21 September 2000. South Antrim was a UUP stronghold and the party's second safest seat. If it lost there, no seat was safe as the next General Election approached. The result was a shock. The UUP candidate lost by 850 votes to its deadly rival, Ian Paisley's DUP. Although the margin was small, the implications of the defeat were momentous. Trimble's opponents within his own party now smelled blood. It was only a matter of time, they calculated, before they could strike the killer blow. The First Minister, on whose shoulders the Agreement survived or fell, was urged by the 'Brits' to stand firm. He was their champion, the linch-pin of the settlement they had striven for the best part of thirty years to achieve.

At his party's annual conference on 7 October 2000, Trimble came out fighting. 'Stop undermining the party. Stop undermining the leadership of the party,' he said with rare passion. 'Will we sleep any sounder in our beds if we are seen to ditch this Agreement? Will there be decommissioning? Will the Union be guaranteed? No, no and no again!'[35] He was cheered and booed in almost equal measure, his party irrevocably split. If David Trimble (and therefore the Agreement) were to survive, he needed two things to retain credibility and power: the British Government had to make concessions on the Patten Report and retain some of the symbols scheduled for destruction, not least the name of the RUC itself; and the IRA had to decommission in earnest to meet the new deadline of June 2001 set by the 'Brits'.

There was no let up in the pressure on the beleaguered First Minister, not least from the dissident faction within his own party now united around Jeffrey Donaldson, who had refused to endorse the Good Friday Agreement the day it was signed. On 28 October 2000, at a specially summoned meeting of the party's governing body, the Ulster Unionist Council, Trimble narrowly saw off a hostile motion tabled by Donaldson and his supporters by 54 per cent to 46 per cent but only did so by declaring that he would exclude Sinn Fein from cross-border Ministerial meetings until there was real progress on decommissioning. As far as General John de

Chastelain's IICD was concerned, decommissioning still meant the *destruction* of terrorist weapons: inspecting and sealing dumps were merely 'confidence building' measures. Ulster Unionists were of the same view. Inspecting a few dumps was not decommissioning. They were thoroughly fed up, believing they had made endless political sacrifices, dividing their party in the process, and got little in return from the IRA. There was a limit to how much longer they were prepared to put up with what they saw as IRA prevarication.

To survive, Trimble had had to seize at least some of Donaldson's ground: he was true to his word and refused to nominate Sinn Fein's Health Minister, Bairbre de Brun, to attend a North–South Ministerial meeting on health in Enniskillen on 4 November 2000. Nevertheless, Ms de Brun attended, as did her Irish opposite number, thereby cocking a snook at what Sinn Fein inevitably called a unionist veto. Unionists dismissed it as 'pantomime politics'. Martin McGuinness warned that the peace process might be facing 'the mother of all crises'.[36] The Education Minister's concern was understandable, given the importance the Republican Movement attaches to the cross-border bodies, which they see as the doorway to a united Ireland.

Although it was insufficient for Trimble, there had been some good news for the 'Brits' on 3 November, the day before the Enniskillen meeting, when Martti Ahtisaari and Cyril Ramaphosa announced that they had re-visited the IRA dumps they had inspected and were able to report that the weapons were still in place – untouched. The revelation that they were still there came as no surprise but the news would have meant far more to the 'Brits' and Trimble had the inspectors been able to announce that they had inspected *more* bunkers. There was, however, some encouragement when the inspectors publicly declared that they believed the IRA were serious about peace. The real test will come in 2001, when, they said, they hoped to make a further inspection. If this turns out to be not an inspection of *new* dumps but merely yet another re-inspection of those already seen, then perhaps Trimble's supporters, faced with a review of progress on decommissioning by the Ulster Unionist Council in early 2001, will indeed see this as the beginning of 'the mother of all crises', calling into question the IRA's sincerity. The early months of 2001, with a possible British General Election in the offing (and the new June target date for decommissioning and the full implementation of the Good Friday Agreement) would probably decide whether the Executive staggered on or collapsed following Trimble's withdrawal (with South Antrim in mind) to avoid melt down at the polls.

As deadlines come and go, time is fast running out, not only for decommissioning but for the Good Friday Agreement itself. Even President Clinton, who made a nostalgic visit to Northern Ireland in the twilight of his Presidency in mid-December 2000, failed to work his magic and resolve the decommissioning conundrum. The omens at the beginning of 2001 looked even worse when the Government was hit by Peter Mandelson's dramatic resignation on 24 January following the allegation that he had made a personal phone call to a junior Home Office minister in 1998 concerning a passport application on behalf of a controversial Indian multi-millionaire, Srichand Hinduja, whose family foundation donated £1 million to the ill-starred Millennium Dome for which Mandelson had responsibility before becoming Northern Ireland Secretary. Blair immediately ordered an inquiry, which reported six weeks later and cleared Mandelson of any impropriety. In his valedictory address outside 10 Downing Street, his final words were about Northern Ireland. 'It has been the greatest privilege of my political life to play a part in the peace process . . . something far bigger and more important than any one individual or his career,' he said. He believed a final settlement was 'so close now' and hoped and prayed that it would come about.[37] Anyone who saw his drawn and wind-blown face knew that he meant it.

Blair moved swiftly to appoint a new Northern Ireland Secretary and surprised Westminster by giving the job to the tough-minded Scottish Secretary, Dr John Reid, (a PhD in economics) who admitted he only had a passing knowledge of Northern Ireland.[38] This was unlikely to cause undue consternation to most of the political parties in the province who knew that the Prime Minister himself had long since taken personal control of the fine threads of the peace process. As Dr Reid took up residence at Hillsborough Castle to begin his sudden and steep learning curve, the shadow of decommissioning, or lack of it, haunted him as it had his immediate predecessors Mayhew, Mowlam and Mandelson. By this time, with growing speculation about an imminent General Election, there were other imperatives closing in on Tony Blair. One of his priorities in the feverish countdown to polling day and his hopes for a coveted second term was to shore up the peace process in which he had invested so much of his time and personal energy. Any dramatic announcement about the final implementation of the Good Friday Agreement seemed out of the question, given the lack of movement in the crucial areas of policing, demilitarization (the scaling down of the army's presence) and, above all, decommissioning. Keeping the show on the road, however unpredictable its run, was vital so that, come election time, the Executive and Assembly would still be functioning, to demonstrate that rumours of their demise were premature. Although the opposing parties could not agree on the resolution of the outstanding issues, they were unanimous in their wish to see the new political institutions survive, a desire with which the British and Irish Governments happily concurred.

On 25 February 2001, hopes of any breakthrough on the decommissioning front appeared to be dashed when Brian Keenan, alleged to be the IRA's contact with General de Chastelain's decommissioning body and one of the hardest of the Provisionals' hard-liners, told a rally in South Armagh that republicans should not fear the collapse of 'this phase' of 'the revolution' if the Good Friday Agreement fell. He reaffirmed his commitment to the Armalite and Ballot Box by saying that violence and political negotiations were both 'legitimate forms of revolution' and that both 'have to be prosecuted to the utmost'. Keenan also killed any hope that the IRA would announce that the 'war' was over. 'I don't know what they're talking about,' he said. 'The revolution can never be over until we have British imperialism where it belongs – in the dustbin of history.'[39] However uncomfortably Keenan's message married with the peaceful professions of Sinn Fein, the 'Brits' knew that there were powerful internal reasons for its delivery at that time. With the Provisionals' grassroots increasingly restless about the impasse in the peace process – not least because of the 'Brits'' insistence on decommissioning – Keenan had to reassure the IRA's rank and file in order to stem any defections to former comrades in the now increasingly active 'Real' IRA. Exactly a week later, on 4 March, the reason for Keenan's defiance became all too clear when the 'Real' IRA exploded a car bomb outside the BBC Television Centre in West London. One person was injured but no one was killed. The explosion was spectacularly captured on film and beamed around the world to show that at least one IRA was still in business.

Then suddenly on 14 March, in a process that has often seen one step forward matched with two steps back, the IRA anounced that its representative (presumably Brian Keenan) had met General de Chastelain's Decommissioning Body to discuss a basis for 'resolving the isue of arms'. How and when the issue might be resolved remained, as for so long, unclear. But at least it seemed like progress and left the way open for David Trimble to remove the ban on Sinn Fein Ministers attending cross-border meetings.

Chapter Thirty-Four

Farewell to Arms?

April–December 2001

Ironically, on 11 September 2001, the 'hand of history' helped break the decommissioning deadlock when Osama bin Laden's suicide bombers flew three hijacked passenger planes into the World Trade Centre and the Pentagon, causing the death of over three thousand civilians. The scenes, watched by the world on live television were literally incredible and millions who switched on thought they were watching some disaster movie. But this was no movie. President George Bush Jr. immediately declared a 'war against terrorism' and against those states who supported and gave succour to the terrorists. Afghanistan's extreme Islamic fundamentalist regime, the Taliban, that had harboured bin Laden's Al-Qaida network and sanctioned its training camps, were the first target. Bush was true to his word as B-52 bombers began their relentless campaign whilst America's unsavoury allies, the Northern Alliance, did the fighting and the killing on the ground – with a little help from the CIA and American and British Special Forces. The SAS were now combing caves and hunting for bin Laden in the mountains instead of scouring the wilds of South Armagh and East Tyrone for the IRA.

In Ireland, the Republican Movement looked anxiously on, concerned that President Bush might restore the IRA to the State Department's terrorist list thus seriously damaging the support, credibility and dollars that Sinn Fein had assiduously reaped from across the Atlantic during the Clinton Administration. It was also concerned that the White House might veto the visas given to prominent Provisionals that made lucrative fundraising events possible. The IRA had been taken off the list following its cease-fire and the last thing it wanted was to see that position restored, thus jeopardising all the political advances they had made over the previous decade. Many Unionists insisted that Bush should never have given the IRA such a reprieve given the atrocities it had committed over the years, citing the carnage of 'Bloody Friday' (1972), the La Mon restaurant (1978),

Remembrance Day in Enniskillen (1987) and the Shankill Road fish shop (1993), to mention but a few.

Nevertheless, in recognition of its commitment to the peace process President Bush did not put the IRA back on his terrorist list. No doubt he was advised by the 'Brits' who saw the danger of the process unravelling and decommissioning vanishing even further over the horizon. Sinn Fein, at the time, had problems enough with the Bush administration since three republicans had been arrested at Bogota airport on 11 August 2001 after consorting with the anti-Colombian government and anti-US guerrillas of the Revolutionary Armed Forces of Colombia (FARC). The guerrillas were Washington's sworn enemies not only because they were determined to overthrow the US-supported Colombian regime but beause they were regarded as 'narco-terrorists' who contributed to the flooding of America with Colombia's biggest cash crop – cocaine. For republicans to be caught in such company was hardly likely to enhance their standing with conservative Irish Americans who were pillars of the business community and hitherto amongst Sinn Fein's strongest financial backers. One of the three men arrested in Bogota was Martin McCauley who had narrowly escaped death at the hayshed near Kinnego in 1982 when it was attacked by undercover RUC anti-terrorist officers [see page 250]. It was a rare moment when Sinn Fein was caught on the back foot in the propaganda war. Unionists were gleeful that in their eyes the hypocrisy of the IRA had finally been exposed at a time when it had declared a cease-fire. It was never established precisely what the visitors were up to but it seemed that British intelligence may have monitored their movements and that they were testing sophisticated new equipment in the vast area of the Colombian jungle controlled by the FARC. There was speculation that the exercise was in preparation for 'a big nudge' in England should the 'Brits', in the IRA's eyes, continue to drag their feet over delivering their side of the peace process on policing, 'demilitarisation' and related matters. The 'Real' IRA was alreadly active in England and the prospect, however unlikely, of the IRA returning to its military campaign in London and elsewhere was causing the intelligence services a considerable headache.

However, just as Sinn Fein was reeling from the Colombian debacle, the spotlight was suddenly turned back onto Belfast and away from the Republican Movement. By the end of June 2001, a bitter confrontation had erupted along the sectarian interface in North Belfast where 7,000 Catholics in Ardoyne face 1,000 Protestants in the Glenbryn estate. Ever since the current conflict began, the area has been a sectarian flashpoint but the two communities were now poliarised as never before. On the face of it, the issue was about a short, 400 yard journey to a girls' primary school.

The problem was that the school, Holy Cross, was Catholic but located in Protestant Glenbryn. Traditionally Catholic mothers from Ardoyne had taken their children to Holy Cross through Glenbryn without a problem, but in the heated atmosphere of yet another of Belfast's 'long hot summers', this was to cease. Loyalists in Glenbryn now declared that Ardoyne's mothers and children could no longer walk the quarter of a mile up the Protestant stretch of Ardoyne Road to Holy Cross. This was Drumcree, where the Catholic residents of the Garvaghy Road did not allow Protestant Orangemen to march down their road, in reverse. But the issue was about much more than a short journey to school. It was about territory and winners and losers. To loyalists, Catholics were getting everything in the peace process whilst Protestants were losing everything. Holy Cross was a line in the sand. Nor were the protests and confrontations entirely spontaneous, any more than they were at Drumcree. With so much at stake in the bigger political picture, Sinn Fein and the loyalist Ulster Defence Association were prominent in organising protests on their respective sides under the banners of different community groups. So savage were the scenes of violence that the RUC officers, clad in black riot gear and looking like Darth Vader, had to escort the children and their mothers to school with soldiers on standby to provide backup. The images of tearful little girls sheltering behind their parents as they ran a gauntlet of loyalist taunts and missiles under heavy police and military escort, shocked not just the United Kingdom and the Irish Republic but other parts of the world. It was as if nothing had changed in thirty years and the peace process and the Good Friday Agreement had never happened. No wonder the 'Brits' despaired. However, on 26 November 2001, loyalists suspended their protest following mediation, realising that the photographs splashed on the front of newspapers worldwide and seen globally by television viewers were only helping republicans and wounding the Protestant cause. Critically, after Colombia, Holy Cross turned the tables and the Provisionals were now seen not as the allies of a South American terrorist group but, as in 1969, the defenders of the nationalist community in Ardoyne and elsewhere from loyalist attack. In that too, nothing seemed to have changed.

Nevertheless, the Colombian arrests and the tragedy of 11 September still threatened to cause the Repulican Movement irreparable damage and reverse the remarkable political progress that Sinn Fein was now making. In the Westminster General Election on 7 June 2001, when Tony Blair won a second Labour landslide victory with a parliamentary majority of 166 seats, Sinn Fein met with unprecedented success, winning four seats and finally eclipsing the SDLP which held onto its three. Pat Doherty won West Tyrone: Michelle Gildernew won Fermanagh and South Tyrone, the seat won by the IRA hunger striker, Bobby Sands, in 1981; and Gerry Adams and Martin McGuinness held their seats in West Belfast and Mid-Ulster respectively. (Previously Sinn Fein had held two Westminster seats with Gerry Adams elected as MP for West Belfast in 1983, 1987 and 1997 – he lost in 1992 – and Martin McGuinness as MP for Mid-Ulster in 1997.) Amid the celebrations, Martin McGuinness MP attributed his party's success to 'Sinn Fein's peace strategy' and declared that it was 'well on the way to becoming the largest political party in the North'.[1] Sinn Fein's rise had indeed been spectacular and Danny Morrison, the former leading Provisional, probably never envisaged just how prophetic his famous 'Armalite and Ballot box' phrase was when he uttered them at Sinn Fein's annual conference in 1981, a few months after Bobby Sand's historic election victory (see page 262–2630). Over the following twenty years, the party had seen its share of the vote in local elections more than double, from 10.1 per cent in 1982[2] to 20.66 per cent in 2001.[3]

But the 'Brits' had little to celebrate: not only did Sinn Fein overtake the SDLP to become the largest nationalist party in the province but Ian Paisley's Democratic Unionist Party (DUP) had trounced David Trimble's Ulster Unionists (UUP). The DUP won a record five seats against the UUP's six after Trimble watched three of his party's seats being washed away by the Paisley tide. The centre, which the Good Friday Agreement of 1998 had been designed to strengthen, caved in to the nationalist and Unionist extremes as a result of the impasse over the full implementation of its provisions, most notably on decommissioning. This strengthening of the extremes was confirmed a few days later when the local election results were announced. (Polling had taken place on the same day as the Westminster election but the count was held over.) Sinn Fein won a further 34 seats, with 20.66 per cent of the vote and the SDLP lost 3 with 19.42 per cent; the DUP won 40 more seats and the UUP lost 31.[4] Nevertheless, encouragingly for the 'Brits', the moderates of the UUP and the SDLP remained the parties with the largest number of seats. Significantly, as a result of the Westminster and local elections of 7 June 2001, the political map of Northern Irealnd changed as the province was effectively re-partitioned along 'green' and 'orange' lines. The nationalists of the SDLP and Sinn Fein now controlled most of the South and West (South Down, Newry and Armagh, Fermanagh and South Tyrone, Mid-Ulster, West Tyrone and Foyle) and the Unionists of the UUP and DUP controlled most of the North and East (Lagan Valley, Upper Bann, South Antrim, East Antrim, North Antrim and East Londonderry). The exception in this Unionist heartland was Gerry Adams who was elected for the fourth time in predominantly nationalist West Belfast.

There were inevitable calls for Trimble's resignation following the

UUP's setbacks at the polls (although the predicted meltdown was avoided) and continuing threats to his leadership by the anti-Agreement factions within his own party, but the First Minister cleverly held them off, walking the tightrope whilst his enemies and friends held their breath to see if he would fall. They watched over the weekend of 30 June 2001 to see if he would stand by the post-dated letter of resignation he had lodged to be acted upon in the absence of any IRA move on decommissioning. No more was offered and so Trimble resigned as First Minister. Copious obituaries were written but, like the report of Mark Twain's death, they were exaggerated.[5] The sword on which Trimble fell was made of cardboard not steel. The Secretary of State, Dr John Reid, then suspended the Executive for six weeks while the parties tried to put a compromise package together. The stalemate was to last much longer.

Trimble's resignation was a tactic to put pressure on the IRA to actually begin the process of decommissioning instead of just talking about it. By late summer, the tactic seemed to be working. On 8 August, the IRA issued a statement that said it had agreed a scheme with General John de Chastelain and his colleagues on the Decommissioning Body to put 'arms completely and verifiably beyond use.' The statement said, 'This was an unprecedented development which involved a very difficult decision by us, and problems for our organisation. While mindful of these concerns, our decision was aimed at enhancing the peace process.'[6] Six days later, however, the IRA withdrew the statement because Trimble and the UUP had rejected it on the grounds that it did not go far enough. Both sides were playing hardball.

The Republican Movement, like Trimble, had to play its cards carefully. Sinn Fein, with two Ministers on the Executive, knew that if the Good Friday institutions collapsed the responsibility for the demise of the Executive would largely be laid at its door because of the IRA's refusal to begin decommssioning. Republicans were in the business of consolidating their political gains and not in the mood to sanction anything that might erode them. Moreover, Sinn Fein's spectacular advances in the Westminster and local elections of 2001 were calculated to be a springboard for the party's campaign in the Republic's General Election due to be held in 2002. The party had its eyes on half-a-dozen potentially winnable seats that might lead to its holding the balance of power in a coalition government in Dublin. Ironically whilst Sinn Fein had been carving such remarkable political inroads in the North, its campaigns in the South had not met with commensurate success. By 2001, the party had 62 local councillors in the Republic and one TD (Member of Parliament), Caoimhghín Ó Caoláin, who represented the border constituency of Cavan/Monaghan. The South's electorate was traditionally wary of a party whose other face was the Provisional IRA. If Sinn Fein were to make significant political advances across the border, then the Republican Movement's long-term strategy would seem to be falling into place with Ministers in government both North and South as a stepping stone to the united Ireland for which the IRA had fought, killed and died. Sinn Fein wanted nationalists on both sides of the border to see it as the party of peace and not as wreckers of a peace process that had brought republicans such great political dividends, not least the release of their prisoners.

Remarkably, by the autumn 2001 as the political wrangling continued, there were signs of movement, driven not by Trimble's resignation but by the events of 11 September. Gerry Adams was clear in his condemnation of the terrorist attacks. Addressing the Northern Ireland Assembly two days after the tragedy he said, 'I unequivocally condemn those who carried out these attacks and have sent my deepest condolences and sympathies to the people of the United States.' He went on to re-affirm his organisation's commitment to the peace process, despite all the remaining problems. 'When viewed in the awful context of other conflicts, or in the enormity of human suffering in New York and Washington, it is true to say that great progress has been made here. Is this to be squandered? . . . I re-dedicated myself and our party to do our very best to resolve the problems that confront us all.'[7] Sinn Fein subsequently announced that all proceeds from its annual 'Friends of Sinn Fein' fund-raising dinner in New York on 1 November 2001, due to be attended by the party's President, Gerry Adams, would go to the families of construction workers killed in the World Trade Centre attack, many of whom had traditionally supported the republican cause.

In the background, under growing pressure not only from the British and Irish governments but from the Bush Administration too, the logjam was gradually being loosened as Adams' spech indirectly suggested. Adams and McGuinness now had to persuade the IRA to move on the most sensitive and difficult issue it faced, even more difficult than the decision to call the ceasefire in 1994 when, although not defeated, it had not won the 'war'. Again, both men proved themselves to be master tacticians. They knew that however convinced their tight circle was that strategically the political course the Republican Movement had embarked upon was correct, many of the IRA's rank and file continued to harbour serious doubts when it came to the issue of decommissioning. If the question were put to a vote amongst Volunteers on the ground, it would almost certainly be rejected. Therefore the presentation of the case, the formulation of the wording and the constitutional mechanism whereby it could be approved by the IRA were absolutely critical if the Republican Movement's peace project was not to founder. The mechanism to circumvent opposition lay hidden in the IRA's Constitution. Section 5 (a) stipulates that the 'Supreme Authority' of the Irish Republican Army is the 'General Army Convention' consisting of delegates from every IRA unit on the island of Ireland. Constitutionally the Convention is scheduled to meet every two years 'unless the majority of these delegates notify the Army Council [the seven member body that runs the 'war'] that they deem it better for military purposes to postpone it'. Adams and McGuinness calculated that if decommissioning or 'putting arms beyond use' were put to delegates at a Convention representing all IRA Volunteers on the ground, there would almost certainly have been a split between the leadership and the rank and file. One split, following the Extraordinary Army Convention in 1997 that led to the emergence of the rival 'Real' IRA, was enough. At that time the Convention had been called to discuss a motion proposed by a small, but powerful dissident faction to oppose the Republican Movement's signing up to the Mitchell principles of non-violence and to propose the ending of the IRA's ceasefire (see page 363). Although the resulting split was relatively small, it was a risk the leadership was not prepared to take again. In practice because of the 'war' the Convention seldom met except to debate and ratify key decisions as above in 1997 and likewise in 1986 when it agreed to end 'abstentionism', thus permitting Sinn Fein to stand for election to the Irish Parliament (Dail Eireann). Again, the decision split the Republican Movement (see page 264). However, the Constitution stipulates that 'when a General Convention is not in session . . . the Army Council shall be the Supreme Authority'. It is this body that then has 'the power to conclude peace or declare war', so[8] without the Convention to discuss the issue of decommissioning, constitutionally the Army Council could make the decision on behalf of the IRA. This is what happened, thus minimising the risk of a split that was likely to have been far more disastrous than the 'Real' IRA split of 1997. The agreed form of words was important as hairs were split with republican precision. The IRA would not be handing over its weapons to the 'Brits' but would be 'putting them permanently beyond use' in a way and at a time of its choosing. Although the decision to do so in principle had already been taken as indicated by the IRA statement of 8 August 2001, there is little doubt that the events of 11 September accelerated the process. Had they not done so, decommissioning would probably have taken place some time before the Irish Republic's election in 2002 as Sinn Fein would have been unlikely to maximise its vote if the electorate knew that the party was still linked to a secret army with its arsenals still buried beneath Irish soil.

At last to the relief of the 'Brits', the IRA fulfilled its promise, or at least began to do so. On 23 October 2001 the IRA issued the statement the 'Brits' and many others had long been waiting for. It was short in length and short on detail but momentous in its historic significance. The IRA had never done anything like this before and, as the statement made clear, it was only doing so now 'to save the peace process and to persuade others of our genuine intentions'.[9] The statement did not detail what the IRA had done other than to confirm that it had acted in compliance with the agreement reached with General de Chastelain in its statement of 8 August 2001. The statement from the General and his colleagues was tantalisingly brief. 'We have witnessed an event which we regard as signifcant in which the IRA has put a quantity of arms beyond use. The material in question includes arms, ammunition and explosives.'[10] There were no reciprocal moves by the loyalist paramilitaries. It was a triumph for the Canadian soldier and diplomat who had so patiently waited, encouraged and eventually helped deliver what most informed observers believed to be impossible and that senior Provisionals had sworn would never happen, except, as one of its leaders once told me, 'never in a million years – in the short term'. What precisely took place was never made clear. Certainly there was no explosion in the forest in the dead of night as an IRA arms dump was blown up, nor was there the sound of grinding machines as weapons were destroyed, nor perhaps even the sound of concrete mixers as dumps were sealed. There were even rumours of locks monitored by Global Positioning Satellites. Nevertheless, the most realistic assessment was that one or more dumps had been sealed in one way or another and weapons thereby rendered 'permanently beyond use'. Tony Blair, who throughout his Premiership had laboured so tirelessly to keep the peace process on track, was delighted and relieved. It was a ray of good news in a world still recovering from the shock of 11 September. He said 'we have worked for this moment for three and half years' since the Good Friday Agreement of 10 April 1998. Perhaps this really was the 'hand of history'.

With the IRA having made its historic move, the road was clear for David Trimble to seek re-election as First Minister. But it was not a foregone conclusion that he would succeed. When two members of his own party failed to support him because they thought he had been hoodwinked by the IRA, Trimble failed by one vote to become First Minster a second time. It was only on 6 November 2001 when the non-sectarian Alliance Party controversially decided to cast its votes as 'Unionist' that Trimble finally made it. But even then, he was not completely out of the woods. The dangerous rumblings from dissidents in his own party plus the belligerent opposition of Paisley's increasingly confident DUP, made Trimble's future and the future of the Executive and Assembly still far from guaranteed. If the IRA was serious, the First Minister's opponents argued, then they must decommission all of their arms. A couple of dumps simply were not enough. The issue, like the writing on the IRA mural, had 'not gone away'

Shortly after the the IRA's symbolic act of decommissioning, the 'Brits' reciprocated by beginning to dismantle some of the army's fortifications in border areas which had caused local people such anger, and the IRA a variety of problems, since most were stuffed with surveillance equipment. One of the first to go was the 'supersangar', the 15 tonne, 22 metres-high watchtower in Newtonhamilton in South Armagh. It was dismantled on 25 October, two days after the IRA statement.[12] The process was unofficially known as 'sequencing' to indicate that the 'Brits' were responding to the IRA's move. At last the Good Friday Agreement seemed to be falling into place, despite the opposition of Paisley's DUP and some members of Trimble's own party.

Progress was also being made in the equally vexed area of policing. On 4 November 2001, the name, the Royal Ulster Constabulary, was consigned to history to the deep regret of its officers, Unionist politicians and their community. As the name went, revered by one section of the community and reviled by the other, the new Police Service of Northern Ireland (PSNI) officially came into being, with Sir Ronnie Flanagan still at its head to oversee the transition prior to his announced retirement in 2002. It was no accident that it was no longer a police 'force' but was now a police 'service'. On that day the first batch of new recruits, selected on a fifty-fifty Catholic/Protestant basis, began their training. Eight thousand people initially applied of whom 550 were deemed to be qualified candidates. Significantly, 154 of them (28 per cent) came from the Catholic community, a figure that would have been unthinkable before the Good Friday Agreement and the Patten Report. This meant that, given the need for a fifty-fifty intake, the new service could recruit around 300 officers, roughly 150 Catholics and 150 Protestants. With the birth of the PSNI, came the body that was to oversee the new service, the 19-member Northern Ireland Policing Board, again as recommended by Patten, that was to hold the Chief Constable and the police to account. Ten were politicians drawn from all the main political parties and nine were independent members. Sinn Fein, however, had refused to take up its two seats on the grounds that the reforms has not been far-reaching enough. Critically the SDLP had agreed to serve on the Board, thus effectively giving approval for Catholics to put on the new police uniform. Had the SDLP not done so, the Policing Board would have been almost meaningless as it would have been seen by nationalists as an almost exclusively unionist preserve, just as they perceived the old RUC. Perhaps it was only a matter of time before Sinn Fein joined in too, but that depended on events. Sinn Fein's Gerry Kelly challenged the SDLP's decision and said it was making a mistake in trusting the 'Brits'

to 'change policing legislation,'[13] and its chairman. Mitchel McLaughlin
had already defended his party's decision to boycott the Board, saying
republicans were not about to buy 'a pig in a poke'. 'If the British
government were moved some distance last year, then let us take some
further time to get it right,' he said 'There is really no point in continuing
with the failure of policing.'[14] As 2001 drew to a close, the omens for
policing began to look good. Remarkably, on 12 December, the Policing
Board reached cross community agreement on a new badge for the new
service, remarkably because such symbols had long excited powerful
emotions on both sides. The new logo had something for everyone. It
featured Saint Patrick's cross surrounded by six symbols: a harp, crown,
shamrock, laurel leaf, torch and scales of justice. Unionists got the harp and
crown, which had been the symbols of the old RUC, and nationalists got
the shamrock. Both sides, it was hoped, would get justice.[15] Then,
suddenly, on the very day the Board was reaching its decision, the past
shook the present with two violent after-shocks from the murky world of
intelligence that most thought and hoped was a thing of the past. Special
Branch operations lay behind both, giving Sinn Fein, who demanded the
Branch's destruction as part of policing reform, propaganda on a plate. One
shock involved a one-off killing, the other mass murder.

Early in the morning of 12 December 2001, William Stobie (51) was
walking to his car outside his home in the Protestant Forthriver area of
North Belfast when he was gunned down. He died almost instantly on the
spot where he fell, hit by five bullets. Stobie was a loyalist and former UDA/
UFF quartermaster for the Shankill Road's 'C' Company, one of whose
leaders was the notorious Johnny Adair. He had not only been in charge of
'C' Company's weaponry but a self-confessed Special Branch agent. The
'Red Hand Defenders', a cover name used by the UDA/UFF, claimed
responsibility for his death, saying he was killed for 'crimes against the loyalist
community'.[16] Once exposed, few informers on either side lived to tell the
tale. Stobie had been recruited by Special Branch sometime in 1987 in
circumstances that were unclear. It may have been after he had been found
in possession of arms or during police inquiries following the UFF's murder
of a young Protestant student, Adam Lambert (19) who was doing work
experience on a building site off the Shankill Road. The killing was in
retaliation for the IRA's Enniskillen bomb that had exploded the day before,
Remembrance Sunday, killing eleven bystanders. The UFF had mistakenly
thought that their target was a Catholic.

By 1989, the 'Brits' had 'C' Company well penetrated. Special Branch
was running William Stobie, and the army's controversial Force Research
Unit (FRU) was running its intelligence chief, Brian Nelson (see pages
287–296). Sometime on the morning of 12 February 1989, Stobie warned

his Special Branch handler that he had provided weaponry for a gun attack later that evening on a prominent republican figure. He did not specify who the target was or where it would take place, but it became clear it was the solicitor, Pat Finucane, whose clients over the years had included many leading republicans, including Bobby Sands. Finucane was gunned down by masked UFF killers later that evening whilst he was having supper with his family. He was hit by fourteen bullets. The question was if Stobie had tipped off his handler earlier that day, why were the killers not stopped? British intelligence, through the agencies of Speical Branch, the FRU and MI5, would have had a pretty good idea who 'C' Company's hit-men were, and could have placed them under surveillance and intercepted them at a 'chance' vehicle checkpoint as had happened on so many occasions. Then Pat Finucane might have lived. One possibility is that to have done so could have risked arousing suspicion over Stobie and exposing him as an agent. Another more conspiratorial explanation, that accords with the standard republican view of 'collusion', is that the 'Brits' were in no hurry to protect Finucane. As news of the killing spread, Sinn Fein described it as 'an unravelling story of collusion which smells of the RUC Special Branch and British military intelligence getting rid of an embarrassment and potential problem.'[17] As we have seen, the republican allegation against the FRU is that it used its agents to remove 'undesirables' and thus do the 'Brits' dirty work for them.

In 1999, in the wake of rising demands for a public inquiry into the killing of Pat Finucane, Sir Ronnie Flanagan asked the Metropolitan Police Commissioner, Sir John Stevens, to investigate the killing and the allegation of collusion, as Stevens had initially investigated the broader allegations of collusion between the security forces and the loyalist paramilitaries in 1989 (see page 293). It was Sir John who brought Stobie's involvement to light with the result that he was charged with involvement in Finucane's murder and the killing of the young Protestant student, Adam Lambert. The case came to trial in November 2001. The key witness was a former journalist, Neil Mulholland, to whom Stobie had spoken, presumably as a means of self-protection. Stobie had also conducted an off-the-record interview in 1990 with the respected Belfast journalist, Ed Maloney. Maloney, however, obeyed the cardinal journalistic principle and refused to give the new Stevens inquiry his confidential notes that were taken at the time. Mulholland, however, did cooperate with the Stevens team and was due to become the chief prosecution witness in the trial at considerable risk to himself. But the case against Stobie collapsed when Mulholland indicated that he did not wish to testify as to do so might severely damage his health. To say he felt under pressure was probably a massive under-statement. As a result, on 26 November 2001, the case collapsed and Stobie walked free from Belfast Crown Court. As he did so, Sinn Fein's Assembly Member for West Belfast, Alex Maskey, who himself had escaped a UFF murder bid in 1994, launched into the 'Brits'. 'The role of the RUC Special Branch and British military intelligence in collusion and running agents within the loyalist death squads has not been explained. Cover up is still the order of the day,' he said. 'Are Stobie's handlers now members of the new policing arrangements? The reality is that Special Branch still exists and exists as a secret police force. Nationalists and republicans will not support policing arrangements with an unaccountable wing, a Special Branch, governed by a culture of silence and operating with no controls, accountability or scrutiny.'[18]

Surprisingly. Stobie did not flee the country as might have seemed sensible given his exposure as a Special Branch agent but returned to the loyalist Forthriver area, having allegedly received assurances from his former UFF comrades that his life was not in danger. Stobie was either naïve or foolhardy or both. On 2 December 2001 the RUC warned him about his personal security. Ten days later he was shot dead, taking his secrets to the grave and fuelling even more vociferous demands for a public inquiry into the killing of Finucane and related loyalist shootings. Ironically Stobie himself had called for a public inquiry, describing himself and Mulholland as 'pawns in a bigger game, caught up in a tangled web spun by very powerful people'.[19]

The day Stobie was gunned down, the second shock hit Special Branch, the Chief Constable, and the new Police Service of Northern Ireland. The implications were potentially even more damaging as the shock involved intelligence provided to Special Branch in advance of the 'Real' IRA's Omagh bombing on 15 August 1998 in which 29 people died in the worst atrocity of the conflict [see pages 372–373]. The dramatic allegation, mirroring that in the Stobie/Finucane case, was that Special Branch had been provided with information by its agents but it had not been acted upon. Ironically, the shock was delivered in-house by the Police Service of Northern Ireland's new Ombudsman, Nuala O'Loan who investigated the Omagh allegation and published her draft report on 12 December 2001. Mrs O'Loan is a former solicitor, law lecturer and member of the now defunct Police Authority. her remit as Ombudsman under the Police (Northern Ireland) Act of 1998 is to provide 'an independent impartial police complaints service in which the public and the police have confidence'. Her office, with a hundred staff and a Chief Investigator on secondment from the Metropolitan Police, opened in November 2000. The Act and the establishment of the Ombudsman's office were vital parts of the post Good Friday Agreement institutions designed to restore public confidence in the police, in particular on the nationalist side.

Mrs O'Loan began her investigation on 17 August 2001 following allegations made by an RUC agent and former British soldier codenamed 'Kevin Fulton' that two or three days before the Omagh bombing he had warned the police that he had heard from a senior member of the 'Real' IRA that there was 'something big on'.[20] He said he suspected the man was making a bomb and passed on the person's name and car registration number. 'Fulton' did not mention Omagh or the precise location and time of the attack. It is said that the officer then logged the warning. It appears that there was an even earlier warning on 4 August 1998, eleven days before the attack, in which Special Branch was told of weapons being brought across the border and into Omagh for an attack on the police on 15 August.[21] The key question that Mrs O'Loan and her team had to investigate was what happened to the intelligence Special Branch received. Was it passed on and could the slaughter of 29 people have been avoided? When Mrs O'Loan published her draft report it made devastating reading:

> The police had received two warnings on 4 and 12 August 1998. The Chief Constable's judgement and leadership were 'seriously flawed'. The result was that the chances of detaining and convicting the Omagh bombers were 'significantly reduced'
> Special Branch officers failed to pass on the warnings.

Besides also being highly critical of the way the RUC had conducted its investigation after Omagh – and the RUC's own internal report into the original investigation had been critical – the Ombudsman's draft report did claim that it was unclear that had action been taken on the warnings, the bombing would have been prevented. It then recommended that a new team of police officers from an outside force should investigate the bombing and the role and fuction of Special Branch should be reviewed.[22] Reaction to Mrs O'Loan's report was predictably split along nationalist and Unionist lines. The Chief Constable, Sir Ronnie Flanagan, was incandescent and hit back saying that the report was 'wildly inaccurate' and even remarking, uncharacteristically, that he would 'commit suicide in public' if it could be proved he was wrong.[23] He attacked its 'basic unfairness' and its 'wild and sweeping allegations'. He said 'Fulton' was unreliable. 'I do not think these people have ever investigated a terrorist incident in their lives,' he said. 'I have to say that I am astounded by the ignorance that they have displayed in terms of how terrorist organisations operate.'[24] He also pointed out that Mrs O'Loan had not conducted a proper, formal interview with him and therefore the report was the case for the prosecution without hearing the defence. Mrs O'Loan said she was 'enormously saddened'[25] by the Chief Constable's response. Tony Blair gave his full support to the Chief Constable who had steered the RUC through its difficult transition to the Police Service of Northern Ireland. Yet, the repercussions of the O'Loan report and the killing of William Stobie were destined to rumble on, and perhaps lift the carpet on still more embarrassing corners of the so-called 'dirty war'.

In Ireland the ghosts of the past seldom rest but return to haunt the future epitomised most painfully by the ongoing Saville inquiry into the events of 'Bloody Sunday'. Despite all the remarkable progress that has been made since the Good Friday Agreement, culminating in the establishment of new political institutions, a new police service and the first verifiable act of IRA decommissioning, the road ahead will still fall under the long shadows cast by the conflict. These shadows will be thrown not only by the raw sectarian hatreds generated once again at Holy Cross but from the murky world of intelligence gathering and the recruitment of informers and agents. The danger is that these shadows may still have the power to destabilise the future. The 'Brits' may have contained the IRA and encouraged it down the political road, even to the extent of giving its four Members of Parliament offices at Westminster, but now they have to consolidate the peace. Changing political institutions is difficult enough but changing hearts and minds is a challenge of a different dimension that will take years and generations to complete. As Tony Blair warned in his words after the IRA's historic gesture on decommissioning, 'We are a long way from finishing our journey but a very significant milestone has been passed'.[26] There are still many more milestones to go before the IRA's last bunker is sealed and a line is finally drawn under the 'Brits' 30 year 'war' against the IRA, thus sealing too the final peace in the centuries-old conflict between England and Ireland. Only then will it truly represent a 'farewell to arms'.

Notes

Chapter One: Into the Mire

1. To many, the terminology used to describe each side in the conflict often seems confusing. Each term has its own particular nuances.

   On the Catholic side, nationalist is the term used to identify those who aspire to a united Ireland but believe that it should only be achieved by peaceful means. Republicans believe that physical force is a legitimate way of reaching the same goal. The mainly Catholic Social Democratic and Labour Party (SDLP), led by John Hume, is a nationalist party. It was founded in 1970 as a radical non-sectarian political party but today only a tiny minority of its members are Protestants. The IRA and its political party, Sinn Fein (roughly meaning 'ourselves alone'), are republicans, as are the IRA's offshoots and their political parties.

   On the Protestant side, unionists believe in maintaining the union with Great Britain (England, Scotland and Wales) and thereby Northern Ireland's place within the United Kingdom (England, Scotland, Wales and Northern Ireland). Loyalists, like the Reverend Ian Paisley, are the more fervent or extreme unionists. The loyalist paramilitaries, most notably the Ulster Defence Association (UDA) and the Ulster Volunteer Force (UVF), believe that they are justified in using violence to defend the union against those who seek to destroy it.

2. *Provos. The IRA and Sinn Fein*, Peter Taylor, Bloomsbury, 1997, p. 8.
3. 'Easter 1916', William Butler Yeats.
4. *The Green Flag. A History of Irish Nationalism*, Robert Kee, Weidenfeld & Nicolson, 1972, p. 575.
5. *The Troubles. The Background to the Question of Northern Ireland*, Richard Broad, Taylor Downing and Ian Stuttard, Thames Futura, 1980, p. 87.
6. *Provos*, op. cit., chapter one. This gives more details of the period, the War of Independence and the Treaty.
7. *Britain and Ireland. From Home Rule to Independence*, Jeremy Smith, Pearson Education Limited, 2000, p. 69. This refers to the so-called Curragh Munity of 20 March 1914 when army officers based at the Curragh military camp in County Kildare were given the choice of putting down unionist resistance in Ulster or being dismissed from the service. Sixty officers chose dismissal. It was hardly a mutiny but it was a warning to the Government that the loyalty of the army in the event of unionist resistance could not be taken for granted.

8. The three counties of the ancient nine-county province of Ulster that were excluded from the new six-county state of Northern Ireland were the border counties of Donegal, Cavan and Monaghan. Each of them had a clear Catholic majority.

9. *Britain and Ireland*, op. cit., p. 97. The revised oath required the new Irish Deputies (MPs) to be 'faithful to H.M. King George V, his heirs and successors by law'.

10. Ibid., p. 96. The Anglo-Irish Treaty of 6 December 1921 also established a Boundary Commission designed to review the borders of the new state of Northern Ireland. Lloyd George assured Collins that this would lead to the 'essential unity' of Ireland as the likelihood would be that the new boundaries would prove unviable and the six-county state would be absorbed by the new Irish Free State.

11. *The Green Flag*, op. cit., p. 741.

12. *Michael Collins*, Tim Pat Coogan, Arrow Books, 1991, p. 403.

13. *Provos*, op. cit., pp. 30–1.

14. *States of Terror. Democracy and Political Violence*, Peter Taylor, BBC Books, 1993, p. 120.

15. *Uncle Remus. Legends of the Old Plantation*, Joel Chandler Harris, 1881, chapter two, the Tar Baby story.

16. *Provos*, op. cit., p. 32.

17. Ibid., p. 22.

18. *Loyalists*, Peter Taylor, Bloomsbury, 1999, p. 53.

19. Since Protestant or 'loyalist' parades play such a central role in the events that unfold, the following is a brief account of the historical origins of the two main organizations that traditionally hold annual marches, the Apprentice Boys of Derry and the Orange Order. Both trace their origins to the religious wars in Europe of the late seventeenth century when Ireland was caught up in the wider power struggle between the European superpowers, Catholic France and Protestant Holland. The Dutch Prince, William of Orange, feared that England under the Catholic King James II was becoming a satellite of his enemy, King Louis XIV of France. He invaded England and seized the throne from King James. William became King William III and proclaimed the 'Glorious Revolution' of 1688 in which the Protestant faith and the Protestant succession to the throne were assured. James fled to France and then with his French allies returned to Ireland to attack England from the rear in the hope of regaining the throne. In 1688, his army prepared to lay siege to Londonderry.

The Apprentice Boys of Derry are the Brotherhood founded at the start of the nineteenth century to cherish the memory of the thirteen young apprentices who closed the gates against the invaders. Whenever the Apprentice Boys march, they are reliving history and drawing strength from the victory of their ancestors. Their annual celebrations begin in December, the month the siege began, when the Apprentice Boys construct and then burn a sixteen-foot effigy of the traitor, Lundy (the Governor of Derry who advocated surrender). They end the following August, in the days after the siege was lifted, when Apprentice Boys' 'clubs' from all over the province gather in Derry to march through the city and around its walls. It was this parade on 12 August 1969 that became the catalyst for the introduction of British troops into the Northern Ireland conflict.

Historically, the Protestants' victory was sealed on 11 July 1690 when their champion, King William, defeated King James at the Battle of the Boyne. (Although Protestants traditionally celebrate their champion's victory on 12 July every year, the battle was actually fought on the 11th. The confusion arose from a misunderstanding of the 1752 calendar reform.) The Protestant succession to the English throne was secured and 'Remember 1690' became another slogan of Protestant defiance.

The Orange Order was founded over a century later in 1795, following a skirmish between Protestants and Catholics near the village of Loughgall in County Armagh. The Protestants won, withdrew to a nearby inn and formed the Orange Order, named after King William of Orange. The huge 'Orange' parades throughout Northern Ireland on 12 July celebrate 'King Billy's' famous victory at the Boyne. Traditionally, many Catholics see these marches as 'triumphalist' which is why loyalist parades have long been a flashpoint.

20. *Loyalists*, op. cit., pp. 59–63.

21. *Violence and Civil Disturbances in Northern Ireland in 1969. Report of Tribunal of Inquiry, Chairman the Hon. Mr Justice Scarman*, HMSO, Cmnd. 566, April 1972, p. 68.

22. *Provos*, op. cit., p. 48. This section gives a more detailed account of the Battle of the Bogside and the participation of some of those who subsequently became prominent IRA leaders in Derry.

23. *Northern Ireland. A Chronology of the Troubles 1968–99*, Paul Bew and Gordon Gillespie, Gill & Macmillan, 1999, p. 14. Bernadette Devlin had been elected to Westminster on 17 April 1969 in the by-election brought about by the death of the sitting Unionist MP, George Forrest. She stood as a unity candidate. The turn out was an astonishing 92 per cent. She was twenty-one at the time and the youngest MP to be elected to the House of Commons for half a century. In the Westminster election of 1 May 1997, Martin McGuinness, standing for Sinn Fein, won the same seat.

Chapter Two: Honeymoon

1. *Provos*, op. cit., p. 50.

2. *Violence and Civil Disturbances in Northern Ireland in 1969*, op. cit., p. 121. This provides the best, most accurate and detailed account of the confused events in Derry and Belfast in the critical days of August 1969.

3. Ibid., p. 127. The Protestant force Paisley referred to was the Ulster Protestant Volunteers, a branch of the Ulster Constitution Defence Committee of which Paisley was Chairman. For more details of both bodies, and Paisley's involvement in them, see *Loyalists*, op. cit., pp. 35 ff.

4. Ibid., p. 131.

5. Republican Movement is the composite term for the IRA and its political wing, Sinn Fein.

6. *Lost Lives. The Stories of the Men, Women and Children Who Died as a Result of the Northern Ireland Troubles*, David McKittrick, Seamus Kelters, Brian Feeney and Chris Thornton, Mainstream Publishing, 1999, p. 34. The book is an indispensable companion to the conflict, detailing the circumstances of every death on every side.

7. *Violence and Civil Disturbances in Northern Ireland in 1969*, op. cit., p. 193.

8. *Loyalists*, op. cit., p. 70.

9. Interview with James Callaghan recorded for *Timewatch*, 'The Sparks that Lit the Bonfire', reporter Peter Taylor, BBC television, 27 January 1992.

10. Interview by the author for 'A Soldier's Tale', BBC television, 7 August 1994.

11. The NLF won the battle to inherit power and formed the Soviet-backed People's Republic of Yemen.

12. *With The Prince of Wales's Own. The Story of a Yorkshire Regiment 1958–1994*, H.M. Tillotson, Michael Russell, 1995, p. 29.

13. *Provos*, op. cit., p. 57.

14. *Law and the State. The Case of Northern Ireland*, Kevin Boyle, Tom Hadden and Paddy

Hillyard, Martin Robertson and Company, 1975, p. 139. The Yellow Card is thought to have been introduced as a result of the army's shooting of nineteen-year-old Daniel O'Hagan during a confrontation with a crowd in Belfast's New Lodge area on 31 July 1970. The circumstances were disputed. The army said he was a petrol bomber. Local people said he was not. The circumstances in which a warning was given were unclear. For details of the shooting of O'Hagan see *Lost Lives*, op. cit., p. 55.

15. *Lost Lives*, op. cit., p. 38. The soldier was Trooper Hugh McCabe of the Queen's Royal Irish Hussars. He was stationed in Germany and home on leave at the time. His family lived in the Divis Flats complex at the city end of the Falls Road. He was killed by an RUC bullet.

16. *Northern Ireland 1968–73. A Chronology of Events. Volume 1. 1968–71*, Richard Deutsch and Vivien Magowan, Blackstaff Press Limited, 1973, p. 47. The three volumes are unique day-by-day accounts of events covering this critical early period. Volume 3 also covers 1974.

17. Interview with James Callaghan for *Timewatch*, op. cit.

18. *Report of the Advisory Committee on Police in Northern Ireland*, Belfast, HMSO, Cmnd. 535, October 1969, p. 12.

19. *Northern Ireland 1968–73. A Chronology of Events. Volume 1*, op. cit., p. 48.

20. '*Exceedingly Lucky*'. *A History of the Light Infantry 1968–1993*, Anthony Makepeace-Warne, Sydney Jary Limited, 1993, p. 39.

21. *Northern Ireland 1968–73. A Chronology of Events. Volume 1*, op. cit., p. 48.

22. '*Exceedingly Lucky*', *A History of the Light Infantry 1968–1993*, op. cit., p. 40.

Chapter Three: Divorce

1. *Provos*, op. cit., p. 67.

2. *Provos*, op. cit., p. 29.

3. Ibid., p. 63.

4. The structure of the IRA goes back to the civil war when, on 26 March 1922, the anti-Treaty forces of the IRA called a General Army Convention at the Mansion House in Dublin. The Convention is made up of IRA delegates drawn from units from all over Ireland, North and South. The Convention elects a twelve-person Army Executive which then elects a seven-person Army Council. The Army Council effectively runs the war under the direction of the person it elects to become its Chief of Staff. However, the IRA's supreme body is the Army Convention and it has to approve all key decisions. In more recent times, these would include the IRA's decision to allow members of the Republican Movement to participate in the power-sharing executive and Stormont assembly that were the result of the Good Friday Agreement of 1998; and the IRA's decision to put its weapons 'beyond use' in 2000.

5. *Provos*, op. cit., p. 67.

6. *Timewatch*, 'The Sparks that Lit the Bonfire', op. cit. From transcript of the original interview with Sir Oliver Wright.

7. *Northern Ireland 1968–73. A Chronology of Events. Volume 1.*, op. cit., p. 42.

8. The Lambeg is a drum almost the size of a man which is struck contrapuntally with flexible drumsticks to produce a thunderous warlike roar. Its origin is unclear.

9. *In Holy Terror. Reporting the Ulster Troubles*, Simon Winchester, Faber & Faber, 1974, p. 31.

10. *Northern Ireland. A Chronology of the Troubles 1968–1999*, op. cit., p. 26.

11. *Northern Ireland 1968–73. A Chronology of Events. Volume 1*, op. cit., p. 63.

12. *Lost Lives*, op. cit., p. 48.

13. *In Holy Terror*, op. cit., p. 57.

14. *Provos*, op. cit., p. 75.

15. *Ulster. New edition – The Story up to Easter 1972*, the *Sunday Times* Insight Team, Penguin Special, Penguin Books, 1972, p. 211.

16. *Provos*, op. cit., p. 76.

17. Ibid., p. 77.

18. *In Holy Terror*, op. cit., p. 63.

19. *Pig in the Middle. The Army in Northern Ireland 1969–1984*, Desmond Hamill, Methuen, 1985, p. 36.

20. *Ulster. New edition*, op. cit., p. 213.

21. *Northern Ireland 1968–73. A Chronology of Events. Volume 1*, op. cit., p. 70.

22. *The British Army in Northern Ireland*, Lieutenant-Colonel Michael Dewar, Royal Green Jackets, Arms and Armour Press, 1985, p. 47.

23. *Lost Lives*, op. cit., p. 53. See also *Ulster. New edition*, op. cit., p. 215.

24. *The British Army in Northern Ireland*, op. cit., p. 47.

25. Ibid.

26. *Ulster. New edition*, op. cit., p. 220.

27. *Provos*, ibid., p. 82.

28. *Before the Dawn. An Autobiography*, Gerry Adams, William Heinemann in association with Brandon Book Publishers Ltd, 1996, p. 141.

29. *Ulster. New edition*, op. cit., p. 220.

30. *Provos*, op. cit., p. 81.

Chapter Four: To the Brink

1. *Freedom Struggle. By the Provisional IRA*. No publisher named, presumably for security reasons. 1973, p. 20.

2. *Lost Lives*, op. cit., p. 56.

3. *Before the Dawn. An Autobiography*, op. cit., p. 145.

4. *Ulster. New edition*, op. cit., p. 244.

5. *Provos*, op. cit., p. 90.

6. *Lost Lives*, op. cit., p. 64.

7. *States of Terror*, op. cit., p. 146.

8. *Provos*, op. cit., p. 90.

9. Ibid., p. 91.

10. *Northern Ireland 1968–73. A Chronology of Events. Volume 1*, op. cit., p. 96.

11. *Northern Ireland 1968–73. A Chronology of Events. Volume 1*, op. cit., p. 98.

12. *Memoirs of a Statesman*, Brian Faulkner, Weidenfeld & Nicolson, 1978, p. 78.

Chapter Five: Crackdown

1. *Law and State. The Case of Northern Ireland*, op. cit., p. 58. The full name of the legislation that covered internment is the Civil Authorities (Special Powers) Act of 1922. It was renewed every year until it was made permanent in 1933. It finally lapsed in 1980.

2. *Provos*, op. cit., p. 21.

3. *Report of the Committee of Privy Counsellors appointed to consider authorised procedures for the*

interrogation of persons suspected of terrorism. Chairman: Lord Parker of Waddington, HMSO, Cmnd. 4901, March 1972, p. 12.

4. Ibid., p. 3.
5. Ibid., p. 12.
6. Ibid., p. 3.
7. *Beating the Terrorists? Interrogation in Omagh, Gough and Castlereagh*, Peter Taylor, Penguin Special, 1980, p. 20.
8. *Report of the Committee of Privy Counsellors appointed to consider authorised procedures for the interrogation of persons suspected of terrorism*, op. cit., p. 12.
9. *Provos*, op. cit., p. 92.
10. *European Commission of Human Rights. Application no. 5310/71. Ireland against the United Kingdom. Report of the Commission (Adopted on 25 January 1976)*, p. 185.
11. *Northern Ireland. A Chronology of the Troubles 1968–1999*, op. cit., p. 116.
12. Ibid., p. 36.
13. *Report of the enquiry into allegations against the security forces of physical brutality in Northern Ireland arising out of events on 9th August 1971, Chaired by Sir Edmund Compton*, GCB, KBE, HMSO, Cmnd. 4823, November 1971, p. 22.
14. Ibid., p. 16.
15. Ibid., p. 12.
16. *Northern Ireland. A Chronology of the Troubles 1968–1999*, op. cit., p. 38.
17. *Report of the enquiry into allegations against the security forces of physical brutality in Northern Ireland arising out of events on 9th August 1971*, op. cit., p. 71.
18. *Report of the Committee of Privy Counsellors appointed to consider authorised procedures for the interrogation of persons suspected of terrorism*, op. cit., p. 5.
19. Ibid., p. 22.
20. *Northern Ireland. A Chronology of the Troubles 1968–1999*, op. cit., p. 115.
21. Ibid., p. 127.

Chapter Six: Aftermath

1. *An Index of Deaths from the Conflict in Northern Ireland 1969–1993*, Malcom Sutton, Beyond the Pale Publications, 1994, p. 6.
2. *In Holy Terror*, op. cit., p. 168.
3. *Provos*, op. cit., p. 114.
4. 'Bloody Sunday: An Open Wound', Peter Taylor, *Sunday Times* Magazine, 26 January 1992, p. 16.
5. 'A Soldier's Tale', BBC documentary, transmitted 7 August 1994.
6. *Northern Ireland. A Chronology of the Troubles 1968–1999*, op. cit., p. 42.

Chapter Seven: 'Bloody Sunday' – The Build-up

1. *Future Military Policy for Londonderry. An Appreciation of the Situation by CLF*, 14 December 1971. 'SECRET'. This is a critically important memorandum marked 'Secret' written by Major-General Robert Ford, Commander Land Forces (CLF), Northern Ireland, to the GOC, Lieutenant-General Sir Harry Tuzo. It was revealed by the Saville Inquiry, the judicial tribunal set up by the British Prime Minister, Tony Blair, on 29 January 1998 to re-examine the events of 'Bloody Sunday'. This chapter contains new material uncovered by the Inquiry.

2. *Provos*, op. cit., p. 115.

3. Ibid., p. 112. More details of the circumstances in which Cusack and Beattie were killed are contained here.

4. *Future Military Policy for Londonderry*, op. cit.

5. *Lost Lives*, op. cit., p. 88.

6. *Future Military Policy for Londonderry*, op. cit.

7. Ibid.

8. *Northern Ireland 1968–73. A Chronology of Events. Vol. 1*, op. cit., p. 145.

9. *Daily Telegraph*, 28 March 2000.

10. *Northern Ireland 1968–73. A Chronology of Events. Vol. 1*, op. cit., p. 145.

11. *Lost Lives*, op. cit., p. 135.

12. *The Situation in Londonderry as at 7 January 1972*. Memo from Major-General Robert Ford to the GOC, Lieutenant-General Sir Harry Tuzo. Marked 'PERSONAL and CONFIDENTIAL'. Revealed by the Saville Inquiry.

13. *Irish Times*, 30 March 2000.

14. *In Holy Terror*, op. cit., p. 189.

15. *Northern Ireland 1968–73. A Chronology of Events. Vol. 2. 1972–73*, Richard Deutsch and Vivien Magowan, Blackstaff Press Ltd, 1974, p. 151.

16. *Lost Lives*, op. cit., p. 143.

17. *Irish Times*, op. cit. Statement provided by Edward Heath to the Saville Tribunal.

18. On 1 February 1972, the Minister of State for Defence, Lord Balniel, confirmed to the House of Commons that 'the arrest operation was discussed by the joint Security Council after decisions had been taken by Ministers here'. *Cain Web Service, Bloody Sunday and the Report of the Widgery Tribunal – Summary and Significance of New Material*, Points 111–150, text by Irish Government, p. 1. This internet site is a valuable repository of much of the 'Bloody Sunday' archive (http//cain.ulst.ac.uk).

19. *Provos*, op. cit., p. 117.

20. *Report of the Tribunal appointed to inquire into the events on Sunday, 30th January 1972, which led to loss of life in connection with the procession in Londonderry on that day, by the Rt Hon Lord Widgery, OBE, TD*, HMSO, 18 April 1972, p. 7.

21. Ibid., p. 7.

22. These are documents released by the various political and security authorities to the Saville Inquiry.

23. *Provos*, op. cit., p. 119.

24. Ibid., p. 118.

25. Ibid., p. 116.

26. Ibid., p. 118.

27. Ibid., p. 119.

Chapter Eight: 'Bloody Sunday' – The Killing Zone

1. *Lost Lives*, op. cit., p. 149. See also *Those Are Real Bullets, Aren't They?*, Peter Pringle and Philip Jacobson, Fourth Estate, London, 2000, p. 92. At the time of writing, this is the most comprehensive and up-to-date account of 'Bloody Sunday'. It contains not only the personal experience of the writers, who investigated 'Bloody Sunday' at the time as members of the *Sunday Times* Insight team, but important material uncovered by the Saville Inquiry.

2. *Report of the Tribunal appointed to inquire into the events on Sunday, 30th January 1972, which led to loss of life in connection with the procession in Londonderry on that day, by the Rt Hon Lord Widgery, OBE, TD*, op. cit., pp. 12–14.

3. *Those Are Real Bullets, Aren't They?*, op. cit., p. 119. The authors make a clear connection between the shooting of Donaghy and Johnson and the shot fired by the Official IRA. They believe that it was fired in retaliation for the shooting of the two men. The Paras, however, insist that the single shot came first.

4. *Eyewitness Bloody Sunday. The Truth*, edited by Don Mullan, Wolfhound Press, 1997, pp. 86–8. This contains much of the new evidence in the form of witness statements that was an important factor in Tony Blair's decision to set up the Saville Inquiry.

5. This is confirmed by Lord Widgery in *Report of the Tribunal appointed to inquire into the events on Sunday, 30th January 1972, which led to loss of life in connection with the procession in Londonderry on that day*, op. cit., p. 13.

6. Ibid., p. 11.

7. *Provos*, op. cit., p. 121.

8. Ibid.

9. Interview from full transcript of interview with 'Phil' for BBC documentary 'Remember Bloody Sunday', transmitted 28 January 1992.

10. *Provos*, op. cit., p. 122.

11. *Eyewitness Bloody Sunday. The Truth*, op. cit. Many of the details of those killed are taken from here and from *Those Are Real Bullets, Aren't They?*, op. cit.

12. The suggestion has been made on the basis of forensic and eye-witness evidence in *Eyewitness Bloody Sunday. The Truth*, op. cit., and by *Channel Four News* in its investigation of 17 January 1997. Shots from the walls were also noted in the Brigade radio log, pirated by an amateur radio enthusiast in the Bogside area. See also *Those Are Real Bullets, Aren't They?*, op. cit., p. 209.

13. *Report of the Tribunal appointed to inquire into the events on Sunday, 30th January 1972, which led to loss of life in connection with the procession in Londonderry on that day*, by Lord Widgery, O.B.E., T.D., op. cit., pp. 8 and 14, respectively.

14. 'Remember Bloody Sunday', op. cit.

15. British Irish Rights Watch 'Bloody Sunday' – Submission to the United Nations Special Rapporteur on Summary and Arbitrary Executions, British Irish Rights Watch, London, 1994.

16. *Provos*, op. cit., p. 123.

17. *Those Are Real Bullets, Aren't They?*, op. cit., p. 224.

18. *Provos*, op. cit., p. 124.

19. *Cain Web Service, Bloody Sunday and the Report of the Widgery Tribunal – Summary and Significance of New Material*, op. cit., p. 6.

20. *Report of the Tribunal appointed to inquire into the events on Sunday, 30th January 1972, which led to loss of life in connection with the procession in Londonderry on that day*, by Lord Widgery, O.B.E., T.D., op. cit., p. 38.

21. Ibid., pp. 35 and 37.

22. *House of Commons Official Report. Parliamentary Debates (Hansard)*, 29 January 2000, columns 501–3.

23. *Guardian*, 'The Bloody Sunday Inquiry: Special Report', John Mullin. Taken from the Guardian news unlimited website. The intelligence documents were revealed by the Saville Inquiry, *Guardian*, 7 April 2000.

24. *Independent*, 28 March 2000.

25. *BBC News Web Site*, www.bbc.co.uk 5 September 2000.

26. *Daily Telegraph*, 19 August 2000.

Chapter Nine: The 'Funny People'

1. *Provos*, op. cit., p. 131.
2. Ibid., p. 131. Responsibility for the Abercorn bombing has never been satisfactorily resolved, although few have any doubt, despite Seán MacStiofáin's denial, that it was the work of the Provisional IRA. The most likely explanation is that it was a Provisional bomb that went off prematurely.
3. *Northern Ireland 1968–73. A Chronology of Events. Volume 2*, op. cit., p. 161.
4. *Provos*, op. cit., p. 133.
5. *Lost Lives*, op. cit., p. 168.
6. *Memoirs of a Statesman*, op. cit., p. 152.
7. *Provos*, op. cit., p. 135.
8. In 1952 General Templer, later Field-Marshal Sir Gerald Templer, was appointed High Commissioner and Director of Operations in Malaya with a brief to direct the civil and military aspects of the campaign against the communist insurgents.
9. *Lost Lives*, op. cit., p. 1,475.

Chapter Ten: Talking to the Enemy

1. *Northern Ireland 1968–73. A Chronology of Events. Volume 2*, op. cit., p. 181.
2. Ibid., p. 185.
3. *Before the Dawn*, op. cit., p. 198.

Chapter Eleven: Piratical Ventures

1. *Who Dares Wins. The Story of the SAS 1950–1992*, Tony Geraghty, Warner Books, 1993, p. 401.
2. *Gangs and Counter-Gangs*, Major Frank Kitson, MBE, MC, Barrie & Rockcliff, 1960, pp. 76ff.
3. *Northern Ireland 1968–73. A Chronology of Events. Volume 2*, op. cit., p. 177.
4. *Lost Lives*, op. cit., p. 182.
5. *Belfast Telegraph*, 3 May 1973.
6. *Lost Lives*, op. cit., p. 269.
7. Ibid., p. 275.
8. Ibid., p. 274.

Chapter Twelve: A Better Parachute

1. The 'back-badge' is a reference to the Gloucesters' right to wear a small badge depicting a sphinx at the back of their berets in addition to the normal badge at the front. The tradition stems from an engagement against the French in 1801 at the Battle of Alexandria. When the French cavalry attacked from the rear, the Gloucesters were given the order, 'Rear rank, right about face!' and, holding their fire until the last minute, shattered the enemy's charge. The Gloucesters thus fought the enemy back to back and the battle was won. Today the 'back-badge' is worn by all members of the Regiment into which the Gloucesters were amalgamated, the Royal Gloucestershire, Berkshire and Wiltshire Regiment.
2. *Lost Lives*, op. cit., p. 378.

Chapter Thirteen: Success

1. *Provos*, op. cit., p. 152.
2. Gerry Kelly was one of the 38 IRA prisoners who escaped from the Maze prison on 25 September 1983. He was subsequently arrested by Dutch police in a flat outside Amsterdam on 16 January 1986 following a tip-off from British intelligence. Another senior IRA figure and Maze escapee, Brendan 'Bik' McFarlane, was arrested with him. In the apartment keys were found to a container parked nearby in which were stored fourteen rifles, 100,000 rounds of ammunition and four huge drums of nitro-benzine, the basic ingredient of many IRA bombs. Kelly and McFarlane were subsequently extradited and returned to serve their sentences in the Maze prison.
3. *Provos*, op. cit., p. 156.
4. *Provos*, op. cit., p. 162.
5. Sinn Fein signed up to the 'Belfast' or 'Good Friday' Agreement of 10 April 1998 in which it agreed to participate in a power sharing Executive with David Trimble's Ulster Unionists.
6. *Loyalists*, op. cit., pp. 127ff.
7. Ibid., p. 136.
8. Ibid., p. 131.

Chapter Fourteen: Changing the Course of History

1. *Lost Lives*, op. cit., p. 1,476.
2. *Northern Ireland 1968–74. A Chronology of Events. 1974 Volume 3*, Blackstaff Press, p. 55.
3. For a more detailed account of the Dublin and Monaghan bombs see *Loyalists*, op. cit., pp. 125 ff.
4. *Northern Ireland. A Chronology of the Troubles 1968–1999*, op. cit., p. 259.
5. *Provos*, op. cit., p. 171.
6. Ibid.
7. *Lost Lives*, op. cit., p. 480.
8. Ibid., p. 490.
9. *The IRA*, Tim Pat Coogan, HarperCollins, 1995, p. 518.
10. *Error of Judgement. The Truth about the Birmingham Bombings*, Chris Mullin, Poolbeg, 1986, p. 207.
11. *Northern Ireland. A Chronology of the Troubles 1968–1999*, op. cit., p. 245.
12. Ibid., p. 96.

Chapter Fifteen: Structures of Disengagement

1. *Provos*, op. cit., p. 175.
2. Ibid.
3. Ibid., p. 176.
4. *Northern Ireland 1968–74. A Chronology of Events. Volume 3*, op. cit., p. 179.
5. For further details of the Republican Movement's minutes and an analysis of the ups and downs of the 'truce', see *Provos*, op. cit., chapter 13.
6. After his first arrest on 30 December 1972, Martin McGuinness admitted IRA membership. He made the following statement to the Court: 'For over two years, I was an officer in the Derry Brigade of the IRA. We have fought against the killing of

our people. Many of my comrades have been arrested and tortured and some were shot unarmed by British troops . . . I am a member of Oglaigh na hEireann [the IRA] and very, very proud of it . . . We firmly believed we were doing our duty as Irishmen.' *Provos*, op. cit., p. 153.

7. *Lost Lives*, op. cit., p. 1,475.
8. For more details of the activities of the 'Shankill Butchers' see *Loyalists*, op. cit., Chapter 13.
9. *Real Lives*, op. cit., p. 574.
10. Ibid., p. 588.
11. Ibid., p. 599.
12. Ibid., p. 568.
13. Extract from original Republican Movement minutes as viewed and noted by the author.

Chapter Sixteen: Enter the SAS

1. *Lost Lives*, op. cit., p. 610.
2. 22 SAS is the Regiment's operational wing and consists of four 'Sabre' Squadrons that do the fighting. They are known as A, B, D and G, each consisting of around seventy men. Each Squadron is divided into four 'troops' of sixteen men which in turn are divided into four four-man teams. To its members, the SAS is known as the 'Regiment' and to its men on the ground as the 'Troop'.
3. *Ambush. The War between the SAS and the IRA*, James Adams, Robin Morgan and Anthony Bambridge, Pan Original, 1988, p. 76.
4. *SAS Terrorism. The Assassin's Glove*, Father Denis Faul and Father Raymond Murray, personal publication, July 1976, p. 6.
5. *Ambush*, op. cit., p. 77.
6. *The SAS in Ireland*, Raymond Murray, Mercier Press, 1993, p. 172.
7. Ibid., p. 173.
8. *SAS Terrorism*, op. cit., p. 16.
9. Ibid.
10. Ibid., p. 32.
11. *The SAS in Ireland*, op. cit., p. 178.
12. Ibid., p. 179.

Chapter Seventeen: Piling on the Pressure

1. *Provos*, op. cit., p. 199.
2. *Northern Ireland. A Chronology of the Troubles 1968–1999*, op. cit., p. 109.
3. *Report of a Committee to consider, in the context of civil liberties and human rights, measures to deal with terrorism in Northern Ireland*, Chairman: Lord Gardiner, HMSO, Cmnd. 5847, January 1975, pp. 5, 7 and 34.
4. *Provos*, op. cit., pp. 198–9.
5. Author's own calculation from statistics.
6. *Lost Lives*, op. cit., p. 664.
7. Ibid., pp. 663–4.
8. Ibid., p. 665.
9. *Paying the Price*, Roy Mason, Robert Hale, 1999, p. 123.
10. Ibid., p. 171.

11. Ibid., p. 171.
12. Ibid.
13. *Northern Ireland. A Chronology of the Troubles 1968–1999*, op. cit., p. 115.
14. *Beating the Terrorists? Interrogation in Omagh, Gough and Castlereagh*, op. cit. This is a detailed account of the use of the emergency legislation and the consequences that led to the IRA hunger strikes of 1980 and 1981.
15. *Beating the Terrorists? Interrogation in Omagh, Gough and Castlereagh*, op. cit., p. 193.
16. Ibid., p. 194.
17. Ibid., p. 71.
18. *Pig in the Middle*, op. cit., p. 220.
19. *Beating the Terrorists?*, op. cit., p. 355. Under the Emergency Provisions Act suspects could be held for questioning for up to three days. Under the Prevention of Terrorism Act, they could be held for up to seven.
20. *Provos*, op. cit., pp. 217–18. This gives the background to 'Life Behind the Wire' and the interview with Desmond Irvine.
21. *Ireland. The Propaganda War. The British Media and the 'Battle for Hearts and Minds'*, Liz Curtis, Pluto Press, 1984, p. 58.
22. Ibid., p. 59.
23. *Paying the Price*, op. cit., pp. 205–6.
24. *Beating the Terrorists?*, op. cit., p. 286.
25. *Paying the Price*, op. cit., p. 213.
26. *Ireland. The Propaganda War*, op. cit., p. 67.
27. *Paying the Price*, op. cit., p. 215.
28. *Beating the Terrorists?*, op. cit., p. 329–32. This is a more detailed account of the impact of the Bennett report on the critical parliamentary arithmetic.

Chapter Eighteen: Shootings and Stakeouts

1. *Provos*, op. cit., p. 201.
2. *Ten Men Dead. The Story of the 1981 Irish Hunger Strike*, David Beresford, Grafton Books, 1987, p. 153.
3. *Lost Lives*, op. cit., p. 716.
4. *Ten Men Dead*, op. cit., p. 158.
5. *The SAS in Ireland*, op. cit., p. 215.
6. Ibid., p. 221.
7. *Big Boys' Rules. The Secret Struggle against the IRA* Mark Urban, Faber & Faber, 1992, p. 62.
8. *Lost Lives*, op. cit., p. 763.
9. *The SAS in Ireland*, op. cit., p. 235.
10. Ibid., p. 244.
11. Ibid., p. 244.
12. *Lost Lives*, op. cit., p. 770.
13. *The SAS in Ireland*, op. cit., p. 241.

Chapter Nineteen: Double Disaster

1. *Future Terrorist Trends* ended up in the hands of the Republican Movement and was published in its weekly newspaper, *Republican News*. This particular copy of Brigadier

Glover's report is thought to have been 'lost' in transit to its destination in the Midlands. It is possible, although highly unlikely, that the loss was deliberate to alert the public and politicians to the threat that lay ahead. Although it is marked 'Secret', it is the analysis that is sensitive not the detail.

2. *Beating the Terrorists?*, op. cit., pp. 345–7.

3. *Northern Ireland. Future Terrorist Trends*, Brigadier J.M. Glover, BGS (Int) DIS, 2 November 1978. Leaked or lost document revealed in *Republican News*.

4. *Lost Lives*, op. cit., pp. 793–5.

5. Ibid., p. 799.

6. *Holding the Line. An Autobiography*, Sir John Hermon, Gill & Macmillan, 1997, p. 102.

7. *Provos*, op. cit., p. 255.

8. Ibid.

Chapter Twenty: The Iron Lady and the Iron Men

1. *The Provisional IRA*, Patrick Bishop and Eamonn Mallie, Corgi Books, 1993, p. 350.

2. *Provos*, op. cit., p. 204.

3. Ibid.

4. *Paying the Price*, op. cit., p. 209.

5. *Provos*, op. cit., p. 219.

6. Ibid., p. 221.

7. *Paying the Price*, op. cit., p. 209.

8. Ibid., p. 210.

9. Ibid.

10. *Provos*, op. cit., p. 222.

11. *Paying the Price*, op. cit., p. 211.

12. *The Downing Street Years*, Margaret Thatcher, HarperCollins, 1993, pp. 389–90.

13. *Provos*, op. cit., p. 229.

14. Ibid.

15. *INLA. Deadly Divisions. The Story of One of Ireland's Most Ruthless Terrorist Organisations*, Jack Holland and Henry McDonald, Torc, A Division of Poolbeg Enterprises Ltd, 1994, p. 173.

16. *Provos*, op. cit., p. 229.

17. *The Downing Street Years*, op. cit., pp. 389–90.

18. Ibid., p. 233.

19. *The Downing Street Years*, op. cit., p. 392.

20. For fuller details of the IRA hunger strikes of 1980 and 1981, see Chapters 16 and 17 of *Provos*, op. cit.

21. Ibid., p. 235.

22. *The Downing Street Years*, op. cit., pp. 390–1.

23. *Provos*, op. cit., p. 237.

24. *Northern Ireland. A Chronology of the Troubles 1968–1999*, op. cit., p. 148.

25. Ibid. The actual figures were Sands 30,492 and West 29,046.

26. *The Downing Street Years*, op. cit., p. 391.

27. Ibid.

28. *The Diary of Bobby Sands. The First Seventeen Days of Bobby's H-Block Hunger Strike to the Death*, Republican Publications, Dublin, June 1981.

29. *Provos*, op. cit., p. 243.

30. Ibid.

31. Ibid., p. 251.
32. *The Downing Street Years*, op. cit., p. 393.

Chapter Twenty-One: 'Firepower, Speed and Aggression'

1. Detailed accounts of John Stalker's inquiry and his subsequent suspension from it are recorded in several books including the author's *Stalker. The Search for the Truth*, Faber & Faber, 1987; John Stalker's own account in *Stalker*, Harrap, 1988; Sir John Hermon's account in *Holding the Line. An Autobiography*, Gill & Macmillan, 1997, and the account of John Stalker's Manchester businessman friend, Kevin Taylor (with Keith Mumby), *The Poisoned Tree. The untold truth about the police conspiracy to discredit John Stalker and destroy me*, Sidgwick & Jackson, 1990. Whilst John Stalker and I do not disagree on the facts, we differ in our interpretations of them. Mr Stalker believes he was the victim of a conspiracy to remove him from his inquiry because he was getting too close to highly sensitive material whereas I believe that he was stood down for other reasons.

2. *Holding the Line. An Autobiography*, op. cit., p. 149.

3. *Lost Lives*, op. cit., pp. 908–10.

4. *Holding the Line. An Autobiography*, op. cit., p. 150.

5. *Lost Lives*, op. cit., p. 927.

6. Ibid., p. 1,347.

7. *Stalker. The Search for the Truth*, Peter Taylor, Faber & Faber, 1987, p. 99.

8. Ibid., pp. 83–4.

9. Ibid., p. 81.

10. Ibid., p. 89.

11. Ibid., p. 41.

12. Ibid., p. 105.

13. Ibid., p. 33. In the wake of the furore Lord Justice Gibson's remarks unleashed, he subsequently issued a qualifying statement in which he said, 'I would wish most emphatically to repudiate any idea that I would approve or the law would countenance what has been described as a 'shoot to kill' policy on the part of the police.'

14. Ibid., p. 71.

15. Kevin Taylor had been under surveillance by the Greater Manchester Police because of his alleged association with a group of Manchester criminals known as the 'Quality Street Gang'. Taylor protested his innocence of any wrongdoing and, after many years of contentious litigation, emerged with his reputation restored but a financially ruined man. To him, the compensation (reported to be £2.4 million, cf., *Sunday Telegraph*, 6 September 1998) he finally received from the Greater Manchester Police Authority's insurers, who deemed it less expensive to settle than fight, was small compensation for the trauma and penury he and his family had endured. The story of Kevin Taylor and his relationship with John Stalker is incredibly complex and covered in detail in the books of the author, John Stalker and Kevin Taylor listed in note 1 above.

Chapter Twenty-Two: Group Activity

1. *The SAS in Ireland*, op. cit., p. 290.
2. *Lost Lives*, op. cit., p. 966.

3. *The SAS in Ireland*, op. cit., p. 290. This is from the account of the SAS soldier given at the inquest.
4. Ibid., p. 290.
5. Ibid., p. 312.
6. Ibid., p. 370.
7. *Lost Lives*, op. cit., p. 1,003.
8. *The SAS in Ireland*, op. cit., p. 329.
9. Ibid., p. 330.
10. Ibid., p. 331.
11. *Lost Lives*, op. cit., p. 1,003.
12. *The SAS in Ireland*, op. cit., p. 333.
13. Ibid., p. 338.
14. Ibid., p. 342.
15. The statistics include the two 'Det' killings referred to in the introduction, 'Frank's Story': Declan Martin and Henry Hogan, killed on 21 February 1984. The other 'Det' killing was of Eugene McMonagle of the INLA, killed on 2 February 1983.

Chapter Twenty-Three: The Political Front

1. *Lost Lives*, op. cit., p. 1,473. The precise overall death toll from 1969 to the end of 1979 was 2,192. The precise security force total – British army, UDR, RUC and RUC Reserve – for the same period was 584.
2. For the complex details of the gun-running scandal in which Haughey and others were charged but acquitted, see *States of Terror. The Politics of Political Violence*, Peter Taylor, BBC Books, 1993, pp. 129–46.
3. *Northern Ireland. A Chronology of the Troubles 1968–1999*, op. cit., p. 141.
4. *Northern Ireland. A Political Directory 1968–1999*, Sydney Elliott and W. D. Flackes, Blackstaff Press, 1999, p. 273.
5. Ibid., p. 273.
6. *Loyalists*, op. cit., p. 174.
7. *Provos*, op. cit., p. 250.
8. Ibid., p. 282.
9. Ibid.
10. Ibid., p. 283.
11. Ibid.
12. Ibid., pp. 283–4.
13. *Lost Lives*, p. 970.
14. *The Provisional IRA*, op. cit., p. 425.
15. *Lost Lives*, op. cit., p. 996.
16. Ibid.
17. Ibid., p. 997.
18. Details of Patrick Magee and quotes from him are taken from an interview conducted by journalist Tom McGurk for the Dublin newspaper *Sunday Business Post*. The interview was published on 27 August 2000.
19. *25 Years of Terror. The IRA's War against the British*, Martin Dillon, Bantam Books, 1994, p. 222.
20. Magee's Open University dissertation was on 'Irish post-colonial representations in popular fiction', i.e. a study of the way that Gerald Seymour, Tom Clancy and many other best-selling authors fictionalized the conflict.

21. *Northern Ireland. A Chronology of the Troubles 1968–1999*, op. cit., p. 186.

22. *The Anglo-Irish Agreement. Commentary, Text and Official Review*, Tom Hadden and Kevin Boyle, Sweet & Maxwell Ltd, 1989, p. 18. The other references to the Agreement are taken from the same source. The *Commentary* is an invaluable guide provided by Professors Hadden and Boyle.

Chapter Twenty-Four: Loughgall

1. For a more detailed account of Loughgall see *Provos*, op. cit., chapter 19. A photograph of Tony Gormley, Eugene Kelly, Seamus Donnelly and Declan Arthurs is included in the photographs. They are shown standing alongside the memorial to Martin Hurson in Cappagh in 1986, the year before the SAS ambush at Loughgall.

2. Ibid., p. 275.

3. *Lost Lives*, op. cit., p. 1,074.

4. *Provos*, op. cit., p. 272.

5. Ibid., p. 275.

6. Ibid., p. 274.

7. *The SAS in Ireland*, op. cit., p. 376.

8. *Provos.*, op. cit., p. 276.

Chapter Twenty-Five: Death in the Afternoon

1. The attack took place on 23 March 1987.

2. *Death on the Rock and Other Stories*, Roger Bolton, W.H. Allen/Optomen, 1990; p. 189.

3. Ibid., p. 190.

4. Ibid., p. 191.

5. Mairead Farrell had been sentenced to fourteen years for a bomb attack on the Conway Hotel, Dunmurry. For a detailed account of her life, see the author's *Families at War*, BBC Books, 1989.

6. *Provos*, op. cit., pp. 259–65. The 'supergrasses' (or 'converted terrorists' in official language) were former members of republican and loyalist paramilitary organizations prepared to give evidence against their former comrades. The phenomenon flourished in the early 1980s, beginning in 1981 when an IRA man from Ardoyne, Christopher Black, agreed to give evidence against thirty-eight people. Thirty-five were convicted and sentenced, many on Black's word alone. In the months that followed, other republican and loyalist 'terrorists' agreed to do the same, invariably on the understanding that they would receive leniency in return. The supergrass system was finally discredited and collapsed in 1986 when the Northern Ireland Court of Appeal quashed the convictions of eighteen republicans who had been convicted on Black's uncorroborated testimony. Savage was alleged by a supergrass to have been a member of the IRA and involved in causing an explosion.

7. *Phoenix. Policing the Shadows. The Secret War Against Terrorism in Northern Ireland*, Jack Holland and Susan Phoenix, Hodder & Stoughton, 1996, p. 134.

8. Cf., *The Oxford Classical Dictionary*, Oxford at the Clarendon Press, 1961, p. 943. The Roman Emperor was Titus Flavius Vespasianus (AD 69–79), who, before being formally appointed as 'Emperor' by the Senate, had stopped a rebellion amongst the Jews in Palestine and established peace in every corner of the Roman Empire.

9. Some of the key Special Branch officers involved were among the twenty-five army, police and MI5 senior intelligence officers killed on 2 June 1994 when the Chinook helicopter in which they were travelling to a security conference in Scotland crashed in fog on the Mull of Kintyre.

10. *Who Dares Wins*, op. cit., p. 287.

11. *Lost Lives*, op. cit., p. 1,112.

12. *Who Dares Wins*, op. cit., p. 293.

13. Ibid., p. 297.

14. Ibid., pp. 567–8.

15. *The SAS in Ireland*, op. cit., p. 402.

16. Ibid., p. 403.

17. There is an important discrepancy in the British and Spanish accounts as to when the white Renault was parked. The British say it was parked on the Sunday. A senior Spanish police officer involved in the surveillance operation told the *Independent* (23 May 1989) it was parked on Saturday, the day before. If this *was* the case, the British would have had plenty of time to establish whether it contained a bomb. The discrepancy is pointed out in *The SAS in Ireland*, op. cit., p. 403.

18. *Who Dares Wins*, op. cit., p. 304.

19. Ibid., p. 306. The following SAS soldiers' accounts are all taken from this source based on their testimonies at the subsequent inquest.

20. *Lost Lives*, op. cit., p. 1,119.

21. Ibid., p. 1,122.

22. Ibid.

23. *The Windlesham/Rampton Report on 'Death on the Rock'*, Lord Windlesham and Richard Rampton QC, Faber & Faber, 1989, p. 54. This is the report of the investigation instigated by Thames Television into the making of the programme. It cleared the programme makers of any impropriety. A full transcript of 'Death on the Rock' is included.

24. *Lost Lives*, op. cit., p. 1,114.

Chapter Twenty-Six: Brian Nelson

1. *Regina v. Brian Nelson Before the Right Honourable Lord Justice Kelly on Wednesday 29 January 1992 at Belfast Crown Court. Evidence of Witness 'Colonel "J"*, transcript p. 1.

2. Ibid., p. 14.

3. 'Time to Come Clean over the Army's Role in the "Dirty War"', John Ware, *New Statesman*, 24 April 1998, p. 16. John Ware did the seminal work on the Brian Nelson story and first revealed the MISR forms.

4. *Loyalists*, op. cit., p. 169.

5. *Deadly Intelligence, State Involvement in Loyalist Murder in Northern Ireland*, British Irish Rights Watch, February 1999, p. 5.

6. *Northern Ireland. A Chronology of the Troubles 1968–99*, op. cit., p. 231.

7. 'Revealed. How the Army Set up Ulster Murders', John Ware and Geoffrey Seed, *Sunday Telegraph*, 29 March 1998.

8. *Regina v. Brian Nelson*, op. cit., p. 53.

9. *Sunday People*, Greg Haskin, 17 September 2000.

10. For a detailed history of the Finucane brothers and family, see *Rebel Hearts. Journeys Within the IRA's Soul*, Kevin Toolis, Picador, Second Edition, 2000, pp. 84 ff. Seamus was arrested and gaoled with Bobby Sands in 1976 for fire-bombing the Balmoral

Furniture Company showroom near the nationalist Twinbrook estate on the outskirts of Belfast. Dermot was sentenced to eighteen years in 1982 for an attack on a security force patrol. He was one of the thirty-eight IRA prisoners who escaped from the Maze in 1983.

11. *New Statesman*, op. cit., p. 17.
12. *Loyalists*, op. cit., p. 207.
13. *New Statesman*, op. cit., p. 17.

Chapter Twenty-Seven: Turning the Screw

1. Although most SAM 7 missiles were found when the *Eksund* was seized, some were included in the previous shipments on board the *Kula* and *Villa*. It is believed that the IRA only fired one, at a helicopter in South Armagh, but it was successfully deflected by its electronic counter-measures (ECM). It is thought that the other SAM 7s were not used either because of a lack of professional expertise or, more likely, technical problems with the firing mechanism.
2. *Phoenix*, op. cit., p. 163.
3. *Lost Lives*, op. cit., pp. 1,473–5. The death toll of British soldiers including the UDR was as follows: 1982 – 39; 1983 – 15; 1984 – 19; 1985 – 6; 1986 – 12; 1987 – 11; 1988 – 34.
4. *Northern Ireland. A Chronology of the Troubles 1968–1999*, op. cit., p. 217.
5. *Provos*, p. 309.
6. *The SAS in Ireland*, op. cit., p. 440.
7. Ibid.
8. *Provos*, op. cit., p. 309.
9. *Lost Lives*, op. cit., p. 1,179.
10. Ibid., p. 1,183.
11. Ibid., op. cit., p. 1,239.
12. *Provos*, op. cit., p. 310.

Chapter Twenty-Eight: The Road to Peace

1. *Lost Lives*, op. cit., pp. 1,473–4. The calculation 1982–1998 is inclusive.
2. *Northern Ireland. A Political Directory 1968–1999*, op. cit., p. 261.
3. The Israeli foreign intelligence service, Mossad, the equivalent of Britain's MI6, tracked down and assassinated those Palestinians it believed were connected with the massacre of Israeli athletes at the Munich Olympic Games in 1972. Mossad was assisted by the Israeli equivalent of the SAS, Sayeret Matkal (*States of Terror*, op. cit., p. 5).
4. *Northern Ireland. A Political Directory 1968–1999*, op. cit., p. 563.
5. *Northern Ireland, A Chronology of the Troubles, 1968–1999*, op. cit., p. 208.
6. *Northern Ireland. A Political Directory 1968–1999*, op. cit., p. 565.
7. *Lost Lives*, op. cit., p. 1,205.
8. *The Politics of Irish Freedom*, Gerry Adams, Brandon Books, 1994, p. 64.
9. Northern Ireland Office Press Notice, 26 September 1988.
10. *Provos*, op. cit., p. 316.
11. Ibid., p. 318.
12. Ibid., p. 321.

13. *John Major. The Autobiography*, John Major, HarperCollins, 1999, p. 238. Chapter 19, 'Into the Mists: Bright Hopes, Black Deeds', is a comprehensive account of Major's critical role in the peace process.
14. *Lost Lives*, op. cit., p. 1,268.
15. *Provos*, op. cit., p. 324. This gives a detailed explanation of the unfortunate circumstances in which it happened.
16. *John Major. The Autobiography*, op. cit., p. 440.

Chapter Twenty-Nine: Secret Talks

1. *John Major. The Autobiography*, op. cit., p. 306.
2. *Provos*, op. cit., p. 328.
3. Ibid., p. 330.
4. For a more detailed account of the messages exchanged between the British and the Provisionals in 1993, see *Provos*, op. cit., pp. 331 ff.
5. *Setting the Record Straight. A Record of Communications between Sinn Fein and the British Government October 1990–November 1993*, published by Sinn Fein, pp. 26–7. These are Sinn Fein's record and minutes of the critical dialogue between the Republican Movement and the British Government in 1993. The quotes in this paragraph are taken from HMG's document submitted to the Provisionals.
6. Ibid., p. 27.
7. Ibid.
8. *Lost Lives*, op. cit., p. 1,317.
9. Ibid., p. 1,314.
10. *Setting the Record Straight*, op. cit., p. 28.
11. According to the Sinn Fein minutes, the Contact had met the British Government Representative on 26 February 1993 when he had passed on the message about HMG being prepared to talk to Sinn Fein on condition that there was a 'no violence' understanding 'over 2/3 weeks of private talks'. For ease of comprehension I have incorporated this in Sinn Fein's account of the meeting between McGuinness and Kelly and the BGR.
12. *Lost Lives*, op. cit., p. 1,318.
13. *John Major. The Autobiography*, op. cit., p. 444.
14. For the involvement of the loyalist UDA/UFF and the UVF in the peace process see *Loyalists*, op. cit., chapter 18, 'Backstage'.
15. For the detail of the involvement of Albert Reynolds in what became known as the 'Hume–Adams' formula, see *Provos*, op. cit., pp. 335 ff.
16. *Lost Lives*, op. cit., p. 1,329.
17. *Provos*, op. cit., p. 338.
18. *Lost Lives*, op. cit., p. 1,329.
19. Irelandclick.com, 10 August 2000.
20. *Provos*, op. cit., p. 340.
21. Ibid., p. 341.
22. *Setting the Record Straight*, op. cit., p. 44.
23. *Provos*, op. cit., p. 342.
24. Ibid., p. 343.

Chapter Thirty: Getting Rid of the Guns

1. *Northern Ireland. A Political Directory 1968–1999*, op. cit., p. 238.
2. *Northern Ireland. A Chronology of the Troubles 1968–1999*, op. cit., p. 287.
3. *John Major. The Autobiography*, op. cit., p. 455.
4. Ibid., p. 457.
5. *Lost Lives*, op. cit., p. 1,475. The figures were: 1994, loyalists 37, IRA 19; 1993, loyalists 47, IRA 36; 1992, loyalists 36, IRA 34.
6. Ibid., p. 1,368.
7. *Provos*, op. cit., p. 346.
8. *Loyalists*, op. cit., pp. 239 ff. The Drumcree 'stand-off' began in 1995 and carried on every year thereafter. The Portadown Orangemen demanded the right to return to Portadown down the nationalist Garvaghy Road following their annual service at Drumcree Church. They insisted this was their 'traditional route'. The residents of the Garvaghy Road objected, with the result that 'Drumcree' became an annual flashpoint. In 1995, David Trimble had joined hands with his DUP rival, Ian Paisley, in celebration at the end of the march down the Garvaghy Road in the teeth of nationalist protests.
9. *John Major. The Autobiography*, op. cit., p. 484.
10. Ibid., p. 483.
11. *Loyalists*, op. cit., p. 237.
12. *Provos*, op. cit., p. 351.
13. *John Major. The Autobiography*, op. cit., p. 486.
14. *Lost Lives*, op. cit., p. 1,389.
15. Ibid.

Chapter Thirty-One: Back to the 'War'

1. *Bandit Country. The IRA & South Armagh*, Toby Harnden, Hodder & Stoughton, 1999, p. 6.
2. Ibid., p. 247.
3. *Lost Lives*, op. cit., p. 1,391.
4. *Northern Ireland. A Chronology of the Troubles 1968–1999*, op. cit., p. 326.
5. *Daily Telegraph*, 3 July 1997.
6. Ibid.
7. *Daily Telegraph*, 5 June 1997.
8. *Daily Mail*, 3 July 1997.
9. *Guardian*, 22 October 1997.
10. *An Phoblact*, 17 February 2000.
11. *Lost Lives*, op. cit., p. 1,399.
12. Ibid.
13. Ibid., p. 1,400.
14. *Death of a Soldier. A Mother's Search for Peace in Northern Ireland*, Rita Restorick, Blackstaff Press, 2000, pp. 1–2. This is Rita Restorick's moving and courageous account of the impact of her son's death and what it drove her to do.
15. *Bandit Country*, op. cit., p. 303.
16. Maginn was also found guilty of the murders of Thomas Gilbert Johnston, a former UDR soldier, in Keady in 1978, and Lance-Bombardier Paul Andrew Garrett, also in Keady, in 1993.
17. *Daily Mail*, 6 October 2000.

Chapter Thirty-Two: Out of the Mire

1. *Northern Ireland. A Chronology of the Troubles 1968–1999*, op. cit., p. 329.
2. Ibid.
3. *John Major. The Autobiography*, op. cit., p. 493.
4. Ibid., p. 489.
5. *Northern Ireland. A Chronology of the Troubles 1968–1999*, op. cit., p. 341.
6. Ibid.
7. Ibid., pp. 341–2.
8. Ibid., p. 345.
9. Ibid., p. 348.
10. For details about the formation of the 'Real' IRA, see the updated paperback edition of *Provos*, op. cit., pp. 355–62.
11. For details of the breaches of the loyalist and IRA cease-fires during the all-party talks, see *Provos*, op. cit., pp. 367–70 and *Loyalists*, op. cit., pp. 244–8.
12. *Loyalists*, op. cit. p. 250.
13. *Irish News*, 10 April 1998.
14. *Loyalists*, op. cit., p. 250.
15. Remarks made by the Prime Minister, Tony Blair, on his visit to the University of Ulster, Coleraine, 20 May 1998, Northern Ireland Information Service.
16. *Provos*, op. cit., p. 373.
17. *The Agreement. Agreement Reached in the Multi-party Negotiations*, HMSO, Cmnd. 3883, April 1998, p. 22.
18. *The Agreement. Agreement Reached in the Multi-party Negotiations*, op. cit., p. 20.
19. Ibid., pp. 8–9.

Chapter Thirty-Three: The Hand of History

1. Remarks made by the Prime Minister, Tony Blair, on his visit to the University of Ulster, Coleraine, op. cit.
2. *Northern Ireland. A Chronology of the Troubles 1968–1999*, op. cit., p. 365.
3. *Provos*, op. cit., p. 377.
4. *Northern Ireland. A Chronology of the Troubles 1968–1999*, op. cit., p. 365.
5. Ibid., p. 368.
6. Ibid., pp. 371–2.
7. *Loyalists*, op. cit., updated paperback edition, p. 260.
8. The former IRA 'supergrass' was Éamon Collins (45) who was battered to death near his home in South Armagh. He had been one of the IRA's fiercest critics and had taken to 'naming and shaming' prominent republicans. He had written a book, *Killing Rage* (1997), in which he had spoken out against the IRA and its works. He had rashly returned to live in South Armagh and had received several death threats. Only fifty people followed his coffin (*Real Lives*, op. cit., p. 1,467).
9. *Real Lives*, op. cit., p. 1,441.
10. RUC Press Release, Omagh bombing, 16 August 1998.
11. *Northern Ireland. A Political Directory 1968–1999*, op. cit., p. 130.
12. Speech of David Trimble MP to the Labour Party Conference, Ulster Unionist Party, 30 September 1998.
13. *Loyalists*, op. cit., p. 256.

14. *Northern Ireland. A Political Directory 1968–1999*, op. cit., p. 133.

15. *Northern Ireland. A Chronology of the Troubles 1968–1999*, op. cit., p. 389.

16. *Loyalists*, op. cit., updated paperback edition, p. 265.

17. Ibid., updated paperback edition, p. 266.

18. Ibid.

19. *Report of the Independent International Commission on Decommissioning*, 2 July 1999, p. 4.

20. Ibid., pp. 3 and 8.

21. *The Way Forward. A Joint Statement by the British and Irish Governments*, 2 July 1999.

22. *Daily Telegraph*, 23 June 1999.

23. World Socialist Web Site. British cabinet reshuffle, 15 October 1999.

24. *Loyalists*, op. cit., updated paperback edition, p. 269.

25. *Guardian*, 22 December 1998. Peter Mandelson, the architect of 'New' Labour's electoral landslide in 1997, had been given a loan of £337,000 by Geoffrey Robinson to buy a £475,000 house in London's Notting Hill. Mandelson had not notified either the Prime Minister or the Permanent Secretary at the Department of Trade and Industry (DTI) of the loan. The matter was controversial because the DTI was investigating Robinson's financial affairs. Mandelson insisted that there was nothing wrong with the loan. 'At all times I have protected the integrity and professionalism of the DTI,' he said. 'Geoffrey Robinson asked for confidentiality and I respected that. I do not believe that accepting the loan was wrong. There is no conflict of interest in this. The loan was always intended to be short-term and I am repaying the remainder of the loan in full with the help of my mother.'

26. *Guardian*, 3 December 1999.

27. Ibid.

28. *Report of the Independent International Commission on Decommissioning*, 31 January 2000, http://www.nio.gov.uk/000211dc-nio.htm.

29. *Report of the Independent International Commission on Decommissioning*, 11 February 2000, http://www.nio.gov.uk/000211dc3-nio.htm.

30. Joint Governmental Statement from the Irish and British governments, 5 May 2000, http://ince.org/assembly/proposal0500.html.

31. Statement on the Inspection of IRA Weapons Dumps – Martti Ahtisaari and Cyril Ramaphosa, 25 June 2000, http://www.nio.gov.uk/000626a-nio.htm.

32. Ibid.

33. *Irish Times*, 24 August 2000.

34. Ibid.

35. *BBC News, Web Site*, www.bbc.co.uk, 7 October 2000.

36. Ibid., 4 November 2000.

37. *Guardian*, 25 January 2001.

38. *Independent*, 26 January 2001.

39. *Daily Telegraph*, 27 February 2001.

Chapter Thirty-Four: Farewell to Arms?

1. *Irish Times*, 9 June 2001.

2. In the Northern Ireland Assembly election of 20 October 1982. It was the first time Sinn Fein had contested a Stormont election.

3. In the local government elections of 7 June 2001.

4. *BBC News Web Site*, www.bbc.co.uk, 12 June 2001.

5. The American writer Mark Twain, author of *Tom Sawyer* and *Huckleberry Finn*, cabled

from Europe to the Associated Press that the report of his death was 'an exaggeration'.

  6. *BBC News Web Site*, op.cit., IRA Statements 1998–2001, 14 August 2001.
  7. *An Phoblacht/Republican News*, 20 September 2001.
  8. Taken from the appendix to the IRA's training manual known as the 'Green Book'.
  9. *BBC News Web Site*, op.cit., 23 October 2001.
 10. Ibid., 23 October 2001.
 11. Ibid., 23 October 2001.
 12. Ibid., 26 October 2001.
 13. Ibid., 7 November 2001.
 14. Ibid., 28 August 2001.
 15. Ibid., 12 December 2001.
 16. *Independent*, 13 December 2001.
 17. Ibid.
 18 *An Phoblacht/Republican News*, 6 December 2001.
 19. *Independent*, op.cit.
 20. *Guardian*, 17 August 2001.
 21. *Irish Times*, 12 December 2001.
 22. *BBC News Website*. op.cit., 12 December 2001.
 23. *Guardian*, 13 December 2001.
 24. *Daily Telegraph*, 13 December 2001.
 25. *Irish News*, 14 December 2001.
 26. *BBC News Web Site*. op.cit., 23 October 2001.

Glossary

ANC	African National Congress
APC	Armoured Personnel Carrier
ASU	Active Service Unit
BGR	British Government Representative
CCTV	Close Circuit Television
CESA	Catholic Ex-Servicemen's Association
CIRA	Continuity IRA
CLMC	Combined Loyalist Military Command
COP	Close Observation Platoon
CQB	Close Quarter Battle
CSM	Company Sergeant Major
DAAD	Direct Action Against Drugs
DCI	Director & Controller of Intelligence
DET	Detachment (of 14 Intelligence Company)
DTI	Department of Trade and Industry
DYH	Derry Young Hooligans
ECHR	European Commission on Human Rights
ECM	Electronic Counter Measures
EOKA	(initials of Greek 'terrorist' organisation)
FARC	Revolutionary Armed Forces of Columbia
FLOSY	Front for the Liberation of South Yemen
FRU	Force Research Unit
GBH	Grievious Bodily Harm
GOC	General Officer Commanding
GPMG	General Purpose Machine Gun
HME	Home Made Explosive
HMG	Her Majesty's Goverment
HMSU	Headquarters Mobile Support Unit
HQNI	Headquarters Northern Ireland

HSB	Head of Special Branch
IBA	Independent Broadcasting Authority
IICD	Independent International Commision on Decommissioning
INLA	Irish National Liberation Army
IPLO	Irish People's Liberation Organization
IRA	Irish Republican Army
IS	Internal Security
LVF	Loyalist Volunteer Force
MISR	Military Intelligence Source Report
MO	Modus Operandi
MOD	Ministry of Defence
MOE	Methods of Entry
MPSB	Metropolitan Police Special Branch
MRF	Mobile Reconnaissance Force
NICRA	Northern Ireland Civil Rights Association
NIO	Northern Ireland Office
NLF	National Liberation Front
OC	Officer Commanding
OIRA	Official Irish Republican Army
OP	Observation Post
ORBAT	Order of Battle
PAC	Provisional Army Council
PIRA	Provisional Irish Republican Army
PLO	Palestine Liberation Organization
POA	Prison Officers' Association
PSNI	Police Service of Northern Ireland
PUP	Progressive Unionist Party
PUS	Permanent Under Secretary of State
QMG	QuarterMaster General
QGM	Queen's Gallantry Medal
QRF	Quick Reaction Force
RIC	Royal Irish Constabulary
RSF	Republican Sinn Fein
RUC	Royal Ulster Constabulary
RV	Rendezvous
RVH	Royal Victoria Hospital
SAM	Surface to Air Missile
SAS	Special Air Service
SASLO	SAS Liaison Officer
SCT	Special Collation Team
SDLP	Social Democratic and Labour Party
SLR	Self Loading Rifle

SOP	Static Observation Post
TCG	Tasking and Co-ordinating Group
TPU	Timer Power Unit
TUAS	Tactical Use of Armed Struggle
UDA	Ulster Defence Association
UDP	Ulster Democratic Party
UFF	Ulster Freedom Fighters
UPNI	Unionist Party of Northern Ireland
UPV	Ulster Protestant Volunteers
UUP	Ulster Unionist Party
UUUC	United Ulster Unionist Council
UVF	Ulster Volunteer Force
UWC	Ulster Workers' Council
VCP	Vehicle Check Point
WPC	Woman Police Constable

Bibliography

Books

Gerry Adams, *Before the Dawn. An Autobiography*, William Heinemann, London, in association with Brandon Book Publishers Ltd, Dingle, 1996.

Gerry Adams, *The Politics of Irish Freedom*, Brandon Books, Dingle, 1994.

James Adams, Robin Morgan and Anthony Bambridge, *Ambush, The War between the SAS and the IRA*, Pan Original, London, 1998.

Don Anderson, *14 May Days. The Inside Story of the Loyalist Strike of 1974*, Gill & Macmillan Ltd, Dublin, 1994.

David Beresford, *Ten Men Dead. The Story of the 1981 Irish Hunger Strike*, Grafton Books, London, 1987.

Paul Bew and Gordon Gillespie, *Northern Ireland. A Chronology of the Troubles 1968–99*, Gill & Macmillan, Dublin, 1999.

Patrick Bishop and Eamonn Mallie, *The Provisional IRA*, Corgi Books, London, 1993.

Roger Bolton, *Death on the Rock*, W. H. Allen/Optomen, London, 1990.

Kevin Boyle, Tom Hadden and Paddy Hillyard, *Law and the State. The Case of Northern Ireland*, Martin Robertson & Company, 1975.

Richard Broad, Taylor Downing and Ian Stuttard, *The Troubles. The Background to the Question of Northern Ireland*, Thames Futura, London, 1980.

Joel Chandler, *Uncle Remus. Legends of the Old Plantation*, 1881.

Tim Pat Coogan, *Michael Collins*, Arrow Books, London, 1991.

Tim Pat Coogan, *The IRA*, revised paperback edition, HarperCollins, London, 1995.

Liz Curtis, *Ireland. The Propaganda War. The British Media and the 'Battle for Hearts and Minds'*, Pluto Press, London, 1984.

Richard Deutsch, and Vivien Magowan, *Northern Ireland 1968–73. A Chronology of the Events. Volume 1. 1968–71*, Blackstaff Press Limited, Belfast, 1973.

Richard Deutsch, and Vivien Magowan, *Northern Ireland 1968–73. A Chronology of the Events. Volume 2, 1972–73*, Blackstaff Press Limited, Belfast, 1974.

Lieutenant-Colonel Michael Dewar, *The British Army in Northern Ireland*, Arms and Armour Press, London, 1985.

Martin Dillon, *25 Years of Terror. The IRA's War against the British*, Bantam Books, 1994.

Martin Dillon, *The Dirty War*, Arrow, London, 1991.

Father Dennis Faul and Father Raymond Murray, *SAS Terrorism. The Assassin's Glove*, personal Publication, July 1976.

Sydney Elliott and W.D. Flackes, *Northern Ireland. A Political Directory 1968–1999*, The Blackstaff Press, Belfast 1999.

Brian Faulkner, *Memoirs of a Statesman*, Weidenfeld & Nicolson, London, 1978.

Robert Fisk, *The Point of No Return. The Strike Which Broke the British in Ulster*, Times Books, André Deutsch, London 1975.

Tony Geraghty, *Who Dares Wins. The Story of the SAS 1950–1992*, Warner Books, London, 1993.

Tom Hadden and Kevin Boyle, *The Anglo-Irish Agreement. Commentary, Text and Official Review*, Sweet & Maxwell Ltd, London, 1989.

Desmond Hamill, *Pig in the Middle. The Army in Northern Ireland 1969–1984*, Methuen, London, 1985.

Toby Harnden, *Bandit Country. The IRA & South Armagh*, Hodder & Stoughton, London, 1999.

Sir John Hermon, *Holding the Line. An Autobiography*, Gill & Macmillan, Dublin, 1997.

Jack Holland and Henry McDonald, *INLA. The Story of One of Ireland's Most Ruthless Terrorist Organisations*, Torc, A Division of Poolbeg Enterprises Ltd, Dublin, 1994.

Jack Holland and Susan Phoenix, *Phoenix. Policing the Shadows. The Secret War against Terrorism in Northern Ireland*, Hodder & Stoughton, London, 1996.

Robert Kee, *The Green Flag. A History of Irish Nationalism*, Weidenfeld & Nicolson, London, 1972.

Major Frank Kitson, MBE, MC, *Gangs and Counter-Gangs*, Barrie & Rockliff, London, 1960.

David McKittrick, Seamus Kelters, Brian Feeney and Chris Thornton, *Lost Lives. The Stories of the Men, Women and Children Who Died as a Result of the Northern Ireland Troubles*, Mainstream Publishing, Edinburgh, 1999.

John Major, *John Major. The Autobiography*, HarperCollins, London, 1999.

Antony Makepeace-Warne, *'Exceedingly Lucky', A History of the Light Infantry 1968–1993*, Sydney Jary Limited, Bristol, 1993.

Roy Mason, *Paying the Price*, Robert Hale, London, 1999.

Don Mullan (ed.), *Eyewitness Bloody Sunday. The Truth*, Wolfhound Press, Dublin, 1997.

Chris Mullin, *Error of Judgement. The Truth about the Birmingham Bombings*, Chris Mullin, Poolbeg, Dublin, 1986.

Peter Pringle and Philip Jacobson, *Those Are Real Bullets, Aren't They?*, Fourth Estate Limited, 2001.

Provisional IRA, *Freedom Struggle. By the Provisional IRA*, (no publisher given), 1973.

Rita Restorick, *Death of a Soldier. A Mother's Search for Peace in Northern Ireland*, Blackstaff Press, Belfast, 2000.

Jeremy Smith, *Britain and Ireland. From Home Rule to Independence*, Pearson Education Limited, Harlow, 2000.

Sunday Times Insight Team, *Ulster. New edition – The Story up to Easter 1972*, Penguin Special, Penguin Books, Harmondsworth, 1972.

Malcolm Sutton, *An Index of the Deaths from the Conflict in Northern Ireland 1969–1993*, Beyond the Pale Publications, Belfast, 1994.

Peter Taylor, *Beating the Terrorists? Interrogation in Omagh, Gough and Castlereagh*, Penguin Special, Penguin Books, Harmondsworth, 1980

Peter Taylor, *Loyalists*, Bloomsbury, London, 1999.

Peter Taylor, *Provos. The IRA and Sinn Fein*, Bloomsbury, London, 1997.

Peter Taylor, *States of Terror, Democracy and Political Violence*, BBC Books, London, 1993.

Peter Taylor, *Stalker. The Search for the Truth*, Faber & Faber, London, 1987.

Margaret Thatcher, *The Downing Street Years 1979–90*, HarperCollins, 1993.

Tillotson, H.M., *With the Prince of Wales's Own. The Story of a Yorkshire Regiment 1958–1994*, Michael Russell, Norwich, 1995.

Kevin Toolis, *Rebel Hearts. Journeys Within the IRA's Soul*, Picador, 2nd edition, 2000.

Mark Urban, *Big Boys' Rules. The Secret Struggle against the IRA*, Faber & Faber, 1992.

Simon Winchester, *In Holy Terror. Reporting the Ulster Troubles*, Faber & Faber, London, 1974.

Articles

John Ware and Geoffrey Seed, 'Revealed. How the Army Set up Ulster Murders', *Sunday Telegraph*, 29 March 1998.

Peter Taylor, 'Bloody Sunday: An Open Wound', *Sunday Times*, 26 January 1992.

John Ware, 'Time to Come Clean over the Army's Role in the "Dirty War"', *New Statesman*, 24 April 1998.

Web Sites

CAIN Web Service, *Bloody Sunday and the Report of the Widgery Tribunal – Summary and Significance of New Material*, http://cain.ulst.ac.uk.

Reports and transcripts and Government publications.

British Irish Rights Watch
Deadly Intelligence, State Involvement in Loyalist Murder in Northern Ireland, British Irish Rights Watch, February 1999.

European Commission of Human Rights
European Commission of Human Rights. Application no. 5310/71. Ireland against the United Kingdom. Report of the Commission (Adopted on 25 January 1976).

Hansard
House of Commons Official Report. Parliamentary Debates (Hansard), 29 January 2000, Columns 501–3.

Regina v. Brian Nelson
Regina v. Brian Nelson Before the Right Honourable Lord Justice Kelly on Wednesday 29 January 1992 at Belfast Crown Court. Evidence of Witness 'Colonel "J"'.

HMSO
The Agreement Reached in the Multi-party Negotiations, HMSO, Cmnd. 3883, April 1998.

Report of a Committee to consider, in the context of civil liberties and human rights, measures to deal with terrorism in Northern Ireland, Chairman: Lord Gardiner, HMSO, Cmnd. 5847, January 1975.

Report of the Advisory Committee on Police in Northern Ireland, Belfast, HMSO, Cmnd. 535, October 1969.

Report of the enquiry into allegations against security forces of the physical brutality in Northern Ireland arising out of events on 9th August 1971, Chaired by Sir Edmund Compton, GCB, KBE, HMSO, Cmnd. 4823, November 1971.

Report of the Privy Counsellors appointed to consider authorised procedures for the interrogation of persons suspected of terrorism. Chairman: Lord Parker of Waddington, HMSO, Cmnd. 4901, March 1972.

Report of the Tribunal appointed to inquire into the events on Sunday, 30th January 1972, which led to the loss of life in connection with the procession in Londonderry on that day, by the Rt Hon Lord Widgery, OBE, TD, HMSO, 18 April 1972.

Violence and Civil Disturbances in Northern Ireland in 1969. Report of Tribunal of Inquiry, Chairman the Hon. Mr Justice Scarman. HMSO, Cmnd, 566, April 1972.

Independent International Commission

Report of the Independent International Commission on Decommissioning, 2 July 1999 (www.nio.gov.uk/000211dc-nio.htm).

Joint Governmental Statement from the Irish and British Governments, 5 May 2000 (http://ince.org./assembly/proposal0500.html)

Sinn Fein

Setting the Record Straight. A Record of Communications between Sinn Fein and the British Government October 1990–November 1993, published by Sinn Fein.

Statement on the Inspection of IRA Weapons Dumps – Marti Ahtissari and Cyril Ramaphosa, 25 June 2000 (http://www.nio.gov.uk/00062a-nio.htm.)

The Way Forward. A Joint Statement by the British and Irish Governments, 2 July 1999.

The Windlesham/Rampton Report on 'Death on the Rock', Lord Windlesham and Richard Rampton QC, Faber & Faber, London, 1989.

Documents

Future Military Policy for Londonderry. An Appreciation of the Situation by CLF, 14 December 1971, Memo from Major-General Robert Ford to the GOC, Lieutenant-General Sir Harry Tuzo. Saville Inquiry.

The Situation in Londonderry as at 7 January 1972, Memo from Major-General Robert Ford to the GOC, Lieutenant-General Sir Harry Tuzo. Saville Inquiry.

Northern Ireland. Future Terrorist Trends, Brigadier J. M. Glover, BGS (Int) DIS, 2 November 1978. Leaked or lost document revealed in *Republican News*.

Television

Peter Taylor, 'A Soldier's Tale', BBC documentary, transmitted 7 August 1994.

Peter Taylor, 'Remember Bloody Sunday', BBC documentary, transmitted 28 January 1992.

Index

NOTE: Ranks and titles are generally the highest mentioned in the text

Provos Peter Taylor
£6.99   0 7475 3818 2

'This is the book of Peter Taylor's excellent television series on the IRA. During
the last twenty-five years Taylor has built a justified reputation as by far the
most knowledgeable British – or Irish – television reporter on Northern Ireland
affairs ... it will certainly become the standard reference work for the next few
years ... as the most accurate account of the republican side of the conflict so
far' Irish Times

'Excellent ... by far the most revealing account of IRA strategy yet published'
Observer

'Diligent research, a sceptical eye and fine reporting' The Times

'The background and culture of the IRA, old and new, are extremely well set-out'
Daily Telegraph

Never before has an outsider had such access to record the remarkable history of
the Provisional IRA and Sinn Fein – the 'Provos' – from their dramatic beginnings
to the critical juncture they have reached today.

To order from Bookpost PO Box 29 Douglas Isle of Man IM99 1BQ www.bookpost.co.uk
email: bookshop@enterprise.net fax: 01624 837033 tel: 01624 836000

bloomsburypbks

bloomsburymagazine.com